Psychology of Language

Language

Second Edition

Psychology of
Language

Second Edition

David W. Carroll
University of Wisconsin–Superior

Brooks/Cole Publishing Company
Pacific Grove, California

I(**T**)**P**® The ITP logo is a registered trademark under license.

Brooks/Cole Publishing Company
A division of International Thomson Publishing Inc.

Printed in the United States of America
10 9 8 7 6 5

Library of Congress Cataloging-in-Publication Data
Carroll, David W.
    Psychology of language / David W. Carroll. — 2nd ed.
      p.   cm.
    Includes bibliographical references and index.
    ISBN 0-534-21300-6
    1. Psycholinguistics. I. Title
BF455.C268 1994
401'.9—dc20   93-26969
                                    CIP

Sponsoring Editor: *Vicki Knight*
Editorial Assistant: *Lauri Banks Ataide*
Production Coordinator: *Fiorella Ljunggren*
Production: *Melanie Field, Bookman Productions*
Manuscript Editor: *Betty Berenson*
Permissions Editor: *Lillian Campobasso*
Interior Design: *Suzanne Montazer, Bookman Productions*
Cover Design: *Laurie Albrecht*
Cover Art: *James Scott Taylor*
Art Coordination: *Bookman Productions*
Interior Illustration: *Ryan Cooper*
Photo Research: *Bookman Productions*
Typesetting: *Weimer Graphics, Inc.*
Cover Printing: *Phoenix Color Corporation*
Printing and Binding: *Arcata Graphics/Fairfield*
(Credits continue on p. 461.)

This book is dedicated to my parents,
Mary M. Carroll and Patrick E. Carroll.

Brief Contents

Contents

Preface

I had two goals when I wrote the first edition of this textbook. The first was to present the principles of psycholinguistics in an accessible manner. Although many students are fascinated with the study of language, the field is complex and can be intimidating at times. I felt there was a need for a presentation of basic concepts and principles that would make the field more accessible to students. To that effect, I used a combination of carefully worked out examples, activities that demonstrate psycholinguistic principles, and various pedagogical devices.

My second goal was to discuss fundamental psycholinguistic issues in a balanced way. It is important that students understand that questions such as the role of the environment in language acquisition and the interaction of syntax and semantics in language comprehension can be approached in a number of ways. I attempted to present issues such as these from a variety of perspectives (different theoretical positions, different research strategies, and so on) and invited the reader to think through the competing claims.

These goals continued to guide my efforts in preparing this second edition, and I hope that enough of the first edition has been retained for those who have used the book in the classroom and were pleased with it. At the same time, various substantive, organizational, and stylistic problems with the first edition have been pointed out to me by reviewers, and I have tried to respond to these concerns.

Much has changed in the eight years since the first edition of the book. I have been selective in representing these changes, preferring to focus on those that highlight important and enduring concerns. As one example, this second edition includes discussion of connectionist models of language in the chapters on both perception and production of language. These models are important because they embody some assumptions that challenge traditional views of language processes. Connectionist models assume a greater amount of interaction between language levels than is assumed in modular approaches and emphasize parallel, not serial, processing. I have not tried to resolve or settle these disputes; rather, I have attempted to clarify the different positions as well as the kinds of data that may be helpful in evaluating each of them.

The book has been reorganized as well. Part 1 (General Issues) still contains three chapters, but Chapter 3 of the first edition (Biological Foundations of Language) has been moved to the back of the book. The old Chapter 2 has been divided into two chapters, one on linguistics and one on information processing. Chapter 2 discusses basic grammatical concepts. There is less emphasis on transformational grammar than in the first edition and more emphasis on current grammatical theories such as lexical-functional grammar and government-binding theory. The chapter also discusses the grammatical features of American Sign Language, a topic that is returned to throughout the book. Chapter 3 focuses on basic concepts of information processing and how they may apply to language. The overriding goal of Part 1 is to introduce the notion of a cognitive approach to language processes, an approach that emphasizes the interrelationships among language, memory, and cognition.

This approach is then applied to various aspects of language processing. Part 2 (Language Comprehension) is similar to the first edition, with chapters on perception, the lexicon, sentence processing, and discourse processing. Part 3 (Language Production and Conversational Interaction) contains, as before, one chapter on language production and one on conversation, but both have been updated and enlarged.

Part 4 (Language Acquisition) still contains three chapters, but the organization is different than in the first edition. Chapters 10 and 11 discuss early and later language acquisitions, respectively. Whereas the previous version of these chapters interweaved data on child language with theory, the current chapters are mainly data, and a new Chapter 12 discusses theoretical issues in language acquisition in an integrated manner. Part 5 (Language in Perspective) is new. It includes Chapter 13, which is the revised chapter on biological foundations, and Chapter 14, which discusses language, culture, and cognition, with particular attention to the Whorf hypothesis. These last two chapters are somewhat broader in scope than most of the earlier ones and help put basic psycholinguistic processes (comprehension, production, and acquisition of language) into biological and cultural perspective.

Some stylistic changes have also been made. The fact that in the first edition both psycholinguistic terms and linguistic examples were printed in italic generated some confusion. To eliminate the problem, now the terms are printed in boldface. And when a linguistic example is of sentence length or longer, I have generally used the convention of numbering the example and setting it apart from the text. For shorter examples, italics are used. Quotation marks are employed when a term is used in an unusual or ironic manner.

This edition, like the previous one, includes a number of pedagogical features that will be of help to students. Chapters begin with a list of about four to six main points that the student should expect to learn. Interim summaries occur after each major section of the chapter, so that readers may assess their learning before going on. Each chapter concludes with two sets of questions. Review questions are directly related to the material in the chapter, and students should be able to answer them if they have read the chapter carefully. Thought questions are intended to stimulate thinking about the material in the chapter. Although the answers to these questions cannot be found directly in the chapter—indeed, most have no single "correct" answer—the material presented provides a basis for beginning to examine these questions. Finally, this edition of the book includes a glossary. What I have not done is avoid difficult or difficult-to-explain topics. Rather, I have provided students with the tools that should enable them to master even complex material.

I would be delighted to hear from students or professors who are using this book. You can reach me at the Department of Psychology, University of Wisconsin–Superior, Superior, WI 54880. I can also be reached via INTERNET at dcarroll@wpo.uwsuper.edu

Acknowledgments

I am pleased to acknowledge the assistance of many people in the preparation of this second edition. A number of reviewers read and commented on one or more chapters, and their efforts have greatly contributed to the book. They are David Dodd of the University of Utah, Don MacKay of the University of California–Los Angeles, Dorothy Piontkowski of San Francisco State University, and Lawrence Schoen of Chestnut Hill College. I thank them for their generosity and for their comments. Of course, I didn't always listen: any problems that remain are strictly my responsibility.

I would also like to thank a number of individuals at the University of Wisconsin–Superior for their assistance. Jan Kuldau arranged some adjustments in my teaching schedule that gave me time to work on the book. The staff at Jim Dan Hill Library assisted me in several ways. Dick Heim helped me identify relevant books and articles, and the interlibrary loan staff (Laura Kremer, Eileen Wasyliszyn, Shelley Oenes, and Jodie Wright) tracked them all down. In addition, students in several classes read early drafts of several chapters and made a number of useful suggestions.

The staff at Brooks/Cole was once again most helpful. Vicki Knight showed interest in the revision, attracted some excellent reviewers, and demonstrated skill in the care and treatment of this author. She was extremely patient at the appropriate times and gently prodding at others. Fiorella Ljunggren and Melanie Field expertly guided the production process and were a pleasure to work with. Betty Berenson edited the manuscript carefully and suggested many changes that improved the clarity of the writing.

Finally, I want to thank my wife, Deb, for her patience and support. The timing of this edition was not ideal, but she sacrificed her own needs gracefully and allowed me the time to complete the project. Without her, this book would not have been possible.

David W. Carroll

part 1

General Issues

1

Introduction: Themes of Psycholinguistics

- Psycholinguistics is the study of how individuals comprehend, produce, and acquire language.
- The study of psycholinguistics is part of the field of cognitive science. Cognitive science reflects the insights of psychology, linguistics, and, to a lesser extent, fields such as artificial intelligence, neuroscience, and philosophy.
- Psycholinguistics stresses the knowledge of language and the cognitive processes involved in ordinary language use.
- Psycholinguists are also interested in the social rules involved in language use and the brain mechanisms associated with language.
- Contemporary interest in psycholinguistics began in the 1950s, although important precursors existed earlier in the century.

Introduction

This book is about how people use language. There are few things that play as central a role in our everyday lives as language. It is our most important tool in communicating our thoughts and feelings to each other. Infants cry and laugh, and their facial expressions surely give their parents some notion of the kinds of emotions they are experiencing, but it is not until children are able to articulate speech that we gain much understanding of their private thoughts.

As we grow, language comes to serve other functions as well. Most young people develop jargon that is more meaningful to those of the same age than to older or younger individuals. Such specialized language serves to bind us more closely with our peers while at the same time excluding those who are not our peers. Language becomes a badge of sorts, a means of identifying whether or not a person is within a social group. Similar processes are at work in gender and social class differences in language use.

Over time, for many of us, language becomes not merely a means to an end, but an end in itself. We come to love words and word play. So we turn to writing poetry or short stories. Or to playing word games, such as anagrams and crossword puzzles. Or to reading novels on a lazy summer afternoon. A tool that is vital for communicating our basic needs and wants has also become a source of leisurely pleasure.

The diversity of how we use language is daunting for psychologists who wish to study language. How can something so widespread and far-reaching as language be examined psychologically? An important consideration is that although language is intrinsically a social phenomenon, psychology is principally the study of individuals. The psychology of language deals with the mental processes that are involved in language use. Three sets of processes are of primary interest: language comprehension (how we perceive and understand speech and written language), language production (how we construct an utterance, from idea to completed sentence), and language acquisition (how children acquire language).

The psychological study of language is called **psycholinguistics.** This book explores the principles of this field along with selected applications. This introductory chapter deals with two questions: What is psycholinguistics? and How has this field evolved over the last century?

The Scope of Psycholinguistics

Psycholinguistics is part of the emerging field of study called **cognitive science.** Cognitive science is an interdisciplinary venture that draws upon the insights of psychologists, linguists, computer scientists, neuroscientists, and philosophers to study the mind and mental processes (Johnson-Laird, 1988; Stillings et al., 1987). Some of the topics that have been studied by cognitive scientists include problem solving, memory, imagery, and language. Anyone who is seriously interested in any of these topics must be prepared to cross disciplinary lines, for the topics do not belong to any one field of study but, rather, are treated in distinctive and yet complementary ways by various disciplines.

As the name implies, psycholinguistics is principally an integration of the fields of psychology and linguistics, although like most interdisciplinary fields, psycholinguistics has a rich heritage that includes contributions from diverse intellectual traditions. These contrasting approaches have often led to controversies in how to best think of or study language processes. We will consider many of these issues in the pages to come. For now, let us begin our survey of psycholinguistics by examining some of its central themes.

Language Processes and Linguistic Knowledge

At its heart, psycholinguistic work consists of two questions. One is: What knowledge of language is needed for us to use language? In a sense, we must know a language in order to use it, but we are not always fully aware of this knowledge. A distinction may be drawn between **tacit knowledge** and **explicit knowledge.** Tacit knowledge refers to the knowledge of how to perform various acts, whereas explicit knowledge refers to the knowledge of the processes or mechanisms used in these acts. We sometimes know how to do something without knowing how we do it. For instance, a baseball pitcher might know how to throw a baseball 90 miles an hour, but might have little or no explicit knowledge of the muscle groups that are involved in this act. Similarly, we may distinguish between knowing how to speak and knowing what processes are involved in producing speech. Generally speaking, much of our linguistic knowledge is tacit rather than explicit. Reading this book will make you more aware of various things you know about language, and will therefore transform some of your tacit knowledge into explicit knowledge.

Four broad areas of language knowledge may be distinguished. **Semantics** deals with the meanings of sentences and words. **Syntax** deals with the grammatical arrangement of words within the sentence. **Phonology** deals with the system of sounds in a language. **Pragmatics** deals with the social rules involved in language use. It is not ordinarily productive to ask people explicitly what they know about these aspects of language. We infer linguistic knowledge from observable behavior.

The other primary psycholinguistic question is: What cognitive processes are involved in the ordinary use of language? By ordinary use of language, I mean such things as understanding a lecture, reading a book, writing a letter, and holding a conversation. By cognitive processes, I mean processes such as perception, memory, and thinking. Although there are few things we do as often or as easily as speaking and listening, we will find that there is considerable cognitive processing going on.

Four Language Examples

The interplay of linguistic knowledge and language processes is a continuing theme throughout this book. Because these concepts play a central role in psycholinguistic work, the following two chapters explore the knowledge and process questions in greater depth. Chapter 2 discusses linguistic insights into our tacit knowledge, whereas Chapter 3 discusses psychological mechanisms of information processing and how these processes may be used in language processing. For now, it will be helpful to consider various examples of language and language processes. The following examples are intended to illustrate how the aforementioned themes apply to specific situations as well as to convey some of the scope of psycholinguistic research.

Garden path sentences   What happens when we comprehend a sentence? We get a hint of what is involved when the process breaks down. For example, consider sentence (1):

(1) The novice accepted the deal before he had a chance to check his finances, which put him in a state of conflict when he realized he had a straight flush. (Adapted from Foss & Jenkins, 1973)

Sentences such as this are sometimes called **garden path sentences** since the subjective impression is that of following a garden path to a predictable destination until it is obvious that you were mistaken in your original interpretation and thus are forced to "backtrack" and reinterpret the sentence. That is, in terms of knowledge, we have stored in our memory at least two different meanings of the word *deal*. One is related to a business transaction and the other, relevant in this case, pertains to card games. This knowledge of the two meanings of *deal* is part of our semantic knowledge of the language. Another part of our semantic knowledge is knowledge of the relationships among words, such as *deal* and *finances*. From a process standpoint, we appear to select the one that is most appropriate, and we have little or no conscious awareness of the alternative (or how else would we have the garden path experience?). That is, we are able, by some process, to focus our attention on what we believe is the relevant meaning of *deal*. Studies of ambiguity are examined in Chapters 5 and 6; we will find that there is more to garden path sentences than what we are immediately aware of. The point for now is that in the course of comprehending language we are making decisions—we are doing mental work.

Indirect requests   Consider now a sentence such as (2):

(2)   Can you open the door?

Literally, this sentence asks if we have the ability to open the door, but everybody assumes that the speaker is asking us to open the door in an indirect manner. Why is the request phrased indirectly? Part of the reason is that we have learned certain rules about the use of language in social settings, including rules of politeness. A request is, by definition, an attempt to change another person's behavior. This can be perceived as intrusive or threatening at times, so we soften it with indirect speech. An indirect request is more polite than a direct command such as sentence (3):

(3)   Open the door!

We know this, as it is part of our pragmatic knowledge of our language. Some of us know it better than others, to be sure (studies discussed in Chapter 9 indicate that women and girls are more likely to use indirect speech than are men and boys).

From a processing standpoint, a speaker takes this pragmatic knowledge into account when producing a sentence such as (2) in a social situation. That is, the speaker utters the sentence with the understanding that it will be taken as a request. The listener presumably shares this aspect of pragmatic knowledge and interprets the sentence as a request rather than in a literal manner, although the exact processes by which the listener arrives at the nonliteral meaning are not fully clear (see Chapter 6).

Indirect requests are an aspect of language that forces us to consider language in a social context. The study of the relationships between language and social behavior is called **sociolinguistics.** Sociolinguists remind us that language activities always take place in a social world. Sociologists and anthropologists study how language varies with social groupings, how it influences social interaction, and how it is used as an instrument of culture (as in the transmission of cultural traditions). All of these aspects are well beyond those of the psychologist, who is principally interested in the behavior of individuals. Yet even when studying individuals, it is necessary to recognize the social dimension of language.

Language in aphasia   Although our primary focus is on language processes in normal individuals, we can learn a great deal about language by studying individuals with impaired language functioning. An **aphasia** is a language disorder due to brain damage. One type of aphasia, called **Wernicke's aphasia,** involves a breakdown in semantics. For example, consider excerpt (4):

(4)   Before I was in the one here, I was over in the other one. My sister had the department in the other one. (Geschwind, 1972, p. 78)

The semantic relationships between words in this excerpt are seriously disrupted, suggesting that the patient's semantic knowledge has been impaired by the brain damage. In contrast, phonological knowledge was spared; the speech, although devoid of meaning, was articulated smoothly, and with appropriate pausing and intonation. It also displays appropriate syntactic structure, which is typical in Wernicke's aphasia.

The study of the relationship between the brain and language is called **neurolinguistics,** which is discussed more fully in Chapter 13. Although the details of the links between brain structures and language elude us, what is presently known is both fascinating and instructive. Depending upon the exact location of the injury, its severity, and many other factors, an individual who has suffered from a brain injury may display a wide variety of reactions. One individual may have normal comprehension but be deficient in language production. Another individual may have no loss of ability with sentence structure but have greater than normal problems finding words. Still other individuals may be unimpaired in comprehension and production but be unable to repeat exactly what they have heard and understood. In normal individuals with intact brains, various facets of language—sentence structure, meaning, sounds—appear to form a smoothly coordinated system of communication; however, in brain-damaged individuals, this system is revealed to be a combination of separate parts, for the deficits in such persons are nearly always selective rather than total. Thus, brain injuries enable us to analyze an apparently unified program of language abilities into its separate components and raise questions about how such abilities become integrated in the normal adult in the first place.

Language in children   An area of considerable concern to psycholinguists is language acquisition. As difficult as it is to infer linguistic knowledge in adults, the problem is even more intractable with children. An example may help here. Imagine a young child, about 1 year old, interacting with her mother. Typically, children around this age produce one word at a time. When the mother leaves the room and then returns with the child's favorite doll, the child says *doll,* not *Mother.* Later, when the mother is helping her with lunch, the child points at the milk and says *more.* Still later, when the child is struggling with her shoes and the mother asks her what she is doing, the simple response is *off.* What can we conclude from these observations?

For starters, the child might know, at least in a tacit manner, some of the rules of language in order to use words appropriately. We could infer that she uses *more* not as an isolated word or imitation, but as a request that the mother bring the milk closer. *Doll* is less clear; the child might be making a comment on her environment by labeling a thing she finds interesting, or she may be requesting the doll. How do we determine what she is trying to say? One way is to see what happens if the mother does nothing. If the word were meant as a request, the child will probably become more insistent, perhaps by repeatedly pointing at the doll and saying *doll*; whereas if it were meant as a comment, the child's behavior should end with mother's mere acknowledgement of the object. Thus, the child may have learned certain pragmatic rules to guide her choice of words.

You may complain that this is reading a good deal, perhaps too much, into a single word. Granted, the inferences made about this stage of development are terribly difficult. Yet, although there is disagreement over exactly how much knowledge to attribute to young children, it appears that children know more than they say. Children somewhat older than the one in the example commonly express themselves with two words at a time, as in *baby gone*, by eliminating the **function words** (prepositions, conjunctions, and so on) in favor of **content words** (nouns, verbs, adjectives). This pattern suggests that children have an intuitive understanding of these two grammatical classes, which is a part of their syntactic knowledge.

An analysis of children's comprehension and production abilities cannot be divorced from the social context in which the child masters language. Parents may set up situations in which one word is sufficient for communication. With the adult's query, *What are you doing with your shoe?*, as the base, the child's simple, economical *off* is instantly comprehensible. Parents do other things as well, such as simplifying their speech to children and teaching specific words. Is the orderly pattern of development observed in child language the result of an orderly biological program or of an orderly social environment? This issue is addressed in Chapter 12.

Summary

Psycholinguistics is part of an interdisciplinary field known as cognitive science. Two primary psycholinguistic questions are: What mental processes are involved in language use? And, What linguistic knowledge is involved in language use? These questions reemerge in different forms in studies of adult language comprehension, the social use of language, language use in aphasia, and language in children.

The Historical Context

In this section we consider some historical developments in the study of psycholinguistics. I have not attempted to be comprehensive here. The history of psycholinguistics has been treated in detail elsewhere (see, for example, Blumenthal, 1970, 1987; Kess, 1991; McCauley, 1987; Reber, 1987), and if you are interested, you are advised to consult these sources. My discussion here is simply meant to put succeeding chapters in a little bit of historical perspective.

Blumenthal (1987) has observed that the interdisciplinary field of psycholinguistics flourished twice: once around the turn of the century, principally in Europe, and once in the middle of this century, principally in the United States. In both instances, it was a somewhat asymmetrical marriage of disciplines. In the early decades of this century, linguists turned to psychologists for insights into how human beings use language. In the later period, psychologists turned to linguists for insights into the nature of language. In between these two periods, behaviorism dominated both fields, each of which practiced a form of benign neglect toward one another. We will look at the events of each of these periods, and I will add some observations on the current directions in the field.

Early Psycholinguistics

From the development of the first psychological laboratory, at the University of Leipzig in Germany in 1879, until the early 1900s, psychology was defined as the science of mental life. A major figure in early scientific psychology was Wilhelm Wundt (1832–1920), a man who was trained in physiology and who believed that it was possible to investigate mental events such as sensations, feelings, and images by using procedures as rigorous as those used in the natural sciences. Moreover, Wundt believed that the study of language could provide important insights into the nature of the mind. Blumenthal (1970) refers to Wundt as the master psycholinguist because Wundt wrote extensively about many different aspects of language. His concerns included grammar, phonology, language comprehension, child language acquisition, sign language, reading, and other topics of contemporary concern.

One of Wundt's contributions to the psychology of language was developing a theory of language production. He regarded the sentence, not the word, as the primary unit of language and saw the production of speech as the transformation of a complete thought process into sequentially organized speech segments (comprehension was thought to be basically the same process in reverse). Wundt described speech production in the following terms:

> When I construct a sentence, an isolated concept does not first enter consciousness causing me to utter a sound to represent it. That it cannot be this way is shown by the phenomenon of phonetic induction which occurs when a vocal element on the verge of being expressed is already affecting the form of a sound being spoken at the moment. And similarly, an articulation that has just occurred influences the succeeding sound. . . . The sentence . . . is not an image running with precision through consciousness where each single word or single sound appears only momentarily while the preceding and following elements are lost from consciousness. Rather, it stands as a whole at the cognitive level while it is being spoken. If this should ever not be the case, we would irrevocably lose the thread of speech. (Wundt, 1912, cited in Blumenthal, 1970, p. 21)

These two notions—the view that speech production is a word-by-word process and that it begins with a whole sentence—continue to be of interest to language researchers. As we shall see in Chapter 3, this distinction is a precursor of a contemporary distinction between bottom-up and top-down processing.

Some significant developments were also being made in measuring various language processes. An example comes from the 1908 work of Edmund Huey (1968), who examined reading from the perspective of human perceptual abilities. Huey, who regarded the achievement of reading as "the most remarkable specific performance that civilization has learned in all its history" (p. 6), employed the **eye voice span** (the lag between eye position and voice when reading aloud, about six or seven words) and the **tachistoscope** (a machine that presents visual stimuli for very brief periods of time) in his studies. Interest in eye-movement and tachistoscopic data remains very strong to this day.

Behaviorism and Verbal Behavior

In the first few decades of this century in the United States, there was mounting opposition to the focus on mental life as a goal for psychology. By the 1920s, **behaviorism** took over the mainstream of experimental psychology. Behaviorists favored the study of objective behavior, often in laboratory animals, as opposed to the study of mental processes. Moreover, behaviorists had a strong commitment to the role of experience in shaping behavior. Emphasis was placed on the role of environmental contingencies (reinforcement and punishment) and on models present in the immediate environment.

From the 1920s to the 1950s, psychologists expressed relatively little interest in language. When behaviorists were able to pull themselves away from rats to study human language, they preferred instead to speak of "verbal behavior." The behavior of speaking correctly was, it was assumed, the consequence of being raised in an environment in which correct language models were present and in which children's speech errors were corrected. The manner in which parents shape their children's utterances was described by the behaviorist B. F. Skinner in his book *Verbal Behavior:*

> In teaching the young child to talk, the formal specifications upon which reinforcement is contingent at first greatly relaxed. Any response which vaguely resembles the standard behavior of the community is reinforced. When these begin to appear more frequently, a closer approximation is insisted upon. In this manner, very complex verbal forms may be reached. (Skinner, 1957, pp. 29–30)

Although this analysis may seem straightforward or even obvious, we will find in Chapter 12 that the role of adult speech in child language acquisition is both more controversial and more complex than is suggested in this excerpt.

About the time Skinner's book appeared, behavioristic research was providing evidence for its most basic premise, that verbal behavior could be conditioned by reinforcement. Verplanck (1955) found that the opinionated statements of college students in free conversation increased in frequency when they were followed by verbal reinforcers such as *mm* or *good*. Related studies showed that the frequency of a grammatical class, such as plural words, could be increased by reinforcing only words from that class (Greenspoon, 1955). In a similar way, subtle signs of approval (such as nods) probably influence our choice of words in conversations.

Another major topic of research was meaning. A number of behavioristic accounts of meaning were developed, most of which emphasized associations among words. Noble and McNeely (1957) constructed an index of the "meaningfulness" of individual words by measuring the number of associations a person could produce in a designated period of time. Later studies showed that high-meaningfulness words such as *kitchen* were more easily learned in a variety of tasks than low-meaningfulness words such as *icon* (Underwood, 1966). It was also about this time that Osgood and his associates developed the **semantic differential,** a tool for measuring the associative meanings of words by asking people to rate words on dimensions such as good/bad and strong/weak (Osgood, Suci, & Tanenbaum, 1957).

Similar developments were occurring within linguistics. Linguists of this period tended to emphasize behavioristic treatments of language, in which reference to mental states or processes was meticulously avoided. However, despite the similarities between the two fields, there was little interdisciplinary interest or activity. One striking example of this is the work of linguist Leonard Bloomfield. Bloomfield was once a student of Wundt's and published a book in 1914 that emphasized many Wundtian themes. However, his more widely known 1933 text took a more behaviorist view. In his preface to the later book, Bloomfield tried to distance himself not only from Wundt but from psychology as a whole:

> In 1914 I based this phase of the exposition on the psychologic system of Wilhelm Wundt, which was then widely accepted. Since that time there has been much upheaval in psychology; we have learned, at any rate, what one of our masters suspected thirty years ago, namely that we can pursue the study of language without reference to any one psychological doctrine, and that to do so safeguards our results and makes them more significant to workers in related fields. (Bloomfield, 1933, p. vii)

Thus, despite the inherent interconnections between the fields, psychology and linguistics "divorced" for a period of several decades.

Later Psycholinguistics

By the early 1950s, psychologists and linguists became interested in talking to one another. Tanenhaus (1988) describes the events in the following way:

> In 1951 the Social Science Research Council sponsored a conference that brought together several leading psychologists and linguists. . . . The proceedings of the conference outlined a psycholinguistic research agenda that reflected a consensus among participants that the methodological and theoretical tools developed by psychologists could be used to explore and explain the linguistic structures that were being uncovered by linguists. (p. 4)

A second, larger conference occurred 2 years later and included anthropologists and communications engineers as well as psychologists and linguists. It was out of these exchanges that the term "psycholinguistics" first came into use (Osgood & Sebeok, 1965). Not everyone was fond of the term. One of the participants at the first conference, Roger Brown, complained that a "psycholinguist" sounded more like a deranged polyglot than a psychologist interested in language (R. Brown, 1958), but the name stuck.

The second period of interdisciplinary psycholinguistics really took hold in the late 1950s, beginning with the emergence of the linguist Noam Chomsky. Chomsky is generally regarded as the most influential figure in twentieth-century linguistics, and Newmeyer (1986) has characterized the Chomskyan influence within linguistics as a revolution. Chomsky also played a powerful role in how psychologists perceived language because he argued that the behaviorists' accounts of language were inadequate (Chomsky, 1957, 1959).

Let us look at some of his arguments. One theory advanced by behaviorists is called the **associative chain theory,** which states that a sentence consists of a chain of associations between individual words in a sentence. Put another way, each word in a sentence serves as a stimulus for the next word, and thus the entire sentence is produced left to right. Lashley (1951) had earlier argued against such a view, claiming that there is something more to the structure of a sentence than the associations between adjacent words.

Chomsky (1957) advanced this notion further. Consider the following sentences:

(5) Colorless green ideas sleep furiously.

(6) Furiously sleep ideas green colorless.

(7) George picked up the baby.

(8) George picked the baby up.

Chomsky suggested that associations beyween words could not possibly explain the existence of sentences such as (5). Even though the associations between these words are almost nonexistent, the sentence is syntactically acceptable. But, if the words are presented backward, as in (6), it is not a sentence at all. Now consider sentences (7) and (8). It is part of our intuitive knowledge of the language that these sentences are synonymous, but this simple fact poses problems for the associative chain theory. Clearly, there is a relationship between *pick* and *up* in these sentences, but the relationship is more complex in the second sentence because the words are separated. In order to comprehend the sentence, we must somehow know that these words are part of a linguistic unit, or **constituent.** Linguists call separate units, like those in sentence (8), **discontinuous constituents,** and their existence suggests that there are long-range dependencies among words in a sentence. Again, a theory that stresses a simple association between adjacent words is inadequate.

Chomsky has also argued that language acquisition cannot be explained in terms of children's language experience. His primary argument is called the **poverty of stimulus argument** (Chomsky, 1980). This argument states that there is not enough information in the language samples given to children to fully account for the richness and complexity of children's language. Sentences (9) through (12) [from Caplan and Chomsky (1980)] illustrate the point:

(9)   John believes he is incompetent.
(10) John believes him to be incompetent.
(11) John wants him to win.
(12) John wants Bill to see him.

Our knowledge of the language tells us that the *he* in sentence (9) and the *him* in sentence (12) could refer to John, though they need not. In contrast, the *him* in sentences (10) and (11) cannot refer to John. It is doubtful that anyone's parents systematically distinguished between the *him* in sentences (10) and (11) versus the *him* in sentence (12). In fact, most people wouldn't know how to explain such a difference. Still, we recognize the difference and, moreover, can make a great number of other linguistic discriminations about much more complex aspects of language that we are similarly unable to explain in an explicit manner. Chomsky's argument is this: the language children acquire is intricate and subtle, and the sample of speech given to them during the course of language development is anything but. Therefore, although parents may assist the child's language development is some ways and influence the rate of development somewhat, the pattern of development is not based on parental speech but on innate language knowledge.

The Chomskyan revolution had a powerful effect on psychological thinking about language. In the late 1960s, Chomsky (1968) noted that "the study of language may very well, as was traditionally supposed, provide a remarkably favorable perspective for the study of human mental processes" (p. 98) and that linguistics could be profitably viewed as a branch of cognitive psychology. That is, linguists were examining the kinds of linguistic knowledge needed for ordinary language use and realized that this knowledge must be used, in some way, by those who use the language. As Slobin (1971, p. 3) puts it, a person who has learned a language has formed something that is "psychologically equivalent" to a grammar. Thus, psychologists became very interested in linguistics in general and in Chomsky's transformational grammar in particular (see Chapter 2).

The psychologist George Miller played an important bridge between psychology and linguistics by introducing psychologists to Chomsky's ideas and their psychological implications. Miller collaborated with Chomsky on several articles and papers in the early 1960s (for example, G. A. Miller & N. Chomsky, 1963) and was at the forefront of research during this period to determine the psychological reality of linguistic rules (see, for example, G. A. Miller & S. Isard, 1963).

Language development became an especially popular topic for investigation during this period. Several **longitudinal investigations** of child language, in which a sample of a child's speech is collected at several points over a period of years, emerged in the early 1960s (Braine, 1963; W. Miller & S. M. Ervin, 1964), and various "grammars" for child language were written, modeled after adult grammars but differing in the specific rules (Bloom, 1970; R. Brown, 1973a). The major questions for language acquisition researchers were posed in the following way: What set of rules governs the child's developing grammar and when does this set develop?

Theoretical analyses of language development emphasized the role of innate factors. Together with Chomsky, the most influential person in this regard was Eric Lenneberg, whose 1967 book *The Biological Foundations of Language* pulled together evidence from aphasia, studies of delayed language development (for example, mental retardation), and the available neurophysiological information into an elegant argument for the role of innate factors in language development. Another strong advocate of innate factors is David McNeill (1966, 1970), who has proposed a theory of development based on the concept of language universals.

The revolution of the 1960s and early 1970s emphasized the role of linguistic theory in psycholinguistic research and the role of innate mechanisms in language acquisition. These themes continue to be influential, but there are indications that psychological interest in linguistic theory has waned. Reber (1987) examined the number of references to Chomsky in psycholinguistic studies and found that they rose sharply in the late 1960s, peaked in the middle 1970s, and then fell off by the early 1980s. Although it might be interesting to look at citations of other linguists, these data nonetheless appear to reflect the trend among psychologists to shy away from directly incorporating linguistic concepts into psychological research. Reber cites several reasons for these changes. One was that throughout the 1960s and 1970s there were rapid and (to psychologists, at least) confusing changes in linguistic theories (see Newmeyer, 1986). These changes made it difficult for psychologists to base their studies on any particular linguistic view, and some psychologists become wary of linguistics, preferring instead to develop a psychological view of language that was not tied to any specific linguistic theory. As Blumenthal (1987) has observed, there is a historical symmetry in these reactions—60 years ago, linguists such as Bloomfield pulled away from psychology for much the same reasons.

Reber also points out the growing realization that the two fields were quite distinct in their methodologies. A distinction may be drawn between two intellectual traditions, **rationalism** and **empiricism.** To some extent, this distinction is reminiscent of the familiar one between heredity and environment, or nature and nurture: rationalists emphasize the role of innate factors in human behavior, whereas empiricists stress the role of experience in behavior. But there is another difference between the two traditions that deals with the mode of inquiry. Rationalists emphasize the use of argument, whereas empiricists favor the collection of data as a means of evaluating hypotheses. For the most part, linguists approach language in a rationalistic manner; psychologists, even those who are sympathetic with the notion of innate factors, favor the empirical method. As a consequence of these differences, ideas tend to be evaluated somewhat differently in the two fields (Pylyshyn, 1972, 1973; Watt, 1970). In retrospect, it may have been too unrealistic to expect that two disciplines with their own histories and methodologies would mesh very easily.

Current Directions

Where do things stand now? It is always more precarious to describe events that are currently in progress than those well in the past, but it is possible to discern several themes of psycholinguistic work over the last 15 to 20 years. One is that the field has become more interdisciplinary. In particular, as noted earlier in the chapter, psycholinguistics has increasingly been viewed as a portion of the interdisciplinary field of cognitive science, which includes contributions from computer science, philosophy, neuroscience, and related fields.

Second, the wave of interest in syntax that occupied psychological interest after the Chomskyan revolution has spurred interest in other aspects of language. One currently lively area of research deals with how people understand, remember, and produce **discourse,** units of language larger than the sentence, such as paragraphs and stories. Another is the **lexicon,** or mental dictionary—studies of individual words have become much more prominent in the last decade. And both areas, while of considerable theoretical importance, have also had practical applications. Studies of discourse have provided insights into conversational processes in psychotherapy (see Chapter 9), and studies of the lexicon have already been useful in increasing our understanding of how children learn to read (see Chapter 11).

One final theme concerns the ways psycholinguists look at child language acquisition. Interest in innate language mechanisms has been complemented by a resurgence of research of the child's linguistic environment. Adults speak to children in ways that are phonologically, semantically, syntactically, and pragmatically distinct from their speech to adults, and much research has examined the role of these language lessons in children's language acquisition.

On balance, psycholinguistics is a more diverse field than the one that existed a few decades ago. Neither psychology nor linguistics is dominated by a single theoretical viewpoint, and the input from other fields within cognitive science has added new perspectives and insights that have been incorporated into this growing field. At the same time, tangible progress has been made in applying psycholinguistic research to topics such as reading (Just & Carpenter, 1987), bilingualism (Hakuta, 1986), and language disorders (Caplan, 1987). These advances have been made possible by integrating the insights from different disciplines within cognitive science. For instance, Just and Carpenter's book on reading comprehension integrates linguistic theories of sentence structure, computer simulations of reading, and psychological experimentation on eye movements. These results give us reason to believe that interdisciplinary work on language, although it can produce tensions between different approaches, can ultimately be fruitful (see, especially, G. A. Miller, 1990).

Summary

The history of psycholinguistics can be divided into two periods of interdisciplinary activity separated by several decades of behaviorism. The first period was dominated by Wundt, who presented a cognitive view of language. The behaviorist position then held that verbal behavior can be explained in terms of the environmental contigencies of reinforcement and punishment. This view was criticized by Chomsky, leading to a second wave of psycholinguistic activity. This period was characterized by an effort to incorporate linguistic theory in psychological research as well as by the view that innate linguistic mechanisms are necessary to explain child language acquisition. Psycholinguistics is presently a more diverse field of study that draws insights and methodologies not only from psychology and linguistics but from adjacent fields of study as well.

Review Questions

1. Identify the two major questions that psycholinguists are interested in.
2. Define semantics, syntax, phonology, and pragmatics.
3. Distinguish between tacit and explicit knowledge.
4. What is a garden path sentence?
5. What aspects of linguistic knowledge appear to be disrupted in Wernicke's aphasia and what aspects are intact?
6. Summarize Wundt's theory of language production.
7. Why did behaviorists prefer to talk of verbal behavior instead of language?
8. When did the term psycholinguistics arise?
9. What arguments did Chomsky give against behaviorist views of language?
10. How does the field of psycholinguistics currently differ from the field of the 1960s?

Thought Questions

1. In sentence (1), our misreading of *deal* forces us to backtrack and do a good deal of extra mental work at the end of the sentence. Why don't we simply entertain both meanings of an ambiguous word until we know which one is appropriate?
2. If you discovered a person who spoke a language that no one else could understand, how would you go about trying to understand what the person was trying to say?

Linguistic Principles

- Linguists have attempted to identify those grammatical features that appear in all languages. Four properties that are pervasive are: duality of patterning, phrase structure, morphology, and linguistic productivity.
- American Sign Language shares these linguistic properties with spoken languages. Sign language differs from spoken language in its iconicity and simultaneous structure.
- A language consists of an infinite set of sentences. A person who knows a language knows its grammar, which consists of a finite set of rules.
- Transformational grammar distinguishes between two levels of sentence structure: deep structure and surface structure. Phrase-structure rules generate deep structures, and transformational rules operate on deep structures to produce surface structures.
- Lexical-functional grammar emphasizes the role of the lexicon in language use and deemphasizes the role of transformational rules.
- Government-binding theory assumes that our knowledge of language is a set of modules, each of which is dedicated to a particular aspect of language.

Introduction

The focus of this book is on how people process language—how we comprehend and produce spoken and written language—and how these skills are acquired. In order to understand these language processes, we need to understand the major properties of language as well as the processing characteristics of the individuals who use it. Chapter 3 examines what is presently known about how humans process information. This chapter deals with the structure of language.

As we saw in Chapter 1, being a fluent speaker of a language does not guarantee that one has any explicit knowledge of the language. For most of us, speaking is easy—it's an activity akin to breathing that we do without much thought or effort. We might then assume, erroneously, that anything so easy must be pretty simple. The study of language proves otherwise. As we learn how languages are organized, we realize how truly complex they are.

This chapter is organized into four sections. The first presents some basic grammatical concepts common to a number of linguistic theories. The second examines American Sign Language and considers whether the concepts introduced in the first section apply to a language in the visual modality. The third section discusses a historically significant theory of grammar called transformational grammar. Some of the problems in the theory are discussed as well, and these have led to newer theories, which are presented in the fourth and final section of the chapter.

Basic Grammatical Concepts

Anyone who has tried to learn a second language is well aware that the languages of the world differ in a number of respects. When learning Spanish, for instance, we must put aside the association we have learned between the sounds *see* and their meaning in English because the same sounds mean *yes* in Spanish. There are also aspects of other languages that do not correspond to anything in English; for instance, nouns in Spanish are masculine or feminine and take corresponding pronouns. These differences between languages are as apparent as the frustration in learning they sometimes produce.

Despite these differences, linguists have identified underlying similarities among languages. In particular, they have attempted to identify features that are found in all human languages but are not present in animal communication systems. What follows is a short list of properties that are commonly agreed to be pervasive among the world's languages and are of significant psychological interest.

Duality of Patterning

A grammatical concept that is basic to the study of language is called **duality of patterning** (Hockett, 1966). At one level, there is a large amount of meaningful elements, or words. At another level, there is a relatively small number of meaningless elements that are combined to form the words. In spoken languages, these meaningless elements are individual speech sounds. As Hockett notes, this form of duality does not appear to exist in animal communication.

Phones and phonemes   In order to explore this duality, we need to make a few distinctions. **Phones** are speech sounds. Two sounds are different phones if they differ in a physically specifiable way. For example, consider the *p* in the words *pill* and *spill*. There is a puff of air, known as **aspiration,** in *pill* that is not present in *spill*. You can tell the difference easily by placing a lighted match a few inches in front of your mouth as you pronounce the two sounds. Phones are indicated by brackets: the aspirated sound is symbolized as [p^h], the unaspirated as [p].

Phonemes are differences in sound that make a contribution to meaning; they are indicated by slashes. For example, the sounds /b/ and /d/ are considered to be different phonemes in English because they contribute to the difference in meaning between *big* and *dig*. Phonemes may be thought of as categories of phones; each phone is a physically distinct version of the phoneme but none of the differences between phones makes a difference to meaning. Notice that these phonemic categories vary from language to language. In English, aspiration is not phonemic, although it is in Thai, which would represent the sounds as /p^h/ and /p/.

Distinctive features   We can understand these patterns better if we think of phonemes as combinations of distinctive features. A **distinctive feature** is a characteristic of a speech sound whose presence or absence distinguishes the sound from other sounds. The phoneme /b/ is similar to the phoneme /p/ except that the vocal cords vibrate during the production of /b/ but not /p/. In distinctive feature theory, contrasts are binary with presence of the feature indicated by + and its absence by − . The phoneme /b/ is said to be + voicing whereas /p/ is − voicing. In a similar vein, /b/ is + bilabial, which means that the sound is articulated at the lips, and is + stop, meaning that the airflow from the lungs is completely stopped during production. Distinctive feature theory (Jakobson, Fant, & Halle, 1969) claims that these are independent units that are combined to form phonemes.

Let us turn to the question of how these small linguistic units are combined. The sequence of phonemes that may occur in any given language is constrained. Consider the sounds *port*, *plort*, and *pbort*. We easily recognize that the first one is a word, the second could be, and the third could not be, at least not in English. As a first approximation, we can state a phonological rule that explains these patterns in the following way.

(R 1) /p/ cannot be followed by /b/ at the beginning of a word.

The problem with this rule is that it is stated too narrowly. There are a number of other sequences in the language, such as *pt, bg, td, kb*, and many others, which are not allowed either. We must look for a broader generalization.

The concept of distinctive features is helpful here, since *p, t, b, g, d*, and *k* are all + stop. This enables us to reformulate the rule more generally.

(R 2) A word cannot begin with two stop consonants.

In the same vein, we may notice that aspiration is predictable in English. The pattern noted with *pill* and *spill* also applies to other voiceless stop consonants, such as *t* (*till/still*) and *k* (*kill/skill*). The aspirated sound occurs only at the beginning of the word; otherwise the unaspirated sound is pronounced. The proper rule is:

(R 3) Voiceless stop consonants are aspirated when they occur at the beginning of a word.

Thus, distinctive features are useful in identifying how to formulate linguistic rules.

A study by Miller and Nicely (1955) demonstrated that these distinctive features have psychological validity. Miller and Nicely constructed a set of syllables that consisted of one of 16 consonants followed by the vowel [a]. The syllables were presented to subjects under difficult listening conditions, with "white noise" (a hissing sound) in the background. The white noise was at a consistent level of loudness whereas the speech varied over seven levels of loudness. Subjects were asked to identify the sounds that they heard. They made more errors when the speech was softer. When errors were made, subjects tended to incorrectly hear a sound that was similar to the target sound in most features but differed in only one. For instance, if [b] was presented, subjects were more likely to err by identifying the sound as [d], which shares all features with [b] except + bilabial, than [f], which differs in a number of respects from the target.

Duality of patterning appears to be a universal property of language. Languages differ in their phonemes and in the rules by which the phonemes may be combined to form words. However, all languages have duality: a level at which there is a relatively small number of basic, meaningless elements and another level at which there is a large number of meaningful elements. And all languages have a systematic set of rules for combining the former into the latter.

Phrase Structure

A second central concept in grammatical description is **phrase structure.** Intuitively, we know that sentences can be divided into groups of words, or **constituents.** Consider the simple declarative sentence (1).

  (1) The drunken sailor saluted the puzzled cat.

Think about how you might put these words into groups. The primary break in the sentence is between *sailor* and *saluted.* This can be indicated by parentheses, as in sentence (2).

  (2) (The drunken sailor)(saluted the puzzled cat).

We can further subdivide the last group as follows:

  (3) (The drunken sailor)(saluted (the puzzled cat)).

The items in parentheses are the constituents of this simple declarative sentence. The first is a noun phrase (NP), which consists of a determiner (*the*), an adjective (*drunken*), and a noun (*sailor*). The second constituent is a verb phrase (VP), which consists of the verb (*saluted*) and then a second NP.

  Phrase-structure rules are syntactic rules that specify the permissible sequences of constituents in a language. Each phrase-structure rule "rewrites" a constituent into one or more other constituents. By using a series of rules, we can derive a sentence from top to bottom (that is, from the largest to the smallest constituent).

  A list of phrase-structure rules sufficient to generate this sentence is shown in Table 2-1. Phrase-structure rule 1 (PS 1), S $\longrightarrow$ NP + VP, is read "A sentence may be rewritten as a NP and a VP." Rule PS 2 means that NPs are rewritten as determiner and noun, with optional adjectives indicated by parentheses placed between the article and the noun. We can now expand each of these items on the left side and ultimately work our way through the entire sentence. The final four

Table 2-1. A Simple Set of Phrase-Structure Rules

PS 1 S (sentence)	$\longrightarrow$	NP + VP
PS 2 NP (noun phrase)	$\longrightarrow$	det + (adj) + N
PS 3 VP (verb phrase)	$\longrightarrow$	V + NP
PS 4 N (noun)	$\longrightarrow$	*sailor, cat, horse*
PS 5 V (verb)	$\longrightarrow$	*saluted, kissed*
PS 6 adj (adjective)	$\longrightarrow$	*drunken, puzzled, gregarious*
PS 7 det (determiner)	$\longrightarrow$	*a, the*

Table 2-2. Steps in the Derivation of *The drunken sailor saluted the puzzled cat*

1. Rule PS 1 NP + VP
2. Rule PS 2 det + adj + N + VP
3. Rule PS 3 det + adj + N + V + NP
4. Rule PS 2 det + adj + N + V + det + adj + N
5. Rule PS 7 *the* + adj + N + V + *the* + adj + N
6. Rule PS 6 *the* + *drunken* + N + V + *the* + *puzzled* + N
7. Rule PS 4 *the* + *drunken* + *sailor* + V + *the* + *puzzled* + *cat*
8. Rule PS 5 *the* + *drunken* + *sailor* + *saluted* + *the* + *puzzled* + *cat*

rules, called **lexical-insertion rules,** put words into the structure that has been built. The entire sequence of rules that produces the sentence is called a **derivation.** The step-by-step derivation of this sentence is shown in Table 2-2. The resulting phrase structure is shown in Figure 2-1.

Phrase-structure rules provide a good account of one type of sentence ambiguity called **phrase-structure ambiguity.** This type of ambiguity is illustrated by sentences such as (4):

(4) They are eating apples.

In these sentences, the assignment of words to constituents is ambiguous, and more than one tree structure, or phrase marker, could be made for each case. In (4), *eating* could be either a part of the verb or an adjective modifying apples. The two phrase markers for this sentence are shown in Figure 2-2.

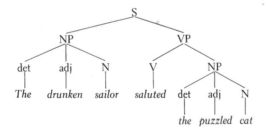

Figure 2-1. Tree diagram (phrase marker) for *The drunken sailor saluted the puzzled cat.*

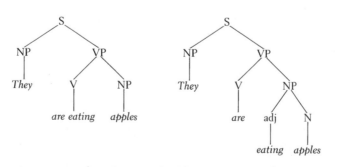

Figure 2-2. Tree diagrams for *They are eating apples.*

Morphology

We have discussed the words of a language in two ways. First, the phonemes and distinctive features that comprise words were defined. Next, we saw how these words are, in turn, combined to form phrase structures. Yet another important way in which we use words is to use different forms of the same word to convey different shades of meaning. The system of rules that governs this aspect of language is referred to as **morphology.**

The smallest meaningful unit in a language is referred to as a **morpheme.** Some words, such as *truck,* consist of only a single morpheme. Others, such as *bedroom,* consist of two or more morphemes. We may also distinguish between **free morphemes,** which may stand alone, and **bound morphemes** (also called grammatical morphemes), which, although contributing to word meaning, are not words themselves. Some of the major grammatical morphemes in English are shown in Table 2-3. Notice that these categories intersect. For instance, the intersection of tense and aspect produces the present perfect (5), the past perfect (6), the present progressive (7), and the past progressive (8):

(5) I have read the book.

(6) I had read the book.

(7) I am reading the book.

(8) I was reading the book.

Although all languages have a morphological system, languages differ in the grammatical distinctions they make and in the way in which they make them. When we use English correctly, we are, at some level, paying attention to these properties. For instance, we must pay attention to the number of both pronouns and verbs because they must agree for a sentence to be grammatical in English. When choosing tense, we must decide when in time a given action took place. In Chapter 14, we will consider the idea that these subtle linguistic differences influence the thought patterns of the individuals who speak the language in such a way that speakers of different languages have distinct world views.

Linguistic Productivity

There is no limit to the number of sentences in a language. The vast percentage of sentences we utter are novel but grammatically acceptable arrangements of

Table 2-3. Major Grammatical Morphemes in English

Morpheme	Distinction(s)	Examples
Number	Singular, Plural	Nouns: *ball, balls* Pronouns: *he/she, they* Verbs: *is, are*
Person	First, Second, Third	Pronouns: *I, you, he/she* Verbs: *I walk, you walk, he/she walks*
Tense	Present, Past, Future	Verbs: *I jump, I jumped, I will jump*
Aspect	Perfect, Progressive	Verbs: *I have read the book, I am reading the book*

words (the main exceptions being clichés, proverbs, and the like). Our ability to create and comprehend novel utterances is called **linguistic productivity** (or linguistic creativity). This notion was discussed by Hockett (1966) but has been emphasized most strongly by Chomsky (1957, 1966, 1980). One way to get a sense of this concept is to take an ordinary sentence, from conversation or from a written source, and then look for the identical sentence from another source (you will be looking for quite a while).

Given that the human brain is obviously finite, the problem of explaining how we can master a language with an infinite set of sentences remains a vexing problem for psycholinguists. It is not possible, for instance, to store an infinite set of sentences somewhere in the brain for later use. Most current psycholinguistic accounts make the assumption that instead of storing sentences, we store rules for creating sentences. The number of rules needed is finite, but the rules can be combined to form an unlimited number of sentences.

An example will clarify the point (Lasnik, 1990). A way to construct longer and more complex sentences is to embed one sentence inside another. We have already seen that we can rewrite a VP into V + NP, but it is also possible to rewrite a VP as follows:

(PS 8)   VP $\longrightarrow$ V + S

That is, the material following the verb can be a complete sentence, as in (9):

(9)   The child thinks the man left.

The phrase marker for (9) is shown in Figure 2-3. Furthermore, we can continue the process and embed more and more sentences (for example, *The woman knows the child thinks the man left*) into the earlier ones, until the sentences become quite difficult to comprehend.

This process can be described through the use of phrase-structure rules. We can combine PS 1 and PS 8 to get PS 9:

(PS 9)   S $\longrightarrow$ NP + V + S

Notice that S is on both sides of the arrow. A rule such as this, which refers to itself, is said to be **recursive**. Recursion is closely related to language productivity

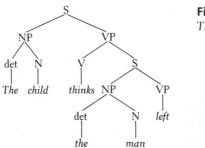

Figure 2-3.   Tree diagram for *The child thinks the man left.*

for, as we have seen, there is no limit to the number of times we can embed one sentence into another. Recursion appears to be a resilient property of human language use. Goldin-Meadow (1982) has shown that children provided with very little exposure to language nonetheless create language that has this property (see Chapter 12).

Linguistic productivity distinguishes human language from animal communication systems, which consist of a small number of discrete signals. In contrast, all human languages are open communication systems in which new words are coined as they are needed. Moreover, not only can we create new words, but we can, as we have seen with recursion, combine existing words in new combinations. These productive processes provide a measure of how complex and open-ended our language faculty is.

Not all aspects of language are productive. There are some aspects of language that are not rule-governed and so must be mastered by rote learning. One instance is the existence of strong verbs, which are verbs that are morphologically irregular. The most common in English are verbs that are irregular in the past tense, such as *went*, *fell*, and *ate*. Children trip over these forms early in their language development, preferring to overuse the past tense marker (for example, *goed*). Interestingly, most strong verbs are rather frequently used in the language, which is precisely what we would expect to see if children needed to learn each one in a rote manner.

Summary

Four basic grammatical concepts are: duality of patterning, phrase structure, morphology, and linguistic productivity. Words are composed of phonemes, which, in turn, are composed of distinctive features. In each instance, the smaller units are combined in a rule-governed manner to produce the larger units. Phrase-structure rules codify our intuitions about the groupings of words in a sentence. Some sentences are ambiguous and may be grouped in more than one way. Words consist of one or more units of meaning, or morphemes. The system of grammatical morphemes in a language provides speakers with a way of signaling subtle differences in meaning. Linguistic productivity refers to the fact that there is no limit to the number of sentences in a language. One type of phrase-structure rule, that of recursion, is responsible for some of this productivity.

Insights from Sign Language

We now consider some of the linguistic properties of American Sign Language (ASL). Unlike speech, signs are expressed in visual or spatial form. This enables us to examine the extent to which the grammatical concepts we have just considered generalize to language in a visual modality.

American Sign Language is sharply distinguished from manual forms of English that translate English sounds into signs. The best known is fingerspelling, which, as the name indicates, translates English words letter by letter into manual form. It is a secondary gestural system, derived from the English language. In contrast, ASL is independent of English, and is derived from French Sign Language (Frishberg, 1975). Although in the past, ASL was regarded as mere pantomime or grammatically deficient in various ways, several decades of scholarly research on ASL have put these ideas to rest.

Even if we accept the notion that ASL is an autonomous language, we still must ask what is its relation to spoken languages. We will begin to answer this question by considering some of the differences between signed (especially ASL) and spoken languages and then some of the similarities.

Differences Between Signed and Spoken Languages

Iconicity and arbitrariness   In English, as with most spoken languages, the principle of **arbitrariness** holds: there is no intrinsic relationship between the set of sounds and the object to which the sounds refer. For instance, there is no relation between the size of a word and the size of its referent; we have big words for small objects (for example, *caterpillar*) and small words for big objects (for example, *train*). According to Hockett (1966), this is a universal feature of human language.

American Sign Language, in contrast, possesses a high degree of **iconicity**: many of the signs resemble the objects or activities to which they refer. For example, the sign for *attention* is to hold both hands parallel to one another in front of one's face and then move them away from one's body. This suggests the act of putting on blinders to keep out distractions. Another iconic sign is the sign for *judge*, which is to place one's hands in front of one's body and then repeatedly move one up as the other goes down. This resembles a balancing scale that weighs various thoughts (Klima & Bellugi, 1979).

Interestingly, different sign languages have developed in different parts of the world. Examination of ASL, Danish Sign Language, and Chinese Sign Language indicates that even though all have iconic signs, the signs differ from language to language in the actual details. For example, the sign for *tree* in ASL is to hold the forearm upright with the hand spread wide, which suggests a tree trunk and its branches. In Danish Sign Language, the hands outline the rounded top of the tree and then the shape of the trunk, whereas in Chinese Sign Language, the hands portray the trunk and then move upward (Klima & Bellugi, 1979). Thus, even though ASL is iconic, this property does not automatically determine the form of the sign. Each language represents the object iconically in different ways.

Frishberg (1975) has claimed that the degree of iconicity has declined in ASL over the past 200 years. An example of this is the sign for *home*. Originally, this was a combination of two other signs, one for *eat* and one for *sleep*. The sign for *eat* involves holding one's hand in a cup form near the mouth. The sign for *sleep* involves laying a flat hand against one's cheek and tilting the head. Just as each of these individual signs are iconic, so was the original sign for *home*: eat followed by sleep. Over time, the sign shortened and became more conventionalized, so that its present form is a hand in cup form touching two different locations on the cheek, which is not as transparent in meaning as the original signs.

Thus, although many ASL signs are iconic, ASL has an increasing degree of arbitrariness. American Sign Language now has a dual system of reference—part iconic, part arbitrary.

Simultaneous and sequential structure A second difference between signed and spoken languages deals with the distinction between simultaneous and sequential structure. The structure of spoken languages is largely sequential in nature. We have rules that specify the correct order of phonemes within syllables, syllables within words, and words within sentences. Sign language differs in that it is organized spatially more than temporally. The meaning of utterances is not specified primarily by the order of signs (although order does matter) but by the combination of features simultaneously present in the sign.

Similarities Between Signed and Spoken Languages

Duality of patterning As with English, signs are composed of smaller elements that are meaningless. The three major parameters of signs are hand configuration, place of articulation, and movement (Stokoe, Casterline, & Croneberg, 1976). Stokoe and colleagues have identified 19 different values of hand configuration, or handshapes. These include an open palm, a closed fist, and a partially closed fist with the index finger pointing. Place of articulation, which has 12 values, deals with whether the sign is made at the upper brow, the cheek, the upper arm, and so on. Movement refers to whether the hands are moving upward, downward, sideway, toward or away from the signer, in rotary fashion, and so on, and includes 24 values. Although these values are meaningless in themselves, they are combined in various ways to form ASL signs. Thus, ASL has duality of patterning.

Figure 2-4 shows a series of minimal contrasts involving these three parameters. The top line shows three signs that differ only in hand configuration (that is, the signs are identical in place of articulation and movement). The second and third lines show minimal contrasts for place and movement, respectively. Notice how a change in a single parameter value can change the entire meaning of a sign.

It is also possible to analyze parameter values into distinctive features. Two such features for handshapes are index, which refers to whether the index finger is extended, and compact, which refers to whether the hand is closed into a fist or not. Among the signs in the top line of Figure 2-4, *candy* is + index, − compact, *apple* is + index and + compact, and *jealous* is − index and − compact. In order to determine if signers' perceptions of ASL are related to features such as these, Lane, Boyes-Braem, and Bellugi (1976) presented deaf subjects with a series of signs under conditions of high visual noise (a video monitor with a lot of "snow"). The subjects were asked to recognize the signs on the monitor. The researchers found that the large majority of recognition errors involved pairs of signs that differed in only one feature. That is, signs with similar patterns of distinctive features were psychologically similar to one another.

Morphology American Sign Language has a rich morphological system that signals various grammatical distinctions. For instance, the distinction between first

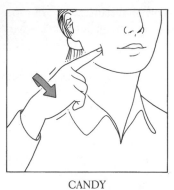

CANDY   APPLE   JEALOUS

(a)   Signs contrasting only in hand configuration

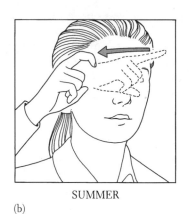
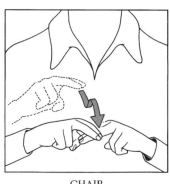
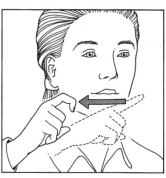

SUMMER   UGLY   DRY

(b)   Signs contrasting only in place of articulation

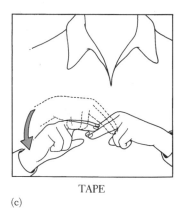
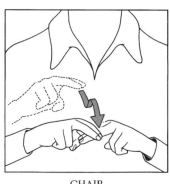

TAPE   CHAIR   TRAIN

(c)   Signs contrasting only in movement

Figure 2-4. Minimal contrasts of signs illustrating major parameters. (From E. S. Klima and V. Bellugi, *The Signs of Language*. Cambridge, MA: Harvard University Press, 1979.)

and second person is marked on a sign such as *ask*. When the utterance is in the first person (*ask me*), the movement of the sign is toward the signer, whereas when it is in the second person (*ask you*), the movement is away from the signer and toward the addressee. In addition to person, ASL marks number, aspect, and reciprocity (Poizner, Klima, & Bellugi, 1987). **Reciprocity** deals with the distinction between *they pinched them* and *they pinched each other*; that is, whether there is a subject that is the agent of the action and an object that is its recipient or whether there is mutual interchange between subject and object. In English, this distinction is made with pronouns. In ASL, there is a reciprocity morpheme on the verb so that *pinched each other* is conveyed by movement back and forth across the signer's body. Again, in all of these instances the marking of these distinctions is sequential in English and simultaneous in ASL.

Linguistic productivity   The property of embedding one sign into another also occurs in ASL (Poizner et al., 1987). Figure 2-5a shows the basic or uninflected sign for *give*. Figure 2-5b shows the durational form of the sign, which means to give on a continuous basis; c shows the exhaustive form, which means to give to each. It is then possible to combine both of these meanings into a single sign by embedding one into the other, as shown in d and e. Notice that these last two differ, just as *The woman knows the child thinks the man left* differs from *The child thinks the woman knows the man left*.

Phrase structure   As we have seen, English marks grammatical categories, such as subject and verb, via word order. American Sign Language sometimes does this as well; for example, with transitive verbs (verbs that require a direct object), the order in which the constituents are signed is subject–verb–object (SVO) (Poizner et al., 1987). Thus, ASL makes some use of temporal order.

American Sign Language also uses spatial processes to convey syntactic distinctions. For example, ASL marks nouns with a given location in space that is initially arbitrary but retained in subsequent references to the noun. Other nouns are given other unique locations. A sentence with the same signs in the same order will have different meanings if there are different spatial indices (Poizner et al., 1987). This system actually reduces some of the ambiguity in language. For example,

(10)   He said he hit him, and then he fell down.

is ambiguous in English, but since each pronoun has its own spatial index, the sentence has a clear interpretation in ASL.

Significance of Sign Language

This introductory survey of ASL reveals some clear differences between ASL and spoken languages as well as some underlying similarities. This combination of properties makes it especially significant for several aspects of psycholinguistics. I

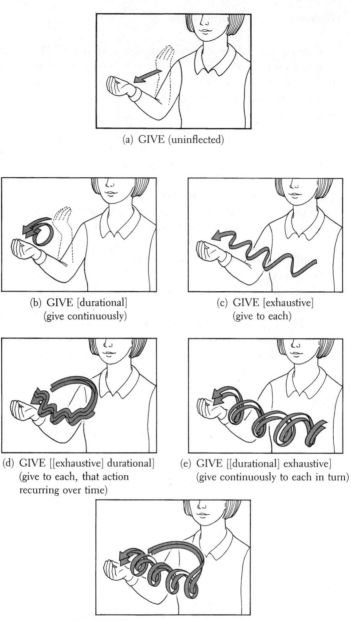

(a) GIVE (uninflected)

(b) GIVE [durational]
(give continuously)

(c) GIVE [exhaustive]
(give to each)

(d) GIVE [[exhaustive] durational]
(give to each, that action
recurring over time)

(e) GIVE [[durational] exhaustive]
(give continuously to each in turn)

(f) GIVE [[[durational] exhaustive] durational]
(give continuously to each in turn,
that action recurring over time)

Figure 2-5. Recursive nesting of morphological processes in ASL. (a) The uninflected sign *give*. (b, c) *Give* under single inflections. (d) One combination of inflections (exhaustive in durational). (e) Another combination of inflections (durational in exhaustive). (f) Recursive applications of rules (durational in exhaustive in durational). (From H. Poizner, E. S. Klima, and U. Bellugi, *What the Hands Reveal about the Brain.* Cambridge, MA: MIT Press, 1987.)

will simply note here several differences that we shall consider in the coming chapters.

One is the topic of language production. Although speech is produced using the same channel as we use for breathing, ASL is independent of breathing. Sign production can occur entirely in parallel with, and unimpeded by, respiratory activity. Because some of the pauses we make during speech are for respiratory purposes and others are for cognitive and linguistic purposes, we might expect some interesting differences in the way the two languages are produced (see Chapter 8).

Another area of research that has gained from sign language research concerns language acquisition. This is in part because, unfortunately, many deaf children are not exposed to a consistent language model in their early years since most deaf children have hearing parents who do not know ASL. This provides a basis for understanding the role of the environment in language development (see Chapters 10 and 12).

Finally, the link between language and the brain could well be different in speech versus sign. It is commonplace these days to hear of differences between the two hemispheres of the brain, with the left being regarded as verbal and the right as skilled at spatial tasks. What then might be the neurological arrangement of a spatial language? (See Chapter 13.)

Summary

American Sign Language has its own set of grammatical rules and is a language that is independent of English. Our preliminary look at ASL indicates some striking similarities in its grammatical organization, suggesting that some of the basic concepts we have been discussing might be universal. At the same time, there are significant differences between ASL and English, and we will examine these further.

Because the similarities and differences between ASL and spoken languages are so intriguing, we will return periodically to the study of ASL throughout this book.

Transformational Grammar

Transformational grammar was an influential theory of grammar formulated by Chomsky in the late 1950s (Chomsky, 1957). Chomsky revised this theory several times, most notably in 1965, before developing his current approach, government-binding theory. Despite the fact that it is no longer considered a viable model of language, transformational grammar commands our attention for two reasons. One is that this theory inspired a great deal of psycholinguistic work, and we need to understand the theory in order to understand the basis for the psycholinguistic studies. The second reason is that transformational grammar provides a basis for understanding more current grammatical theories. Several of the key assumptions underlying transformational grammar appear, in somewhat modified form, in later views.

Language and Grammar

Before discussing transformational grammar, we need to understand the relationship between grammar and language a little more precisely. A **language** can be defined as an infinite set of well-formed sentences. As we have seen, there is no limit to the number of sentences in a language. A **grammar** is a formal device with a finite set of rules that generates the sentences in the language. This notion of generation is similar to the notion of deduction in mathematics or logic: we can deduce the sentences in a language by using the rules of the grammar. Grammars thus are theories of language, composed of more specific hypotheses about the structure or organization of some part of the language.

Evaluation of grammars   If a grammar is a theory of language, how do we evaluate how good a theory it is? Chomsky (see Greene, 1972, for a lucid discussion) has suggested three criteria. First, the grammar must specify what is and what is not an acceptable sequence in the language. This criterion is referred to as **observational adequacy,** and it applies at several levels of language. We know at the phonological level that *pbort* is not an acceptable sequence; a grammar is observationally adequate (at the phonological level, at least) if it generates all the acceptable sequences in a language and none of the unacceptable sequences. Similarly, at the syntactic level we want the grammar to have rules that generate grammatical sentences without also generating strings of words we would regard as ungrammatical.

The second criterion is that the grammar must specify the relationships between various sequences in the language, a criterion known as **descriptive adequacy.** It is not enough for the grammar to mark a sequence as permissible; it must also explain how it relates to other sentences that are similar in meaning, opposite in meaning, and so on. If, for example, two sentences are similar in meaning but differ in syntax, the grammar should be able to explain this fact.

The third criterion is called **explanatory adequacy.** Chomsky points out that it is theoretically possible for a number of grammars, all based on different principles, to attain these two forms of adequacy. How then does the linguist determine which of all of descriptively adequate grammars is the best? Chomsky's answer pertains to language acquisition in children. He suggests that the child learning a language is presented with samples of the language and must determine the grammar from these samples. Chomsky notes, however, that even though the incoming data may be consistent with any number of grammars, children choose one particular grammar. This implies that there are certain innate language constraints that enable the child to deduce the correct grammar. These innate language mechanisms would presumably be related to linguistic universals common to all languages. Thus, the final level of adequacy goes beyond the ability to describe patterns in a particular language; instead, it involves the ability of a grammar to explain the role of linguistic universals in language acquisition.

These criteria have played a significant role in the development and evaluation of linguistic theories. In fact, Chomsky (1957) initially developed transformational grammar because of the descriptive inadequacy of a grammar based on phrase-structure rules. Let us now turn our attention to transformational grammar.

Deep and Surface Structure

A crucial insight into language is that sentences have more than one level of structure. In transformational grammar, this insight is captured in the distinction between deep structure and surface structure. These are both tree structures, differing in emphasis. **Deep structure** is the underlying structure of a sentence that conveys the meaning of a sentence. **Surface structure** refers to the superficial arrangement of constituents and is closer to how the sentence is actually pronounced. There are three basic arguments for the usefulness of this distinction. First, consider sentence (11):

(11)   Flying planes can be dangerous.

This sentence is ambiguous, but not in the sense that the constituents may be grouped in more than one way, as in sentence (4) (page 26). Here the ambiguity comes from the (optional) deletion of certain elements of the sentence (or, more precisely, the deep structure of the sentence). The sentence may be paraphrased roughly as *The act of flying planes can be dangerous* or *Planes that are flying can be dangerous*. This type of ambiguity, called **deep-structure ambiguity,** comes from a single surface structure that is derived from two distinct deep structures. It cannot be explained by phrase-structure rules.

A second reason for the distinction is that some pairs of sentences are similar in their phrase structure but not in their underlying structure. Consider, for example, sentences (12) and (13).

(12)   John is easy to please.
(13)   John is eager to please.

These sentences are apparently similar, but their paraphrases reveal their dissimilarity. We can explain this by observing that *John* is the object of the deep structure in (12) and is the deep-structure subject in (13).

Third, other pairs are quite distinct in their surface arrangement but similar in their deep structure, such as the following sentences in active (14) and passive voice (15).

(14)   Arlene played the tuba.
(15)   The tuba was played by Arlene.

In this case, the active and passive sentences are considered two manifestations of the same deep structure.

Transformational Rules

Within transformational grammar, the entire derivation of a sentence is a two-part process. First, phrase-structure rules are used to generate the underlying tree structure we have referred to as the deep structure. Second, a sequence of **transformational rules** (sometimes simply called **transformations**) is applied to the deep structure and the intermediate structures (those between the deep and surface structure), ultimately generating the surface structure of the sentence. Unlike phrase-structure rules, which apply to only one constituent at a time, transformations apply to entire strings of constituents. They transform them by adding, deleting, or moving constituents.

Let us look at a few transformations and see how they work. One is called the **particle-movement transformation.** We know that the following two sentences mean the same thing.

(16)   John phoned up the woman.
(17)   John phoned the woman up.

The concern is with the placement of the particle *up*; in these sentences, the particle may occur either just before or just after the noun phrase. Accordingly, we might write two different phrase-structure rules for the two instances, the first conforming to

(PS 10)   VP $\longrightarrow$ V + (part) + NP

and the second to

(PS 11)   VP $\longrightarrow$ V + NP + (part)

The problem with this approach is that it does not reveal the similarity between the two sentences; they are derived separately, using different phrase-structure rules. An alternative approach is to assume that the two sentences have the same deep structure and to apply the particle-movement transformation to (16). The transformational rule looks like this:

(T 1)   V + part + NP $\longrightarrow$ V + NP + part

Consider now the following sentences:

(18)   John phoned up the interesting woman.
(19)   John phoned the interesting woman up.
(20)   John phoned up the woman with the curly hair.
(21)   John phoned the woman with the curly hair up.

Notice that in each case the particle is shifted around the entire NP—two words in (17), three in (19), and six in (21). The point is that the particle movement is defined in terms of constituents, not words. This condition gives transformational grammar tremendous power to apply to an infinite number of NPs. Instead of stating the rule in terms of the number of words, which will vary from sentence to sentence, we state it in terms of grammatical structures such as NPs. Because the movement is dependent upon the grammatical structure, rules such as this are said to be **structure-dependent.**

A second example is **passive transformation.** Simplified somewhat, the rule is as follows:

(T 2) $NP\,1 + V + NP\,2 \longrightarrow NP\,2 + be + V + \text{-}en + by + NP\,1$

This complex transformation, which might be involved in the derivation of sentences such as (8), contains several elementary operations. Let us begin with the active sentence (22) and then add the transformations needed to produce the passive sentence. First we invert subject and object, a transformation that produces (23). (Sequences that are not grammatically acceptable are, by convention, marked with an asterisk.) Then we insert the preposition *by* in (24). Finally, we add the auxiliary verb to (25):

(22)   Arlene played the tuba.
(23)   *The tuba played Arlene.
(24)   *The tuba played by Arlene.
(25)   The tuba was played by Arlene.

One final property of transformational rules deserves mention. These rules may be blocked under certain circumstances. For example, the particle-movement transformation does not work with pronouns:

(26)   John called them up.
(27)   *John called up them.

These restrictions on transformations would be specified in the description of the rule. The rule would operate under specified conditions, but would be blocked when these conditions did not apply.

Psychological Reality of Transformational Grammar

As indicated earlier, much psycholinguistic research in the early and middle 1960s was based on transformational grammar. This research was guided by the belief that the structures and rules of transformational grammar were psychologically real; that is, that they were a part of how people comprehend and produce language. One assumption that was made was that the surface structure was the starting point for comprehension and that the deep structure was the endpoint;

the roles were assumed to be reversed for production. If so, then it would be reasonable to assume that the distance between surface and deep structure, as measured by the number of transformations in a sentence's derivation, would be an accurate index of the psychological complexity of the sentence. This view was called the **derivational theory of complexity,** or DTC.

Early studies were encouraging. A variety of studies showed that negative sentences such as

(28)   The sun is not shining.

were more difficult to comprehend than the corresponding affirmative form such as

(29)   The sun is shining.

But these sentences differ in meaning as well as transformational complexity, so this is hardly conclusive. Later studies directly contradicted DTC. Sentence (30) is, for example, transformationally more complex than (31):

(30)   The boy was bitten.
(31)   The boy was bitten by the wolf.

That is, sentence (30) requires a deletion transformation, but neither intuition nor experiment has revealed any relationship to processing difficulty. Similarly, there is no psychological difference between sentences that have undergone particle-movement transformation and those that have not. These studies have been reviewed extensively elsewhere (Cairns & Cairns, 1976; Fodor, Bever, & Garrett, 1974; Slobin, 1971).

As Berwick and Weinberg (1983) point out, these results do not necessarily mean that the linguisic theory of transformational grammar is faulty. It could be that the linguistic theory is correct but some of the psychological assumptions guiding DTC are faulty. However, in recent years attention has turned away from transformational grammar and toward newer models of language.

Summary

Transformational grammar assumes that sentences have a deep structure and a surface structure. The deep structure is derived by a series of phrase-structure rules, and the surface structure is derived from the deep structure by a series of transformational rules. This approach generated considerable psycholinguistic research, not at all of which provided sympathetic results. Nonetheless the transformational approach has influenced current grammatical theories, to which we now turn.

Current Grammatical Theories

There are a number of linguistic theories that have been developed since the decline of transformational grammar (Newmeyer, 1986). Two are of special interest to psychologists: **lexical-functional grammar** and **government-binding theory.**

Lexical-Functional Grammar

Lexical-functional grammar (LFG) was developed as an alternative to transformational grammar by Bresnan (1978). It consists of a constituent structure, a functional structure, and lexical entries.

Constituent structure The constituent structure in LFG is similar to the phrase structure we have already considered except that it is generated by phrase-structure rules only; no transformational rules are involved.

Functional structure The functional structure of a sentence compiles all of the information needed for semantic interpretation. The functional structure, simplified somewhat, for sentence (32) is presented below (from Pinker, 1984).

> **(32)**   John told Mary to leave Bill.

Pred	*"tell* (subj, obj, V-comp)"	
Tense	past	
Subj	*John*	
Obj	*Mary*	
V-comp	pred	*leave*
	subj	*Mary*
	obj	*Bill*

This sentence is referred to as a complement construction because a verbal complement (*to leave Bill*) rather than a direct object completes the verb phrase. The functional structure is generated by phrase-structure rules and the lexical entries. The pred (predicate) listing indicates the main verb and what other grammatical elements are required by this verb (*tell* requires a subject, an object, and the complement). In addition, the functional structure indicates the tense of the main verb, the subject and object of the sentence, and the verb, subject, and object of the complement.

Lexical entries The role of the lexicon is, as one might expect, significant in LFG. In most grammars, the entry for a word includes its meaning, its spelling, its pronunciation, and syntactic characteristics such as part of speech. In LFG, lexical entries also include the various forms of the word (for example, *kiss, kissed, kissing*) and the different kinds of sentences into which each form would fit. For verbs, this includes the arguments or semantic roles, such as the **agent** (the person doing the action) and the **patient** (the one to whom the action is done) that are associated with the verb as well as the surface structure designation, such as subject or object, which goes with it.

Consider sentences (33) and (34):

(33)   Mary kissed John.
(34)   John was kissed by Mary.

The lexical entry for *kiss* would indicate its underlying semantic structure as

kiss: (agent, patient)

That is, the verb requires both an agent and a patient (*John kissed* is not a grammatical sentence). In addition, the entry includes various forms of the word, including

kiss: agent = subject; patient = object

and

(be) kiss: agent = object; patient = subject

The first verb form, used in sentences in the active voice, assigns the agent role to the surface-structure subject, and the patient to the surface object. The second form, used in passive sentences, assigns the patient to the subject, and the agent to the object of the preposition *by*.

By storing this additional information in the lexical entry, the derivation of passive sentences becomes shorter than in traditional transformational grammar. When the surface structure includes a form of the verb *kiss*, that lexical entry is retrieved and fitted into the sentence. The grammatical information in the entry allows us to interpret the sentence semantically (that is, to interpret *John* as patient). The constituent structure of a passive sentence in LFG looks like a passive sentence, not like an active sentence, and no passive transformational rule is involved. The meaning relation between these two sentences is preserved through lexical rules that specify the relation between different forms of a word, not by transformational rules.

The major significance of LFG is the shunting of most of the explanatory burden onto the lexicon and away from transformational rules. We will see the psychological basis for this in the next chapter. In addition, we will consider the LFG account of sentence comprehension in Chapter 6.

Government-Binding Theory

Government-binding theory (GB), proposed by Chomsky (1981), has also been called universal grammar, reflecting Chomsky's consistent emphasis on innate grammatical mechanisms.

Grammar as modular   One of the characteristics of GB is that grammar is seen as the interaction of several independent subsystems, or modules. Imagine a subsystem dedicated to performing one aspect of a complex task. Each of the modules may be relatively simple, but if there are enough of them and if they interact, the resulting overall system can be quite complex. In government-binding theory, the grammar is composed of seven modules, of which government and binding are two (Newmeyer, 1986).

The contrast with earlier transformational grammar is instructive. In transformational grammar, there was a one-to-one correspondence between a linguistic rule and various constructions. There was a passive rule for the passive construction, a negative rule for negative sentences, and so on. These rules were specified in highly specific ways. In contrast, in government-binding theory, the rules are simple and general (for example, there is a rule that allows movement of a constituent from one location in a sentence to another). These rules then are constrained in a variety of ways by one or more of the subsystems in the grammar.

Binding theory   One of the subsystems in government-binding theory is called **binding theory,** and it deals with how grammatical elements such as pronouns and names are related (or bound) to their antecedents in discourse. For example, consider sentences (35) and (36):

(35)   Helen reminded herself of the appointment.

(36)   Helen reminded her of the appointment.

In (35), our intuitions about the sentence are that *Helen* refers to an individual and that *herself* refers to the same individual. We may say that the pronoun and name are **coreferential.** In (36), in contrast, *Helen* and *her* are not coreferential. Another way of saying the same thing is to say that *herself* is bound to *Helen* but *her* isn't.

Lasnik (1990) provides some examples that illustrate some of the subtleties of binding. Consider sentences (37) and (38):

(37)   John thinks he won.

(38)   He thinks John won.

Notice that *John* and *he* may be coreferential in sentence (37), although it is possible that the two expressions refer to different individuals. In sentence (38), in contrast, *he* and *John* are not coreferential; *he* clearly refers to someone other than *John*.

As a first approximation account of these patterns, consider the following rule:

(GB 1)   If a pronoun precedes a full noun phrase, then the two expressions may not be coreferential.

This rule is consistent with sentences (37) and (38), but it is not difficult to find counterexamples, such as sentence (39):

(39)   After he ate lunch, John left.

Here, *he* and *John* may be coreferential, even though the pronoun precedes the name in the sentence. So, clearly, GB 1 is insufficient.

The difference between sentences (38) and (39) is in the degree of embedding of the pronoun in the phrase structure of the sentence. Figure 2-6 shows the phrase structure tree for (38). A phrase category (NP, VP, S, and so on) dominates another if the former is at a higher level in the tree structure than the latter. Notice that *he* is dominated only by the higher S category, whereas *John* is dominated by the lower S and VP, as well as the higher S, categories. Figure 2-7 shows the phrase-structure tree for sentence (39). Here *he* is dominated by a lower S, a PP (prepositional phrase), and a higher S category. *John* is dominated by a different lower S and the higher S categories.

We may now introduce a pair of rules that accounts for these patterns. Consider first GB 2:

(GB 2)   One noun phrase binds another if every category that dominates the former also dominates the latter.

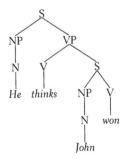

Figure 2-6.   Tree diagram for *He thinks John won.*

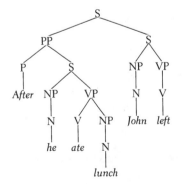

Figure 2-7.   Tree diagram for *After he ate lunch, John left.*

If we apply this rule to sentence (37), we find that *John* binds *he*, which accords with our intuition that *John* and *he* may be coreferential. If applied to sentence (38), the rule indicates that *he* binds *John*, which is not consistent with intuition. The reason for this is rule GB 3:

(GB 3) A pronoun may not bind a full noun phrase.

GB 3 blocks the normal binding process in sentence (37); the sentence is still grammatical, but only on the interpretation that *he* refers to a person other than *John*. Interestingly, (38) is not blocked in the same way because *he* and *John* are dominated by a different set of phrase categories.

In short, coreferentiality does not depend simply on whether the pronoun precedes the name. It depends crucially on whether or not these grammatical elements are embedded deep in the phrase structure. It is only when the pronoun is at a high level in the structure that the restrictions in GB 3 apply. These principles of binding are another example of the structure-dependent nature of linguistic rules.

Implications Obviously these grammatical facts are rather subtle. Chomsky (1965, 1980) has argued from these and related observations that there must be an innate grammatical mechanism that guides language acquisition. Moreover, Chomsky (1975) has argued that it is unlikely that any recourse to general principles of cognition can explain these linguistic patterns, as they appear to be quite specific to language.

As noted earlier, Chomsky's theory is sometimes referred to as universal grammar. In recent treatments, he has emphasized the notion of **parameters.** He claims that we all inherit a universal grammar that can be set to different parameter values corresponding to different languages. As we gain experience with our native language, we acquire these values and thus the language upon which they are based. One example is the **null-subject parameter** (sometimes called the pro-drop parameter). In English, sentences are required to have a subject, but in languages such as Italian and Spanish it is grammatically acceptable to drop the subject of a sentence. This parameter, then, has two values: subject and null-subject. It has been suggested that children begin with this parameter "set" to the null-subject value (Hyams, 1986). Children learning English would then have to be exposed to a certain amount of English sentences in order to "reset" this parameter to the subject value. This view carries the interesting implication that children acquiring English would initially drop their subjects just as Italian and Spanish children (correctly) do. This hypothesis has been the subject of considerable recent research in language acquisition (see Chapter 12).

Summary

Lexical-functional grammar and government-binding theory represent two new ideas in grammatical theory. The former is a response to transformational grammar that deemphasizes transformational rules and increases the role of enriched lexical entries in the grammar. These entries include different forms of a given verb that might be used in different sentences. These verbs are retrieved from the lexicon as the corresponding sentence frames are recognized. The latter GB conceives of grammar as a set of interacting modules that are dedicated to performing one aspect of the complex task of language. One module is binding theory, which explains the patterns of reference from pronouns and other terms to antecedents in discourse.

Review Questions

1. What is aspiration, and how is it related to the distinction between phones and phonemes?
2. What is wrong with a rule that states that a word cannot begin with two stop consonants?
3. Distinguish between free and bound morphemes.
4. How is duality of patterning represented in American Sign Language?
5. Why is American Sign Language of interest to psycholinguists?
6. Define grammar, and state its relation to language.
7. Distinguish between phrase-structure rules and transformational rules.
8. What is the current status of the derivational theory of complexity?
9. In lexical-functional grammar, what is the advantage of storing syntactic information in the lexical entries of words?
10. Define binding.

Thought Questions

1. Is productivity an attribute of human language, or of the human mind generally, or both?
2. Is a stereo system modular? Is a car? What might be the advantages or disadvantages of a modular organization of language?
3. The discussion of American Sign Language indicates that it is becoming progressively less iconic and more arbitrary. Speculate as to why this might be occurring.

3

Psychological Mechanisms

- The acts of comprehending and producing language are performed within the constraints of our information processing system. This system consists of three structural components—sensory memory, working memory, and permanent memory—along with a set of control processes that govern the flow of information within the system.
- A number of issues regarding language processing have been raised. These include whether we primarily use serial or parallel processes, whether we tend to use top-down or bottom-up processes, whether language processes are primarily automatic or controlled, and the extent to which language processing displays modularity.
- Children appear to process information very differently than adults, but studies of the development of the processing system suggest that most of the system is developmentally invariant.

Introduction

The linguistic perspective sketched in Chapter 2 provides an important yet incomplete view of the psychology of language. This perspective places a strong emphasis on linguistic structures of various sorts, such as phrase structure, distinctive features, and morphological structure. To be sure, these ideas are advanced with the belief that a fuller understanding of human language will reveal deep insights into the human mind. The notion of productivity, to take but one example, is a property not only of language but of language users. This implies that the means to generate an unlimited number of sentences is present, in some form, in the human mind. It is clear that this perspective has enriched our knowledge of human cognitive functioning and will continue to do so.

At the same time, there are some important issues not fully addressed in most linguistic accounts. Linguistic investigations have typically focused on what we have called the knowledge question: what kinds of knowledge underlie ordinary language usage? There has been relatively less attention paid to the process question of how this knowledge is utilized. That is, linguistic structure does not determine language processing. Given a particular phrase structure, there are still any number of ways we might comprehend or produce a sentence with that structure. More to the point, some of these ways might be preferred over others for purely psychological reasons: they might be easier, or pose less burden on memory, and so on.

In this chapter, we will discuss the psychological mechanisms that are involved in using language. Together with the linguistic principles presented in Chapter 2, these mechanisms provide the basis for an integrated understanding of language use. Language processing is a joint product of linguistic principles and psychological mechanisms.

This chapter consists of three sections. The first presents an overview of the human information processing system. This provides a framework for understanding human cognition, whether it operates within the linguistic sphere or not. The second section applies these concepts more directly to language processing and examines a series of issues that arise in this context. The final section sketches the development of the processing system and examines the question of which portions of the system may be present at the time that most children acquire their native language.

The Information Processing System

A general model of information processing is shown in Figure 3-1. According to this interpretation of mental functioning, environmental information is successively encoded, stored, and retrieved by a set of distinct mental structures. The emphasis is on the flow of information through the system. Environmental stimuli—the constellation of sights, sounds, and other sensory events to which we are constantly exposed—are represented in each structure in a particular way. We assume that this system is used in a wide range of activities, including remembering lists of numbers, solving mathematical problems, and, of course, using language.

The model consists of three mental structures and a set of processes that move information from one structure to another. Let us first examine each of these structures and then consider their interrelationships.

Sensory Stores

The **sensory stores** take in the variety of colors, tones, tastes, and smells that we experience each day and retain them, for a brief period of time, in a raw, unanalyzed form. It is assumed that we have one sensory store for each sensory system, although only the visual and auditory sensory stores have been studied in any detail.

The visual sensory store has been studied by Sperling (1960). He presented subjects with arrays of letters or digits for very brief periods of time, such as 50 milliseconds (one-twentieth of a second). A typical array consisted of twelve

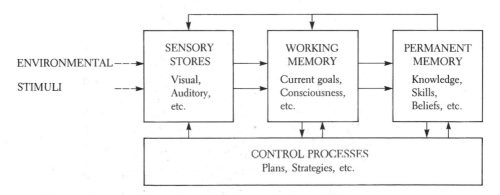

Figure 3-1. A general model of information processing.

letters in a 3 × 4 array (four columns and three rows). Subjects saw these arrays briefly and then were asked to report what they saw. Typically subjects could report only about four or five of the twelve letters. However, many reported subjectively that they could see all of the letters in the array but lost some of them by the time they had reported the others.

This finding provided a challenge for Sperling, for if subjects did indeed retain all of the items for such a brief period of time, then the procedure of having subjects report all of the items (a procedure known as whole report procedure) was likely to underestimate their retention. Sperling's response to this problem was ingenious. He devised a **partial report technique** in which the subjects had to report only a portion of the entire array. Subjects were presented with a high-pitched tone if they were to recall the top row of the array, a medium-pitched tone for the middle row, and a low-pitched tone for the bottom row. The tone was presented immediately after the array was removed. Sperling's reasoning was that if subjects did not know which row they were to report, then they would have to retain the entire array for a brief time. The results were that subjects reported about three-fourths of the row under the partial report conditions, suggesting that they were able to retain about three-fourths of the entire array. Sperling concluded that a considerable amount of information in a stimulus array is available immediately after it is presented.

Further studies examined the duration of storage in the visual sensory store. This was done by delaying the presentation of the tone signal. When the tone was delayed for only 1 second, the performance in the partial report condition declined to 36%, which was approximately the level of performance in the whole report condition (Sperling, 1960). Sperling thus inferred that information in the visual sensory store persisted for approximately 1 second.

Comparable studies of the auditory sensory store (Darwin, Turvey, & Crowder, 1972) have found that the advantage of partial report over whole report persists for approximately 4 seconds. This difference might well be important in language processing. When we are processing language visually (typically in reading), we can always go back and reread, but this is not possible with speech. The relatively longer duration of the auditory store may enable us to reanalyze auditory messages that were not understood initially.

As the first step in the information processing sequence, the sensory stores represent information in a literal, unanalyzed form. Most of the information in these stores disappears very rapidly because it is not germane to our current goals. But the processes of taking in new information, identifying it, and choosing whether or not to process it more extensively, although rapid, take a measurable amount of time. The sensory stores perform the invaluable function of preserving this information long enough for more extensive processing to be initiated.

Working Memory

The second type of memory has been traditionally referred to as **short-term memory** and more recently as **working memory**. Although the meanings of the terms are similar, there is a subtle difference between them. Let us begin with short-term memory and then examine the more current term.

The need for short-term storage is easy to state. The contents of the sensory stores are held for at most a few seconds, but many cognitive acts require that we hold onto information for longer periods of time. Many apparently simple acts, such as solving problems in your head, mentally retracing a path after losing your keys, and remembering the topic of a conversation after a distraction, are in fact a complex series of decisions, and it is necessary to have a temporary holding place for intermediate decisions.

Short-term memory is severely limited in size; it can hold approximately seven plus or minus two items of information. As a consequence, we cannot take in a string of digits such as 71539260932168352370 and repeat it verbatim unless we reduce the strain on short-term memory. One way to do this is by **chunking,** in which we group individual pieces of information into larger units. With a little practice, nearly everyone can learn to chunk a 20-digit number into units such as 715-392-6093 and 216-835-2370. This arrangement is much easier to remember, at least for me, since these are the phone numbers of two of my friends.

Working memory differs from short-term memory in that the term conveys a more dynamic view of memory processes. Whereas short-term memory has usually been viewed as a passive repository of information, working memory has both storage and processing functions. The storage functions are similar to those credited to short-term memory—we hold onto a limited amount of information for a limited amount of time. The processing functions are related to the concept of processing capacity. **Processing capacity** refers to the total amount of cognitive resources we may devote to a task, and this is assumed to be limited. When tasks are new or difficult, they require more processing capacity, thereby leaving less space available for the storage function.

An example will clarify these concepts. Suppose you are asked to multiply 8 times 4 in your head. This would pose no problem. But if the numbers were 84 and 67, the task would be much more difficult. Part of your processing capacity would be devoted to performing the arithmetic operation of multiplying 4 by 7, and part of this capacity would be needed to retain the result in temporary storage while you then multiplied 8 by 6. Ultimately these two functions would be in conflict with one another, competing for the same limited pool of resources.

Permanent Memory

Permanent memory, which is also known as long-term memory, is a repository of our knowledge of the world. This includes general knowledge, such as the rules of grammar or of arithmetic, along with personal experiences, such as memories of your childhood. Permanent memory holds all of the information we have retained from the past that is not currently active (that is, in working memory). These memories are used to interpret new experiences and, in turn, the new events may later be added to this storehouse of information.

Tulving (1972) has distinguished between two types of permanent memory—semantic memory and episodic memory. **Semantic memory** refers to our organized knowledge of words, concepts, symbols, and objects. It includes such broad classes of information as motor skills (typing, swimming, bicycling), general knowledge (grammar, arithmetic), spatial knowledge (the typical layout of a house), and social skills (how to begin and end conversations, rules for self-disclosure). Semantic memory holds all of the information in permanent memory that is not tagged for a particular time or place. It holds the information that horses have four legs and a tail but not the memory of the last time you went horseback riding.

The latter event is held in your **episodic memory,** which holds traces of events that are specific to a time and a place. This is the memory that we use to keep a record of our personal experiences. It thus varies from person to person and time to time (it is constantly updated), whereas semantic memory is relatively stable. Episodic memory includes such items as what you had for breakfast this morning, what you were doing when you learned of the *Challenger* tragedy, and where you got your first job.

Semantic and episodic memory interact in our processing of information. Semantic information is used to interpret and recognize events and patterns in our environment by retrieving time-independent and context-free representations of stimulus patterns that are then matched with incoming information. That is, when information is stored in permanent memory, it involves both episodic and semantic information. For example, the knowledge that the Blue Jays won the 1992 World Series will be stored in our semantic memory as part of our general knowledge of baseball history, and our memory of how we learned about this event will be part of our episodic memory. Although not all of our semantic memory is derived from such episodes, much of what is there is a condensation of a number of experiences. We can often use an episodic trace to retrieve semantic information, as when we remember where a concept was presented on a page in a textbook and this memory helps us recall the concept itself. In other cases, we lose the episodic tags and all that remains is the general, semantic information about the event.

Relevance for Language Processing

Now let's explore the application of these concepts to the problem of how we comprehend spoken language. In comprehension, we may assume that as we hear a sentence the sounds are first stored briefly in the auditory sensory store. The sounds are held there for about 2 to 4 seconds, which gives us time to recognize the auditory pattern. **Pattern recognition** occurs when information from one of the sensory stores is matched with information retrieved from permanent memory. In order to recognize speech sounds, we must identify some of the acoustic cues that are presented in the speech signal, such as the frequency of some of the sounds. At some point, after recognizing the sounds, we are able to organize them into syllables and eventually words, although it is not clear exactly how or when that happens.

As noted, working memory is only able to hold about seven units of information. This could simply be seven words, but since many sentences are longer than this, we need some way to deal immediately with more than seven words. One way we do this is to chunk the words into grammatical constituents such as noun and verb phrases, thereby reducing the storage burden to perhaps two or three constituents. The processing function of working memory is used to organize the words into the constituents.

Permanent memory plays several roles. Semantic memory contains information on the speech sounds and words that we retrieve during pattern recognition. And while this process is going on, we are also building up an episodic memory representation of the ongoing discourse. That is, once we complete the processing of a given sentence, we might extract the gist of it and store that in episodic memory. Permanent memory would also be involved in finding antecedents for expressions such as pronouns; this would involve holding some information from previous sentences in memory long enough to establish coreferences.

Throughout this discussion, I have indicated that some processing could take place or might occur in a given way. In truth, a great deal remains to be learned regarding exactly how language processing takes place. The information processing system presented in this section leaves as many questions unanswered as it answers. It is best thought of as a framework for exploring how language processing takes place by providing a vocabulary for framing the important questions.

Summary

The general strategies by which the human mind encodes, stores, and retrieves information can be described independently of language. Three mental structures (sensory stores, working memory, and permanent memory) and a set of control processes are general features of human cognitive functioning.

Incoming sensory information is held in a literal or unanalyzed state in our sensory stores while information from permanent memory is retrieved to recognize the incoming patterns. The identified information, if relevant to the current activity, is held temporarily in working memory. As new information enters working memory, some of the older information is reorganized into larger units, other information is lost, and still other information is sent to permanent memory. The resulting permanent memory trace has both episodic and semantic attributes.

These concepts provide a framework for understanding how language processing occurs. Although it is generally agreed that we encode, store, and retrieve linguistic information along the general lines sketched here, the specific processes have yet to be addressed. We now turn our attention to these processes in the next section.

Central Issues in Language Processing

In this section we examine several alternative ways in which linguistic information can be handled by the information processing system. After discussing each of these processes individually, we will apply them to an extended example of language processing.

Serial and Parallel Processing

If a group of processes takes place one at a time, it is called **serial processing.** If two or more of the processes take place simultaneously, it is called **parallel processing.** Serial models have been influential in the study of language and cognition over the past quarter century, in part because many of the models were based on the electronic computer, which tends to execute processes rapidly in a serial manner.

Suppose we wish to develop a model of language production. We could take as our starting point the idea that the speaker wishes to convey. The ending point would be the actual articulation of the idea. But what happens in between? A serial model would divide the process into stages: there might be a stage devoted to developing the phrase structure of the sentence, another to retrieving the lexical items that are inserted into the structure, and still another to determining the correct pronunciation of these lexical items. The serial model would assume that these stages occur one at a time, with none overlapping (Fromkin, 1971). If, on the other hand, we assume a parallel model, all of these processes could take place at the same time (Dell, 1986). That is, we could be phonetically specifying one word while we search for the next word or both of the processes could take place as we flesh out the syntactic structure.

Rumelhart, McClelland, and the PDP Research Group (1986; McClelland, Rumelhart, & the PDP Research Group, 1986) have presented a version of a parallel model that they call **parallel distributed processing** (PDP). This model views the mind as "massively parallel"; that is, as simultaneously processing a large amount of information at the same time.

Some language examples are shown in Figure 3-2. In the first instance, we interpret the middle letter as an *h* in one word but as an *a* in the other despite the fact that the letter is physically identical in the two cases. The remaining four examples show degraded letters, with features of one or more of the letters being obscured. It is not difficult to identify what the word is in each case. At first glance, this may appear to be paradoxical. It seems reasonable to say that we are using the context to help decide the identity of the obscured letter. However, that context is a word and we normally think of first identifying the letters and then identifying the word. How can we use the word to help identify the letter? Rumelhart and McClelland suggest that the answer lies in parallel processing. Assume that we are identifying the individual letters and, at the same time, actively trying to fit the letters into various possible words. Some of the identified letters enable us to recognize the word as a familiar word, and then we identify the obscured letter from our knowledge of the spelling of the word. Thus, we are processing at the letter and word levels simultaneously.

Parallel distributed processing models have been described as neurally inspired because they use the brain, rather than the computer, as the dominant metaphor. There is a great deal of neural activity occurring throughout the brain at the same time. We know some properties of neural networks. We know that neurons can affect neighboring neurons in either an excitatory manner (causing the neighbor to become active, or "fire") or an inhibitory manner (reducing

Figure 3-2. Some ambiguous displays. Note that the second line shows that three ambiguous symbols can each constrain the identity of the others. Lines 3, 4, and 5 indicate that each of these characters is ambiguous and can assume other identities in other contexts. (From D. E. Rumelhart, J. L. McClelland, and the PDP Research Group, *Parallel Distributed Processing: Vol. 1. Foundations.* Cambridge, MA: MIT Press, 1986.)

the likelihood of the neighbor firing). Rumelhart and McClelland theorized a cognitive model built along the same lines—a vast, interconnected network of information nodes with each node influencing and being influenced by a large number of adjacent nodes. At present, PDPs are an important alternative to serial models.

Top-Down and Bottom-Up Processing

Suppose you are listening to a lecturer, trying to comprehend what is being said and remember the main points of the lecture. We can view your language processing as occurring on a set of levels. At the lowest level, the phonological level, you are identifying the phonemes and syllables that the lecturer is using. At a higher level, the lexical level, you are using the identification of phonemes and syllables to retrieve the lexical entries of the words from your semantic memory. At the next level, the syntactic level, you are organizing the words into constituents and forming a phrase structure for the sentence. Finally, at the highest level, the discourse level, you are linking the meaning of a given sentence with preceding ones, and organizing sentences into higher-order units.

We may now define **bottom-up processing** as that which proceeds from the lowest level to the highest level of processing in such a way that all of the lower levels of processing operate without influence from the higher levels. That is, the identification of phonemes is not affected by the lexical, syntactic, or discourse levels, the retrieval of words is not affected by syntactic or discourse levels, and so on. But, as we have already seen in Figure 3-2, there is some reason to doubt that a strict bottom-up model will provide a comprehensive account of how we understand language.

A **top-down processing** model, in contrast, states that information at the higher levels may influence processing at the lower levels. For instance, a sentence context may influence the identification of words within that sentence. Speaking more intuitively, a top-down model of processing is one in which one's expectations play a significant role. If you know where a lecturer is going—based on previous experience with the instructor or maybe even by reading the text in advance of the lecture—then you can generate some expectations regarding what the next point might be. If you are correct, then you are using the higher levels of processing to facilitate lower levels of processing.

I should hasten to add that not all top-down processing is facilitative. There are times when the content or structure of a lecture clashes with our expectations. Under these circumstances, the expectations may actually interfere with learning new material. It might be better to abandon one's preconceptions and simply use a bottom-up approach.

The distinction between top-down and bottom-up processing is similar in some respects to the distinction between serial and parallel processes. In fact, a top-down process is often a parallel process and a bottom-up process is usually serial. But the distinctions are not synonymous; a top-down process is not necessarily parallel. Let's take lexical and syntactic processing as our example. Suppose we identified each word of a sentence and then began a tentative phrase structure of the words to that point, with the incomplete structure guiding our identification of subsequent words. We would, in effect, be cycling back and forth from lexical to syntactic levels. It would be a top-down process, but serial in nature.

Automatic and Controlled Processes

Earlier, when discussing working memory, I introduced the notion that we may have a fixed processing capacity for handling information. This has been a central assumption in a variety of accounts of human cognitive functioning. It is an important concept when considering human performance on complex tasks, such as language processing. When the task is complex, one part of the task may draw substantial resourses from this limited pool of resources, thereby leaving insufficient resources for the other parts, resulting in overall impaired performance.

Tasks that draw substantially from this limited pool of resources are called controlled tasks, and the processes involved in these tasks are referred to as **controlled processes.** Tasks that do not require substantial resources are called automatic tasks; processes that do not require extensive capacity are referred to as **automatic processes.**

Various criteria have been used to determine whether a task is automatic or controlled (Hasher & Zacks, 1979). These include sensitivity to developmental and strategy effects. Developmental effects refer to whether there are differences in performance due to the age of the individual. Strategy effects pertain to whether the adoption of a particular strategy influences performance on the task.

In both of these instances, controlled tasks are more sensitive than automatic tasks. That is, automatic tasks appear to be unrelated to the age of the individual or to the strategy employed.

Certain automatic tasks appear to be biologically built into our cognitive equipment. We have, for example, an automatic process in which we are able to roughly estimate the frequency of an event (Hasher & Zacks, 1979). Most of us can correctly judge that red automobiles are more common than yellow ones. This "frequency counter" does not require conscious effort; it is simply a by-product of processing a stimulus in some way. Other tasks become automatic as a consequence of our degree of practice with them. Many of the tasks we perform automatically, such as tying our shoelaces, have been done thousands of times. They were more demanding when we were young and have become automatic through practice.

One language processing task that is automatic, at least for adults, is recognizing common words. This is undoubtedly due to our large amount of experience with words. In contrast, developing a phrase structure for a sentence is a controlled process. Recognition of this processing distinction was a major factor in the development of lexical-functional grammar, introduced in Chapter 2. Bresnan (1978) reasoned that the process of working our way through syntactic structure places heavy burdens on working memory, which has a fixed capacity. By comparison, the process of lexical retrieval is far easier. Thus, if grammatical information was stored in the lexicon, it would simplify overall language processing.

Modularity

We also discussed the notion of modularity earlier, in connection with Chomsky's universal grammar. There the emphasis was on the independence of the different linguistic subsystems within the grammar. Within cognitive psychology, **modularity** has a slightly different meaning. Here the concern is with the degree of independence of the language processing system, taken as a whole, from the general cognitive system we have sketched so far in this chapter. The modularity position is that the language processing system is a unique set of cognitive abilities that cannot be reduced to general principles of cognition. This is the position that Chomsky has taken in a number of writings (for example, Chomsky, 1975). The alternative position stresses the interconnections between language and cognitive processes by emphasizing the role of concepts such as working memory, automatic processing, and parallel processing in language comprehension, production, and acquisition.

Perhaps the best candidate for the status of a special language module is speech perception. As we shall see in greater detail in Chapter 4, there are certain properties of how we perceive speech that appear to be distinctive, or domain specific. That is, they apply to the perception of speech but not to the perception of, say, music or visual art.

The notion that speech is modular is related but not identical to the argument that our language faculty is biologically innate. Certainly one way to talk about modules is to talk about innate modules, but this is not a necessary property. A module is dedicated to performing one aspect of a complex task. Whether this assignment is biologically given or acquired through experience is a separate issue.

An Example of Language Processing

We have discussed four distinctions that are relevant to language processing. Let us now consider a specific example and see how these distinctions might apply. Consider the following sentence (from Clark & Clark, 1977, p. 81):

(1) I was afraid of Ali's powerful punch, especially since it had already laid out many tougher men who had bragged they could handle that much alcohol.

This is another example of a garden path sentence (see Chapter 1). The key word here is *punch*, which can mean either an alcoholic beverage or a boxing punch. The subjective impression for most people at the end of the sentence is having assumed the wrong meaning and then backtracking. If we were to flesh this out into a more complete processing model, it might look like this: when we encounter a word that has more than one meaning, we survey the immediate environment of the word, make a rapid decision as to the most appropriate meaning, and then stay with that meaning unless it becomes obvious that we are in error.

This model corresponds reasonably well with subjective impressions, but are these impressions accurate? The model assumes serial processing (one meaning at a time), with top-down processing playing only a limited role (decision is based on the immediate context, not the entire sentence). Because the emphasis is on decisions the comprehender must make during the course of comprehension, the model emphasizes controlled processes more than automatic processes. Finally, this approach can safely be described as nonmodular. It relies on our general ability to figure things out, not on a specialized capacity that is related to language; it might even be described as common sense.

We could, however, develop a completely contrasting model. We could begin with the assumption that people routinely and simultaneously activate more than one meaning of an ambiguous word from semantic memory. Moreover, we could assume that the retrieval of multiple meanings is a fixed property of the lexicon—that it is automatic, modular, and not related at all to the sentence context (that is, it is bottom-up).

Although the latter model may sound counterintuitive, there is some psychological evidence for it. It does indeed appear that we automatically activate all of the meanings of an ambiguous words at least briefly (Foss, 1970). At the same time, it also appears that we decide among the choices rather quickly, perhaps within three or four words (Cairns & Kamerman, 1975). Thus, there may be two stages of processing: an automatic stage in which all meanings are retrieved and a more controlled stage that is more top-down in nature.

The notion that we might have two different ways of approaching a sentence with an ambiguous word is not limited to this one example. This state of affairs is the rule in human information processing, in which we nearly always have multiple ways of doing things and in which we generally employ the easiest, fastest, or most efficient strategy that will work. Nor should it be entirely surprising that our subjective impressions of this sentence may be a rather poor guide. One point that I have made a couple of times already but which perhaps bears repeating is that our knowledge of language is, for the most part, tacit rather than explicit. Considering the complexity of language and the sheer amount of information processing that is taking place in just a few seconds, it is sometimes a wonder that we have any conscious awareness of these processes at all. If we are to develop a solid knowledge of how language processing takes place, we will need to rely not on introspection but rather on systematic experimentation.

Summary

This section raises a number of issues regarding language processing. These include the distinctions between serial and parallel processing, top-down and bottom-up processing, and automatic and controlled processes, as well as the issue of modularity.

It should be clear that we have a number of ways of processing linguistic information. That is, language processing is not just determined by linguistic structure but jointly by that structure and by processing considerations that are independent of language. The manner in which our cognitive processing system interacts with linguistic structures is a central concern of much psycholinguistic research.

Development of the Processing System

As noted in Chapter 1, one of the main themes of psycholinguistics is how children acquire language. In order to understand language acquisition, it will be helpful to understand the cognitive abilities children bring to the task of acquiring their native language. In the present context, the primary question is to what extent the information processing system sketched in this chapter is operating during the first few years of life, when most normal children acquire language.

It is clear enough that children encode, store, and retrieve a great deal of linguistic information in their first few years. They are constantly being presented with new lexical items to remember. Grammatical rules such as the English past tense, with its many irregular forms, require children to commit many terms to memory. Children may come to understand productive grammatical rules by noticing patterns in different sentences, retaining them, and then organizing them into a single rule.

We may begin by assuming that the information processing system as we have discussed it in this chapter is, for the most part, developmentally invariant. I say "for the most part" because some components, by definition, must change. The episodic portion of permanent memory is a repository of one's experience and thus will clearly grow with experience. But, on the whole, we may tentatively assume that the sensory stores, working memory, and capacity limitations we have emphasized are present to the same extent in newborn infants as in mature adults.

This may seem an unlikely hypothesis, for we ordinarily think of children and especially infants as cognitively very different creatures than adults. Recent research, however, has suggested that there are some important cognitive similarities between children and adults.

Perceptual Processing

Although virtually no research has addressed the development of the sensory stores per se, there is a substantial literature on perceptual processing defined more broadly. The discussion here will be limited to vision and audition.

Prior to the early 1960s, it was generally believed that infants perceive the world in a disorganized or haphazard way. The view was captured memorably by James (1890):

> The baby, assailed by eyes, ears, nose, skin, and entrails at once, feels it all as one great blooming, buzzing confusion (p. 488).

The research of Fantz (1963), however, indicates otherwise. Babies were shown various forms while observers recorded how long the infants looked at each one. The infants looked at some patterns more than others, which Fantz interprets as meaning that the infants could distinguish among the forms and preferred some to others. Fantz found that young infants preferred patterns, such as faces or checkerboards, over plain stimuli.

The infants' preference for the human face has provoked a good deal of discussion and research. It should be noted that even if infants prefer faces to plain figures, it does not mean that infants have an innate ability to perceive human faces. A large percentage of the eye fixations infants display toward faces is toward certain high-contrast areas, such as the eyebrows or the hairline, so it is likely that the infant visual system is programmed to attend to high-contrast stimuli of various kinds, not just faces. It appears that infants are not able to respond to a face as a whole until they are about 4 months of age.

Just as the human face, for whatever reason, fascinates infants, so does the human voice. Infants are biologically prepared to distinguish between speech and other sounds. For instance, Condon and Sander (1974) have shown that infants make synchronized movements to individual speech sounds shortly after birth. These movements included raising a finger, kicking a leg, and so on. Frame-by-frame analysis of these movements indicated that they were synchronized with the syllables in the speech signal. Newborns displayed this synchrony with different languages but not with nonspeech sounds, such as the tapping of a pencil.

Eimas, Siqueland, Jusczyk, and Vigorito (1971) have found that infants make distinctions between different speech sounds very early in life. These researchers examined infant perception of the voicing contrast in English. For example, the vocal cords vibrate during the production of [ba] but only after the production of [pa]. More precisely, the sounds differ in the time between when the sound is released at the lips and when the vocal cords begin vibrating. With voiced sounds, the vibration occurs immediately; with voiceless sounds, it occurs after a short delay. This lag, which is called **voice onset time** (VOT), is an important cue in the perception of voicing.

If you were presented with a sound with a 0-millisecond (ms) VOT, you would always hear it as [ba], and if presented with a 40-ms VOT, you would hear it as [pa]. With a speech synthesizer, we can examine the way that people perceive the intermediate cases. Adult listeners hear the VOT differences up to + 25 as the voiced [ba] and values above that point as [pa].

Eimas and colleagues used a technique known as **habituation** to study infant responses to these stimuli. Habituation refers to the decline in a response to a stimulus following repeated presentation of the stimulus. The response studied is referred to as nonnutritive sucking and involves a special pacifier that is connected to a machine that measures the number of sucks an infant makes. When a stimulus with a VOT of + 20 ms ([ba]) was initially presented, the infant showed great interest and the sucking rate was high; but with repeated presentations, the sucking decreased. At this point, a new stimulus was presented. On some occasions it was a stimulus from the [ba] category (a VOT of + 0 ms) and on other occasions it was from the [pa] category (a VOT of + 40 ms). The interesting result observed was that sucking returned briefly to a high level (a phenomenon referred to as dishabituation) if the new stimulus was from a different category, but not if the new stimulus was from the same category. Eimas and colleagues conclude that infants as young as 1 month are sensitive to the distinction between voiced and voiceless sounds.

Taken together, studies of perceptual processing by infants reveal infants to have rather sophisticated perceptual skills at or shortly after birth. These results suggest that infants are well equipped at birth to process linguistic stimuli.

Working Memory

A second aspect of the cognitive system that has been examined developmentally is short-term memory. A common test of short-term memory in grade school children is the simple memory span test: children are presented with a list of numbers and asked to recall them, sometimes in forward and sometimes in backward order. It is clear that there are significant differences between older and younger children on this task (Dempster, 1981). In fact, the simple memory span test is a standard feature on intelligence tests for that very reason.

These results, however, do not tell us much about the development of working memory. Recall that working memory consists of both storage and processing functions, and these compete for limited resources. Thus, a developmental change in either of these functions would affect the other. In particular, if children become more efficient in processing numbers, fewer resources would be needed for that function, thereby leaving more resources available for storage. In this way, simple memory span might improve without any change in the total size of working memory.

A series of elegant experiments by Case, Kurland, and Goldberg (1982) has confirmed this analysis. In their first experiment, 3- to 6-year-olds were given a storage and a processing task. The storage task was a simple memory span task of remembering seven words. The processing task was a repetition task, in which the children had to repeat auditorily presented words. The investigators measured the time between the presentation of the word and the onset of the child's vocal response. The same words were used in both tasks. Case and colleagues found a negative correlation between the two tasks; as response time increased, memory span decreased. Older children remembered more words than younger children, but when their reaction time was taken into account, there were no differences between the two age groups.

A second experiment presented adults with the same two tasks, using nonsense words. The use of nonsense words was significant because adults have no familiarity with them. Adult reaction time to the nonsense words was slow, comparable to the younger children's reaction time to real words. If memory span depends upon processing speed, then adult recall of the nonsense words should also be similar to the younger children's recall of real words, and it was. The studies thus demonstrate that when adults are slowed down to children's speed of processing, memory span differences disappear.

Case and colleagues conclude that there is no substantial increase in overall working memory capacity with development, at least from 6 years to adulthood. Under this interpretation, simple memory span shows a functional increase in storage due to the greater efficiency of processing. As we shall see in Chapter 11, this notion of developmental changes in processing efficiency is highly relevant to understanding early reading by children.

Sensorimotor Development

The information processing perspective introduced in this chapter is the primary organizational framework used throughout this book to discuss cognitive processing. An alternative perspective on cognitive development, one that challenges the notion of invariance, has been described by the Swiss scholar Jean Piaget, who constructed a theory of development over a research career that lasted well over 50 years. Piaget claimed that children's thinking processes are qualitatively different from those of adults. Adults do not merely think faster or more accurately than children, but in a different way. Piaget referred to the concepts that we use to organize our experience as schemas.

A well-documented example is **object permanence,** which refers to children's understanding that objects continue to exist even when they cannot be perceived. Very young infants (4 months or younger) operate on an "out of sight, out of mind" principle. When an attractive toy is taken from them and placed behind an adult's back, the infant may protest briefly but rapidly appears to forget completely about the object. When the object is reintroduced to the child, the infant is again joyous. Thus, the infant remains interested but does not search for the object because the infant, according to Piaget, does not know that the object still exists.

Object permanence develops in a series of stages. Children of about 8 months will actively search for the hidden object if it is only partially covered.

Somewhat older infants will search for objects that are fully obscured. The final crowning achievement is the ability to handle invisible displacement tasks. In this task, the infant is shown a small attractive object, such as a key, which is then put into the adult's hand. The adult makes a fist, thereby taking the key out of view, and while still in a fist, the hand is placed under a blanket and the key deposited there. In order to find the object, the infant must be able to mentally imagine the invisible object being displaced from one location to another and then search the latter. Infants typically solve this problem between 18 and 24 months.

The acquisition of object permanence is not an isolated cognitive skill. At about this time, two related skills are emerging. One is **pretend play,** in which a child may use an object in a playful and unconventional manner (for example, using a toy rake to comb a doll's hair). The second skill is **deferred imitation,** in which the child imitates a behavior seen some time before. A famous example is from Piaget's daughter Jacqueline, who observed a tantrum in a playmate and then imitated it very closely a day later (Piaget, 1962). These two developments, along with object permanence, define the transition from the earliest period of development (in Piaget's theory, the sensorimotor period) to the second period, which Piaget called the preoperational period. These achievements indicate that the child is able to symbolically represent objects in the immediate environment. No longer at the mercy of immediate stimuli, infants can behave on the basis of past events or the products of their imagination.

Piaget's interpretation of these developments has not gone unchallenged. An alternative interpretation of object permanence is that the infant knows that the object continues to exist but has forgotten where it is and therefore does not search for it. A study by Diamond (1985) supports this view. Diamond varied the amount of time between when the object was hidden from the infant and when the infant was allowed to begin searching for it. Although object permanence should not depend on this variable, she found that infants' search behavior was affected by the delay. When they were allowed to search immediately, infants as young as $7\frac{1}{2}$ months searched for an object in its correct location, whereas with a delay of only 2 seconds, infants searched the wrong place. These results indicate that at least some of the problems infants have with object permanence tasks stem from memory difficulties. As we have already seen, memory limitations may appear when a new task requires significant processing capacity. It may be that the novel task of searching for hidden objects places a demand on processing that leads to storage problems.

Put more generally, observed differences between children and adults on cognitive tasks have more to do with the use of information processing resources than with qualitative shifts in thinking. The major change over time is an increase in efficiency, or a decrease in the amount of cognitive capacity required for a task. Increased efficiency enables a child to simultaneously do two or more tasks (or a complex task with two or more components). This is directly pertinent to language acquisition, for to acquire a language a child must ultimately perform correct analyses simultaneously on the phonological, semantic, syntactic, morphological, and pragmatic levels. A child of 3 may approach the task in a way that is similar to adults, but less efficient. When working on new syntactic structures, a demanding

Complex tasks such as riding a bicycle or using language involve a number of individual skills. It takes time to coordinate these components.

task, the child may compensate by attending less to phonological specification. Perhaps only later, when the syntax comes a little easier, will the child be able to master both levels simultaneously.

Summary

This section has explored research into the development of the information processing system. Young children and infants are inherently difficult to study, so we must be careful in drawing conclusions, but a number of clever studies have shown several cognitive similarities between young children and adults. Infants appear to be preprogrammed to distinguish between speech and nonspeech and between different speech sounds. Memory differences occur from early childhood through adulthood on short-term memory tasks, but these appear to be related to automaticity rather than to increases in storage capacity per se. Increases in efficiency may result in a functional increase in storage capacity.

An alternative view, suggested by Piaget, emphasizes qualitative changes in cognitive organization throughout development. But at least one of the major developments studied by Piaget, object permanence, can be interpreted as a failure in memory rather than a qualitative shift in thinking. Both the Piagetian and the information processing accounts of cognitive development have merit and both have influenced studies of language acquisition. We shall pursue the connections between language and cognitive development more fully in Part 4.

*R*eview Questions

1. What evidence indicates that we store more information in sensory memory than we are able to report?
2. Why might the duration of the auditory sensory store be longer than that of the visual sensory store?
3. How does working memory differ from short-term memory?
4. Distinguish between episodic memory and semantic memory.
5. Cite one piece of evidence that suggests some limitations of a purely serial model of language processing.
6. Identify one aspect of language processing that qualifies as being automatic.
7. Distinguish between two senses of the term modular.
8. What experimental evidence suggests that infants can perceive speech sounds?
9. What conclusions can be drawn from the study by Case and colleagues on the development of working memory?
10. Cite two explanations of the object permanence phenomenon.

*T*hought Questions

1. Does the existence of limits of human information processing imply the impossibility of a language that contains sentences whose length or complexity violates these limits? Are there psychological limits on the set of languages that could be used by human beings?
2. The text indicates that some language processing is done automatically. What factors might influence the extent of automatic processing?
3. The text provides two interpretations of object permanence. How might a study be designed to distinguish between these views?

part 2

Language Comprehension

4

Perception of Language

- The study of speech sounds is called phonetics. Articulatory phonetics refers to the study of how speech sounds are produced. Acoustic phonetics refers to the study of the resulting speech sounds.
- Speech exhibits characteristics not found in other forms of auditory perception. The phenomenon of categorical perception suggests that speech is a special mode of perception.
- Perception of speech sounds is influenced by the contexts in which they appear. We use top-down processing to identify some sounds in context.
- Visual perception of language is achieved through a succession of processing levels. Perception of letters in a word context is superior to perception of isolated letters.
- Recent models of the perception of language assume that we process information at multiple levels in an interactive way. These models can account for several findings in speech perception and visual word perception.

Introduction

In this chapter and the three that follow, we will examine language comprehension at a number of levels. This chapter deals with the phonological level. Chapters 5, 6, and 7 present the lexical, syntactic, and discourse levels, respectively.

This analysis of language comprehension into four levels of processing is for convenience of exposition; it does not necessarily mean that we process language in a strictly serial manner. As you might have anticipated from our discussion in Chapter 3, the question of serial versus parallel processing has been a major interest of researchers studying the perception of language. We will return to this issue at several points during this chapter.

Another issue of importance is the relationship between comprehension of oral and written language. Obviously, the peripheral equipment is different and, just as obviously, speech is temporal whereas print is spatial. Nevertheless, we may ask whether there are fundamental similarities between listening and reading that lurk beneath these surface differences.

This chapter is divided into four sections. The first considers the linguistic structure of speech. Next, we consider the way we identify different speech sounds when they are presented in isolation, followed by a discussion of the means by which we extract these individual sounds from the continuous stream of speech. The final section provides a selective overview of research on the perception of written language.

The Structure of Speech

The process of speech perception seems simple enough. Listeners must, in effect, categorize the sounds that they hear into one of the many classes of sounds that exist in their language. In fact, the task is an extraordinarily complex one, and for two major reasons. First, the environmental context often interferes with the speech signal. Under normal listening conditions the speech we hear is in competition with other stimuli for our limited processing capacity. Other auditory signals, such as a conversation across the room or someone's sneezing or burping, can interfere with the fidelity of the speech signal. Moreover, visual signals often serve as sources of distraction.

Even if the environmental conditions are ideal, however, the perception of speech presents a second major problem: the variability of the speech signal itself. There is no one-to-one correspondence between the characteristics of the acoustic stimulus and the speech sound we hear. There are a number of factors that influence or distort the acoustic stimulus that reaches our ears. These include the voice of the speaker (that is, high versus low pitch), the rate at which the speaker is producing speech, and the phonetic context.

How, then, do we achieve stable phonetic perception when the acoustic stimulus competes with other stimuli and contains a good deal of inherent variability? The ease with which we recognize phonetic segments suggests that listeners make a series of adjustments in the course of perceptual recognition. Some of these adjustments are based on the implicit knowledge of the way speech sounds are produced. It is appropriate, then, to begin our discussion of speech perception by examining how speech is produced.

Articulatory Phonetics

The study of the pronunciation of speech sounds is called **articulatory phonetics**. All of the sounds of a language can ultimately be described in terms of the movements of the physical structures of the vocal tract (see Figure 4-1). Air is emitted from the lungs and passes over the vocal cords and into the oral cavity or the nasal cavity. In some languages, speech sounds can be made by sucking in air instead of expelling it, but not in English.

Speech sounds differ principally in whether or not the airflow is obstructed and, if so, at what point and in what way. Although vowels are produced by letting air flow from the lungs in an unobstructed way, consonants are produced by impeding the airflow at some point.

Place of articulation Some consonants, such as [b] and [p], are articulated at the lips and are called **bilabial** consonants. Others, such as [d] and [t], are formed by placing the tongue against the alveolar ridge; these are called **alveolar** consonants. Still others, such as [g] and [k], are produced in the back of the mouth; since the tongue is placed against the velum at the back of the mouth, these are called **velar** consonants.

Manner of articulation Consonants also differ from one another in terms of the manner in which they are produced. **Stop** consonants obstruct the airflow completely for a period of time, then release it. All of the examples in the preceding paragraph are stop consonants. **Fricatives** are produced by obstructing without completely stopping the airflow, as in [f] or [s]. The passage in the mouth through

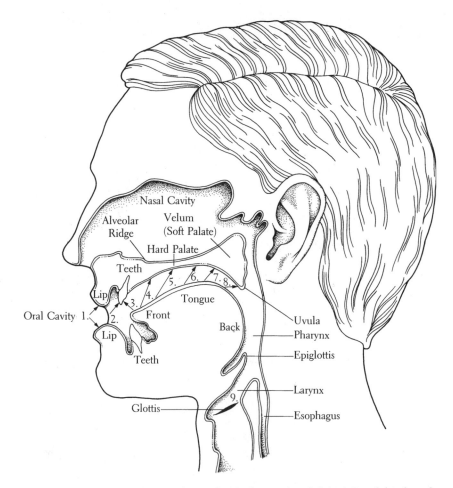

Figure 4-1.   The vocal tract: places of articulation: 1 = bilabial, 2 = labiodental, 3 = dental, 4 = alveolar, 5 = palatoalveolar, 6 = palatal, 7 = velar, 8 = uvular, 9 = glottal. (From V. Fromkin and R. Rodman, *An Introduction to Language.* New York: Holt, Rinehart & Winston, 1974.)

which air must travel becomes more narrow, and this narrowing causes some turbulence. Another type of consonant, the **affricate,** is produced by a stoplike closure followed by the slow release characteristic of fricatives. The first sounds in *church* (phonetically represented as [č]) and *judge* ([ǰ]) are affricates.

Voicing   A final distinction among consonants concerns whether or not the vocal cords are together or separated when the lung air travels over them. The opening between the vocal cords is called the **glottis.** If the cords are together, the airstream must force its way through the glottis, causing the vocal cords to vibrate. The resulting sound is called a **voiced** speech sound, as in [b]. If the cords are separated, the air is not obstructed at all, and the sound is called a **voiceless** sound, as in [p]. These characteristics of English consonants are summarized in Table 4-1,

Table 4-1.   English consonants

Manner of Articulation		Bilabial	Labiodental	Dental	Alveolar	Palatal	Velar	Glottal
				Place of Articulation				
Stops	Voiceless	p (*p*at)			t (*t*ack)		k (*c*at)	
	Voiced	b (*b*at)			d (*d*ig)		g (*g*et)	
Fricatives	Voiceless		f (*f*at)	Θ (*th*in)	s (*s*at)	š (*f*i*sh*)		h (*h*at)
	Voiced		v (*v*at)	ð (*th*en)	z (*z*ap)	ž (a*z*ure)		
Affricatives	Voiceless					č (*ch*urch)		
	Voiced					ǰ (*j*udge)		
Nasals		m (*m*at)			n (*n*at)		ŋ (si*ng*)	
Liquids					l (*l*ate)	r (*r*ate)		
Glides		w (*w*in)				y (*y*et)		

Source: S. Glucksberg and J. H. Danks, *Experimental Psycholinguistics: An Introduction* (Hillsdale, NJ: Erlbaum, 1975).

which shows the place of articulation, manner of articulation, and voicing characteristics of these and other English consonants.

Table 4-2 shows a similar chart of English vowels. Vowels are distinguished from one another chiefly by whether they are produced in the front, center, or back of the mouth and whether the tongue position is high, middle, or low. As with the consonants, we can best appreciate these phonetic distinctions by practicing these sounds and comparing the positions of the articulators, particularly the tongue. Notice that with the front vowels [i], [I], [e], and [ae], the front part of the tongue becomes progressively lower. With [u], [o], and [a], it is the back of the tongue that changes position.

This description of speech sounds in terms of the details of their articulation suggests that it might be possible to describe the entire inventory of phonetic segments by constituent features based on their mode of production. As we

Table 4-2.   English vowels

	Front	Center	Back
High	i (b<u>ee</u>t)		u (b<u>oo</u>t)
			U (b<u>oo</u>k)
	I (b<u>i</u>t)		
		ɚ' (b<u>ir</u>d)	o (b<u>o</u>de)
	e (b<u>a</u>by)		
Middle		ə (sof<u>a</u>)	
	ɛ (b<u>e</u>t)		ɔ (b<u>ou</u>ght)
	æ (b<u>a</u>t)	ʌ (b<u>u</u>t)	
Low			
			a (p<u>a</u>lm)

Source: S. Glucksberg and J. H. Danks, *Experimental Psycholinguistics: An Introduction* (Hillsdale, NJ: Erlbaum, 1975).

discussed in Chapter 2, Jakobson, Fant, and Halle (1969) devised a system of distinctive features in which each segment is defined in terms of the presence or absence of various elementary features such as voiced/voiceless or nasal/oral, which refers to whether or not sounds are produced with a lowered velum, which directs the airflow to the nasal cavity. The utility of distinctive features is that they allow us to describe the relationships that exist among various speech sounds in an economical manner.

Acoustic Phonetics

One practical application of understanding the way people process speech signals is in devising reading machines for the blind. Applied research along this line (see Liberman, 1982) has proved to be unexpectedly difficult. In the 1940s and 1950s, research was beginning to identify the relationships between the acoustic properties of the speech signal and the perceptual experience of the listener, and it was thought that the application of this knowledge to reading machines was just around the corner. It has turned out, however, that although it is possible to convert visual information into speech signals intelligibly enough to be of some value to the blind, the result does not sound like speech. That is, taking an individual letter, attaching the sound that goes with the letter, and then putting it together with other sounds in the sentence can be done, but it doesn't sound much like natural speech.

It appears that an implicit assumption underlying this early speech research—that there was a parallel between phonetic segments and letters of the alphabet—was largely invalid and that we process speech differently from letters of the alphabet. One indication of this is the sheer speed with which we perceive language. It has been estimated that we can encode up to 25 to 30 phonetic segments per second while listening to speech (Liberman, 1970), a rate that far surpasses that of other forms of auditory perception. For example, if we were to hear a series of recognizable sounds (say, a tone, a buzzer, a click, and a siren), we would hear an indistinct blur if they were played at a rate approaching that of conversational speech.

Some clues as to how we perceive speech segments so rapidly may be found in the acoustic structure of the speech signal. The examination of these acoustic properties of speech sounds is called **acoustic phonetics.**

Spectrograms   One of the most common ways of describing the acoustical energy of speech sounds is called a **sound spectrogram.** It is produced by presenting a sample of speech to a device known as a **sound spectrograph,** which consists of a set of filters that analyze the sound and then project it onto a moving belt of phosphor, producing the spectrogram. Some typical spectrograms are shown in Figure 4-2. The frequency of the speech sounds is represented on the vertical axis, the time on the horizontal axis, and the intensity in terms of the darkness of the spectrogram at various locations. Each of the spectrograms contains a series of dark bands, called **formants,** at various frequency levels. These appear horizontally on the spectrogram, with the first formant being the one with the lowest frequency and higher formants being roughly parallel. In *tool,* the first formant is

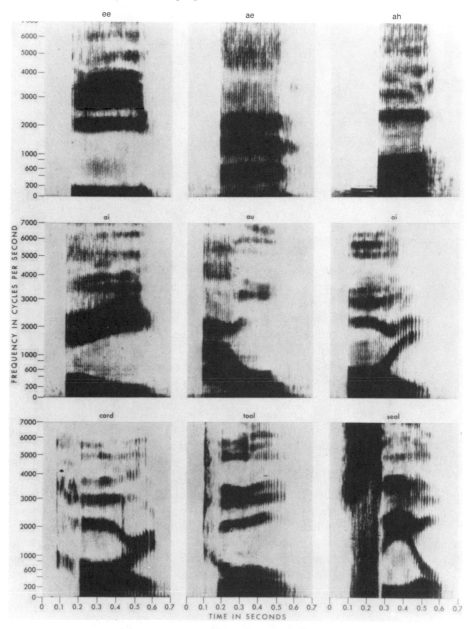

Figure 4-2. Typical speech spectrograms. [From P. D. Denes and E. N. Pinson, *The Speech Chain* (Baltimore: Bell Telephone Laboratories, 1963).]

about 1000 hertz (Hz) (or cycles per second), the second roughly 2000 Hz, and the third 3000 Hz.

Two aspects of formants have been found to be important in speech perception. **Formant transitions** are the large rises or drops in formant frequency that occur over short durations of time. In *card*, the first formant is rising and the second one falling in frequency near the end of the word. These transitions nearly always occur either at the beginning or the end of a syllable. In between is the formant's **steady state,** during which formant frequency is relatively stable. It is a bit oversimplified but basically correct to say that the transitions correspond to the consonantal portion of the syllable, and the steady state to the vowel.

Parallel transmission   We are now in a position to examine some of the acoustic properties of the speech signal. One, called **parallel transmission,** refers to the fact that there is no sharp physical break between adjacent sounds in a syllable. Rather, the acoustic signal is essentially continuous. The [t] in *tool* runs into the [u], which runs into the [l]. We hear three distinct phones, but inspection of the spectrograms reveals that they are not physically distinct in the speech signal.

Context-conditioned variation   A related characteristic, **context-conditioned variation,** describes the phenomenon that the exact spectrographic appearance of a given phone is related to (or conditioned by) the speech context. The clearest example is the way that the spectrogram of a consonant is conditioned by the following vowel. This is shown in Figure 4-3 for the simplified spectrograms for [di] and [du]. (They are simplified in that although they are sufficient to produce a sound that most people would be able to identify, they leave out other natural characteristics of speech.) In Figure 4-3, both the formant frequency and the formant transitions vary with the subsequent vowel context. In [di], the second formant is approximately 2400 Hz with a sharply rising transition. In [du], the frequency is near 1200 Hz with a falling transition. Nevertheless, we hear both as [d]. This phenomenon, along with parallel transmission, suggests that we do not process speech sounds one at a time. It appears that the information for each phonetic segment is spread throughout the syllable.

Context-conditioned variation is closely related to the manner in which syllables are produced. The [d] sound is produced by constricting the airflow by placing the tongue at the roof of the mouth or alveolar ridge. The [u] sound is made with the back of the tongue near the top of the mouth and with the lips rounded. The [i] is produced with the tip of the tongue near the roof of the mouth and with spread lips. We can conceive of the process of producing sounds as one in which the vocal tract "aims" at a series of articulatory targets, while the actual site of articulation varies somewhat with the speech context. That is, the exact manner in which [d] is produced varies with the following vowel. The phenome-

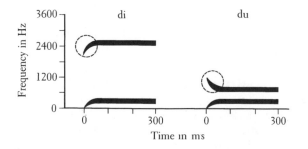

Figure 4-3.   Simplified spectrographic patterns sufficient to produce the syllables [di] and [du]. [From A. M. Liberman, "The Grammars of Speech and Language," *Cognitive Psychology* 1 (1970):301–323.]

non of producing more than one speech sound at a given time is called **coarticu-lation;** it reveals the important point that production, like the physical signal that results from it, tends to vary with the phonetic context.

Prosodic Factors

The phonetic context is not the only source of variability in the speech signal. In addition, **prosodic factors** such as stress, intonation, and rate influence the acoustic structure of speech. Prosodic factors are sometimes called **suprasegmentals.** *Supra* means to be above something, and these aspects of speech lie over speech segments (phones), providing a kind of musical accompaniment to speech. The same phrase or sentence may be expressed prosodically in different ways, and these variations become important cues to the speaker's meaning and emotional state.

Stress refers to the emphasis given to syllables in a sentence. We use stress to distinguish between the noun and verb forms of various words, such as *project* and *pervert*, and between pairs such as *black bird* and *blackbird*. **Intonation** refers to the use of pitch to signify different meanings; the pitch pattern of a sentence is called its **intonational contour.** An example sometimes found in men's restrooms is: "We aim to please. You aim too, please" (Fromkin & Rodman, 1974). Finally, **rate** refers to the rate at which speech is articulated. We modify our rate of speech by altering the number and length of pauses during utterances, as well as the amount of time articulating speech segments. The rate of speech sometimes conveys meaning. Consider how we would produce the sentence *Take your time* versus the sentence *We've got to get going!* (Bolinger, 1975).

Prosodic factors add to the variability of the speech signal in that they alter the acoustic cues that listeners use to identify speech segments. For instance, J. L. Miller (1981) has documented the acoustic consequences of speaking rate. As we speed up our speaking rate, vowel duration is reduced, and the duration of cues that signal various consonants is also modified. The frication noise found in fricatives and affricates is reduced, and the onset of vocal cord vibration that distinguishes voiced from voiceless consonants is also altered. Later in the chapter, we will consider how listeners take prosodic factors such as rate of speech into account when identifying speech segments.

Summary

Speech may be described in terms of the articulatory movements needed to produce a speech sound and the acoustic properties of the sound. Vowels differ from consonants in that the airflow from the lungs is not obstructed during production; consonants differ from one another in terms of the manner and place of the obstruction, as well as the presence of vocal cord vibration during articulation.

The acoustic structure of speech sounds is revealed by spectrographic analyses of formants, their steady states, and formant transitions. The spectrographic pattern associated with a consonant is influenced by its vowel context and is induced by the coarticulated manner in which syllables are produced. Moreover, prosodic factors such as stress, intonation, and speech rate also contribute to the variability inherent in the speech signal.

Perception of Isolated Speech Segments

Levels of Speech Processing

We may roughly distinguish the process of speech perception into three levels (Studdert-Kennedy, 1976). At the **auditory level,** the signal is represented in terms of its frequency, intensity, and temporal attributes (as, for example, shown on a spectrogram) as with any auditory stimulus. At the **phonetic level,** we identify individual phones by a combination of acoustic cues, such as formant transitions. At the **phonological level,** the phonetic segment is converted into a phoneme, and phonological rules are applied to the sound sequence. These levels may be construed as successive discriminations that we apply to the speech signal. We first discriminate auditory signals from other sensory signals and determine that the stimulus is something that we have heard. Then we identify the peculiar properties that qualify it as speech, only later recognizing it as the meaningful speech of a particular language.

Some work has been done on the phonological level of processing (see Day, cited in Clark & Clark, 1977); however, most interest has focused on the similarities and differences between speech and nonspeech perception, and hence on the auditory and phonetic levels of processing. A controversial issue in the study of speech perception is whether and to what extent general principles of auditory perception can explain what we have learned about speech perception.

Speech as a Modular System

As we saw in Chapter 3, the concept of modularity is an important concept in contemporary cognitive psychology. Some criteria for modularity have been advanced by Fodor (1983). A cognitive system is modular if it: (1) is domain specific (that is, if it is dedicated to speech processing but not, less us say, to vision), (2) operates on a mandatory basis, (3) is fast, and (4) is unaffected by feedback. These are merely some of the most basic criteria; Fodor discusses several others.

Why is the question of modularity important? The main reason is that it is related to the question of the organization of the brain for language, which is, in turn, related to questions concerning language development and language disorders. If speech is a modular system, then we might expect it to have a specialized neurological representation. This representation would not be based on general cognitive functioning (that is, working memory, episodic memory, and so on) but would be specific to language (or, possibly, specific to phonetic processing). This module might be the basis for the perception of language in very young infants and, if damaged, the reason why certain individuals suffer quite specific break-downs in language functioning.

The problem of invariance   We have already seen, from the phenomenon of con-text-conditioned variation, that the relationship between acoustic stimulus and perceptual experience is complex in the case of speech. The fact that there is no one-to-one correspondence between acoustic cues and perceptual events has been termed the **problem of invariance.** This is a significant problem, for if there are no invariant cues for phonetic segments, how is the listener to determine these sounds and thereby reconstruct the speaker's intended message? According to researchers at Haskins Laboratory in New Haven, Connecticut (Liberman, 1970; Liberman, Cooper, Shankweiler, & Studdert-Kennedy, 1967; Mattingly, Liberman, Syrdal, & Halwes, 1971), the lack of such an invariant relationship suggests that the perception of speech segments must occur through a process that is different from and presumably more complex than that of "ordinary" auditory perception. In other words, speech is a special mode of perception.

Before going on, we should bear in mind that context dependence applies to some but certainly not all of the acoustic cues for speech sounds. In fact, the relative preponderance of invariant and context-dependent cues is a matter that has generated considerable research (see Blumstein & Stevens, 1979; Cole & Scott, 1974). It appears that speech percepts are based on both invariant and context-conditioned cues. As an example, Cole and Scott (1974) point out that the nasal consonants [m] and [n] are distinguished from other consonants by a single bar of low-frequency energy along with a complete lack of high-frequency energy; these characteristics appear to be distinctive in various vowel contexts. However, in order to distinguish between [m] and [n], vowel information (that is, formant transitions) is needed. Thus, it appears that earlier reports may have exaggerated the extent of, if not the problems caused by, variability in the acoustic stimulus.

Categorical perception   A number of experimental findings have been advanced to support the view that speech is perceptually special, but the one that has received the most attention has been the phenomenon of **categorical perception.** Thus, we will look in some detail at what it is, the procedures used to demonstrate it, and its implications for the modularity theme.

Ordinarily when we perceive objects or events in our world, we are capable of making some fine discriminations between one color and another, one odor and another, and so on. Moreover, this discriminative capacity is largely continuous in the sense that we can perceive a series of quantitative changes in stimuli lying on a continuum, such as tones of varying degrees of intensity. The task of the listener in speech perception is different. In order to comprehend speech, we must impose an absolute or categorical identification on the incoming speech signal rather than simply a relative determination of the various physical characteristics of the signal. That is, our job is to identify whether a sound is a [p] or a [b], not whether the frequency or the intensity is relatively high or low. Certainly, such auditory cues such as frequency and intensity will play a role, but ultimately the result of speech perception is the identification of a stimulus as belonging to one or another category of speech sounds.

Categorical perception refers to a failure to discriminate speech sounds any better than you can identify them. This may be illustrated with an experimental example. On a speech spectrogram it is possible to identify the difference between the voiced sound [ba] and the voiceless sound [pa] as due to the time between when the sound is released at the lips and when the vocal cords begin vibrating. With voiced sounds, the vibration occurs immediately; however, with voiceless sounds it occurs after a short delay; this lag, the voice onset time (VOT), is an important cue in the perception of the voicing feature.

As we noted in Chapter 3, if we were presented with a sound with a 0-millisecond (ms) VOT, we would always hear it as [ba], although if the sound were presented with a 40-ms VOT, we would hear it as [pa]. With a speech synthesizer, we can examine the way that people perceive the intermediate cases. If synthesized sounds varying in VOT are constructed and people are asked to identify what they have heard, the results are clear-cut. As VOT varies continuously, the perception changes abruptly from one consonant to the other. That is, we tend to hear the sound as either a [ba] or a [pa], and the dividing line between the two is quite sharp indeed.

The second part of the experiment is to perform a discrimination task. Subjects are given three stimuli, with the third one matching one of the first two. The subjects' task is to indicate whether the final sound matches the first or the second one. When the two sounds are taken from two sound categories, performance is excellent in this task, but when the two sounds are taken from the same phonetic category, performance drops to chance level (Figure 4-4). Thus, there are two criteria for categorical perception: the presence of sharp identification functions and the failure to discriminate between sounds within a given sound class.

Subsequent research has examined whether the phenomenon holds for other kinds of stimuli as well or only for speech. Mattingly, Liberman, Syrdal, and Halwes (1971) have investigated which aspects of the speech signal might be sufficient to produce categorical perception. They constructed synthesized speech syllables containing the first two formants and formant transitions along with synthesized nonspeech sounds. One nonspeech sound was based only on the second formant transition; another was based on the second formant transition plus steady state. The former sounds like "chirps" of differing pitch. The authors refer to the latter as "bleats" (Figure 4-5). The experiment consisted of the usual procedure for categorical perception, done with synthesized syllables, chirps, and bleats, along with backward versions of all sounds. The researchers found there was categorical perception for the synthesized syllables but not for the chirps, bleats, or backward sounds. That is, subjects were unable to distinguish one chirp or bleat from another. These results show that formant transitions (especially the second formant transition) provide important information for producing the special mode of speech perception.

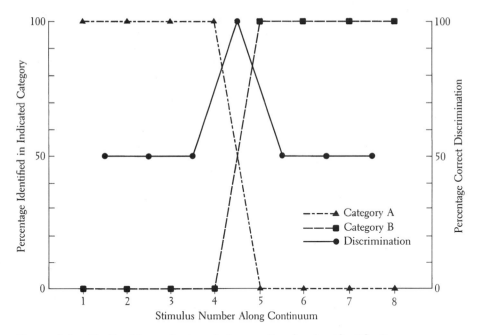

Figure 4-4. Idealized form of categorical perception showing identification performance for two categories and discrimination performance between categories. (From D. B. Pisoni, "Speech Perception," in W. K. Estes (ed.), *Handbook of Learning and Cognitive Processes, Vol. 6: Linguistic Functions in Cognitive Theory.* Hillsdale, NJ: Erlbaum, 1978.)

Studies of the perception of vowels contrast sharply with those of consonants (see, for example, Fry, Abramson, Eimas, & Liberman, 1962) since vowel perception is continuous and noncategorical, of the type typically associated with nonspeech stimuli. These results have been attributed to some basic differences between consonants and vowels (Studdert-Kennedy, 1974). Recall that the steady-state portion of a format, which contains most of the cues for vowels, is much longer than the formant transitions that are so important in the perception of consonants. It has been argued that the transient nature of the stimulus cues for consonants forces listeners to impose a categorical identity upon these stimuli more rapidly than for vowels. Thus, after the stimulus has been identified, the acoustic cues that led to that identification are lost, and only the coded stimulus remains. This relationship implies that vowels are processed more at the auditory level than are consonants, because of their relatively longer duration. Moreover, it suggests that categorical perception is a reflection of the phonetic level of processing in which a phonetic identity is imposed and all other acoustic features are lost (thus leading to especially poor performance on within-category discrimination tests).

The role of memory in categorical perception has been investigated by Pisoni (1973). Pisoni varied the delay interval (from 0 to 2 seconds) in a simple

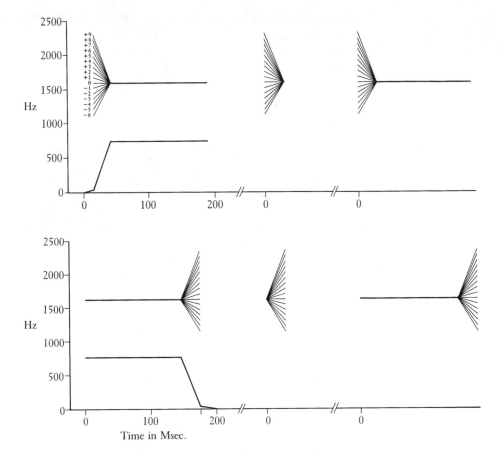

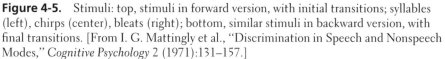

Figure 4-5. Stimuli: top, stimuli in forward version, with initial transitions; syllables (left), chirps (center), bleats (right); bottom, similar stimuli in backward version, with final transitions. [From I. G. Mattingly et al., "Discrimination in Speech and Nonspeech Modes," *Cognitive Psychology* 2 (1971):131–157.]

same/different task involving vowel and stop consonant continua. The delay interval had relatively little effect for consonants but significantly impaired the within-category performance for vowels. Pisoni argued on the basis of these and related results that the relatively strong discrimination performance within categories for vowels was not due to the absence of a conversion to a phonetic mode but to the greater longevity of the auditory mode for vowels. These results are nicely summarized by Studdert-Kennedy (1975):

> Stop consonants are indeed perceived differently than vowels. For while the vowel, carrier of stress, rhythm, and prosody, leaves a rapidly fading "echo," the consonant leaves none. The initial sound of [da], for example, is difficult if not impossible to hear: the sound escapes us and we perceive the event, almost instantly, as phonetic. (p. 12)

Attentional processes   Categorical perception is not the only evidence for the modularity of speech perception. Rand (1974) performed an experiment in which a formant transition was presented to one ear and its steady-state portion was presented to the other ear. Although neither of these stimuli was speech, Rand reported that listeners could "integrate" these two signals into a meaningful speech signal.

The intriguing feature of this procedure is that it enables researchers to identify the characteristics of the signals coming into the two ears separately and to examine the process by which listeners integrate them into a speech sound. Figure 4-6 shows the normal **binaural** procedure: presenting the base (steady states plus first and second formant transitions) and the third formant transitions together to both ears. In the **duplex perception** procedure, the base is presented to one ear and the third formant transiton to the other. Mann, Madden, Russell, & Liberman (1981) found that different discrimination performances could be obtained simply by instructing the listener to attend to the chirp or to the integrated speech sound. When attention was directed to the speech, categorical-like performance was found (sharp discrimination peaks at category boundaries).

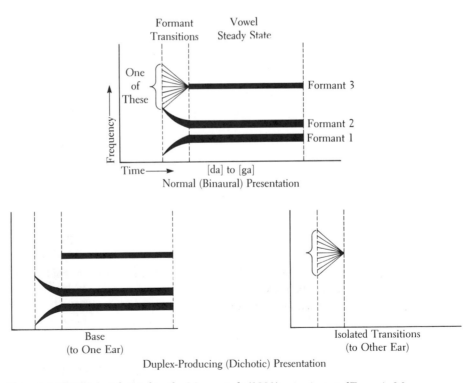

Figure 4-6.   Materials used in the Mann et al. (1981) experiment. [From A. M. Liberman, "On Finding that Speech Is Special," *American Psychologist* 37 (1982): 148–167.]

However, the discrimination performance was flat when attention was directed to the nonspeech chirp. Moreover, the presentation of a vowel context influenced only the speech side of the dichotic signal.

These results suggest that the distinction between speech and nonspeech modes is clear, but that the conditions necessary to obtain the phonetic mode involve the deployment of attention and not just the presence of certain acoustic cues. Listeners are perfectly capable of directing their attention to the nonspeech qualities of the stimulus. Nonetheless, when they direct their attention to the speech qualities, distinctive results are obtained.

Another recently discovered phenomenon is related to the relative equivalence of various cues in the perception of speech. It has been known for some time that our perception of consonants is aided by a number of cues present in the speech signal. For example, the detection of the [p] in *split* versus *slit* depends in part on the VOT but also on the second formant transition. Fitch, Halwes, Erickson, and Liberman (1980) examined the role of these two cues by *trading* them off: the relative value of one cue was changed in one direction while the other cue was changed in the opposite direction. Thus, researchers can determine how much of one cue is needed to obtain the same effect as the other cue. They found that the role of formant transitions is accomplished by approximately 20 milliseconds of silence following the release of the [p].

The main point, however, is that these trading relations are sensitive to the listener's deployment of attention. In particular, it has been found that these relations only exist when the stimuli are perceived as speech (Best, Morrongiello, & Robson, 1981). When, as before, the synthetic stimuli may be perceived as either speech or nonspeech, the distinctively phonetic trading relations hold for the speech mode only.

The Motor Theory of Speech Perception

Shortly after the initial discovery of categorical perception (Liberman, Harris, Hoffman, & Griffith, 1957), Liberman and his colleagues developed a theory of speech perception based on the notion that perception proceeds "by reference" to production (Liberman, Cooper, Shankweiler, & Studdert-Kennedy, 1967). The notion is that listeners use implicit articulatory knowledge—knowledge about how sounds are produced—as an aid in perception. To some extent, this approach is motivated by the economy of using the same mechanisms for both perception and production. But the main rationale for the motor theory is that it deals effectively with the problem of invariance discussed earlier. Liberman and colleagues (1967) argue that although the relationship between acoustic structure and perception is quite complex, the link between articulation and perception is more direct: sounds produced in similar ways but with varying acoustic representations are perceived in similar ways.

There does appear to be a link between perception and production. Students taking foreign language classes are often encouraged to practice articulating new sounds as a means of hearing them better. Anecdotal evidence suggests that teaching students to produce sounds silently aids them in the identification of new sounds (Catford et al., 1991). As Catford points out, this activity might encourage new learners to attend to subtle motor processes that would otherwise be over-shadowed by auditory sensations.

There is also some experimental evidence for the theory. Studies of the role of visual information in speech perception suggest that we may use articulatory knowledge during speech perception. McGurk and MacDonald (1976) showed that when visual information and auditory information are in conflict, perceivers use both sources of information to arrive at a stable perception. When the lips of the speaker indicate the velar consonant [ga] while the synchronized speech is the bilabial stop [ba], perceivers report hearing [da], an alveolar stop that retains some of the phonetic features of the other two sounds. In a subsequent study, MacDonald and McGurk (1978) demonstrated that place of articulation (especially the lips) is cued primarily by eye and that manner of articulation is cued more by ear. These reports indicate that listeners use information about the way a sound was produced from both auditory and visual modes in the process of speech perception.

Recently, Liberman and Mattingly (1985) updated the motor theory with regard to current thinking in cognitive psychology. In the revised theory, the claim is that the objects of speech perception are the intended phonetic gestures of the speaker. Phonetic gestures include such movements as rounding of the lips, raising the jaw, and so on. By intended phonetic gestures, Liberman and Mattingly are referring to invariant motor commands sent from the brain to the structures in the vocal tract. According to the revised theory, the conversion from acoustic signal to intended phonetic gesture is done rapidly and automatically by a phonetic module.

The motor theory is not without its critics. MacNeilage (1991) has suggested that the concept of phonetic gesture is too abstract, and that, consequently, the motor theory is not directly testable. Liberman and Mattingly (1985) acknowledge that these neural commands do not result in invariant configurations of the vocal tract. Because of context-conditioned variation, the actual configurations vary with the phonetic context.

Despite these problems, the motor theory remains interesting, more than 20 years after its initial formulation, because it contains some far-reaching implications about language. In particular, the theory makes some testable claims about the brain mechanisms associated with language. Generally, it has been held that the areas responsible for language perception and production are distinct and separate. The motor theory would expect a closer neurological link between these functions. Ojemann (1983) provides some support for the idea that the perception and production areas of the brain are closely related and, thus indirectly, for the motor theory. (We will discuss the brain mechanisms responsible for language in Chapter 13.)

In addition, the theory has some interesting implications regarding language acquisition. Recall from Chapter 3 that infants can hear certain phonetic distinctions well before they are able to produce them. If the phonetic mode of perception depends upon a link between perception and production, as the motor theory presumes, then the link might also be present shortly after birth. Liberman and

Mattingly (1985) speculate that infants in their first year may be sensitive to the acoustic consequences of all language gestures significant in *any* language, and only over time narrow down to their own language. If so, the phonetic module, which links these perceptual and productive skills, may be an important innate mechanism in the acquisition of language. (We will discuss language acquisition processes more fully in Chapter 12.)

On balance, then, the motor theory has been a useful theory. Beyond its specific contributions to our understanding of speech perception, it provides links with related aspects of language study in ways that suggest a more comprehensive view of language.

Summary

Speech may be processed at the auditory, phonetic, or phonological levels of processing. The auditory level is characteristic of the way all sounds are perceived, whereas the phonetic level is assumed to be specific to speech, and the phonological level specific to a particular language.

Various investigators have argued that speech is perceived through a special mode of perception. Part of the argument rests on the failure to find invariant relationships between acoustic properties and perceptual experiences, and part is supported by the empirical phenomena of categorical perception, duplex perception, and phonetic trading relations.

The motor theory of speech perception claims that we perceive speech sounds by identifying the intended phonetic gestures that may produce the sounds. Although the status of the concept of phonetic gestures is somewhat controversial, the theory has been supported by studies of visual processing during speech perception. In addition, the theory has implications for neurolinguistics and language acquisition in children.

Perception of Continuous Speech

Up until now we have dealt with the convenient fiction of the speech sound in isolation. Under normal listening conditions, however, speech sounds are embedded in a context of fluent speech. Since we know that the acoustic structure of a speech sound varies with its immediate phonetic context, it seems likely that broader aspects of context, such as adjacent syllables and clauses, may play a significant role in our identification of speech.

This point was demonstrated by Pollack and Pickett (1964), who recorded the conversations of women who were waiting to participate in a psychology experiment in a soundproof room. Individual words were spliced out of these tape-recorded conversations and presented individually to a separate group of subjects. Although the words were perfectly intelligible in the context of fluent speech, only about one-half of the words were correctly identified when presented in isolation. Thus, acoustic information may be insufficient by itself to permit identification of speech sounds; we may need to appreciate the context in which a speech sound is uttered in order to interpret it correctly.

This context consists of many factors, but only the two main factors will be considered here. First, we will examine the role of prosodic factors in perception. Next, we will consider the role of higher order semantic and syntactic factors.

Prosodic Factors in Speech Recognition

There is little doubt that prosodic factors such as stress, intonation, and rate influence the perception of speech. They provide a source of stability in perception since we can often hear these superimposed qualities at a distance that would tax our ability to identify the individual speech segments. For instance, we can detect the moods of persons talking down the hall from the intonational contours of their speech but still not be able to identify what they are saying. Similarly, other prosodic factors, such as speech rate or tempo, are relatively easy to detect. The sheer availability of prosodic information suggests that it probably plays some role in the identification of segmental information. Let us look at two cases of the way prosodic and segmental information interact: stress and rate.

Stress   It appears that we perceive stress by a combination of acoustic cues along with our knowledge of the stress rules of the language (Lieberman, 1965). One of the main acoustic cues to stress, in addition to pitch and duration, is the intensity of the sound. We distinguish between the two meanings of *blackbird*, for example, by detecting the relative loudness of the first and second syllables. In addition to loudness, the rate at which syllables are produced can influence perceived stress. Bolinger and Gerstman (1957) demonstrated that a brief pause between the /t/ and /h/ in *light house keeper* can change the perceived stress. Without the pause, the primary stress was heard on *light*, secondary on *keeper*, and tertiary on *house* (that is, a keeper of lighthouses). When the pause was introduced, the primary stress was shared by *light* and *house*, with *keeper* having secondary stress (a house-keeper who does light housekeeping).

Martin (1972) has argued that the stress pattern of speech provides cues for listeners to anticipate what is coming next and that listeners tend to organize their perception around stressed syllables. An experimental demonstration of this point was provided by Shields, McHugh, and Martin (1974). They presented speech passages to listeners who had to detect the presence of a particular speech segment, such as [b]. The researchers found that the detection rates were faster with stressed syllables than with unstressed syllables, but this occurred only for speech. When the same words were embedded in a list of nonsense words, the difference between stressed and unstressed syllables did not appear. This suggests that we tend to interpret continuous speech in terms of stress patterns.

Rate   Speakers modify their rates of production by the number and length of pauses during utterances, as well as by the amount of time spent articulating the utterance (Grosjean & Lane, 1981). J. L. Miller (1981) has documented the acoustic consequences of changes in speaking rates. As we speed up, vowel duration is reduced, and the duration of the cues that signal various consonantal distinctions is also modified.

As we have seen, VOT is an important cue for voiced versus voiceless stop consonants. Short VOTs are associated with voiced sounds; longer VOTs are found with voiceless sounds. These VOT values, however, are sensitive to the rate at which the words are spoken. As the speech rate increases, there is a tendency for VOT values to decrease (Summerfield, 1974, cited in J. L. Miller, 1981). Consequently, VOT values do not serve as invariant cues for voicing but are, like most of the cues we have examined, context-dependent.

Summerfield (1975, cited in J. L. Miller, 1981) has demonstrated that when a target syllable is preceded by a precursor syllable articulated at a slow, normal, or fast rate of speech, listeners hear the constant target syllable as different sounds. With faster rates, the perceived boundary between voiced and voiceless sounds shifted toward smaller VOT values. With [g] and [k], for instance, a sound that would be perceived as [g] with a normal rate of speaking would be perceived as [k] with a faster rate. Exactly the opposite occurred with slower rates.

This process of taking information about speech rate into consideration when identifying individual speech segments is referred to as **rate normalization** and has been demonstrated for a number of phonetic distinctions (see J. L. Miller, 1981, for a review). Listeners appear to operate under the assumption that the acoustic cues for various sounds must be adjusted to what is known about the circumstances under which the sounds are produced. The rate of production is one case. Another is the size of the vocal tract of the speaker, which also influences the exact values of various acoustic cues. There is evidence that listeners use the pitch of the speech signal as a cue for vocal-tract size and make perceptual adjustments on this basis, too (Diehl, Souther, & Convis, 1980). This is called **speaker normalization.** Both types of normalization are consistent with the earlier conclusion that implicit articulatory knowledge may aid in the perception of speech.

Semantic and Syntactic Factors in Speech Perception

Context and speech recognition   As we have seen, a word isolated from its context becomes less intelligible (Pollack & Pickett, 1964). It follows that if we vary semantic and syntactic aspects of this context, then we should find changes in the perceptibility of the speech passage.

The role of higher order contextual factors in speech recognition has been convincingly demonstrated by George Miller and his associates. Miller, Heise, and Lichten (1951) presented words either in isolation or in five-word sentences in the presence of white noise (hissing sound). Performance was better in the sentence condition at all levels of noise. Apparently, listeners were able to use the syntactic and semantic constraints of continuous speech to limit the number of possibilities to consider. Further research (G. A. Miller & Isard, 1963) isolated the influence of syntactic and semantic information in this process. In this study, three different types of sentences were presented in continuous speech: (1) grammatical strings, (2) anomalous strings that preserved grammatical word order, and (3) ungrammatical strings:

(1)   Accidents kill motorists on the highways.

(2)   Accidents carry honey between the house.

(3)   Around accidents country honey the shoot.

The results indicated that people were most accurate with grammatical strings, somewhat less accurate with anomalous strings, and even less able to recognize ungrammatical strings. It would appear that the more predictable a passage is, the better it is recognized.

These results are consistent with our discussion of top-down processing in Chapter 3. Top-down processing proceeds from the semantic level of processing to the sensory levels. Thus, our knowledge of the general organization of the input enables us to predict some of the sensory features that are to follow. Top-down processing of continuous speech seems most likely when the speech context is semantically reasonable and familiar to the listener.

Phonemic restoration   A most dramatic demonstration of the role of top-down processing of speech signals comes from what is called the **phonemic restoration effect,** studied by Warren (1970; Warren and Warren, 1970). The first /s/ in the word *legislatures* in sentence (4) was removed and replaced with a cough:

(4)   The state governors met with their respective legislatures convening in the capital city.

This procedure led to a striking auditory illusion: listeners reported hearing the excised /s/! In addition, when told that a sound was missing and asked to guess which one, nearly all listeners were unsuccessful. Restoration has also been found in a variation of the procedure in which a noise is added to but does not replace the speech sound (Samuel, 1981).

Subsequent studies have shown that it is the context that helps determine how phonemic restorations take place. When Warren and Warren (1970) presented the following four sentences to listeners, they found that the restorations that were made were related to the subsequent context: **eel* was heard as *wheel, heel, peel,* or *meal,* depending on the sentence.

(5)   It was found that the *eel was on the axle.

(6)   It was found that the *eel was on the shoe.

(7)   It was found that the *eel was on the orange.

(8)   It was found that the *eel was on the table.

Phonemic restoration is closely related to the fact that we normally listen to speech when lots of other events are taking place: people are knocking things over, other conversations are taking place, the television is on, and so on. There are many segments of the speech signal that are impossible to identify in isolation because of masking from other sounds, indistinct or mumbled production, and related factors, yet we are generally able to achieve perceptual recognition by actively using higher order contextual factors. Phonemic restoration is a particularly dramatic demonstration of top-down processing since it shows that the perception may occur in the complete absence of bottom-up information. In most situations, however, the two forms of processing interact. We will now look at several instances of this interaction.

Mispronunciation detection   What happens when a perfectly ordinary sentence contains a minor phonetic error? For example, if you heard sentence (9), would you have noticed that the first phoneme in the fourth word has been mispronounced? (You might try reading it aloud to a friend.)

(9)   It has been zuggested that students be required to preregister.

Our subjective impression is that minor errors in pronunciation tend to be ignored, as we "know" what the person was trying to say. Still, some mispronounced sounds do get detected. Cole (1973) found that the likelihood of detection depends upon the place in a word or sentence. Detection performance was better for mispronunciations at the beginning of a word compared to those later in a word, and better earlier in a sentence than later on.

Marslen-Wilson and Welsh (1978) extended these results by combining the mispronunciation detection task with a shadowing task. A **shadowing task** is one in which subjects have to repeat immediately what they hear. Marslen-Wilson and Welsh examined the conditions under which listeners would repeat a mispronounced sound exactly, as opposed to restoring the "intended" pronunciation. They found that restorations were associated with greater fluency than were exact repetitions; in particular, less pausing was observed for restorations. Moreover, restorations tended to occur when the context was highly predictable, but reproductions were more likely with low levels of contextual predictability.

It is as if when we "know" what a person is going to say, we barely listen for the actual words and need only check for broad agreement of sounds with expectations. In contrast, when uncertainty is higher, we are less likely to have a firm basis upon which to make these restorations. Moreover, the fluent nature of the restorations suggests that semantic and syntactic constraints are naturally integrated with incoming speech during language processing. These are not "guesses" but rather are heard, like phonemic restorations, just as clearly as if they were really there. Our immediate awareness thus seems to be a combination of an analysis of incoming sounds with an application of semantic and syntactic constraints.

The interactive nature of the perceptual process is revealed in another aspect of Marslen-Wilson and Welsh's study. They examined the relative proportion of restorations in cases in which the target ("intended") phoneme and presented phoneme differed in one, two, or three distinctive features. The percentage of restorations was far higher (74%) when only one feature differentiated target and presented phoneme than when three features differentiated them (24%). So bottom-up processing plays a role here, too. Even if the context strongly implies that a word is appropriate, if the expected phoneme is not sufficiently similar to the presented one on phonetic grounds, restoration is not likely to occur. Under these conditions, listeners are prone to pause, as if to make these comparisons, then repeat the presented word.

The TRACE Model of Speech Perception

Much of our discussion so far in this chapter may be summed up with reference to the **TRACE model** of speech perception presented by McClelland and Elman (1986; Elman & McClelland, 1988). The TRACE model challenges the assumption, found in the modularity view, that phonemic processing is unaffected by higher levels of processing. In contrast, it assumes that several levels of processing—distinctive features, phonemes, and words—are simultaneously active during speech perception and interact with each other.

Let us look at the TRACE model more closely. McClelland and Elman assume that there is a cognitive unit for each feature (for example, nasality) at the feature level, for each phoneme at the phoneme level, and for each word at the word level. At any given time, all of these units are activated to a greater or lesser extent, as opposed to being all or none. When units are activated above a certain threshold, they may influence other units at the same or different levels. These effects may be either excitatory or inhibitory; that is, they may increase or decrease the activation of other units. The entire network of units is referred to as the trace, because "the pattern of activation left by a spoken input is a trace of the analysis of the input at each of the three processing levels" (McClelland & Elman, 1986, pp. 66–67). The network is active and changes with subsequent input.

McClelland and Elman claim that the TRACE model can explain most of the facts about speech perception we have considered, including categorical perception, trading relations, top-down processing, and coarticulation effects. Let us look at coarticulation in particular. Consider the phrases *foolish capes* and *Christmas capes*. The word *foolish* ends with the /š/ sound, which is made at the front of the mouth. In contrast, the final sound in *Christmas* is /s/, which is made by shortening the lips and thus the vocal tract as a whole. These articulatory differences influence the perception of the initial phoneme of the subsequent word (Mann & Repp, 1981). If the first phoneme of the next word were ambiguous, for example, between a /t/ and a /k/, listeners heard it as /t/ when preceded by /š/ but as /k/ when following /s/.

Elman and McClelland (1988) found that similar coarticulation effects occurred even when the final phoneme of the initial word was not present. They presented listeners with pairs of words such as *fooliX capes* and *ChristmaX capes*, in which X represented an ambiguous sound. Once again, the first phoneme of the second word was ambiguous, and the word could be heard as *capes* or *tapes*. Elman and McClelland found coarticulation effects similar to those found by Mann and Repp (1981) despite the fact that the /š/ and /s/ phonemes were not present. They concluded that they found evidence of top-down processing in phonemic processing and that activation of word units influenced phonemic units.

It appears that the TRACE model provides a good account of many facts about speech perception. Still, it is likely that both interactive and modular approaches will play a role in a complete account of language processing. This is because there may well be limits on the kinds of interaction among levels that takes place. For instance, Connine (1987; Connine & Clifton, 1987) recently found that the sentence level did not influence the perception of phonemes, although the word level did. Future research seems likely to uncover the limits as well as the promises of interactive models.

Summary

Contextual information powerfully influences the perception of individual speech segments. Prosody is used to organize incoming speech and to adjust acoustic cues for various speech sounds. Phonemic restoration and mispronunciation data suggest that higher levels of processing may influence the perception of phonemes. Our perception of speech segments in continuous speech appears to be an interaction of various levels of analysis that proceed simultaneously in the course of language processing.

Perception of Written Language

In this section we examine the early stages of visual language processing during reading. Reading, clearly, is a multifaceted and complex process, and we cannot do full justice to this complexity here. Rather, our approach will be selective in attempting to identify points of similarity and difference with the early stages of auditory language processing. Visual processing of larger units of language, such as sentences and discourse, will be treated in subsequent chapters.

Levels of Written Language Processing

As with speech perception, the perception of written language can be understood at a number of levels. We may distinguish among feature, letter, and word levels of processing.

At the **feature level,** the stimulus is represented in terms of the physical features that comprise a letter of the alphabet. For instance, the letter *K* may be represented as a vertical line and two diagonal lines; *R* may be coded as a vertical line, a diagonal line, and a curved portion, and so on. At the **letter level,** the visual stimulus is represented more abstractly as an identity separate from its physical manifestation. That is, a stimulus may be represented as an *F* regardless of whether it is typewritten or handwritten. Finally, there is a **word level** of processing, in which an array of features and letters is recognized as a familiar word. As the word is recognized, various properties of the word, such as its spelling, pronunciation, and meaning, become available to us.

These distinctions raise several important questions concerning the perception of written language. First, how do we go about extracting these elements of the written word? Is there any evidence that we identify the features of words prior to word identification? Second, is the order of levels of processing invariant? Do we always need to identify the constituent letters of a word before identifying the word? We will tackle the first question first, as we next examine the pattern of eye movements that occurs as we read written language.

Eye Movements during Reading

The study of reading is one of the oldest topics in experimental psychology, and some of the earliest investigators discovered that it was fruitful to examine the role of eye movements during the reading process (for example, see Huey, 1968). Modern technology has made tremendous advances in this area, and we now have the capacity to monitor these eye patterns closely and to examine the role they may play in a wide variety of psychological processes (Just & Carpenter, 1976).

Some representative data on eye movements during reading for various grade levels are shown in Table 4-3. The average college student reads leisure material, such as a magazine article, at about 280 words per minute. This rate obviously varies with the material. It would be greater for children's stories and less for an anatomy textbook. Table 4-3 also reveals that rate is sensitive to reading skill, or at least grade level, since it more than triples from first grade to college.

Table 4-3. Components of Eye Movements as a Function of Grade Level

	Grade												
	1	*2*	*3*	*4*	*5*	*6*	*7*	*8*	*9*	*10*	*11*	*12*	*C*
Average duration of fixations (in seconds)	0.33	0.30	0.28	0.27	0.27	0.27	0.27	0.27	0.27	0.26	0.26	0.25	0.24
Regressions per 100 words	52	40	35	31	28	25	23	21	20	19	18	17	15
Fixations (not including regressions) per 100 words	172	134	120	108	101	95	91	88	85	82	78	77	75
Number of words per fixation	0.58	0.75	0.83	0.93	0.99	1.05	1.10	1.14	1.18	1.22	1.28	1.30	1.33
Rate with comprehension in words per minute	80	115	138	158	173	185	195	204	214	224	237	250	280

Source: S. E. Taylor, H. Frackenpohl, and J. L. Pettee, *Grade Level Norms for the Components of the Fundamental Reading Skill* (Huntington, NY: Educational Development Laboratories Research and Information Bulletin No. 3, 1960).

Although the overall reading rate gives us some idea of the way a person has processed a chunk of reading material, a clearer understanding of information processing during reading comes from an analysis of various contributors to the overall reading rate.

Saccades   The movements of the eyes during reading are called saccadic eye movements, or **saccades.** The saccades take approximately 10 to 20 milliseconds in duration, and it has been established that our eyes are moving too quickly for us to pick up any visual information from the printed page during these saccades (Haber & Hershenson, 1973). Rather, we just perceive a blur. These movements traverse approximately 10 letters on the average and may proceed in either forward or backward directions.

Regressions   Saccades that move backward (leftward in English, rightward in Hebrew) are called **regressions.** About 15% of the eye movements of mature readers are regressions. It is generally believed that they are an indication that a reader has misperceived or misunderstood some portion of a text and has gone back to reanalyze it. As seen in Table 4-3, the proportion of regressive eye movements is considerably higher in the lower grade levels than in the college population.

Fixations   The time that we spend at a given location between eye movements is termed a **fixation.** It is possible, through eye-monitoring equipment, to determine the exact point on the printed page at which a person's eye fixates. Typically, these fixations last about 250 milliseconds, but fixation duration varies with both the difficulty of the content and the skill of the reader. Moreover, there is some variability in fixation durations for a given reader of a given text; a person might fixate one segment for 200 milliseconds, and then the next for 300 milliseconds. It is generally believed that these fluctuations in fixation duration reflect the transient changes in processing difficulty across sentences and paragraphs. It has been shown, for example, that the time taken to read a given portion of a story is related to the ease or difficulty associated with integrating that portion with previous sentences and paragraphs (Daneman & Carpenter, 1980). Thus, fixation duration is one index of the difficulty of information processing during reading.

One aspect of enduring concern (Huey, 1968; Woodworth, 1938) has been the size of the area from which a reader picks up visual information, or the **span of fixation.** The role of peripheral cues in reading has been probed in a series of ingenious studies by Rayner (1975). The basic methodology is to have a person read a passage displayed on a computer screen while, unknown to the individual, certain words from the passage are being replaced by other words and letter strings. These replacements always take place during the saccades. As noted earlier, no visual information is extracted during this time. The replacements are set up in such a way that the peripheral view is of the original word whereas, when the string is fixated, another set of letters is present.

Rayner (1975) reasoned that if the letters in peripheral view were extracted, then a change when the letters were fixated should increase processing time, and hence fixation duration. One of the sentences he used was (10):

(10)   The captain granted the pass in the afternoon.

The key word here is *granted*. Upon fixation the reader saw *granted*, but the peripheral information was either another word (*guarded*), a nonword that was visually similar (*gnarbed*), or a nonword that was visually dissimilar (*pmavbcd*). Readers saw one of the three alternatives to *granted* in the periphery, but all saw *granted* during fixation. Rayner found that both visual and semantic inconsistencies increased fixation duration, indicating that peripheral information is used during reading. However, the size of the area from which information is derived is limited to 7 to 12 character spaces for visual information, and 1 to 6 for semantic information. Thus, we extract information from the periphery during reading, but there are some rather strict limits on the size of this area.

Perception of Letters in Isolation

Let us return to the issue of whether the levels of processing we have identified proceed in a fixed order or whether there is more flexibility in how we extract features, letters, and words during reading. If studies of speech perception provide any clue, we would expect some degree of interaction between higher and lower order levels (that is, top-down processing) on the basis that a skilled reader might well be able to anticipate what is coming next and thus might be less reliant on the bottom-up visual information.

This issue has been addressed primarily in studies of word perception with individual letters and words presented tachistoscopically. A **tachistoscope** is a device that permits the rapid visual presentation of a stimulus. In a typical study, a stimulus might be presented for 50 milliseconds or less, with subjects asked to report what they see.

Participation in a tachistoscopic task can be a humbling experience. Although there are few things we do as well or as often as recognizing letters, when the stimuli are presented briefly and in isolation we often find ourselves uncertain of what we have seen. We may have a fleeting image of an *R* or was that a *K*? Perhaps it was even a *P*, but it certainly wasn't a *Z*. Studies of tachistoscopic perception have shown that the constituent features of letters are a significant determinant of performance. In particular, perceivers confuse letters with similar features, such as *E* and *F* or *R* and *P* (Rumelhart, 1970). This finding suggests that under conditions of brief presentation without word context, we can extract some but not all of the features associated with that letter.

Independent evidence of the role of features in the visual detection of letters comes from a task in which individuals searched an array of letters for a prespecified target letter, such as *K* (Neisser, 1964). Figure 4-7 shows two such arrays; you can get a feel for the experiment by scanning each for the letter *Z*. Studies have shown that detection time is faster when the array is made up of letters with different features (as in the first list) than when it consists of letters with features similar to *Z*, as in the second list (Neisser, 1964). This suggests that we identify letters from a variable number of features, depending on the other letters that are present. If the letters have vertical and diagonal lines, a careful scrutiny of the

ODUGOR	IVMXEW
OCDUGO	EWVMIX
COOGRD	EXWMVI
OUGCDR	IXEMWV
URDGQO	VXWEMI
GRUODO	MXVEWI
DUZGRO	XVWMEI
UCGROD	MWXVIE
DORCGU	VIMEXW
ODOCGU	EXVWIM
CGUROQ	VWMIEX
OCDURO	VMWIEX
UOCGOD	XVWMEI
RGOCOU	WXVEMI
GRUDQO	XMEWIV
GODUCO	MXIVEW
OCURDO	VEWMIX
DUCOQG	EMVXWI
CGRDOU	IVWMEX
UDRCOQ	IEVMWX
GOCORU	WVZMXE
GOQUCD	XEMIWV
GDOUOC	WXIMEV
URDCGO	EMWIVX
GODROC	IVEMXW

Figure 4-7.   Stimuli used by Neisser (1964). [From U. Neisser, "Visual Search," *Scientific American* 210 (1964):94–102.]

visual array is necessary, but when the array is less confusing, the target seems to "jump out." In that instance, the number of features needed for identification is much smaller.

It might be noted that the case for feature analysis in human perceptual performance is not limited to behavioral studies. Physiological investigations by Hubel and Wiesel (1965) have shown that cells in the visual cortex of cats are selectively responsive to visual stimulation such as vertical lines, edges of lines, and edges of a certain length moving at a certain rate. It is quite possible that a similar arrangement exists in the human nervous system.

Perception of Letters in Word Context

The word-superiority effect   An early study of word perception was conducted by Cattell (1886), who compared performance on individual letters with letters in word context. His results were striking. Whereas people were able to report only about three or four unrelated letters, they could report as many as two short words that were not semantically or syntactically related to one another.

Cattell's report was the first to demonstrate superior performance for words over nonword letter strings, but it suffered from methodological problems. Specifically, he instructed his subjects to report everything that they remembered from the briefly presented array. This method can lead to two problems. First, as we saw in Chapter 3, it has been shown that more information is retained in sensory memory than can be reported (Sperling, 1960), so forgetting may be partly responsible for these results. Second, and more important, response factors such as guessing can play a role in these results. To see this, consider the difference between perceiving *yelv* and *read*. Even if perceivers could identify only the second and third letters from these two arrays, they might still perform better with the word array because of prior knowledge of words that have the form _ea_. Moreover, if one or more features of the initial *r* in *read* were extracted, subjects might be able to guess that the last letter was a *d* even if they had not picked up any visual information at all from that position. Of course, they might also guess wrong and choose *l*, but a nonword string doesn't provide any basis for guessing at all. Thus, although Cattell's results are interesting, they don't clearly show that the difference between words and letter strings is due to perceptual rather than response factors.

Surprisingly, it took more than 80 years for these problems to be corrected, and with it, renewed interest in what was now called the **word-superiority effect** was stimulated.

Clear evidence that the word-superiority effect can occur when response factors are controlled was first documented by Reicher (1969). Individuals were tachistoscopically presented with a word (*word*), a nonword (*owrd*), or a letter (*d* or *k*). Immediately after the display was removed, the subjects were given a recognition test on one of the letters from the display. For example, they might be asked whether the letter in the final position was a *d* or a *k*. Reicher found that accuracy was greater when a word was presented than when a nonword or a single letter was presented. The results are especially significant since *d* and *k* would both result in a word (*word* or *work*), so guessing can be ruled out as a possible explanation. This study provided the first clear evidence that the word-superiority effect was perceptual in nature. The results seem to suggest that we process letters more efficiently within words, implying that word processing aids letter identification, rather than the other way around.

The superior performance of words in relation to nonwords found by both Cattell and Reicher clearly indicates that our experience with words makes a big difference in this task. Numerous investigators (Baron & Thurston, 1973; N. F. Johnson, 1975; Smith & Spoehr, 1974; Wheeler, 1970) have suggested that we process words in higher order units, although there is no consensus quite yet on just what these units may be. Some investigators suggest that whole words, especially if used frequently, may be encoded as a single unit. Others emphasize the role of linguistic knowledge in establishing intermediate units of processing, such as letter groups and syllables.

The Interactive Activation Model

Now that we have discussed some of the processes involved in the perception of letters and words, let us turn to how we might explain perceptual processing. I will concentrate primarily on the interactive activation model introduced by McClelland and Rumelhart (1981). (The model draws upon earlier efforts: Adams, 1979; Johnston & McClelland, 1980; and, especially, Morton, 1969.)

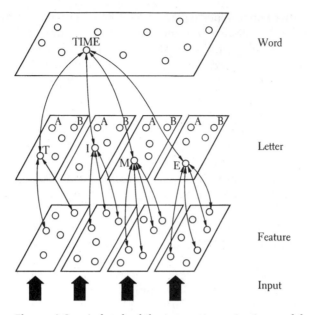

Figure 4-8. A sketch of the interactive activation model of word perception. Units within the same rectangle stand for incompatible alternative hypotheses about an input pattern and are all mutually inhibitory. The bidirectional excitatory connections between levels are indicated for one word and its constituents. [From J. L. McClelland, "Putting Knowledge in Its Place: A Scheme for Programming Parallel Processing Structures on the Fly," *Cognitive Science* 9 (1985):115.]

McClelland and Rumelhart's model is based on three main assumptions. The first is that processing occurs at three different levels: feature, letter, and word (see Figure 4-8). The second assumption is that all of these levels are operating in parallel. That is, processing is occurring simultaneously on all three levels. Finally, there is interaction among the three levels. The interaction may be either excitatory (in which the activation at one level increases the activation at another level) or inhibitory (in which activation at one level decreases the activation at another level). For example, activation of the letter detector for *E* may excite word detectors that contain an *E* but inhibit word detectors that don't. Notice that in this case, a lower level influences activation at the higher level, but the model assumes that higher levels influence lower levels as well.

The model provides an interesting account of the word-superiority effect. Consider the case of the word *work*. As some of the letters are detected, they activate detectors for words that are consistent with the recognized letters. As these words are activated, they provide feedback to the letter level, which increases the strength of activation of the individual letters. As a consequence of this top-down effect, letters embedded in words receive more activation than single letters or letters in nonword strings. The model also accounts for the fact that letters in pronounceable nonwords (pseudowords) are perceived better than letters in nonpronounceable nonwords (Baron & Thurston, 1973). McClelland and Rumelhart assume that pseudowords (such as *mave*) activate detectors for words that share more than one letter (such as *more* and *mate*). These word-level activations then feed back to the letter level, enabling us to perceive letters in pseudowords almost as well as letters in words.

McClelland and Rumelhart suggest that there are two reasons for the success of their model. One is the "architecture"; that is, the assumption that processing is distributed among three different levels of processing appears to be an important assumption. The other main reason they cite is that the model assumes that processing is "massively parallel." It is similar to the TRACE model of speech perception (Elman & McClelland, 1988; McClelland & Elman, 1986) that we have already discussed as well as a model of speech production (Dell, 1986) that we will consider in Chapter 8. These models are often called **connectionist** models because they explain complex processes in terms of the connections among elementary units.

One measure of the importance of a theory is the amount of criticism it inspires. Richman and Simon (1989) claim that a sequential model can explain context effects in letter perception as well as the interactive activation model. In contrast, Healy, Oliver, and McNamara (1987) and Allen and Madden (1990) retain the parallel processing assumption but argue that different levels of processing do not interact with one another. All of these models have merit, and all of them can explain some facts that the others cannot. The interactive activation model is complex; it will take some time to identify which of its assumptions are crucial for explaining the important facts about letter and word perception.

Summary

Processing of written language exists at three main levels: the feature, letter, and word. All three pieces of visual information are extracted through a series of eye movements. Reading speed is determined by the duration of our fixations, the span of material that is fixated, and the proportion of regressive eye movements. Regressions typically reflect a reanalysis of previous material, whereas fixation duration is a sensitive barometer of the difficulty we have in integrating the fixated material with previous material.

There is clear evidence that featural and letter informations influence subsequent stages of processing. The notion that the stages operate in invariant order, however, is called into question by the word-superiority effect, in which the perception of individual letters is facilitated by the presence of a word or a wordlike context. These and related aspects of letter and word perception have been explained in terms of the interaction between detectors at different levels of processing.

On balance, the conclusions that have arisen from our survey of reading are congruent with those we reached when discussing listening. Although there are some visual phenomena, such as regressions and saccades, which have no direct auditory counterpart, these cases appear to be restricted primarily to the feature and letter levels. At the word level, there is much similarity between oral and written language. We now turn to a fuller discussion of words in Chapter 5.

Review Questions

1. Describe the place and manner of articulation for the phonetic segments [b], [d], [g], [p], [t], and [k].
2. Describe what a spectrogram is, and include descriptions of formants, formant transitions, and steady states.
3. What is categorical perception, and why is it more prominent for consonants than for vowels?
4. What is the motor theory of speech perception?
5. What is rate normalization?
6. Why does phonemic restoration show that a purely bottom-up model of speech perception is inadequate?
7. What is the TRACE model of speech perception?
8. Define the levels of processing we go through in the perception of written language.
9. Define the word-superiority effect.
10. How does the interactive activation model account for the word-superiority effect?

Thought Questions

1. On the basis of your understanding of categorical perception, do you think that this phenomenon would occur if you heard sounds from a foreign language? Why or why not?
2. If a person suffered from a congenital physical condition that disrupted motor control of speech organs, would the person's speech perception also be impaired?
3. The text discusses normalization based on two aspects of speech: its rate and the pitch of the speaker's voice. Can you think of any other basis for normalization? Discuss your choice.
4. As a student, you may have had experience listening to a nonnative lecturer whose English was somewhat limited. Relate your experience as a listener to the concepts of top-down and bottom-up processing.

5

The Internal Lexicon

- A word's meaning includes both sense and reference. Sense refers to a word's relationships with other words, whereas reference pertains to the relationships between a word and an object or event in the world.
- The organization of word knowledge in permanent memory is called the internal lexicon. Four hypotheses about the structure of the internal lexicon have been advanced: semantic features, prototypes, semantic networks, and mental models.
- Studies of semantic verification have been used to test various models of the lexicon. The findings of this research have tended to support a semantic network model called the spreading activation model.
- The process by which we activate our knowledge of words is termed lexical access. Lexical access is influenced by the frequency of a word, its morphology, whether it is ambiguous, and whether a semantically similar word has just been encountered.

Introduction

This chapter is about words—what they consist of and how we find them, use them, and relate them to each other. Of all the levels of language we will discuss, words are the most familiar, for a good share of our daily activity involves the playful manipulation of words. If any indication of our voracious appetite for word play is needed, consider the enduring appeal of puns, anagrams, crossword puzzles, and television game shows. Let's look at one case of word play and see what it tells us about the way words are understood and used.

In one popular game show, teams of two contestants are chosen, and one member of each team is designated as the sender while the other is the receiver. The purpose of the game is to communicate a specific target word to the receiver by using other, related words. The teams alternate taking turns. One sender might begin with the cue word *elephant,* to which the receiver responds with *large*. If the response is not correct, the other sender uses another word, say, *vivid*, and receives a response, say, *bright*. The process continues with new cues until one of the receivers identifies the target word.

To understand how this game is performed, we must distinguish between the process of retrieving information about words and the storage of words in memory. The distinction is similar to the one between the information about words that is contained in a dictionary and the processes (flipping pages, and so on) by which we find the information. Psycholinguists refer to the representation of words in permanent memory as our **internal lexicon.** When a given word in our lexicon has been found, the properties we associate with the word become available for use. These properties include the meaning of the word, its spelling and pronunciation, its relationship to other words, and related information. Much of this is the stuff of which dictionaries are made, but our internal lexicon also contains information that is not strictly linguistic. A part of our knowledge of elephants is that they are said to never forget things, but this is not part of the meaning of the word per se.

The process by which we activate these meanings is called **lexical access.** A word in our internal lexicon may be activated in several ways. One way is as a result of the perception of the word; if we see *elephant* on a printed page, we identify it as a recognizable, familiar word and bring our knowledge of the word to bear on the task of comprehension. Alternatively, as in the game show, we activate meanings through other words, since all words conjure up the image of related words to varying degrees. In this chapter we begin by examining some issues pertaining to the meaning of words, then consider competing ideas about how the internal lexicon is arranged. In the final section, we discuss the role of a number of variables in lexical access.

Meaning

What is meaning? What is it that we know when we know the meaning of a word? And how is that meaning represented mentally? Linguists, philosophers, and psychologists have identified several important aspects of word meaning. Let us begin by looking at some of these distinctions.

Aspects of Meaning

Sense and reference　　The relationship between words and things in the world is termed the **reference** of a word; the things in the world are called the **referents** of the word. This aspect of meaning is crucial for determining whether or not given utterance is truthful. For instance, consider sentence (1):

(1)　　There is a brown cow grazing in the field.

When we understand the meaning of this sentence, then we grasp its **truth conditions,** the conditions under which the sentence may be said to be true. In this instance, there must be a cow, it must be brown, and it must be grazing in the field. That is, we must assess whether the events in the world correspond to the referents of the words *cow, brown, grazing,* and *field.* Reference concerns what the world should be like if a given utterance is true.

Not all reference is so easy. Some words clearly have meaning but it is difficult to know what they refer to. This group includes abstract words, such as *justice, plausibility,* and *relativity.* Other words are meaningful but have no real referents, such as *unicorn* or *minotaur.* But even though the reference of these words is unclear, they communicate meaning. One way to explain this is to assume that we can construe reference not only within the real world as we know it, but also in the context of possible worlds, worlds that do not exist but might possibly exist. In this context, the word *unicorn* might refer to an object in another, hypothetical world. The process of referring to imaginary worlds plays an important role in literature (Pavel, 1986).

Reference is a part of meaning, but there is more to meaning than reference. Two different words or expressions may have the same reference but not mean the same thing. For instance, the reference of the two noun phrases *The prime minister of Great Britain* and *The leader of the Conservative party* is currently the same, namely, John Major. But the meanings of the two expressions are different, as can be seen when a different party comes to power. Similarly, sentence (2) is currently true, but may not be after the next election. The truth value of the sentence will vary with the referents of the two noun phrases, but the meaning of the phrases and of the sentence will remain the same.

(2)   The leader of the Conservative party is the prime minister of Great Britain.

The part of meaning that is not its reference is termed its **sense.** The sense of a word means "its place in a system of relationships which it contracts with other words in the vocabulary" (Lyons, 1968, p. 427). Linguists have identified several important relations. **Synonymy** exists when two words or expressions mean the same thing, as in *fear* and *panic*. **Antonymy** refers to opposition of meaning, as in *big* and *small*. **Incompatibility** occurs when one word contradicts the other. This relation is found in words denoting color; for example, sentence (3) is incompatible with sentence (4):

(3)   Rebecca wore a red dress.
(4)   Rebecca wore a green dress.

Finally, **hyponymy** deals with the notion of class inclusion; that is, *dog* is a subordinate of *animal*, a coordinate (or cohyponym) of *cat*, and a superordinate of *German shepherd.*

These sense relations rest on the notion of implication. **Implication** exists when if one expression is true, then another must be true. For instance, sentence (5) implies (6):

(5)   Bob is a bachelor.
(6)   Bob is not married.

Each of the sense relations in the previous paragraph may be described in terms of implication. Synonymy, for instance, may be thought of as a bilateral implication in that each word in a synonym pair implies the other. In contrast, to say that Fido is a dog implies that he is an animal, but here the implication is only in one direction; to be an animal does not imply that one is a dog. I leave it to the interested reader to define the other relations in terms of implication.

Sense and reference are complementary aspects of meaning. Sense pertains to the relationships that exist between a word and other words in the language. Reference deals with the relationships between a word and what it stands for in the world. To use language in a meaningful manner, we need to pay attention to both properties.

Denotation and connotation   We have been speaking of the **denotation** of a word, which is the objective or dictionary meaning of the word. A word also has a **connotation.** It suggests certain aspects of meaning beyond that which it explicitly names or describes. Two words may have the same denotation but differ in their connotations.

For instance, consider the terms *bachelor* and *spinster* (E. E. Smith, 1978). From the standpoint of a dictionary definition, the terms are comparable: both refer to an adult who has never been married. But there are other aspects of meaning that the dictionary definition does not fully capture. For most people, *spinster* connotes an older woman who is past the society's definition of the standard age for marriage. *Bachelor* does not carry this connotation and, indeed, may be associated with the opposite preconception: a young man, of eligible age. If you told a friend that an acquaintance of yours, Annie, is a spinster, and then mentioned that she is married, your friend would have reason to believe that you simply don't know what *spinster* means. In contrast, if you said she was a spinster, but also a young, energetic, and attractive woman, your friend would be surprised and perhaps feel misled. In this latter case, the word is being used in a way that is consistent with its denotation but not with its connotation, at least as conventionally defined in our society.

Mental Representation of Meaning

These notions reflect our tacit knowledge of what words mean. A major psycholinguistic question is how this knowledge is stored or mentally represented in semantic memory. We shall consider several proposals here.

Semantic features   In Chapter 4, we discussed the idea that phonemes are composed of distinctive features such as voicing. A similar approach to word meaning asserts that words are bundles of semantic features. According to the semantic feature view, our mental representation of a word is a bundle of semantic features. One attractive aspect of this view is that word meaning is seen as acquired feature by feature, as opposed to all or none. This appears to provide a natural explanation for some semantic errors children make in the course of their language development.

This view also helps to understand words within a given semantic domain. One is the domain known as **verbs of possession,** which includes verbs such as *give, receive, pay, trade, buy, sell,* and *spend* (Gentner, 1975). Clearly, any mature speaker of the language knows what these words mean. On a more subtle level, we have intuitive knowledge of some of the relations that exist between these words. Consider the following pairs of sentences:

(7a)   Hal sold the piano to Sally.
(7b)   Sally paid Hal for the piano.
(8a)   Megan gave the book to Darren.
(8b)   Darren received the book from Megan.

(9a)   Willie traded his bike for a camera.

(9b)   Willie owns a bike.

Notice that (7a) implies (7b), (8a) and (8b) are synonymous in meaning, and (9a) and (9b) are incompatible.

How do we explain these relations of meaning between sentences? According to the semantic feature notion, we can identify semantic elements that the words have in common. For example, the word *own* involves the notion that a person possesses some object. Verbs such as *give* and *receive* also involve possession, but, in addition, there is a change of possession of an object from one person to another. Another semantic element found in these words is the notion of a contract. Verbs such as *buy* and *sell*, unlike *give* and *receive*, involve the idea that changes in possession occur in such a way that both parties are obligated to each other in some way.

Notice how semantic features may illuminate the relations between sentences. We can see how (7a) implies (7b) since *paid*, like *sold*, involves the notion of a contract. Similarly, (8a) and (8b) are synonymous because both involve possession and change of possession. Sentence (9a) is incompatible with (9b) since the former but not the latter implies change of possession. Thus, by understanding the semantic features of a word we can understand some of the relations it has with other words.

Prototypes   One problem that confronts the theory of semantic features is that it assumes that there are defining features for the words that we use, but there are many words for which this is not the case. The problem was described lucidly by the philosopher Wittgenstein (1953):

> Consider for example the proceedings that we call "games." I mean board-games, card-games, ball-games, Olympic games, and so on. What is common to them all?— Don't say: "There *must* be something common, or they would not be called 'games' "—but *look and see* whether there is anything common to all.—For if you look at them you will not see something that is common to *all*, but similarities, relationships, and a whole series of them at that. To repeat, don't think but look! (p. 31)

Wittgenstein went on to characterize these similarities as **family resemblances**:

> And the result of this examination is: we see a complicated network of similarities overlapping and criss-crossing: sometimes overall similarities, sometimes similarities of detail.
>
>   I can think of no better expression to characterize these similarities than "family resemblances"; for the various resemblances between members of a family: build, features, colour of eyes, gait, temperament, etc., etc., overlap and criss-cross in the same way.—And I shall say: 'games' form a family. (p. 32)

An example of family resemblance is shown in Figure 5-1. Notice that most of the Smith brothers have dark hair, large ears, a large nose, a moustache, and

Figure 5-1. An example of family resemblance. [From S. L. Armstrong, L. R. Gleitman, and H. Gleitman, "What Some Concepts Might Not Be," *Cognition* 13 (1983):263–308.]

eyeglasses. With one exception, however, no brother has all of these features. All of the brothers have some of the features, but each brother has a different set of features. This is what Wittgenstein means by family resemblance. Brother 9 is the exception, in that he has all the attributes of the Smith brothers.

According to prototype theory, some members of a meaning category are, like brother 9, better instances of that category. Most people would agree that a collie or a German shepherd is a better example of the category *dog* than is a chihuahua, and that an armchair is a better example of the category *furniture* than is a footstool. The category instances that appear to be the best instances of that category are referred to as **prototypes.** It appears that prototypes have a privileged status in memory, as we are more adept at retrieving prototypes than other members of a category (Rosch, 1973; Rosch & Mervis, 1975; but also see Armstrong, Gleitman, & Gleitman, 1983).

The appeal of the prototype view relative to the semantic feature view is related to the distinction between denotation and connotation. Although features capture the logical or dictionary definition of a word well, they do not appear to be as successful in capturing the connotations of words as we use them. One value of the prototype view is that it captures both aspects. That is, *chihuahua* denotes an animal that is properly described as falling within the category of dog, but also one that differs from the dog protoype in several respects.

Networks   Some words naturally cause others to spring to mind. *Bread* calls forth *butter*, *table* leads to *chair*, and *dog* beckons *cat*. These rapid, strong associations between words may obscure the more indirect and subtle connections that exist between words. For example, how are *butter* and *smooth* alike? In an attempt to describe these relationships, we might resort to a spatial metaphor and say that all words are closer to some words than to others and that the distance between words is associated with their degree of similarity or relatedness.

This intuitive concept has been sharpened somewhat in the concept of a **semantic network**. According to this view, words are represented in memory through a rich network of sense relations. Each word concept is represented as a distinct node in the network and is connected to other words by means of various labeled relations or links. For example, *dog* is a subordinate of *animal*, a coordinate of *cat*, and a superordinate of *collie*.

Semantic network models have played a significant role in psychological research on the internal lexicon in recent years. We will have much more to say about them in the remainder of this chapter.

Mental models   Johnson-Laird, Herrman, and Chaffin (1984) have criticized the notion of a semantic network on the grounds that it pays exclusive attention to the relations between words and none at all to the way words are related to objects or events in the environment. That is, semantic networks are all sense and no reference. The point is well taken, and may be applied to feature and prototype views as well. Psychologists have not had much to say about referential relationships.

Johnson-Laird (1983) has suggested that the concept of a mental model might be fruitfully applied to the problems of reference. A **mental model** is an internal cognitive structure that represents some aspect of our environment. Such models are not limited to linguistic aspects. We have, for example, a model of our visual environment, in the form of a mental image, which allows us to navigate our way through our environment. If I blindfold you and then take you into a room in your house, you would probably be able to find your way around fairly well. But suppose I move the furniture while you are blindfolded. You would have a great deal of trouble moving around. However, if I warned you when you were about to run into something, you would in short order form vivid images of each piece of furniture in its new location (Johnson-Laird, 1988).

In a similar vein, we may have mental models of those aspects of the environment that correspond to words. When we hear a sentence, we may construct "a mental model of the particular state of affairs characterized by the utterance" (Johnson-Laird et al., 1984, p. 311). This model can then be used to evaluate whether the sentence is true or not, by comparing the model with perceptual evidence, at least for those sentences that refer to our immediate environment. The truth value of a sentence is an important aspect of referential relations, and one that is not easily handled within network accounts of meaning.

The mental model approach is relatively new. Most psychological work on word meaning has focused not on referential relations, but on sense relations.

Nevertheless, any theory of meaning that hopes to be complete will need to address some of the issues raised by Johnson-Laird and his associates.

Summary

Psychologists have proposed several theories as to how meaning is represented in permanent memory. Each of these proposals places emphasis upon different aspects of meaning. The semantic feature approach and network approaches emphasize the denotation of a word in general and sense relations in particular. The prototype view complements the emphasis on denotation with greater attention to connotative meaning. The theory of mental models focuses on referential relations. It is likely that some combination of these approaches will be necessary for a comprehensive account of meaning.

Structure of the Internal Lexicon

In this section, we discuss experimental research that examines the organization of the lexicon. We will consider some of the major findings, along with their implications for models of the lexicon. These models emphasize the notions (features, prototypes, networks) we have just considered.

The most common experimental procedure is known as a **semantic verification task**. In this task, a person is presented with a statement of the form *An A is a B*, such as sentence (10), and is asked to determine as quickly as possible whether the sentence is true or false.

(10) An apple is a fruit.

Since extremely few errors are made on this task, the time taken to answer is usually what is measured. This time is thought to reflect the organization of information in the internal lexicon. That is, even though these decisions are made very rapidly, they take a measurable amount of time, and the assumption is that the time that is taken might be a measure of the "distance" between different words in the internal lexicon.

It might give you a better idea of the kinds of data we will be discussing if you do a little experiment. Find a friend and read the statements listed in Table 5-1 one at a time: Ask your friend to quickly decide whether each statement is true or false and say so aloud. You should be forewarned that this task will probably reinforce your friend's preconception that psychology experiments are a little weird.

If your results are similar to those of others, you will probably find that some of your friend's answers are very fast. Others may provoke a little laughter. Still others may be a little slower and with perhaps a little less confidence. You might

Table 5-1.   Sample Items in a
Semantic Verification Task

A robin is a bird.
A butterfly is a bird.
A robin can fly.
A goose is a computer.
A horse is a mammal.
A tomato is a vegetable.
A mouse has teeth.
A monkey can read.
A pickle has fingernails.
Thomas Edison invented the telephone.
An octopus runs on batteries.
Abraham Lincoln had a beard.

try to develop some statements of your own and see what responses they get. This work will give you a better idea of the kinds of data that we will discuss in this section.

Hierarchical Network Models

Network models are those that assume that our memory for word concepts forms a system of interconnected elements. A network is hierarchical if some of these elements stand above or below other members of the network. The research of Collins and Quillian (1969, 1970, 1972) stands as the prototype of this approach.

Collins and Quillian model   The model of language representation used by Collins and Quillian is shown in Figure 5-2. Notice that concepts similar to the word are represented as distinct nodes in a network of category and property relations. Category relations are those that deal with hyponymy (that is, relations of subordination and superordination). Property relations indicate what characteristics (for example, can breathe, can fly, and so on) may be attributed to the items at various levels in the network. A key assumption made by these researchers deals with the concept of **cognitive economy.** They assumed that the space available for the storage of semantic information was limited, so that some information that could conceivably be stored in more than one place would be stored only at the highest possible node. For instance, the information that birds can breathe is stored at the animal level since it is true of all animals. Rather than store it at all of the nodes, the researchers suggest that we store the information just once but make it available to other nodes through the network of relations. Since we are capable of drawing inferences, the notion of saving storage space has some merit. This occurs only when the information is redundant; the information that birds can fly would be stored directly at the bird node.

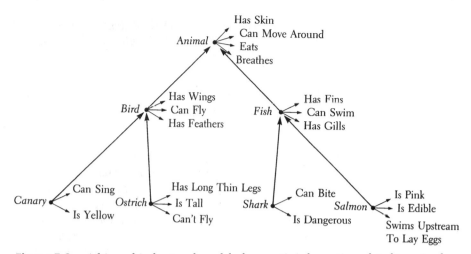

Figure 5-2. A hierarchical network model of semantic information related to animals. [From A. M. Collins and M. R. Quillian, "Retrieval Time from Semantic Memory," *Journal of Verbal Learning and Verbal Behavior* 9 (1969):240–247.]

In order to derive testable predictions from the model, Collins and Quillian had to make some additional assumptions about the way semantic information is retrieved. Consider what happens in the typical semantic verification task. If we were presented with sentence (11), the sentence would activate both the bird node and the animal node.

(11)   A bird is an animal.

The process of deciding whether the sentence is true or false is based, according to Collins and Quillian, on a mechanism known as **intersection search.** Once these two nodes are active, it would take a brief period of time to travel from one node to another. They assumed that we continue to search for relevant information until the two items in the sentence intersect. Finally, we would check to make sure that the relation depicted in the sentence fits the relation in the lexicon. In sentence (12), there would be an intersection, but a check of the relations would indicate that the sentence contradicts the information in the lexicon.

(12)   An animal is a bird.

Taken together, cognitive economy and intersection search yield the prediction that making decisions of the form A *bird is an animal* or A *bird can breathe* takes longer than deciding about An *animal is an animal* or An *animal can breathe.* In each case, it is because we must mentally traverse one relation in the network to decide whether the statement is true or false for birds, but no relations need to be followed to determine this for animals. The early work of Collins and Quillian and others (Landauer & Meyer, 1972) found just this relationship in the verification times. They called this the **category-size effect:** in a statement of the form *An A is a B* or *An A has B*, the higher the location of B in the hierarchy in relation to A, the longer the reaction times.

Evaluation of the Collins and Quillian model   Two major problems soon became apparent with this model. One was that the major result that supported the model, the category-size effect, was cast into doubt. Conrad (1972) found that the frequency with which a property is associated with a concept is another important factor in determining response times and that, more important, when frequency is controlled, the category-size effect disappears. For example, the statement that a bird has feathers may be verified more rapidly than the statement that a bird can eat, not because of their relative positions in a hierarchy of semantic relations but simply because *bird–feathers* is a more frequent combination than *bird–eat*. To distinguish between these two factors, Conrad had a different group rate the degree of associative relationship between various words, revised the verification study with this factor controlled, and found no evidence for the category-size effect. Conrad's study suggests a problem with Collins and Quillian's assumption of cognitive economy. It may be that commonly used properties are stored redundantly in the lexicon, perhaps in the highest applicable level plus other commonly used levels.

The second major problem was that the original Collins and Quillian model assumed that all items on a given level of the hierarchy were more or less equal. *Canary* and *ostrich*, for example, were both subordinates of *bird* and one link away from *bird*, so they should take equal time to verify. In fact, they do not. It seems that this is generally true; some instances of categories are usually verified faster than others. Smith, Shoben, and Rips (1974) carefully examined the effect of category similarity on verification times and concluded that similarity reduces verification times for true statements and increases it for false statements. That is, (13) takes less time than (14); moreover, (15) takes longer than (16).

(13)   A robin is a bird.
(14)   An ostrich is a bird.
(15)   A whale is a fish.
(16)   A horse is a fish.

This has generally been called the **typicality effect:** items that are more typical of a given superordinate take less time to verify than atypical items in true statements; the opposite is true for false statements.

The main point here is that we have found it necessary to supplement the emphasis on hyponymy in the Collins and Quillian model with more functional aspects of word meaning. That is, what we know about words such as *dog* is not only where they fit into an overall classificatory scheme but also reflects aspects of the word that pertain more directly to its everyday use. When we say the word *dog*, a typical member of the class is activated in our mind, and this information must be fit into our description in our internal lexicon.

Semantic Feature Models

In the Collins and Quillian model, individual words were represented discretely, as complete units. An alternative approach is to represent words as bundles of semantic features. A model of this form has been developed by Smith and colleagues (1974).

The Smith, Shoben, and Rips model   These investigators distinguish between two types of semantic features: defining and characteristic. A **defining feature** is one that must be present for an instance to be a member of the concept. **Characteristic features** are those that are, strictly speaking, not necessary for category membership but are nonetheless typically associated with the word. For example, two defining features for birds are that they must have feathers and must be animate. A characteristic feature is that a bird can sing. The inclusion of characteristic features makes this model similar to the prototype view we discussed earlier.

The model assumes that semantic verification decisions are made by a two-stage process (see Figure 5-3). At the first stage, all features of the subject and predicate term are retrieved and compared to derive an overall estimate of the

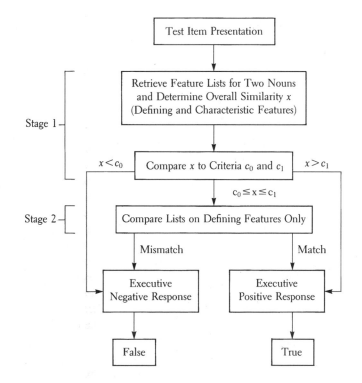

Figure 5-3.   A semantic feature model of semantic verification performance. [From E. E. Smith, E. J. Shoben, and L. J. Rips, "Structure and Process in Semantic Decisions," *Psychological Review* 81 (1974):214–241.]

similarity of the two terms. If they are highly similar, we respond true. If they are highly dissimilar, we respond false. If the degree of similarity is moderate, we go to a second stage, in which only defining features are considered.

This simple model has been found to be useful in explaining a number of results from verification studies. The typicality effect is assumed to be due to the operation of characteristic features during the first stage. For example, consider sentences (13) through (16) again. Sentence (13) leads us to retrieve characteristic features that are generally similar for robins and birds. This increases the likelihood that the overall similarity between the two will be high enough to skip stage 2, and thus response time is reduced. In contrast, sentence (14) might take longer because the overall similarity is lower and thus stage 2 might be needed.

Similar considerations apply to false statements. Sentence (15) might lead to a moderate level of similarity at stage 1, and hence stage 2 would be needed to register a false response. A statement such as (16), however, would be immediately rejected as false. According to the model, this occurs because the similarity at stage 1 is very low, and therefore stage 2 is skipped.

Evaluation of the Smith, Shoben, and Rips model   The main problem with this model is that it relies so heavily on the distinction between defining and characteristic features, and this distinction has a problematic status. It is difficult to know how to determine what is a defining feature of any object, and since stage 2 of the model hinges on this determination, the point is absolutely crucial for the model. As we saw earlier, functional concepts such as *game* may not have any defining features at all (Wittgenstein, 1953).

The manner in which characteristic features are determined is also a source of concern. Usually this process involves giving people groups of words and asking them to rate them in terms of how "essential" or "typical" they are for a given class (Rips, Shoben, & Smith, 1973). The problem that this creates is that it turns experimental findings into correlational findings: word ratings are correlated with response times. As with any correlation, this leads to difficulties of interpretation. It may be that ease of access is due to similarity, or that similarity judgments are influenced by ease of access, or that perhaps some third factor is responsible for the observed correlation. Indeed, McCloskey (1980) has argued that the familiarity of the category pairs, not their similarity, is the most significant factor in the study by Smith and colleagues (1974).

A final problem with semantic feature models is that it is not yet clear whether they can be extended to larger units of language such as sentences or discourse (but see Rips, Smith, & Shoben, 1978). That is, we need to know how word meanings fit into the larger context of language processing. If our knowledge of words is in terms of their constituent features, how do these features combine to form the meaning of an entire sentence or paragraph? At the present time, semantic feature models have not clearly specified the way that this process occurs.

Spreading Activation Models

In recent years, a variation on network models called **spreading activation models** has become popular in cognitive psychology (Anderson, 1983; Collins & Loftus, 1975). Since the Collins and Loftus model was specifically advanced to respond to the criticisms of the earlier Collins and Quillian model, I will use this model as an example of this class.

The Collins and Loftus model   Collins and Loftus assume that words are represented in the internal lexicon within a network of relationships, but the organization is not strictly hierarchical as in the original model. In contrast, the organization is closer to a web of interconnecting nodes, with the distance between nodes determined by both structural characteristics such as categorical relations and functional considerations such as typicality and the degree of association between various concepts. Thus, the model incorporates some aspects of both the Collins and Quillian and the Smith and colleagues approaches. The notion that concepts are stored as interconnected links is retained, but the view that all such relations are equal is revised by assuming that some nodes are more accessible than others and that the degree of accessibility is related to factors such as frequency of usage and typicality.

The concept of cognitive economy is also modified; Collins and Loftus distinguish between a strong version of cognitive economy and a weak version. The strong version states that all properties are stored just once in the network. As we have seen, this claim is inconsistent with the research of Conrad (1972). The weak claim is that properties are not stored in all of the places they are applicable. Perhaps when we encounter certain relationships often enough, we store them—redundantly—where useful. The weak version of cognitive economy is that such properties are still not stored in other portions of the internal lexicon where they are also applicable.

The process by which semantic information is retrieved is also revised in this model. Instead of an intersection search throughout the network, Collins and Loftus argue that retrieval occurs by a process of **spreading activation**: activation begins at a single node and then spreads in parallel form throughout the network. This activation attenuates over distance, thus ensuring that closely related concepts are more likely to be activated than distant concepts (see Figure 5-4). The process of spreading activation has been likened to the effect of dropping a rock into a pool of still water (Wessells, 1982). The disturbance spreads out in all directions from the point of entry, with its magnitude determined by factors such as the intensity of the initial stimulus, the distance between a part of the pool and the part the rock was dropped into, and the time elapsed since the rock was dropped.

The process of arriving at decisions in semantic verification tasks is rather complicated and depends upon a variety of influences operating at a single node. Collins and Loftus assume that there is a threshold for the activation of a given

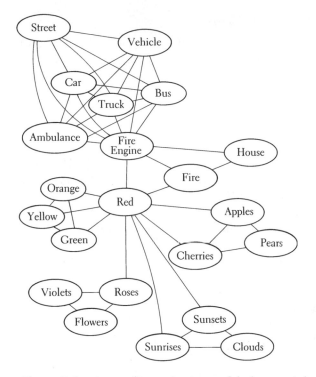

Figure 5-4. A spreading activation model of semantic knowledge. [From A. M. Collins and E. F. Loftus, "A Spreading-Activation Theory of Semantic Processing," *Psychological Review* 82 (1975):407–428.]

node and that the node becomes active when a variety of influences accumulate to a level beyond this threshold. When this occurs, we become aware of the word or concept. For example, the verification of a statement such as sentence (17) depends in part on the closeness of the two concepts in the network; these two concepts are reasonably close since bats have some of the characteristic features of birds.

(17)   A bat is a bird.

But the verification also depends upon categorical information that is inconsistent with this statement. Categorical links take precedence over other types of semantic information in this task, and thus the response is false. The model attempts to account for typicality effects by assuming that the distance between chicken and bird, for example, is greater than that between robin and bird. Here the categorical information is the same in the two cases, but relatedness information enables *robin-bird* to be verified faster.

     The model also can explain the **context effect,** in which the nature of the filler items influences the verification times of interest. For example, consider the following sentences:

(18)   Robbery is a crime.

(19)   Murder is a crime.

(20)   Libel is a crime.

McCloskey and Glucksberg (1979) found that reaction times to (18) were faster when (19) was used as a filler item than when (20) was used. This is presumably because the activation of *murder* has spread to the similar item *robbery*.

To sum up, the Collins and Loftus model is more complex and provides a more comprehensive view of word knowledge than either of the other approaches we have considered. One way to compare it with its predecessors is to note the relationship between denotative and connotative meaning in each model. The original Collins and Quillian model was faulted for ignoring the importance of typicality, which is an aspect of connotative meaning. The semantic feature model sharply distinguished between the two forms of meaning. In the Collins and Loftus approach, they are integrated into a single semantic network.

Evaluation of the Collins and Loftus model   Compared with the earlier model, this approach is more realistic, less rigid, and more complicated. It specifically recognizes that there is a diversity of information in a semantic network and realistically assesses the complexity of semantic decision making by presenting a series of decision procedures instead of a single one. But the problem with this approach, according to some detractors (McCloskey & Glucksberg, 1979; Smith, 1978), is that it leads to a less testable model. With so many different assumptions built into it, deriving testable predictions from the model is difficult.

Collins and Loftus respond by arguing that models of the lexicon should not be evaluated solely on their ability to account for verification results. These experiments, after all, were intended to provide data upon which we could build models of semantic processing; a model that can only account for the data that gave rise to the model is not worth much. Rather, they argue, the acid test of a more generally useful model of lexical information processing is whether or not it can illuminate other lines of research with words, such as the way individual words are accessed and the way word access contributes to our understanding of language comprehension at levels of sentence and discourse.

Summary

Three approaches to semantic organization in the lexicon have been discussed. The hierarchical network model postulates that we have stored our knowledge of words in the form of a semantic network, with some words represented at higher nodes in the network than others. The semantic feature approach regards the lexical representation of a word as a set of semantic features. The spreading activation approach is a revision of the hierarchical view that stresses the diversity of semantic relations within the network. Whereas earlier approaches tended to focus on categorical information, recent models have recognized the need to mix in typicality information to provide a psychologically realistic approach to the lexicon.

Although most models of the lexicon have been evaluated on the basis of semantic verification results, any truly general theory of word storage must integrate a growing body of research results beyond verification studies. In the following section of the chapter, as we explore further the properties of the internal lexicon, we will be in a better position to evaluate the general usefulness of these approaches.

Lexical Access

The process of accessing or retrieving lexical information from memory is influenced by a number of factors. Among such factors are the frequency of the word, its morphological structure, whether a semantically related word has just been encountered, and whether or not the word is ambiguous.

Word Frequency

The role of word frequency in lexical access has been demonstrated in a **phoneme-monitoring** study by Foss (1969). In this task, subjects listen for a continuous speech passage and do two things: comprehend the passage and listen for a target phoneme such as /b/. In some instances, the target phoneme followed a high-frequency word, and in other instances, it followed a low-frequency word. The results were clear-cut: monitoring times increased slightly after a low-frequency word. Foss interpreted this result as evidence of an increasing processing load for low-frequency words due to the difficulty associated with accessing them.

Frequency has also been investigated in **lexical decision tasks,** in which the subject sees a string of letters and must decide whether the string is a word or not. Ordinarily in lexical decision studies the stimuli are presented one at a time, but you can get an idea how these studies are performed by looking at Table 5-2. Both list 1 and list 2 consist of words and nonwords. For each item on each list, you should say yes aloud if it is a word and no if it is a nonword. Find a stopwatch with a second hand, and time yourself on how long it takes to complete each list.

List 1 will take a few more seconds to complete than list 2 because the words in list 1 are lower in frequency than the corresponding words in list 2. A number of studies have shown that frequency influences response time in this task, with higher frequency words having shorter times (Rubenstein, Garfield, & Milliken, 1970; Whaley, 1978).

Rayner and Duffy (1986) have found that word frequency also plays a role in normal reading. They measured eye fixations to words during reading and found that low-frequency words were fixated for about 80 milliseconds longer than high-frequency words. The magnitude of the differences between high- and low-frequency words is similar to that found in the lexical decision studies. This is important because tasks such as lexical decision and phoneme monitoring are

Table 5-2.   A Lexical Decision Experiment

List 1

---

gambastya, revery, voitle, chard, wefe, cratily, decoy, puldow, raflot, oriole, voluble, boovle, chalt, awry, signet, trave, crock, cryptic, ewe, himpola

---

List 2

---

mulvow, governor, bless, tuglety, gare, relief, ruftily, history, pindle, develop, gardot, norve, busy, effort, garvola, match, sard, pleasant, coin, maisle

---

Note: See text for instructions.
Source: K. Hirsh-Pasek, L. M. Reeves, and R. Golinkoff, "Words and Meaning: From Primitives to Complex Organization," in J. B. Gleason and N. B. Ratner (eds.), *Psycholinguistics* (Orlando, FL: Harcourt Brace Jovanovich, 1993), pp. 133–197.

sometimes criticized for being "artificial" or not reflecting language processes as they occur outside the laboratory. But the purpose of such tasks is to isolate one aspect of normal reading processes, not to create a task that has nothing to do with ordinary reading. Rayner and Duffy's results suggest that since similar results are found in reading and in more specialized tasks, the latter tasks tap into normal reading processes.

Two main approaches have been taken to explain word frequency and related effects on lexical access. In Morton's (1969) model, each word in the lexicon is represented as a **logogen,** which specifies the word's various attributes (semantic, phonological, and so on). The logogen is activated by sensory input and by contextual information. With regard to sensory input, each time a word is encountered, the threshold for that logogen is temporarily lowered. That is, after the word *heart* is presented, less sensory information (for example, a less-audible sound) would be needed to recognize the word again. With high-frequency words, the recovery from the lowering of the threshold is less complete than with low-frequency words, so less sensory information is needed for recognition. The role of contextual information in the logogen model will be discussed later in this chapter.

An alternative approach based on an active search process has been presented by Forster (1976). Here, information about a word is organized into a master file, and access to this information occurs through a series of access files, one for orthographic information, one for phonological information, and so on. A key assumption is that words are stored in these files according to the frequency with which they are encountered in ordinary language. High-frequency words are stored higher in the files than low-frequency words, and the search process begins at the top of the files. Accordingly, lexical access is more rapid for high-frequency words.

Morphological Structure

From a processing standpoint, it would make sense to distinguish between the affixes (prefixes and suffixes) of a word and the base or root word. This is because the set of morphemes or affixes is relatively small and is used over and over in ways that are semantically similar. As a matter of fact, new linguistic examples occur regularly (for example, *desensitize*) and are easily interpreted.

These considerations have led several investigators to argue that morphological information and base word information are organized separately in the mental lexicon (MacKay, 1978; Taft, 1981; Taft & Forster, 1975). In this view, a word such as *decision* would be stored as the base word *decide* with a separate representation for *-ion*. In retrieving *decision*, the base word and morpheme are united, and phonological processes result in the final phonological form *decision*. One argument for this kind of arrangement is that it achieves some storage economy since we would not have to store all the various forms of a word but only the base and the set of morphemes used throughout the language. But to store multimorphemic words in terms of their base morphemes complicates the processing of these words. Thus, we seem to have to trade off storage economy with processing economy.

Some evidence for the independent storage of base word and morpheme has been provided by MacKay (1978), who presented people auditorily with verbs (*decide*) and asked them to produce a related noun (*decision*) as quickly as possible. MacKay found that the time taken to make these responses varied with the derivational complexity. The suffix *-ment* is linguistically simpler than *-ence*, which in turn is simpler than *-ion*. The suffix *-ion* is most complex because, unlike the other two, the shift from verb to noun involves an alternation of vowels. And *-ence*, in turn, is more complex than *-ment* because it often involves a regrouping of syllables. Notice that the /n/ in *government* remains at the end of the syllable (*go-vern-ment*), whereas the /t/ in *existence* shifts from the end of a syllable to the beginning of a syllable (*ex-is-tence*). MacKay found that the times taken to produce words such as *government, existence,* and *decision* reflected their linguistic complexity.

Taft and Forster (1975) have drawn similar conclusions. They assume that a word is analyzed into its morphological components and then the base word is accessed. A single-morpheme word would be accessed directly. A prefixed word, however, would go through an initial prefix-stripping stage. After the prefix has been stripped, a search for the base word is undertaken. If successful, the final stage compares the prefix and base word to see whether they are compatible. Some evidence for this multistage process has been found in lexical decision experiments. Snodgrass and Jarvella (1972) found that response times were greater for affixed words than for words without affixes, lending support for the assumption of a prefix-stripping stage.

In addition, Taft (1981) found that lexical decision times were shorter for prefixed words (such as *remind*) than for words with "pseudoprefixes" (such as *relish*). According to the Taft and Forster model, when we see *relish*, the pseudoprefix *re* would be stripped off and then a search would be made for *-lish*. After this search was unsuccessful, *re* would be reattached to *-lish*, and a search for the word *relish* would be successful. The unsuccessful search is presumably responsible for the longer decision times. Lima (1987) found a similar result using eye fixations during reading. Pseudoprefixed words received longer fixation times than prefixed words. The result held even when the two groups of words were similar in frequency, length, syntactic category, and other variables known to influence lexical access.

Although decomposing words into their morphological components appears to be a useful strategy on occasion, some reports suggest that it may not be used all of the time (Rubin, Becker, & Freeman, 1979). Rubin and colleagues found a difference in lexical decision times between prefixed and pseudoprefixed words only when the stimulus list contained 50% prefixed words. When the percent of prefixed words in the list was only 10%, no difference between prefixed and pseudoprefixed words appeared. This suggests that the process of analyzing a word into its morphological components depends to some extent on the frequency of occurrence of various types of words. It may be that some frequently encountered words (such as *impossible*) are represented as single lexical items in memory and that less common words (such as *imperceptible*) are stored as base plus affixes. If so, this would be consistent with the notion of weak cognitive economy we discussed in the last section.

Semantic Priming

I have already mentioned that once a word has been presented, the threshold for recognition of the word at a later time is reduced. **Semantic priming** occurs when a word presented earlier reduces the threshold for accessing a second word.

The priming task consists of two phases. In the first phase, a priming stimulus is presented. Often no response to the prime is required or recorded; in any event, the response to the prime itself is of little interest. In the second phase, a second stimulus (the target) is presented, the subject makes some response to it, and the time taken to make this response is recorded. The response could take many forms, but two of the most commonly used tasks are to ask people to name the word or to decide whether the string is a word or not. The times to respond to the target in the priming condition are then compared to a condition in which no priming stimulus or a different priming stimulus was presented.

An example is provided in a study by Meyer and Schvaneveldt (1971). They used a lexical decision task and found that the time needed to classify the target *butter* as a word varied with the priming stimulus. Times were shorter when the prime was *bread* than when it was *nurse*. In terms of the spreading activation model of the lexicon, these results make a good deal of sense. It would be assumed that *bread*, unlike *nurse*, spreads its activation to the closely associated concept of *butter*, thus reducing its threshold for activation.

Priming studies have become popular in recent years because the size of the priming effect appears to provide a sensitive index of the closeness of the relation between various concepts in a semantic structure (McKoon & Ratliff, 1980) and the degree to which various concepts automatically trigger activation of related concepts (Dosher & Corbett, 1982). It is clear that a given word activates related words, but the extent of the spread of activation remains to be determined.

Lexical Ambiguity

The form of ambiguity in which a single word may be interpreted to have more than one meaning is referred to as **lexical ambiguity**. The study of lexical ambiguity has generated a substantial amount of research because it raises a number of intriguing questions. Do ambiguous words have more than one node or logogen in semantic memory? Do we consider multiple meanings of ambiguous words when we hear or see one? And how might the sentence context influence how lexically ambiguous words are processed? As we shall see, ambiguity is a significant property of language, and so it is vital that any theory of language processing come to grips with the processes through which ambiguous meanings are processed and resolved.

Introspection is of little help in this regard, for we generally do not recognize or remember the multiple meanings of words that we hear. But there are some exceptions. Read sentence (21) orally to a friend, and ask for a reaction.

> **(21)**   Rapid righting with his uninjured hand saved from loss the content of the capsized canoe.

Most people hear the second word as *writing*, presumably because it is a more common meaning. Moreover, there is nothing in the sentence that refutes this interpretation until we get to the end. Subjectively, the impression is that we have seized upon a single meaning at the outset and carry it through until we discover the error (Lashley, 1951). But do experiments bear out this subjective impression?

Foss (1970) was the first to apply the phoneme-monitoring technique to the study of lexical ambiguity. He presented listeners with sentences containing ambiguous words, such as in sentence (22):

> **(22)**   The man started to drill before the truck arrived.

The response times to monitor the first phoneme of the very next word (here, the /b/ in *before*) increased ever so slightly (by about 50 milliseconds) after an ambiguous word. Foss attributed this result to a process of activating more than one meaning of an ambiguous word.

Cairns and Kamerman (1975) extended this result. They varied the time between the ambiguous word and the phoneme that was to be monitored and found that the increased processing load associated with lexical ambiguity was very short lived. If the phoneme was delayed by as little as two syllables, the result disappeared. These results suggest that although multiple meanings of an ambiguous word are briefly entertained, the ambiguity is quickly resolved.

Role of frequency of meaning   One factor that seems to be important in any discussion of lexical ambiguity is the relative dominance or frequency of usage of various word meanings. Some words have multiple meanings that, in the absence of any biasing context, are roughly equivalent in commonality. In other instances, one meaning is clearly dominant over the others. Given our prior discussion of word frequency, it makes sense to assume that, all other factors being equal, common meanings should be easier to access than uncommon meanings.

Hogaboam and Perfetti (1975) constructed sentences with ambiguous words in which either the primary or the secondary meaning of the word was appropriate. The word *letter*, for example, contains two different meanings: a note sent by one person to another (the postal meaning) or an element of the alphabet (the alphabet meaning). A sentence such as (23) requires the activation of the presumably dominant postal meaning, whereas (24) requires activation of the secondary sense for comprehension.

(23)　The jealous husband read the letter.

(24)　The antique typewriter was missing a letter.

Hogaboam and Perfetti gave subjects a series of sentences such as these and asked them to decide whether the final word in the sentence was ambiguous. Decision times were faster when the sentence required the secondary sense than when it required the primary meaning.

Though this result may sound counterintuitive, consider what is involved in deciding whether a word is ambiguous. Suppose the various meanings of an ambiguous word are stored in separate locations in the lexicon. In this task, we must not only find the primary meaning but also discover whether it has a less common meaning. Presumably the common meaning is easily activated, so the time taken to find the other meaning is more directly related to response time in this task. In sentence (24), the context provides cues for the secondary meaning, and if we assume that the primary meaning is accessible all of the time, then response times should be relatively fast. However, in sentence (23), both context and meaning frequency point in the same direction, so it may be difficult to find the second meaning of the word.

As Hogaboam and Perfetti point out, these results are consistent with both the active search and spreading activation views of the internal lexicon. According to the active search view, more common or frequent meanings are stored higher in a list of meanings associated with that word than are less common meanings. Consequently, if an active search process begins at the top of the list, common meanings are more easily recovered. Alternatively, the different meanings of an ambiguous word may have separate logogens in the lexicon (Morton, 1979). If it is further assumed that these logogens are arranged in a semantic network in which activation spreads from one logogen to neighboring ones (Collins & Loftus, 1975), then the results of this experiment can be accommodated. More frequent meanings, like more frequent words, would have a lower threshold for activation. Furthermore, the contextual information in the sentence should serve to prime one meaning more than another. As a consequence, frequency of meaning and contextual information combine to produce a pattern of activation of the various meanings that a word has (Simpson, 1984).

To return to sentence (21), it should be clear that both context and frequency favor the handwriting meaning of the word over the meaning having to do with setting something right. Moreover, when we consider that these decisions concerning the appropriate meaning are made very rapidly, and that the biasing context (*capsized canoe*) occurs much later, it is not surprising that we choose the wrong meaning in this instance.

Role of prior context   What might happen if the biasing context occurred before an ambiguous word? As we saw earlier, there is evidence that we activate multiple meanings of lexically ambiguous words (Cairns & Kamerman, 1975; Foss, 1970). Can a prior semantic context override this process? In particular, can a context that is biased toward one or another meaning of an ambiguous word selectively activate the appropriate meaning? This is a specific form of a general question we have already pursued—the relative importance of top-down and bottom-up processes in language comprehension. Here the top-down processes are represented by possible contextual (sentential) effects on the perception of individual lexical items, whereas bottom-up processes refer to multiple activation of even inappropriate word meanings. The question, then, is whether we activate inappropriate word meanings even when there is contextual reason not to do so.

Swinney (1979) examined this question with a cross-modal lexical decision task. Subjects listened to sentences containing lexical ambiguities in strongly biasing semantic contexts. Simultaneously, they performed a lexical decision task on visually presented letter strings. Some of these letter strings were semantically related to one of the meanings of the ambiguous word. For example, subjects might hear sentence (25):

(25)   Rumor had it that, for years, the government building has been plagued with problems. The man was not surprised when he found several spiders, roaches, and other bugs in the corner of his room.

Here the ambiguous word is *bug*, and the biasing context favors the insect meaning over the espionage meaning. As the subjects heard the word *bug*, they saw a contextually related word (*ant*), a contextually inappropriate word (*spy*), or an unrelated word (*sew*). Swinney found that lexical decision times for visual words related to either meaning of the ambiguous word were shorter than for unrelated words when the visual words immediately followed the ambiguity. When the visual words were presented four syllables after the ambiguity, however, only the contextually appropriate meaning was facilitated. These results suggest that even in the presence of a strong biasing context, multiple meanings of ambiguous words are briefly activated.

The role of semantic context in lexical ambiguity was clarified further by Seidenberg, Tanenhaus, Leiman, and Bienkowski (1982), who found evidence of contextual facilitation only when the context contained words that were semantically associated with or identical to the target word. When no word was individually associated to the target, but the sentence as a whole was, no contextual facilitation was found. This suggests that the "sentence" priming might be reducible to lexical priming, or as Seidenberg and colleagues state:

> We found no evidence that subjects could use their knowledge of a language or knowledge of the world to restrict access to one reading. The only contextual effect was due to lexical priming, an automatic, nondirected, intralexical process that is a consequence of the organization of semantic memory. (p. 523)

This process may sound rather inefficient. After all, why activate aspects of meaning that turn out to be irrelevant? Why not just selectively activate the meaning that is appropriate? According to Forster (1979), the key is found in the processing demands of various stages of language comprehension. The lexical processor may be conceived of as a nearly automatic processor that "performs highly specific tasks in a quite inflexible manner" (p. 33). The alternative, to use the context to guide lexical processing, might involve the activation and testing of hypotheses about the fit between word and sentence and thus might be very demanding. It might be easier, ultimately, to retrieve in nearly effortless form more information than is needed and then let the sentence processor sort it out later.

In any event, accessing words in an automatic manner saves resources for other aspects of language processing that, it is generally agreed, are very cognitively demanding. Once a word is activated, it may be used in combination with other words to establish and test hypotheses about the syntactic structure of the sentence. (We discuss sentences and sentence processing in Chapter 6.)

Summary

Lexical access is influenced by a variety of factors, including the frequency of a word, its morphological structure, the presence of semantically related words, and the existence of alternative meanings of the word. Common words and meanings appear to be in a state of greater readiness than less often used words and meanings. We rely upon morphological structure when encountering unfamiliar words. Two main approaches to lexical access have been developed: an active search model, which states that we search through lists of words (or meanings), and a logogen model, which claims that a word's spot in the lexicon is activated when sensory and contextual information reach a threshold for that word.

It appears that we briefly consider all of the meanings of an ambiguous word, then quickly decide upon the appropriate meaning or suppress the inappropriate meaning. Evidence also suggests that prior context may influence the activation of lexically ambiguous words. These context effects may be plausibly attributed to automatic spreading activation stemming from words in the context that are semantically related to target words.

Review Questions

1. Why is there more to meaning than reference?
2. Distinguish between the denotation and the connotation of a word.

3. What semantic elements are involved in the meaning of *pay* and *trade*?

4. Why is the notion of family resemblances a problem for the concept of defining features?

5. What is a mental model?

6. What are the advantages and disadvantages of storing redundant information, such as *a bird can breathe*, in the internal lexicon?

7. How does typicality influence semantic verification times in opposite ways for true and false statements?

8. Describe in what way a logogen for the word *table* would respond to the presentation of: (a) the word *table*; (b) a semantically similar word, *chair*; and (c) a semantically distant word, *game*.

9. What evidence suggests that we store the morphemes in a multimorphemic word as separate units in memory?

10. Why are we not likely to carry more than one meaning of an ambiguous word throughout a long sentence?

Thought Questions

1. Analyze a television game show using the concepts from this chapter. What aspects of meaning are being utilized? How are they accessed?

2. Try giving sentences like those in the list on page 110, or others of your own choice, to another friend. What responses did you get, and what can you conclude from them?

3. Do you think that a fluent bilingual would have two internal lexicons, one for each language, or would there be a single lexicon? Explain your decision.

6

Sentence Comprehension and Memory

- Parsing is the process of assigning elements of surface structure to linguistic categories. Because of limitations in processing resources, we begin to parse sentences as we see or hear each word in a sentence.
- We use syntactic, semantic, and pragmatic knowledge to comprehend sentences. An ongoing debate is whether we use these forms of knowledge simultaneously or whether we process syntactic information first.
- The meaning of sentences is often related to the context in which they appear. We use context, along with shared assumptions about communication, to understand nonliteral and metaphorical sentences.
- We ordinarily remember the gist of a sentence and quickly forget its surface form. An exception is pragmatically significant statements, such as insults, whose exact wording is often well remembered.

Introduction

We hear thousands of sentences every day and respond to many, perhaps most, with barely any notice of their structure. In others, the wording is so cumbersome that we find ourselves struggling to unravel what has been said. And still others are clearer in meaning than in intent: when a coworker asks over coffee whether you are feeling all right, you may perfectly well understand the question without knowing precisely what the person means by it. We often forget the exact words a person uses to convey a message, but some sentences linger in our memories for years. In short, we respond to sentences in a variety of ways. In this chapter, we will try to identify and understand the many facets of the way we comprehend sentences.

Comprehending a sentence involves attention to syntactic, semantic, and pragmatic factors. Consider a simple active declarative sentence, such as *The actor thanked the audience.* At the syntactic level, we identify the constituent or phrase structure of the sentence; that is, we identify *the actor* as a noun phrase (NP), *thanked* as a verb phrase (VP), and *the audience* as another NP. At the semantic level, we identify the semantic or thematic roles played by various words in the sentence. *Actor* is the agent and *audience* the recipient of the action. At the pragmatic level, we probably have some knowledge about the real world circumstances in which this sentence would make sense. It might, for instance, describe the end of a play after an actor has taken a bow.

It is one thing to say that these factors are involved in comprehension and quite another to identify what part each factor plays. Do we use our syntactic, semantic, and pragmatic knowledge simultaneously when we comprehend a sentence? Or do certain factors take priority at various stages of the comprehension process? And what kinds of cognitive processes are involved when a sentence, unlike this simple declarative one, is complex enough to be a burden for working memory? These are some of the issues we will be looking at in this chapter. In the first section, we look at how we identify the syntactic structure of a sentence. Then we discuss the role of the semantic and pragmatic context in sentence comprehension. Finally, in the last section, we discuss memory for sentences.

Immediate Processing of Sentences

Parsing

A first step in the process of understanding a sentence is to assign elements of its surface structure to linguistic categories, a procedure known as **parsing.** The result of parsing is an internal representation of the linguistic relationships within a sentence, usually in the form of a tree structure or **phrase marker.** Figure 6-1 depicts some of the successive points in parsing a sentence. We recognize *the* as a determiner, which signals the beginning of a noun phrase (Kimball, 1973). Our knowledge of noun phrases is that they take the form NP ⟶ det + (adj) + N, so at this point we are looking either for an optional adjective or a noun. We recognize the next word, *actor,* as a noun and add it to the noun phrase. The remaining items are added as shown in Figure 6-1.

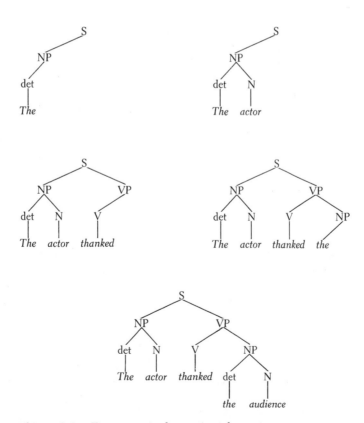

Figure 6-1. Five stages in the parsing of a sentence.

We may think of parsing as a form of problem solving or decision making, in the sense that we are making decisions (although not necessarily in a conscious manner) about where to place incoming words into the phrase marker we're building. Just and Carpenter (1980) suggest that we make these decisions immediately as we encounter a word, a principle they call the **immediacy principle.** According to this view, when we first see or hear a word, we access its meaning from permanent memory, identify its likely referent, and fit it into the syntactic structure of the sentence. The alternative to immediate processing is to take a "wait and see" approach: to postpone interpreting a word or phrase until it is clearer where a sentence is going. However, there is considerable evidence for the immediacy principle. Although we sometimes postpone decisions, more often than not, we interpret the words as we hear or see them.

The primary reason why we use immediate processing is that the number of decisions involved in understanding even a single sentence can be quite large and thus can overload our cognitive resources. Suppose we heard sentence (1).

(1)   John bought the flower for Susan.

This sentence is syntactically ambiguous. It might mean that John bought the flower to give to Susan, or that John bought a flower as a favor for Susan, who intended to give it to another person. This ambiguity is encountered when we hear the word *for.* Suppose further that we kept in mind both meanings of the sentence. But then *flower* has more than one interpretation also. It could mean *flower* or *flour* (remember, the sentence was heard). One approach to these multiple possibilities is to take a wait-and-see approach; that is, to wait for further information before deciding which interpretation to use. There is, however, a major disadvantage in such an approach. If we retained two or more interpretations at each of the several choice points, we would rapidly overwhelm our working memory (see Singer, 1990).

Although immediacy of processing reduces memory load, it may lead to errors in parsing. For example, consider sentence fragment (2).

(2)   The florist sent the flowers . . .

Where might this sentence be going? At this point it looks like a simple declarative sentence, but suppose it continues as indicated in (3).

(3)   . . . was very pleased.

Although it at first appears to be ungrammatical, in fact this is a grammatical sentence with an embedded relative clause (a clause that modifies a noun). One of the reasons why the sentence is difficult to comprehend is that the embedded clause is a reduced relative clause; it is not signaled with a relative pronoun, as in sentence (4):

(4)   The florist who was sent the flowers was very pleased.

Another reason is that declarative sentences are more familiar than relative clauses, so we are more likely to "place our bets" on that outcome. If we took a wait-and-see approach, we would not be surprised by the continuation in (3). But we are surprised, so it appears that we immediately interpret the fragment in (2).

Parsing Strategies

If we are making decisions about where words fit into the syntactic structure of a sentence, what are these decisions based upon? Much work has been done on the strategies we use in parsing. Strategies are thought of as approaches to parsing that work much of the time, although they are hardly foolproof. We will discuss two strategies that have gathered considerable empirical support.

Late closure strategy   One parsing strategy is called the **late closure strategy.** This strategy states that, wherever possible, we prefer to attach new items to the current constituent (Frazier, 1987; Frazier & Fodor, 1978; Kimball, 1973). A primary motivation for this strategy is that it reduces the burden on working memory during parsing (Frazier, 1987).

One example of late closure is sentence (5):

(5) Tom said that Bill had taken the cleaning out yesterday.

Here the adverb *yesterday* may be attached to the main clause (*Tom said* . . .) or the subsequent subordinate clause (*Bill had taken* . . .). Frazier and Fodor (1978) argue that we tend to prefer the latter strategy. Another example is (6), in which the prepositional phrase *in the library* could modify either the verb *put* or the verb *reading.* We tend to prefer attaching the prepositional phrase to the latter verb (Frazier & Fodor, 1978).

(6) Jessie put the book Kathy was reading in the library . . .

Further evidence for the late closure strategy comes from Frazier and Rayner (1982), who examined eye fixations of subjects reading structurally ambiguous sentences, such as (7):

(7) Since Jay always jogs a mile seems like a very short distance to him.

The ambiguity in this sentence is a little artificial because it lacks a comma after *jogs.* Nonetheless, the subjects' eye fixations were interesting. Frazier and Rayner found that fixation times on the last few words were longer than on the earlier ones, implying that readers had misinterpreted the phrase *a mile* and had to make some later adjustments.

Sentences such as (7) are **garden path sentences.** As we saw in Chapter 1, in a garden path sentence, we interpret a sentence in a particular way only to find out near the end that we misinterpreted it. The subjective impression is that of being led down a garden path until discovering at the end that we took the wrong path and have to retrace our efforts. The garden path experience lends further support to the immediacy principle, for if we did not commit ourselves to an immediate interpretation, we would not have found ourselves in this predicament.

Minimal attachment strategy   A second strategy is referred to as **minimal attachment strategy,** which states that we prefer attaching new items into the phrase marker being constructed using the fewest syntactic nodes consistent with the rules of the language (Frazier, 1987; Frazier & Fodor, 1978). For example, a sentence fragment such as (8) could be interpreted as either a noun phrase conjunction (that is, both Marcie and her sister were recipients of a kiss) or as the beginning of a new noun phrase. According to minimal attachment, we prefer the former interpretation (Frazier, 1987).

(8)   Ernie kissed Marcie and her sister . . .

Frazier and Rayner's (1982) study cited earlier also found evidence for the minimal attachment strategy. For example, consider sentences (9) and (10):

(9)   The city council argued the mayor's position forcefully.
(10)   The city council argued the mayor's position was correct.

Sentence (9) is consistent with minimal attachment in that the adverb *forcefully* is attached to the current constituent, the VP (see Figure 6-2a). In contrast, sentence (10) is a complement construction that requires building a new constituent (Figure 6-2b). Frazier and Rayner found that reading times were faster for (9) than for (10).

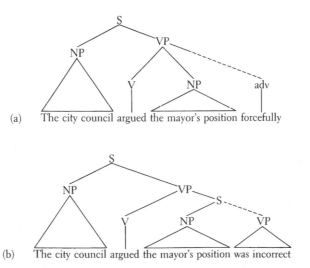

Figure 6-2.   Tree diagrams for (*a*) *The city council argued the mayor's position forcefully,* and (*b*) *The city council argued the mayor's position was incorrect.* [From L. Frazier and K. Rayner, "Making and correcting errors during sentence comprehension: Eye movements in the analysis of structurally ambiguous sentences," *Cognitive Psychology* 14 (1982):178–210.]

Issues in Sentence Processing

The parsing mechanism that has emerged from the research we have considered so far has some clear characteristics. For one thing, it is assumed to be based on structural preferences, such as minimal attachment and late closure (which are themselves presumably based on information processing limitations). For another, it can be described in modular terms; that is, it does not directly interact with other parts of the language comprehension system. Each of these points has been debated extensively in recent years.

Structural versus lexical preferences   The assumption so far has been that the parsing mechanism has certain structural preferences that guide the parsing process. An alternative approach is to give greater emphasis to lexical preferences. In this view, the linguistic structure of individual lexical items includes knowledge of the kinds of syntactic arrangements in which they may participate. An early idea along this line was reported by Fodor, Garrett, and Bever (1968). More recently, advocates of the lexical approach have examined parsing within the context of lexical functional grammar (see Chapter 2).

Ford, Bresnan, and Kaplan (1982) have argued that a sentence is initially analyzed in accordance with the strongest or preferred lexical form of the verb (and other heads of phrases). Look at sentences (11) and (12):

(11) The woman positioned [the dress] on that rack.

(12) The woman wanted [the dress on that rack].

Although the sentences appear to be similar, the interpretation favored in (11) is that of a simple noun phrase, whereas the verb *wanted* tends to favor a more complex NP. These results suggest that lexical preferences may influence parsing (see also Shapiro, Nagel, & Levine, 1993).

The matter is not fully resolved, however. Frazier (1987) has argued that these results could also be explained by a process in which lexical preferences do not influence the initial parsing, but instead are used later to identify whether a previous analysis is correct. Some evidence for this latter idea is presented in Mitchell (1987), who employed a self-paced reading task. Subjects were presented with sentence fragments such as (13a) and (14a) and were instructed to press a bar when they had finished reading the fragment. The time they took to read the fragments was recorded. Upon finishing the first fragment, they saw the remainder of the sentence, (13b) and (14b), respectively, and again their reading times were recorded.

(13a) After the child had sneezed the doctor . . .

(13b) . . . prescribed a course of injections.

(14a) After the child had visited the doctor . . .

(14b) . . . prescribed a course of injections.

The lexical view would make specific predictions based on the types of verbs in these sentences. In (13), *sneezed* is an obligatorily intransitive verb (that is, it does not take a direct object). In (14), the verb *visited* is optionally transitive; it may, but is not required to, take an object. According to the lexical view, these attributes should be stored in the lexical entry and guide parsing. If so, we might expect a garden path phenomenon for (14) but not (13). Mitchell indeed found that (14b) took longer to read than (13b), which suggests that readers were forced to reanalyze (14) near the end of the sentence. More interestingly, it was also discovered that (13a) took longer to read than (14a), suggesting that readers initially analyzed (13a) as a transitive, then reanalyzed it. In effect, a garden path effect was found with both sentences, although the clarifying information occurred earlier in (13) than in (14). These results are consistent with the view that initial parsing is based on the minimal attachment principle. At a later stage, the parsed sentence is then examined to determine if it is compatible with the lexical information subsequently made available.

The distinction between whether lexical factors operate in initial parsing or at a subsequent stage is one that is difficult to assess. As Frazier (1987) points out, data from other languages may be helpful here. English is a "head-first" language. This means that the head of the construction (for example, the verb in a verb phrase) tends to occur first. Frazier notes that in a head-final language, we would have to postpone processing a verb phrase, if the lexical view is correct, because we could not entertain lexical biases before encountering the verb. In effect, in a head-final language, we would have to choose between lexical-based parsing and the immediacy principle. Relatively little research has been done on cross-linguistic aspects of parsing (but see Cuetos & Mitchell, 1988).

Modularity versus interactive parsing   The parsing strategies identified by Frazier are consistent with the modular approach to language comprehension in which comprehension as a whole is the result of many different modules, each devoted to a particular aspect of comprehension (Fodor, 1983). In this view, parsing is performed initially by a syntactic module that is not influenced by higher order contextual variables such as the meaning of the sentence or by general world knowledge. Frazier, for example, claims that parsing is executed by a syntactic module and these contextual factors influence comprehension at a later stage.

The alternative view is that syntax and semantics interact during the comprehension process (Britt, Perfetti, Garrod, & Rayner, 1992; Crain & Steedman, 1985; Taraban & McClelland, 1988; Tyler & Marslen-Wilson, 1977). In the Tyler and Marslen-Wilson (1977) study, subjects heard sentence fragments containing structurally ambiguous phrases, with the first clause of each fragment biasing the listener to one of the readings. For example, two of the fragments were (15) and (16).

> **(15)**   If you walk too near the runway, landing planes . . .
> **(16)**   If you've been trained as a pilot, landing planes . . .

The semantic context suggests different interpretations of *landing planes* in these two fragments. At the end of the fragments, a word was presented visually that either was or was not an appropriate continuation of the sentence: *are* is appropriate for the first fragment and *is* for the second one. The time the subjects took to name the words presented visually was recorded. Tyler and Marslen-Wilson found that latencies were shorter for appropriate words than for inappropriate words, suggesting that the subjects were able to use the context to assign one or another structural meaning to the sentence immediately.

However, several other studies have supported the modular view (Ferreira & Clifton, 1986; Rayner, Carlson, & Frazier, 1983; Shapiro, Zurif, & Grimshaw, 1989). Rayner and colleagues examined whether the plausibility of real world events influenced the immediate parsing of sentences. They used reduced relative clause sentences such as (17) and (18).

(17)   The florist sent the flowers was very pleased.

(18)   The performer sent the flowers was very pleased.

When we discussed sentence (17) earlier, you may have wondered whether the garden path effect is related to the fact that we expect florists to send flowers, not receive them. In sentence (18), the interpretation that the performer received the flowers is considerably more plausible. Rayner and colleagues measured eye fixations on segments of these sentences and found that initial analyses of the sentences were unrelated to the plausibility variable. Clear garden path effects were found with both plausible and implausible sentences.

These results were extended by Ferreira and Clifton (1986), who examined whether a paragraph context would override the minimal attachment strategy:

(19)   The editor played the tape and agreed it was a big story.

(20)   The editor played the tape agreed it was a big story.

(21)   John worked as a reporter for a big city newspaper. He sensed that a major story was brewing over the city hall scandal, and he obtained some evidence that he believed pretty much established the mayor's guilt. He gave a tape to his editor and told him to listen to it.

(22)   . . . He ran a tape for one of his editors, and he showed some photos to the other.

They presented subjects with sentences that could (19) and could not (20) be parsed by means of minimal attachment. In some instances, the paragraph context biased the reader toward a minimal attachment interpretation of the target sentence, as in (21). In other instances, (22), the context primed the nonminimal attachment interpretation. Despite these context differences, the researchers found that readers continued to use the minimal attachment principle. Reaction times for the critical region of the sentence (*agreed*) were longer for sentences that violated minimal attachment than for those that didn't, but no differences were observed between different paragraph contexts. These results suggest that the parser operates with structural biases that are not influenced by prior semantic context.

These results converge with those we saw in Chapter 5 regarding the role of semantic context in understanding lexically ambiguous words (Swinney, 1979). We saw, counterintuitive though it may be, that we automatically activate more than one meaning of an ambiguous word even if a context that biases one of the meanings is available prior to the ambiguous word. Ferreira and Clifton (1986) make an analogous point. The parsing mechanism may be viewed as a syntactic module that operates on specific input (a string of words) to produce a specific output (a tree structure). The role of context, in this view, is not directly related to the initial parsing of a sentence but rather to its subsequent interpretation. In the next section of the chapter, we will look at this latter process more closely.

Summary

As a result of processing limitations, we begin to analyze sentence structure as soon as we see or hear the first words. These words activate syntactic processing strategies that are used to organize the words into a phrase marker. These strategies indicate that we prefer to attach incoming words onto the most recent constituent as opposed to attaching them to earlier constituents or developing new ones. These strategies, although generally useful, sometimes lead to errors and subsequent reanalyses of syntactic structure. These reanalyses are costly in terms of processing resources and lead to difficulties in comprehension.

Current work leaves several important questions unanswered. These include the extent to which parsing is based on lexical versus structural preferences, the extent to which parsing is modular, and whether principles of parsing are universal versus specific to a particular language.

Comprehending Sentences in Context

The parsing mechanism we have just considered has as its output a syntactic structure of the incoming sentence. This provides a basis for determining the literal meaning of the sentence. But many of the sentences we use on an everyday basis are not meant to be taken literally. For instance, suppose we heard someone say sentence (23):

(23)   Can you pass the salt?

It is literally a question of one's ability, but it is taken, in most contexts, as a polite form of a request. Similarly, sentence (24) may at first appear to be a meaningless statement, but if preceded by a discussion of some of the emotional problems that may beset a relationship, it may be successfully understood as a metaphor:

(24)   Some marriages are iceboxes.

These sentences suggest that there is often a difference between the meaning of a sentence and the meaning that a speaker is conveying with the sentence. This is a rich area in the study of language, one that brings semantic and, especially, pragmatic factors into play.

This section of the chapter will examine how we may use the communicative context to understand sentences. We begin by discussing the notion that we interpret utterances in context by means of communicative conventions. Then we turn to two important and interesting types of sentences: indirect speech acts and metaphors.

Conventions

It is generally held that linguistic communication takes place within a context of shared assumptions about communication (Bach & Harnish, 1979; Grice, 1975). These implicit assumptions are referred to as **conventions.** Grice identified four conventions (which he calls maxims) governing conversations (Table 6-1). According to Grice, we strive to be informative, clear, relevant, and truthful.

Of course, these conventions provide no more than ground rules for successful conversations; all of us, from time to time, are uninformative, unclear, irrelevant, and deceitful. Grice's point is that these conventions provide a basis for interpreting what others mean because we generally assume, unless we have information to the contrary, that such conventions will be observed. A simple example of what can happen when a convention is violated is provided by Clark and Clark (1977):

Steven:	Wilfred is meeting a woman for dinner tonight.
Susan:	Does his wife know?
Steven:	Of course she does. The woman he is meeting is his wife.

Did Susan jump to an erroneous conclusion, or did Steven mislead her? It depends on your assumptions. According to Grice, Steven's initial comment violates the convention of quantity and, by failing to provide enough information for Susan to understand what was being said, misled her.

As a second example, suppose you heard the following pair of sentences:

(25) Harold was in an accident.

(26) He had been drinking.

Table 6-1. Four Conventions for Conversations

1. Quantity: Make your contribution as informative as is required, but not more informative than is required.
2. Quality: Try to make your contribution one that is truthful. That is, do not say anything you believe to be false.
3. Relation: Make your contribution relevant to the aims of the ongoing conversation.
4. Manner: Be clear. Try to avoid obscurity, ambiguity, wordiness, and disorderliness in your use of language.

Source: H. P. Grice, "Logic and Conversation," in P. Cole and J. L. Morgan (eds.), *Syntax and Semantics: Vol. 3. Speech Acts* (New York: Seminar Press, 1975), pp. 41–58.

More than likely, you would consider Harold's drinking as a factor in his accident. However, if you think about it, the drinking might have been unrelated to the accident; he might have been driving safely although intoxicated when another driver ran a red light. For that matter, Harold might have been a passenger in the car, or might have been drinking soft drinks. All of these possibilities would be given little or no consideration by most comprehenders. Most would think, quite naturally, that if these scenarios were what was meant, then the pair of sentences is misleading. Another way of saying the same thing is to say that we are led, by the convention of relation, to assume that there is a relationship between the events in the two sentences. It is this convention that guides us to a particular interpretation of these events.

Similar examples can be constructed for the other conventions identified by Grice. Collectively, the conventions represent some shared assumptions about how we communicate with others, and these conventions guide our comprehension.

Speech Acts

Austin (1962) inspired a good deal of research into the various ways a speech utterance might function. He was especially interested in certain utterances that do not seem to communicate much information but, instead, serve as an action. When we use phrases such as *I promise . . .* , *I apologize . . .* , and *I congratulate . . .* , the very act of uttering the sentence is a kind of action. These are quite different than utterances in which assertions are made. That is, it makes sense for someone to say *No, that's not true* to an assertion such as (27), but it makes no sense at all to respond in this manner to a sentence such as (28).

(27)   It is going to be cold today.

(28)   I congratulate you on your award.

In discussing such sentences, it will be helpful to use some of Austin's terminology. The act of saying something is referred to as the **locutionary act.** The **illocutionary force** of an utterance is the action that is performed by saying the sentence. In sentence (28), the illocutionary force is a congratulation; the act of saying the sentence performs this act. An utterance with an illocutionary force is commonly referred to as a **speech act.** Finally, we may distinguish each of these from the **perlocutionary effect** of the utterance, which is the effect of the utterance on a listener. This may or may not coincide with the illocutionary force; for instance, I may apologize, but you may not accept my apology.

There have been several attempts to classify speech acts into different categories. Bach and Harnish (1979) distinguished four types of speech acts. **Constatives** occur when a speaker expresses a belief with the intention of creating a similar belief in the listener. Verbs such as *deny* and *report* serve this function. **Directives** occur when the speaker expresses an interest in the listener's future action, using such verbs as *ask* and *request*. **Commissives** occur when the speaker is obligated, by virtue of the speech act, to do something, as when using *promise* and *offer.* **Acknowledgements** occur when the speaker expresses feelings for the listener by using, for example, *apologize* and *congratulate.*

One type of speech act that has drawn considerable interest is the **indirect speech act,** which is a speech act in which the communicative meaning does not correspond to the literal meaning of the sentence. An example is sentence (29), which is conventionally understood as an indirect or polite form of a request.

(29)   Can you shut the door?

An interesting fact about indirect speech acts is that although there is no direct relationship between the form of the sentence and its intended meaning, listeners apparently have little trouble comprehending these speech acts.

There are several common ways of making an indirect request. One is to question the ability of the person who is asked to perform the action, as in sentence (29). Another is to refer to the listener's willingness to perform the desired action, as in sentence (30):

(30)   Will you shut the door?

Still another is to indicate the reason why such an action needs to be done, as in sentence (31):

(31)   It is getting cold in here.

Whether or not the person addressed has the ability or willingness to perform the desired action and the reason why the action is necessary are referred to as **felicity conditions.** When a speech act meets most of these conditions, it is generally regarded as sincere or valid. When these conditions are not present, the speech act is typically viewed as odd or socially inappropriate, as it would be if we addressed (29) to a person in a wheelchair.

How do we comprehend indirect speech acts? Searle (1975) claims that we use several stages, of which three are most relevant here. In stage 1, the listener extracts the literal meaning of the sentence. In stage 2, the listener decides whether the literal meaning is what the speaker intended, based on the context and on communicative conventions. For instance, a literal reading of sentence (29) may be viewed as a violation of the convention of relation. If in stage 2 the listener decides the literal meaning was not intended, then the listener computes in stage 3 an indirect meaning based on communicative conventions and the direct speech act. In this view, literal meaning necessarily precedes nonliteral meaning.

This model was tested in a study by Clark and Lucy (1975). On each trial, subjects were presented with a request and a picture and were asked whether the two matched or didn't match. Relying upon previous studies that indicated that negative sentences take longer to comprehend than affirmative sentences (Clark, 1974), Clark and Lucy examined the effects of negation on both literal and non-literal meaning. For example, sentence (32) is positive in terms of both the indirect meaning and its surface expression; sentence (33), although expressed positively, conveys the negative meaning that the speaker would like the door to remain closed. In contrast, sentence (34) is a request to open the door but is expressed in negative form.

(32)   Can you open the door?

(33)   Must you open the door?

(34)   Why not open the door?

Clark and Lucy found that positive requests behaved as affirmative sentences, requiring less time to comprehend than negative requests. Moreover, when the request was phrased in negative form, it also increased comprehension time. They took this result to mean that subjects computed the literal meaning of the sentence first, just as predicted in Searle's model.

Gibbs (1979) challenged this view. He presented individuals with sentences such as (35) either in a story context or as an isolated sentence. This sentence might be interpreted literally, as in (36), or as an indirect request, as in (37).

(35)   Must you open the window?

(36)   Need you open the window?

(37)   Do not open the window.

One story context matched the first interpretation:

> Mrs. Smith was watering her garden one afternoon. She saw the housepainter was pushing a window open. She didn't understand why he needed to have it open. A bit worried she went over and politely asked, "Must you open the window?"

Another matched the second one:

> One morning John felt too sick to go to school. The night before he and his friends got very drunk. Because of this he caught a bad cold. He was lying in bed when his mother stormed in. When she started to open the window John groaned, "Must you open the window?"

Individuals either read the isolated sentence or the sentence in one of the two story contexts. After reading the key sentence, they were shown another sentence and asked whether it was a true or false paraphrase of the key sentence. The time needed to make this judgment was recorded. When the sentences were presented in isolation, indirect requests took longer than literal sentences, replicating the results of Clark and Lucy. However, when the sentence was in a story context people took longer to comprehend literal meanings than indirect meanings.

Gibbs concluded that it is not always necessary to compute a direct meaning prior to indirect meaning. In natural discourse, previous sentences may have activated enough information in semantic memory to comprehend the nonliteral meaning directly, without first considering the direct speech act. The three-stage procedure suggested by Searle and found by Clark and Lucy (and Gibbs, in the no-context condition) may be a special strategy used when an indirect speech act is presented to us either in a way that does not fit with previous discourse or with no context at all.

Metaphors

When someone says that *Jim's head is full of rocks,* we instantly recognize it as a **metaphorical statement.** The comprehension of metaphorical language poses some very interesting problems for a general theory of language comprehension. For one thing, metaphors and other forms of figurative language are ubiquitous features of language and thus cannot be dismissed as a peripheral concern. Moreover, the apparent ease of comprehension of most metaphors suggests a link with the processes of language comprehension we have discussed throughout this chapter. Yet, the manner in which word meanings are combined to form novel metaphors seems to extend our understanding of comprehension, for metaphors are invariably literally false. Thus, the question to be pursued here is in what way we comprehend a meaning that is literally anomalous but metaphorically not just meaningful but often amusing, thought-provoking, or poignant.

Metaphors consist of three main parts. Consider, for example, sentence (38):

(38)   Billboards are warts on the landscape.

The topic or **tenor** of the metaphor is *billboards*. The **vehicle** is what is predicated of the tenor; here it is *warts*. The **ground** of the metaphor is the implied similarity between tenor and vehicle. Thus, we could say that the ground, in this metaphor, is that both billboards and warts are "ugly protrusions on some surface" (Verbrugge & McCarrell, 1977). In terms of comprehension, this analysis suggests that comprehenders use the tenor and vehicle to infer the ground.

Why do we choose to use a metaphor rather than a literal statement to express a thought? Ortony (1975) has suggested that metaphors are often used to communicate continuous experiential information, especially information that is otherwise difficult or impossible to express. Ortony argues that whereas the range of human experience is continuous, words are intrinsically discrete. This argument implies that there is a gap between concepts derived from experience and the words used to describe that experience and that the use of metaphor is an attempt to fill that gap by extending the meanings of various words. Thus, sentence (39) is a good metaphor because it would be difficult to express the thought literally. In contrast, sentence (40) is not as good because the ground could have been expressed literally: both are round.

(39)   The thought slipped my mind like a squirrel behind a tree.
(40)   Oranges are the baseballs of the fruit lover.

Comprehension of metaphor   Let us now turn to the comprehension of metaphors. Verbrugge and McCarrell (1977) have convincingly shown that people comprehend and retain the ground of metaphors they have heard. The researchers orally presented a series of metaphors to students and later tested the students' recall by prompting them with the topic, the vehicle, or the ground. (Remember that the ground, unlike the other two elements, is not explicitly stated in a metaphor.) Thus, in sentence (41), the ground might be *are very tall compared to surrounding things.*

(41)   Skyscrapers are the giraffes of the city.

The interesting result was that grounds were found to be as effective as (and sometimes even more effective than) topics or vehicles as recall cues for the sentences. This result strongly suggests that we identify the underlying similarity relation between tenor and vehicle during the comprehension process.

Given this result, much of the recent research on metaphor comprehension has been devoted to the issue of exactly how this relation is recovered. It has been suggested that we do so by means of a series of stages (Grice, 1975; G. A. Miller, 1979; Searle, 1979). We first recognize that the sentence is not literally true. Then, guided by the convention of quality, we search for another possible meaning. This leads us to transform the sentence into an implicit similarity statement of the form A *is like* B. This view implies that the literal interpretation of an utterance always precedes the metaphoric interpretation and that the metaphoric meaning is optional in the sense that it comes into play only if we decide that the literal meaning is defective or inappropriate. Let us look at each of these points in turn.

The idea that the literal meaning is understood before the metaphoric meaning implies that metaphors should always take more time to comprehend than literal sentences. Ortony, Schallert, Reynolds, and Antos (1978) directly compared the comprehension time for literal statements and for metaphors. They found that when no context preceded the metaphor, metaphorical statements took longer to comprehend than literal statements. However, with 45-word contexts, metaphors required no more or less time to understand than literal statements.

Glucksberg, Gildea, and Bookin (1982) examined the notion that metaphoric readings are optional. They used a paradigm in which subjects were asked to decide if a sentence was literally true or not. Some of these sentences were metaphors, such as (42), and were metaphorically true but literally false.

(42)   All jobs are jails.

Glucksberg and colleagues reasoned that if the metaphoric reading was automatically available at the same time as the literal reading, it would slow down the subjects' response times on the task. They found that when metaphoric interpretations of literally false sentences were available, the subjects took longer to decide that the sentence was false. The researchers concluded that we cannot ignore metaphors, even when metaphoric readings are irrelevant to the task.

In a related study, Gildea and Glucksberg (1983) studied the effect of context on the comprehension of metaphor, using a task similar to that used by

Glucksberg in the earlier study. Gildea and Glucksberg distinguished between metaphors that may be easily understood in isolation, such as in sentence (42), and metaphors that require some degree of contextual support, such as in sentence (43). The purpose of the study was to determine the minimal amount of context needed to comprehend the latter type of metaphor. The subjects were given metaphors such as (43) preceded by figurative primes (44), literal primes (45), or no prime at all, and the subjects' task was to determine if the sentence was literally true or false.

(43) All hands are medicine.

(44) Some arms are soothing.

(45) Some songs are soothing.

If the primes facilitated the understanding of the metaphor, and if—as in the previous study—the presence of the metaphoric reading slowed response time to the literal reading, then the facilitating context should slow down times further. Gildea and Glucksberg found that it took the subjects longer to make literal true/false decisions when either type of prime was present, relative to the no-prime condition. Apparently both literal and figurative priming contexts facilitate metaphor comprehension.

Metaphors and "normal" comprehension processes   Taken together, these results suggest that metaphor is not merely a special case—something we do when "normal" comprehension doesn't work—but rather fundamentally similar to "normal" comprehension processes. In support of this notion, Glucksberg and Keysar (1990) argue that metaphors may be viewed as class-inclusion statements. That is, when we see a metaphor such as (46), we understand it as analogous to the kinds of class-inclusion statements we studied in Chapter 5, such as (47):

(46) My job is a jail.

(47) All dogs are animals.

To determine if either of these sentences is true, we must retrieve the lexical representations of the appropriate nouns and assess whether the class-inclusion relation is applied appropriately.

But how can we assess this relation if the statement is not literally true? Glucksberg and Keysar suggest that the term *jail* belongs not to just one but to several different superordinate categories. It belongs to the category of punishments, including related notions of fines, tickets, and spankings. It is a member of the category of buildings, which also includes hotels, hospitals, and dormitories. It also may be considered a member of a category that does not have a conventional name but includes situations that are regarded as unpleasant, confining, or stifling. It is this latter category that may include the term *job*.

Some might complain that this is not what *jail* ordinarily means. And yet even the literal meanings of words vary with the context. Consider, for example, the differences in the meaning of *container* in sentences (48) and (49):

(48)   The container held the apples.

(49)   The container held the cola.

In (48), most people develop a concrete meaning along the lines of a basket; in the second, something closer to a bottle or glass would be appropriate. In either case, we seem to be identifying a general term with a specific meaning, a process known as **instantiation** (Anderson & Ortony, 1975).

In a similar way, metaphors also require a selective activation of information from the lexicon. Only certain aspects of billboards and giraffes are important; others are irrelevant. Glucksberg and colleagues (1982) argue that certain "stock" metaphors such as *is a butcher* call forth a core of meaning from the lexicon that is used in different situations. For example, what do sentences (50) and (51) have in common?

(50)   The pianist is a butcher.

(51)   The surgeon is a butcher.

Certainly, the statements involve a negative evaluation in either case and imply gross incompetence. The exact type of incompetence varies with the topic, but, as we have seen with instantiation, this is generally true in literal comprehension.

Thus, the emerging view of metaphor comprehension is that we understand metaphors much the way we understand literal speech—by retrieving information from the lexicon, selecting the part that is germane, and identifying a relationship between the lexical representations that have been retrieved.

Summary

We comprehend sentences in light of the sentential and nonverbal context and with reference to various conventions regarding how language is ordinarily used. Metaphors are primarily used to convey ideas and feelings that are difficult to express, and indirect speech acts are often employed to state a request in a polite way. These conventions are generally shared by members of the linguistic community and are used during the comprehension process.

It has been proposed that we comprehend indirect speech and metaphor by a multistage process in which we first consider and reject the literal meaning and then use communicative conventions to construct the speaker's intended meaning. Recent research on both indirect speech acts and metaphors fails to support this view. On the contrary, we tend to comprehend such sentences directly, in a manner analogous to, rather than dependent upon, literal language.

Memory for Sentences

What do we remember after one exposure to a single sentence? As we have seen, the processing activities devoted to even a single sentence can be quite complex, and there is reason to believe that substantial processing leads to durable retention

(Craik & Lockhart, 1972). But in natural discourse, one sentence follows rapidly on the heels of another, then another, and it is unlikely that we can retain all of them accurately. Perhaps some stand out more and are used to help recall some of the others. Or perhaps they become blended into a single general idea of what the other person said. In this section of the chapter, we will examine what we do and what we don't remember from sentences and the way sentences are ultimately stored in permanent memory.

Memory for Meaning versus Surface Form

A basic idea in studies of sentence memory concerns whether we retain the exact or verbatim wording of a sentence or simply its meaning. Most of the early research on this issue suggested that only meaning was retained. Fillenbaum (1966) presented people with a long list of unrelated sentences and later gave them a multiple-choice test of each of the sentences. In one example, the sentence was (52), and the options were sentences (53) to (55):

(52) The window is not closed.
(53) The window is closed.
(54) The window is not open.
(55) The window is open.

The alternatives were structured to permit some inferences about the basis of sentence retention. Both sentences (53) and (54) are superficially similar to (52), but sentence (55) is closer to the original in meaning. Fillenbaum found that most people correctly remembered sentence (52) as what they heard, but if they made an error, they were much more likely to choose sentence (55) than either (53) or (54). Apparently, the meaning similarity of *closed* and *not open* enabled subjects to infer one from the other.

Fillenbaum was careful to distinguish between adjectives such as *open* and *closed*, which are contradictories, and *tall* and *short*, which are contraries. Whereas the negation of a contradictory implies its opposite, this does not happen for contraries (*not short* does not imply *tall*). People in his study drew inferences from contradictories but not from contraries.

A clever experiment by Wanner (1974) also examined surface form versus meaning retention. People often bring to psychological experiments special strategies that are not representative of language processing under more natural circumstances. Wanner sought to get around this problem by giving the subjects fairly routine instructions to an experiment, then giving them a surprise test on the instructions themselves. The key sentence was (56):

(56) When you score the results, do nothing to your correct answer but mark carefully those answers which are wrong.

Seconds after hearing this sentence, the subjects were tested on one of two parts of it. Some were tested on the wording *your correct* and were given a recognition test with the choice of the original wording and *correct your*, which changes the meaning of the sentence. Others were tested on their ability to distinguish between *mark carefully* and *carefully mark,* which mean the same thing. Wanner found excellent memory for meaning (100% correct on *your correct*) but only chance performance on wording (50% correct on *mark carefully*). Thus, when people listen to sentences without knowing they are to be tested on them, they primarily retain the meaning, not the surface form.

Time course of retention   Studies like those we have been discussing have been used to support the idea that we ordinarily use the syntactic structure of a sentence to extract the underlying meaning. A classic study by Sachs (1967) examined the time parameters within which these processes might operate.

Sachs asked subjects to listen to tape-recorded passages. At various intervals she interrupted the passage and tested the subjects on a sentence they had heard previously. She varied two factors: the types of test sentences and the **retention interval** (the time between presentation and test). For each sentence in the passage, there was a set of four possible test sentences: the original, two that changed wording but not meaning, and one that changed wording and meaning. When the tape was stopped, the subjects were given one of the four sentences and asked whether it was identical or changed from the one they heard before. When the test sentence was presented immediately after the study sentence, retention of both form and meaning was excellent, but memory for form declined substantially with 40 syllables of retention interval (about 12.5 seconds) and even more with 80 syllables of delay. In contrast, memory for meaning was relatively durable over this time period.

This result has proved to be reliable. Sachs (1974) repeated the study with visual presentation of sentences and had essentially the same results. Even more impressively, Hanson and Bellugi (1982) replicated the study, using American Sign Language. American Sign Language, like English, conveys both lexical and morphological information, but unlike English, it does so simultaneously (see Chapter 2). Despite this difference in the manner of expression, Hanson and Bellugi found results that were strikingly similar to those of the original study. On an immediate test, deaf subjects recognized semantic, inflectional, lexical, and formal changes; but in a delayed test, those that changed meaning (semantic and inflectional) were recognized better than those that didn't (lexical and formal). Thus, the tendency to store only the meaning of a sentence seems to be a general characterisic of the way we use language.

Pragmatic factors   There are, however, situations in which we seem to remember the exact form of what was said to us. Perhaps it was puzzling or confusing or irritating, and we found cause to mull it over a bit. A few studies have examined the way pragmatic factors interact with semantic and syntactic considerations in sentence memory.

Keenan, MacWhinney, and Mayhew (1977) examined memory for sentence form and content in natural conversations. They recorded luncheon discussions by researchers (who did not know they were being recorded) and constructed recognition memory tests from these recordings. The researchers' key finding was that the **interactional content** of an utterance is an important factor in its retention under naturalistic conditions. Some utterances only convey information to the listener; others convey the attitude of the speaker toward the listener. These latter types of utterances are high in interactional content and include figures of speech, jokes, insults, and the like. Keenan and colleagues found that subjects had excellent retention of form as well as meaning of statements that were high in interactional content; but they showed no memory for surface form and less memory for meaning of statements low in interactional content. Moreover, when such statements were pulled out of context and presented individually in a separate study, these differences in retention disappeared. Thus, it is not the syntactic or semantic aspects of high-interactional statements that make them memorable but rather the pragmatic function they play in the conversational context. Bates, Masling, and Kintsch (1978), who reported similar results, conclude that "the probability that a given surface form will be retained will, at least in part, be a function of the pragmatic role that surface form plays in a given context" (p. 196).

Inferences and Sentence Memory

The notion that greater elaboration of processing leads to better retention has received a substantial amount of support in psychological studies of words, sentences, and discourse. **Elaboration** is thought of as a process by which incoming information is related to information already stored in permanent memory, thereby enriching the memory representation of the new material. We have just seen how information pertaining to the pragmatic functions of everyday speech may serve as the basis for elaboration. We now turn to elaborations based on our general knowledge of the world, information that is not specifically linguistic in nature.

A particular form of elaborative processing is the drawing of **inferences.** Bransford, Barclay, and Franks (1972) have argued that we routinely draw inferences in the course of comprehending new events and that these inferences become incorporated into our memory representation of the event. With the passage of time, it becomes increasingly difficult to distinguish what was presented from what was inferred.

Inferences and false recognition errors   The general experimental procedure used by Bransford has been to present people with long lists of sentences and to later probe their tendency to make **false recognition errors:** errors that people make by believing that they saw or heard something that was actually not presented. A long list is necessary to encourage subjects to attend to the meaning, not just the form, of the sentences.

In one study (Bransford, Barclay, & Franks, 1972), the subjects were presented with sentences such as (57). In this sentence, *them* refers to the turtles. Now compare sentence (57) with sentence (58).

(57)   Three turtles rested beside a floating log, and a fish swam beneath them.

(58)   Three turtles rested on a floating log, and a fish swam beneath them.

The only difference is the words *on* and *beside*. In explicit form, this latter sentence conveys that the fish swam beneath the turtles but also conveys implicitly that the fish swam beneath the log since the turtles were on the log.

After presentation of these sentences, the researchers gave their subjects a surprise memory test. The critical test item replaced *them* with *it*. The results showed that the *on* group was more likely to recognize the test sentence falsely than the *beside* group. People appear to make inferences (here, based on spatial knowledge) spontaneously during the comprehension of a sentence and to store the inference with the sentence meaning. Since the test came a few minutes after the presentation of the study items (much longer than the 80 syllables used by Sachs), and since the test itself was a surprise (as with Wanner), it is not surprising that the subjects appeared to remember only what they took a sentence to mean at the time, not the actual wording.

In a similar study, Johnson, Bransford, and Solomon (1973) examined people's comprehension and retention of sentences such as (59):

(59) John was trying to fix the bird house. He was looking for the nail when his father came out to watch him and to help him do the work.

The passage does not specifically state that John used a hammer, but it is part of our general knowledge that is retrieved in the course of comprehension. Later, subjects who heard sentence (59) falsely believed that they had heard sentence (60):

(60) John was using the hammer to fix the bird house when his father came out to watch him and to help him do the work.

Once again, this suggests that an inference about the instrument used in fixing the bird house was drawn during comprehension. Other studies have shown that although we do not automatically draw instrument inferences during comprehension (Dosher & Corbett, 1982), we tend to do so when the inferences aid in the integration of sentences in a passage (McKoon & Ratliff, 1981).

It is at least a little misleading to call these patterns "errors." In normal circumstances, these inferences are adaptive in enabling us to tie sentences in discourse together (see Chapter 7). In effect, Bransford and his colleagues have devised some clever ways of revealing the ways in which these inferences may produce "errors" in a laboratory setting in which, quite unlike natural language use, we are asked to remember the exact form of what was said.

Role of inferences in advertising   Our inability to distinguish easily between linguistic messages and the inferences we draw from them is a matter of considerable practical concern. This is especially true in advertising, for advertisers are highly skilled at creating impressions about products that are not actually stated in a commercial. Psychological studies have explored the question of whether our tendency to draw inferences from the material we see and hear influences our beliefs about commercial products.

In one study, Harris (1977) instructed students to listen to 20 commercials about various products and later asked them to determine whether statements about the products were true, false, or of indeterminate truth value. Some of the claims were directly stated, but others were merely implied:

> "Wouldn't it be great," asks the mother, "if you could make him coldproof? Well, you can't. Nothing can do that (boy sneezes). But there is something that you can do that may help. Have him gargle with Gargoil Antiseptic. Gargoil can't promise to keep him cold-free, but it may help him fight off colds. During the cold-catching season, have him gargle twice a day with full-strength Gargoil. Watch his diet, see he gets plenty of sleep, and there's a good chance he'll have fewer colds, milder colds this year." (Harris & Monaco, 1978, p. 18)

Despite disclaimers and hedges such as *you can't, can't promise,* and *a good chance,* all 15 subjects in this study agreed with sentence (61):

(61)   Gargling with Gargoil Antiseptic helps prevent colds.

In general, Harris found that people were not very good at distinguishing between claims that were directly asserted and those that were implied.

These results have implications for the way advertisers do their work. Advertisers are prevented, on legal grounds, from making false statements about their products, but making false implications is less dangerous. From an advertiser's perspective, implied messages are extremely attractive because they can create the same impression as explicit messages without the same legal repercussions. Moreover, it would be extremely difficult to protect the general public from false implications because, in most situations, unlike the Gargoil commercial, only some people draw the misleading inference. If only half of the people draw a false conclusion from a commercial, should the advertiser be held responsible?

An alternative approach to dealing with misleading claims is to focus on the processing activities of the comprehender. People don't ordinarily distinguish between assertions and implications, but they can do so under certain conditions. Harris (1977) found moderate improvement in performance when people were explicitly warned not to interpret implied claims as assertions. Moreover, Bruno (1977, cited in Harris, 1977) found that a 20-minute training session involving written exercises and student/teacher interaction improved performance for junior high school students and for adults. Thus, training directed at understanding the dangers of drawing unwarranted inferences can reduce our susceptibility to misleading claims.

Propositions and Sentence Memory

Let me sum up what we have learned about sentence memory. It appears that we generally store the gist of what another person has said, rather than the exact form of the sentence. An exception is statements that are pragmatically striking, such as those that require a response from us or flout the normal conventions of everyday discourse. In these cases, we often draw some inference based on what a person has said and store this enriched meaning along with the surface form of the utterance. Moreover, other forms of inference that we draw are not based on purely linguistic knowledge but rather on general world knowledge. These inferences are drawn in the process of comprehension and are, after a period of time, increasingly indistinguishable from the exact sentences to which we were exposed.

All of these considerations suggest that a linguistically based representational system (such as deep structure in transformational grammar) is a poor candidate for a model of sentence memory. It appears that the exact linguistic form is often not well retained and, moreover, additional, nonlinguistic information may play a major role in the retention process. Alternatively, investigators have developed propositional models of sentence representation (see, for example, J. R. Anderson, 1976; Kintsch, 1974; Norman, Rumelhart, & LNR Research Group, 1975). All of the proposals assume that a sentence can be represented as a proposition consisting of one or two lexical items and some form of relation between them. Thus, sentence (62) could be represented as (63). The passive form of the sentence (64) or, for that matter, other forms, such as (65) and (66), despite their superficial dissimilarities, all convey the same proposition.

(62)   George hit Harry.
(63)   Hit (George, Harry).
(64)   Harry was hit by George.
(65)   It was Harry who was hit by George.
(66)   The one who hit Harry was George.

More complex sentences convey more than one proposition. Sentence (67) could be represented as three separate propositions [(68) through (70)]. Once again, these propositions may be realized linguistically in a very large number of ways.

(67)   George got into an argument with Harry, hit him, and then left the bar.
(68)   Initiated (George, Harry, argument).
(69)   Hit (George, Harry).
(70)   Left (George, bar).

A rough description of the way a propositional representation of a sentence might be set up during comprehension is as follows. When we first encounter a sentence, we extract its meaning and construct a proposition that represents this meaning. At the same time, the surface form of the sentence is being retained in working memory. Since the meaning is usually of greater interest, more processing resources are devoted to the meaning (which persists for a period of time) than to the surface form (which fades over a briefer interval). If the surface structure is pragmatically significant, more attention is given to it, with consequently better retention. This might lead to the drawing of additional propositions (inferences), which are stored along with the propositions of the presented sentences. On memory tests, the memory representation(s) of a sentence are consulted. Unless the sentence was pragmatically striking or the retention interval was very short, only the propositional representation along wih any inferences that were drawn will still be stored. As a consequence, our memory for meaning is excellent, but we are susceptible to remembering inferential material falsely.

An important advantage of propositional models is that they can be extended naturally to discourse since the meaning representation of two one-proposition sentences is equivalent to that of one two-proposition sentence. In natural discourse, we generally recall the meaning that a sentence contributes to the overall discourse meaning. In the next chapter, I will have much more to say about the role of propositions in discourse comprehension and retention.

Summary

Our memory for sentences is a mixture of the meaning of the sentences, their wording, and the inferences that we draw at the time of comprehension. Numerous studies show that meaning predominates in our retention of sentences. Inferences may be seen as embellishments to a core of meaning we have extracted from the sentences. After a period of time, we have some difficulty distinguishing between what was presented and what we inferred, a tendency that leaves us somewhat vulnerable to misleading advertising. Yet, with careful attention, we can distinguish between assertions and implications. Similarly, by focusing attention on the exact form of the sentences we hear, we can retain this form for a long period of time. This may occur if the speech is insulting, humorous, or pragmatically significant in some other way.

Review Questions

1. Define parsing.
2. What is the basis for the immediacy principle?
3. What is the minimal attachment principle?
4. What evidence suggests that initial parsing decisions are based on syntactic but not semantic or pragmatic information?
5. What is a communicative convention, and how is it used in the comprehension process?
6. Is it necessary for us to understand the literal meaning of an indirect speech act before we understand the intended meaning?
7. How do we identify the ground of a metaphor?
8. Under what conditions do we remember the exact wording of a sentence we have seen or heard?

9. Describe the results and conclusions of psychological studies of inferences in advertising.

10. What considerations make propositional models of sentence memory more attractive than linguistic models?

Thought Questions

1. Think of a recent example of a misunderstanding that occurred during a conversation. Using the conventions of Grice, identify the basis of the misunderstanding.

2. We saw in Chapter 2 that linguistic productivity is a basic linguistic concept. To what extent are the principles of parsing discussed in this chapter equipped to handle an infinite number of sentences?

3. Using the discussion of inferences as your foundation, discuss the way in which a political candidate might use language to exploit our tendency to accept false implications.

4. Is there any limit to the number of inferences a person can draw from a sentence? How are the inferences based on communicative conventions to be differentiated from the wider class of conclusions that an imaginative listener might reach?

5. Metaphor is often used to express thoughts that are difficult or impossible to express literally. What does this suggest about the possible role of metaphor in linguistic evolution?

7

Discourse Comprehension and Memory

- Connected discourse is coherent if its sentences can be related to one another. These relationships exist on both local and global levels.
- Comprehenders use a variety of strategies to understand discourse in a coherent manner. These strategies are related to assumptions about the use of given and new information.
- We represent discourse in memory in three different ways: a verbatim representation, a propositional representation, and a situational model. Retention of discourse is closely related to working memory capacity.
- Comprehension of the global structure of discourse is guided by schemata, which are structures in semantic memory that depict the general sequence of events.

Introduction

This chapter deals with the ways we comprehend and remember units of language larger than the sentence—that is, **connected discourse.** In our everyday lives, we process a number of different types of discourse, for example, stories, lectures, and sermons. Each form has its own characteristics, to be sure, but we will find in this chapter that there are certain properties that all types of discourse share.

Research on discourse has grown significantly in recent years, for several reasons. For one, since we rarely speak in isolated sentences, discourse is a more natural unit of language to investigate. Also, sentences are often ambiguous or obscure apart from their discourse context. Just as we need to examine sentence structure to fully appreciate word processing, so we must understand discourse structure to appreciate sentence processing. Finally, discourse provides a rich source of material for those interested in the cognitive processes used in language. Discourse imposes a considerable burden on our working memory while at the same time drawing heavily from our permanent memory.

We begin our investigation by discussing the ways discourse is organized and how this organization influences comprehension strategies. I will describe several processing strategies that we use to produce a coherent discourse structure. Then, we turn to memory for connected discourse and examine the structures that are built into memory after we have understood a passage. We will discover that three types of memory representation are implicated in discourse processing. Finally, I will point out some of the educational implications of research on discourse comprehension and memory.

Discourse Coherence and Comprehension Strategies

Local and Global Discourse Structure

Comprehension of connected discourse depends less on the meanings of the individual sentences than on their arrangement. Indeed, it is entirely possible for a group of meaningful sentences to be thrown together in a way that makes no sense at all:

> Carlos arranged to take golf lessons from the local professional. His dog, a cocker spaniel, was expecting pups again. Andrea had the car washed for the big wedding. She expected Carlos to help her move into her new apartment.

In contrast, the following passage is much easier to follow:

> John bought a cake at the bake shop. The cake was chocolate with white frosting, and it read "Happy Birthday, Joan" in red letters. John was particularly pleased with the lettering. He brought it over to Greg's house, and together they worked on the rest of the details.

What makes some passages easy to understand and others virtually incomprehensible?

Part of the reason that the second story is easier to comprehend is that the sentences in John's story are connected in conventional ways. It is customary, for example, to use the indefinite article *a* when readers have not yet been introduced to the object, person, or event, and the definite article *the* when these have already been mentioned. Notice, then, that *a cake* in the first sentence is replaced by *the cake* in the second sentence. Similarly, the pronoun *it* is incomprehensible without a preceding context. In John's story, we are able to determine that *it* refers to the cake in the second and fourth sentences. In the story about Carlos, events are mentioned as if we knew about them already, but we don't really know that the cocker had had pups, who is getting married, or that Andrea is moving. The only basis of coherence in the story, the repeated references to Carlos and Andrea, is quite insufficient for purposes of comprehension.

It is not necessary to be explicit all of the time. Sometimes we leave out some of the connections between sentences if we think readers are able to infer them. For example:

> John bought a cake at the bake shop. The birthday card was signed by all of the employees. The party went on until after midnight.

Here it is assumed that the cake, the card, and the party all correspond to the same event, a birthday party. How do we make this judgment so easily? We know a good deal about birthdays and what typically happens at birthday parties, and this knowledge allows us to fill in some of the gaps in the tale. Yet, note that *the* is used to introduce both the card and the party, thus signaling that we should know which card and which party. This serves as a cue to use some of that information in memory (party? what party?) to draw these inferences, which ties together the loose strings of the passage so that its overall meaning is unified and coherent.

The contrast between the last two passages illustrates an important point— that we must look beneath the surface to understand discourse structure. Superficially, the last passage is incomplete, but the overall result in readers' minds may be quite complete.

The three passages discussed illustrate two aspects of discourse structure. The story about Carlos differs from the first John story in its **local structure** (sometimes called its **microstructure**)—that is, in the relationships between individual sentences in the discourse. Texts also have a **global structure** (or **macrostructure**), and it is our knowledge of the structure corresponding to birthdays that enables us to understand and remember the shorter passage about the birthday. Both levels of structure contribute to the **coherence** of a text, the degree to which different parts (words, sentences, paragraphs) of a text are connected to one another. We will begin with the local structure and work our way up to global aspects of discourse.

Cohesion

At the local level, a discourse is coherent if there are semantic relationships between successive sentences. A central concept is the notion of **cohesion.** Halliday and Hasan (1976) define cohesion as referring to "the range of possibilities that exist for linking something with what has gone before" (p. 10). They studied cohesion in English and discovered the categories in Table 7-1.

Categories of cohesion   One type of cohesion is called **reference.** This is a semantic relation whereby information needed for the interpretation of one item is found elsewhere in the text. We often use pronouns such as *she, he, it, his, hers,* and *theirs* to refer to earlier items. In the example in Table 7-1, *she* in the second sentence refers back to *her little boy* in the first sentence. This gives cohesion to the two sentences, and we may then integrate them into a connected whole. We also use demonstratives such as *the, this, that,* and *those* for referential purposes; in the table, *that* refers to a particular exam. Another type of reference is comparative reference, in which we use terms such as *same, different,* and *similar* to relate current objects with those of the past.

Table 7-1.   Categories of Cohesion

Category	Example
Reference	
Pronominal	*The woman lost track of her little boy at the mall. She became very worried.*
Demonstrative	*That was the worst exam I had all term.*
Comparative	*It's the same band we heard last week.*
Substitution	*My computer is too slow. I need to get a faster one.*
Ellipsis	*I wish I had more talent. My sister has a lot more than I do.*
Conjunction	*Melissa flunked out of school, so she is looking for a job.*
Lexical	
Reiteration	*I saw a boy win the spelling bee. The boy was delighted afterward.*
Synonymy	*I saw a boy win the spelling bee. The lad was delighted afterward.*
Hyponymy	*I saw a boy win the spelling bee. The child was delighted afterward.*

Source: Adapted from M. A. K. Halliday and R. Hasan, *Cohesion in English* (London: Longman, 1976).

Halliday and Hasan identify several other categories of cohesion. In **substitution,** we replace one lexical item with another as an alternative to repeating the first. For example, *one* substitutes for *my computer.* **Ellipsis** is a form of cohesion that is really a special case of substitution in which we "substitute" one phrase with nothing. Notice that the word *talent* could be repeated after the word *more* in the second sentence; in ellipsis, this repetition is assumed. In **conjunctive** cohesion, we express a relationship between phrases or sentences by using conjunctions such as *and, or, but, yet,* and *so.* In **lexical** cohesion, a tie is made between one sentence or phrase and another by virtue of the lexical relationships between certain words in the sentence. In the simplest instance, we merely reiterate the same word used earlier. Other forms of lexical cohesion may be based upon relationships such as synonymy and hyponymy.

Cohesion plays an important role in discourse. One way to see this is to look at a paragraph in which the sentences have been scrambled:

(1) However, nobody had seen one for months.

(2) He thought he saw a shape in the bushes.

(3) Mark had told him about the foxes.

(4) John looked out of the window.

(5) Could it be a fox?

Look at sentences (1) through (5) and try to unscramble them. You will find that the cohesive ties between sentences are an important clue (from Crystal, 1987).

Anaphoric and cataphoric reference   In all of these examples, cohesion consists of relating some current expression to one encountered earlier. This is called **anaphoric reference.** When we use an expression to refer back to something previously mentioned in discourse, the referring expression is called an **anaphor,** and the previous referent is called an **antecedent.** In the first example in Table 7-1, *she* is the anaphor, and *her little boy* is the antecedent. Alternatively, we sometimes use referring expressions to point forward, which is called **cataphoric reference.** *This* in sentence (6) serves this function.

(6) This is how you do it. You let the herbs dry and then grind them up in a food processor.

Of all of these forms of cohesion, it is anaphoric reference that has commanded the greatest interest among psychologists. One reason why anaphoric reference has been of interest is that it enables us to explore the role of working memory in discourse comprehension. In order to understand a simple pair of sentences, we must hold the antecedent in working memory long enough to link it with the anaphor. All of the examples so far have been of relations between successive sentences in discourse, but this is not always the case. Sometimes the distance between antecedent and anaphor is much longer, imposing a burden on working memory and ultimately disrupting comprehension.

The use of anaphors also illuminates the role of communicative conventions in discourse. We discussed some of Grice's (1975) notions about communication in Chapter 6, and they are relevant here as well. To communicate successfully, we need to use language in conventional ways. If as a speaker or writer we place a large distance between antecedent and anaphor, it is not only cognitively difficult for the comprehender but also an unexpected burden as well. As we shall see in Chapter 9, the failure to attend to such conventions is one reason why schizophrenic speakers are so difficult to comprehend.

Strategies Used to Establish Coherence

Let us now turn to psychological investigations related to the comprehension of anaphoric expressions. A good deal of the research on discourse comprehension strategies has been stimulated by the work of Clark and Haviland (Clark, 1977; Clark & Haviland, 1977; Haviland & Clark, 1974). This work is based on the distinction between given and new information. **Given information** refers to information that an author or speaker assumes the reader or listener already knows, whereas **new information** is information that the comprehender is assumed to not know. Most sentences contain both given and new information. For example, sentences (7) and (8) below are similar in their grammatical structure but convey different expectations, with (7) assuming that readers already know that the bank was robbed (the given information) but do not know who did it (the new information), and (8) assuming that readers know that Steve robbed something but not what it was he robbed.

(7)   It was Steve who robbed the bank.

(8)   It was the bank that Steve robbed.

Given/new strategy   In an explicit extension of Grice's (1975) maxim of relation, Clark and Haviland (1977) suggest that readers expect authors to use given information to refer to information the readers already know or can identify and to use new information to refer to concepts with which they are not already familiar. A model of sentence integration called the **given/new strategy** is derived from these assumptions. According to this strategy, the process of understanding a sentence in discourse context consists of three subprocesses or stages: (1) identifying the given and new information in the current sentence, (2) finding an antecedent in memory for the given information, and (3) attaching the new information to this spot in memory. The primary usefulness of this model has been in examining the various possibilities that can occur during stage 2. Sentences that mark information as given but have no obvious antecedent from previous sentences should pose comprehension difficulties.

The method most often used to examine the relative ease with which we relate sentences is a reading-time paradigm. Subjects are shown a sentence and are asked to press a button when they think they have understood it. The time from when the sentence is first presented until the subject presses the button is measured. This is an essentially subjective determination of comprehension time, since we are relying on the subjects' reports of comprehension. A more rigorous technique would be to require subjects to perform some task that depends on the meaning of the sentence, such as generating a plausible next sentence or verifying the sentence as true or false in relation to another sentence. Since the results of these more controlled studies generally corroborate the studies using simple comprehension time, we will restrict our discussion to the latter for ease of exposition.

In this context, our interest is not in the time necessary to comprehend a single sentence but rather the time needed to understand the sentence as a function of one or more previous sentences. Thus, experiments have kept the target sentence (the one whose reading time is measured) constant and have varied the preceding context sentence(s). When a target directly follows from the context, stage 2 should be relatively simple, and comprehension should be fast. Let us go through some cases to illustrate the varieties of sentence relations we typically encounter.

Direct matching   The simplest case is surely that in which the given information in the target sentence directly matches an antecedent in the context sentence:

(9)   We got some beer out of the trunk.

(10)   The beer was warm.

In comprehending the target sentence, we first divide it into given and new information. The definite article *the* marks *the beer* as given and *was warm* as new. We then search our memory for a previous reference to beer and find it in the context sentence. Finally, we attach the information that the beer was warm to the previously stored information.

Even though direct matches are the simplest case of sentence relations, they are not so simple that they can be reduced to merely searching for a specific word. Finding a prior antecedent for given information in a target sentence resembles searching for a concept more than searching for a word. This distinction is clarified in the following sentences:

> Zak hopped into a waiting car and sped around the corner. He swerved to avoid the parked car and smashed into a building.

Here the reference to *car* in the second sentence is not taken as a reference to Zak's car. In contrast, in the following passage, it is:

> Zak hopped into a waiting car and sped around the corner. The old car lost a wheel and smashed into a building.

What counts is not the repetition of words but the repetition of concepts in the underlying discourse, which may be referred to in any number of ways. When we speak of direct matches, then, we are talking of matches of underlying concepts previously introduced into the discourse (see Yekovich & Walker, 1978).

Bridging   In some cases, we don't have a direct antecedent for the given information but can still tie the sentences together:

(11)   Last Christmas Eugene went to a lot of parties.

(12)   This Christmas he got very drunk again.

Here, we must make a **bridging** inference, such as that Eugene got very drunk at last year's parties, to make sense of the word *again.* In contrast, a direct antecedent pair such as

(13)   Last Christmas Eugene became absolutely smashed.

(14)   This Christmas he got very drunk again.

requires no such bridge for comprehension. Haviland and Clark (1974) have shown that target sentences that require bridges take longer to comprehend than those for which there is a direct match of antecedents.

Reinstating old information   The best way to understand this strategy is to compare the following two passages:

I am trying to find a black dog.
He is short and has a dog tag on his neck that says Fred.
Yesterday that dog bit a little girl.
She was scared but she wasn't really hurt.

Yesterday a black dog bit a little girl.
It got away and we are still trying to find it.
He is short and has a dog tag on his neck that says Fred.
She was scared but she wasn't really hurt.

You probably found that the target sentence in the first passage was easier to comprehend. Since a direct antecedent for *she* is presented, we do not need to resort to bridging. The problem in the second passage is simply that the antecedent is too far removed from the target. Using Chafe's (1972) terms, the dog is in the **foreground** and the girl is in the **background** by the time we see the target sentence, whereas the girl is in the foreground in the first passage. When a sentence refers to something or someone already introduced but no longer in the foreground, the comprehender must **reinstate** the information that is to be matched with the target information. Several studies have shown that reinstatements increase comprehension time (Clark & Sengul, 1979; Lesgold, Roth, & Curtis, 1979).

Identifying new topics of discourse   We have discussed three cases so far. When there is a direct match between given information in the target and an antecedent immediately preceding it, the given/new strategy is performed without any prob-

Figure 7-1. A memory representation.

lem. If we cannot find an antecedent readily, we might form a bridge between the antecedent and target, or we might search information recently entered in permanent memory for antecedents that could be reinstated. In general, we form bridges when we believe the author intends for us to find a relationship between the context and the target but has not spelled it out explicitly. Reinstatements are more likely to be used when we think our failure to find a unique antecedent has been caused by the carelessness of the author.

All of these strategies share the implicit assumption that part of a target sentence should relate to earlier information, but sometimes the information is all new and the target is meant to establish a new topic of discourse. This is easy to detect when explicit markers such as *Now, I want to move on to* . . . or *This concludes our discussion of* . . . are used. Unfortunately, we know very little about the way comprehenders use more subtle cues to detect topic shifts.

The given/new strategy provides a sensible framework within which we can examine a number of cases of integration among sentences. The focus up until now has been almost entirely on stage 2 of the strategy. Let us now consider stage 3, the process of attaching new information to the memory location defined by antecedents. Note that the process of adding new information to given information subordinates the former to the latter. That is, the new information is generally taken as an elaboration, sometimes a small detail, of the given information. Once introduced, this new information may itself serve as an antecedent for later sentences, which are subordinated to it. Thus, the natural result of this integration process is a hierarchical structure in episodic memory. Using the example given at the start of the chapter, the memory representation for the passage might look like Figure 7-1.

The next section of the chapter examines these memory representations in greater detail. We thus turn from the question, How do we put sentences together? to What is the result once we have done so? As you might have expected from the last chapter's discussion of sentence processing, the relationships between comprehension and memory for discourse are quite intimate.

*S*ummary

A discourse is coherent if its elements are easily related to one another. At the local or microstructural level, coherence is achieved primarily through the appropriate use of cohesive ties between sentences. New sentences are easier to integrate when they have a clear relation to prior material while presenting new information.

The given/new strategy specifies a three-stage process of comprehending sentences in discourse: identifying the given and new information in the sentence, finding an antecedent for the given information, and attaching the new information to the memory location defined by the antecedent. When we can find no unique antecedent for the given information, we resort to a variety of strategies for bringing the current information in line with previous information.

Memory for Discourse

Many times we read or listen to discourse with no intention of remembering its content, as when reading a newspaper or listening to a casual conversation. In such instances, our primary cognitive activities are to identify the topic of discourse, tie sentences together, and follow the flow of what is being said. On other occasions, as when reading a textbook or listening to a particularly interesting speech, we wish to remember some or all of the passage. Since comprehension and memory are closely related, much of the work needed to remember a passage is accomplished when we understand it well. Approaching discourse with the intention of recalling it, however, usually calls up other processes designed to strengthen and reinforce what has already been understood.

Perhaps the best way to get a feel for these matters is to participate in a prototypical experiment. The simplest and easiest method of assessing memory for discourse is immediate free recall. Read the passage below, going over it until you think you understand it, and then put it away and try to recall its content in your own words. Don't worry about remembering the exact words. Instead, concentrate on remembering the meaning. Feel free to recall the information in any order that you wish. Go to it.

Pyramids

When an Egyptian died, friends heaped stones on the body. The stones covered the body decently and kept it from being destroyed by desert animals. Kings prepared piles as high as hills for their graves before they died. These piles were the pyramids. They were intended to impress future generations with Egyptian glory, and, indeed, the pyramids are still admired today by students of architecture and lovers of antiquities. (Kintsch, Kozminsky, Streby, McKoon, & Keenan, 1975, pp. 196–214)

Done? The data you have collected, to which we will return several times in this chapter, may be used to address some basic questions about memory for discourse: What do people remember when they read a passage? What parts stand out in one's memory? Are the important parts remembered best? Do different people remember the same or different things?

Propositions

To examine these questions, we need a way of defining what is remembered. At first glance, it might appear that we could simply count the number of words that are correctly recalled. This method will not work, however, for it does not give proper credit for paraphrases. For example, *Friends and neighbors collected rocks and placed them on the corpse after an Egyptian was killed* retains the central idea from the passage, although the words and sentence structure vary from the original. We want a measure of content, not verbatim, recall.

An alternative approach is to analyze the text, and your recall, in terms of propositions. A proposition, as we saw in Chapter 6, consists of a predicate plus one or more arguments. A predicate is usually expressed by a verb, adjective, or conjunction. Arguments are usually expressed linguistically as a noun or pronoun. Essentially, the arguments are what the proposition is about, and the predicates are what is asserted about the arguments. Some sentences consist of just a single proposition, but, more commonly, there are usually several propositions in a single sentence, as in *The Egyptian king prepared an impressive pyramid*, which contains three propositions:

Proposition 1: Predicate = EGYPTIAN; Argument = KING
Proposition 2: Predicate = PREPARE; Arguments = KING, PYRAMID
Proposition 3: Predicate = IMPRESSIVE; Argument = PYRAMID

Each of these propositions may be verbalized in a single sentence, such as *The king was Egyptian*, *The king prepared a pyramid*, *The pyramid was impressive*, and in numerous other ways.

We still need a way to determine if a person's recall includes the most important propositions in a passage. That is, we need to define importance in an objective manner. Kintsch (1974) has suggested that propositions are connected to one another if they share a common argument. Thus, proposition 2 is connected to proposition 1 because they share the argument KING. The notion of levels of discourse is introduced by the assumption that any proposition that repeats some or all of the arguments of a previous proposition is subordinated to it. This is known as the **repetition rule**. Proposition 2 is subordinated to proposition 1 since it repeats KING, and proposition 3 is subordinated to proposition 2 because it repeats PYRAMID. (This is equivalent to saying that when we identify new information in a sentence, we attach it and subordinate it to given information already in memory.) We can then go through the entire text and identify the level of each proposition by this rule. In "Pyramids," the proposition that kings prepare piles is a level 1 (superordinate) proposition because it does not repeat previous arguments, whereas the notion that these piles are pyramids is level 2 (repeats PILE), and the idea that pyramids impress later generations is a level 3 proposition since it repeats an argument, PYRAMID, which was introduced at level 2. Some paraphrases of propositions from several levels of "Pyramids" are given in Table 7-2.

The analysis of texts into propositions gives us an objective method of determining recalled content. Moreover, the notions of propositions, arguments, and levels practically invite experimentation to ascertain whether they have some measure of psychological validity. Do propositions make a difference in the recall of discourse?

Table 7-2.   Examples of Various Propositional Levels from "Pyramids"

Level	Example
Level 1	Friends heaped stones on body, Egyptians died, kings prepared piles
Level 2	Piles were high, piles were for grave, students admire pyramids
Level 3	Animals were from desert, piles were as high as hills, students study architecture
Level 4	The generations to be impressed were in the future, the glory was Egyptian glory

Role of Propositions in Discourse Processing

Psychological validity of propositions   The earliest studies by Kintsch and his colleagues were aimed at determining the role of propositions in the immediate processing and retention of prose. Using very simple texts, Kintsch and Keenan (1973) showed that the number of propositions influences the time required to read a passage when preparing to recall it. For example, the following two sentences have about the same number of words:

> **(15)**   Cleopatra's downfall lay in her foolish trust in the fickle political figures of the Roman world.
>
> **(16)**   Romulus, the legendary founder of Rome, took the women of the Sabine by force.

However, sentence (15) is more complex propositionally (eight propositions) than (16) (four propositions). The researchers found that a proposition added about 1.5 seconds to the reading time. Later studies (for example, Graesser, Hoffman, & Clark, 1980) provide somewhat lower estimates of the time needed to encode a single proposition but support the general approach of the earlier studies.

The levels effect   Further evidence for the hierarchical organization of our memory for discourse comes from the **levels effect**. This refers to the fact that propositions at a higher level are recalled better than lower level propositions. This is a reliable finding, having been observed in a variety of studies that differed in methodological details (for example, McKoon, 1977; Meyer, 1975).

Activation of propositions in discourse   According to the repetition rule, discourse is stored as a network of propositions that are linked by arguments. After reading or listening to a passage, we can use this memory structure in a variety of ways, such as recalling the passage, answering questions about it, summarizing it, and so on. As we do these tasks, different portions of the memory structure become active. Recall from Chapter 5 the concept of **spreading activation,** in which the activation of one concept in a structure spreads to related concepts, with the greatest effect being on those items closest in the memory structure.

McKoon and Ratliff (1980), in an elegant series of experiments, used this notion to examine the memory representations of discourse. Students were given passages such as the following:

Early French settlements in North America were strung so thinly along the major waterways that land ownership was not a problem. The Frenchmen were fur traders, and, by necessity, the fur traders were nomads. Towns were few, forts and trading posts were many. Little wonder that the successful fur trader learned to live, act, and think like an Indian. Circulation among the Indians was vital to the economic survival of the traders.

Later the students participated in a priming task in which one proposition (the context or prime) from the passage was presented and followed by a second proposition (the target). The time taken to decide whether the target was true or false, in relation to the passage, was recorded. (Reaction time to the target should decrease if the context primes it, with closer items showing a larger priming effect.)

The most interesting aspect of McKoon and Ratliff's study was their comparison of two definitions of "close": the number of intervening words in the surface structure versus the number of intervening propositions in the discourse structure. The discourse structure for this passage, simplified somewhat, is shown in Figure 7-2. Pairs of sentences that were close in the discourse structure but not in surface structure, such as (17) and (18) (see below), produced larger priming effects than pairs that were close in surface structure but not in discourse structure, such as sentences (19) and (20):

(17) Circulation among the Indians was vital.

(18) The fur traders were nomads.

(19) Land ownership was not a problem.

(20) The fur traders were nomads.

These results suggest, once again, that we have a propositional structure, not a verbal representation, in episodic memory after we have understood a passage.

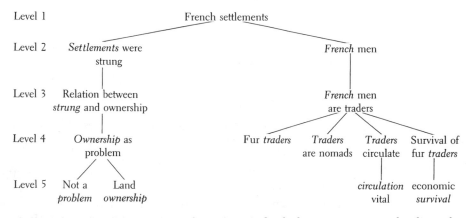

Figure 7-2. Discourse structure of a passage. Individual propositions are subordinated to others whose argument they repeat. Repeated arguments are in italic. [From G. McKoon and R. Ratliff, "Priming in Item Recognition: The Organization of Propositions in Memory for Text," *Journal of Verbal Learning and Verbal Behavior* 19 (1980):369–386.]

Inferences and Discourse Representation

You may have already noted, in comparing your recall with the original version of "Pyramids," that you included some information that was not explicitly presented in the passage. It appears that some inferences are routinely drawn as we comprehend discourse. Purely on the grounds of the frequency with which they are made, inferences must be taken seriously in any comprehensive view of discourse.

Inferences and discourse structure   From the perspective outlined in this chapter, inferences are not mere recall errors, nor are they random, spurious contributions by imaginative readers. Inferences are intrinsic to discourse structure. Authors leave out information they think readers will be able to figure out. This technique does no harm to discourse coherence since implicit propositions (those the comprehender supplies) restore the coherence lost when explicit propositions are omitted. Once again, it is useful to bear in mind that coherence has a greater association with the unitary impression of a passage in the comprehender's mind than with the completeness of a set of words sitting on the printed page.

The ability to restore discourse coherence requires more than knowing the way to make connections between explicit propositions. It also demands the ability to detect when an inference should be drawn, which can be a subtle matter. We must see a gap before we are motivated to fill it. From this perspective, inferences are not drawn simply because they are available, but because they are necessary. For example, consider sentences (21) and (22):

> **(21)**   Paul walked into the room.
> **(22)**   Paint was all over his shirt.

This pair demands an inference because otherwise our conventions regarding the use of given and new information are violated. From a communication standpoint, an inference is a proposition in the underlying discourse structure that is intended but not explicitly expressed by the author and thus must be drawn by the reader.

An alternative view presented by Rieger (1975) is that we draw all inferences that are available, whether or not they are needed. This seems quite implausible. Not only is such a view fundamentally incompatible with the notion of discourse structure outlined to this point, but it is also inconsistent with some of the data that have been collected on inferences in discourse. For example, Glenn (1978) has found that subjects make more inferences in short, elliptical texts than in longer ones. Presumably, this is because more inferences are needed to supply coherence to the shorter texts.

The view that we draw only certain inferences is supported as well by a recent, thorough analysis by McKoon and Ratliff (1992). They concluded, on the basis of a number of studies, that we automatically draw inferences during reading only when two conditions are present. One condition is the one we have been discussing: the inference must be necessary to make a text locally coherent. Their second condition is that the information upon which the inference is based must be easily activated (either from explicit statements in the text or from general knowledge). When these conditions applied, McKoon and Ratliff found that readers automatically drew inferences. Other inferences may be drawn as well, but are not drawn automatically.

Representation of inferences   If inferences are special kinds of propositions that the author lets readers form, it is natural to ask how they are represented in memory in relation to explicit propositions. Are implicit propositions stored with explicit propositions, or are they put into a separate store? The answer, it turns out, is yes on both counts.

A series of studies by Kintsch and his associates have cleverly shown the way that inferences are integrated into the existing discourse structure and have provided additional evidence that this structure is propositionally based. Kintsch (1974) presented subjects with passages that required inferences or their explicit counterpart. For example, an explicit version is sentences (23) and (24), whereas an implicit version is sentences (25) and (26):

(23)   A carelessly discarded burning cigarette started a fire.
(24)   The fire destroyed many acres of virgin forest.
(25)   A burning cigarette was carelessly discarded.
(26)   The fire destroyed many acres of virgin forest.

The subjects' task was first to read the passage and then perform a verification task. On the verification task, they were given sentences such as A *discarded cigarette started a fire* and their reaction time to respond true or false was recorded.

The results are shown in Figure 7-3. Note that although the verification times for explicit propositions are faster when given an immediate test, there is no

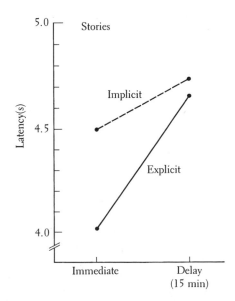

Figure 7-3.   Reaction times to verify explicitly presented test sentences. (From W. Kintsch, *The Representation of Meaning in Memory.* Hillsdale, NJ: Erlbaum, 1974.)

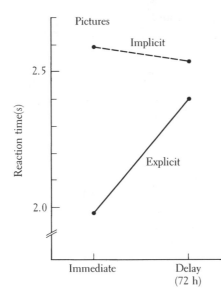

Figure 7-4. Reaction times to verify explicitly and implicitly presented test pictures. [From P. Baggett, "Memory for Explicit and Implicit Information in Picture Stories," *Journal of Verbal Learning and Verbal Behavior* 14 (1975):538–548.]

difference between explicit and implicit propositions when the test is delayed by 15 minutes. Kintsch explains the results by arguing that, like sentences, there are two types of representations for prose material: a short-term verbatim representation that decays or is otherwise lost very quickly and a long-term propositional representation. Implicit propositions have only a propositional representation, and it is assumed that consulting a verbatim representation is quicker than retrieving a propositional representation. The immediate test taps both representations, so there should be an advantage for the explicit propositions. However, since this verbatim representation is lost with a longer retention interval, there is no difference between explicit and implicit propositions in the delayed test.

Baggett (1975) found a similar effect with picture stories. She constructed a series of four pictures that depicted a common event (for example, getting a haircut). Subjects were then given a verification test on either propositions that were one of the four pictures or must have been inferred. The results, shown in Figure 7-4, are similar to those for verbal stories except that the delay needed to produce equivalence of explicit and implicit propositions is much greater with pictures, 72 hours. This reflects the fact that visual scenes are much more enduring than verbal memories.

Taken together, these studies show that stories have both surface and underlying forms. When the latter is accessed, it appears that implicit propositions are stored in a manner similar to explicit propositions in a single discourse structure in memory.

Situational Models

Recent work indicates that in addition to surface and propositional representations, we have a third memory representation of discourse that is called a

situational model (Johnson-Laird, 1983; van Dijk & Kintsch, 1983). Unlike propositional representations, which represent the meaning of a text, situational models represent the state of affairs that a text refers to. That is, the assumption is that as we comprehend the propositions of a text, we construct a mental or situational model of the world as described by the text.

Research on situational models is just beginning, but some interesting results have been obtained (see Bower & Morrow, 1990; Morrow, Bower, & Greenspan, 1989). Morrow and colleagues asked subjects to memorize a map of a research center and then read narratives about characters at various locations in the center. Some of the sentences described the characters' movements through the rooms in the center. After each of these "motion sentences," the subjects were presented with pairs of objects from various rooms. The researchers found that the subjects' response times were faster when the objects were from the goal room (the room to which the character was going) than the source room (where the character came from) or the path room (which the character moved through to get to the goal room). This was true even when the goal room was not explicitly mentioned in the narrative. These results suggest that the subjects constructed mental models of the center during the course of reading.

The Role of Working Memory

Earlier in the chapter, we discussed the notion of cohesive relationships between sentences. In order to have an integrated understanding of a passage, we must relate current propositions with those that have come before. This implies a central role for working memory—we must temporarily store propositions in working memory in the course of comprehension. It should be no surprise, then, that a considerable amount of research has been done on the relationship between working memory and discourse comprehension. In the next few pages we will look at some of these studies, with an eye on individual differences in working memory and in comprehension.

The Kintsch and van Dijk model   An influential model of discourse processing was presented by Kintsch and van Dijk (1978; see also Kintsch, 1988; van Dijk & Kintsch, 1983). They assumed that we cannot process all of the propositions in even a short paragraph at once. Instead, we work our way through the text in cycles of about 6 to 12 propositions. In each cycle, the overlap of propositional arguments is noted automatically. If there is no overlap between an incoming proposition and the propositions currently in working memory, then more time-consuming processes of inference and reinstatement are executed.

An important consideration is the selection of a subset of the propositions in a cycle to go into working memory. Kintsch and van Dijk assumed that whenever a proposition is selected for working memory, its probability of being reproduced (for instance, in a free recall task) increases. Although several selection strategies may be plausible, Kintsch and van Dijk suggest that selection depends mainly on the level and recency of a proposition. That is, we scan the cycle of incoming propositions for level and choose the most recent proposition at each of the highest levels in the text so far. We then put these in working memory and use them to comprehend the next series of propositions. A given proposition may be carried over from one cycle to the next.

This model provides an interpretation of the levels effect we discussed earlier. In each cycle of propositions, priority is given to recent, high-level propositions. Thus, high-level propositions are held in working memory longer and are elaborated more fully than other propositions, resulting in better reproduction in a free-recall task. Since the levels effect is attributed to successive processes over a period of time rather than to increased processing at the time of encoding, the model is consistent with the general failure to find encoding differences related to propositional level (see, for example, Britton, Meyer, Simpson, Holdredge, & Curry, 1979).

Readability   The emphasis on comprehension processes has some interesting implications for the concept of **readability**. Readability has traditionally been viewed as a characteristic of a text, measurable in terms of the superficial aspects of a passage, such as word frequency and sentence length. In contrast, Kintsch (Kintsch & Vipond, 1979; J. R. Miller & Kintsch, 1980) have argued that readability might be construed in terms of the discourse processing operations that are needed to comprehend a text. Two such operations are reinstatement searches and inferences. Reinstatement searches are needed when new information is not related to any information currently in working memory; the relevant proposition must be reinstated from permanent memory before the new proposition can be understood. Inferences are used when the antecedent of a new proposition was not actually presented earlier.

Kintsch suggests that when readers must perform these operations during the comprehension of a passage, the readability of the passage—in essence, the number of propositions recalled divided by reading time—decreases. Moreover, since the necessity of these operations depends upon the skills of the reader, the readability of a passage is not necessarily the same for different individuals. As one example, individuals with smaller working memory capacity are less likely to have a particular antecedent in working memory when it is needed. As a consequence, when a new proposition refers to the antecedent, that reader must either do a reinstatement search (which takes time) or fail to make the cohesion between propositions (which reduces comprehension and recall). Either way, readability for that individual suffers.

Individual differences   As noted, there are individual differences in working memory and these differences influence discourse comprehension (Carpenter & Just, 1989; Daneman and Carpenter, 1980; Singer, Andrusiak, Reisdorf, & Black, 1992). Daneman and Carpenter (1980), for example, distinguish between the storage and processing functions of working memory. The limited resources of working memory are allocated to processing certain tasks as well as to temporarily storing the results of these tasks. As a result, we sometimes find ourselves in a trade-off position. When a task has considerable storage and processing demands, we may be unable to perform both functions satisfactorily.

Daneman and Carpenter developed a complex **reading span task** to examine this trade-off. The researchers had subjects read aloud a series of sentences (processing function) and then recall the final word in each sentence (storage function). The task began with only two sentences in a series and progressed until a subject could not recall the final words in each sentence. For their subjects, the reading spans (the number of final words recalled) varied from two to five. The researchers then gave a reading comprehension task to each subject: the subjects read a passage and then answered a few questions about it. Daneman and Carpenter found a significant correlation between reading span and reading comprehension. Some of their results are shown in Figure 7-5. This figure shows performance on pronoun reference questions as a function of reading span and of the distance between the pronoun and the referent noun. Note that all the individuals performed well when the pronoun referred back only two to three sentences, but with medium and large distances, performance dropped off, especially for those with smaller reading spans. Daneman and Carpenter's interpretation of these results was that individuals with smaller reading spans had smaller working memory capacity, which made it difficult for them to comprehend references more than a

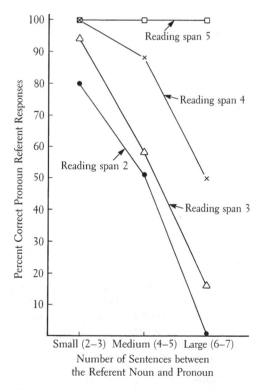

Figure 7-5.   Percent of correct responses to the pronoun reference questions as a function of the distance between the pronoun and the referent noun. [From M. Daneman and P. A. Carpenter, "Individual Differences in Working Memory and Reading," *Journal of Verbal Learning and Verbal Behavior* 19 (1980):450–466.]

few sentences back (but see Daneman & Tardif, 1987, for a somewhat different interpretation of these results).

Daneman and Carpenter also found that their reading span measure correlated significantly with their subjects' verbal SAT scores. In contrast, a simple span test (simple recall of words, which requires resources for storage but not processing) did not correlate significantly with either pronoun reference or verbal SAT. It appears that both the reading comprehension test the researchers devised and the verbal SAT tap working memory processes.

These results have been extended recently by Whitney, Ritchie, and Clark (1991). They had two groups of individuals who differed in working memory read difficult passages aloud and think out loud during the reading. Whitney and colleagues were particularly interested in the inferences that occurred during the thinking-out-loud procedure. Both groups produced inferences, but high-memory-span readers tended to do so toward the end of a passage whereas low-memory-span readers distributed their inferences more evenly throughout the passage. In addition, low-span readers developed more specific elaborations that were definite interpretations of ambiguous aspects of the passage, whereas high-span readers used more general inferences that left the interpretation more open-ended. Apparently, the difficulty in retaining so much information in working memory led some low-span readers to form concrete, specific inferences, some of which later turned out to be wrong. By keeping their options open, high-span readers were able to make these decisions later in the passage, when they are more likely to be correct.

Working memory capacity, of course, is not the only individual characteristic that influences discourse comprehension. Another is the background knowledge that the individual may have of the subject matter in the passage. When we encounter unfamiliar passages, it is more difficult to draw appropriate inferences. In contrast, when we have information in permanent memory that helps us interpret the information, it is easier to draw inferences. In the next section, we shall examine more closely the kinds of knowledge we use during discourse comprehension.

*S*ummary

The meaning that is extracted during comprehension of discourse is organized into an episodic memory structure that captures the gist of the passage. Like sentences, discourse is held in verbatim form for a short period of time, but its long-term memory representation is believed to be propositional.

Research aimed at revealing the properties of this propositional representation has shown that (1) the time required to read a prose segment is influenced by the number of propositions in the segment; (2) superordinate propositions are retained better than subordinate propositions; (3) the activation of a proposition from discourse spreads to other propositions, especially to those closest in the discourse structure; and (4) inferences are drawn during the comprehension process and are stored in propositional form.

Comprehension and memory for discourse are closely related to the concept of working memory. We hold certain propositions in working memory, which permits us to more easily connect earlier and later portions of a text. Studies have indicated that individuals with greater working memory capacity do better on reading comprehension tasks than those with smaller capacity. These notions have been incorporated into a model of readability which states that the readability of a text is a joint function of the characteristics of the text and the characteristics of the comprehender.

Schemata and Discourse Processing

I have described at some length the way we, as comprehenders, achieve discourse coherence by identifying the propositions of a text, connecting them by argument repetition, and creating a hierarchically organized structure. All of this activity pertains to local discourse structure. We now turn to global discourse structure— the overall organization of discourse.

Genres

It is helpful to distinguish between different types of global structures. A type of discourse that has a characteristic structure is referred to as a **genre.** We have genres for, among other things, lectures, sermons, opinion articles, presidential inauguration speeches, and comedy monologues. Genres are important because they provide us with general expectations regarding the way information in a discourse will be arranged. Let's consider a few examples.

The organization of a news article in a newspaper can be thought of as an inverted pyramid. The most important points are introduced in the headline and at the beginning of the article. As the article progresses, less important details are brought in. This structure is directly related to the way news stories are edited. If there is not enough space for the entire article as written, the editor typically deletes paragraphs near the end of the story. Consequently, journalists arrange their stories so that the more important pieces of information are higher in the story (van Dijk & Kintsch, 1983).

Psychology students are familiar with another genre, the format that the American Psychological Association uses in its journal articles. The article begins with an abstract, followed by an introduction, the method, the results, and the discussion. Students encountering a journal article for the first time frequently report that it can be very difficult to understand. Gradually, as students become aware of where to find various pieces of information in the article, comprehension improves.

One genre that has been studied a great deal in discourse research has been narrative stories. Typically, stories begin with the introduction of characters and setting. The main character sets out with some sort of a goal, runs into some obstacles, and ultimately resolves the dilemma. There are many different genres for stories; in fact, there are different ones for detective stories, fairy tales, and romances. Detective or suspense stories, for instance, create interest in a crime and supply possible motives for usually several suspects along the way. A skilled writer will drop enough clues for readers to anticipate some but not all of the details of the ending. In a well-constructed story, readers can imagine many different outcomes at the beginning, but these become fewer in number as we go along and ultimately at least part of the ending can be predicted. It has been said that in the beginning of a story everything is possible; in the middle, some things become probable; but in the end, one result is necessary.

The Role of Schemata in Discourse Processing

A **schema** (plural: **schemata**) is a structure in semantic memory that specifies the general or expected arrangement of a body of information. The notion of schema is not new in psychology. It is generally associated with the early work on story recall by Bartlett (1932). In some imaginative studies that are still cited very frequently, Bartlett attempted to show that remembering is not a rote or reproductive process but rather a process in which we retain the overall gist of an event and then reconstruct the details from this overall impression. Bartlett conducted experiments that were conducive to memory errors—unusual, bizarre stories that were repeatedly recalled over long time intervals—so that he could examine the guiding function of schemata in the reconstruction process. He found that when subjects were given unusual stories that were inconsistent with their schemata, recall was usually distorted in the direction of the schemata. Bartlett suggested that when we encounter an event that is discrepant from our usual understanding, we have difficulty fitting it into our existing schemata, and subsequently tend either not to remember it or to "normalize" it, altering its details until it is congruent with existing schemata.

Bartlett's ideas were relatively unappreciated at the time but have taken on new significance recently as psychologists have developed new techniques to explore the way people comprehend and remember stories. Bartlett's notion of a schema, although appealing, was rather vague, and modern extensions of his work have focused primarily on two issues: characterizing schematic knowledge more precisely and determining how this knowledge is used during discourse comprehension and memory. Let us look at the second issue first.

Activation of appropriate schemata   As a starting point, we consider some studies that have tested variations on the hypothesis that we must activate the appropriate schema to properly comprehend a story.

The simplest case is the one in which we lack the appropriate schema. Bartlett's early studies indicated that British college students had a very hard time understanding Eskimo folktales and tended to modify many of the details in their recall efforts, producing, in Bartlett's words, "a more coherent, concise, and undecorated tale" (1932, p. 127). It appears that comprehension and memory are poor when we do not have a schema that corresponds to the story that is unfolding, because it is nearly impossible to see the significance of the events being described.

In other instances, we may have an appropriate schema in memory but fail to activate it for one reason or another. A series of studies by Dooling and colleagues (Dooling & Lachman, 1971; Sulin & Dooling, 1974) and by Bransford and Johnson (1973) have convincingly demonstrated that comprehension and memory will be poor when the passage is written so obscurely that we cannot determine what might be the right schema. An example is:

> With hocked gems financing him, our hero bravely defied all scornful laughter that tried to prevent his scheme. "Your eyes deceive," he had said, "an egg not a table correctly typifies this unexplored planet." Now three sturdy sisters sought proof, forging along sometimes through calm vastness, yet more often over turbulent peaks and valleys. Days became weeks as many doubters spread fearful rumors about the edge. At last from nowhere welcome winged creatures appeared signifying momentous success. (Dooling & Lachman, 1971, p. 217)

Persons who read this passage without a title as context remembered very little of what was presented, whereas those who were told that the title was "Christopher Columbus Discovering America" did much better. Clearly, it is not enough to have an appropriate schema in memory; we must also be able to activate it at the proper time.

Reconstruction of schema-specific details   One of Bartlett's notions was that the activated schema serves as a retrieval plan, summoning up certain details rather than others by virtue of their centrality to the schema. Studies of comprehension with and without titles support this notion. For example, Kozminsky (1977) found that subjects who read a passage with one or two possible appropriate titles tended to emphasize different details in their recall. Thus, the perspective provided by the schema activated at the time of encoding seems to play an organizational role in our retrieval efforts.

Similar results have been found at the time of retrieval. Pichert and Anderson (1977) gave subjects a text about a burglary and asked them to recall it from either the perspective of the homeowner or that of the burglar. After this first recall effort, the subjects were asked to switch perspectives and try to recall any details that they may have failed to note earlier. Pichert and Anderson found that the subjects were able to recall previously unrecalled propositions after shifting perspective and that the specific details newly recalled were more central to the second schema than to the first one.

These studies provide evidence of the directive function of schemata in discourse processing. It is clear that the schema that is in effect during comprehension has a powerful organizing effect on recall. Moreover, information central to the schema is well remembered, but other details seem to be misplaced, although they can be revived with a shift of perspective. All told, the evidence that schemata influence discourse processing is quite impressive.

Story Comprehension and Memory

Let us now look at the question of defining the concept of schema more precisely. One type of schema that will serve as a case in point is the story schema, which has been the subject of extensive research.

Story grammars   Some of Bartlett's ideas have been formalized by contemporary researchers into the concept of a **story grammar** (see, for example, Mandler & Johnson, 1977; Rumelhart, 1975, 1977; Stein & Glenn, 1979; Thorndyke, 1977). A story grammar is a schema in semantic memory that identifies the typical or expected arrangement of events in a story. Mandler (1984) drew up a set of rules that are similar to phrase-structure rules or rewrite rules (see Table 7-3).

These rules use several conventions. Nonterminal units are in uppercase—these are units that can be rewritten into other units. Terminal units are those that can be expressed by a sentence or phrase from the story and are represented in lowercase. Rule 1 states that a story consists of a setting and an episode (which is then rewritten into other units). Rule 2 states that an episode consists of a beginning followed by a development followed by an ending. Subsequent rules rewrite each of these into terminal units. In some cases, a unit may be used recursively and it is then marked with a superscript *n*. Thus, there may be one or more

Table 7-3.   Rewrite Rules for the Structures of Simple Stories

Rule			
1	STORY	$\longrightarrow$	Setting and EPISODE
2	EPISODE	$\longrightarrow$	$\begin{cases} \text{BEGINNING cause DEVELOPMENT cause ENDING} \\ \text{EPISODE} \left(\begin{Bmatrix} \text{and} \\ \text{then} \end{Bmatrix} \text{EPISODE} \right)^n \end{cases}$
3	BEGINNING	$\longrightarrow$	$\begin{cases} \text{Beginning event} \\ \text{EPISODE} \end{cases}$
4	DEVELOPMENT	$\longrightarrow$	$\begin{cases} \text{COMPLEX REACTION cause GOAL PATH} \\ \text{Simple reaction cause action} \\ \text{DEVELOPMENT (cause DEVELOPMENT)}^n \end{cases}$
5	COMPLEX REACTION	$\longrightarrow$	Simple reaction cause Goal
6	GOAL PATH	$\longrightarrow$	Attempt cause OUTCOME
7	OUTCOME	$\longrightarrow$	$\begin{cases} \text{Outcome event} \\ \text{EPISODE} \end{cases}$
8	ENDING	$\longrightarrow$	$\begin{cases} \text{Ending event} \\ \text{EPISODE} \end{cases}$

Source: J. M. Mandler, *Stories, Scripts, and Scenes: Aspects of Schema Theory* (Hillsdale, NJ: Erlbaum, 1984).

episodes (rule 2) and one or more developments (rule 4). Parentheses indicate optional elements, so both forms of recursion are optional.

Mandler (1984) applied this story grammar to various children's stories. One of them is this one:

(1) All the animals at the zoo receive very good carc.

(2) A zookeeper stays up each night to watch over them.

(3) One night the lions starting making a lot of noise.

(4) One by one they started to roar and growl fiercely.

(5) The keeper was worried that they were sick or hurt.

(6) He wanted to see if something was wrong with them.

(7) He carried his bag of medicine into the lions' pen.

(8) The keeper fully checked over each one of the lions.

(9) He soon discovered that they were not sick at all.

(10) They were just trying to keep the other animals up.

(11) The zookeeper finally got them to go back to sleep.

(12) Soon things were quiet, and the zoo was calm again.

(13) Later on the elephants all got into a water fight.

(14) They used their trunks to toss water at each other.

(15) The keeper was mad because they were making a mess.

(16) He wanted them all to be quiet and peaceful again.

(17) He ran after the frisky elephants with a big stick.

(18) He shouted angrily at them to stop the water fight.

(19) They paid no attention to him and just ran faster.

(20) They squirted lots of water all over the poor man.

(21) They made an awful muddy mess in the elephant yard.

(22) The zookeeper worked for three days cleaning it up.

A tree structure for the story, simplified somewhat, is shown in Figure 7-6. The numbers in the figure correspond to the propositions in the story. According to Mandler's story grammar, this is a well-formed story. It consists of a setting [sentences (1) and (2)], and two episodes [sentences (3) to (12) and (13) to (22)]. According to this view, once we understand the story, we should have something similar to Figure 7-6 in memory.

Episodes as chunks   The story grammar model places strong emphasis upon the concept of an **episode**. There are several sources of evidence that episodes are an important unit in our memory for stories. One is that episodes tend to be recalled in an all-or-none fashion, as if they are stored in separate chunks in working memory (Black & Bower, 1979; Glenn, 1978). Black and Bower showed that the length of one episode does not influence the recall of another. Similarly, Glenn reported that the episodic structure of recall is unaffected by the length of the episodes.

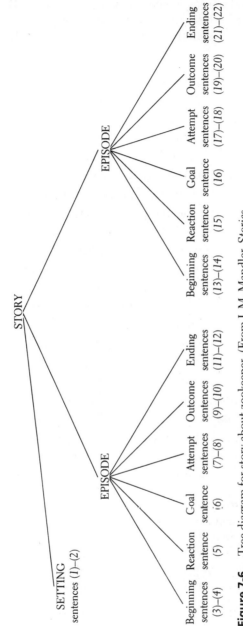

Figure 7-6. Tree diagram for story about zookeeper. (From J. M. Mandler, *Stories, Scripts, and Scenes; Aspects of Schema Theory.* Hillsdale, NJ: Erlbaum, 1984.)

An implication of the view that episodes are processed as separate chunks is that the boundaries between the episodes should be areas of high processing load. Haberlandt, Berian, and Sandson (1980) have argued that the ends of episodes require summing-up processes that increase the processing load. The researchers presented subjects with a reading task in which sentences from a story were shown one at a time on a computer terminal. The time the subjects took to read each sentence was recorded. After the final sentence, the subjects were asked to recall the story.

Haberlandt and colleagues found that reading times were longer at the beginnings and the ends of episodes. The researchers suggest that cognitive activities at the boundaries of the episodes were responsible for the increased reading times. At the beginnings of episodes, readers were assumed to be initiating a new episode, identifying the new topic of discourse, and forming expectations for the remainder of the episode. [You can simulate this by reading sentence (3) from the zoo story to a friend and asking for an idea of what is likely to follow.] At the end of an episode, readers summarize the episode and rehearse some of its propositions. The researchers assume that readers have tacit knowledge of episodes as a unit of stories and that readers organize their reading efforts around this unit.

Haberlandt and colleagues also studied the recall of stories and found that some story constituents are recalled better than others. In particular, beginnings, attempts, and outcomes are recalled better than reactions, goals, and endings. Similar results were reported by Mandler and Johnson (1977). It appears that in a free recall task, subjects prefer to emphasize the objective aspects of a story as opposed to the internal cognitive and emotional responses that they may infer from the objective events. For example, subjects are more likely to recall that a dragon roared at some children than they are that the children were afraid. In a similar vein, endings (including the ubiquitous *And they lived happily ever after* of children's stories) are predictable from the outcomes most of the time.

Cross-cultural investigations   Mandler, Scribner, Cole, and DeForest (1980) have examined whether these patterns of story recall are similar or different in different cultures. There is relatively little evidence on this issue. As we saw earlier, Bartlett had presented Eskimo folktales to British college students and found that their recall was very poor. Presumably, this was because their story schemata did not match the schemata implicit in the folktales.

Mandler and colleagues took a different approach. They presented stories that are coherent from the standpoint of the story grammar shown in Table 7-3 to a sample of children and adults in Liberia. Liberia is a country in northern Africa in which formal education is not required. As a consequence, the subjects varied in their degree of literacy and education. Some had no formal education and were not literate, some had some degree of school experience but could not read, and still others were both schooled and literate. The results for these groups as well as comparable U.S. groups are shown in Figure 7-7. The left side of the figure shows recall patterns for U.S. and Liberian adults, and the right side shows children's recall. Clearly, there is a substantial degree of similarity in the recall patterns. All groups recalled settings, beginnings, attempts, and outcomes better than reactions

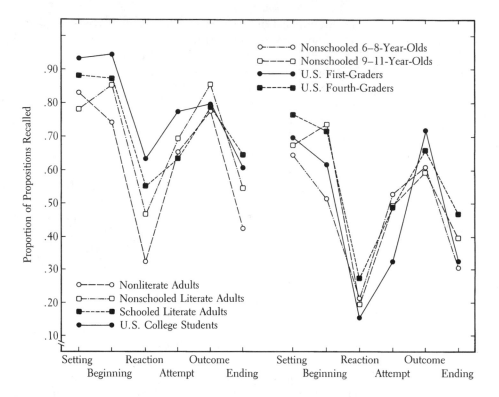

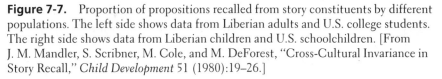

Figure 7-7. Proportion of propositions recalled from story constituents by different populations. The left side shows data from Liberian adults and U.S. college students. The right side shows data from Liberian children and U.S. schoolchildren. [From J. M. Mandler, S. Scribner, M. Cole, and M. DeForest, "Cross-Cultural Invariance in Story Recall," *Child Development* 51 (1980):19–26.]

and endings. Children in both cultures show a lower level of recall, but the patterns are similar.

These results suggest that a story grammar of the type described by Mandler could be a universal schema rather than one that is specific to our culture. This does not necessarily mean that there are no cultural differences in story schemata, only that there are certain schemata that are culturally invariant. As Mandler (1984) has said, "At this point, the best evidence we have is that the human mind and its limitations on memory are such that certain forms of storytelling regularly emerged in various cultures around the world" (pp. 52–53).

Summary

Our processing of discourse is governed by some conventional notions of how passages are typically organized. Different genres are associated with different types of schemata, which are structures in semantic memory that specify the usual arrangement of information in a text. The general notion that schemata direct and guide discourse processing is well established: we have difficulty understanding passages when we do not have or cannot activate the appropriate schemata, and we tend to pay greater attention to parts of a story that are central to the schema under which we are operating.

Studies of comprehension and recall of stories provide support for a specific type of schema, the story grammar. We tend to store the episodes of a story in separate chunks in memory, and we use the ends of episodes as cues to summarize the episode as a whole. In addition, the results to date are consistent with the notion that the story schema prevalent in studies with U.S. college students is a universal schema.

*E*ducational Implications

What does research on discourse have to say about how well we are able to learn from textbooks and lectures? In many cases, what is clear to one person is "Greek" to another, and hence the question for the latter becomes, What must I do to make this passage clear to me? As I have emphasized several times, coherence is achieved during the course of comprehension, not given in the words on the printed page. This implies that the comprehension activities we engage in when reading or listening to prose play a crucial role in the way we understand—and misunderstand—what is being said.

To learn a text's content, we must store its underlying structure. The studies cited earlier confirm that, under ordinary laboratory conditions, people hold both a surface and a deep representation of a text for a short period of time, but the long-term representation is propositional. But it is sometimes different in educational situations. Students don't always remember the most important points in a lecture or passage. Although this result is sometimes due to deficiencies of either student or author/lecturer, the more interesting and, I think, more common instance is the one in which a reasonably well constructed passage is not understood very well despite a considerable effort at comprehension. Since comprehension is poor, memory is usually poor as well. All that is remembered are isolated details, not necessarily the most important ones, and not connected to other, intrinsically related points. In short, a coherent body of information presented to an able and conscientious comprehender ultimately is stored in incoherent and fragmented form. Why?

One obvious factor is familiarity. Much of what we study is material for which we have no available schema. As the studies of Bartlett and others have shown, this state of affairs has predictably negative effects on performance, for, without the appropriate perspective, appreciating the significance of even those concepts that are learned and remembered is often difficult. Nevertheless, identifying lack of familiarity as a contributing element is only the beginning, not the end, of a satisfactory explanation. We need to describe the way we process familiar and unfamiliar texts.

When we deal with familiar material, we are scarcely aware of the multiple ambiguities, missing elements, and irrelevant, potentially distracting details, for we are able to resolve most of them rather easily. All discourse processing involves both local and global structure. With familiar texts, we tend to rely more on our knowledge of the global structure to guide our way through a text, which frees us from some of these details. Unfortunately, we are not able to do this with unfamiliar texts because we don't have the relevant schema. Thus, in the absence of schematic guidance, local cohesive relations must play a relatively more important role in making sense out of connected discourse. Careful processing of these local relations can, to a considerable degree, overcome the disadvantage of lack of familiarity.

The research on discourse comprehension suggests several strategies that may be helpful in improving comprehension and memory. The following discussion highlights five strategies.

Actively Processing Discourse

One general strategy that has a good deal of merit is to actively process textual material. **Active processing** refers to a collection of activities that include relating new material to information we have in permanent memory, asking questions of the material, and writing summaries or outlines of the material. When we read or listen more passively, we generally retain less information.

An example of active processing comes from a study by Palincsar and Brown (1984, cited in Just and Carpenter, 1987). The researchers studied junior high school students who were very poor readers but were not mentally retarded. The researchers taught the students to formulate questions that would be answered by the most important point in a passage. In this way, the students would be trained to identify the main theme of the passage. The study showed that students receiving training rose from 30% on a comprehension test before training to about 80% on a comprehension posttest. In addition, the students were able to maintain these gains after the training was completed. A control group of similar youngsters showed no gains in comprehension.

The exact type of active processing may be individually designed, of course. When I was an undergraduate student, I developed a complex system of notations that I put in the margins of the textbooks I was reading. A vertical line signified what I regarded as an important point. A line with an asterisk next to it was especially significant. Another symbol indicated a point of the author's that I disagreed with. As I look over some of my old texts, it sometimes appears that I wrote as much as the authors did! Still, it was an effective strategy because it forced me to make decisions about whether the information was important or not, whether I agreed with it or not, and so on, and these decisions promoted retention. Much psychological research has shown that when we process information at this deeper semantic level, we remember more of what we read (see, for example, Craik & Lockhart, 1972).

Connecting Propositions in Discourse

As we have seen, an intrinsic characteristic of discourse is that sentences overlap in content and that given information is used to introduce new information. At the beginning of a text, nearly everything is new, but once introduced, newly defined concepts are specifically linked, at least in well-structured texts, to later concepts. There are sequential dependencies in learning from texts; we must know, for example, what a proposition is before the repetition rule can make any sense at all. Attempting to understand the new without fully understanding (as opposed to being vaguely familiar with) what led up to it ensures the same result as trying to run with a football before catching it.

All of this implies that we would benefit from a strategy of explicitly looking for relationships between concepts in discourse. This includes such actions as paying close attention to anaphoric references and noting where inferences have to be drawn. There are several benefits that result from this strategy. First, it produces a network of interrelated propositions in which each concept may serve as a retrieval cue for many others. Second, even if we do not have the information needed to draw an inference, explicitly searching for such relationships between propositions deepens the level of processing and hence promotes the retention of individual propositions. Finally, as propositions are connected to one another, they are also subordinated or superordinated to one another, thus leading to a hierarchical memory structure that may be used to organize our recall of the text or to summarize it.

Identifying the Main Points

Careful attention to the local structure of discourse helps, but it can still be difficult to figure out what an instructor or author regards as the main points. Kintsch and Bates (1977), in a study of recall of lecture material, found that their students not only recalled as many details as main points but also remembered extraneous comments such as jokes and asides better than anything else!

Several studies indicate that the difficulty in determining main points may be traced to the presence of distracting and often confusing details. Meyer, Brandt, and Bluth (1980) found that when the key points of a passage are signaled explicitly, performance improves. An example of an explicit sentence is (27); the implicit version is (28):

(27) A problem of vital concern is the prevention of oil spills from supertankers.

(28) Prevention is needed of oil spills from supertankers.

These researchers found that the signals improved the immediate retention performance of readers whose comprehension was otherwise poor (those who did not share the schema of the author) but did not affect the retention of good comprehenders.

Reder and Anderson (1980) tried a different approach. Instead of highlighting the main points, they eliminated many of the details from the passage. This is the idea behind publications such as *Cliff Notes*, which present condensed versions of plays and novels. Reder and Anderson found that retention was better when the material was presented in a condensed version rather than in a standard textbook version.

Building Global Structures

Devices that highlight the main points of a passage are certainly helpful in the short run, but ultimately we need to identify important points even when they are not so explicitly marked. As we become more familiar with the content and structure of an author's prose, we can gradually induce the author's schema.

One good test of whether we have successfully done this is to write a summary for a portion of the text. This requires us to select specific propositions as the most important ones and to generalize some of the individual propositions into broader thematic statements. For example, a summary of the zookeeper story might be (29):

(29)   The animals in the zoo kept the zookeeper busy at night.

By comparing our summary with the author's, we can see how close we have come to extracting the gist of the text. As we become more proficient, we can shift to a greater reliance on global processing strategies.

Tailoring Comprehension Activities to Tests

One final principle that deserves discussion is that we should always try to match our comprehension activities to the types of tests we may have to take. Memory researchers have established that retention is best when we study material in a manner similar to the way we must encode it at the time of a test (Tulving & Thomson, 1973). Most strategies for improving discourse performance work some but not all of the time. Their success often depends upon whether they are appropriate for a particular test.

An example is from a recent study by Mannes and Kintsch (1987). Students studied an outline of relevant background information before reading a text. For some students, the organization of the outline was consistent with the organization of the text. For others, the outline was inconsistent with the text. As might be expected, consistent-outline students performed better on memory for the information in the text. However, the inconsistent-outline group showed superior performance on an inference verification task and on a difficult problem-solving task that required a deep understanding of the passage.

The point is that it is not appropriate to say that the presence of a consistent outline improved discourse performance. We need to consider what aspect of performance is being measured. We need to know what we will be asked to do with information before we can decide on a comprehension strategy that makes sense.

Summary

This section of the chapter has addressed the implications discourse studies may have for understanding or improving students' learning from lectures and textbooks. A good general strategy is to process the passage in an active way. Some difficulties in learning are traceable to differences in schemata between students and authors/lecturers. In the absence of a familiar schema, we must pay closer attention to local discourse structure. It is easier to identify the main points if they are highlighted or if other details are omitted, but ultimately our comprehension is dependent upon our ability to induce the schema of the author.

Review Questions

1. Distinguish between coherence and cohesion.
2. Why is anaphoric reference of interest to psychologists?
3. Identify the three steps in the given/new strategy.
4. What is the levels effect?
5. Describe the role of inferences in achieving discourse coherence, and explain the way inferences are stored in permanent memory.
6. Define situational model.
7. Discuss how individual differences in working memory may influence discourse processing.
8. What evidence suggests that the activation of an appropriate schema may influence how well we are able to remember a passage?
9. Define story grammar.
10. How might failures of learning in an educational system be viewed as a joint function of the student and the text/lecturer?

Thought Questions

1. How might the enduring appeal of soap operas be explained in psycholinguistic terms? Although they have a very stereotyped schema, soap operas (unlike many other stereotyped events) draw strong feelings. More generally, how might degrees of deviation from one's schema be related to the attractiveness of a story?
2. Sometimes, in the course of reading a story or article, information that was earlier identified as of little importance takes on greater importance, and vice versa. How might such reversals of higher level and lower level status be explained in the Kintsch and van Dijk model?
3. Are story grammars grammars in the same sense as sentence grammars? Do the rules in Table 7-3 represent our story knowledge in the same way that phrase-structure rules represent our sentence knowledge?
4. If comprehension is a joint function of the text and the individual's information-processing abilities, is it ever possible to say that a given text is not written clearly?

part 3

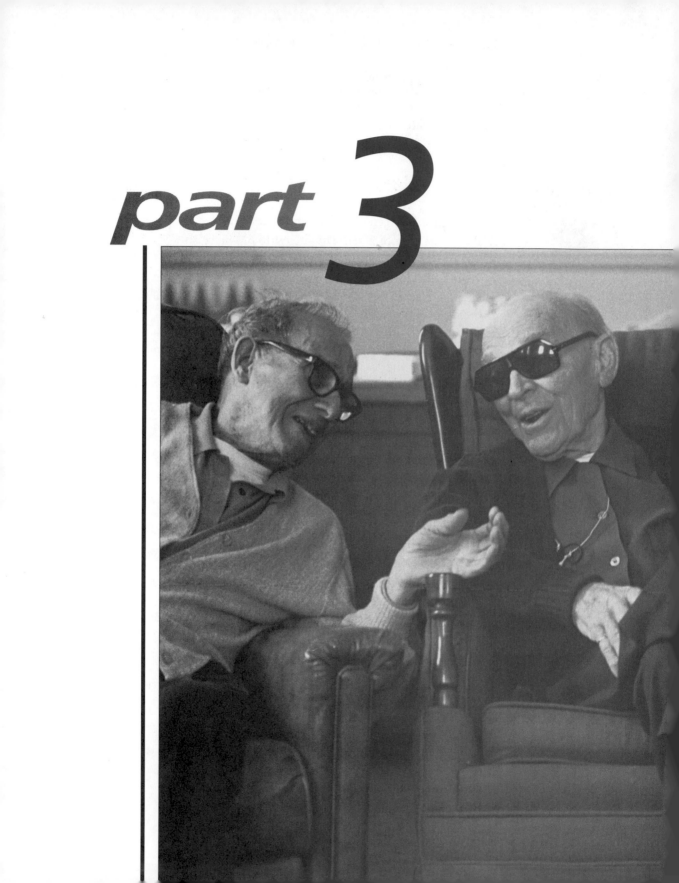

Language Production and Conversational Interaction

8

Production of Speech and Language

- Speech production consists of four major stages: conceptualizing a thought to be expressed, formulating a linguistic plan, articulating the plan, and monitoring one's speech.
- Spontaneous speech errors (slips of the tongue), although infrequent, reveal planning units in the production of speech. Slips tend to occur in highly regular patterns.
- Both serial and parallel models of speech production have been developed, and each has its merits. It appears that we plan one portion of our utterance at the same time that we are producing another portion.
- We edit and correct our utterances when we err. The form and timing of self-corrections occur in systematic ways.
- Comparisons of the production of signed and spoken language reveal both similarities and differences.

Introduction

Language production, which is our concern in this and the following chapter, is an intrinsically more difficult subject to study than language comprehension, and, as a consequence, far more is presently known about receiving language than producing it. This is primarily because it is easier to study the process of going from speech to thought than the other way around. Although speech is observable, the ideas derived from or leading to speech are far more elusive. In comprehension, it is relatively easy to specify the ideas that a person extracts from a segment of speech; one can, for example, compare the recall of a text with its original version. To understand the process of production, as opposed to merely identifying the physical features of the resulting speech, involves understanding where ideas for speech come from. It is no wonder that progress is comparatively slow.

Researchers have responded to this dilemma by using convergent measures. Some investigators have made detailed and systematic analyses of naturally occurring errors of production, and others have given speakers, under laboratory conditions, more or less specific instructions on what to produce. Despite these differences in approach, the findings from these varied investigations are beginning to yield useful fruit, and the outline of an overall model of production is becoming clearer. Following Levelt (1989), we may distinguish four stages of production: conceptualizing, formulating, articulating, and self-monitoring. First, we must conceptualize what we wish to communicate. Second, we formulate this thought into a linguistic plan. Third, we execute the plan through the muscles in the speech system. Finally, we monitor our speech, to assess whether it is what we intended to say and how we intended to say it.

This outline has the value of directing our attention to problems in need of further study. Do these stages occur invariably in the given order? Are there substages for any of the processes? Do the levels or stages interact in the production of a given utterance, as was seen to some extent in the comprehension process? What process has gone awry when we make slips of the tongue? There are a good many more questions than answers in the study of production. We will begin our survey with the study of speech errors and what they tell us about the demands of production.

Slips of the Tongue

The scientific analysis of speech errors, commonly called "slips of the tongue," reemerged in the early 1970s with the seminal publication of an article by Fromkin that examined the way speech errors may be used in the construction of linguistic arguments (Fromkin, 1971). This paper, and those that followed, marked the end of a long period in which speech errors were regarded with suspicion in scientific circles. It has become respectable, even common, for investigators to use errors to examine the role of linguistic units in the production of speech, with many articles and books devoted to the subject (see, for example, Fromkin, 1980). Researchers have painstakingly recorded the speech errors, innocuous and otherwise, of friends and colleagues, within the limits imposed by good taste and a desire to preserve such friendships.

A number of collections of spontaneous speech errors have been made (Fromkin, 1971; Garrett, 1975; Shattuck-Hufnagel, 1979), and it is interesting to determine whether there are consistent patterns in when and how they occur. Although these errors are not common, they appear to be made on an occasional basis by all speakers. Some people are more prone to speech errors than others. The legendary Dr. William Spooner, infamous for his tendency to say such things as sentence (1) to an ungrateful college class, gave speech researchers more than his share.

(1)   You have hissed my mystery lectures. I saw you fight a liar in the back quad. In fact, you have tasted the whole worm.

His peculiar form of speech may have been due to cerebral dysfunction (Potter, 1980).

Most of us make similar errors from time to time. There is anecdotal evidence that such errors are common when we are nervous or under stress, as when performers appear on live television and radio shows; programs devoted to "television's best bloopers" never seem to run out of material. It seems probable that errors are more likely to occur when we are tired, anxious, or drunk. Most research, however, has focused less on the factors that may influence the frequency of speech errors than on the nature of the errors themselves.

Types of Speech Errors

Although speech errors cover a wide range of semantic content, there appear to be only a small number of basic types (Fromkin, 1971; Garrett, 1975; Shattuck-Hufnagel, 1979). Examples of the eight types are given in Table 8-1, with the words that were apparently intended in parentheses.

Table 8-1. Major Types of Slips of the Tongue

Type	Example
Shift	*That's so she'll be ready in case she decide to hits it (decides to hit it).*
Exchange	*Fancy getting your model renosed (getting your nose remodeled).*
Anticipation	*Bake my bike (take my bike).*
Perseveration	*He pulled a pantrum (tantrum).*
Addition	*I didn't explain this clarefully enough (carefully enough).*
Deletion	*I'll just get up and mutter intelligibly (unintelligibly).*
Substitution	*At low speeds it's too light (heavy).*
Blend	*That child is looking to be spaddled (spanked/paddled).*

In **shifts,** one speech segment disappears from its appropriate location and appears somewhere else. **Exchanges** are, in effect, double shifts, in which two linguistic units exchange places. **Anticipations** occur when a later segment takes the place of an earlier one. They differ from shifts in that the segment that intrudes on another also remains in its correct location and thus is used twice. **Perseverations** occur when an earlier segment replaces a later item. **Additions** add linguistic material, whereas **deletions** leave something out. **Substitutions** occur when one segment is replaced by an intruder. These differ from previously described slips in that the source of the intrusion may not be in the sentence. **Blends** apparently occur when more than one word is being considered and the two intended items "fuse" or "blend" into a single item.

If you have closely examined these examples, you probably have noticed by now that these types of errors occur with a number of different linguistic units. In some cases, a single phoneme is added, deleted, or moved, but at other times it may be a sequence of phonemes, morphemic affixes and roots, whole words, or even phrases. As a general rule, errors tend to occur at only one linguistic level per utterance. That is, when a person clearly says the wrong word, as in substitutions, the sentence is syntactically, prosodically, and phonologically intact.

Common Properties of Speech Errors

There are other patterns in these speech errors that we should look at a little more closely. Garrett (1975) has identified four generalizations about speech errors that reappear with striking regularity.

First, elements that interact with one another tend to come from similar linguistic environments, as indicated by examples (2) through (4):

(2) The little burst of beaden (beast of burden).

(3) You're not a poojin pitter-downer, are you? (pigeon putter-downer).

(4) Children interfere with your nife lite (night life).

Notice that phonetic segments in the beginning of a word tend to be exchanged with other initial segments; the same is true for middle and final segments. Moreover, exchanges of segments are more common when the segments that precede them are similar. The exchange of /f/ and /t/ in sentence (4) follows this principle.

Second, elements that interact with one another tend to be similar to one another. In particular, consonants are invariably exchanged or shifted with other consonants, but not with vowels. Errors involving similar sounds, such as in sentence (5), often have little relation to meaning but are based, instead, on phonetic similarity.

(5)   Sesame Street crackers (sesame seed crackers). (Fromkin, 1973)

Third, even when slips produce novel linguistic items, they are generally consistent with the phonological rules of the language. This point can be appreciated by studying blend errors. When a blend such as *slickery* (for *slick* and *slippery*) occurs, the result is a nonword that could be a word. Other, phonologically impermissible forms, such as *slickppery* and *slipkery*, are logically possible but do not occur.

Finally, there are consistent stress patterns in speech errors. Segments that are exchanged for one another typically both receive major stress in the word or phrase in which they reside, or both receive minor stress.

To sum it up simply, speech errors are hardly random; in fact, they occur in highly regular patterns. Let us consider, then, explanations that have been offered for these patterns. What lies behind these linguistic errors?

Explanations of Speech Errors

The Freudian explanation   One intriguing idea is that speakers have more than one idea in mind at a time. During the 1992 campaign, President Bush began his remarks for one speech by saying sentence (6):

(6)   I don't want to run the risk of ruining what is a lovely recession (reception). (*Newsweek*, 1992)

This could be construed as simply a sound error, as the two words are similar phonologically. But it could also be evidence that the president was preoccupied with the recession (and its effect on his campaign). Or consider a student who explains that he wants to postpone an exam with statement (7):

(7)   Last night my grandmother lied (died). (Motley, 1987)

This could be an innocent phonological error but then again, the slip could reveal the student's thinking more than he wishes.

Freud emphasized the role of psychodynamic factors in making certain types of content more available than others. He argued that these errors "arise from the concurrent action—or perhaps rather, the mutually opposing action—of two different intentions" (Freud, 1916–1917/1963, p. 44). One of these actions was thought to constitute the conscious intention of the speaker, whereas the other pertained to a more disturbing thought or intention that interfered with the former. Sometimes, the disturbing comment would be censored, but on other occasions, the outcome of this hypothetical intrapsychic conflict would be a slip of the tongue that expressed some aspects of the less conscious intention. Examples consistent with Freud's position include a general who referred to a group of injured soldiers as *battle scared (scarred)*, and a speaker extolling the achievements of a fellow worker who had just *expired (retired)* (Ellis, 1980).

Freud's position was that virtually all speech errors were caused by the intrusion of repressed ideas from the unconscious into one's conscious speech output. Although the Freudian interpretation may be appealing in cases in which the slip of the tongue results in a word with emotional significance, many slips seem to reflect simpler processes, such as the anticipation (*a meal mystery* instead of *a real mystery*) and perseveration (*he pulled a pantrum* in place of *he pulled a tantrum*) of phonetic segments. In these latter cases, it seems to be unnecessarily complicated and unconvincing to claim that the error originated from intrapsychic conflicts. Still, these more common speech errors demand an explanation.

A psycholinguistic explanation   Most recent psycholinguistic and linguistic research has focused on the insights gained in understanding language mechanisms (not unconscious motivations) from the study of speech errors. In this respect, errors of linguistic performance occupy a role in psycholinguistic theories similar to that played by aphasic disorders (see Chapter 13). The types of language breakdowns that occur in each case provide important insights for normal language functioning.

Fromkin (1971), for example, has showed that many of the segments that change and move in speech errors are precisely those postulated by linguistic theories, lending support to the notion that linguistic units such as phonetic features, phonemes, and morphemes constitute planning units during the production of an utterance. Similarly, Garrett (1975, 1980) has used error data to argue for the existence of an autonomous syntactic processor.

One view of language production is that we produce utterances by a series of stages, each devoted to a different level of linguistic analysis (Dell & Reich, 1981; Fromkin, 1971; Garrett, 1975). If so, speech errors can tell us a good deal about what these specific stages might look like. In the next few sections of this chapter we will examine some of the psychological and physiological processes that take place when we go from idea to articulation.

Summary

Speech errors, the bane of performers on live television and radio live performers, are systematic, and typically fall into one of eight categories: exchanges, substitutions, additions, deletions, anticipations, perseverations, blends, and shifts. Each of these errors occurs at several linguistic levels.

Various hypotheses concerning the basis for such errors have been advanced. One of the most prominent has been Freud's view that errors occur because we have more than a single plan for production and that one such plan competes with and dominates the other. Although a Freudian type of explanation may apply to some speech errors, more recent thinking has focused on the psycholinguistic processes underlying speech errors. The most common interpretation is that we produce speech through a series of separate stages, each devoted to a single level of linguistic analysis. Errors typically occur at one level, but not others, during the production process. In the following section, we will examine this notion of stages of production more closely.

Formulating Linguistic Plans

As noted in the introduction, the production of an utterance may be analyzed into four steps: conceptualizing a message to be conveyed, formulating it into a linguistic plan, articulating (implementing the plan), and self-monitoring. In this section we look at the process up through the completion of the second step.

Very little can be said about the first step. Basically, the questions here are: Where do ideas come from? and In what form do ideas exist before they are put into words? As to the latter question, there is general agreement among psycholinguists and cognitive psychologists that there exists some form of "mentalese"— a representational system that is distinct from language. The notion is that thoughts take form in mentalese and are then translated into linguistic form, but there is little agreement as to the properties of this prelinguistic mental representation (see, for example, Fodor, 1975). The question of the origin of ideas may be even more intractable at this time, although there have been some noteworthy efforts in its study (see Osgood, 1971; Osgood & Bock, 1977; Sridhar, 1989). Thus, we know that the first step occurs but are unable to say much about it.

We are in a better position with respect to the process of organizing thoughts into linguistic patterns, and that process is now our focus.

Serial Models of Linguistic Planning

Fromkin (1971, 1973) and Garrett (1975, 1980, 1988) have each argued that the process of planning speech can be viewed as a series of stages, each devoted to one level of linguistic planning. Fromkin's six-stage model is presented in Table 8-2.

The basic idea of this model is that we begin with the meaning that we wish to express and that subsequent levels of processing are devoted to specific and distinct aspects of the utterance. We set up a syntactic structure of the sentence, which specifies which words will receive major and minor stress and where the content words will fit in. Then the content words are added in, followed by function words and affixes. Finally, we identify the correct phonetic characteristics of the utterance, given its linguistic structure. Overall, the model is a plausible account of the way the mental work of production is distributed.

Table 8-2.   Fromkin's Model of Speech Production

Stage	Process
1	Identification of meaning—a meaning to be conveyed is generated.
2	Selection of a syntactic structure—a syntactic outline of the sentence is constructed, with word slots specified.
3	Generation of intonation contour—the stress values of different word slots are assigned.
4	Insertion of content words—appropriate nouns, verbs, and adjectives are retrieved from the lexicon and placed into word slots.
5	Formation of affixes and function words—function words (articles, conjunctions, prepositions), prefixes, and suffixes are added.
6	Specification of phonetic segments—the sentence is expressed in terms of phonetic segments, according to phonological rules.

Source: V. A. Fromkin, "The Non-Anomalous Nature of Anomalous Utterances," *Language* 47 (1971):27–52.

Let us go through a speech error step by step. One of Garrett's (1975) examples is sentence (8):

(8)   She's already trunked two packs (packed two trunks).

At stage 1, the meaning of the overall utterance is identified. At stage 2, the syntactic structure is laid out, and slots are constructed for the noun or pronoun, adverb, verb, adjective, and object noun. At stage 3, primary stress is placed on the verb with secondary stress on the object noun. At stage 4, the content words *she, is, already, trunk, two,* and *pack* are fitted into the outline. Here is where the error is said to occur, as *trunk* and *pack* are exchanged for one another. At stage 5, the suffixes *-ed* and *-s* are added to their original and correct location. At stage 6, the complete utterance is put into phonetic form.

Independence of planning units   What evidence can be given that the stages hypothesized in Table 8-2 are actually independent of one another? Probably the clearest evidence is that the vast majority of speech errors contain mistakes at only one level of planning. One of Fromkin's examples is sentence (9), which was pronounced *so-er*:

(9)   singing sewer machine (Singer sewing machine)

Here the error is at stage 5, as the suffixes are exchanged for one another. Yet the rest of the utterance—the content words, stress values, and syntactic structure—remained unaltered. An even more striking example of the point is Garrett's sentence (10):

(10)   Stop beating your brick against a head wall (Stop beating your head against a brick wall).

The exchange of content words (stage 4) left the rest of the sentence intact, and it was pronounced with the primary stress on *brick*. Thus, it appears that stages 4 and 5 can each "misfire" in a manner that is independent of other stages.

The point applies to other stages as well. In particular, phonetic errors at stage 5 have been used as evidence of further substages. Some errors involve the breakup of consonant clusters, such as *frish gotto (fish grotto)* and *blake fruid (brake fluid)*. Fromkin (1971) used these examples to argue that phonetic segments are independent units in the planning of speech, for if the cluster were a single unit, the entire *gr* would have been exchanged for *f*, yielding *grish fotto*.

Evidence has also been given that phonetic features are a "psychologically real" planning unit, but here the results are more equivocal. Fromkin (1971) found a case in which a speaker who intended to say *clear blue sky* came out with *glear plue sky*. Note that this is not a simple switch of phonemes. Rather, according to Fromkin, it is a shift of phonological features: the (+ voicing) from /b/ in *blue* has shifted to the /k/ in *clear*. When the voicing feature is lost from *b*, the result is /p/; when it is added to /k/, the result is /g/. Shattuck-Hufnagel and Klatt (1979), however, argue that these types of errors are extremely rare. They examined 70 cases in which target and uttered consonants differed by more than one feature and found evidence for exchanges of individual features in only three cases.

The overall evidence for the view that these stages exist as independent planning units is relatively strong. So, let us look at the order of the stages.

The sequence of planning units   Certain errors indicate that when a speech unit is exchanged or shifted into a different speech environment, certain phonological processes specify the exact phonetic representation. Consider, for example, speech errors (11) through (13), from Garrett (1980):

(11) It certainly run outs fast (runs out).

(12) An anguage lacquisition (a language acquisition).

(13) Easy enoughly (easily enough).

The first example may appear to be a simple shift of a single phoneme. We see, however, that more is involved when we consider the pronunciation of the target and the actual productions. The phonetic form of the plural morpheme varies predictably with its phonetic environment. Normally, when we pronounce *runs*, the final phoneme is /z/, whereas in *outs*, it is /s/. This raises an interesting question: When the plural morpheme is shifted out of its appropriate slot into another slot, does it retain the phonetic form of its original slot or does it take the form appropriate to its displaced slot? The answer is the latter: *outs* is pronounced as /s/, not /z/. This is an example of the phonological process of **accommodation**—elements that are shifted or deleted are accommodated to their error-induced environments. Similar processes are at work in sentences (12) and (13). In (12), the shift of /l/ leads to a change in the phonetic form of the indefinite article from *a* to *an*. In (13), the shift of *-ly* to *enough* leads to a corresponding change in the pronunciation of the final vowel in *easy*; that is, it is pronounced *easy*, not *easuh*.

The significance of accommodation processes in speech errors is that they strongly support the notion that the phonetic representation of the sentence (stage 6) is formulated after the level at which the errors occur, which is stage 5 in these examples. The morpheme that is moved is thus an abstract entity; its precise phonetic specification depends on where it lands, as it were.

There are other indications that the stages devoted to the formulation of syntactic structure precede those devoted to the insertion of lexical items into that structure. Garrett (1975) has carefully examined word exchanges and found that they are distinct from morpheme and sound exchanges in a number of ways. Most sound and morpheme exchanges occur within zero to one word, whereas exchanges of words take place over longer stretches. Moreover, the vast majority of errors occur within the clause, but of those that do not, nearly all are word exchanges. Furthermore, these exchanges tend to preserve the grammatical class of the items. All of these considerations led Garrett to argue that word exchanges reflect a stage of linguistic planning in which functional syntactic relations were being constructed (basically, stage 2 in Fromkin's model) and that the introduction of morphemes and sounds (stages 5 and 6) comes later, when the outline is in place, and involve more local exchanges of material.

The analysis of the syntactic stage has recently been extended to discontinuous dependencies, in which one word in a clause depends upon the form of a nonadjacent word. For example, in sentence (14), the head noun (*time*) controls the correct form of the subsequent verb (*is*), but we sometimes err by using a form of the verb (*are*) that matches the immediately preceding word (*games*).

(14)   The time for fun and games is over.

Bock and Cutting (1992) examined agreement errors as a function of the material that intervened between the head noun and the verb. They found that phrase interruptions, such as sentence (15), led to more agreement errors than clause interruptions, such as (16), even when the number of words was equivalent. In (15), both the head noun (*report*) and the subsequent noun (*fires*) are in the same clause as the verb (*were*); in (16), only the head noun is in the same clause as the verb:

(15)   The report of the destructive fires were accurate.
(16)   The report that they controlled the fires were printed in the paper.

The authors conclude that clauses are planned as complete units even if the words in the clause end up separated in the final utterance. Once a clause is organized, information from another clause, such as *fires* in (16), is less likely to interfere. These results are consistent with the Garrett's notion that clause planning precedes planning at the word level.

Editing Processes

In addition to the stages of planning, there is some intriguing evidence that indicates that editing processes intervene between the planning of an utterance and its articulation. These editing operations might provide a last check to determine whether the planned utterance is linguistically and socially acceptable. It is clear that some monitoring and editing processes occur after a speech segment is uttered; after all, we often spontaneously correct ourselves. The question we want to consider now is whether or not we also have editing processes prior to articulation.

Laboratory-induced speech errors Several studies have examined editing processes by inducing speech errors in laboratory settings. In a typical study, subjects are given a list of word pairs to read silently, although occasionally they receive a cue that they must read one pair aloud. It is possible to induce errors by varying the nature of the word pairs that precede the pair to be read aloud (the target pair). This is known as the **phonological bias technique**. To appreciate the phenomenon best, you should read the following sequence aloud quickly:

> ball doze
> bash door
> bean deck
> bell dark
> darn bore
> RESPOND

The target is *darn bore*, but the preceding four pairs increase the likelihood of the spoonerism *barn door*. In fact, the spoonerism occurs about 30% of the time. As Baars (1980) notes, the technique is something like the children's game of calling out *On your mark—get set—STOP!* or like having someone repeat the word *poke* many times and then ask, *What is the white of an egg called?* In the laboratory technique, one is setting up, through phonological similarity, an alternative speech plan that competes with the plan to produce the target pair.

Evidence for covert editing processes may be found in cases in which such alternative or competing plans are generated but not actually produced. One way to do this is to vary the properties of the resulting speech error. In the previous example, a pair of real words would be produced. In contrast, consider this sequence:

> big dutch
> bang doll
> bill deal
> bark dog
> dart board
> RESPOND

Here the spoonerism, *bart doard,* occurs only 10% of the time (Baars, Motley, & MacKay, 1975). This is referred to as the **lexical bias effect**—induced speech errors that result in words are more frequent than errors that result in nonwords; this is also the case with spontaneous errors (Dell & Reich, 1981). How would the production system "know" that a speech error that has not even been produced would be a nonword? Baars argues that the error is generated covertly but suppressed by an editing process that is sensitive to lexical criteria. In an analogous way, Baars and Motley have argued that editing operations exist for a variety of criteria, including phonological, syntactic, semantic, and situational criteria (Motley, Baars, & Camden, 1983).

These results suggest that during speech we sometimes develop more than a single speech plan and that when this occurs the two plans may compete for production. If this kind of internal competition takes place, then the relatively low frequency of certain types of errors may be understood as evidence of an editing process that operates after the assembly of a sentence but before its articulation.

Another look at Freud's view   The notion of competing plans, you will recall, is a central feature of Freud's view of slips of the tongue. Although contemporary emphasis on linguistic units has superceded Freud's theory, studies of laboratory-induced errors suggests some new ways of testing his hypothesis of intrapsychic conflict. Using the phonological bias technique, Motley (1980) found that spoonerisms that were sexually related, such as *bine foddy* into *fine body,* were more common when a subject's "cognitive set" was predominantly sexual. In one study, more sexual errors occurred when the administrator of the test was a provocatively attired female rather than a male (the subjects were male). In a related study, subjects who scored high on a test of sexual anxiety produced more sexual errors than those who scored low. In both cases, the results were attributed to the cognitive set of the individual at the time of production: ideas that are "on our mind" tend to influence the kinds of speech errors we make.

These studies of editing, particularly those dealing with sexual and social taboos, are not without their problems. A recurrent problem in interpreting Freudian theory is that it is difficult to develop unambiguous predictions. For example, we might expect relatively high levels of sexual errors by those individuals with a high degree of sexual anxiety, for such ideas are more salient to them. Alternatively, if they were more anxious, we might expect them to have editing criteria that would be more stringent than that of other people and so consequently they would produce fewer errors.

Still, the basic idea behind Freud's view is broadly consistent with current psycholinguisic theory. Blends, such as *slickery* and *spaddle,* reveal the presence of multiple plans underlying speech production. Although the nature of Freud's plans differs from those discussed by other researchers, the processes involved may actually be rather similar. It appears that most speech errors can be parsimoniously explained in terms of movement of linguistic units. The question remains whether, in addition to these principles, Freudian principles also play some role.

Parallel Models of Linguistic Planning

An alternative to the serial models advanced by Fromkin and Garrett are parallel models that assume that multiple levels of processing take place simultaneously during the course of language production. This idea has been advanced by several theorists, including Dell (1985, 1986, 1988), MacKay (1982, 1987), and Stemberger (1985). These models are similar in spirit to the TRACE model of speech perception (McClelland & Elman, 1986) and the interactive activation model of visual word recognition (McClelland & Rumelhart, 1981), both of which we discussed in Chapter 4.

Dell (1986) assumes that there are four levels of nodes in permanent memory: semantic, syntactic, morphological, and phonological. There are separate representations of the intended message at each level, much as in the serial models. Unlike the serial models, however, these representations work in parallel. As a node at one level becomes activated, it may activate other nodes at the same level or at other levels.

Consider the following example (from Levelt, 1989). Suppose a person activated the word *reset* at the syntactic level; this simply means that the person intended to place this noun in the syntactic frame being developed. This activation at the syntactic level then triggers activation of the component morphemes, *re* and *set*, at the morphological level. These morphological nodes further spread the activation to the phonological level as well, activating the node for the phoneme /r/.

An important assumption of the model is that there is positive feedback from "later" to "earlier" stages of processing. Once a morphological node is activated, it may spread its activation to a syntactic node. For instance, once *re* is activated at the morphological level, it leads to activation of other words with the *re* prefix, such as *resell*. *Resell* then spreads some of its activation to the morpheme *sell*, and, ultimately, to the phoneme /s/. All of this activation decays exponentially over time, so that eventually activation is reduced to zero.

Dell's model provides an account of the lexical bias effect discussed earlier. The parallel activation model explains this finding in terms of feedback from the phonological to the morphological levels. Note that true words have morphological nodes but that nonwords do not. As a consequence, errors favoring true words may occur by backward spreading but this will not occur for nonwords. This difference, according to Dell, is responsible for the lexical bias effect. Thus, it appears that the spreading activation model can account for effects previously attributed to an editor (Baars et al., 1975) without assuming any special mechanism.

Another example of the model at work concerns the **phonemic similarity effect**—the tendency for intruding phonemes to be phonemically similar in their distinctive feature composition to the target phonemes. If a level of distinctive features is incorporated into the phonological level, Dell's model can explain the phonemic similarity effect fairly easily. Each phoneme that is activated spreads its activation to the corresponding set of distinctive features; in turn, the features then activate a number of phonemes that share one or more of these features. This increases the probability that an intrusion will be phonologically similar to the target.

A final example pertains to speaking rates. The model assumes that parameters of activation dynamics (spreading and decay rates) are constant. Slow speaking rates are generally associated with fewer speech errors because there is more time for activation to spread from the current morpheme to the correct sounds and for the activation of previously activated sounds to decay. Both of these factors increase the likelihood that the correct sound is activated. More interestingly, the model makes specific predictions regarding error patterns at different speaking rates. In particular, the account of the lexical bias effect is based on backward spreading, which takes time. As a consequence, the model predicts that with slower speaking rates there will be a more pronounced tendency for errors to result in existing words and morphemes. In fact, Dell (1985) found that when subjects had to speak quickly, the lexical bias effect disappeared.

Parallel and spreading activation models of speech production provide an interesting alternative to the stage models discussed earlier. Speech production is a very rapid activity, and the parallel structure of these models seem well adapted to explaining various aspects of production. As we shall see in the next section, both serial and parallel processes may have a role to play in language production.

Summary

Speech errors from both spontaneous speech as well as laboratory studies have provided researchers with a body of data about the production of language. Theories of how we proceed from message to linguistic structure come in two types. Serial models assume that we begin with the overall idea of an utterance, followed by syntactic organization, content words, morphemes, and phonology. Slips of the tongue typically involve just one level of planning, with other levels unaffected. There may be a final stage, after the planning of an utterance but before its articulation, that edits the utterance-to-be in a manner not inconsistent with Freud's ideas.

A recent alternative to the stage models are parallel models of production. These models assume that the linguistic message is organized at semantic, syntactic, morphological, and phonological levels. Activation of a node at one level may trigger activation of nodes at other levels, and there may be feedback from morphological and phonological levels back to higher levels of processing. Models organized along these lines have been shown to account for several important research findings.

Implementing Linguistic Plans

Up until now we have considered the first two steps of the production process: the development of a thought to be expressed and the formulation of a linguistic structure for that thought. At this point, we have a linguistic plan for our utterances. In this section, we consider the last two stages of production—articulating and self-monitoring.

Articulating

Once we have organized our thoughts into a linguistic plan, this information must be sent from the brain to the muscles in the speech system so that they can then execute the required movements and produce the desired sounds. Obviously, a thorough explanation of articulatory processes is beyond the scope of the present chapter. However, it is useful to understand certain basic aspects of articulation, in anticipation of our later comparison of the production of signed versus spoken language.

Three systems of muscles   Fluent articulation of speech requires the coordinated use of a large number of muscles. These muscles are distributed over three systems: the **respiratory**, the **laryngeal**, and the **supralaryngeal** or **vocal tract**. The latter two systems are shown in Figure 4-1 in Chapter 4.

The respiratory system regulates the flow of air from the lungs to the vocal tract. The act of producing speech begins by air being pushed out of the lungs. This is accomplished by the action of several muscles near the rib cage that have the combined effect of lifting and enlarging the rib cage (MacNeilage & Ladefoged, 1976).

The laryngeal system consists of the vocal cords or vocal folds, which are two bands of muscular tissue in the larynx that can be set into vibration. This system is responsible for the distinction between voiced and unvoiced sounds. For voiced sounds such as [b], the air expelled from the lungs is turned into acoustic energy by the action of the vocal cords. When a voiced sound is to be produced, the vocal cords are nearly touching one another, and when air passes over them, a suction effect that draws them together occurs. Once they have come together, however, there is no more airflow, and thus no suction effect; this causes them to pull apart and release the tension that has built up beneath them. In contrast, when the sound to be produced is a voiceless sound such as [p], air still passes over the cords, but they are too far apart for the suction effect to occur (MacNeilage & Ladefoged, 1976).

The muscles in and around the laryngeal region produce these changes by manipulating the length, thickness, and tension of the vocal cords. This, in turn, significantly influences the fundamental frequency of the sound that results. In particular, the larynx seems to be involved in the increase in frequency that occurs at the end of yes/no questions such as *Did Tom mow the lawn?* (Lieberman, 1967).

The supralaryngeal system consists of structures that lie above the larynx, including the tongue, lips, teeth, jaw, and velum. These structures play a significant role in the production of speech by manipulating the size and shape of the oral cavity (the mouth and pharynx) and the nasal cavity. Phonetic segments can be distinctly described in terms of the articulatory maneuvers used to produce them. For example, [d] is produced by stopping the airflow temporarily by placing the tongue at the tip of the alveolar ridge.

All of the structures involved in speech production have other functions. The main function of the respiratory system is, of course, breathing. The teeth and tongue are used to chew and swallow food. The larynx operates as a valve, controlling the airflow to and from the lungs, and preventing food from entering the lungs. However, when these structures are used to produce speech, the pattern of coordination is different. A major challenge for speech researchers is to explain how so many different muscles are coordinated so smoothly during the production of speech.

Motor control of speech   Motor control of speech begins with motor commands from the brain. As we assemble a linguistic plan for our utterance, the brain structures responsible for speech production (discussed in Chapter 13) send messages to the muscles in the respiratory, laryngeal, and supralaryngeal systems. Let us focus on the motor commands to the muscles in the vocal tract.

It is generally believed that these motor commands to speech muscles take the form of commands for the articulators (tongue, lips, and so on) to move to a particular location. If the next phonetic segment is [b], the muscles controlling the lips must be brought into action, whereas if it is [g], the muscles controlling the velum are needed. One way to think of the motor commands, then, is that they specify a series of target locations in the vocal tract.

It is a simplification, however, to view articulation as the production of a series of discrete sounds. Recall the concept of coarticulation, which we discussed in Chapter 4. The phenomenon refers to the condition that the shape of the vocal tract for any given sound often accommodates to the shape needed for surrounding sounds. This typically occurs for upcoming sounds (**anticipatory coarticulation**) but may also occur when a sound is influenced by previous sounds (**perseveratory coarticulation**). An example of anticipatory coarticulation is the rounding of the lips in the production of the [b] in *boo* (which anticipates the rounding needed for the vowel [u]) as opposed to their formation in, for instance, *bed*.

The result of coarticulation is the **undershooting** of targets. When an articulator, in anticipation of an upcoming sound, aims for a given location, it does not actually achieve it. The main reason appears to be the distance the articulators must travel to reach a series of rapidly changing targets. When sounds are produced individually, the targets are reached; but when they are articulated in a phonetic context, particularly one that involves antagonistic movements, articulatory undershooting occurs (see Sussman & Westbury, 1981).

These observations suggest that it is not possible to describe the articulatory process fully in terms of the places in which segments are produced since the shape of the vocal tract is constantly changing. This dynamic property of speech production is but one reason why adequate theories of speech articulation have been slow to emerge (for a review, see Levelt, 1989).

Planning and production cycles   What is the relationship between these articulatory processes and the planning processes discussed in the previous section? Several studies have converged on the conclusion that we alternate between planning speech and implementing our plans. Consider first a study performed by Henderson, Goldman-Eisler, and Skarbek (1966). They studied the hesitations and fluent speech of individuals being interviewed. Their results are shown in Figure 8-1. The horizontal axis represents speaking time whereas the vertical axis represents pausing time. Note that there appears to be an alternation of steep parts (primarily pausing) and flat parts (mainly speech). Henderson and colleagues found that all of the subjects showed this cycle of hesitation and fluency, although the ratio of speech to silence varied among speakers. These results are consistent with the notion that we plan our utterance in cycles: we express a portion of our intended message, pause to plan the next portion, articulate that portion, pause again, and so on (see also Beattie, 1983).

One underlying reason why we tend to hesitate during speech production is that linguistic planning is very cognitively demanding and it is difficult to plan an entire utterance at once (Lindsley, 1975). As a consequence, we typically plan only a portion of an utterance at a time. A substantial amount of research has examined some of the linguistic variables that are related to hesitation pauses within sentences. The driving force behind much of the work has been Lounsbury's (1965) contention that we pause at periods of high uncertainty. This hypothesis has been

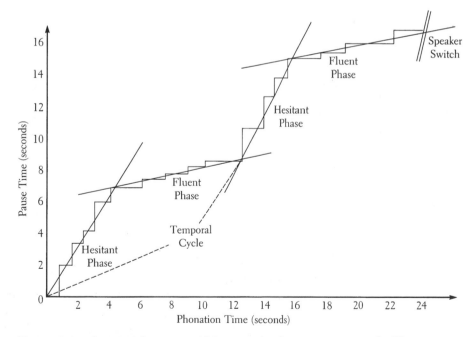

Figure 8-1.   Sequential patterns within a sample of spontaneous speech. (From G. Beattie, *Talk: An Analysis of Speech and Non-Verbal Behaviour in Conversation*. Milton Keynes: England Open University Press, 1983.)

generally supported by studies that have found that variables that influence lexical retrieval also influence hesitation pauses. For instance, Levelt (1983) found that pauses occurred· more often before low-frequency words than before high-frequency words.

We have been talking of planning and production cycles as being in strict alternation, but there are occasions of overlap as well. Although formulating linguistic plans can be demanding, implementing plans once we have formulated them is not intrinsically demanding; in fact, we ordinarily have little conscious awareness of the movements of our articulators. This observation suggests that we might be able to implement some plans while we are in the process of formulating others. This notion, which Kempen and Hoenkamp (1987) call **incremental processing,** can be described in the following way. Suppose we characterize a complete sentence as a series of units. Given this, it is surely the case that we plan unit *x* before we articulate unit *x*. In this sense our implementation of linguistic plans is serial. But, at the same time that we are articulating unit *x*, we are planning unit *x* + 1; in this sense, processing is parallel.

A brief digression: we might reasonably ask at this point what "units" are— are they clauses, phrases, words, syllables, phonemes? The answer is probably all of the above (Foss & Hakes, 1978). At various times in the course of production we treat all of these as processing units. The unit of production depends, in part, on the amount of resources needed for a given portion of the message. An infrequent or difficult word might command a good share of our resources, whereas an entire routinized phrase such as a cliché could be activated as a complete unit. It is therefore not possible to identify any one unit of language as "the" unit of production.

Returning to incremental processing, it is difficult to see how we could be fluent in our speech without at least some parallel processing. Consider what our speech output would be like if we had a strictly serial processing system. First, we would have to generate a complete message to be expressed. Next, we would have to formulate a linguistic structure for that message. Only then could we begin to articulate the sentence. After completing one utterance, we would then have to begin to prepare for the next message. Danks (1977) referred to this strictly serial arrangement as having stages in lock-step succession. If this is how we spoke, there would be long periods of silence, followed by fluent speech. The observations that our pauses are more brief and are internal to the sentence make a parallel model such as incremental processing attractive.

The Kempen and Hoenkamp (1987) model is also an example of a lexically driven approach to sentence production. In this respect it contrasts with a model such as Fromkin's that assumes that the syntactic structure is laid out in advance and then content words are fitted into the structure. According to the lexical approach, the production process may begin with words that are conceptually accessible, which then trigger the syntactic structure, not the other way around. For example, words that are more easily retrieved may be placed early on in a sentence or constituent (Bock, 1982). This lexical approach is consistent with the lexical-functional grammar of Bresnan that we discussed in Chapter 2. Moreover, in emphasizing that the lexical level may influence the syntactic level and not simply vice versa, it is similar in spirit to the spreading activation view of production (Dell, 1986).

Self-Monitoring

Earlier in the chapter, we discussed the notion that we covertly edit our utterances prior to articulation. This notion remains a controversial one. There is no debate, however, over whether we overtly edit what we say. From time to time, we spontaneously interrupt our speech and correct ourselves. These corrections are referred to as **self-repairs.** According to Levelt (1983), self-repairs have a characteristic structure that consists of three parts. First, we interrupt ourselves after we have detected an error in our speech. Second, we usually utter one of various editing expressions. These include terms such as *uh, sorry, I mean,* and so on. Finally, we repair the utterance. Let us consider each in turn.

Self-interruptions   Nooteboom (1980) examined a corpus of 648 speech errors and made several interesting discoveries. He found that 415 of the errors (64%) were corrected. Some errors were more likely to be corrected than others; anticipations were corrected more often than perseverations. In addition, Nooteboom found that most interruptions occurred very shortly after the error. Nooteboom suggested that the timing of self-interruption after detection of an error is based on two competing forces. On one hand, we have an urge to correct the error immediately. On the other hand, we want to complete the word we are speaking. As a consequence, interruptions are predominantly made at the first word boundary after the error.

Levelt (1983) used a somewhat different procedure. Students were shown color patterns such as those shown in Figure 8-2. They were then asked to describe the patterns beginning at the node indicated by an arrow in such a way that another person hearing a tape-recorded version of the description would be able to draw it. The main advantage of this approach, relative to the study of spontaneous errors in conversation, is the greater degree of experimental control. The distribution of interruptions over time is shown in Figure 8-3. Levelt found that 18% of the corrections were within a word, as in sentence (14). Another 51% occurred immediately after the error, as in (15). The remaining 31% of errors were delayed by one or more words; in (16), the correction comes three words later.

(14)   We can go straight on to the ye–, to the orange node.
(15)   Straight on to green—to red.
(16)   And from green left to pink—er from blue left to pink.

Thus, although the speech task studied by Levelt differed substantially from the spontaneous speech errors examined by Nooteboom, the results of the two studies are quite similar.

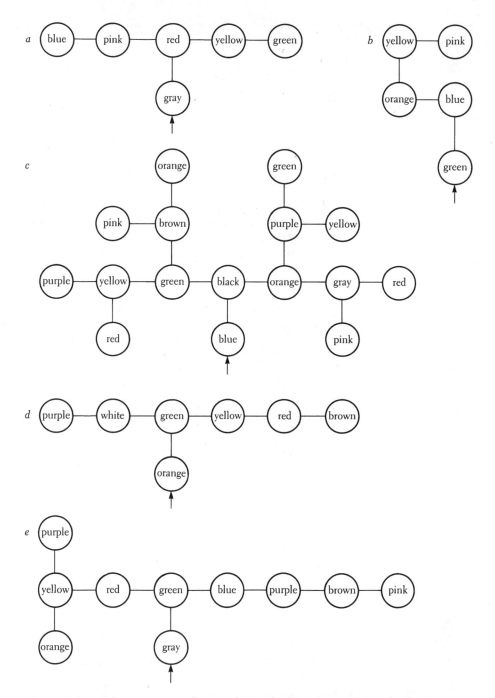

Figure 8-2.   Color patterns used in Levelt's study. (From W. J. M. Levelt, *Speaking: From intention to articulation.* Cambridge, MA: MIT Press, 1989.)

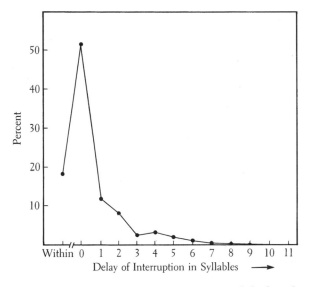

Figure 8-3.   Distribution of interruptions while describing a pattern. [From W. J. M. Levelt, "Monitoring and Self-Repair in Speech," *Cognition* 14 (1983):41–104.]

Editing expressions   Although the matter could use further study, it appears that the editing expression conveys to the listener the kind of trouble that the speaker is correcting. James (1972) analyzed utterances containing expressions such as *uh* and *oh*, and suggests that these convey different meanings. For instance, in sentence (17), the *uh* suggests that the speaker paused to try to remember the exact number of people. In contrast, sentence (18) would be used when the speaker did not know the precise number but was trying to choose a number that was approximately correct.

(17)   I saw . . . uh . . . 12 people at the party.
(18)   I saw . . . oh . . . 12 people at the party.

DuBois (1974) has also analyzed several different editing expressions. The phrase *that is* is typically used to further specify a potentially ambiguous referent, as in sentence (19). *Rather* is used for what DuBois calls nuance editing, as in (20), in which a word is substituted that is similar in meaning to the original, but slightly closer to the speaker's meaning. *I mean* is reserved for true errors, as in (21).

(19)   Bill hit him—hit Sam, that is.
(20)   I am trying to lease, or rather, sublease, my apartment.
(21)   I really like to—I mean, hate to—get up in the morning.

Notice that the use of *that is* in place of *I mean* in (21) would be odd or inappropriate. This suggests that these different editing expressions are not fully interchangeable and that the expression that is used conveys the type of editing that the speaker is doing.

The expression *uh* may differ in some respects from these other expressions. It is the most common expression, and turns up in many different languages. Levelt (1989) argued that it is a symptom of trouble rather than a signal with specific communicative meaning. Speakers may simply utter *uh* when they get stuck in the middle of their utterances. If it does not convey a specific meaning, why say it at all? Perhaps *uh*, along with various nonverbal cues such as averting one's gaze, indicates to the listener that the speaker still has the floor.

Self-repairs   After the interruption and the editing expression comes the correction proper. Levelt (1983, 1989) distinguishes among three types of repairs. **Instant repairs** consist of a speaker's retracing back to a single troublesome word, which is then replaced with the correct word, as in sentence (22):

(22)   Again left to the same blank crossing point—white crossing point.

In **anticipatory retracings,** the speaker retraces back to some point prior to the error, as in (23):

(23)   And left to the purple crossing point—to the red crossing point.

Finally, in **fresh starts,** the speaker drops the original syntactic structure and just starts over, as in (24):

(24)   From yellow down to brown—no—that's red.

Levelt (1989) argues that repairs are systematically different when there is an out-and-out error as opposed to an utterance that is merely inappropriate. Repairs based on social or contextual inappropriateness are those in which the speaker says what was intended but perhaps not in the way intended. Error repairs consisted primarily of instant repairs (51%) and anticipatory retracings (41%), with very few fresh starts (8%). For the most part, error repairs are conservative: the speaker leaves most of the original utterance unaffected but alters the erroneous element. In such a case, the error and revised utterance have a parallel structure with but one difference. In contrast, fresh starts are more likely when the original utterance is contextually inappropriate (44%). When what we have said is technically correct but awkward, we tend to rephrase.

In general, speakers repair their utterances in a way that maximizes listeners' comprehension. The listener's problem when a speaker errs is not only how to understand the correction, but also how to fit the correction into the ongoing discourse. Several aspects of speaker self-repairs recommend themselves as helpful in this regard: speakers interrupt themselves quickly, their editing expressions indicate the type of error, and then the repair itself is systematic. All of these characteristics would appear to make the listener's work easier.

Summary

The production of speech is a complex process that requires the coordination of the respiratory, laryngeal, and supralaryngeal systems. Motor commands from the brain specify the target locations for the articulators in the vocal tract. However, the phenomenon of coarticulation indicates that the process of specifying targets is not context-free but, rather, is based on the preceding and following phonetic context.

Speaker monologues reveal an alternation between fluent speech and hesitation pauses. These pauses are related to various linguistic variables and appear to reflect linguistic planning within the sentence. This planning may take place in parallel with the implementation of previous linguistic plans.

Speakers routinely monitor their utterances to ensure that they are saying what they wanted to and in the way they wanted to. When errors are detected, speakers interrupt their speech nearly immediately and begin editing their utterance. Both the use of editing expressions and the linguistic structure of the repair itself appear to facilitate listener comprehension.

Insights from Sign Language

In the final section of this chapter we look at the production of sign language. The production of signs is important theoretically because it gives us an opportunity to disentangle the cognitive processes involved in translating thought into language from the physical characteristics of our speech apparatus. Speech shares the vocal channel with respiration; in contrast, sign production can occur entirely in parallel with, and unimpeded by, respiratory activity. Thus, consideration of sign production in comparison to speech production can yield insights into some of the biological limits on linguistic form (Bellugi & Studdert-Kennedy, 1980).

We will examine both similarities and differences between the two modes. One striking similarity is that errors occur in signing that strongly resemble those found with speech.

Slips of the Hand

Newkirk, Klima, Pedersen, and Bellugi (1980) have found some fascinating evidence that slips of the hand similar to slips of the tongue take place with deaf signers. They used a corpus of 131 errors, 77 of which came from videotaped signings and 54 of which were reported observations from informants or researchers. Ninety-eight of the errors were judged by the person who made them as errors, either by spontaneous self-correction or by subsequent viewing of the videotapes.

Independence of parameters   As we saw earlier in the chapter, slips of the tongue have provided evidence for linguistically defined units such as phonemes and distinctive features. Moreover, speech errors suggest that these are independent planning units because errors ordinarily occur at only one level of planning at a time. Newkirk and colleagues analyzed the errors in terms of the parameters of American Sign Language (ASL)—hand configuration, place of articulation, and movement—in order to assess whether sign parameters also appear to be independent units of production.

The researchers found errors analogous to exchanges, anticipations, and perseverations. One example of an exchange concerned an individual who apparently intended to sign *sick, bored* (similar to the English *I'm sick and tired of it*). This intended production can be described in the following way:

Sick
Hand configuration: hand toward signer
Place of articulation: at forehead
Movement: with twist of wrist

Bored
Hand configuration: straight index finger with hand toward signer
Place of articulation: at nose
Movement: with twist of wrist

What the signer actually produced was the sign for *sick* with the hand configuration for *bored* and vice versa. The other two parameters were not influenced (see Figure 8-4). Overall, Newkirk and colleagues found 65 instances of exchanges involving hand configuration, of which 49 were "pure" cases (that is, ones in which no other parameter was in error). In addition, 9 of 24 errors related to place and movement parameter were single-parameter errors. These cases provide evidence that ASL signs are not holistic gestures without internal structure; rather, they are subdivided into parameters that are somewhat independent of each other during sign language production.

As we saw in Chapter 2, positions such as "hand toward signer" can be further analyzed into distinctive features. The question then is whether these features are also independent units in sign production. Newkirk and colleagues found some evidence that they are. One example was a signer who intended to convey *must see* (roughly, *I must see about it*). The correct sign for *must* consists, in part, of a hand configuration in which the index finger is bent (Figure 8-5, top). The sign for *see* includes a hand configuration in which the index and middle finger make a V, as in a victory (or peace) sign. In the error, *must* was made in the V hand configuration but with both fingers bent (Figure 8-5, bottom). It appears that the (+ bent) feature of one hand configuration was anticipated in the production of the earlier sign.

Morpheme structure constraints   One final aspect of signing errors concerns whether they obey constraints of morpheme structure that are part of the grammar of ASL. With speech, we have found that errors follow phonological rules. For instance, if a person mispronounced *slip of the tongue*, she would be highly un-

Sick

Bored

Error

Error

Figure 8-4.   Errors of hand configurations. [From D. Newkirk, E. S. Klima, C. C. Pedersen, and U. Bellugi, "Linguistic Evidence from Slips of the Hand," in V. A. Fromkin (ed.), *Errors in Linguistic Performance.* New York: Academic Press, 1980, pp. 165–197.]

likely to utter *tlip of the sung* because *tl* is not phonologically permissible in English at the beginning of a word (Fromkin, 1973).

Similarly, with slips of the hand, most errors result in nonexistent but possible ASL signs (Newkirk et al., 1980). One constraint concerns the possible contacting regions for particular hand configurations. A contacting region is "the part of the hand that serves as a focus for contact or pointing during the movement of a sign" (Klima & Bellugi, 1979, p. 45). In one example, the signer intended *deaf woman*, but signed *deaf* with the hand configuration of *woman* (Figure 8-6). The correct sign for *deaf* includes a hand configuration in which the index finger is extended; the contacting region is the tip of the extended finger. In the error, the

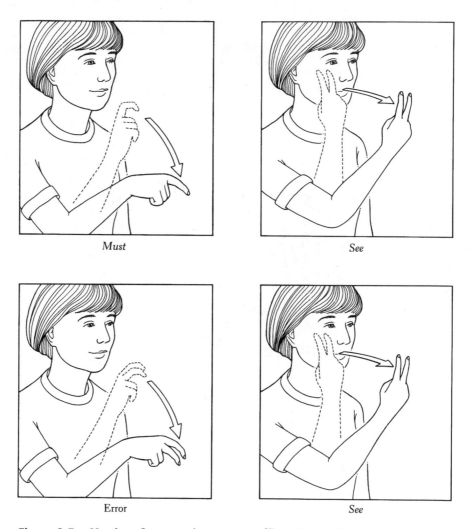

Figure 8-5. Hand configuration feature errors. [From D. Newkirk, E. S. Klima, C. C. Pedersen, and U. Bellugi, "Linguistic Evidence from Slips of the Hand," in V. A. Fromkin (Ed.), *Errors in Linguistic Performance.* New York: Academic Press, 1980, pp. 165–197.]

hand configuration of *woman,* an open palm, is substituted for the index finger. However, the open palm handshape does not permit an index finger contact, so the contacting region was shifted to the tip of the thumb, which is an acceptable contacting region for this hand configuration. In other words, the contacting region of the sign is accommodated to the hand configuration that is (erroneously) used.

In general, slips of the hand strongly suggest that similar principles of organization underlie signed and spoken language, pointing to the possibility that both types of language take the form that they do because of basic cognitive limits on

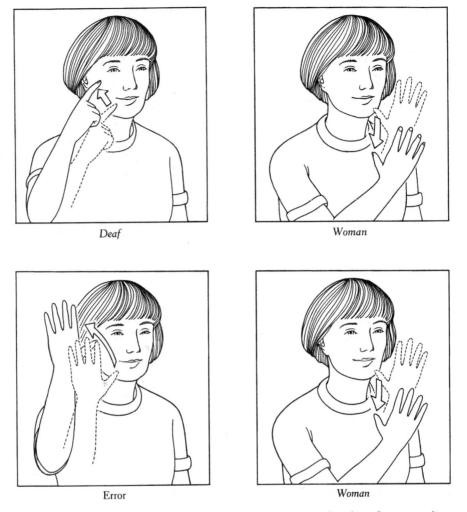

Figure 8-6 (cont.):

Deaf   *Woman*

Error   *Woman*

Figure 8-6. Contacting region substitution accompanying a hand configuration slip. (From E. S. Klima and U. Bellugi, *The Signs of Language*. Cambridge, MA: Harvard University Press, 1979.)

how (or how much) linguistic information may be structured or used. In contrast, some recent studies of the rate at which signs and speech are produced point to some equally interesting discrepancies between the two modes.

Production Rates

As we discussed earlier, spontaneous speech alternates between fluent phases and hesitation phases. These hesitations tend to reflect linguistic planning but also might be related to other factors. One such factor is the need to breathe. Speakers must interrupt their speech in order to breathe, but signers are under no such obligation. It therefore might be interesting to examine whether this difference might cause differences in the rate of speaking and signing.

Bellugi and Fisher (1972) began this line of research by studying three bilingual individuals who were fluent in both ASL and English. They were young hearing adults who had acquired ASL as a native language from deaf parents and had signed throughout their lives. The researchers had these individuals tell a personal story in three versions: one in ASL, one in spoken English, and one simultaneously signed and spoken. Different individuals did the versions in different orders. The results indicated that more time was spent in pausing in speech than in sign. When pauses were taken out, the rate of speech (words per second) was roughly double that of signing (signs per second). The results were slightly different in simultaneous and successive conditions, but the basic patterns were borne out in both conditions.

When, however, the rate of expressing a proposition was examined, the results changed dramatically. A proposition was defined as a simple underlying sentence. Here it was found that the number of seconds taken to express a proposition was highly similar for the two languages (about 1.5 seconds).

Another study of the rate of expression was performed by Grosjean (1979), who was interested in the way various rates of production were achieved in the two modes. He gave signers and speakers either an English passage or an ASL version with an English gloss. The subjects' task was to read aloud or sign the passage at five different rates, four times each. Understandably, the subjects were given some practice at this somewhat unusual task, but with practice they were able to achieve the desired rates consistently.

The results indicated that at normal rates of production, signers spend more of their production time in articulation than do speakers: they articulate more slowly (Grosjean estimates the word-to-sign ratio as closer to 4.5:1 than 2:1) and use somewhat fewer pauses. Moreover, the pauses that do occur in sign are for much shorter durations than in speech. The average pause in speech was 0.46 second; for sign, it was 0.20 second.

Interestingly, different strategies for changing speed were evident in the two modes. Speakers change the frequency but generally not the length of their (relatively long) pauses; signers modify both. Grosjean attributes this difference to respiratory activity: speakers seem to have a minimal pause duration based on respiratory requirements; they take a sufficiently long pause to inhale and then continue, whereas signers can breathe anytime they want.

These interesting results reinforce a central thread in our discussion in this chapter—that the production of speech operates within a matrix defined by cognitive and physiological resources. Variations in speech rate necessitate strategies based closely on these physiological limitations; variations in signing rates, free from respiratory requirements, are relatively more closely attuned to cognitive processes. In both modes, the processes of production are wedded inextricably with the cognitive and physiological resources required to execute linguistic goals successfully.

Summary

Studies of sign language production are valuable because they enable us to distinguish between those aspects of production that are constrained by broad biological forces and those that are specific to speech. Sign language, since it exists in an entirely different mode from speech, might well have differed substantially from speech in terms of grammatical organization. In contrast, basic similarities have been found in the two modes' organization of basic units into words or signs and in the syntactic rules by which words and signs are combined to form sentences. These similarities are illustrated by slips of the hand, which, like those of speech, typically involve a systematic error in a single linguistic unit. These results provide evidence that the parameters underlying signs are planned independently of one another.

Studies of production rate, in contrast, reveal differences between the two modes. Speakers achieve differences in speech rate primarily by varying the number of pauses, whereas signers vary the duration of signed segments and both the duration and number of pauses. These dissimilarities reflect the effects of respiratory functioning on speech but not on signs.

Review Questions

1. Identify and give examples of the following types of speech errors: shifts, exchanges, anticipations, perseverations, additions, deletions, substitutions, and blends.
2. Use Fromkin's model of production to identify the stage at which the following speech errors were made:
   a. A *singing sewer machine*
   b. *I wouldn't buy kids for the macadamia nuts*
   c. *There's a lot of flee floating anxiety*
   d. *At the end of today's lection*
   e. *He's a laving runiac* [double whammy!]
3. What is accommodation? Do errors of accommodation support serial models of language production?
4. Define the lexical bias effect.
5. How does Dell's model of linguistic planning differ from Fromkin's?
6. Describe respiratory, laryngeal, and supralaryngeal contributions to the articulation of speech.
7. What is incremental processing?
8. Are fresh starts more common with nuance errors or with outright errors? Explain.
9. Identify points of similarity between slips of the hand and slips of the tongue.
10. Distinguish between the way signers and speakers speed up their rate of production.

*T*hought Questions

1. Keep a log of naturally occurring slips of the tongue. Identify the date, the setting, the utterance, and what you believe the intended utterance was. Organize them into the categories listed in Table 8-2. Are there any errors that don't fit a category or that appear to fit more than one?

2. It is commonly believed that alcohol and other drugs increase the frequency of slips of the tongue. Do you think they would increase all types of slips across the board, or would certain types of slips be more likely when a person is intoxicated? Explain.

3. Suppose you have been paralyzed in an auto accident. Your only way to communicate is to manipulate a pencil-like instrument with your mouth to push buttons on an apparatus that produces humanlike sounds. How might this type of communication system influence your production of language? Identify similarities and differences with spoken language.

4. How would the frequency and distribution of speech errors and hesitations vary in the following three situations: (a) reading aloud; (b) talking without notes on a topic specified ahead of time; and (c) describing a picture?

9

Conversational Interaction

- Conversation is a form of oral discourse that is distinguished by the absence of explicit rules.
- In place of a formal structure, conversations are governed by a set of implicit conventions regarding the social use of language. These include rules for taking turns in conversations, for maintaining and changing topics, and for the appropriate use of requests.
- Social roles shape conversational processes. Women and men tend to converse in different ways.
- Conversation also varies with the social setting. The setting influences the topics that may be discussed as well as the interpretation given to conversational acts.
- Studies of language production in schizophrenic speakers reveal that although their utterances are grammatically correct, they are often inappropriate from the standpoint of discourse coherence.

Introduction

Conversations, of course, require at least two parties—two individuals to select meanings, form syntactic outlines, and do the other sorts of planning that we discussed in the preceding chapter. When our attention turns from monologue to dialogue, the complexity of processes involved increases tremendously, for a conversation is not simply two monologues side by side or in alternating order, but rather a special form of social interaction with its own rules and dynamics.

Much of our concern in this chapter is on how conversation is organized. That may seem surprising, for conversation can be, among friends, a nearly effortless flow of topics, thoughts, and events that is attractive precisely because it doesn't appear to have any rules. This is an illusion, however, though the rules of conversation are certainly more relaxed than those of, say, a debate. Moreover, the rules, unlike those of other aspects of language, show powerful influences of social and cultural context: the rules of proper conversation vary with the culture. But it is not correct to say that conversation operates without rules; rather, we have internalized them to the point that we need not think of them in order to have a conversation. In this chapter, we will try to identify some of this tacit knowledge explicitly.

Conversation, then, is deeply rooted in a set of shared assumptions about how human linguistic interaction is to take place. What happens when an individual does not acquire this background? In the final section of the chapter, we will take a glimpse at the language of individuals who are cut off from the rest of the social world. The language of schizophrenics has been found to be essentially normal in several respects but fundamentally different in the areas of social patterning and social interaction. A fascinating topic, schizophrenic language provides illuminating insight into language when the links between linguistic structure and social structure are severed.

Conversational Discourse

Some Forms of Discourse

Conversation is but one form of oral discourse. People also engage in debates, interviews, ceremonies, meetings, and so on. It is undoubtedly overly optimistic to hope that a single set of principles can explain language behavior in such diverse settings. Still, we may uncover some common properties in these settings along with each also having its own distinguishing features (see Table 9-1).

Debates, for example, typically have topics specified in advance and rules specifying who can speak at a given time and for how long are also usually agreed upon ahead of time. The turns of each speaker are identified clearly. Speakers typically speak for an extended period of time.

Ceremonies, such as an awards dinner, are also formalized. The topic is specified in advance but not the length of time any given speaker may take. Turns are identified rather clearly, with formal introductions given for each speaker. Again, the length of a given speaker's monologue can be rather long.

Meetings are typically less formal than either ceremonies or debates. While it is not uncommon for specific rules, such as Robert's rules of order, to be used to organize discussions, the discussions themselves vary, as a general rule, more than those of more formal types of discourse. Also, the number of participants is much larger than for debates, and the contributions of different members vary a great deal. It is not uncommon for one member of a committee to dominate the proceedings.

Finally, conversations are the least formal of these four types of oral discourse. The number of participants, the topic, the length of a given's speaker's contribution, and many other factors are left undecided or decided on the spot. The relaxation of formal rules is, of course, one of the prime enjoyments of a good, rich conversation. Yet, in the absence of formal rules we have implicit communicative conventions that help organize everyday conversations.

Table 9-1. Comparison of Four Forms of Discourse

	Form			
Attribute	Debate	Ceremony	Meeting	Conversation
Number of people	Usually two or more	Varies	Varies	Varies
Topic	Fixed	Fixed	Partially fixed	Varies
Turn order	Fixed	Fixed	Varies	Varies
Turn length	Fixed	Varies	Varies	Varies

The Structure of Conversation

Conversations have been studied for some time by researchers interested in language behavior, language acquisition, and social interaction, and some of its main features have been identified (see, for example, Jaffe & Feldstein, 1970; Sacks, Schegloff, & Jefferson, 1974). In the vast number of cases, only one person speaks at a time. This does not mean that there are no times when two (or more) speakers are talking, but these times tend to be brief in most conversations. More precisely, it is simultaneous turns rather than simultaneous talking that is uncommon, for listeners often say things like *um hmm* and nod their heads while listening to a speaker; these are not attempts to speak but merely identify that the listener is following the speaker's train of thought. True points of overlap are most common at turn exchanges, when one speaker's turn is ending and another's is beginning.

Since neither turn order nor turn length is decided ahead of time, it is not surprising that there is considerable individual variation in the number of turns a given speaker will take and the length of each turn. Jaffe and Feldstein (1970) report that the length of a particular speaker's turn was a stable individual characteristic. In contrast, the pauses between vocalizations during a speaker's turn tended to match the pauses of other participants in the conversation. The net effect is to produce a conversation with a certain "rhythm."

In addition to these studies of conversational behavior, there is growing interest in the social conventions involved in conversational discourse and how these conventions give shape and structure to our daily interactions with others (see Gamst, 1982). Let us consider several of these conversational "rules."

Opening conversations   While there are theoretically an infinite number of possibilities for opening conversations, in practice we do so in a limited number of ways (Schegloff, 1972). Most commonly, we address another person (*Hey, Carl*), request information (*Do you know what time it is?*), offer information (*Are you looking for someone?*), or use some form of stereotyped expression (*Hello*) or topic (*Strange weather lately, eh?*). These serve to get the listener's attention and often lead to stock replies. This quickly establishes the alternation of turns that is central to conversation: A asks a question, B replies, followed by a sequence of the form ABABAB.

Since these openers are so predictable, we can often anticipate a conversational response. Schegloff (1972) gives a humorous example from Jewish folklore:

> On the express train to Lublin, a young man stopped at the seat of an obviously prosperous merchant.
> "Can you tell me the time?" he said.
> The merchant looked at him and replied: "Go to hell!"
> "What? Why, what's the matter with you! I ask you a civil question in a properly civil way, and you give me such an outrageous rude answer! What's the idea?"
> The merchant looked at him, sighed wearily, and said, "Very well. Sit down and I'll tell you. You ask me a question. I have to give you an answer, no? You start a conversation with me—about the weather, politics, business. One thing leads to another. It turns out you're a Jew—I'm a Jew, I live in Lublin—you're a stranger.

> Out of hospitality, I ask you to my home for dinner. You meet my daughter. She's a beautiful girl—you're a handsome young man. So you go out together a few times—and you fall in love. Finally you come to ask for my daughter's hand in marriage. So why go to all that trouble. Let me tell you right now, young man, I won't let my daughter marry anyone who doesn't even own a watch!" (Ausubel, 1948, cited in Schegloff, 1972, p. 377)

The humor, of course, is based on our knowledge of conversational processes. The merchant first responds impolitely to a standard opening line, then exaggerates the sense of predictability inherent in conversation by reeling off an entire conversation.

Taking turns in conversations Conversations become more complicated when more than two people are present. Nevertheless, the single most outstanding fact about conversations is that they run so smoothly in the absence of formal rules. How do speakers avoid "bumping into" one another in the course of conversations?

According to Sacks, Schegloff, and Jefferson (1974), turn-taking during conversations operates by three implicit rules. The first rule states that the current speaker is allowed to select the next speaker. This is often done by directing a question to another person. The second rule is that of self-selection: if the first rule is not used, another person may speak up. The third rule states that the current speaker can continue, although she is not obligated to do so. These rules are ordered; the first one takes priority over the second, which takes priority over the third. If speaker A addresses a comment specifically to B while C starts to talk, B has the floor.

This simple set of rules accomplishes a good deal of the organization of conversations. For example, it ensures that most of the conversation takes place with a single speaker, for each of the three rules allocates the next turn to a specific individual. The gaps between speakers will tend to be small since the second rule provides an incentive for starting quickly. Thus, while neither turns nor turn lengths are decided ahead of time, these rules produce an orderly shift from speaker to speaker.

Nonverbal behavior between conversational partners also facilitates an orderly transition from one speaker to another. Duncan (1972) has analyzed the signals given to regulate turns in a conversation. He defines a **turn-yielding** signal as the display of one or more of six behavioral cues that appear to indicate a willingness to conclude one's turn. These six cues are: (1) a drop of pitch; (2) a drawl on the final syllable or final stressed syllable of a final clause; (3) the termination of hand gestures; (4) the use of stereotyped expressions such as *you know, or something*, and *but uh*; (5) a drop in loudness; and (6) completion of a grammatical clause. Duncan found a direct relationship between the number of cues indicating turn-yielding and the probability that a listener would attempt to take a turn: when no such cues were presented, a listener attempted to speak 10% of the time; with three cues, the figure was 33%; and with all six cues, it was 50%.

There are times, of course, when we wish to continue speaking but fail to find the right word or expression. The "trailing off" of our speech is ambiguous to a listener and may appear to indicate that we are finished. Duncan found that in such cases speakers resort to what he calls an **attempt-suppressing signal,** which is the continued use of hand gestures in conjunction with one or more of the turn-yielding cues. When yield cues and attempt-suppressing signals are simultaneously displayed, a listener almost never attempted to take a turn. Cook (1977) found that speakers who were silent but looked away from listeners were seldom interrupted. When speakers look at listeners and stop talking, it is generally a sign for a listener to start. When a speaker looks away, it is often taken as a signal that he is not through with his turn.

The ability to regulate conversational encounters thus requires sensitivity to a wide range of nonverbal behaviors, including but not limited to the following: eye contact, facial expression, body movements (kinesics), hand gestures, paralanguage (nonsemantic aspects of language, such as loudness), and body position or distance relative to others (proxemics). These nonverbal signals are described in a number of sources, including Robinson (1972).

Discourse coherence   It is not enough, however, merely to take turns with others in conversation. As Grice (1975) has noted, there is a strong social convention to "be relevant." In conversations, this means to stick to the topic and to tie one's comments to those of the preceding speaker.

We discussed the notion of discourse coherence in Chapter 7. In particular, recall the discussion of Halliday and Hasan's (1976) categories of cohesion, in which successive sentences in discourse are related by cohesive devices such as reference, ellipsis, conjunction, and lexical ties. In Chapter 7, our interest was with individual discourse, whereas here it is with conversational discourse. With conversation, the notion of coherence becomes a more complex process. How does one person stick to another's topic? Are there, in fact, rules that determine what is an acceptable response to another's statement in a conversation?

Schank (1977) argues that there are, indeed, rules of this kind, although it is probably more accurate to say that they govern rather than severely restrict our responses. This is reflected in the observation that while some responses are clearly odd, there is a wide range of "acceptable" responses to any statement. Which of the following strike you as a reasonable response to *I just bought a new hat?*

    (1)   Fred eats hamburgers.
    (2)   I just bought a new car.
    (3)   There is supposed to be a recession.
    (4)   My hat is in good shape.
    (5)   What color?

Many would describe (1) as an absurd response and (2) as at least odd. Sentence (3) is more relevant but not too polite, while (4) is marginally relevant and (5) seems to be a reasonable response. Clearly, there are many responses similar to (5) that are equally reasonable. For example, the listener might ask, *Oh, where did you get it?* or *How much did you pay?* and so on. Our question then becomes: Is it possible to identify this entire class of "reasonable" responses?

What the responses seem to have in common is that they are faithful to the topic identified by the speaker, but this is not helpful unless we are able to specify the term topic more precisely. Schank (1977) argues that topics in conversation can be defined in terms of the intersection of propositions across sentences. Thus, if speaker A says, *John bought a red car in Baltimore yesterday,* there are numerous propositions being advanced: John bought a car, the car was red, John bought it in Baltimore, John bought it yesterday. If speaker B responds to one of these propositions (for example, *I think a red car would be ugly*), the intersection of these two sentences is the proposition *the car is red.* An implication of this definition of topic is that only conversations, not individual sentences or even speaker turns, have topics.

Suppose, instead, B's response to this sentence is, *You mean he's not going to buy my car?* This response deals with only one proposition of the preceding sentence (John bought a car) and adds a new topic, the selling of B's car. According to Schank, A now has three basic options at this point. A may respond to the new topic directly: *No, he didn't like your car.* Alternatively, A may refer back to that part of the original topic that got a response: *Well, John needed a car in a hurry.* Finally, A can make a more generalized response: *It's always difficult to sell a car.* While all three types of responses preserve the coherence of the discourse, they do so in different ways. The first response effectively enables B to switch the topic of conversation to B's car, while the second response preserves the initial topic but, importantly, does so in a way that is relevant to B's remark. More specifically, it continues the discussion of the topic *John bought a car* but focuses on a reason for John's buying the car that is relevant to B's comment. The third response is somewhat ambiguous from a discourse point of view and permits the conversation to go in several directions. Noncommittal statements that are broadly related to the topic but do not direct further discussion are common when there are "lulls" in a conversation.

Even if a new topic is formed, there seem to be additional rules that govern what kinds of topic shifts can be made. For example, consider the following sequences:

(6) *A:* I just bought a Maserati.
   B: I know someone who had a Maserati.
(7) *A:* I just bought a box of cookies.
   B: I know someone who had a box of cookies.

Sequence (6) is sensible, whereas sequence (7) is absurd, suggesting that the attributes that may be used to form a new topic vary with the object. Schank (1977) has identified some of the attributes of various objects in terms of what is most distinctive of each, and he believes that rules of this sort also play a role in governing our conversations. The task of identifying these attributes may prove to be difficult, however, for many attributes, such as the availability of the object, may vary with the culture.

Since any statement provides multiple opportunities for topic shifts, it can sometimes seem that the flow of conversation is hardly governed by rules at all. This seems especially true of long conversations that cover a number of topics; we often find ourselves wondering, "How did we get from there to here?" Usually, with some effort, the paths can be reconstructed. A close examination of the transcript of a conversation, for example, would reveal the kinds of connections between the topics that we have been discussing.

We still have a great deal to learn about what most people regard as appropriate topics and topic shifts in conversations. As further evidence that there is more than meets the eye in this matter, consider the observation of Jefferson (1972) of a group of children playing a game called Marco Polo. In this game, whoever is "it" closes his eyes and counts to ten while the others hide. Then the person who is it attempts to find the others by saying *Marco* while the others are obliged to say *Polo.* Jefferson observed the following:

Steven:	One, two, three . . . four, five, six . . . eleven, eight, nine, ten.
Susan:	"El*even*"?, eight, nine, ten?
Steven:	Eleven, eight, nine, ten.
Nancy:	"El*even*"?
Steven:	Seven, eight, nine, ten.
Susan:	That's better.

Here two of the children have stepped outside the game temporarily to make a comment about Steven's speech. When he corrects himself, they return to the game. None of the children regarded Susan's response as either irrelevant or a true switch of topics. It would be more accurate to regard it as an intact sequence embedded in the rest of the conversation. Thus, even children's conversations appear to operate on more than a single level at a given time.

Similarly, Polanyi (1989) has analyzed conversational storytelling and has found that it differs in interesting ways from conversational discourse in general. When one person in a conversation tells a story, the ordinary rules of turn-taking seem to be temporarily suspended. If a speaker is in the middle of a story and pauses, it is considered inappropriate for one of the listeners to seize the floor. At the same time, stories must have a point that is relevant to what preceded them. Polanyi discusses several conversational stories in some detail and analyzes how the stories may influence conversational processes in a number of subtle ways.

Requests   A particularly interesting area of discourse analysis deals with the rules under which **requests** (and the responses to them) are seen as appropriate or inappropriate. From the standpoint of social interaction, requests are an especially significant aspect of language, for much of what we do in conversation revolves around our desire to get someone else to do something. While there are certainly contexts in which direct commands are appropriate (the military comes to mind readily here), most of the time we are prone to phrase our requests of others in a more polite, indirect form.

Several attempts have been made to identify the rules for forms of request (Gordon & Lakoff, 1975; Labov, 1970; Labov & Fanshel, 1977; Searle, 1975), and a common theme is that there are certain preconditions that are present in valid requests for action that distinguish them from comments such as *drop dead* or *give the president my regards.* Labov and Fanshel (1977) identify six such preconditions (see Table 9-2).

The left side of the table shows a series of preconditions for a request being regarded as sincere or valid. On the right side are examples of indirect requests that correspond with each of the preconditions. If these preconditions are met, all of the examples are typically heard as indirect requests for action. It would, for example, be pragmatically inappropriate to respond to *Isn't it your turn to dust?* with a simple *Yes.* Moreover, it is not hard to see that many of these indirect requests are also ways of criticizing a person's performance in a particular role.

Other statements are also usually heard as requests. For example, if a person asks a question about the status of an action (*Have you dusted yet?*), its consequences (*This room would look a lot better if it was dusted*), or its time of occurrence (*I guess you'll dust this evening?*), it is usually taken as an indirect request (Labov & Fanshel, 1977).

Requests, like other speech acts, may be embedded in ongoing discourse. If you ask someone, *Are you going to the movies tonight?* and the response is a question such as *What's playing?*, it is usually taken as an indication that the person needs more information before answering the original request. Answering a question with another question is usually pragmatically inappropriate, but when an answer to the original question is given following an embedded question and its answer, it is usually taken as sincere. On the other hand, when an embedded question asks for information that the questioner knows the other person is clearly

Table 9-2. Preconditions for Use of Requests

Precondition	Example
Ability: A believes that B has the ability to carry out the action	*Can you grab a dust rag and just dust around?*
Need for the action: A believes the action should be done	*Don't you think the dust is pretty thick?*
Need for the request: B would not carry out the action unless requested	*Are you planning to dust this room?*
Obligation: B has the obligation to carry out the action	*Isn't it your turn to dust?*
Willingness: B is willing to carry out the action	*Would you mind picking up a dust rag?*
Right: A has the right to tell B to carry out the action	*I'm supposed to look after this place but not do all of the work.*

Source: W. Labov and D. Fanshel, *Therapeutic Discourse: Psychotherapy as Conversation* (New York: Academic Press, 1977).

aware of, then the embedded request becomes a way of putting off the first request.

The proper use of requests, then, is not simply a linguistically significant act but also a socially significant act. Requests reflect shared assumptions about the social nature of conversation and reveal a great deal about how we manage the delicate task of controlling others' behavior in civilized ways. In the following section, we will pursue how social discourse is organized not only to meet linguistic and informational goals but social goals as well.

Summary

Conversations differ from other forms of speech interactions in the number of people and the degree to which topics, turn lengths, and turn orders are specified in advance. Thus, unlike debates, conversations operate without a rigid set of explicit rules. This degree of relaxation, however, is made possible by a set of implicit rules or conventions governing conversational interactions. These include rules for taking turns in conversations, for establishing discourse coherence, and for identifying the proper use of speech acts such as requests. These rules enable most conversations to flow rather easily from one person to another and from one topic to another.

Sociolinguistic Dimensions of Discourse

The concepts we just discussed indicate that conversation has an inherent organization that is different from other forms of discourse. This organization, as we have seen, is revealed through careful observation of the "microstructure" of conversation—how the conversational moves and the nonverbal gestures that each person uses are closely tailored to the immediately preceding actions. These aspects were described without regard to who the participants were and where the conversation was held, factors that seem rather likely to influence the nature of conversation. Here we explore how features of the social context influence conversational processes.

Consider two conversations. In the first you are sitting on a park bench discussing a movie you have just seen with a friend who has also seen the movie. You loved it and she hated it. She points out that the movie was slow and dull compared to the director's previous movie. You listen and reply that this was a different type of movie. You say that your friend probably went in with inappropriate expectations. This movie was more interesting for its characters than its action. She concedes this, but adds that the character of the father was really stupid. You agree, but point to the relationship between the son and the mother as the major selling point of the film. This goes on for some time.

In a second conversation, you are in your family living room discussing some household work with your father. He mentions that the lawn needs to be mowed and that the leaves in the front need to be raked and bagged. You say that you know but that you have to do some work at the campus library before it closes. He asks how long it will take because the yard work needs to be done before it rains. You say it won't take that long, perhaps an hour, since you only have to find a book and Xerox a few articles. He says okay, but don't forget about the stuff that you have to bring to the dump. You say okay, and are on your way to the library.

In both conversations, speakers alternate turns, paying attention to the verbal and nonverbal behavior that signals that the other person is finished. Moreover, in both cases, speakers make an active effort to relate their comments to the agreed-upon topic of conversation. And yet, the conversations are different due to the social relationships of the speakers: the first is a discussion between equals, the second is not. This has a powerful effect on the interpretation of utterances within the conversation. When your father says, *I think we'd better mow the lawn before it rains*, it is generally not a topic for discussion (at least not in the sense of a movie's merits) and he generally means *you*, not *we*.

In short, conversations operate within a particular context, which includes the relationships between conversationalists, the immediate speech setting, and local customs regulating conversations. We shall first attempt to understand this social context by examining the insights of sociolinguists into the social patterning of conversation. Two sociolinguistic concepts stand out as basic: **social roles** and **social situations.**

Social Roles

Social roles refer to behaviors prescribed for or expected from individuals in a particular position in a social structure. The list of roles would include pastor, salesperson, mother, neighbor, and many others. Social relationships are relationships that we enter into with specific other individuals, beyond those specified by social roles. Intimate relationships and friendships are clear examples of social relationships.

Both roles and relationships are displayed clearly in speech. R. Brown and A. Gilman (1960) have studied the use of pronouns in how French, Italian, and German speakers refer to one another. In English, we use *you* regardless of the relationship. In French, however, a child speaking to his mother uses *vous* while the mother uses *tu* in speaking to the child. Similar distinctions occur in German and Italian. Brown and Gilman suggest that this asymmetrical use of personal pronouns reflects what they call the **power semantic,** the use of different forms of speech to mark asymmetrical power relationships. It thus turns out that persons in positions of authority, such as employers, use *tu* and receive *vous* when conversing with those who are subordinate.

In addition to the power semantic, Brown and Gilman identified a **solidarity semantic.** Individuals who have attended the same school or practice the same profession or have other similar backgrounds and interests tend to use *tu* when speaking to one another, while those less familiar with one another use *vous*. Interestingly, the solidarity semantic seems to be gaining in strength relative to the power semantic in recent centuries. When there is a conflict between the two semantics, the solidarity appears to be more influential. For example, according to both principles, parents should address their children as *tu*, yet the child would use *vous* if following the power semantic but *tu* if using the solidarity principle. Linguistic evolution has favored the child's use of *tu*, reflecting the ascendancy of the solidarity semantic. One striking example of this principle in action is the observation that mountaineers shift to the use of *tu* when they reach that altitude where "their lives hang by a single thread" (Brown & Gilman, 1960, p. 262).

Although this distinction between pronouns has evolved out of the English language, all languages have multiple means of signifying role relationships. R. Brown and M. Ford (1961) studied the use of proper names in a set of modern plays and in business meetings. They found a series of address forms that varied in familiarity and power: title only, title and last name, last name only, first name, multiple naming. The two most common forms of address—title and last name, and first name—clearly reflected social reality. In asymmetric power situations, the superior typically used the first name of the subordinate while the subordinate used the title and last name of the superior. Two equals who were not familiars used title and last name, while first names were used by equal and familiar individuals.

It often happens that social roles and relationships are ambiguous or unclear and we may not feel comfortable in expressing these roles so clearly. A case in point is when a graduate student's doctoral dissertation is accepted. The social norms indicate that she may now refer to her teachers (and now colleagues) on a first-name basis, but many people have difficulty making such a rapid adjustment after treating these academic authority figures with linguistic respect for years. Fortunately, English offers us the choice of using the neutral *you* until we can summon up the courage to be on a first-name basis.

Social Situations

Speech roles provide a source of constancy, but conversational behavior varies with the physical and social setting. One attribute of a situation is its formality. While the interaction between a professor and student might be reasonably formal during a classroom lecture, a more casual form of discourse could be expected between the two in a private conversation in the professor's office or in a chance meeting at the cafeteria.

A good example of the way in which situational characteristics influence speech is provided by Labov (1969). He was interested in the linguistic characteristics of Black English and recorded the speech of a black child (C) in interaction with a friendly white interviewer (A):

> *A:* Tell me everything you can about this.
>   (12 seconds of silence)
> *A:* What would you say it looks like?
>   (8 seconds of silence)
> *C:* A space ship.

> *A:* Hmmmm.
> (13 seconds of silence)
> *C:* Like a je-et.
> (12 seconds of silence)
> *C:* Like a plane.
> (20 seconds of silence)

The speech behavior of this 8-year-old boy did not change measurably when a familiar black adult did the interview. But crucial changes occurred when Labov (1) brought along a supply of potato chips, changing the interview into more of a party, (2) brought along the boy's best friend, (3) reduced the height imbalance by getting down on the floor, and (4) introduced taboo words and taboo topics. This resulted in changes in the speech behavior of the boy (C), his friend (F), and the black adult (A):

> *A:* Now, you said you had this fight now, but I wanted you to tell me about the fight you had.
> *C:* I ain't had no fight.
> *F:* Yes, you did!
> *A:* You said you had one! You had a fight with Butchie . . .
> *F:* An' he say Garland . . . an' Michael.
> *A:* An' Barry . . .
> *C:* I di'n; you said that, Gregory!
> *F:* You did
> *C:* You know you said that!
> *F:* You said Garland, remember that?

The same child who engaged in monosyllabic answers after long pauses now is actively competing for the floor with his friend, almost ignoring the adult.

Code Switching

A good example of the joint influence of roles and situations on conversational behavior is the phenomenon of **code switching,** which refers to switching of languages, dialects, or styles of discourse (for example, formal versus casual) during a conversation. Blom and Gumperz (1972) suggest that there are two distinct types of code shifting. In one, which they call **metaphorical switching,** the shift occurs because of a topic change in the conversation. Bilinguals may be more proficient in one language than another, so may switch to the more fluent language when their ability in the other language is taxed. Similarly, many who learn English as a second language know only formal English; thus, when a conversation turns informal, such a bilingual may return to her native tongue (Scotton, 1976).

The second type of code switching, **situational switching,** occurs when a change in the social situation occurs, one that influences the rights and obligations of the speakers. Blom and Gumperz (1972) investigated this latter type of code shifting in a small community in northern Norway called Hemnesberget. The commonly used dialect is Ranamål, which enjoys great prestige. Formal education, in contrast, is always carried out in one of the standard languages, Bokmål. Bokmål is used for official transactions, religion, and mass media.

These two languages are used in different ways. Lecturers use the standard language during their formal presentations, but switch to Ranamål when they want to encourage discussion. Similarly, the dialect is used for more private conversations. Thus, it is revealing when speakers switch between the languages in the middle of a conversation:

> The case of the local who, after finishing his business in the community office, turns to a clerk and asks him to step aside for a private chat further illustrates the contrast between metaphorical and role switching. By their constant alternation between the standard and the dialect during their business transaction, they alluded to the dual relationship which exists between them. The event was terminated when the local asked the clerk in the dialect whether he had the time to step aside to talk about private affairs, suggesting in effect that they shift to a purely personal, local relationship. The clerk looked around and said, "Yes, we are not too busy." The two then stepped aside, although remaining in the same room, and their subsequent private discussion was appropriately carried on entirely in the dialect. (Blom & Gumperz, 1972, pp. 425–426)

Thus a shift in language effectively indicates a shift in a social situation, with corresponding changes in roles and expectations for each person.

Summary

Conversations are governed at one level by a set of general rules concerning the taking of turns, the selection of topics, and the formulation of requests. These rules appear applicable to a wide variety of conversational situations, but there are other features of conversations that are related to the social context in which they take place. Two relevant sociolinguistic concepts are the social roles played by conversational participants and the social situation in which the conversation takes place. The phenomenon of code switching reveals the operation of both factors.

Gender, Language, and Conversation

Let us take a closer look at how social roles shape conversational processes. One sociolinguistic variable of interest is the gender of the conversational participants. Those who have studied the issue agree that there are significant differences between the speech of women and men (Lakoff, 1975; Tannen, 1990).

Gender Differences in Language

We will begin with the observations of Lakoff (1975), whose work has been influential in redirecting scholarly attention to issues of gender and language. She suggests that women are socialized to speak in different ways than men. She identifies a number of linguistic differences, but we will focus on three main areas.

One is related to politeness. Women use more particles such as *oh, dear* than men do, who are more likely to utter *oh, shit*. Women also, according to Lakoff, use more indirect speech, including indirect requests. As we have seen earlier, questions such as *Can you open the door?* are generally regarded as polite ways of making a request.

Lakoff also claims that women's speech contains more linguistic expressions of uncertainty than men's speech does. Women tend to use **tag questions** (*John is here, isn't he?*) and hedges (*sort of*). They also tend to use more question intonation patterns in declarative sentences than men do. For example, women would be more likely to utter *So, we will meet at eight* with a rising intonation at the end of the sentence. All of these manners of expression suggest a degree of uncertainty.

Finally, women's speech contains features that may be viewed, especially by men, as trivial or irrelevant. According to Lakoff, women talk more about the color of the objects in their environment and use more different types of color terms than men do. They also tend to use more intensifiers (such as *so* in *That sunset is so beautiful*). In contrast to alternatives such as *very* or *extremely, so* is less a precise statement about the sunset than an indication of the speaker's emotional reaction to it. This may be regarded as irrelevant.

Lakoff suggests that girls are exposed to these linguistic lessons and that there are important consequences attending to how well they learn them:

> If a little girl "talks rough" like a boy, she will normally be ostracized, scolded, or made fun of. In this way society, in the form of a child's parents and friends, keeps her in line, in her place. . . . If the little girl learns her lesson well, she is not rewarded with unquestioned acceptance on the part of society; rather, the acquisition of this special style of speech will later be an excuse others use to keep her in a demeaning position, to refuse to take her seriously as a human being. Because of the way she speaks, the little girl—now grown to womanhood—will be accused of being unable to speak precisely or to express herself forcefully. (Lakoff, 1975, pp. 5–6)

It should be emphasized that Lakoff's conclusions were not based on empirical research but, instead, on anecdotal observations. There have been relatively few empirical studies related to these points. However, one study, by McMillan, Clifton, McGrath, and Gale (1977), analyzed the speech of men and women in same-sex and mixed-sex problem-solving groups. The women used intensifiers six times more often than the men, and tag questions twice as often. The researchers also found that the women used modal constructions, such as *can, could, shall,* and *might* (which can express doubt), about twice as often. These results are generally consistent with Lakoff's views. The researchers also found that the men used all of these linguistic constructions somewhat more often when speaking to women than when speaking to men. The authors speculate that men may be more sensitive in the presence of women and that "women's language" conveys sensitivity well.

Some authors, however, have criticized Lakoff's ideas. For instance, DuBois and Crouch (1977) questioned Lakoff's points on tag questions. They compared the use of tag questions by men and women in a formal professional conference and found that the men used tag questions more. As West and Zimmerman (1985) point out, however, Lakoff was careful to distinguish between different contexts for tag questions. There are some occasions in which it is contextually appropriate to express doubt. When one does not or cannot know whether an assertion is true, a tag question such as (8) is perfectly appropriate. Similarly, tag questions are often used when small talk is desired (9).

(8)   I had my glasses off. He was out at third, wasn't he?

(9)   Sure is hot in here, isn't it?

Lakoff (1975, p. 16) specifically addressed the situation in which the speaker's opinion was the issue at hand and argued that in this context women were more likely to use tag questions than men. That is, she argued that tag questions were indicative of women's speech in this conversational situation, not in all situations. Since formal professional meetings differ in several respects from ordinary conversation—they tend to elicit an "academic style" of language, which expresses caution and uncertainty more than everyday language—the results of DuBois and Crouch's study do not bear directly on Lakoff's thesis.

Nor is it the case that the use of men's speech by women (and vice versa) necessarily invalidates Lakoff's view. She stated that although there are speech norms for men and women, these norms (like all norms) are sometimes violated. She discussed, in particular, the tendency of homosexual men to use some aspects of women's speech, and suggested that this is a reflection of their lack of acceptance of the traditional male role. By the same token, women sometimes use male speech. The presence of norms does not mean that they are never violated; it means that when they are violated, that act is culturally meaningful.

Gender Differences in Conversation

Let us now turn from the characteristics of women's speech to the characteristics of speech interactions between men and women. If it is true that men and women approach speech situations in different ways, then we might expect some important differences to emerge when they are holding a conversation together.

One area of conversational interaction that has received attention in recent years is that of interruptions. A line of research by Zimmerman and West (1975) suggests that men are more prone to interrupt women in conversations than vice versa. They place their work in the context of the Sacks, Schlegoff, and Jefferson (1974) model of speech interaction discussed earlier in the chapter. Sacks and coworkers claim that we have several rules for holding conversations, including those that the current speaker has the power to select the next speaker but that

Men and women have different styles of conversation.

another speaker may self-select by speaking up when there is a pause. The researchers suggest that these rules minimize the degree of conflict and conversational overlap between participants.

Zimmerman and West (1975) tape-recorded and transcribed conversations in natural settings such as coffee shops and drug stores. They identified three speech behaviors of interest. **Overlaps** were defined as periods of simultaneous speech during the last word of the speaker's projected closing. Overlaps appear to be consistent with the second of the Sacks et al.'s rules; since the first person to speak during a silence gains the floor, there is an incentive to be quick. **Interruptions** were defined as periods of simultaneous speech more than one word before the speaker's projected completion point. Zimmerman and West viewed interruptions as violations of the speaker's turn. They also discussed **minimal responses,** which were remarks such as *uh huh* and *um hmm*. These were not viewed as interruptions but, rather, as a listener's display of interest in a speaker's topic.

In their initial study, Zimmerman and West (1975) found that 96% of the interruptions were by the male speakers. Ten of the eleven males interrupted at least once. In contrast, interruptions were less frequent and were symmetrically distributed in same-sex conversations. A second major result was that many of the responses by males to female topics were delayed minimal responses, in which there was a delay of several seconds before the listener's minimal responses.

Zimmerman and West (1975) concluded that "men deny equal status to women as conversational partners with respect to the rights to the full utilization of their turns and support for the development of topics" (p. 125). They further suggest that this pattern of verbal interaction is a reflection of the power difference between men and women in our culture. In support of this notion, their second study (1977) found that children are treated by parents in ways that are similar to the ways women are treated by men; that is, 12 of 14 interruptions in parent/child interactions in a physician's office were initiated by the parent.

West and Zimmerman are careful to point out that these differences have emerged in the communication situations they have investigated; they do not claim that the differences occur in all speech interactions between men and women. This is fortunate, for at least one study (Beattie, 1981) found no differences in interruptions between men and women in university tutorial classes. It remains to be seen under what circumstances men do more interruptng than women.

There is also the matter of interpretation. The distinction between overlaps, which are regarded as minor intrusions, and interruptions, which presumably reflect an attempt to dominate a conversation, is based on the projected completion of a speaker's turn. This is difficult to assess just from transcripts. As we saw earlier, there are a host of nonverbal signals that accompany the ends of speakers' turns, such as eye contact and a drop in pitch (Duncan, 1972). It would be useful to base the definition of interruptions on videotaped conversations as well as on transcriptions.

Development of Gender Differences

If these gender differences in language and conversation are due to socialization, then we would expect to see both different linguistic socialization practices applied to boys and girls as well as evidence that they are acquiring these lessons in socialization. A number of studies have addressed these issues.

As for socialization practices, Cherry and Lewis (1976) examined verbal interactions between mothers and their 2-year-old children in a play situation. Mothers of girls talked more, asked more questions, repeated children's utterances more often, and used longer utterances relative to mothers of boys. Gleason and Greif (1983) report that both parents are more likely to interrupt girls than boys. Bellinger and Gleason (1982) also found that fathers use imperatives more than mothers.

There is also good evidence that children learn these lessons. Andersen (1984) found that girls are more likely to use indirect requests than boys and that girls are more likely to show exaggerated intonation than boys. Edelsky (1976) studied children's awareness of these linguistic patterns. She gave first-graders, third-graders, sixth-graders, and adults a series of statements and asked respondents to decide who would most likely make each statement (men generally, women generally, or equal likelihood). The statements included *Won't you please get me the pencil?, I was just furious, Damn it, I lost my keys,* and *They did the right thing, didn't they?* The results showed that even the youngest children answered in ways that were similar to the adults, indicating an awareness of "proper" speech for boys and girls.

Summary

Men and women's speech differ in some specific ways. Women tend to be more polite, to express greater uncertainty, and to use linguistic terms such as intensifiers more than men. Developmental studies converge on the conclusion that both men and women encourage these patterns of speech in young children. Moreover, men interrupt women more than women interrupt men, and both parents are more likely to interrupt young girls than young boys. Although these differences are not absolute (for instance, men will sometimes use "women's speech" and vice versa), they do indicate that gender is a significant factor in conversational processes.

Analyses of Two Conversational Situations

As we have just seen, social roles such as gender roles may play a significant role in our conversations. What about the social situation? Is there any reason to think that our choice of conversational topics, our use of turn-taking devices, and our responses to requests might be related to the social situation in which a conversation takes place?

To examine this, we need to study different kinds of conversational situations and identify both their similarities and their differences. Moreover, we need to study precisely those kinds of settings that demonstrate these sociolinguistic dimensions. Here we will focus on two types of conversations that have been studied—those between tutor and student and those between therapist and client. Although both operate within a particular, well-defined context, there are some salient differences. While both student and client are in a position of inferiority, this relationship is primarily cognitive for the student, but carries more emotional implications for the client. Consequently, the role of a client in psychotherapy may be a more difficult one to maintain, and some may resist playing it fully. Thus, we can see to what extent these sociolinguistic concepts play a role in the dynamics of the two conversational exchanges.

Tutorial Dialogues

Conversations between tutors and students have been studied by Collins and his colleagues (Collins, Warnock, & Passafiume, 1975). They recorded a number of tutorial dialogues that differed from one another in a variety of ways. The tutors varied in teaching experience, degree of preparation, and teaching strategies, while the students varied a great deal in their knowledge of the topics covered. While the topics covered a limited domain (factual information about geography and population density), the dialogues revealed much about how tutor behavior— giving hints, selecting topics, correcting errors, and so on—is flexible and responds to the needs of the student.

One area of tutor behavior that was studied was the selection of topics. In general, the order in which topics and subtopics were brought up was closely related to the structure of the tutor's knowledge. For example, one tutor organized geography facts into the topic South America, with subtopics names and locations of countries, geographical features such as rivers and mountains, climate and terrain in different regions, and so on. The conversation tended to pursue each area systematically up to a certain depth—that is, up to the point at which most of the important facts had been covered—and then move on and do the same for another subtopic. Other tutors structured the material somewhat differently, but used substantially similar processes.

Although all tutors organized their material in some way, they did not appear to be following a prespecified agenda. Rather, they did some of the organization as they went. In particular, the answers given by the students sometimes became the new subtopic for a period of time. As the student-initiated area was dwelled on, its features, like those of the tutor-initiated topics, were covered in the order of their importance. When such discussions drifted into insignificant (defined in terms of the tutor's knowledge) aspects, the tutors would switch topics, but those tutors who had prepared most for the session did this more promptly than the less-prepared tutors. The latter tended to let discussions wander somewhat aimlessly at times, controlled more by the immediately preceding statement than by an overall goal for the session.

Experienced tutors also seemed to be sophisticated in their use of questions. A simple view of the role of questions in tutorial dialogues might be to say that the tutor should first present the material, then should ask the student some questions about it. In contrast, the Collins team (1975) found that the tutors they studied interweaved presentations and questions in such a way that questions sometimes preceded as well as followed presentations of new material. Tutors often employed questions when introducing a new topic, for two reasons. First, questions about new topics tended to be relatively easy ones (*Where is Brazil?*) so the student would experience some success. Second, the answers to such basic-level questions gave the tutor a way to assess the sophistication of the student; indeed, experienced tutors can "calibrate" their questions so as to be close to but just beyond the student's current level of understanding.

Questions were also used sometimes to encourage students to interrelate and interpret information. One tutorial strategy was to ask a series of review questions about apparently disparate material, thus encouraging the students to see the topics as an interrelated whole. Another, often called the Socratic method, involved giving the student a series of yes or no questions. Thus, if a student said that the reason why rice grows in one area is that it receives enough rain, the tutor might ask, *Do they grow rice in Ireland?* (They don't, even though Ireland gets a lot of rain.) The juxtaposition of the questions with the student's earlier statements leads to a contradiction. The net result of the Socratic series is that it brings the student, ultimately, to the tutor's conclusions, in such a way that the student finds the connections him- or herself.

Research into tutorial conversations has some promise in helping us evaluate the teaching effectiveness of various tutorial strategies for different students, topics, and tutors. Collins, Adams, and Pew (1978) developed a computer program based on the tutorial exchanges they recorded and have established that the program leads to better student retention than more traditional approaches. Further work of this type may enable us to sort out how specific features of a tutorial conversation lead to specific aspects of student learning.

From a sociolinguistic perspective, this tutorial situation is well structured and stable: the tutor's role is to impart information to the student and the student's is to learn it. Moreover, both participants accept these role assignments. Consequently, the considerable complexity of this conversation stems mainly from the inherent difficulties in assessing another's level of knowledge and in teaching to that level, not from any uncertainty or qualms about the roles each person is to play in the interaction. As we shall see, this is not the case at all in therapeutic conversation.

Psychotherapy as Conversation

A second, and very different, specific type of conversation is the talk that occurs between client and therapist in a psychotherapy session. Building upon earlier analyses (Pittenger, Hockett, & Danehy, 1960; Scheflen, 1973), Labov and Fanshel (1977) have provided the first systematic analysis of therapeutic discourse. Although many people regard therapeutic insight as an art rather than a science and therefore a skill that can be acquired but not learned, Labov (a linguist) and Fanshel (a therapist) joined forces in the belief that a better description of what actually is said during therapy would benefit both fields.

Labov and Fanshel analyzed a single therapeutic session between a 19-year-old woman with a history of anorexia nervosa and her therapist, who was also a woman. This was their 25th session together, so they had developed consistent ways of communicating with one another. A primary issue in the psychotherapy was the client's difficulty in asserting herself with her mother and aunt, with whom she lived. The client was overwhelmed with housework and schoolwork. The therapist had urged the client to ask her mother and aunt to help with the housework, but the client had found the suggestion threatening. Labov and Fanshel recorded the speech and paralinguistic features (such as intonation and pitch) of both the therapist and client. Then they drew upon principles of discourse analysis and upon the special characteristics of therapeutic roles to interpret the multiple levels of communication in this setting.

Labov and Fanshel found that three different styles (or fields, as they called them) of discourse occur in therapy. First, there is the **everyday style** in which the client presents recent events in a fairly neutral, objective, and colloquial style. These provide the "raw data" for the session's conversation. Next, there is the **interview style,** which is loaded with jargonish terms such as *relationship, interpretation, guilt,* and so on. This style, which is used by clients as well as therapists, serves to evaluate or interpret the emotions and behaviors that have been brought up. Finally, there is the **family style,** in which the client speaks of family members and daily events, often in an emotionally charged manner.

In the conversation analyzed by Labov and Fanshel, the client begins in interview style:

I don't . . know, whether . . I—*think* I did the right thing, jistalittle . . situation came up . . . an' I tried to uhm . . . . . . well, try to . . . . use what I—what I've learned here, see if it worked. (p. 119)

It is interesting to note that there is no "small talk" at the beginning of the conversation; the client is expected to begin the session with an event that illustrates understanding of the principles the therapist has been working at (this conversation occurred after a number of sessions had taken place). The client responds, appropriately, to this social convention by beginning to describe a relevant event, but does so in a halting, tentative sort of speech that includes several qualifying expressions, several long pauses, and contrastive stress on the word *think*. It would appear that this tentativeness is closely related to the roles of client and therapist; while the client can claim to be an expert on what occurred, she cannot, in this context, interpret these events as consistent with some therapeutic principle without that interpretation being evaluated and perhaps challenged by the therapist. Thus, she hedges. Of course, the content itself probably has something to do with the form of speech used. It would be interesting to see how she would recount the same event to a friend.

One of the features that repeatedly occurs in this conversation is that the client answers requests with narratives. For example, the therapist's suggestion, which is put in qualified form, that the client attempt to work out a disagreement by talking with her aunt is followed by a narrative:

Therapist: But what would happen if you—um—you know—tried to arrive at some working relationship with her . . .

Client: Sso-like-las' night—like, on Wednesday night is my late—one o' my late nights—

Therapist: Mm.

Client: I have two late nights, Tuesday and Wednesday.

Therapist: Mm. (pp. 215–217)

The client goes on to describe the behavior of her aunt in some detail, but does not respond directly to the implicit request of the therapist. Yet, she appears to be cognizant of the fact that her response is pragmatically inappropriate, for her speech is laden with paralinguistic cues of tension and emotion. The therapist notices the nonanswer and later repeats the request in even more mitigated form. When this does not succeed, the therapist reverses positions and agrees with the client that it would not be useful to talk to the aunt as a means of solving the overall problem.

The tendency of the client to respond to requests, suggestions, and challenges in narrative form is instructive. These narrative responses appear to be defensive maneuvers, attempts to shift the conversation to topics that are both emotionally safer and in which the client has greater expertise. Since the therapist does not have access to the events themselves, the options available are either to take in the comments without evaluation or to break in and insist upon a response, which would be a disruptive communicative event. So the therapist has chosen to put the request in an indirect form, which softens its effect but also enables the client to ignore it, at least on the surface. Thus, conversational processes in a therapeutic interview may be discussed at a number of different levels.

Some appreciation of the skills of a therapist emerges from this discourse. The therapist repeatedly shows sensitivity to the responses of the client by couching the most threatening actions (challenges, requests, and so on) in mitigated form. The form of the therapist's comments is closely related to the therapist's judgment of the client's emotional state; when a given request is posed too threateningly, it may be rephrased or even abandoned. The therapist must be sensitive to the fact that while her task is to increase the client's insight into her emotional problems, this cannot be done in a way that is too threatening, for that puts the entire therapeutic work into peril.

In contrast, when the client is obscure in reporting some details yet draws a conclusion from them, the therapist repeatedly challenges the client to clearly say what happened, and ultimately rejects the client's conclusion. Why might the therapist be so challenging in one case and so careful in another? It may be because in order for the therapist to be of any help, she must help the client separate what occurred from what it means, which is the area of expertise of the therapist. While the therapist dare not challenge the accuracy of the client as a reporter—this would deprive their conversation of the necessary data base—she is willing to challenge the client's interpretation of these events. Thus, the significance of a particular speech act depends upon its relevance for the roles of the conversational participants.

What emerges, then, is the view of a skilled participant who uses a variety of conversational strategies that are closely tailored to the immediate context and the responses of the client. In this respect, the skills of a therapist are similar to those of a tutor. The difference lies in that in addition to the cognitive processes involved in tutorial exchanges, therapeutic discourse elicits communication processes at a deeper emotional level. This additional level of complexity is present precisely because of the personal and social tensions associated with the roles of therapist and client; if such tension existed in the tutorial environment (for example, if the student failed to accept the tutor's authority), some of the challenges and defense manuevers of therapeutic discourse would appear, probably in muted form.

It is clear, in any event, that therapeutic discourse provides a wealth of information for those wishing to analyze conversational processes in real life situations. Though Labov and Fanshel's fascinating account is of only a single session, it provides a basis for identifying what skilled therapists actually do and thus for improving instruction for future therapists.

Summary

We have seen a number of ways in which the conversational setting influences conversational processes. The salient features of the setting influence the range of appropriate discussion topics, the choice between language options exercised by the speaker, and the interpretation of any given speech act by the listener. The types of discourse we have discussed differ from casual conversations in that both tutor and therapist occupy a position of authority in the conversation. The role assumptions in therapeutic discourse, however, are more complex and meet with greater resistance than the assumptions in a tutoring session, and this influences the flavor of the conversational interaction.

Language Production in Schizophrenia

This section examines the discourse of mentally ill individuals. Here we will look at the discourse of schizophrenic speakers and attempt to identify patterns of language use that coincide with or differ from normal practice. These studies, while providing important applications of psycholinguistic principles, also offer an opportunity to assess the generality of the principles themselves.

Descriptions of Schizophrenic Language

Schizophrenia is a form of mental illness that involves disorders of the thought process, flattened affect, withdrawal from social situations, bizarre behavior, attentional deficits, and sometimes delusional thinking. Schizophenia is not a unitary disorder and, in fact, is subdivided into a number of distinct types, but these details will not concern us here (for further information, see Cromwell, 1975).

What is of direct concern here is the language of schizophrenia. There is no single form of speech that can be characterized as schizophrenic speech because schizophrenics differ just as other speakers do. Moreover, many schizophrenic patients are lucid some of the time but not at others. Nevertheless, there are certain types of language commonly found, at least intermittently, in schizophrenia.

First, some prosodic aspects of schizophrenic speech are sometimes unusual. Bleuler (1911/1950) described schizophrenic speaking patterns vividly:

> The intonation in the patients' speech is often peculiar. In particular, there is often an absence, exaggeration or misplacement of modulation. Speech may be abnormally loud, abnormally soft, too rapid, or too slow. Thus one patient speaks in a falsetto voice, another mumbles, a third grunts. A catatonic speaks in precisely the same fashion during inspiration as during expiration, another has no intonation at all. Sometimes, the voice will change with the set of ideas . . . when the patients think of themselves as different persons, they utilize a correspondingly different tone of voice. (pp. 148–149)

Prosodic factors are often used to convey emotions through language, so perhaps we should not be too surprised that schizophrenia, which includes an affective disturbance, is associated with unusual prosodic features.

Second, schizophrenic speech sometimes is characterized by degrees of **perseveration** (or repetition) not found in most speech. Speakers may repeat a particular word again and again, as in (10). Others may repeat grammatical morphemes; in sentence (11), we see a repetition of morphemes, such as *sub-*, *mis-*, and *un-*.

(10) Kindly send it to me at the hospital. Send it to me Joseph Nemo, in care of Joseph Nemo and me who answers by the name of Joseph Nemo will care for it myself. Thanks everlasting and Merry New Year to Metholatum Company for my nose, for my nose, for my nose, for my nose, for my nose, for my nose. (Maher, 1972, p. 14)

(11) The subterfuge and the mistaken planned substitutions for that demanded American action can produce nothing but the general results of negative contention and the impractical results of careless application, the natural results of misplacement, of mistaken purpose and unrighteous position, the impractical serviceabilities of unnecessary contradictions. (Maher, 1972, p. 13)

Some investigators have suggested that these speakers may suffer from an attentional deficit in which they have difficulty pulling attention away from stimuli to which they are attending (Chapman, Chapman, & Miller, 1964).

Third, schizophrenics appear to be less likely than other speakers to spontaneously edit their own utterances when they have made a minor speech error (Chaika, 1974). As we saw in the previous chapter, ordinary speakers edit their utterances in a number of ways (for instance, distinguishing between nuance errors and outright errors) that appear to be helpful to the listener. The failure of self-editing may reflect a lack of attention to, or interest in, the needs of the listener.

Finally, it has sometimes been claimed that schizophrenic language is disordered at the syntactic level (Chaika, 1982; Hoffman, Hogben, Smith, & Calhoun, 1985). Schizophrenics may use **word salads,** which are sentences in which the words are thrown together in seemingly random fashion, as in sentence (12):

(12) the house burnt the cow horrendously always (Vetter, cited in Chaika, 1974)

It is not clear, however, that the prevalence of these kinds of errors is greater than that found in normal speakers (Fromkin, 1975).

Even when the syntax is normal, schizophrenic speech may be difficult to comprehend. Pavy (1968) notes:

> It is frequently observed that though schizophrenics use proper words and produce reasonably well-formed sentences, one is unable after having heard a series of such sentences, to comprehend what has been said. (p. 175)

Similarly, Cohen, Nachmani, and Rosenberg (1974) comment on one schizophrenic speaker, "He seems to be speaking ordinary English, but I can't tell what in the world he's driving at" (p. 1). If the sentences are (relatively) clear, then why is comprehension so hard? As Pavy (1968) suggested some time back, perhaps the best linguistic models for understanding schizophrenic language will come from units of language larger than the sentence.

Discourse Production in Schizophrenia

As we saw in Chapter 7, we ordinarily use a number of cohesive devices, such as pronominal reference, to make our discourse coherent to a listener. Rochester and Martin (1979) examined schizophrenic discourse from the standpoint of cohesion. They were interested to see whether there were differences in the use of cohesive devices between normal and schizophrenic speakers and the extent to which such differences influence the comprehensibility of schizophrenic language.

The researchers compared the speech of schizophrenic speakers with that of normal individuals. They subdivided the schizophrenic group into two subgroups: those who manifested a thought disorder (as identified by clinicians) and those who didn't (although they displayed other characteristics of schizophrenia). Then the three groups were given three tasks: an interview task, a cartoon task, and a narrative task. In the interview, subject and interviewer sat facing each other and discussed any topic that the subject cared to discuss, with the interviewer suggesting topics if necessary. In the cartoon task, they were shown 10 cartoons and asked to describe them and explain why they were supposed to be funny. In the narrative task, they read a 108-word story and told it back to the investigator.

A number of interesting results were found. There was a relative lack of cohesive ties in the speech of the thought-disordered (TD) schizophrenics compared to the other two groups. The researchers used Halliday and Hasan's (1976) method for determining cohesion (see Table 7-1) and averaged over all forms of cohesion to find that TD speakers linked their present speech to previous speech considerably less than normal speakers. When they did provide ties, the ties were most often in the form of simple lexical ties, which often involve repeating words used previously. Here is a response to the interviewer's question, *A stitch in time saves nine. What does that mean?*.

> Oh! That's because all women have a little bit of magic to them. I found that out and it's called, it's sort of good magic and nine is sort of a magic number like I've got nine colors here you will notice. I've got yellow, green, blue, gray, orange, blue, and navy and I've got black and I've got a sort of clear white. The nine colors to me they are the whole universe and they symbolize every man, woman and child in the world. (Rochester & Martin, 1979, pp. 94–95)

The speaker appears to be making an effort to answer the question with the use of the word *that* in the first two sentences but quickly gets sidetracked. Yet the successive statements are lexically related to one another. The connections are first made through the word *magic*, then *nine*, and still later *color*. These relations are achieved, however, only at a superficial level since most people would regard a shift from nine as a magic number to nine colors as an abrupt change of topic. Thus, while there are some links between adjacent utterances, the overall answer is an incoherent response to the question.

Another difference was that while normal speakers varied their output in the three tasks, TDs did so less readily. Normal speakers, for example, referred primarily to previous verbalizations rather than to nonverbal characteristics when describing the cartoons, but began using more references to the nonverbal situation when in an interview. This pattern also held for nonthought disordered (NTD) schizophrenics, but it didn't hold for the TD schizophrenics. Reference to the immediate context makes a good deal more sense in an interview setting than when describing a cartoon.

Underlying these inappropriate uses of discourse seems to be an impairment of understanding the needs of the listener. One interesting discussion in Rochester and Martin (1979) concerns the appropriate use of bridging in discourse. Bridging, as we saw in Chapter 7, is where a speaker links one utterance or proposition to another by means of an inference that is drawn by the listener. For example, in *The speaker walked to the podium. She adjusted the microphone*, it is appropriate to refer to *the microphone* instead of *a microphone* since it is reasonable to assume that the listener can make the bridging inference that podiums sometimes have microphones. When setting up a bridge, the time elapsed between the previous comment and the present one is crucial. If the time lapse is long, it may be difficult for the comprehender to retrieve the previous proposition, and thus comprehension breaks down. Apparently, TD speakers are not good judges of how easy it may be to form a referential link and casually make comments that are difficult, but not impossible, to connect with previous speech. In this regard, Rochester and Martin make the intriguing suggestion that TD speakers tend to use the informal mode of interview discourse in a variety of circumstances, as if they have difficulty understanding that speech appropriate to one situation is inappropriate in another.

Implications for Diagnosis

The diagnosis of many psychiatric disorders requires close attention to the language used by the patient. A series of studies by Hoffman and his colleagues have examined the implications of schizophrenic language for diagnosis. In particular, Hoffman (1986) has suggested that the deficiencies of discourse structure found in schizophrenic speech may increase the processing requirements for listeners and lead to variability of interpretation and diagnosis. It is thus possible that a linguistic analysis of schizophrenic discourse may assist standard clinical diagnosis.

Hoffman, Kirstein, Stopek, and Cicchetti (1982) compared the effectiveness of discourse analysis and clinical judgments in the diagnosis of schizophrenia. Eleven schizophrenic and nine nonschizophrenic psychiatric patients were given a brief interview consisting of open-ended questions such as *Tell me about your first day of school* and *What is it like where you live?* Two passages from each interview were randomly selected for analysis.

In the discourse analysis, examples of discourse failure such as statements that lacked a supporting context, statements that were pragmatically ambiguous, and statements that showed upward branching were identified. **Upward branching** is illustrated in the following set of statements:

(13a)   I've not been able to find a book for an awfully long time.
(13b)   Finally last week Martha recommended this new release by X.
(13c)   I actually got around to reading it.
(13d)   It was a really good book.
(13e)   Honesty is not one of his weaknesses.
(13f)   He plagiarized magnificently.

Although many of these sentences are related to one another, the text as a whole is somewhat disjointed. Hoffman and his colleagues attribute this to the double meaning of statement (13d). On the one hand, it follows naturally from statements (13a) to (13c) as a statement about a book that was recommended, read, and then evaluated. On the other hand, the book's goodness in (13e) and (13f) refers to the author's expert plagiarism. Graphically, the discourse may be represented as

```
a
 \
  b
   \
    c  e
    \/ \
    d  f
```

with the transition from (d) to (e) as an awkward upward branch.

For the discourse analysis, similar instances of discourse incoherence were identified and tabulated. For comparison, four psychiatrists were given the transcripts and made clinical judgments of whether or not the speaker was thought disordered.

The psycholinguistic analysis of discourse, when pitted against clinical judgments, did a better job of discriminating between schizophrenic and nonschizophrenic groups. More specifically, the analysis of passages into cohesive and noncohesive was 80% accurate in identifying schizophrenic versus nonschizophrenic groups, while the percent of correct classifications by the four clinicians varied between 36% and 82%. Moreover, those clinicians who were most accurate were those whose judgments correlated most strongly with the discourse analysis. These results suggest that an analysis of schizophrenic discourse would be a useful supplement of traditional clinical judgment in the diagnosis of schizophrenia.

Some Unresolved Issues

Normal versus abnormal language   There are several questions that arise from these observations. One is whether the differences between schizophrenic language and normal language are primarily quantitative or qualitative. If the difference is merely quantitative, then schizophrenic speakers might organize their output in a manner similar to normal speakers but display more errors in production. The discussion of bridging in Rochester and Martin (1979) implies a possible quantitative difference since both normal and schizophrenic speakers appear to function with the assumption that it is appropriate to refer back to earlier discourse, but schizophrenic references cover a larger chunk of discourse.

In contrast, it could be argued that schizophrenic language is fundamentally different than normal language. Deese (1978, 1980) has analyzed the discourse of normal, well-educated speakers in town meetings and in graduate seminars. He found that all such discourse is consistent with the notion of a strong hierarchy. This means that individual propositions are fitted into an overall discourse structure in such a way that each proposition is presented only once and lower level propositions modify or elaborate higher level propositions. This form of hierarchical organization, according to Deese, is nearly always present in the discourse of normal speakers. Moreover, such organization usually influences the manner in which speech is produced, with speakers proceeding in a "top-down" manner.

Hoffman, Kirstein, Stopek, and Cicchetti (1982) observed that schizophrenic discourse is not organized hierarchically, since schizophrenics often switch topics unpredictably. The fact that they later return to their original point raises an interesting question: Are schizophrenic speakers deviant in the way they organize discourse, the way they express it, or both? Are they like a lecturer with a well-organized lesson who can't seem to stay on the topic, pursuing digressions until his listeners are totally exasperated? Or are they more like a lecturer without a well-organized plan in the first place? Is the flaw in the plan or in its delivery? It is too early to tell. Although further research will be needed to pinpoint the exact nature of these differences, it appears that the production of discourse in schizophrenics is qualitatively different in some respects from the discourse production of normal speakers.

Abnormal language versus abnormal thought   A second issue that has interested investigators of schizophrenic language has been whether the disorder, however it is ultimately to be characterized, is one of language or of thought. Chaika (1974) argues that schizophrenic speech is a form of aphasia and that its symptoms are attributable to temporary aphasic interruption of normal speech. She has identified six symptoms of schizophrenic language, which, she claims, are outside the normal kinds of errors most speakers make, including the tendency to be distracted by the phonological form of words, the failure to apply discourse rules, and the failure to monitor one's speech errors. Further evidence for this view may come from studies of brain function in schizophrenics. Aphasia typically is due to deficits in the left hemisphere (see Chapter 13 for a fuller discussion of aphasia), so if schizophrenia is related to a disfunction of the brain mechanisms involved with language, we would expect to see left hemisphere deficits in schizophrenia. And there is some evidence of such deficits (see, for example, Gur, 1978).

This view is rejected by Fromkin (1975) and R. Brown (1973b). Fromkin argues that these characteristics of schizophrenic language are not unique and can be found in normal individuals from time to time. Fromkin, noting the preponderance of semantic, pragmatic, and discourse violations are greater than violations of syntax and phonology, considers schizophrenic production as an aberration of thought processes rather than a linguistically based deficit. Brown presents a similar view. He had conversations with schizophrenics over a period of 3 weeks and found little evidence of impairment in phonology or grammar. In contrast, the patients with whom he spoke showed thought disorders. Brown cites an example of a young man who said that when he left the hospital he was going to go to Scotland to try out for the lead in the film *Fiddler on the Roof*. The problems in thinking were manifest: the film had already been made, Scotland was never a likely location for that movie, the man was not the right age for the lead role, and so on. So Brown argues that schizophrenia is a disorder of thought more than of language.

The matter is not settled. In arguing that linguistic rules operate normally in schizophrenia, Brown restricted his attention to phonological and grammatical rules. Although some of the examples of schizophrenic speech errors that we have seen are at one of these levels, more commonly the level of discourse has been implicated. And it is in discourse, as well as semantics, that the lines between thought and language become blurred. Certainly a clarification of this issue will be a high priority for future research on schizophrenic language.

Summary

Schizophrenics display intermittent problems with various aspects of language, including prosody, perseveration, editing, and possibly syntactic processing. In addition, schizophrenic discourse differs in some systematic ways from "ordinary" discourse. Schizophrenic speakers are less attentive than most speakers to the cohesive ties between different parts of a discussion and appear to have an impaired understanding of the pragmatic side of language. The research efforts may well have practical benefits for the clinician, as the analysis of discourse structure has been found to be a significant aid in the diagnosis of schizophrenia.

Scrutiny of schizophrenic discourse may also increase our understanding of normal conversational discourse. In particular, the flexibility and context dependence of ordinary discourse seem peculiarly lacking in schizophrenic production. Schizophrenic language gives us a glimpse of what language looks like when words and sentences are divorced from discourse—language that is grammatically correct but socially aberrant and ultimately dysfunctional.

Review Questions

1. Distinguish between the major properties of debates, ceremonies, meetings, and conversations.
2. Identify the three rules for taking turns in conversations, and explain why they are ordered rules.

3. Explain the way in which a topic is defined in a conversation.
4. How are topic shifts accomplished within the principle of coherence?
5. What role do preconditions play in our use of requests?
6. How do the power semantic and the solidarity semantic jointly determine our choice of pronouns?
7. In what ways does women's speech differ from men's speech?
8. How is therapeutic discourse similar to and different from tutorial dialogues?
9. Identify the salient characteristics of schizophrenic language production.
10. Describe the controversy surrounding whether schizophrenia reflects a disorder of language or of thought.

Thought Questions

1. Schank's model of topic shifts is based on relationships between adjacent statements in conversation. Yet we often refer to something that was said much earlier. How might we formulate conversational rules pertaining to the coherence of nonadjacent statements?
2. Do you think it is ever appropriate for a man to use women's speech? Is it ever appropriate for a woman to use men's speech? Explain.
3. Would a conversation with your physician regarding your chronic high blood pressure be more similar to a tutorial or to a therapeutic conversation? Why?

part 4

Language Acquisition

10

Early Language Acquisition

- Children's construction of language emerges from their understanding of communication prior to language. Their comprehension and production of gestures reveal a basic understanding of communication processes.
- Although children first acquire the sound system of their native language independently of meaning, they eventually merge it with communicative gestures to form productive speech.
- The development of one-word speech comprises two important developments: the acquisition of the lexicon and the use of single words to express larger chunks of meaning.
- Children's first word combinations reveal a structure that is neither an imitation of adult speech nor fully grammatical by adult standards. With further development, children acquire the grammatical categories of adult speech.
- Early stages of acquisition are similar in signed and spoken languages.

Introduction

It is little wonder that parents take such joy in observing their children's first steps in the acquisition of language. In the space of little more than a year, a child limited to babbling has come to label objects in the immediate environment, identify names of important people, and form simple sentences. These rapid advances make children much more active participants in the daily affairs of the home, as they learn how to ask for desired objects and participate in simple conversations, and as parents come to expect more, verbally, from their children. And, bit by bit, children's language comes to resemble the language of their everyday environment.

These developments have come under intense scrutiny by psychologists and linguists over the last 30 years. Some investigators have followed individual or small groups of children over a period of years, recording their linguistic development with painstaking accuracy. Others have used the more conventional methods of assessing development by comparing children of different ages. What has arisen out of this substantial research effort is a wealth of detail about how children acquire their first language. Many important questions, however, remain unanswered. For example: Why do children acquire speech at this particular point in development? What role does the child's environment play in language development? Do all children acquire language in the same way?

This chapter and the two that follow will chart children's progress in first language development. This chapter will examine children's development up until they have mastered the basic linguistic structures of the language, at about 3 years of age. We begin with a discussion of the infant's communication skills prior to language. Next we turn to how children master the phonology of their native language. Then we address children's first one-word utterances, followed by their early attempts to acquire the grammar of their language. Finally, we compare and contrast the acquisition of English and American Sign Language.

Prelinguistic Communication

Up until the early part of their second year, infants communicate with their world primarily in nonverbal ways: they tug at people's clothes, point at desired objects, and wave bye-bye. These gestures, though basic, reveal a good deal about the infant's understanding of how communication works. It appears that the emergence of these communication skills is made possible by advances in the child's understanding of how actions can be used as means for achieving desired goals. These advances take place in the first year of life, suggesting that infants' understanding of communication precedes and facilitates much of the child's acquisition of phonology, syntax, and semantics.

This section traces children's development from the earliest communicative acts to their first steps in language development. Though a child's language development undergoes dramatic changes in form and complexity over the first few years of life, there are some important underlying functional similarities in the communication skills of younger and older children. These communication skills are best seen where they originate, in the prelinguistic infant.

The Social Context of Preverbal Infants

Let us first look at the social environment of the prelinguistic child. Well before children begin to speak in comprehensible ways, they are exposed to the social uses of language by their caregivers (Sachs, 1993).

Speech to children prior to birth   These lessons begin even before birth. Anecdotal evidence from mothers-to-be has suggested that children in utero hear their mother's speech and may respond to it (for instance, by kicking). Some experimental evidence supports this view. DeCasper and Spence (1986) asked mothers-to-be to read a Dr. Seuss book aloud during the last 6 weeks of their pregnancies. A few days after the children were born, the babies were tested using a special pacifier that measured their rate of sucking. Half of the babies heard the story that their mothers had read, and the others heard a new story. The babies that heard the familiar story modified their sucking rate when they heard the Dr. Seuss story but the other group did not. The investigators concluded that the infants had heard and retained the stories presented to them in utero.

Newborns also prefer their mother's voices over those of strangers (DeCasper & Fifer, 1980). It is not clear what the limits of this phenomenon might be. We do not know how well if at all the baby can hear other voices or at what gestational age the baby is mature enough to perceive speech. At the very least, these studies suggest that newborns are prepared to perceive speech at birth.

Speech to children in the first year of life   After birth, caregivers speak to children in distinctive ways. **Child-directed speech** (also called **baby talk** and **motherese**) differs in many ways from the speech adults direct to other adults. Early in life, the phonological differences seem to be paramount. Child-directed speech tends to be higher in pitch, more variable in pitch, and more exaggerated in its intonational contours than adult-directed speech. All of these characteristics would appear to be likely to get and maintain the attention of very small infants.

Recent evidence, indeed, suggests that infants prefer to listen to baby talk rather than adult-directed speech. Fernald and Kuhl (1987) had 4-month-old infants sit on their mothers' laps and reinforced them for turning their head one way or the other. A head turn in one direction produced child-directed speech (higher pitch), while a turn in the other direction produced adult-directed speech (lower pitch). Fernald and Kuhl found that the infants preferred to listen to the child-directed speech. In everyday life, it may be that the signs of inattention that babies display when adults use ordinary speech lead the adults to make these phonological adaptations. We will discuss the syntactic aspects of baby talk in Chapter 12.

Another aspect of the early speech behavior of caregivers is that they encourage infants to participate in conversations. Snow (1977) noticed that when mothers spoke to their babies they tended to interpret the infants' vocalizations and sounds as conversational turns. Consider the following sequence between a mother and her 3-month-old daughter (p. 12):

Ann:	(smiles)
Mom:	Oh, what a nice little smile! Yes, isn't that nice? There. There's a nice little smile.
Ann:	(burps)
Mom:	What a nice wind as well! Yes, that's better, isn't it? Yes. Yes.
Ann:	(vocalizes)
Mom:	Yes! There's a nice noise.

Note that the mother is counting the child's burps, passing of wind, and so on as an attempt to take a turn in a conversation. In this sense, the caregiver is pulling intentionality out of a preintentional child. The caregiver is encouraging the child to think of language as a social activity with rules, and as an activity that we engage in intentionally to communicate with one another. It seems likely that these early conversational lessons, along with the child's own cognitive maturation, enable the child to communicate in a more purposeful manner later in the first year.

Prelinguistic Gestures

Despite the richness of the language infants receive in the first year of life, it is some time before they are able to speak themselves. Before they use language to communicate, they communicate through gestures.

Well before 10 months of age, children engage in a lot of vocal behavior that appears to have some communicative value. Children's smiles and (most definitely) cries elicit parental behavior. Moreover, different cries are discriminated by parents and these yield responses that differ in urgency as well as type. Still, these sounds are not true forms of intentional communication because infants do not display flexible, goal-directed behavior. For example, if a cry is ineffective in obtaining adult attention, young infants do not turn to another behavior, such as banging an object against the side of the crib. Thus, while infants' cries generally elicit parental responses, the infant is not using the cry for that purpose. Rather, it is simply a built-in response with predictable consequences.

Development of communicative intent   At around 8 months of age, infants begin to use gestures, such as pointing and showing, in a communicative manner. It is not easy to determine if a behavior is meant to communicate something or is simply a behavior that an infant enjoys. However, psychologists have developed criteria to determine if a behavior displays an intent to communicate (Bruner, 1975; Harding, 1982). The major criteria are: (1) waiting, (2) persistence, and (3) development of alternative plans. For example, suppose an infant tugs at her parent's leg, waits for the parent to look down, and then points at a toy. The fact that the infant waited for the adult to pay attention suggests that the infant was operating on the assumption that we first have to get an adult's attention and then we can point out what we want. As presented, the child's desires are somewhat ambiguous. Sometimes children merely want to point to an object that interests them and have the adult acknowledge that this is an interesting object. But if the adult does so and the child persists, then most adults would infer that the child wants to have the toy given to her. Caregivers make these inferences about what an infant wants all the time; the above criteria are an attempt to describe more systematically how we make these inferences.

I noted earlier that infants appear to be developing communicative intent at around 8 months of age. It is likely that this ability develops at this time because of the child's cognitive development. As we discussed in Chapter 3, Piaget (1952) has argued that children go through a series of stages of cognitive development in the first 2 years of life. Piaget's stage 3 (about 4 to 5 months) and stage 4 (about 8 to 12 months) are relevant here. At stage 3, children show little understanding of goal-directed behavior. They display what Piaget calls "making interesting sights and sounds last." If a child is given a rattle, shakes it, and enjoys the sound, he may continue to shake the rattle. If he accidentally drops the rattle and it makes an interesting sound, he may repeat that behavior. The child shows no advance plan; he merely stumbles upon something interesting and repeats it.

At about 8 months of age, infants become more purposeful in their behavior. They begin to show problem-solving behavior in which they experience a problem, wait, and then try to solve the problem. Piaget describes the behavior of his son, Laurent, in which the child was shown a bell that was partially covered by a cushion. Laurent moved the cushion with one hand and then grasped the bell with the other (Piaget, 1952). The child appeared to have a goal in mind and combined two existing behaviors in order to achieve the goal.

At this point, children are now able to approach individual goals with a sense of purpose and with a degree of flexibility not present earlier. So far, however, our focus has been exclusively on individual goals and we have ignored social goals. The next step is to see how children use these newly acquired cognitive abilities to communicate with others.

Beginnings of intentional communication   True intentional communication occurs when children apply their understanding of means and ends relationships to social goals. Early prelinguistic gestures have been studied by Bates, Camaioni, and Volterra (1975), who focused on two communicative acts: **assertions** (or declaratives)—the use of an object as a means of obtaining adult attention, and **requests** (or imperatives)—the use of adults as means to an object.

Bates and her colleagues used the total communicative context to help determine the meaning of the child's nonverbal behavior:

> Carlotta, unable to pull a toy cat out of the adult's hand, sits back up straight, looks the adult intently in the face, and then tries once again to pull the cat. The pattern is repeated three times, with the observer refusing to yield the cat, until Carlotta finally manages to pull the object away from the adult. (p. 215)

Earlier on, Carlotta repeatedly tried to take a box out of her mother's hand without at any time looking at her mother's face. By stopping and looking at the adult, she appears to have begun to understand that the adult can be of some use in getting an object. The act of looking at the adult thus can be considered as a request.

The child also uses objects to gain adults' attention:

> At 9;6 [9 months, 6 days], Carlotta is in her mother's arms, and is drinking milk from a glass. When she has finished drinking, she looks around at the adults watching her, and makes a comical noise with her mouth (referred to in some dialects as "the raspberries"). The adults laugh, and Carlotta repeats the activity several times, smiling and looking around in between. Her parents explain that this behavior has been discovered earlier in the week, and that Carlotta now produces it regularly at eating and drinking times, always awaiting some response from the adult. (p. 216)

At this stage, the child is using familiar behavior for novel ends: making sounds and gestures in order to get adult attention, provoke humor, and so on.

It wasn't until about a month later that Carlotta began to use novel means to achieve familiar goals:

> At 10;18, we observed the first instance in which Carlotta extends her arm forward to show an object to the adult. She is playing with a toy already in her hand; suddenly, she looks toward the observer and extends her arm forward holding the toy. In the next two to three weeks, this behavior increases and stabilizes until we observe Carlotta looking around for objects not already in her grasp, and immediately presenting them while awaiting adult response. At this stage "showing" does not seem to involve any intention to give the object. In fact, several times when the adult tries to take the exhibited toy, Carlotta refuses to let go, and often pulls her arm back. (p. 216)

The child's communicative advances seem to be a result of fundamental changes in cognition during infancy. Shortly after children understand intentionality in nonsocial contexts, they use prelinguistic gestures in a social, communicative manner.

The pointing gesture, which serves either as assertion or request depending upon the context, came a few months later for Carlotta. Again, communicative pointing gestures differ from noncommunicative pointing mainly in flexibility. A child who points as an assertion, to get an adult's attention, will now look at the adult's face to confirm that the adult is looking at the right thing, whereas earlier there was no such attempt at confirmation. Children's comprehension of others' gestures follows a similar pattern. They respond to others' pointing by looking in the right direction and not at the "speaker's" face (Clark & Clark, 1977).

It is an open question as to how much parents can assist or influence these processes. It is apparent that ordinary parent/child interaction requires parents to interpret ambiguous or vague child messages, as in distress cries, and parents routinely interpret messages. Parental input could assist the child, perhaps by helping him figure out what he wants to "say." Bruner (1975) discovered that parents often mark the segments of actions by the use of a word or phrase after the child's actions. Thus, the child takes food from a spoon and the mother exclaims, *Good boy!* It could be that these parental messages help the child segment his own continuous stream of behavior into discrete units that may be repeated or used later in a different context.

To sum up, prelinguistic children use gestures to get the receiver's attention and to communicate. The transition to speech acts can then be viewed as learning how to do with words what has already been done without words. A child who looks at a ball and says *ba* might be making an assertion, telling the adults to look at the ball. In contrast, *Mama* accompanied by a whine and reaching for an object out of reach appears to be a request. In the latter instance, the child is more insistent about a response.

Communicative competence and early comprehension   The discussion so far has focused on how simple types of **communicative competence**—knowing how to use gestures and words to show off objects, to make assertions, to make requests, and the like—figure into the child's prelinguistic gestures and early speech acts. There is somewhat less information available on how this knowledge influences early comprehension activities, but what little there is suggests that young children also use these communicatively based strategies for comprehension prior to developing full mastery of the various structures of their language. Children seem to comprehend language in a manner similar to how they produce it, with attention given to concrete manipulations of objects in the immediate environment.

Shatz (1978) has shown that young children often respond to complex speech by using a simple, action-based comprehension strategy. The strategy is merely to respond to an utterance by performing an action on the object that is specified in the utterance. For example, if a parent wanted her daughter to put a doll in a toy swing and said, *Why don't you put the doll in the swing?*, the child could respond correctly by merely identifying one or two key words in this complex, interrogative sentence and then doing the most obvious thing that could be done with these objects. Suppose, instead, that the child were asked, *Do you want to put the doll in the swing?* Here the sentence calls for an informing response, as Shatz calls it, rather than an action response. Shatz reasoned that if a child were using the simple action strategy, then the syntactic form of the sentence, which specifies the appropriate response, would have little effect on the child's response. Shatz's subjects, who were 19 to 34 months of age, followed this pattern in their responses to sentences about toy objects. For example, 70% of the responses to the simple imperative *Put the dog in the car* were action responses, which are correct responses to an imperative. Yet 64% of responses to *Do you want to put the dog in the car?* were also action responses, when here an informing response is called for. Shatz found a consistent preference for action responses across a wide range of sentence types.

It is easy to overestimate the specific linguistic competence of the young child because we are oblivious to strategies such as these. It appears that young children use their understanding of the cognitive meaning of situations to help figure out what adults are saying. The general thesis that children use meaning as a clue to language has been stressed by other researchers. Macnamara (1972), for example, claims that "infants learn their language by first determining, independent of language, the meaning which a speaker intends to convey to them, and by then working out the relationship between meaning and language" (p. 1). The evidence presented here is consistent with this view. Meaning—that is, a primitive system of intentions—precedes and guides both comprehension and production.

Summary

Children are born into a social world. Adults speak differently to children than to adults, and these speech patterns introduce infants to the use of language as a social instrument. For their part, infants appear to be well prepared to benefit from these lessons, given that they have at least some ability to perceive speech prior to birth.

Children seem to be cognitively ready to communicate intentionally by about 8 months of age. Although their speech is not well developed at this time, they utilize gestures in flexible ways to communicate their needs to their caregivers. Moreover, children's communicative knowledge influences how they interpret the speech of others. We now turn to how these communication skills may figure in the child's acquisition of phonology.

Early Phonology

Children's acquisition of the sound system of their language does not occur in isolation of the communicative processes we have just discussed. Rather, children come to the task of learning phonology with some knowledge of how to communicate in nonverbal ways. The prelinguistic infant knows how to use gestures to make assertions and requests, and once early speech sounds are mastered, they are quickly used for these same communicative functions. The child's first attempts at producing sounds, however, appear to have more to do with practicing with the sound system than with communicating with others. Eventually, the abilities to communicate without words and to vocalize without meaning merge into productive and communicative speech.

The task of identifying what the child knows about phonology is difficult, for the ways in which phonological knowledge is expressed can often be rather indirect. As evidence of this point, consider the following case.

Our next door neighbor's child, a preschooler, is hard to understand because she tends to make phonological substitutions. Eventually we were able to figure out her system. When she asked about our son, Michael, she called him *Mytul*; when talking about our dog, Zeke, she said *Zete*; and when interested in our cat, she would inquire as to the whereabouts of our *titty*. By paying attention to the patterns of her substitutions and to the context of her utterances (for example, when she announced she had *tate* for dinner), some semblance of understanding could be achieved. As a check on whether we were right, we sometimes tried to repeat what she said, but we quickly learned that we had to repeat our version, not hers. For example, if we said *Mytul*, she would appear irritated at this adult silliness:

Child:	Where is Mytul?
Adult:	You mean Mytul?
Child:	No, Mytul!
Adult:	Oh, Michael?
Child:	Yes, Mytul!

Further conversation revealed a curious discrepancy between her natural and her imitated speech. After hearing her use the term *Zete* once too often, we asked her to listen carefully and repeat the word *Zeke*. Surprisingly, she did so accurately. Nevertheless, moments later, while talking about one event or another, she went right back to *Zete*.

There are several points about phonological development that are evident in this little interchange. First, while young children make many errors in their speech, the errors are systematic, not random. This girl consistently substituted /t/ for /k/ and deleted the initial /s/ in a word. Second, apparently children can produce a distinction in imitation that cannot be made accurately in natural conversational speech. Third, apparently a child can perceive a distinction that she cannot produce, an occurrence that has been christened the **fis phenomenon** after a child who called fish *fis* (Berko & Brown, 1960).

Our survey of phonological development begins with the child's perception of speech, then turns to the production of speech.

The Development of Speech Perception

Categorical perception in infancy   A considerable amount of research indicates that young infants display perceptual skills that are similar to the phenomenon of categorical perception. Recall from Chapter 4 that categorical perception refers to the inability to perceive sounds any better than we can identify them. In adults, this phenomenon is studied by giving listeners an identification test followed by a discrimination test. In the identification test, a series of sounds are presented and the listener must identify the phonemic category of the sound. For instance, the sounds /b/ and /p/ differ in voice onset time (VOT)—the time between when the sound is released at the lips and when the vocal cords begin vibrating. Typically, English-speaking listeners hear VOTs of less than 25 milliseconds as /b/ and those greater than 25 milliseconds as /p/. In the discrimination test, listeners are presented with two different sounds, then a repetition of one of them, and must say which of the first two sounds the third sound matched. In some instances, the first two sounds come from the same phonemic category (such as 0 and 20 millisecond VOTs), and in other cases, the sounds come from different categories (such as 20 and 40 millisecond VOTs). Adult listeners perform very well when the sounds come from different phonemic categories, but very poorly when the sounds are from the same phonemic category.

A series of fascinating studies have explored infant categorical perception of speech sounds. The first study, which we discussed in Chapter 3, was performed by Eimas, Siqueland, Juscyzk, and Vigorito (1971). They presented 1- and 4-month-old infants with pairs of speech sounds. One pair consisted of sounds with VOTs of 20 and 40 milliseconds (heard by adults as /ba/ and /pa/, respectively). The second pair consisted of VOTs of 0 and 20 milliseconds (heard by adults as /ba/), and the third included VOTs of 60 and 80 milliseconds (heard by adult as /pa/). Infants were attached to a pacifier that recorded their sucking responses. Each time an infant responded, one member of a pair was presented. When the infants grew tired of the same stimulus (that is, when the level of response fell below a predetermined level), the other member of the pair was presented. When the infants were presented with the second member of either of the last two pairs, there was no change in the sucking rate, and the infants appeared not to notice the difference. When the second member came from a different phonemic category, however, their rate of sucking increased sharply, indicating that the infants perceived the change. Eimas and colleagues suggest that these results indicate that infants are born with perceptual mechanisms that are attuned to speech categories.

It should be noted that the procedures used to study infant categorical perception are not identical to those used in studies of adults. In adults, one needs to compare identification and discrimination performance in order to determine if a stimulus has been perceived categorically. There is no corresponding way to assess identification of speech sounds in infants, so we are left with their discrimination performance. It is ordinarily assumed that the discriminations that infants make reflect comparisons across phonemic categories (see, for example, Eimas, Miller, & Jusczyk, 1987, p. 167; see also Kuhl, 1987). This appears to be a reasonable assumption, although it is not clear how to test it.

In any case, these results have been extended by Lasky, Syrdal-Lasky, and Klein (1975), who studied several phonemic contrasts in Guatemalan infants born into Spanish-speaking homes. The infants were between 4 and 6½ months of age. The study included three pairs of VOT contrasts. The first was between 20 and 60 milliseconds, which corresponds to the distinction between voiced and voiceless sounds in English. The second was a distinction between **prevoiced** sounds (in which vocal cord vibration precedes consonantal release) and voiced sounds. The VOTs were − 60 and − 20 milliseconds. (The prevoiced/voiced distinction is phonemic in Thai but not in English or Spanish.) The third pair included VOT values of − 20 and 20 milliseconds; Spanish speakers, unlike speakers of English and many other languages, perceive the voiced/voiceless distinction as falling between these two values. Lasky and colleagues found that the Guatemalan infants perceived the first two distinctions but not the third. That is, they perceived two distinctions that are not part of their language but did not perceive the one that is. Similarly, infants from English-speaking environments perceive the prevoiced/voiced distinction categorically (Aslin, Pisoni, Hennessy, & Perey, 1981).

These and related studies (Streeter, 1976) suggest that infants are born with the ability to perceive a number of phonemic distinctions. Perhaps the most interesting aspect of these studies is that they clearly demonstrate that infants are not limited to those distinctions that are phonemic in the language to which they are exposed. Thus, it seems quite unlikely that these perceptual abilities would have arisen out of the brief linguistic experience they have had. On the contrary, the observation that infants perceive phonemic categories from other languages but not their own suggests that categorical perception is innate.

The role of language experience   The ability to perceive phonemic distinctions from other languages declines in strength during the first year of life. Werker, Gilbert, Humphrey, and Tees (1981) compared 6- and 8-month-old infants from English-speaking communities, English-speaking adults, and Hindi adults. All three groups demonstrated the ability to distinguish between voiced and voiceless sounds, a distinction that is recognized in both Hindi and English. But only the Hindi adults and the infants were capable of distinguishing between pairs of Hindi sounds. It appears as if we lose some of our perceptual abilities over time.

Werker and Tees (1984) have demonstrated that this developmental decline occurs by 1 year of age. They examined the perception of a phonemic contrast in Salish/Thompson (a language spoken in British Columbia) and a Hindi contrast in three groups of infants from English-speaking families. The youngest group (6 to 8 months) showed considerable sensitivity to these contrasts, but there was considerable decline at the middle (8 to 10 months) and especially the older (10 to 12 months) age ranges. Infants in the oldest group showed essentially no ability to perceive these nonnative contrasts.

Werker and Pegg (1992) argue that the developmental changes they have observed are best described as a form of perceptual reorganization as opposed to a complete loss of earlier abilities. This view is supported by a study by Best, McRoberts, and Sithole (1988), who found no perceptual decline in the ability to distinguish sounds from Zulu click consonants. These consonants, which are very dissimilar to English sounds, were discriminated successfully by English-speaking adults and by 12- to 14-month-old infants from English-speaking homes. Best and her colleagues suggest that the decline found in earlier studies reflects a process of phonological reorganization in which phones are organized into the phonemic categories of the native language. Phones that do not fit into any of these categories (such as click consonants) presumably do not undergo this reorganization and, consequently, there is no decline in discriminating them.

The role of prosodic factors   We have been discussing infants' perception of speech segments, but there is also the question of how well they can perceive suprasegmentals or prosodic factors. A recent study by Mehler and colleagues (1988) found that infants could distinguish between utterances in their maternal language and those in another language by 4 days of life. The researchers suggest that these discrimination abilities are based on prosodic cues such as intonational contours. It is interesting to note in this light that children develop the ability to use intonation in their own utterances quite rapidly.

The Development of Speech Production

We have seen that during a period that is often called prelinguistic, the first year of life, infants can demonstrate some sophisticated speech perception abilities. We now turn to their production of speech.

Babbling   Children's early vocalizations pass through a series of stages (Oller, 1980; Stark, 1980). By the end of the second month, infants begin to do a lot of cooing. Coos are acoustically more varied than cries, as infants exercise some control over their articulatory organs to produce a greater variety of sounds. Coos tend to be made in the back of the mouth and are similar to back vowels and velar consonants.

A little later, by about 6 to 7 months, babbling, or sounds that approximate speech, begin. Infants first use **reduplicated babbling,** in which they repeat a consonant-vowel sequence, such as *babababa*. Similar tendencies have been found in various languages (Oller, 1980; Stark, 1980). By 11 to 12 months, infants use **variegated babbling,** in which syllable strings consist of varying consonants and vowels, such as *bigodabu*. It is also about this time that infants begin to impose an sentence-like intonational contours on their utterances, and their vowels begin to sound similar to those in their native language (Boysson-Bardies, Halle, Sagart, & Durand, 1989). These developments, along with the decline of categorical perception of nonnative contrasts, suggest that infants are beginning to acquire the phonology of their native language by late in their first year.

Babbling is thought to be a form of language play by the infant, a form of play in which various sounds are practiced and mastered before they are used in communicative ways. There are several reasons to think that babbling is fundamentally noncommunicative early on. One is that sounds made during babbling are similar to, but phonologically more sloppy than, the corresponding sounds made later on. While the *ma* of the 7-month-old and the 18-month-old may sound similar, when the two utterances are examined spectrographically, the earlier sound is generally "sloppier" and exhibits a greater range of acoustic properties than true speech. Another reason is that infants have been found to babble more often when an adult is not present than when one is present (Nakazima, 1975). For instance, babies often babble in the crib when awakening and before falling asleep. Since no one else is present, it is difficult to see these as communicative acts.

Transition to speech   By the end of the first year, two aspects of the infant's development—the use of gestures to convey messages and the mastery of speech sounds in noncommunicative situations—begin to merge. Now the child is capable of using speech sounds to communicate meaning.

Children come to use "true" words due to several processes. There is greater motor control of the speech apparatus, which enables infants to make sounds in a more precise way. There is cognitive maturation, as we saw in the previous section, that enables infants to express communicative intent. And there is the dawning awareness that specific objects are represented by specific symbols in the language: things have names!

Before children fully grasp this latter point, they sometimes invent their own symbols to refer to objects or events in their environment. These personalized words are called **idiomorphs.** Interestingly, children at this stage of development use their idiosyncratic sounds in a highly consistent way. My daughter Rachel, when she was about a year old, referred to milk as *ca ca*. It took us a while to understand what she was saying, but once we did, communication proceeded smoothly.

Another example of an idiomorph is reported by Reich (1986), who told of a child who referred to ice cream as *ABCDE*. Although his parents were initially puzzled, they eventually figured it out. They tended to spell out certain words that they didn't want the child to know, so they might ask each other, *Would you like some I-C-E C-R-E-A-M?* The child couldn't spell it, so he simply used the only letters he knew! But my favorite example comes from Hakuta (1986), who reported that a child said *Whew!* as a way of saying hello to guests who came to the house. It turns out that the mother often greeted the child in the morning in this way, along the lines of *Whew! You must have some load in your pants!*

As these examples suggest, children appear to draw from their language experience in forming these idiomorphs. Sometimes the idiomorphs are simplifications of adult speech or relate to the sounds of the objects to which they refer (as opposed to the sounds of the words used to refer to the objects).

Idiomorphs underline several important aspects of development. First, they indicate that children's language is creative. Children do not simply imitate the language they hear, but, instead, sometimes take this language and use it in novel ways. We will observe several other aspects of children's linguistic creativity throughout this and the following two chapters. Second, idiomorphs indicate that children have learned that it is important to be consistent when referring to objects. Only a short while earlier, they might well have used various sounds in random combinations and hoped for the best. The consistency of idiomorphs suggests that infants know that it is important to be consistent even if they have not yet grasped that there are conventional sounds in languages. Or perhaps they know this, but don't know the names of these objects. In either case, idiomorphs are a transitional stage between babbling and true words, one that indicates, once again, that children's awareness of communicative processes may precede their knowledge of language structure.

Phonological processes in early words   Shortly after their first birthday, children begin to produce recognizable words. Some simple words may be pronounced correctly from the start. But, as we saw earlier in this section, in other instances children's versions of words differ from adult versions. By examining these differences, we can draw some inferences about children's phonological processes.

Let's look at some of the regularity in children's pronunciation of adult words. Table 10-1 lists four processes that commonly occur. **Reduction** occurs when children delete or eliminate sounds. It is common for preschool children to have difficulty with consonant clusters and to reduce clusters when they occur at the beginning of a word, such as saying *tore* for *store*. They may also reduce later segments of words, such as saying *baw* for *bottle*. **Coalescence** occurs when phonemes from different syllables are combined into a single syllable. In the example in Table 10-1, the *f* in the third syllable is combined with the rest of the first syllable. **Assimilation** occurs when children change one sound to make it similar to another sound in the same word, such as saying *nance* for *dance* or *fweet* for *sweet*. In the second example, the *f* is articulated closer to the front of the mouth than *s*, making it more similar to the bilabial *w*. **Reduplication** occurs when one syllable of a multisyllabic word is repeated, as in *dada* for *daddy*. These processes are common but not invariant in child language; different children may use different processes to varying extents.

Why do children make these errors? A simple explanation states that the child cannot discriminate between the sounds that are confused. For example, the child might actually hear *stop* as *top*. Much anecdotal evidence, such as children's objections to adult imitations of their utterances as "silly," argues against this

Table 10-1. Phonological Processes Used by Children

Type	Examples
Reduction	*Tore* for *store*
	Baw for *bottle*
Coalescence	*Paf* for *pacifier*
Assimilation	*Nance* for *dance*
	Means for *beans*
Reduplication	*Titty* for *kitty*

Sources: L. Bloom and M. Lahey, *Language Development and Language Disorders* (New York: Wiley, 1978) and L. Menn and C. Stoel-Gammon, "Phonological Development: Learning Sounds and Sound Patterns," in J. B. Gleason (eds.), *Language Development*, 3rd ed. (New York: Macmillan, 1993), pp. 65–113.

view. Also, this view cannot explain why errors are typically made in only one direction. If the child cannot tell the difference between two sounds, then she should substitute one or another equally often, but generally this is not what happens. More often than not, the errors are only in one direction.

Another possibility is that the child simply cannot produce the omitted sounds. While somewhat plausible, this view cannot account for studies of imitation that show that many errors made in spontaneous speech are not made in imitation (Eilers & Oller, 1975, cited in Dale, 1976). It also cannot explain a situation such as the one described by N. V. Smith (1973), who heard a child say *puddle* as *puggle*, yet say *puddle* in place of *puzzle*. Here the child is capable of producing *puddle* but nevertheless fails to do so in the correct context. Something more than articulatory difficulties seems to be involved.

A third possibility is that these simplification errors are part of a more general linguistic process (Dale, 1976; Oller, 1974). Children mastering a phonological system must also pay attention to the syntactic, semantic, and pragmatic features of their utterances. A complex phonological sequence might "overload" their information processing capacity. This position would predict deviations from adult speech in the direction of simpler consonant-vowel sequences, particularly in spontaneous speech. When the child is merely imitating speech, however, less attention needs to be given to these other levels of language.

It is not possible at present to firmly conclude that any of these ideas are correct. Although there are reasons to reject a perceptual explanation and doubt a production explanation, the evidence in favor of the processing-load explanation is somewhat indirect.

Summary

Infants demonstrate the ability to perceive various speech distinctions, including some not in their native language, shortly after birth. The ability to perceive most nonnative contrasts declines by the end of the first year.

Infants progress through a series of stages in speech production during their first year. Later forms of babbling reflect the child's linguistic experience more closely than earlier forms. The child's mastery of the sound system of the language proceeds largely independently of communication processes. Sound and meaning merge with the development of the first words, at about 1 year of age.

Children's renditions of adult words vary systematically from the adult target. Several phonological processes are commonly found in early child speech, including reduction, coalescence, assimilation, and reduplication.

One Word at a Time

Children usually utter their first words at around 12 months of age, and for the next few months most of their utterances consist of single words produced in isolation. Not until the latter half of the second year do they produce simple multiword combinations. The single-word stage of speech that occupies most of the first half of the second year is the focus of this section.

At this period, several developments begin to take shape at once. Children come to master certain words as labels for regular features of their environment, such as common toys, members of the family, and favorite events. In short, the child begins to acquire the lexicon of the language. The ability to label the immediate, concrete environment brings a degree of tangibility to the child's interaction with the social world, since it is now possible for parents to directly tutor their children in the acquisition of vocabulary, the appropriate use of various words, and in the correct pronunciation of them.

At the same time, children are developing the ability to make comments about the world around them. Since the child has only one word at his disposal, it is often difficult for parents to discern what the child means, but it is clear that children at the one-word stage are capable of expressing meanings that would be conveyed, by a more mature speaker, in a longer utterance. Precisely what the child means and what prevents him from expressing these thoughts more fully are questions that child language investigators have pursued.

Lexical Development

Estimates of children's vocabulary growth indicate that children typically have acquired 14,000 words by age 6 (Carey, 1978). If we assume that children learn words from roughly 18 months on, this amounts to an average of 8 words per day. Although this is an impressive accomplishment, it is useful to remember that all of us, including children, "know" words in different ways. As we saw in Chapter 5, words have a number of attributes. Words have reference as well as meaning, and have connotations as well as denotations. The lexical entries for words in our internal lexicon includes semantic, syntactic, phonological, and orthographic attributes. It will take years for children to master many of these features.

Early words   Children begin by focusing on words related to the here and now, an observation that fits well with Piaget's description of the sensorimotor period of cognitive development. Many of their early words consist of nominals that refer to concrete aspects of their environment. They learn the names of the toys they play with, the clothes they wear, and the food they eat. Children have a bias toward objects that change or move in response to their actions; they are more likely to learn the word *ball* than the word *chair*.

Their early vocabulary, however, is not limited to nominals. As Nelson (1973) has shown, children use words from various grammatical classes early on. Nelson found that general nominals such as *ball* and *car* were most prevalent, followed by specific nominals (*Mommy*), action words (*up, go*), modifiers (*dirty, pretty*), personal and social words (*please, want*), and function words (*what, for*). As Reich (1986) has noted, names for articles of clothing that the child cannot easily manipulate (such as *diaper*) as well as objects in the environment that do not move (*tree*) are conspicuously absent on this list.

Overextensions and underextensions   One portion of lexical development is referential learning, the process of learning what objects in the world various words refer to. As children begin to learn these words, they often make errors in their assignment of new objects to word classes. Sometimes, they include too many items into their word classes, a phenomenon referred to as **overextension.** Examples are when children refer to all four-legged animals as dogs or all round objects as moon. Typically, these errors occur when the child identifies one attribute of a complex stimulus with the name and then applies the name to another object with the same attribute. Rescorla (1980) has studied children's overextensions and found that some, like the examples above, are based on perceptual similarities between objects. Others are based on other kinds of similarity, such as functional (a child referring to a shirt stuck on a person's head as a *hat*), contextual (calling a crib blanket a *nap*), and affective (referring to a forbidden object as *hot*).

Children also use **underextensions,** in which they use a word in a more restrictive way than adult usage. Reich (1986) provides an interesting example. When his son, Quentin, was asked *Where's the shoes?* when he was in his parents' bedroom, he would crawl to his mother's closet and play with her shoes. If other shoes were between Quentin and the closet, he would crawl around them to get to his mother's shoes. Similarly, his father's shoes did not count. Reich found that Quentin's notion of *shoes* gradually expanded to coincide with adult usage.

There are several possible reasons why children use overextensions and underextensions. On some occasions, their conceptual categories may actually differ from those of adults; children may, for instance, initially regard cows and dogs as part of the same category until being told otherwise. On other occasions, they may know perfectly well that a cow is not a dog, but not know what it is called (or be able to retrieve the name). In this instance, a child might deliberately mislabel an object as a learning strategy; that is, the child might intentionally use an inappropriate name in order to be corrected and hear the appropriate name. On still other occasions, the child's misuse of words may reflect an attempt at humor.

The role of adult speech   When a child's speech is incorrect, the caregiver has an opportunity to provide the correct name. A general characterization of this process has been made by Brown (1958), who referred to it as the **original word game.** In this game, the child points at an object, often saying *What's that?*, and the adult supplies the name. Then the child attempts to say the word, and the adult corrects the child if needed. Alternatively, the adult may point at an object and supply the name. In either case, the child comes to learn the name typically associated with a given object.

This game may sound simple, but there are several ways in which the process can go awry. The basic problem is that there is no one-to-one association between a word and its referent. For example, more than one word may apply to same referent. Consider the following situation. You are sitting in your home with your child on your lap, reading a book together. You come to a picture of an ostrich. Do you call it an *ostrich* or a *bird*? People may reasonably differ as to what is most appropriate. Some may feel that it is unnecessary for children to learn complicated or detailed words and that it suffices for the child to simply know that it is a kind of bird for now. Others think that it is confusing for a child to be told that it is a bird and later told that it is an ostrich, so one should call it by its correct name from the outset. This dilemma reappears in many contexts: Do we call it *banana* or *fruit*? *Penny* or *money*? *Car* or *vehicle* or *Toyota*?

It turns out that caregivers are very systematic in how they go about dealing with this matter (Mervis & Mervis, 1982). They tend to choose the **basic level** term. Basic level terms, as discussed by Rosch and her colleagues (Rosch, Mervis, Gray, Johnson, & Boyes-Braem, 1976), are those in which broad similarities exist across exemplars of that category. In general, basic level terms are intermediate in a hierarchy. Thus, after children have learned these terms, caregivers are able to move up in the hierarchy as well as move down. Ultimately the child comes to acquire the kind of semantic network we discussed in Chapter 5.

Book reading provides an opportunity for parents to teach their children the names of objects.

There is another, related problem confronting the child. Just as a given referent may be named by several words, it is also possible that a given word may apply to more than one referent. Bloom and Lahey (1978) give an example of a child who calls a window pane *water*. What might lead to such an error? Bloom and Lahey suggest that if initially shown a glass of water and told that it was *water*, the child, reasonably enough, might think that the caregiver was referring to the glass and subsequently generalize the concept to window panes.

It is also possible for children to think that the referent is only one part of an object rather than the whole object. If an adult points at a dog and supplies the name, how is the child to know whether the name refers to the entire animal or to only to, say, the dog's tail? Once again, it appears that the naming practices that caregivers use in talking to young children assist them. Ninio (1980; Ninio & Bruner, 1978) examined the types of **ostensive definitions** that caregivers provide for infants. An ostensive definition is a statement of the form *That is an x*. Note that such definitions are inherently ambiguous, as they could refer to the whole object, part of the object, or an action performed by the object. Certainly if caregivers were inconsistent in the level of reference, such definitions would have little didactic value. Ninio found that 95% of the definitions she observed referred to the entire object, and on these occasions where only parts were referred to, the whole object was named immediately afterward. Moreover, *What's that?* questions were typically used to elicit the name of the whole object, not a part.

Other studies have examined the role of gestures in early lexical development. Both Murphy (1978) and Ninio and Bruner (1978) studied mother/child interactions during book reading and found that infants' pointing gestures were typically followed by the mother labeling the indicated pictures. Masur (1982) examined how mothers responded to such child gestures as pointing, extending objects, and open-handed reaching. Mothers were especially sensitive to children's pointing gestures, usually reciprocating with word labels. The children, in turn, come to respond with more object labels to pointing than other gestures. Thus, caregivers appear to provide a model for naming objects that children later mirror.

These studies suggest that adult naming practices guide children through lexical development. Adults tend to have clear preferences for where to begin the learning process and focus on these aspects early on to prevent undue confusion. Later on, adults branch out to other aspects of meaning. All things considered, the manner in which caregivers play the original word game seems ideally suited to promoting the child's lexical development.

Cognitive constraints   Studies of adult naming practices have been complemented by investigations of the role that **cognitive constraints** may play in lexical development. As children are exposed to adult words for the objects, there are many possible referents for these words (Quine, 1960). It seems unlikely that children explore every possible meaning of a given word, given what we have learned about the speed of lexical acquisition. Adult naming practices help the child, but some theorists believe that the child must have certain expectations about word learning in order to maximally benefit from these lessons.

The notion of cognitive constraint is that children are constrained to consider only some of these possibilities, or at least give priority to them over others (Markman, 1989).

Recent studies suggest several possible constraints. One is called the **whole object bias:** when children encounter a new label, they prefer to attach the label to the entire object rather than to part of the object. To return to the earlier example, when someone points to an object and says *dog*, the child assumes that the word is a label for the entire object rather than the dog's tail. In addition, children seem to use a **taxonomic bias:** they will assume that the object label is a taxonomic category rather than a name for an individual dog (Markman & Hutchinson, 1984). For example, they will assume that *dog* is a label for a group of animals, not just Fido.

A third constraint is called **mutual exclusivity bias:** it refers to the fact that, if a child knows the name of a particular object, then the child will generally reject applying a second name to that object. Several experimental studies by Markman and Wachtel (1988) have supported the notion that children use mutual exclusivity in acquiring new words. In one, 3-year-old children were presented with pairs of objects. One member of each pair was an object for which the child already had a label (such as a banana, toy cow, or spoon), and the other was an object for which the child did not have a label (such as a lemon wedge press or a pair of tongs). The children were then asked by a puppet to *Show me the x* (*x* was a nonsense syllable). The children were much more likely to select the novel object. A subsequent study presented children with novel labels for objects for which they already had labels, such as *claw* for *hammer*. In this instance, the children interpreted the novel term as applying to only one part of the object.

Let us try to reconstruct the children's thinking. In the first study, the whole-object bias would lead the child to look for a whole object as the referent for the nonsense term. The mutual exclusivity bias would block the term being used for the familiar item, hence the child would infer that the novel term named the other object. In the second study, the whole object bias leads the child to find an object that is being named, but the object present already has a name. Since it would be a violation of mutual exclusivity to give it a second name, and since there is no other object present, the child comes to apply the new term to a part of the object.

These results suggest that children have some clear biases or preferences in learning new words. However, this is not to say that there are not violations of these principles. We have already seen one: we use *dog, collie,* and *mammal* to refer to the same animal. In order to acquire these terms, children must violate the principle of mutual exclusivity. Thus, children appear to use these constraints to guide their lexical acquisition, much as if the biases are working assumptions (Merriman & Bowman, 1989). That is, children continue to use the biases until there is evidence to the contrary.

Together with the studies of how caregivers play the original word game, these studies of cognitive constraints indicate that although children learn words very rapidly throughout the preschool period, there are numerous opportunities for error. That children make as few errors as they do is a testimony to the structure of their learning environment and the structure of their learning approach, in some combination.

Holophrases

A **holophrase** has been defined as a single-word utterance that is used by a child to express more than the meaning usually attributed to that single word by adults (Rodgon, 1976). This tendency to use single words to apparently express broader meanings has long been noted in studies of language development:

> When a very young child says *water*, he is not using the word merely as the name of the object so designated by us, but with the value of an assertion something like *I want water*, or *there is water*. (Stevenson, 1893, p. 120, cited in Barrett, 1982)

If holophrases are single words that "stand for" complete assertions, they represent an important sense of continuity with prelinguistic gestures, on the one hand, and more grammatically complex (and less ambiguous) speech on the other. Although it is generally agreed that holophrases indeed refer to more than a single lexical item, there is less agreement on exactly what they mean.

Approaches to holophrases   One early approach was to consider the holophrase as an implicit sentence. McNeill (1970) has argued that children at the holophrase stage have some knowledge of certain syntactic relations but are not able to formally express them in their speech. In this view, a single word such as *dog* might refer to the subject in the complete sentence *The dog is drinking water.*

If so, then this fuller grammatical knowledge would be likely to appear in other situations, notably in the comprehension of language. Indeed, several studies have shown that one-word speakers can comprehend more complex language than they can produce (see, for example, Shipley, Smith, & Gleitman, 1969). But these studies are hardly conclusive, for it is possible to comprehend a sentence on the basis of a combination of lexical knowledge and attention to the nonverbal context. In fact, studies have found that young children are unable to comprehend the relational meanings of simple speech (Benedict, 1978, cited in Barrett, 1982). For example, one child responded to *get Mommy's shoe* by getting a toy shoe and giving it to his mother.

A somewhat different approach was presented by Greenfield and Smith (1976). They claimed that young children use their single words as adults use sentences, but do not actually have the grammatical knowledge implicit in a sentence. By carefully examining the contexts in which children spoke, they were able to identify the different semantic relationships that were expessed in single-word speech. These relationships, in their order of occurrence, are shown in Table 10-2. Thus, *dada*, when used in a context in which the child's father has just arrived home, would express the agent relationship. If, instead, *dada* were said when the infant pointed at the father's chair, it would be an example of the

Table 10-2.   Semantic Relations in One-Word Speech

Relation	Instance
Naming	*Dada*, looking at father
Volition	*Mama*, looking at mother and at bottle of milk, whining
Agent	*Dada*, hearing someone come in
Action	*Down*, when he sits or steps down
Object	*Ball*, while throwing it
State of object	*Down*, having just thrown something down
Associated object	*Cracker*, pointing to room where crackers are kept
Possessor	*Lara*, upon seeing Lauren's empty bed
Location	*Box*, putting crayons in box

Source: P. M. Greenfield and J. H. Smith, *The Structure of Communication in Early Language Development* (New York: Academic Press, 1976).

possessor relationship. Greenfield and Smith conclude that children, in effect, use the environment as the rest of their utterance.

This more functional view of holophrases fits well with studies that have shown that one-word speakers are capable of using either intonation or gesture to accompany their single words (Barrett, 1982; Dore, 1975). In essence, the argument is that there is greater continuity in development at the functional level than at the structural level; although the child has little grammatical knowledge, she is able to express complete thoughts that will later be expressed with grammatical phrases and sentences by selectively expressing those aspects of a situation that are most unusual, interesting, or informative (see Greenfield, 1982).

Summary

Children's lexical development shows rapid gains during the second year of life. Most of their early words refer to concrete aspects of the immediate environment. Adult naming practices appear to facilitate lexical development by emphasizing whole objects over parts of objects, and basic level terms. In addition, various cognitive constraints enable children to understand otherwise ambiguous terms in an unambiguous manner.

Children at this stage also tend to use a single word to express meanings that mature speakers would express in a phrase or sentence. Holophrases appear to be precursors of multiword utterances, but it is not clear what grammatical knowledge children have at the holophrase stage.

Early Grammar

Children begin to speak in word combinations by about 2 years of age, and over the course of the next few years they make impressive advances in grasping the grammar of their native language. These aspects of grammar, of course, differ from language to language. Children learning English must pay close attention to word order, which is the primary way in which meaning is signaled. Those acquiring a more inflected language, such as Turkish, must spend a relatively greater amount of time learning the different forms or conjugations of verbs. These language differences surely play an important role in child language acquisition.

There are, however, important similarities in children's early grammatical efforts. Slobin (1985) has suggested that at least the early stages of grammatical development are similar in all of the world's languages. Studies have now been conducted on dozens of different types of languages, and these have found that what Slobin calls **basic child grammar** is a universal construction of children learning their native language. In this section, we will consider the structure of basic child grammar and some ideas researchers into child language have developed as to what rules comprise this grammar as well as review evidence that indicates individual differences in early language acquisition.

Measures of Syntactic Growth

We begin with the question of how we measure the child's syntactic development. Researchers have found it necessary to construct an index of the child's language progress in order to facilitate comparison of children at the same level of language development. You might think that the child's chronological age is a good enough index, but there are considerable differences in children's rate of language development (which may or may not be related to later language gains). In fact, two children at the same age may display very different language skills.

Researchers have developed two measures of syntactic development. The best known and most widely used is to measure the **mean length of utterances in morphemes (MLU)**. The method, as discussed by Brown (1973a), consists of taking 100 of the child's spontaneous utterances and counting the number of morphemes (meaningful units) per utterance. The MLU is a conservative index of the child's ability to combine morphemes in a productive manner. Brown counts some words that are multimorphemic in adult speech, such as *birthday*, as one morpheme for children unless there is evidence that the child understands the constituent morphemes, *birth* and *day*, and then combines them.

Using MLU, Brown divided language development into five MLU-defined stages. Stage I, consisting mainly of one- and two-word utterances, lasts until an MLU of 1.75. Stages II through V correspond to upper-limit MLUs of 2.25, 2.75, 3.5, and 4.0, respectively. Because children within normal limits vary in their rate of development, the MLU is a more useful index of a child's language growth than his or her age is. Most children, for example, are in stage I at about 24 months, but variations in either direction are not unusual. It is more informative to compare two children with similar MLUs but different ages than the other way around. Figure 10-1 shows the relationships between age and MLU for a sample of children studied by Miller and Chapman (1981).

Brown has indicated that these MLU-defined stages provide a global view of what aspects of language the child is currently mastering. Children at Stage I are putting words together. At Stage II, they are learning to modulate the meaning of

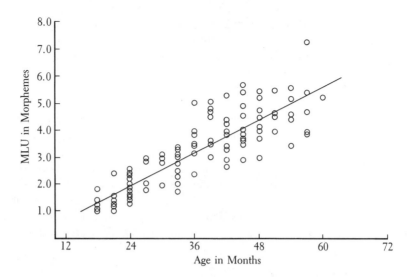

Figure 10-1.   Relationship between age (± 1 month) and mean length of utterance (MLU) in morphemes for 123 children. [From J. F. Miller and R. S. Chapman, "The Relationship between Age and Mean Length of Utterance in Morphemes," *Journal of Speech and Hearing Research* 24 (1981): 154–161.]

their utterances by the use of grammatical morphemes. Stages III and IV are devoted to learning more complex constructions, such as questions and negatives. Most research into children's grammatical development has focused on Brown's first two stages. In fact, it is generally agreed that the MLU loses its value as an index of language development beyond about 4.0 (Tager-Flusberg, 1993).

A newer measure called the **Index of Productive Syntax (IPSyn)** has been developed to better assess later development (Scarborough, 1990). This approach counts the child's use of various noun phrases, verb phrases, questions, negatives, and sentence structures. It measures the emergence of these structures, not their mastery; Scarborough gives the child credit for each occurrence of each type of structure over a corpus of 100 utterances. Preliminary evidence suggests that the IPSyn is a valid measure of grammatical development. For instance, the IPSyn scores of children at 30 months of age were found to predict subsequent reading disabilities (Scarborough, 1990).

We will examine the acquisition of complex sentences more thoroughly in Chapter 11. For now, our focus is on children's first grammatical acquisitions. A central question is how children acquire the grammatical categories of adult speech, such as subject and predicate.

Emergence of Grammatical Categories

The structure of early utterances   It may seem odd to talk of two-word utterances as sentences having a grammatical structure. After all, early utterances such as *allgone baby* and *more crayon* are hardly grammatical by adult standards and may appear to be little more than random combinations of previously acquired words. Most investigators of child language, however, agree with Sachs (1976) that "the two-word utterances he [the child] says are neither simple imitations of adult utterances nor random combinations of the words he knows. Rather, they follow from the system that the child is using to express meanings at that time" (p. 156). There are several lines of evidence in support of this view.

First, when children first put words together, they tend to combine content words and leave out function words, thus producing utterances such as *More milk, Push truck,* and so on. This is similar to the way adults phrase utterances when sending a telegram where there is a premium on word cost: *lost money, send cash,* and so on. This suggests that the child has an understanding of this grammatical distinction as well as an intuitive appreciation that content words may be more informative than function words.

Second, as children put words together, there are regular patterns to which words go in which positions in the sentence (Braine, 1976). A child, for example, is much more likely to say *Allgone sock* than *Sock allgone.* Thus, the child is not merely stringing together separate words that she knows but is putting them together in a systematic way.

Interpretations of early multiword utterances　　There is therefore a good deal of structure in the child's early multiword utterances. However, it is one thing to say that children put words together in a systematic way and quite another to identify the nature of this system. A considerable amount of research has pursued the question of how to best describe the linguistic system that governs the child's early utterances.

Consider a simple utterance such as *Baby cry.* We can describe this in syntactic terms as a subject followed by a predicate. Alternatively, we can describe it in semantic terms as an agent (an animate being who is the instigator of an action) and an action. Although these two characterizations may appear to be similar, they differ in degree of abstractness (Bowerman, 1973). The subject of a sentence may be an agent, but could also be an object (*The book is on the table*), an instrument (*The nail pierced the wood*), or a location (*Dallas is dull*). If we attribute the syntactic notion of subject to a child, we are implying that the child grasps the similarity between the subjects in such diverse sentences, which seems unlikely.

Alternatively, Brown (1973a) has claimed that these early utterances are expressing semantic relations. Brown developed a list of 11 semantic relations that, he says, comprise 75% of children's two-word utterances (see Table 10-3). Several of these are similar to the relations expressed in one-word speech (compare with Table 10-2); but the agents, actions, and locations of younger children are in separate utterances, while older children are able to combine these elements in a single utterance. These semantic relations also appear in other languages, such as Russian, Finnish, and Samoan (Slobin, 1970).

Braine (1976) has criticized the semantic relation approach and has argued that children's early rules tend to be more limited in scope. Some correspond to semantic properties, such as actor and action and possessor and possessed, but Braine argues that most nouns in child speech express a more narrow range of semantic content than the adult versions.

Other rules noted by Braine (1976) are even more limited and simply reflect children's preference for putting certain words in specific positions in a sentence.

Table 10-3.   Semantic Relations in
Two-Word Speech

Relation	Instance
Nomination	*That ball*
Recurrence	*More ball*
Nonexistence	*Allgone ball*
Agent and action	*Daddy hit*
Action and object	*Hit ball*
Agent and object	*Daddy ball*
Action and locative	*Go store*
Entity and locative	*Book table*
Possessor and possession	*Daddy chair*
Entity and attribute	*Big house*
Demonstrative and entity	*That box*

Source: R. Brown, A *First Language: The Early Stages* (Cambridge, MA: Harvard University Press, 1973).

Thus, common rules are "more plus recurring element" (*More car, More hot,* and so on) and "want plus desired entity" (*Want car, Want truck,* and so on). The comparison of Braine's treatment of such utterances with Brown's is revealing. Although Brown would regard *Want car* as an instance of a action-object relation, Braine's claim is that it is merely the word *want* in the first position attached to any number of desired objects. That is, in Braine's view, the child has not yet acquired the general concept action, let alone the syntactic category verb, but has merely a rule that identifies a particular word with a particular position in the sentence. These rules are not so much syntactic or semantic as merely positional.

Acquiring grammatical categories   Ultimately the child must grasp categories that are defined in syntactic terms, and there has been much debate concerning how the child does this. One suggestion is that children use their knowledge of semantic relations to learn syntactic relations. This process is known as **semantic bootstrapping** (Bowerman, 1973; Pinker, 1987). As Bowerman (1973) puts it:

> children launch their syntactic careers by learning simple order rules for combining words which in their understanding perform semantic functions such as *agent, action,* and *object acted upon,* or perhaps other even less abstract semantic functions. Through additional linguistic experience a child may begin to recognize similarities in the way different semantic concepts are formally dealt with and to gradually reorganize his knowledge according to the more abstract grammatical relationships which are functional in the particular language he is learning. (p. 213)

For instance, children ordinarily use sentences in which the grammatical subject is the semantic agent. Then they use this correspondence to begin learning the grammatical category of subject. As children become more linguistically experienced, they induce grammatical concepts from the semantic-positional configurations already acquired. Exactly how this is done is still very much up in the air, but Maratsos (1982; Maratsos & Chalkley, 1980) has provided evidence that children acquire some of the concepts during the preschool years. Maratsos suggests that children do this by paying attention to the grammatical operations that given linguistic forms take. For example, while *like* and *fond* are similar semantically, *like* takes the grammatical morpheme *-ed* while the past tense of *fond* is formed with the auxiliary *be* (*was fond*). These two are also distinct in their present tensing, with *like* taking the *-s* morpheme and *fond* taking the auxiliary. According to Maratsos, children analyze the correlations in grammatical operations between linguistic forms and regroup forms with similar operations into more abstract and differentiated grammatical classes.

Comprehension and Production

Most of the emphasis here has been on children's language production, but language comprehension at this period of development has also been studied. The relationship between comprehension and production in language development has often been a matter of considerable interest. To parents, it appears that children comprehend certain types of utterances before they are able to produce such utterances themselves. What does the research say concerning this issue?

Various attempts have been made to assess children's language comprehension. Most studies have presented children with sentences and then had them indicate through nonverbal behavior their comprehension. Some have children act out sentences presented to them (for example, *Make the doll kiss the duck*), whereas others present children with sentences and have them choose by pointing to the picture that corresponds to the sentence (for example, *The dog is chasing the cat*). Although there are some discrepancies in these studies, in general the results corroborate the notion that comprehenson is in advance of production (see Tager-Flusberg, 1993, for a review).

Individual Differences

It was once thought that all children acquire language in pretty much the same way (Lenneberg, 1964). To be sure, some children might develop a little quicker than others, but the stages of development and strategies used to acquire language were assumed to be similar. Studies over the last 20 years have, however, found evidence for individual differences in language styles and strategies. Attention has now turned to the best way to characterize these differences.

On the basis of a longitudinal study of children between 1 and 2 years of age, K. Nelson (1973) has suggested two different strategies for acquiring language. Most of the children Nelson studied approached language using a **referential** strategy of attempting to learn words—mainly nouns but also some verbs, proper names, and adjectives—which referred to aspects of their immediate environment. In contrast, some children used an **expressive** strategy that emphasized social interaction. Expressive children had more diverse vocabularies, including social routines, such as *Stop it* and *I want it*, which were apparently learned as complete, unanalyzed units. They were also more likely to utter whole sentences than were referential children; they did so with poor articulation of the words but with an overall sentence intonation pattern that makes the meaning clear (Peters, 1977). Moreover, expressive children were more likely to use "dummy terms" in their early sentences (these are terms that do not carry meaning but play a role in the entire sentence). Whereas referential children seemed to regard language as a process of naming objects, expressive children appeared to be more interested in the interpersonal aspects of language.

These differences implicate different processes later in development. Referential children begin with words and combine them to form sentences, whereas expressive children eventually break down their longer utterances into individual words. In other words, referential children go from part to whole whereas expressive children go from whole to part. Once expressive children analyze their utterances into words, they may then combine the words into new utterances (Lieven, Pine, & Barnes, 1992). This suggests that the two styles of language learning may well merge later in development. K. Nelson (1975) provides some evidence for this view. She examined the later language development of her original sample of children. She found that referential speakers used a high proportion of nouns in their early utterances, whereas expressive speakers used a mix of nouns and pronouns. As their MLUs increased, referential children used fewer nouns, whereas expressive children used more. Thus, over time, the two styles began to merge. Bloom, Lightbown, and Hood (1975) found similar results.

These individual differences raise several questions. One question is how to best characterize these differences. It is not clear if they represent different degrees of competence in various language components or if they are better described as preferences. For example, are expressive children less able to learn and retain object names, or are they able to do so but prefer a style of language that will more likely elicit adult reactions?

Another question of considerable interest is the cause of the individual differences. K. Nelson (1981) has reviewed the evidence pertaining to the role of hemispheric differences, cognitive style, and environmental factors in these differences. As for environment factors, there is evidence that both the amount (Huttenlocher, Haight, Bryk, Seltzer, & Lyons, 1991) and the type (Della Corte, Benedict, & Klein, 1983) of maternal speech influences children's language styles. Della Corte and colleagues found that mothers of referential children produced more descriptive utterances and fewer prescriptive utterances than mothers of expressive children. Goldfield (1987) extended these results by showing that children's lexical preferences were influenced by both child and caregiver variables. Children who more often used objects to elicit maternal attention and whose mothers more often labeled and described toys were more likely to use referential language. Those children low on both of these variables were more likely to use expressive language.

These results show that there is more than one way to piece the puzzle of language together. Moreover, these differences serve as a useful reminder that the components into which we dissect language—syntax, semantics, phonology, and pragmatics—are not neatly separated in the child's experience. In contrast, the child must acquire one in relation to the others, as when using newly formed syntactic structures for appropriate pragmatic ends. What these individual differences suggest is that there are a number of ways of doing this.

Summary

Children begin to put words together in systematic ways, preferring some words to others, and some orders to others. A substantial amount of research has been devoted to identifying the nature of the child's grammatical development when multiword utterances begin to be produced. It is generally agreed that children know more than they are able to express, but there is a difference of opinion as to whether this knowledge can be characterized as underlying syntactic relations, underlying semantic relations, or merely positional regularities.

There are reliable individual differences in early language acquisition. Some children emphasize the referential function of language whereas others use language in a social way. These two styles of learning may merge later in development, with referential children using more pronouns and expressive children using more nouns than earlier. The styles appear to reflect characteristics of both the child and the child's caregivers.

Acquisition of Sign Language

We return in this last section to the study of American Sign Language (ASL). Throughout this book, we have periodically examined similarities and differences between signed and spoken language. In this section we discuss how children acquire American Sign Language.

As we discussed in Chapter 2, there are both similarities and differences between ASL and English. The two languages share some basic grammatical features, such as duality of patterning and linguistic productivity. At the same time, there are some differences between the two languages. We saw that ASL is more iconic than English, that it has a richer morphology, and that linguistic information is more often conveyed simultaneously in ASL than in English. And, of course, there is a difference in modality between a visual and an auditory language. These similarities and differences suggest that a comparison of the acquisition of ASL and that of speech may be illuminating. In particular, it may help clarify which aspects of language acquisition are universal, which are specific to certain types of language, and which are specific to languages in a particular modality.

We will focus on children of deaf parents who have been exposed early in life to ASL. For the most part, these children have normal hearing. These children are of interest because the conditions under which they acquire ASL are most similar to those of hearing children acquiring speech: language is presented to the child, from birth, in the context of daily events by those to whom the child is emotionally attached. Therefore, any differences that may be observed between the acquisition of ASL and English may be attributed to differences in the two languages or in modality, but not in the conditions of exposure.

Our discussion thus is not directly applicable to most deaf children. It has been estimated that only 5% to 10% of deaf children are born to deaf parents (Meier & Newport, 1990). The remaining 90% to 95% of deaf children are not typically exposed to ASL early in life. Moreover, deaf children are not likely to benefit fully from exposure to speech. It is in this sense that Meadow (1980) has commented that the basic deprivation of profound congenital deafness is one not just of sound but of language. Since hearing parents are unprepared to teach ASL to their deaf infants, many deaf children are not systematically exposed to sign language in the early years. Many deaf persons, in fact, learn sign language much later in life—from peers, not parents. Other deaf and hearing-impaired individuals use other methods of communication. These may include oral training (teaching children to speak and understand oral language) or training in manual English. Various forms of manual English express English grammar in sign form, unlike ASL, which is a separate language from English. In general, language acquisition in all of these groups is poor relative to hearing children acquiring speech (see Quigley & King, 1982).

To return to ASL, the main question we want to consider is whether developmental milestones found in oral language—babbling, one-word stage, two-word stage—have any correlates in the acquisition of sign language. As for babbling, Petitto and Marentette (1991) recently studied deaf infants acquiring ASL as a first language. The infants, born to deaf parents, were studied when they were between 10 and 14 months of age. Petitto and Marentette found that the deaf infants engaged in two types of manual activity: gestures and syllabic manual babbling. Gestures, such as raising one's arms to be picked up, were meaningful and similar to those of infants exposed to speech (discussed earlier in the chapter). In contrast, manual babbling was typically not meaningful; infants combined values of ASL parameters (handshape, location, and movement) into signs that were permissible but nonexisting forms in ASL. On the basis of these and other observations, Petitto and Marentette conclude that manual babbling is similar to vocal babbling.

The investigators also studied manual activity in hearing infants of hearing parents. Interestingly, both groups of infants used both gestures and manual babbling. However, whereas the quantity and type of gestures were similar in the two groups, manual babbling was far more common in the deaf infants.

Turning to the one-word stage, Prinz and Prinz (1979) observed a bilingual hearing child who learned English from a hearing parent and ASL from a deaf parent. This child produced her first sign at 7 months of age. By 12 months of age, the child had produced five signs but only one word. Thus, if anything, there appeared to be earlier acquisition of signs than of speech. Bonvillian, Orlansky, and Novack (1983) replicated this result with a larger group of infants. They studied the sign language of 11 children (10 hearing, 1 deaf) with deaf parents over a period of 16 months and found that these children, on the average, produced their first recognizable sign at 8.5 months, approximately 2 to 3 months before first words are recognizable.

The role of iconicity in ASL acquisition has been studied by Orlansky and Bonvillian (1984). They examined the prevalence of iconic signs in the early language of hearing children of deaf parents. Iconic signs were those in which there is a clear, transparent relationship between the sign and its referent. An example is the sign for *eat*, which involves moving one's hand back and forth into one's open mouth, as if feeding oneself. Metonymic signs, on the other hand, are those in which there is a more obscure relationship between sign and referent, one not likely to be apparent to most observers. Arbitrary signs reveal no discernible relationship between sign and referent. Orlansky and Bonvillian examined the children's sign language at two points in development: when the children had attained 10 signs (about 13 months) and again at 18 months. At the earlier period, only 31% of the signs were iconic, 34% were metonymic, and 35% were arbitrary. These percentages were very similar at 18 months. If iconicity aided early acquisition, we might expect that there would be a higher percentage of iconic signs at 13 months. Orlansky and Bonvillian concluded that iconicity is not a major factor in the precocious acquisition of sign language.

The extent and significance of a sign advantage over speech have been discussed by Petitto (1988) and by Meier and Newport (1990). Petitto contends that early signs are actually gestures used by all children, such as pointing and reaching, or are imitations of adult models. Folven and Bonvillian (1991) addressed this issue. They found that children's initial recognizable signs occurred at 8.2 months of age (replicating Bonvillian et al., 1983). However, children did not use signs referentially (that is, to name objects) until they were 12.6 months, after they had demonstrated communicative pointing; this age is comparable to the first signs of referential speech. Earlier signs were imitations of adult signs, signs used in interactive routines, and requests for familiar items.

Meier and Newport (1990) argue that the advantage for sign is only in early lexical development and does not extend to syntactic development. In addition, they suggest that peripheral differences in the two modalities may explain the earlier emergence of signs. That is, the visual system may be more developed than the auditory system at 10 months of age, the age at which, under this hypothesis, children are cognitively able to acquire lexical items.

Newport and Ashbrook (1977) examined early multisign utterances. They found that deaf children used semantic relations similar to those found in English (Bloom, Lightbown, & Hood, 1975). Moreover, the relations emerged in sign language in about the same order as was found in previous studies of English. Also, children at the two-sign stage use sign order, not morphology, to signal meaning (Newport & Ashbrook, 1977); this, of course, is similar to the first multiword utterances of young speakers. Thus, children acquiring ASL do not initially exploit the morphology of ASL when beginning to put signs together. Instead, they primarily use sign order to convey meaning, just as children do in diverse spoken languages.

On balance, these studies indicate that the course of language development is similar for signed and spoken languages, at least through the two-word stage. The only difference of note, the earlier acquisition of signs at the one-word stage, appears to reflect differences in modality, not language. Moreover, the linguistic feature most likely to lead to early sign acquisition, iconicity, apparently plays little role. These observations are consistent with the view that the early milestones of language development, in sign as in speech, are under biological control.

This is not to say that there are no differences between signed and spoken languages later in acquisition. Although children do not initially use ASL morphology in their utterances, they eventually acquire it (Bellugi, 1988; Newport & Meier, 1985). More generally, languages diverge later in development, and children acquire the rule systems of their particular language. We will discuss the later stages of language acquisition more fully in Chapter 11.

Summary

Although ASL differs from English in linguistic features such as iconicity and morphological structure, there are more similarities than differences in the early stages of acquisition of ASL and English. The primary difference is that infants acquire their first signs 2 to 3 months earlier than infants typically acquire their first words.

Review Questions

1. How can you tell whether a child is using a pointing gesture intentionally or not? What criteria are necessary for an act to be considered intentional?
2. Define communicative competence and explain the way in which it influences the child's early comprehension of speech.
3. What evidence suggests that infant perception of speech changes by about 1 year of age?
4. Give an example of each of the following: coalescence, assimilation, reduction, reduplication.
5. Why might children make phonological errors in spontaneous speech that they do not make in imitative speech?
6. How do adult naming practices assist the child's vocabulary development?
7. What is mutual exclusivity and what role does it play in the child's acquisition of words?
8. What evidence suggests that children's early grammatical categories are not equivalent to adult grammatical categories?
9. Distinguish between referential and expressive styles of language learning.
10. Compare and contrast the acquisition of American Sign Language and English.

*T*hought Questions

1. Do you think that you could promote a child's language development by pretending not to understand her? Could you retard it by quickly responding to immature forms of speech? Explain.

2. How could you interpret what a child means by a single word? What procedure would you use?

3. Children typically comprehend language at a more advanced level than they are able to produce. Why might this be so? Are there any cases in which production precedes comprehension?

4. How might the language development of a child exposed to two languages in the home differ from that of a monolingual child? In what ways might their development be similar?

11

Later Language Acquisition

- Children's grammatical development in the late preschool years includes the acquisition of grammatical morphemes and complex syntactic structures.
- Children are increasingly aware of the language that they are using. Greater linguistic awareness is related to several linguistic achievements, such as the use of metaphor and the understanding of verbal riddles.
- Children's skills as narrators and conversationalists grow during the preschool years. As they enter school, children are able to communicate in flexible ways.
- Children expand and modify their linguistic skills as they enter into formal schooling. Classroom discourse differs from discourse out of school, and written language poses different challenges than oral language.

Introduction

There was a time when attention to child language acquisition was restricted to the first few years of life. In recent years, later acquisitions by the child and, in fact, language development through the life span have become increasingly popular as topics of study. In this chapter we will discuss children's later language acquisition, roughly corresponding to developments in the late preschool and early school years.

One major theme of this period of development is that children elaborate the grammatical structures they have already acquired. They begin to embellish their simple utterances with function words and grammatical morphemes and begin to master more complex sentence constructions. A second theme is that children become more aware of language units and processes. For instance, although children may arrange words in a syntactically correct order, they may have little awareness of the syntactic rules that they are using. Awareness of language comes gradually throughout the preschool years.

The developments in linguistic awareness may affect other aspects of language as well. It is also during this period that children become able to size up different communication situations and thereby employ their linguistic resources to the best advantage. And these skills also are important when children get to school and are confronted with written language.

The organization of this chapter is as follows. We begin by surveying the acquisition of complex syntactic and semantic structures. Next we examine the child's increased awareness of language structure and language processes, especially comprehension processes. Following this we discuss the development of discourse processes, including narrative and conversational skills. Finally, we consider the special kinds of language used in the school and discuss how the child adjusts to these new demands.

Later Grammar

As we saw in the previous chapter, children make impressive strides in their acquisition of grammar in their first 2 to 3 years. They develop the ability to form simple, functional utterances such as *Daddy chair* that express their meaning relatively directly. Later grammatical acquisitions are built upon earlier accomplishments. In this section we look at two such acquisitions: grammatical morphemes and more complex sentence constructions.

Acquisition of Morphology

Grammatical morphemes   Grammatical morphemes are conspicuously absent in children's early word combinations. Children initially use word order to convey meaning, even those children acquiring highly inflected languages. But as their mean length of utterances in morphemes (MLU) approaches 2.5, morphemes such as the past tense and plural inflections and prepositions such as *in* and *on* begin to appear. Brown (1973a) notes that these morphemes "like an intricate sort of ivy, begin to grow up between and upon the major construction blocks, the nouns and verbs" (p. 249). It takes children years to fully acquire the morphological system of their language.

The first major study of the acquisition of grammatical morphemes was conducted by Brown and Cazden (Brown, 1973a; Cazden, 1968) as part of an extensive longitudinal study of three children. The researchers looked at 14 morphemes in the English language; these are shown, in their order of emergence, in Table 11-1. The procedure was as follows: they looked closely at the linguistic and nonlinguistic context of child utterances to determine whether a grammatical morpheme was obligatory in that context. For instance, suppose an adult holds up a book and asks a child *What is this?* and the child responds *That book*. It may be inferred that the child meant to say *That is a book* and thus omitted two obligatory grammatical morphemes, the copula *is* and the article *a*. Brown and Cazden used

Table 11-1.   Average Order of Acquisition of Grammatical Morphemes

Order	Morpheme	Example(s)
1	Present progressive	*I driving*
2–3	Prepositions	*in, on*
4	Plural	*balls*
5	Irregular past tense	*broke, fell, threw*
6	Possessive	*Daddy's chair*
7	Uncontractible copula	*This is hot*
8	Articles	*a, the*
9	Regular past tense	*She walked*
10	Third person present tense, regular	*He works*
11	Third person present tense, irregular	*She does*
12	Uncontractible auxiliary	*The horse is winning*
13	Contractible copula	*He's a clown*
14	Contractible auxiliary	*She's drinking*

Sources: R. Brown, *A First Language: The Early Stages* (Cambridge, MA: Harvard University Press, 1973) and J. G. de Villiers and P. A. de Villiers, *Language Acquisition* (Cambridge, MA: Harvard University Press, 1978).

a stringent criterion for when a child was considered to have acquired a morpheme—when the child used it in 90% of its obligatory contexts. Brown (1973a) concluded that the order in which children acquire these grammatical morphemes was similar across different children. De Villiers and de Villiers (1973) replicated this study by examining the order of morpheme acquisition in 21 children between 16 and 40 months of age. Their findings were highly similar to Brown's.

Brown considered several possible explanations for this sequence of development. One was the frequency with which the child hears these morphemes in adult speech. Although it might be expected that the frequency of exposure would be correlated with the ease of acquisition, Brown found no correlation between the two. For instance, definite and indefinite articles appeared with the greatest frequency in the parents' speech for all three children but ranked eighth in order of acquisition for the children. Conversely, the earliest acquisition, the present progressive, was third, fourth, and sixth in frequency, respectively, for the three sets of parents. Thus, Brown rejected the notion that frequency could explain the acquisition of grammatical morphemes.

Moerk (1980, 1981) presents an alternative view. Using a more refined measure of parental speech—frequency of parental use of morphemes just prior to the child's acquisition of the morphemes—Moerk found a relationship between frequency and order of acquisition. Moerk concludes that the relationship between frequency of exposure and morpheme acquisition may have been dismissed prematurely by Brown. Moerk's work has, in turn, been criticized by Pinker (1981), who argues that Moerk restricted his analysis to those morphemes that would be favorable to his hypothesis. Pinker found that when a different subset of morphemes was considered, the correlation between frequency and order of acquisition dropped sharply. Although the issue is far from settled, it appears that parental frequency of morphemes may be related to some extent to the child's acquisition of morphemes.

Brown also investigated the relationship between linguistic complexity and order of acquisition. He defined linguistic complexity in two ways: **semantic complexity** (also called **conceptual complexity**) refers to the complexity of the ideas expressed, whereas **syntactic complexity** (also called **formal complexity**) refers to the complexity of the expressions used to convey the idea. For instance, to assess the role of semantic complexity, Brown identified several meanings that were entailed by various morphemes. For example, the plural morpheme entails the notion of number; that is, in order to use the morpheme correctly, a speaker must attend to whether there is one or more than one of the object referred to. The third person regular entails both number (since the morpheme is used with singular but not plural subjects) and time (since it is used with the present but not the past tense). Finally, both forms of the auxiliary include these two semantic notions plus a third: temporary duration, or the notion that something is currently happening (the auxiliary is always accompanied by *-ing*). On the basis of cumulative semantic complexity, Brown predicted that the plural would be acquired before the third person regular, which would in turn be acquired before the auxiliary. As you can see in Table 11-1, the results corresponded to these predictions. Unfortunately, the syntactic analysis yields identical predictions. Using a form of transformational grammar as the measure of syntactic complexity, Brown determined that the plural, third person regular, and auxiliary required, respectively, two, three, and four transformations in their derivations. In general, both forms of complexity appeared to be related to the order of the morphemes, but Brown was unable to tease them apart.

The distinction between formal and conceptual complexity is useful, however. For one thing, it can also be applied not only to grammatical morphemes but also to different grammatical constructions in the language. For another, languages differ in the formal complexity with which they mark various notions. Thus, the distinction is relevant for understanding differences in how children acquire both morphology and syntax in different languages.

Productivity in morphology   Once children acquire morphemes, they begin to use them in productive ways. This was demonstrated by a famous study by Berko (1958). Berko showed children novel creatures and actions that were given invented names. The children were then given the opportunity to supply appropriate morphemes for these invented words (see Figure 11-1). Berko found that preschool and first-grade children showed productive control of several grammatical morphemes (plural and possessive inflections for nouns; progressive, past tense, and third person present tense for verbs). This study suggests that children are not merely learning these morphemes in rote fashion but are acquiring morphological rules.

An aspect of children's morphological productivity that has been intensively studied is the presence of **overregularizations** in their speech (Cazden, 1968; Ervin, 1964; Slobin, 1973). An overregularization is the child's use of a regular morpheme in a word that is irregular, such as the past tense morpheme in *breaked* and *goed*. The acquisition of irregular verbs typically goes through three stages. First, the child uses the word correctly. Second, the child overregularizes the word.

This is a wug.

Now there is another one.
There are two of them.
There are two _____.

Figure 11-1.   Item used to test for the plural morpheme in Berko's study. [From J. Berko, "The Child's Learning of English Morphology," *Word* 14 (1958):150–177.]

Finally, the irregular form reappears. It appears that children analyze linguistic forms that were previously unanalyzed. That is, *broke* was initially learned rote, not as an instance of an irregular past tense verb but simply as a single lexical item. Later, as the child comes to better understand the regular past tense morpheme, it is overapplied to the irregular cases. Then, when the irregular form reappears, it is with a new status, that of an exception to a general rule.

Rumelhart and McClelland (1986) provide an alternative view of how children acquire the past tense in English. Their approach is based on their parallel distributed processing model, which we discussed in Chapter 4. They argue that the mental representation of verbs is a set of connections in a network rather than rules such as the past tense rule. That is, instead of assuming that children explicitly learn grammatical rules, these researchers assert that children form associations between sound sequences in a complex network. Moreover, different sequences are in competition at any given time. It does appear that different forms of the same word compete with one another in children's language; for example, children sometimes alternate a correct form (*went*), an overregularized form (*goed*), and perhaps an amalgam (*wented*). The essence of Rumelhart and McClelland's model is that the strength of these connections gradually changes over time, partly in response to the language models to which the children are exposed. Thus, the correct form gradually overtakes the others. However, certain assumptions made by Rumelhart and McClelland, including assumptions about the speech to which children are exposed, have been questioned by Pinker and Prince (1988).

Later Syntactic Development

Children acquire grammatical morphemes gradually, over a period of years. During this time, their sentences get longer and more complex. Some of the changes in sentence length reflect the fact that children are now able to express agent, action, and object in a single sentence. For instance, whereas a younger child might express agent and action or agent and object in a sentence, a somewhat older child can express all three, as in *Daddy throw ball.*

Children also develop the ability to use different types of sentences. We will look at several emerging sentence constructions: negatives, questions, passive sentences, and complex sentences.

Negation   Although young children clearly understand the concept of negation (see, for example, L. Bloom, 1970), mastery of the negative sentence structure comes relatively late for most children. This is primarily because the syntactic structures that must be acquired are rather complex. For example, consider the negative sentence (1):

(1)   I won't be coming for dinner on Friday.

In comparison to the affirmative, this negative involves the introduction of a new element, *not* in *will not*, as well as the contraction of this phrase into *won't.*

Klima and Bellugi (1966) found that negatives come in a series of stages. The first step is simply to attach a negative word to an affirmative sentence, as in sentences (2) and (3). The second step occurs when children begin to incorporate negatives into affirmative sentences such as (4). Interestingly, this is when children first begin to use contractions, as in (5). They don't, however, use the uncontracted form of the expression (*does not*), suggesting that the *doesn't* is an isolated achievement at this point, unrelated to a general ability to form contractions of verbs. The third stage occurs when internal negatives occur, as in (5), along with the affirmative forms in (6).

(2) No wipe finger.

(3) No doggie bite.

(4) Doggie no bite.

(5) Doggie doesn't bite.

(6) Doggie does bite.

L. Bloom (1970) has questioned the first of these stages. Bloom observed that in some sentences the negative element may be properly placed at the beginning of the utterance. Consider, for example, an utterance such as (7):

(7) No mommy do it.

This could be an instance of a negative morpheme attached to an utterance, meaning *Mommy won't do it*. Alternatively, the *no* may be anaphoric, referring back to a previous utterance, meaning *No, let mommy do it*. On the basis of this and other reports, de Villiers and de Villiers (1985) concluded that the use of the external negative was not a universal stage, although some children may adopt this approach.

Questions   There are several types of questions in English. One is the **yes/no question,** which is a question that can be answered yes or no. An example is sentence (8):

(8) Can your baby walk?

The yes/no question is formed by inverting the subject with the auxiliary verb. Children have considerable difficulty with this rule and often simply use the declarative form with question intonation, as in sentence (9):

(9) Your baby can walk?

Another type of question is the **wh-question,** which is a question that begins with one of the *wh*-words (*who, what, where, when, why*). An example is sentence (10):

(10) Why won't you let me go?

According to transformational grammar (see Chapter 2), there are three syntactic operations used in this sentence: *wh*-preposing, noun phrase–auxiliary inversion, and negation. Using the sentence *You will let me go* as the starting point, these three transformations add a *wh*-word at the beginning of the sentence, invert the noun phrase (*you*) and the auxiliary verb (*will*), and add a negative element (*not* added to *will*, then contracted to *won't*).

Once again, it has been proposed that children acquire these sentences in a series of stages (Klima & Bellugi, 1966). In the first stage, which occurs about the first half of the third year, children master the *wh*-preposing operation, but without the inversion. This produces questions such as (11):

(11)   Where I should put it?

The sentence is usually produced with an intonational rise at the end which, together with the context, makes it easy to interpret as a question. The next stage (at about 3.5 to 4 years) involves both *wh*-preposing and inversion, but only for affirmative sentences. Thus, the child correctly handles the affirmative question (12) but fails to correctly invert the noun phrase and auxiliary in negative, producing sentences such as (13):

(12)   What will you do now?
(13)   Why you can't sit down?

Klima and Bellugi suggest that children's processing capacity is too limited at this point in development to control all three operations at once, or even two operations if one of them is highly demanding. Thus, while they show mastery of inversion with *wh*-preposing, which had been acquired earlier, they fail to invert with negatives, a later acquisition. The last stage (4 to 4.5 years) occurs when children invert both affirmative and negatives, as in sentence (14):

(14)   Why won't you let me go?

As with negation, this orderly pattern of development may occur for individual children but is not necessarily true for all English-speaking children. There appear to be individual differences in the acquisition of the inversion operation (de Villiers & de Villiers, 1985). In addition, Kuczaj and Brannick (1979) found that children's knowledge of the rule regarding auxiliary placement was acquired at different points for different *wh*-words.

Passive sentences   A **passive sentence** is one in which the agent of the action is the syntactic object of the sentence, as in sentence (15):

(15)   The cat was chased by the dog.

Passives are much less common than active sentences in English but are often used to highlight or give focus to the recipient. There has been considerable interest in the acquisition of passives, in light of the significance of the passive in transformational grammar.

Preschool children find passives difficult. Bever (1970) studied the comprehension of passives by children between 2 and 5 years of age. Children performed at better than chance level between 3.5 and 4 years of age, but children who were slightly older did slightly more poorly. Maratsos (1974) replicated these results. Maratsos found that children about 3 to 3.5 years understood the passive voice, but that children from 3.5 to 4 years had difficulty with it.

The apparent regression in development is certainly interesting and suggests that children who initially analyzed passive sentences correctly subsequently misinterpreted them. In particular, Bever contends that older children tend to interpret an incoming string of noun plus verb plus noun as agent plus action plus object, a strategy that will work for active sentences but not for passive ones. The tendency to overapply a comprehension strategy is reminiscent of the process of overregularization of morphological rules discussed earlier.

Complex sentences   A **complex sentence** is one that expresses more than one proposition. Passive sentences convey a single idea in linguistically complex form. Other sentences, such as coordinations, complements, and relative clauses, express more than one idea.

A **coordination** is a construction in which two simple sentences are conjoined, as in sentences (16) and (17):

(16)   Jill loved rock and Sally loved jazz.

(17)   Hal will bring his wife or she will come in a separate car.

Children combine their sentences using a variety of conjunctions, including *but, because, then, so,* and *if* in addition to *and* and *or.* Bloom, Lahey, Hood, Lifter, and Fiess (1980) studied children's acquisition of *and* and found that acquisition was related to semantic factors. Early on, children used *and* in an additive fashion; one phrase was added to another, with no dependency relation between them, as in sentence (18). Later, they used *and* in a temporal context, as in (19). Still later, they used *and* to express causal relations, as in (20):

(18)   Maybe you can carry that and I can carry this.

(19)   Jocelyn's going home and take her sweater off.

(20)   She put a Band-Aid on her shoe and it maked it feel better.

Some of the children used *and* in still other ways.

A **complement** is a noun phrase that includes a verb. The phrase *to go home* in sentence (21) is a complement.

(21)   I want to go home.

Another example is *I see you sat down,* in which *you sat down* is a complement. These sentences are more semantically complex than comparable sentences without complements, such as (22), because they express more than one idea or proposition.

(22)   I want ice cream.

Children tend to acquire complement constructions between MLUs of 3.5 and 4.0, which is about 3 years of age (Reich, 1986). They first use complements as objects in their sentences; subject complements, such as sentence (23) (from Reich, 1986), come much later.

(23)   That she likes him surprises me.

Finally, a **relative clause** is a *wh*-clause that modifies a noun. When a *wh*-clause modifies the object of a sentence, it is called an object relative clause. One of my daughter's earliest examples is sentence (24), in which *what you just did* modifies *the thing* (I stretched my arms, then she imitated me). There are also subject relative clauses, such as sentence (25) in which *who was lost* modifies *the boy*.

(24)   I did the thing what you just did.
(25)   The boy who was lost was found unharmed.

Children's first relative clauses tend to be object relatives (Limber, 1973). Subject relative clauses may be more difficult because of processing limitations (Goodluck & Tavakolian, 1982). Notice that the subject relatives require a speaker to interrupt a clause to modify the subject, then return to complete the clause. It is likely that such constructions overload young children's working memory.

Crosslinguistic Differences in Later Grammar

Our discussion here has been on the acquisition of English constructions. Many of these aspects of development have been studied for other languages, and there are many differences. For example, a recent study by Demuth (1990) indicates that children acquiring Sesotho, a language spoken in southern Africa, master the passive voice earlier than English-speaking children. Demuth attributes the advancement to the frequency with which the passive is used in Sesotho.

There are also differences that appear to be attributable to the formal complexity of grammatical structures in different languages. For instance, Eyal (cited in Berman, 1985) found that Hebrew-speaking children produced well-formed questions with MLUs between 1.2 and 2.6 (at approximately 21 to 30 months). By comparison, English-speaking children are only beginning to master questions at MLUs of approximately 3.5 (at roughly 38 months). Berman suggests that the relative structural simplicity of questions in Hebrew may explain this difference. In Hebrew, yes/no questions merely require speakers to use a rising intonation with a declarative sentence, as opposed to the subject-verb phrase inversions that cause such difficulty for English-speaking children.

These examples merely scratch the surface of what is known about cross-linguistic differences in language acquisition. Much of the literature on this subject has been pulled together by Slobin (1985), and you are urged to consult this source.

Summary

Children acquire grammatical morphemes gradually throughout the preschool years. As children acquire morphemes, they use them in productive ways, sometimes producing errors such as overregularizations. Complex syntactic constructions such as negatives, questions, and relative clauses are also developed during the preschool years. Ease of acquisition appears to be related to the formal and conceptual complexity of the construction, along with certain processing limitations in the child.

The Emergence of Linguistic Awareness

Throughout most of this book I have emphasized how much of our language knowledge and language processing exists at a level beneath our conscious awareness. We are scarcely aware of most of the grammatical rules of our language and of the processing strategies that we use to comprehend and produce speech. We have some awareness of linguistic units, though, which appears when we attempt to analyze and dissect language, to reflect upon it—in short, when we think about language rather than merely use it. The distinction between the ability to use language and the ability to analyze it is significant and was described well by Cazden (1976):

> It is an important aspect of our unique capacities as human beings that we can not only act, but reflect back on our actions; not only learn and use language, but treat it as an object of analysis and evaluation in its own right. Meta-linguistic awareness, the ability to make language forms opaque and attend to them in and for themselves, is a special kind of language performance, one which makes special cognitive demands, and seems to be less easily and less universally acquired than the language performances of speaking and listening. (p. 603)

It is likely that the developmental course of **metalinguistic** skills may be very different than that of the "primary" linguistic skills of speaking and listening, as Cazden's last sentence implies. Metalinguistic skills are almost surely acquired later than the corresponding "primary" skills that provide the raw data for linguistic analysis. Let us begin by tracing some of the child's achievement in this area, then assessing its significance for language development.

Awareness of Linguistic Units

Researchers, as we have seen, have attempted to identify the child's grammatical system for expressing meanings by examining the types of utterances children make at various ages. A fundamental limitation of this method is that there is no direct way of determining what types of utterances a child might consider to be ungrammatical at a given age. With adults, we can not only note what adults say but can ask them questions about utterances they have not or would not say. So we can ask them, *Is 'The firefighter ankle broke the while saving the young child' a grammatical sentence?* With children, such metalinguistic judgments are more difficult to secure. Witness this early observation:

Experimenter:	Adam, which is right, "two shoes" or "two shoe"?
Adam:	Pop goes the weasel! (Brown & Bellugi, 1964, p. 134)

Nonetheless, over the past 20 years, a number of clever studies have discovered ways to explore young children's linguistic awareness.

The first study that was able to elicit judgments of grammaticality from young children was performed by Gleitman, Gleitman, and Shipley (1972). They first had 2-year-old children listen as their mothers read grammatically acceptable and unacceptable sentences to the experimenter, who either said *good* and repeated the sentences or said *silly* and corrected the sentences. After a short while, the children were eager to play the judge. These children showed an ability to discriminate between acceptable and unacceptable sentences (although they did accept about 50% of the unacceptable sentences) but were generally unable to correct the deviant sentences without recourse to semantics. For example, they changed *box the open* to *get in the box* rather than dealing with the syntax alone, as a change to *open the box* would be.

The significance of this study was that it showed for the first time that even very young children have some metalinguistic skills. Further research has examined other aspects of their language awareness and has attempted to sketch developmental progressions in children's awareness of language.

One group of studies has explored children's awareness of the arbitrary nature of words. When do children understand that there is no intrinsic relationship between the size of an object and the length of the word that refers to it? Berthoud (cited in Sinclair, 1982) found that 4- and 5-year-old children, when asked to give an example of a long word, will respond with words such as *train*. Similarly, Osherson and Markman (1975) found that while preschool children understand that the names of objects may change, they believe that when they do, the properties of the object cling to the name when it is transferred. So, a child will agree that a dog can be called *cat* but, if so, it will meow, or that a dog called *cow* will have horns. Thus, young children's concepts of words are not as yet separate from their referents.

Another topic of inquiry has been children's awareness of phonological units. Bruce (1964) gave a word (*snail*) and asked the children to take off the *n* and say what word is left. Children younger than 6 years were baffled by the task. In a similar vein, Zhurova (1973) placed a sentry on a bridge over which toy animals had to cross. The investigator was the sentry and the children could pick up various toy animals and try to cross the bridge. The children had to say the first letter of the toy's name in order to get across the bridge (*b* for *bear*, and so on). The children were unable to deal with this game successfully until they were 5 or 6 years of age.

Phonological awareness is not an all-or-none affair. Rather, certain aspects develop more rapidly than others, with some acquired as early as 3 years of age (Chaney, 1992; Smith & Tager-Flusberg, 1982). Stanovich, Cunningham, and Cramer (1984) studied several phonological awareness tasks, some of which are shown in Table 11-2. They gave these tasks to kindergartners and determined the relative difficulty of each task. Try yourself to rank the task from easiest to hardest. Your ability to make these judgments is itself a metalinguistic ability and thus should give you some idea of the kinds of skills that young children are mastering. The answer is given at the end of the chapter.

Awareness of Linguistic Processes

Up until now, we have concentrated on children's awareness of linguistic units and structures. A concurrent advance is the child's development of explicit knowledge about language processes, especially comprehension processes. The term **comprehension monitoring** refers to a person's ability to gauge her level of comprehension (Markman, 1981). For example, when we daydream while reading a textbook, we often keep on reading until it dawns on us that we have little understanding of what we've read. It is a self-reflective process in which we assess the satisfaction of our current level of comprehension according to some criterion.

There is clear evidence that young children often fail to realize when they don't understand. In an ingenious study, Markman (1977) asked children to give

Table 11-2.   Five Phonological Awareness Tasks

Task	Description
Supply rhyme	Given a word (for example, *fish*), supply a rhyme
Strip initial consonant	Given a word (for example, *task*), identify what is left when the first consonant is removed
Identify different initial consonant	Given four words (for example, *bag, nine, beach, bike*), choose the word with the different initial consonant
Identify different final consonant	Given four words (for example, *rat, dime, boat, mitt*), identify the one with a different final consonant
Supply initial consonant	Given two words (for example, *cat, at*), identify the sound present in one that is missing in the other

Source: Adapted from K. E. Stanovich, A. E. Cunningham, and B. B. Cramer, "Assessing Phonological Awareness in Kindergarten Children: Issues of Task Comparability," *Journal of Experimental Child Psychology* 38 (1984):175–190.

advice to someone who was writing instructions for a new children's card game. First-, second-, and third-graders were shown cards with letters of the alphabet on them and were told that an equal number of cards would be dealt to each player. Then they were given the following instructions: *We each put our cards in a pile. We both turn over the top card in our pile. We look at the cards to see who has the special card. Then we turn over the next card in our pile to see who has the special card this time. In the end, the person with the most cards wins the game.* Despite some glaring omissions in the instructions—there was no indication of what the special card was, nor how players accumulated the cards—the children professed to understand the instructions.

In a later study, Markman (1979) showed that older elementary school children also displayed failures of comprehension monitoring. Third-, fifth-, and sixth-graders were given brief essays that contained explicitly inconsistent information, such as the following information about baked Alaska: *To make it they put the ice cream in a very hot oven. The ice cream in baked Alaska melts when it gets that hot.* Later, the children heard, *When they make baked Alaska, the ice cream stays firm and it does not melt.* Despite the fact that the essays were read twice and the children demonstrated the ability to recall the relevant information, they claimed that the passages made sense and that they understood them.

Under certain conditions, children can be encouraged to recognize that their level of comprehension is low. In the earlier study, children were more prone to recognize the omissions if the instructions were demonstrated for them or if they attempted to carry them out. It appears, then, that children have the capacity to monitor their comprehension but don't do so spontaneously. Unlike adults or older children, young children realize they don't understand only when they are faced with the implications of their level of understanding.

The significance of this research is that unless people are aware that they do not understand what they have read or heard, they will not make any attempt to remedy the situation by rereading or asking questions. Moreover, simply asking a child whether he understands is not likely to be informative. A more useful approach is to encourage children to act on their understanding—thereby revealing gaps—and to give them practice in drawing inferences from the given information.

Related Linguistic Achievements

The emergence of increased awareness of linguistic units and processes plays a significant role in other aspects of language development. As children increasingly appreciate that language is a tool that can be used for a variety of purposes they are able to extend their intentional use of language to riddles, jokes, and metaphors. We now consider two aspects of language that are made possible by, or facilitated by, linguistic awareness.

Metaphor   As children gain insight into linguistic units, they are able to intentionally manipulate them for metaphorical purposes. We tend to use metaphor when we are unable to express a thought or experience in any other way (Ortony,

1975). Given this, and the fact that preschool children still have much to learn about the structure of their language, it is not surprising that metaphor is a pervasive feature of language development from the very beginning. Chukovsky (1963) reports some delightful examples of young children's spontaneous metaphors such as *Look Daddy, your pants are sulking!* Such uses of language often derive from the child's partial understanding of the lexicon, as when he uses a novel way to express a thought that could actually be expressed in a single word. Presumably, the child had not yet learned the word. In other cases, metaphorical expressions arise when a child's knowledge of word is incomplete, as with under- and overextensions. Metaphors spring naturally from the child's knowledge of language at any point in development.

The earliest systematic investigation of children's ability to comprehend metaphoric language was performed by Asch and Nerlove (1960). They studied the ability of children from 3 to 12 years of age to understand the dual functions of adjectives such as *soft, hard, sweet,* and *bitter.* In particular, the researchers were interested in whether children could understand that such words may have both physical and psychological referents. They first examined children's literal comprehension by presenting two objects (say, a cube of sugar and a powder puff) and asking which was *soft* or *sweet.* Once the children's literal comprehension was verified, they were asked questions pertaining to the metaphorical meaning, as in *Are people cold? What do they say or do when they are cold?* Asch and Nerlove found that children below the age of 6 had little awareness of psychological meanings. They suggest that children first learn the literal use, later the metaphorical, and only later do they realize the dual function of a word.

Using more simplified tasks, however, other investigators have found that even young children have some grasp of metaphor. Gardner (1974) used similar stimuli to those of Asch and Nerlove and had children match descriptive terms across different modes. For example, they were given two sounds and told that one was cold and the other was warm and could they identify which was which? Gardner found that children of 3.5 years of age were able to match adjectives across domains. While these results may seem to contradict those of Asch and Nerlove, the conflict is more apparent than real. While Asch and Nerlove asked their subjects to describe their understanding of metaphors, Gardner merely required them to demonstrate their understanding. In other words, the Asch and Nerlove study required a higher degree of metalinguistic skill than the Gardner study. It is possible that 3-year-old children are as metaphorically sensitive as 12-year-olds but are able to demonstrate their understanding only in a limited array of tasks. More likely, as children develop further linguistic awareness of phonemes, words, and grammar, they probably achieve greater understanding of the metaphoric aspects of words.

Winner, Rosenstiel, and Gardner (1976) examined three stages in children's development of metaphor understanding. At the **magical** stage, the interpretation of a metaphor is made literal by the child mentally imagining an appropriate scenario. For example, in the sentence *The prison guard was a hard rock,* a magical response would be to turn the guard into a rock. The **metonymic** stage assumes that the terms of the metaphor are associated in some way, as if the guard worked in a prison with rock walls. The **primitive metaphoric** stage reveals the first glimpses of metaphoric understanding. At this stage, children would regard the guard as physically tough or hard. Winner and colleagues found that 6- to 8-year-olds made mainly metonymic and primitive metaphorical responses, with some magical replies, while 10- to 14-year-olds gave mainly genuine metaphorical responses, with fewer magical responses.

Humor   Children's use of and response to linguistic humor is also closely related to their development of metalinguistic skills. McGhee (1979) reviewed what children consider to be humorous at various stages of development. He notes that preschool children often play with the phonological structure of the language, by changing a phoneme in a word (*watermelon, fatermelon*) or adding a nonsensical ending to a word (*pajoodles* for *pajamas* or *rhinoceropiple* for *rhinoceros*).

The appreciation of riddles, which are based on a child's awareness of lexical ambiguity, comes during the elementary school years. Riddles of the following form separate preschoolers from children in the early school years (Fowles & Glanz, 1977; Shultz, 1974):

> **Question:**   Do you believe in clubs for young people?
> **Answer:**   Only when kindness fails. (Van Kleeck, 1982, from W. C. Fields)

Still later, children's awareness of morpheme boundaries enables them to appreciate the following type of riddle, which requires them to recombine the final two morphemes of the answer into a single, two-morpheme word *selfish*.

> **Question:**   Why is the man in the fish market stingy?
> **Answer:**   Because his job makes him sell fish. (Van Kleeck, 1982)

Van Kleeck (1982) suggests that children do not appreciate such riddles until they are approximately 12 years of age.

Individual Differences in Metalinguistic Skills

We saw in Chapter 10 that there are reliable individual differences in how children approach early language acquisition. There also appear to be significant differences between children in linguistic awareness and related linguistic skills. Several factors have been suggested as possibly contributing to these differences, although their relative importance is not presently well understood.

Horgan (1981) suggests that the prevalence of language games in the home encourages children to adopt a playful attitude toward language and consequently develop metaphoric skills more rapidly. Horgan found that a number of linguistically based jokes and riddles appeared spontaneously in the language of one young girl between the middle of her second year to the beginning of her fourth year. The child was the first-born daughter of a philosopher and a psycholinguist, and it is clear that rhyming and games involving the violation of linguistic rules and categories were common in the home.

Another factor that may enhance metalinguistic awareness is bilingualism in the home. One possibility is that bilingual children understand the arbitrariness of the word-referent relationship. The notion is that children who have acquired more than a single label for an object will more easily appreciate the fact that there is an arbitrary relationship between the two. Studies that have examined the relationship between bilingualism and word awareness have, however, had mixed results (see, for example, Ianco-Worrall, 1972; Rosenblum & Pinker, 1983). More recently, Galambos and Hakuta (1988) found a relationship between bilingualism and young children's ability to notice ungrammatical utterances and detect syntactic ambiguities.

Still another factor is the child's cognitive development. Related developments are taking place in children's understanding of (nonlinguistic) cognitive processes, such as how memory works (Kreutzer, Leonard, & Flavell, 1975). Van Kleeck (1982) argues that the development of metalinguistic skills is related to Piaget's stage of concrete operations (see also Abrahamsen, 1982).

Regardless of the factors that give rise to it, the emergence of linguistic awareness has a significant impact on several aspects of language we will discuss later in this chapter. One is the child's communication skills. In order to communicate effectively with a diverse group of people, a speaker must learn to select words that are appropriate to the situation and to the listener. This ability is related to the speaker's metalinguistic ability to analyze words and their communicative effects. Also, we will find that children's ability to read is closely related to linguistic awareness, in particular their phonological awareness. In the next section, we discuss the discourse and communication skills of young children.

Summary

While a good deal of our linguistic knowledge is tacit, explicit awareness of linguistic units and processes is essential for writing, reading, metaphor, and many other aspects of language. The emergence of metalinguistic awareness takes place after the child's basic grammatical system is organized, in the later preschool and early school years. With increased awareness, children are able to recognize ambiguous expressions, determine that the relationship between word and referent is arbitrary, and appreciate metaphorical uses of language. The basis of individual differences in these skills is not presently well understood.

Discourse Processes in Children

In this section we consider two aspects of children's discourse skills. First, we look at children's narrative skills, their ability to tell a story in a comprehensible way. Then we look at conversational skills and children's ability to relate their linguistic goals to those of their conversational participant.

Narrative Skills

As we saw in Chapter 7, discourse coherence operates at two levels: the local level, at which there are cohesive ties between successive sentences in discourse (Halliday & Hasan, 1976), and the global level, at which the discourse as a whole fits a particular genre. Both forms of coherence have been studied in children's narrative production.

The most common way to examine children's narrative skills is to ask them to relate a personal story (Peterson & McCabe, 1983; Sutton-Smith, 1986). Young children often have considerable difficulty telling a story in a comprehensible way. They sometimes use pronouns ambiguously, such as using *she* to refer to a particular character when it may refer to several characters. Their narratives are also weak in linkages between successive sentences in the discourse. These and related skills develop gradually during the preschool years.

However, even very young children can use cohesive devices to connect successive sentences in their narratives (Bennett-Kastor, 1983; Peterson & Dodsworth, 1991). Peterson and Dodsworth examined the acquisition of cohesive devices in a longitudinal study of children from 2 years of age to 3 years 6 months. The children were asked to narrate a personal experience. The investigators then examined the narratives for the presence of cohesive devices such as reference, ellipsis, substitution, conjunction, and lexical cohesion (see Chapter 7, Table 7-1). They found that even these very young children used all of the forms of cohesion identified by Halliday and Hasan. Six of the nine devices they studied (reference pronouns, reference demonstratives, verbal ellipsis, clausal ellipsis, conjunctions, and lexical cohesion) were present at the start of the study, indicating that they are acquired prior to 2 years of age. The remaining devices (comparative reference, nominal ellipsis, and substitution) appeared with increases in age and MLU.

Peterson and Dodsworth also found some changes in the use of cohesive devices over time. The total number of cohesive ties increased with both age and MLU, and the relative proportion of different cohesive devices shifted. Pronominal reference and conjunctions increased, whereas clausal and verbal ellipsis declined. Overall, the cohesive device most often used by children was lexical cohesion, the simplest form of which is just to repeat lexical items. Lexical cohesion constituted 42% of the children's cohesive links. This percent is higher than the percent (30%) found in adult speech (Rochester & Martin, 1979). In contrast, adults use a relatively higher proportion of referential ties than children do. Thus, we would expect to see improvements in referential cohesion as the children develop.

Pratt and MacKenzie-Keating (1985) studied referential cohesion in 4- and 6-year-old children. They told stories to the children and then asked them to retell the stories to peers. The preschool children were much more likely to make errors when introducing new referents. They sometimes treated a new referent as if it were already given information, an error that was very uncommon for the first-graders. However, once a referent was introduced into the discourse, even the younger children correctly referred back to it, as opposed to reintroducing it. The 6-year-old children made few errors on either given or new information.

Some work has also been done at the global level. Peterson and McCabe (1983) collected 1124 personal narratives of children from 3.5 to 9.5 years of age. The researchers found age-related changes in the overall narrative structure. The youngest children often produced lists of unrelated sentences. By 6 years of age, most children were able to produce a good story: they provided the listener with a setting, identified a problem or complication, and described how the problem was resolved. Some children were able to produce complex narratives, such as stories with multiple or embedded episodes. In addition, the children provided remarks that clarified the point of the story and the narrator's evaluation of the story events.

Children, of course, differ somewhat in these narrative skills. In a more recent study, McCabe and Peterson (1991) argue that these individual differences are related to parental strategies for eliciting narratives in the home. The researchers were particularly interested in parental strategies that encouraged children to extend or elaborate their narratives, such as the use of open-ended and clarifying questions. McCabe and Peterson found that these strategies were positively correlated with the length of the children's subsequent narratives to experimenters. In contrast, parental topic switching was related to shorter subsequent child narratives. McCabe and Peterson conclude by noting that "we did not find any 'natural storytellers' at age 2. We only found parents who differed in the extent to which they tried to get their children's stories and in the manner in which they went about such collaboration" (p. 250).

Hicks (1990, 1991) is one of the few investigators who have examined children's acquisition of the differences between narratives and other genres. Hicks studied first-graders' ability to perform three different tasks. The children were shown a short silent film, *The Red Balloon*, and were asked to (a) describe the events as they rewatched a portion of the film (similar to a sportscaster describing events as they occur), (b) provide a factual news report, and (c) tell the film's events as a story. The children shifted their language from one genre to another. When doing the first task, they used the present tense, whereas they used the past tense for the other two tasks. In the news-reporting task, the children preferred to stick to a factual and detailed rendition of the events in the film. In the storytelling task, however, they provided more evaluative remarks, sometimes telling events out of temporal sequence, and concentrated more on the internal motivations of the characters. These results suggest that these children are beginning to grasp the difference between describing facts and telling a good story.

Conversational Skills

As we saw in Chapter 9, conversational discourse involves a number of implicit rules related to taking turns, sharing conversational topics, taking the needs of the listener into account, and formulating requests in a socially appropriate manner. Let us see how the child masters each of these.

Taking turns Conversations need a speaker and at least one listener. Becoming competent in these roles includes grasping some elementary notions such as not speaking when another person is and making one's contributions related to the contributions of the other person. In a sense, conversations are games with certain broad rules. Fillmore (cited in Bloom, Rocissano, & Hood, 1976) depicted two versions of a conversational game. In the first version, person A picks up a ball and throws it in the air. Person B catches it and then throws it back. In the second version, A picks up a ball and throws it. B waits for A to finish, then picks up a ball and throws it to A. Both versions embody two concepts—namely, that only one ball (topic) should be in the air at a time and that a person should throw a ball after the other person finishes throwing his. The first version contains a third concept that is missing in the second version, that balls are meant to be shared— our contribution should be topically similar to our partner's.

Fillmore's two games provide a convenient organizational device for the discussion of conversational discourse. Coherent conversational discourse occurs when our contributions are related to the shared topic of discussion [note the similarity with Grice's (1975) convention of relation, discussed in Chapter 6]. A developmentally simpler form of conversation is the mere alternation of turns. This primitive form of turn-taking might be learned through parent/child interactions. As we saw in Chapter 10, very early in life, mothers treat babies as active conversational partners by interpreting their burps and other sounds as conversational turns (Snow, 1977).

Sharing conversational topics Let us now look at how young children begin to make the transition to Fillmore's first game. Keenan (1974) has presented evidence that children begin to do this by attending to the form of a speaker's utterance. Some of the time her children (aged 2 years 9 months) engaged in sound play, in which they attended to the phonological properties of the other's speech, usually in a playful spirit. Children of this age also tend to repeat some or all of the previous utterance (*flower broken* to *flower*), to expand it (*big one* to *I got big one*), or to substitute one or more items (*two moths* to *many moths*). These repetitions are similar to the lexical ties young children use when recounting personal narratives. While these are extremely simple modifications, Keenan's observations show that before children are able to do much with others' speech, they behave as if they are aware of a conversational requirement to make one's speech relevant.

Bloom, Rocissano, and Hood (1976) examined the nature of adult/child discourse and came up with several interesting conclusions. First, they classified all child utterances into one of five categories (see Table 11-3). Note that the broadest classification is between adjacent and nonadjacent utterances and that noncontingent, imitative, and contingent utterances are three types of adjacent utterances. Bloom and her colleagues studied a group of children at periodic intervals from the time the children were 19 months of age until they were 38 months. When the children were between 19 and 23 months of age, they played a game that is similar to Fillmore's second version. A large percent of their utterances (69%) were adjacent, but few were contingent. Among the adjacent utterances, noncontingent (31%) were most common at this age, followed by contingent (21%), and finally imitative utterances (17%).

Table 11-3.　Categories of Child Utterances

Category	Definition
Nonadjacent	Those utterances that occurred without a previous adult utterance, or with a definite pause after a previous adult utterance
Adjacent	Those utterances that occurred right after an adult utterance
Noncontingent	Those utterances that did not share the same topic as the preceding adult utterance
Imitative	Those utterances that shared the same topic with the preceding utterance, but did not add information; that is, all or part of the preceding utterance was repeated with no change
Contingent	Those utterances that both shared the same topic with the preceding utterance and added information to it

Source: L. Bloom, L. Rocissano, and L. Hood, "Adult-Child Discourse: Developmental Interaction between Information Processing and Linguistic Knowledge," *Cognitive Psychology* 8 (1976):521–552.

By the time the children were between 35 and 38 months of age, several developmental trends were apparent. The overall percent of adjacent utterances declined (to 64%). However, the percent of contingent utterances, one type of adjacent utterance, more than doubled (to 46%). The percent of noncontingent and imitative utterances dropped sharply to 16% and 2%, respectively. It appears that between 2 and 3 years of age, children are developing both the ability to respond appropriately to another's topic of conversation (that is, contingent utterances) and the ability to select their own conversational topics (that is, nonadjacent utterances).

These studies bear on the question of how children integrate different forms of linguistic knowledge. Two-year-old children, as we saw in Chapter 10, have acquired quite a bit of semantic and syntactic knowledge. However, they do not apply this knowledge right away in conversations. Rather, children seem to "fill their slot" by making a comment of some sort, one that is not necessarily related to the previous utterance. By 3 years of age, children have come a long way toward integrating linguistic knowledge and pragmatic knowledge, and they begin to use their conversational turns in semantically appropriate ways.

Adapting one's speech to the listener　　Another important aspect of conversational skill is the skill to adapt our speech to the conversational situation. One aspect of this is to adapt our speech to the listener's perceived linguistic skills. In particular, we tend to speak in more simplified form when talking to a person we view as less linguistically sophisticated.

A **referential communication task** is one in which a child must formulate a message to refer to an object or picture, as opposed to communicating the ideas, needs, or emotions of the speaker. Developmentally, the interesting aspect of this task is that it forces the speaker to prepare a message that fits the situational context and/or the perceived receptive abilities of the listener. For a long time, psycholinguists, influenced by the work of Piaget, believed that young children could not alter their speech in socially appropriate ways. According to Piaget, children are unable to adopt the vantage point of another person until they reach the cognitive stage known as concrete operations (about 7 years of age). Although some early studies tended to support Piaget's claim (Glucksberg, Krauss, & Weisberg, 1966; Piaget & Inhelder, 1948/1967), later work (Borke, 1975; Maratsos, 1973; Shatz & Gelman, 1973) has indicated that even very young children can switch codes under certain conditions.

A comparison of these tasks is instructive. In the study by Glucksberg and coworkers, two children were seated on opposite sides of a partition and were asked to stack a set of objects the same way, even though they could not see the other stack. Thus, they had to verbally instruct each other on how to construct the pile. The results showed that when familiar objects were used (that is, ones whose names were readily available), 3-year-olds did well, yet they performed miserably when unfamiliar, novel objects were used. Adults did well in both situations. The young children gave private, idiosyncratic names to the unfamiliar objects, but these names did not communicate very much to their partner.

Shatz and Gelman (1973) examined whether 4-year-old children could code switch when talking to 2-year-olds as opposed to adults. The 4-year-olds were asked to tell a partner about a toy. When the partner was a 2-year-old, the older children used shorter and simpler sentences. With peers or adults, they used longer and more complex sentences. This result occurred whether or not they had a younger sibling at home. In other words, code switching was a spontaneous adapation to a communication situation, not merely an imitated response.

Why did these later studies show young children to be communicatively competent when the earlier results so consistently showed incompetence? It is not just that the later studies used simpler tasks. Gelman (1978) argues convincingly that children must have available alternative responses to a communication situation before it is fair to ask whether they will choose one over the other as a result of another person's perspective. In the Glucksberg and colleagues (1966) task, correct performance required not only that the subjects formulated messages that were appropriately communicative but also that they labeled new objects in a distinctive way. The latter skill is a difficult one for most young children. Even if they had the idea that they should formulate their message to the needs of the listener, they are unable to do so. In contrast, Shatz and Gelman indexed their subjects' communicative skills in terms of syntactic complexity. Gelman (1978) explains:

> Why syntactic measures? Because 4-year-olds have a remarkably rich repertoire of syntactic constructions and it is therefore *possible* for them to select among these when talking to different listeners. Not that they necessarily will. It's just that they could, should they be so inclined, modify messages as they confront listeners with different needs. (p. 315)

The significance of this rise in referential communication skills is that the young speaker is now more capable of taking the listener into account. Children can now adjust their speech to the perceived level of comprehension of the listener, greatly enhancing their ability to communicate effectively with a wide range of listeners.

Part of learning to communicate is adapting one's speech to different listeners.

Formulating requests   Requests are an interesting aspect of language because they represent one way a person seeks to control the behavior of another. Sociolinguistic factors such as being polite and making the request reasonable thus come into play, and it is intriguing to watch how children gain command of these interpersonal aspects of language. Several authors have advanced the notion that requests have a particular structure and that adherence to this structure improves the chances of the request being satisfied. We have already seen the ideas of Labov and Fanshel (1977, see Chapter 9), who regard a sincere or valid request as one that fits most or all of several preconditions. Similarly, it has been suggested that requests include several steps (Garvey, 1975).

Children are flexible in their use of the multiple steps of the request form. Garvey distinguished between obligatory steps, which were nearly always included, and optional steps, which were added when communication broke down (see Table 11-4). Garvey's subjects, children between the ages of 3 years 6 months and 5 years 7 months who were observed in unstructured play in a room with many toys, appeared to appreciate this distinction. The request form consists of three obligatory steps. First, the speaker must prepare the listener for the request by identifying the object(s) involved in the request. It is not surprising that children master this step since it is similar to the distinction between given and new information that prelinguistic children seem to understand. The second obligatory step is the request itself. The third obligatory step is some acknowledgement of the request on the part of the listener. While the listener may choose not to comply with the request, it is not conversationally appropriate to ignore it altogether. Compliance

Table 11-4. Six Steps in the Request Form

Step	Example
1. Preparation of the propositional content (obligatory)	S: *You see that hammer there?* [preparation] L: *Yeah.* S: *Hand it to me.* [request]
2. Adjunct to the request (optional)	S: *That's where the iron belongs.* [adjunct] S: *Put it over there.* [request]
3. Request (obligatory)	S: *Roll this tape up for me.* [request] S: *I can't do it.* [adjunct]
4. Clarification of the request (optional)	S: *Hand me the truck.* [request] L: *Which one?* [clarification] S: *The dump truck.*
5. Acknowledgement of the request (obligatory)	S: *Come on, get on.* [request] L: *As soon as I finish putting out this roaring fire.* (Plays firefighter) [acknowledgement] S: (Waits) L: (Comes to car)
6. Acknowledgement of the acknowledgement (optional)	S: *Give it to me.* [request] L: *Here it is.* [acknowledgement] S: *Thanks.* [acknowledgement of acknowledgment]

Note: S = speaker (requester), L = listener (addressee)
Source: C. Garvey, "Requests and Responses in Children's Speech," *Journal of Child Language* 2 (1975):41–63.

is usually marked with a simple *okay* or *all right.* Noncompliant acknowledgements were divided into temporary noncompliance and outright refusal. When the noncompliance is temporary, the listener often explains that he is presently unable to carry out the request (step 5). Even if the listener refuses outright, the refusal is often accompanied with an explanation.

Children's use of the optional steps is even more revealing. The essential, obligatory steps are not run off in fixed, rigid form. When the basic steps are insufficient for some reason, both speaker and listener respond flexibly. Adjuncts, which appear either just before or just after the request itself, are often useful for explaining why the request is being made. Clarifications are used by listeners if the request was not heard or fully understood. Finally, the speaker or requester sometimes acknowledges the response of the listener, usually with a simple *thanks.* Children's use of these optional steps, especially the adjuncts and clarifications, reveals a sensitivity to the informational needs of conversational partners at each point in the sequence.

Garvey's study is a splendid example of how the detailed analysis of a single aspect of language can yield conclusions of general interest. It is clear that the speaker and the listener share a number of interpersonal meanings in the request situation, and these elements are used again and again in justifying, refusing, repeating, and paraphrasing requests. The entire sequence takes place within the context of a shared set of beliefs: that the speaker's request was motivated by a reason, that the listener would be willing to perform the action but wouldn't do so unless asked, and so on. Thus, in mastering the request form, children show a remarkably sophisticated understanding of the roles and responsibilities of participants in a conversations.

Summary

Children as young as 2 or 3 years are able to tell stories and participate in conversations, albeit in limited ways. During the subsequent preschool years, they become more flexible and skilled conversationalists and storytellers. They use a greater variety of cohesive devices, learn new genres, adapt their speech to different listeners, and formulate and justify requests of others. As children enter school, they have an impressive repertoire of communication skills.

Language in the School

The language skills that children bring to the school setting are important since language is the predominant means of instruction in a wide variety of subject matters. But the language of the school is different from the language of the home and of the playground, and adapting to these differences provides a major challenge for children as they enter formal schooling. We will begin with a discussion of oral communication in the classroom, then discuss the relationships between reading and language development.

Communicating in the Classroom

The classroom environment contains a wealth of verbal interaction that has been explored by sociolinguists, psycholinguists, and educational researchers (Cazden, 1986; Mehan, 1979; Wilkinson, 1982). Classrooms, like other communication situations, have implicit conventions for how oral discourse should take place, and it is likely that some children will be better able than others to discern these "rules of the game." The causes and consequences of these individual differences have been the focus of much research.

Classroom discourse　　There are several distinguishing characteristics of classroom discourse. One is that the language in the classroom is **decontextualized** (Cook-Gumperz & Gumperz, 1982). In most communicative situations outside of formal education, there is a close relationship between the utterances of conversational participants and the immediate context. In formal education, however, it is common for children to be asked *Who discovered America?* or *What is 5 times 5?* questions that have nothing to do with the immediate environment.

Teachers' use of questions diverges from everyday discourse in another way. Teachers frequently ask children questions as a way of gauging the students' learning rather than learning the answer to the question. These questions function more like an exam than a true question (Searle, 1969). One form of discourse that enables teachers to assess student learning is the **initiation–reply–evaluation** sequence, in which a teacher poses a question to a student, receives a student reply, and then evaluates the student's answer (Mehan, 1979). Children are unlikely to have much experience with this type of discourse outside of school.

Teachers' language to children is also more formal than most language to which children are accustomed. In a study of classroom teachers and their language behavior, Feldman and Wertsch (1976) found differences in the styles of speech in the classroom and the lunchroom. When away from children, teachers used expressions such as *It seems to me . . . , I certainly expect . . .* , and other ways of qualifying one's speech. These devices are used to distinguish personal opinion from factual content. In the classroom, these qualifiers were absent. Teacher language in the classroom thus is somewhat formal relative to everyday, colloquial speech.

One final aspect of classroom discourse is the teacher's inability to attend to every child at the same time. As Merritt (1982) puts it, the teacher's attention is a scarce resource. If so, then how is this attention distributed? Several studies of classroom interaction have found that a fundamental rule is that teachers, as authority figures, determine how conversational turns are allocated. This is generally done by the teacher specifically addressing one member of the class. Typically, most student comments are in direct response to the query. Spontaneous student comments are relatively rare (DeStefano, Pepinsky, & Sanders, 1982; Mehan, 1979).

An important issue is the role these communication rules play in classroom interaction and, ultimately, in learning. Some observers agree that academic success depends upon communicative competence as much as intellectual competence. The point is put well by Mehan (1979):

> Students not only must know the content of academic subjects, they must learn the appropriate form in which to cast their academic knowledge . . . They must know with whom, when, and where they can speak and act, and they must provide the speech and behavior that are appropriate for a given classroom situation. Students must also be able to relate behavior, both academic and social, to varying classroom situations by interpreting implicit classroom rules. (p. 133)

Acquiring classroom skills   Research has examined how children use requests for information and action during group reading assignments (Wilkinson & Calculator, 1982; Wilkinson, Clevenger, & Dollaghan, 1981). In these studies, first-grade children read aloud or silently in groups and then completed a workbook, drew pictures, or otherwise demonstrated their understanding of what they read. As the teacher moved from group to group around the room, there were opportunities for students to ask each other for assistance. Wilkinson and colleagues found that requests were often accompanied by justifications of why the request

A teacher's attention is a scarce resource. Children must learn the rules of the classroom in order to be granted a conversational turn.

was made (for example, *Can I use your eraser for a minute, Sandy? I made a boo-boo.*) and clarifications of exactly what was requested. Moreover, the children often spontaneously revised their questions when the question didn't produce the desired response. These results are highly similar to those found by Garvey (1975) with preschool children.

Wilkinson and Calculator (1982) also found individual differences in peer group interactions. Those children who were found to be the most effective speakers were those whose responses were direct, sincere, relevant to the task at hand, and addressed to a specific listener. Children who used this form of speech received a much higher degree of compliance than those who didn't. Other studies indicate that children, like adults, respond positively to individuals whose messages are informative and clear. Pratt, Scribner, and Cole (1977) found that children who were effective speakers were those most often selected by children to be teachers.

Moreover, teachers' interactions with students are related to teachers' perceptions of students' communication skills. Several studies have shown that students perceived as higher in communicative competence gain the floor more often (Cherry, 1978; Michaels, 1981). Cherry (1978) found that teachers tended to request more information from those they considered to be high in communication skills.

The notion that communicative skills enable children to gain access to the floor more often is particularly relevant for understanding the classroom performance of minority children. Michaels (1981) studied student narratives during "sharing time" (sometimes called "show and tell"), in which students are encouraged to describe an object brought from home or give a narrative account about some past event to the entire class. Michaels found that lower-income black and middle-income white children used different narrative styles. White children used a topic-centered approach that focused on a single topic or a series of related topics, whereas black children used a topic-associating style, a discourse that consisted of a sequence of implicitly associated anecdotes. Gee (1989) suggests that white teachers may have difficulty appreciating the latter style and understanding the implications of asking children to change their style of speech. More generally, the home backgrounds of some children may not prepare them to participate in a classroom that emphasizes a different style of discourse (Michaels, 1991).

Reading and Language Development

There is, of course, another major difference between language in the school and language before school. Schooled language is increasingly written language, and the demands of written language pose a considerable challenge for most children entering formal schooling.

The beginning reader is already a fluent language user. Many of the comprehension skills that have been acquired to deal with oral language are also applicable to reading. These include the ability to extract the meaning of a sentence, to interpret that sentence in a given communicative context, to draw inferences from individual statements, and to monitor one's own comprehension. These may be referred to as general comprehension skills.

In addition, learning to read involves mastering other skills that are specific to the written language. These include using eye movements to scan sentences in a text, extracting the visual features of letters and words, reading from left to right on a page (in most languages), and relating printed language to spoken language in some way. It is likely that some of these skills may be acquired rather easily, but others may take substantial time and effort.

What this suggests is that reading involves a variety of skills that are well coordinated only in the mature reader. That is, the early reader is consumed with the task of identifying even familiar words in a new and unfamiliar mode. Early readers thus are less able to attend to the overall meaning of a text and to apply those comprehension strategies acquired in the acquisition of oral language. As children master reading-specific skills, they are increasingly able to bring their substantial repertoire of linguistic skills to bear on the task of reading.

Phonological awareness and reading One skill that is specific to reading is the task of linking printed letters (called **graphemes**) to phonemes. This task is difficult for young children, for several reasons. For one, there is a lack of one-to-one correspondence between phonemes and graphemes. The grapheme *c* is sometimes pronounced as /k/, as in *coffee*, and sometimes as /s/, as in the first phoneme in *circus*. In addition, the child must learn that some graphemes are pronounced in ways that are difficult to anticipate, such as the *ph* in *phoneme*. Moreover, the young reader will have to confront words with silent letters, such as *house*.

Phoneme-grapheme linkage is also difficult because children tend to be weak in metalinguistic awareness of phonemes. The young reader's metalinguistic skills do not appear to be sufficient for this type of analysis of language. Several authors (for example, Mattingly, 1972) have suggested that reading is a secondary language skill, like literary analysis, which is intrinsically more difficult than spoken language because it involves conscious awareness of linguistic units. A startling study by Rozin, Bressman, and Taft (1974) shows the extent of young children's ignorance in this regard. Children were shown word pairs such as *mow* and *motorcycle* and were told that one was *mow* and the other *motorcycle*. Then they were asked which one was *mow*. Only 10% of inner-city kindergartners performed to the criterion (7 of 8 correct). This appears to indicate that these children were unaware of a fundamental relationship between sound and writing: that words that take longer to say have more letters.

As awareness of the sound system grows, some levels are more accessible than others. In particular, some research indicates that awareness is particularly hard to acquire at the phonemic level. Liberman, Shankweiler, Fischer, and Carter (1974) examined phonemic and syllabic awareness in 4-, 5-, and 6-year-old children. The researchers had one group of children listen to words and then indicate, by tapping a wooden dowel on a table, the number of syllables (one, two, or three) in the word. A separate group identified the number of phonemes in a word. Thus, the first group would tap three times to *hospital* and the second group three times to *bag*. The phoneme-segmentation task proved to be much harder than the syllable-segmentation task for all three age groups. In fact, none of the 4-year-olds and only 17% of the 5-year-olds could segment phonemically. In contrast, nearly half (48%) of the 5-year-olds could segment a word into syllables.

The special difficulty of phonemes is probably related to the way in which phonemes are encoded into syllables (see Chapter 4). In a word such as *ball*, the information pertaining to the initial /b/ is spread throughout the syllable. The syllable is thus, in this sense, a more natural (that is, more accessible) linguistic unit than the phoneme. As a consequence, some researchers have suggested that it would be easier for children to begin reading by analyzing words into syllables, and only later to break syllables into phonemes (Gleitman & Rozin, 1977).

In any event, it is clear that phonological awareness is causally related to the development of reading skill (Bradley & Bryant, 1983; Gibb & Randall, 1988; Stanovich, Cunningham, & Cramer, 1984). And, if this is so, then training in metalinguistic skills should lead to reading improvement, and several recent studies support this assertion (Ball & Blachman, 1991; Lundberg, Frost, & Petersen, 1988). Lundberg and colleagues developed a training program of metalinguistic games and exercises designed to improve phonological awareness. The researchers provided daily training sessions for 155 Danish preschool students over a period of 8 months. The program produced significant gains in several metalinguistic tasks, including phonemic segmentation. Moreover, the metalinguistic gains led to reading improvement that was sustained over a period of time.

Top-down and bottom-up processes   As a result of these metalinguistic problems, children often find it difficult to identify printed words. One strategy for overcoming this problem is to encourage children to use the sentence context to help figure out the meaning. For instance, if a child is stuck on the last word of a sentence, the child may be asked to figure out a likely ending to the sentence by generating possible words. Once a set of words is constructed, the child can return to the troublesome item with greater semantic support, and it may now be possible for the child to recognize the word through a combination of semantic and orthographic cues (spelling).

Although in the short run this may be a useful approach, most good readers eventually "crack the code" and learn to identify words based solely on their spelling and not on contextual factors. A study by Allington and Strange (1977) illuminates the point here. Fourth-grade children identified as good versus poor readers on standardized reading tests were given a task in which they had to read aloud various sentences. Five percent of the sentences contained an error, such as *The frog hopped oven the snow.* The question of interest was whether students would read *oven* as it was printed or would spontaneously correct it to *over,* and, if so, which group of readers would do so more often. It turned out that the poor readers said *over* more often than the good readers. These results suggest that better readers rely less, not more, on top-down processing to recognize individual words (see Stanovich, 1980, for a review of pertinent studies).

These results may sound counterintuitive. We sometimes think of good readers as those who attend to meaning whereas less successful readers go word by word. And, of course, the ultimate goal of reading is to comprehend the meaning of a printed passage. But our intuitions may not be reliable here, for many reading processes are long since automatic in mature readers. We may be more aware of the results of our reading efforts than we are of the processes we use to obtain these results.

From an information processing vantage point, the notion that good readers rely on bottom-up processing to recognize words makes good sense. Word recognition has often been regarded as an automatic process in mature readers (see Chapter 5), whereas many other important processes in reading—such as noting cohesion between sentences, drawing inferences, and summarizing paragraphs—are controlled processes for most of us. With limited overall processing resources, the more automatic lower level processes are, the more processing capacity is available for higher level processes. The end result should be better comprehension.

These results may be related to the observation that children who are read to more often in the preschool period eventually become better readers (Snow, Barnes, Chandler, Goodman, & Hemphill, 1991). There may be several reasons for this relationship. Listening to stories is often a pleasurable experience for young children, and it may foster positive attitudes toward reading later on. Another reason may be that early exposure to printed words facilitates children's later ability to recognize them automatically. These ideas are not mutually exclusive; both may play a role. In any event, exposure to printed language, even in adults (Stanovich & West, 1989), promotes reading skills.

Summary

The linguistic skills needed for success in formal schooling differ from those that children have acquired during their preschool years. Classroom discourse requires students to learn the "rules of the game," and children's academic success is related to how well they learn these communicative lessons. In particular, children must learn to formulate requests clearly and express themselves in the formal style of discourse recognized in the classroom.

Although children come to school with oral language skills and with experience with printed materials, successful reading requires children to rapidly identify written words, a reading-specific skill that depends upon metalinguistic processes. Successful reading requires a mix of top-down and bottom-up processes. The ability to automatically identify words, an asset in reading, enables readers to devote resources to higher level processes, thereby promoting comprehension.

Review Questions

1. Identify the factors that are related to children's acquisition of grammatical morphemes.
2. Distinguish between formal and conceptual complexity.
3. Why do children regress in their ability to comprehend passive sentences?
4. What evidence suggests that metalinguistic skills do not develop all at once?
5. Define comprehension monitoring.
6. How do children's narrative skills change during the late preschool period?
7. Discuss the relative frequency of contingent, noncontingent, and imitation speech in children's discourse.
8. What are referential communication tasks, and why might young children do poorly on these tasks?
9. How might differences in communication skills influence the classroom learning of different children?
10. Discuss the relationship between phonological awareness and early reading.

Thought Questions

1. Identify some caregiver activities that might foster metalinguistic skills and explain why they might be effective.
2. Relatively little research has been done on children's learning to write. On the basis of the text's discussion of how children learn to read, how might learning to write be related to speech production? Would similar stages be involved? Explain.

3. Would a child who has moved from one school district to another several times be more or less likely to learn the "rules of the game" of a particular classroom? Justify your answer.

4. De Villiers and de Villiers (1978) have suggested that one index of a child's metalinguistic skill is the ability to tell a lie. How might this "achievement" be related to linguistic awareness?

Answer to Table 11-2: The tasks, from easiest to hardest, are: supply rhyme, identify different initial consonant, supply initial consonant, identify different final consonant, and strip initial consonant.

Processes of Language Acquisition

- Language acquisition has been studied in relation to three classes of variables: environmental factors, cognitive processes, and innate linguistic mechanisms.
- Studies of feral and isolated children indicate that gross environmental neglect or abuse may retard language acquisition. The precise aspects of the environment necessary for normal language growth are not clear.
- Nonlinguistic cognitive processes are correlated with language milestones at various points in development. There is some evidence that cognitive achievements facilitate language development.
- Children given only impoverished linguistic input are able to create communication systems that are similar to early child language, suggesting some innate guidance in early language acquisition.

Introduction

In Chapters 10 and 11, we surveyed some of the more important facts of language development. Although all normal children achieve mastery of language in a few short years, we have seen that it is not a simple achievement.

This chapter examines the question of how language is acquired. One way to think about the factors that play a role in language acquisition is to identify necessary and sufficient conditions. A **necessary condition** is one that must be present in order for language to occur in a normal way. A **sufficient condition** is one that, if present, ensures that language will develop normally. It is rare for a complex behavior to have a single sufficient condition. On the contrary, it may have several necessary conditions, none of which is sufficient by itself to ensure a positive outcome.

Three classes of variables have been proposed as necessary or sufficient conditions for language acquisition. These are environmental, cognitive, and innate factors. Although each of these is sometimes discussed to the exclusion of the other two, it is likely that all three classes of variables are needed for a complete account of language acquisition. If so, a successful theory of acquisition will be one that explains the interactions among these factors.

This chapter is organized in the following way. The beginning section examines the role of the environment on language acquisition. We consider children who receive little or no exposure to language and also consider the special modifications adults make when speaking to children acquiring language. The second section discusses cognitive contributions to language acquisition. The final section addresses the question of whether, in addition to environmental and cognitive factors, there are innate constraints that guide the child's journey to language mastery.

The Linguistic Environment

The effect of experience on human nature has been a source of fascination for philosophers, psychologists, and laypeople. It is most commonly expressed nowadays in terms of the familiar heredity versus environment, or nature versus nurture arguments. What is most responsible for our knowledge and behavior, our biological predispositions or the shaping done by our environments? These arguments have typically evoked passionate reactions and not uncommonly extreme positions, and this is no less true of language than of other aspects of behavior.

Rather than pit nature against nurture, it might be more productive to begin by looking at the language environment into which children are born and then assess to what extent the acquisitions we discussed in the last two chapters can be accounted for in environmental terms. There are many questions related to the role of the environment in language acquisition: Is exposure to language needed for language acquisition? Does the exposure have to be within a particular time frame? What types of language input are most useful?

Feral and Isolated Children

The first question has been addressed through studies of feral and isolated children. **Feral children** are those who have grown up in the wild. Lane (1976) presents a detailed description and analysis of a boy named Victor, who was found in the woods of France in 1797. Peasants spotted the boy running naked through the woods, searching for potatoes and nuts, and he was subsequently captured by some hunters and brought to civilization. They called him the Wild Boy of Aveyron, after the province in which he was found.

The Wild Boy came to the attention of Jean-Marc-Gaspard Itard, a young physician. At the time of his capture, Victor was thought to be about 12 or 13 years old. He had no speech, although his hearing was normal and he uttered some sounds. Other physicians thought that Victor was deaf and retarded, but Itard was optimistic that he could be trained to be socialized and to use language. Itard worked intensively with Victor for 5 years, using techniques of language training and behavior modification similar to those used by modern researchers. For example, he taught Victor to name objects such as milk by presenting the object and then the French word for it. Victor would name objects that were presented, but would not request them by using their names.

Victor had other problems with language. One was that he developed a gestural communication system that interfered with the language training. Lane suggests that the signs might have supplanted his need to acquire spoken language. Another problem was Victor's understanding of words. Victor associated a particular name with a particular object, rather than with a class of objects. For instance, when taught the word for book, he initially applied it to only one book. Only with considerable effort could Itard teach Victor to generalize names for classes of objects.

In general, Victor's language progress was poor. There are several competing explanations for this fact. Some observers believed that Itard's techniques were defective and that Victor might have acquired more language if given better instruction. Others embraced the hypothesis that Victor was past the critical period for language acquisition. This view holds that exposure to language must occur within a specified time period (for example, by puberty) in order for language to be acquired normally. Although no one is sure, Victor was believed to be about 16 years old when Itard's training began. Finally, some scholars believe that Victor was either mentally retarded or autistic from the beginning and that he was perhaps abandoned in the woods for that reason. Lane (1976) disputes the latter point and tends to agree with Itard's analysis that Victor was normal when born and that the symptoms he displayed were a consequence of his isolation in the wild.

Isolated children are those who grow up with extremely limited human contact. The best-documented case is of a child who experienced extreme social and physical isolation from 20 months of age until about age 13½ years (Curtiss, 1977, 1981; Curtiss, Fromkin, Krashen, Rigler, & Rigler, 1974; see also Rymer, 1993). The child is referred to in the scientific literature as Genie.

Some understanding of Genie's family background is helpful. Despite the fact that her father was adamant about not having children, Genie's mother became pregnant 5 months into their marriage. Late in the pregnancy, the father-to-be viciously beat and tried to kill his wife. Later, after the child was born, the father kept her in the garage to avoid hearing her cry. The child died at 2½ months of pneumonia and overexposure. A second child, a boy, was born the following year and died within 2 days. Another son was born 3 years later. The child's development was slow, and eventually his paternal grandmother took him into her home.

Three years later Genie was born. She was average in birth weight, but suffered from a congenital hip dislocation that required a splint. Pediatric checkups for the next few months indicated essentially normal development, but by the eleventh month—6 months after the last checkup—she weighed only 17 pounds. Shortly after that, she developed an acute illness that required her to be brought to another pediatrician, who indicated that she showed signs of possible retardation. This statement had tragic consequences, for it was used by Genie's father to justify extreme neglect and isolation on the grounds that he believed the child to be profoundly retarded.

Curtiss (1977) reports the conditions under which Genie lived:

> Genie was confined to a small bedroom, harnessed to an infant's potty seat. Genie's father sewed the harness, himself; unclad except for the harness, Genie was left to sit on that chair. Unable to move anything except her fingers and hands, feet and toes, Genie was left to sit, tied-up, hour after hour, often into the night, day after day, month after month, year after year. At night, when Genie was not forgotten, she was removed from her harness only to be placed into another restraining garment—a sleeping bag which her father had fashioned to hold Genie's arms stationary (allegedly to prevent her from taking it off). In effect, it was a straight jacket. Therein constrained, Genie was put into an infant's crib with wire mesh sides and a wire mesh cover overhead. Caged by night, harnessed by day, Genie was left to somehow endure the hours and years of her life. (p. 5)

Genie had very little exposure to language during her imprisonment. Her father apparently did not speak to her, and he prevented other family members from entering the room. There was no TV or radio. The room was in the back of the house, so that Genie probably heard very little speech or noise from the street.

Her father responded to her few sounds by beating her. Eventually she learned to suppress all vocalization.

Genie was ultimately rescued, when she was 13½ years old, by accident. After a violent argument with her husband, Genie's mother took Genie and escaped to her own mother's home. Shortly afterward, Genie's mother, who was almost blind, went to a family aid building to check into services for the blind. She brought Genie with her, and a worker noticed the frail child and alerted her supervisor. After questioning the mother, they called the police, who took Genie into custody. After charges were filed against the family, Genie's father committed suicide.

At this point, Genie was severely undernourished and displayed almost no social skills. She had no language skills at all. After being placed in a program of language remediation, Genie began to show some language gains, but her development was uneven. Phonologically, she showed signs of using intonation appropriately, but also showed many substitutions of speech sounds. Her semantic development was rapid and extensive. She begin acquiring vocabulary within 2 months of entering the hospital, and her first words included a wider variety of concepts than that typically found early in language development (for example, words for colors, numbers). Once she began putting words together, she used semantic relations similar to those found in normal children. However, her syntactic development was slow. She displayed few grammatical morphemes and no complex syntactic devices (for example, relative clauses). What she did was to string together content words with little grammatical structure, albeit with relatively clear meaning, as in sentence (1):

(1)   I like hear music ice cream truck. (Curtiss, 1981, p. 21)

Her cognitive development appeared to be well in advance of her language development since she sometimes expressed subtle or complex ideas with rudimentary syntax, as in sentence (2):

(2)   Think about Mama love Genie. (Curtiss, 1981, p. 21)

A puzzling aspect of Genie's language development was that she appeared to process language in the right hemisphere, even though she was right-handed and had no discernible damage to the left hemisphere. Ordinarily, right-handed individuals process language principally with the left hemisphere (see Chapter 13). Curtiss and her colleagues speculated that Genie's left hemisphere may have suffered "functional atrophy" from lack of use, forcing her to acquire language with the right hemisphere.

Although there are many other reports of feral or isolated children (see Reich, 1986), the cases of Genie and Victor are representative. It is clear from these two instances that the overall prognosis for acquiring language after prolonged isolation from other humans is quite bleak. Given the extreme circumstances of their early years, it is perhaps remarkable that they were able to do as well as they did.

However, these reports leave many unanswered questions. They are consistent with the notion that children must be exposed to language early in life in order to develop language properly, but we do not know how early this experience must be. Studies by Newport (1990) indicate that the age at which children acquire certain aspects of language is correlated with the level of acquisition: the earlier the acquisition, the higher the level of learning. On the basis of this research, it seems reasonable to infer that the prognosis for Victor and Genie might have been considerably better had they been given language instruction at a younger age. But these case studies do not provide us with a precise idea of the kinds of language to which a child must be exposed. All we can conclude is that severe isolation for prolonged periods of time produces gross deficits in a child's language.

Motherese

Another line of research that has examined how the linguistic environment might shape language development deals with the way adults speak to young children. Adult-to-child language, which has been called **motherese,** differs in a number of ways from adult-to-adult language (see Table 12-1). In general, speech to children learning language is shorter, more concrete, more directive, and more intonationally exaggerated than adult-directed speech. Although it would appear that such properties would assist children in their language development, data on this basic question are relatively scarce, and widely different opinions exist on the matter (DePaulo & Bonvillian, 1978; Hoff-Ginsburg & Shatz, 1982; Marshall, 1980; Snow, 1979).

The motherese hypothesis (Gleitman, Newport, & Gleitman, 1984) states that there is a relationship between the speech adjustments adults make and children's language development. The strong form of the hypothesis claims that these features are necessary for language to develop properly; if so, the absence of these features would be predictive of a child's language difficulty. The weak form of the hypothesis claims that these linguistic features assist a child's development.

There have been two approaches to testing the motherese hypothesis. One is the correlational approach. Mothers naturally vary in their use of the features

Table 12-1. Some Characteristics of Adult Speech
to Children

Language Level	Characteristic(s)
Phonological	Exaggerated intonation Clear articulation
Syntactic	Shorter sentences
Semantic	Use of diminutives (for example, *doggie*) Concrete referents
Pragmatic	Preponderance of directives and questions

shown in Table 12-1, and it is possible to exploit this normal range of variation by correlating mothers' tendency to use these aspects of language with measures of their children's language progress.

In general, correlational studies have found limited relationships between parental speech and child language. Newport, Gleitman, and Gleitman (1977) tape-recorded the speech of 15 girls aged 12 to 17 months with their mothers in two sessions that were conducted 6 months apart. Most aspects of child language were unrelated to any characteristics of the mothers' speech. Others were related to specific aspects of maternal speech. The clearest example was verb auxiliaries, which were related to the frequency of yes/no questions in maternal speech, such as *Did you eat?* Mothers who used more yes/no questions had children who used more auxiliaries. This result has been replicated by Furrow, Nelson, and Benedict (1979) and by Gleitman and colleagues (1984). As Gleitman and colleagues note, the observation that the most robust correlation deals with a complex aspect of language does not fit with the idea that "simplifying" adult speech promotes child language. In this instance, it is the presence of a complex aspect of language that is facilitating the child's progress.

Of course, there are problems in interpreting correlational studies. A positive correlation between parental speech and child speech does not mean that the parental speech causes the child speech. It is also possible that the parent's speech is contingent upon child behavior, such as signals that the child is not understanding or is bored. Bohannon and Marquis (1977) have demonstrated that adult speech to children is related to child responses. The alternative to the correlational approach is to use an experimental approach, in which different groups of children are randomly assigned to different types of adult speech. While early experimental attempts were unsuccessful (Cazden, 1965), there is now clear evidence that such adult speech input can influence development.

Nelson, Carskaddon, and Bonvillian (1973) found that language development can be facilitated if children are presented with new syntactic information that is related to the child's previous sentence. These children, between 30 and 40 months of age, were seen regularly for 13 weeks and were assigned to one of three groups. The recast-sentence group received new sentences related to the child's sentence; for example, if the child said *Allgone truck*, the experimenter would expand it into a grammatical sentence such as *Yes, the truck is all gone*. The new-sentence group received relatively short, grammatical sentences that excluded the content words of the child's previous utterance. A control group received no special treatment. The children's progress in five aspects of language (MLU, sentence imitation, noun phrases, verb phrases, and auxiliary verbs) was assessed. The results indicated that the recast-sentence group showed marginally more linguistic advancement than the new-sentence group on the two measures of verb development, but the two groups performed the same on the three other measures. The recast-sentence group outperformed the control group on the two verb measures as well as on the test of imitation.

A later study by Nelson (1976) showed that the effects of linguistic input can be quite specific. He arranged for one group of children to hear recasts of negative *wh*-questions (*Why don't you play on the swing?*) and for another to hear recasts of complex verb constructions. The finding was that each group showed advances only in the type of speech they heard.

These studies provide a more direct link between adult speech and child language development than in correlational studies, but they are limited in several respects. First, although they indicate that adult speech may influence child speech, they do not demonstrate that such speech modifications are necessary for normal language acquisition. Thus, they provide support only for the weak form of the motherese hypothesis. Second, the studies are limited in the number of grammatical constructions that have been used. As noted earlier, Newport, Gleitman, and Gleitman (1977) examined a number of maternal characteristics and found that most were not correlated with child speech.

This pattern of results may be interpreted in light of the distinction between universal and particular characteristics of language. Certain aspects of language, such as the semantic categories of agent, action, object, and so on, appear to be universal, whereas others, such as auxiliaries and *wh*-questions, vary from language to language. This distinction might be expected to influence the extent to which a grammatical property is sensitive to environmental variables. Particular features must be learned and hence it is reasonable to expect them to be related to appropriate environmental variables, such as frequency of occurrence. Recall that children's acquisition of auxiliaries was related to the mothers' use of yes/no questions in several correlational studies. One feature of yes/no questions in English is that the subject and the auxiliary are inverted, thus placing the auxiliary verb at the beginning of the sentence. It seems likely that this position is more salient for the child and therefore might lead to improved performance on auxiliaries because of the attention it receives. In contrast, universal features may not be learned at all, but might be part of the child's innate equipment.

In any event, the distinction between universal and particular linguistic features makes sense both linguistically and psychologically. It suggests that there are some fragile aspects of language that are sensitive to environmental variations and more sturdy aspects that need less support. Goldin-Meadow (1982) makes an apt analogy to gardening: some properties of language are like weeds that grow under any conditions and other properties are like hothouse orchids that need rather specialized conditions.

Summary

Studies of varying methodology have addressed the role of the environment in child language acquisition. Case studies of children who have undergone severe isolation indicate grossly delayed language and imply that exposure to language is a prerequisite for normal language growth. Correlational and experimental studies of motherese suggest that at least certain aspects of the speech adjustments adults make when speaking to children may influence the child's language development. However, some aspects of language appear to be impervious to variations in maternal language.

Cognitive Processes

In the preceding section, we saw that parents provide a structured environment for children who are acquiring language. Although some of these speech adaptations facilitate development, they are not sufficient to explain language acquisition. In order to benefit from these language lessons, children must have certain cognitive prerequisites. These include procedures for registering, storing, and analyzing linguistic information.

A simple analogy may be helpful here. Suppose you are taking a course in philosophy. The instructor is well prepared, lectures well, and is available when students have problems. Although all of these characteristics are beneficial, they do not guarantee the desired learning outcome. A course in philosophy typically requires students to think abstractly and to write analytical essays. Students who lack these skills may have considerable difficulty even if the course material is presented in an organized fashion.

The same is true for the child learning language. A structured environment is only helpful if the child has the ability to take advantage of the structure that is provided. In this section we will look at the cognitive skills children bring to the language learning task.

Operating Principles

One of the most productive approaches to this question has been Slobin's work on operating principles (Slobin, 1973, 1985). We may think of **operating principles** as children's preferred ways of taking in (or operating on) information. An early list of operating principles is shown in Table 12-2.

These principles have proven useful in explaining certain patterns in early child grammar. For instance, children in virtually all languages use fixed word order to create meanings, even though some languages have much freer word order than others. This early pronounced tendency seems related to Slobin's Principle C. We have already seen some of the major developments in the acquisition of grammatical morphemes. Children must first segment words into free and bound morphemes; this is presumably done by noticing different versions of the same

Table 12-2. Operating Principles Used by Young Children

A Pay attention to the ends of words.
B The phonological forms of words can be systematically modified.
C Pay attention to the order of words and morphemes.
D Avoid interruption or rearrangement of linguistic units.
E Underlying semantic relations should be marked overtly and clearly.
F Avoid exceptions.
G The use of grammatical markers should make semantic sense.

Source: D. I. Slobin, "Cognitive Prerequisites for the Development of Grammar," in C. A. Ferguson and D. I. Slobin (eds.), *Studies of Child Language Development* (New York: Holt, Rinehart & Winston, 1973), pp. 175–208.

word (Principle B) and by noticing the kinds of linguistic elements that may serve as bound morphemes (Principle A). And we know that when children come to learn a grammatical morpheme, they often overregularize it (Principle F).

Several of the principles are also useful in understanding children's acquisition of complex sentences. When first attempting to form negatives and questions, children often simply place the negative or question marker at the front of a simple declarative sentence. This seems to reflect a desire to avoid breaking up intact linguistic units (Principle D). Similarly, there is a tendency for children, when forming relative clauses, to do so first by simply attaching the clause to the end of the sentence. Only later do they embed the clause within the sentence.

These operating principles are first approximations to the kinds of cognitive prerequisites a child must have in order to benefit from linguistic experience. In his later work (Slobin, 1985), Slobin presents a revised list of principles, making them more specific and more numerous.

One problem with the notion of operating principles is that it is open to the charge of circularity. The evidence for operating principles is found in children's language patterns and then the principles are assumed to account for the patterns. Independent evidence of these operating principles would be helpful. It might be possible to see evidence of some of these principles in cognitive domains other than language, but, as written, they tend to be fairly specific to language. Slobin is noncommittal on the question of whether these processes are specific to language (modular) or whether they can be understood in terms of general cognitive processes. We turn now to cognitive processes that are more clearly independent of language.

Induction

Induction is the process of reasoning from the specific to the general. We use induction when we notice similarities among several instances and draw a generalization based on these similarities. Induction may come into play at both the lexical and the grammatical levels of language development.

At the lexical level, children must be able to derive the meaning of *dog* from their experiences with specific dogs. These, of course, vary in size, shape, color, and many other attributes. In order to induce the category, the child must be presented with both positive evidence (examples of the category) and negative evidence (nonexamples). These are usually supplied by parents, who are only too happy to tell children *Yes, that's a dog, a German shepherd* and *No, that's a cow.* Although this may sound very simple, it actually implies a great deal of cognitive processing. The child must remember the positive and negative instances, formulate hypotheses, and determine whether the evidence presented is consistent with the hypotheses being entertained. All of this may cause a significant memory burden.

In Chapter 10, we discussed the evidence regarding lexical induction. In brief, we found that the process of inducing lexical categories is related to both environmental and cognitive variables. On the environmental side, parents typically structure the word-learning environment for their children by providing positive and negative instances of concepts and by using consistent naming practices, such as naming the whole object before the parts (Ninio, 1980). In addition, children appear to be operating with the notion of cognitive constraints, such as the notion that a given object can only be assigned a single word label (Markman, 1989). These constraints serve to limit the number of hypotheses that the child must consider. On balance, it appears that a combination of a structured environment and a structured approach to learning greatly facilitates the child's acquisition of the lexicon.

This discussion has been entirely at the level of the lexicon. As it turns out, the role of positive and negative evidence in the area of grammar is quite controversial, and I will postpone that discussion until the end of the chapter.

Sensorimotor Schemata

Recall from Chapter 3 that another way of characterizing the child's cognitive system comes from the work of Piaget, who expressed the belief that children undergo several qualitative shifts in their thinking throughout development. Piaget (1952) referred to the first 2 years as the sensorimotor period of development because the schemata the child uses to organize experience are directly related to taking in sensory information and acting on it. Sensorimotor schemata include banging, sucking, and throwing. The major development that culminates near the end of the sensorimotor period is the acquisition of object permanence, the notion that objects continue to exist even when they cannot be perceived. Once acquired, the child is no longer at the mercy of immediate stimuli but can respond on the basis of stimuli no longer present.

We would certainly anticipate that developments of this magnitude would be related to the child's language development. More specifically, we can make two predictions about child language. One is that the very young infant, who has not yet acquired object permanence, should use words that refer to concrete objects in the immediate environment and especially to objects that are easily manipulated by the infant. This appears to be the case, as early child language consists of a large number of "here and now" words.

A second prediction is that infants who have mastered object permanence should begin to use words that refer to objects or events that are not immediately present. Two such words are *allgone*, as in *allgone truck*, and *more*, as in *more milk* (when referring to milk that is no longer present). One way to express the idea behind this prediction is to use the metaphor of a waiting room (Johnston & Slobin, 1979). Imagine a room with two doors, one an entry door and the other an exit door. The entry door refers to the achievement of the cognitive prerequisite; this puts the child in the waiting room. Opening the exit door depends upon noncognitive factors, such as the amount of exposure to the linguistic item and the linguistic complexity of the item. Depending upon these and other factors, the length of stay in the waiting room (the time between the cognitive achievement and the corresponding linguistic achievement) will vary.

This hypothesis has been tested in a number of experiments. Most research has found that the predicted delay between object permanence and the acquisition of *more* and *allgone* has held in some instances, but not all (Corrigan, 1979; Gopnik, 1984; Tomasello & Farrar, 1984). For instance, Tomasello and Farrar report varying delays of from 0 to 8 months, depending upon the criteria used for object permanence and on the child. Gopnik (1984) suggests that object permanence develops simultaneously with these words. The idea is that just when children are acquiring what is, for them, a difficult concept, they begin to notice linguistic expressions that refer to the concept. These expressions are salient to the child because they are relevant to what the child is learning at the time. Thus, the words are acquired with a very short cognitive-linguistic lag, or none at all.

Although these results are not entirely supportive of the second hypothesis, they do generally support the cognitive approach to language acquisition. In particular, the results stress the importance of the child's cognitive level in determining how a child responds to linguistic input. The suggestion is that it is not enough for the child to be presented with a given lexical item—the child must be cognitively ready to learn the item before it will be given much attention.

Impairments of Language and Cognition

Our knowledge of the relationships between language and cognition has also been advanced by studies of children and adolescents with cognitive or linguistic impairments. The notion that there is a close relationship between language and cognition has generally been supported by studies of individuals with Down's syndrome (reviewed by Rosenberg, 1982). These individuals tend to have language delays that are proportionate to the severity of the cognitive disability. However, in certain individuals, there can be significant discrepancies between the level of cognitive functioning and the level of linguistic functioning.

Some individuals display cognitive skills that are advanced relative to the individual's linguistic skills. Curtiss (1981) contrasts the language development of mentally retarded children with that of Genie, whom we discussed earlier in the chapter. The children who were mentally retarded tended to produce sentences with appropriate and sometimes complex syntax but with relatively rudimentary meaning, as in (3). In contrast, Genie expressed herself in sentences that were often grammatically rudimentary but semantically and conceptually more advanced, as in (4).

(3) *Adult:* Does your Daddy stay home all day and cook?
    Child: Nope. He was not comin' home.
(4) *Adult:* Why aren't you singing?
    Genie: Very sad.
    Adult: Why are you feeling sad?
    Genie: Lisa sick.

Although Genie's linguistic skills were rudimentary, her cognitive development appeared to be more age-appropriate. If so, this would provide evidence against the thesis that cognition is sufficient for language.

The hypothesis that cognition is necessary for language has not fared much better. Recently, Bellugi and her colleagues (Bellugi, Bihrle, Jernigan, Trauner, & Doherty, 1990) have studied individuals with Williams syndrome, a rare disorder that is characterized by an "elfin-like" facial appearance, mental retardation, and cardiac defects. Despite their cognitive impairment, these individuals' syntactic skills were found to be normal. The failure to find syntactic delays in individuals with Williams syndrome is not consistent with the notion that cognition is necessary for language.

Some may complain that this condition, in which there is sparing of syntax in the presence of cognitive deficits, is rare. But if normal cognitive development is necessary for normal language development, it should not happen at all. Together with the lukewarm support for the cognitive thesis in object permanence studies, these results suggest that we need to look beyond cognitive factors in our efforts to explain the course of language development. In particular, we must look at factors that are not part of general cognitive skills but rather are specific to language.

Summary

Research on cognitive prerequisites for language development has proceeded on the assumption that certain cognitive processes must be in place for the child to benefit from structured language lessons. We have considered three types of cognitive processes that may assist or guide language development. Operating principles are preferred ways of taking in linguistic information. Induction refers to the process of drawing general patterns from specific examples. Object permanence is the knowledge that objects do not depend on our perception of them for their existence. The general prediction that the cognitive position makes is that children with a given cognitive prerequisite should acquire corresponding aspects of language more rapidly than those without the prerequisite. This hypothesis has only been directly assessed in the area of object permanence, where it has received some support.

Finally, we saw that in certain individuals there are dissociations between language and cognition: relatively strong cognitive skills with weak linguistic skills or strong linguistic skills with weak cognitive skills. These observations suggest that cognitive development, although it is generally associated with language development, may not be either necessary nor sufficient for it.

Innate Mechanisms

In this final section of the chapter we consider the role of innate mechanisms in language acquisition. These are easily the most controversial of the processes we have considered in this chapter. Although it is generally agreed that environment and cognition play some role in a full account of development, the notion that these processes are constrained by innate properties of the human mind is greeted with diverse reactions. It is thought to be a necessary assumption by some, met with skepticism by others, and with downright hostility by still others. In this section we will examine the reasons why some theorists have assumed innate constraints and assess their merits of their arguments.

The Language Bioprogram Hypothesis

One version of how innate processes operate in child language has been called the **language bioprogram hypothesis** by Bickerton (1981, 1983, 1984). Bickerton's claim, in brief, is that we, as children, have an innate grammar that is available biologically if our language input is insufficient to acquire the language of our community. It is something like a linguistic backup system.

Pidgins and creoles   In order to understand this idea more fully, we have to make a few distinctions. A **pidgin** is "an auxiliary language that arises when speakers of several mutually unintelligible languages are in close contact" (Bickerton, 1984, p. 173). Typically this occurs when workers from diverse countries are brought in as cheap labor in an agricultural community. Immigrant workers come to speak a simpler form of the dominant language of the area—just enough to get by. A **creole** occurs when the children of these immigrants acquire a pidgin as their native language. Since access to native speakers of the dominant language is usually limited, these children receive the impoverished pidgin version as their primary linguistic input.

Bickerton (1983) observed that the conditions necessary to produce creoles have existed numerous times between 1500 and 1900 when various European nations developed labor-intensive agricultural economies in isolated, underpopulated tropical islands throughout the world. Bickerton's studies have focused on creoles in Hawaii. Although Hawaiian contact with Europeans goes back to the 18th century, it was not until 1876 that a revision of the U.S. tariff laws led to a large influx of indentured workers to harvest Hawaiian sugar. Since Hawaiian creole developed between 1900 and 1920, it was possible for Bickerton to study the development of the creole by studying the speech of people who are still living. In particular, he examined the language of immigrants who moved to Hawaii and that of their children who were born in the first two decades of this century.

The speech of pidgin speakers was rudimentary. In many cases, there was no recognizable syntax and the language resembled a linguistic free-for-all. Some speakers used one word order and others another; the word orders were often related to the speaker's own native language. Moreover, there was an absence of complex sentences in pidgin: pidgin sentences had no subordinate clauses, and even single-clause utterances often lacked verbs. In addition, there was no consistent system of anaphora (see Table 12-3).

The language bioprogram   Despite this impoverished linguistic input, the children of immigrants developed a creole that was fairly sophisticated. It included consistent word order, the use of complex sentences with relative clauses, and the distinction between definite and indefinite articles. Unlike pidgins, the creoles

Table 12-3.   Examples of Hawaiian Pidgin and Hawaiian Creole English

Pidgin	Hawaiian Creole English
Building—high place—wall part—time— nowtime—and then—now temperature every time give you.	*Get one* [There is an] *electric sign high up on da wall of da building show you what time an' temperature get* [it is] *right now.*
Now days, ah, house, ah, inside, washi clothes machine get, no? Before time, ah, no more, see? And then pipe no more, water pipe no more.	*Those days bin get* [there were] *no more washing machine, no more pipe water like get* [there is] *inside house nowadays, ah?*
No, the men, ah—pau [finished] *work— they go, make garden. Plant this, ah, cabbage, like that. Plant potato, like that. And then—all that one—all right, sit down. Make lilly bit story.*	*When work pau* [is finished] *da guys they stay go make* [are going to make] *garden for plant potato an' cabbage an' after little while they go sit down talk story* ["shoot the breeze"].
Good, this one. Kaukau [food] *any kind this one. Pilipin island no good. No more money.*	*Hawaii more better than Philippines, over here get* [there is] *plenty kaukau* [food], *over there no can, bra* [brother], *you no more money for buy kaukau* [food], *'a'swhy* [that's why].

Source: D. Bickerton, "Creole Languages." In S-Y. Wang (eds.), *The Emergence of Language: Development and Evolution* (New York: W. H. Freeman, 1983).

resembled the structural rules of other languages. From these observations, Bickerton concluded that children have an innate grammar that, in the absence of proper environmental input, serves as the child's language system. He called this system the **language bioprogram.**

However, there are other possible interpretations of Bickerton's research. One is that the sophistication found in the children's creoles was based on their access to English, the language of the plantation owners. Bickerton points out, however, that contact between immigrant families and owners was limited and that the Hawaiian creole differed in several respects from English. Another possibility is that linguistic features not attributable to English could be derived from the original native languages of the parents. For example, children whose parents were Portuguese might incorporate some Portuguese elements into their creoles. Again, the evidence provided by Bickerton suggests otherwise; he found that Hawaiian creole was strikingly similar to creoles created by children in very different parts of the world.

The language bioprogram hypothesis has been further buttressed by studies of language development in congenitally deaf children by Goldin-Meadow and her colleagues (Feldman, Goldin-Meadow, & Gleitman, 1978; Goldin-Meadow, 1982; Goldin-Meadow & Mylander, 1990). The children were between 13 months and 4 years at the start of the study, and were studied every 2 to 4 months for about a year and a half. None of these children were exposed to conventional sign language; most were educated by the oral method, which emphasizes lipreading, and some were not in any educational program. Nevertheless, the children invented a form of gestural language that was similar in many respects to the language of children with normal hearing. They acquired aspects of language in the same sequence, and at roughly the same age, as hearing children. One-sign utterances appeared at about 18 months, followed by two- and three-sign utterances. Moreover, they expressed semantic relations that were similar to those used by children at the two- and three-word stages. They also used gestures that were similar morphologically to sign language. Thus, when linguistic input is minimal, deaf children may create a gestural language that is similar in many respects to normal child language.

We have been discussing how the proposed bioprogram might operate in the absence of ordinary linguistic stimulation. What happens if children are given appropriate linguistic input? Bickerton suggests that under these circumstances the bioprogram is suppressed and children instead learn the native language. In particular, he claims that children use what he calls the **preemption principle:** "If you hear people using a form different from the one you are using, and do not hear anyone using your form, abandon yours and use theirs" (Bickerton, 1984, p. 186). This principle is based on assumptions found elsewhere in language development: the assumption that there is one unique form for a given function (Pinker, 1984) and the assumption that alternative candidates for that form are in competition with one another (Rumelhart & McClelland, 1986).

Bickerton's research provides a fascinating perspective on the nature of biological limits on language learning. We have seen throughout this text that Chomsky and other nativists have emphasized the task-specific or modular nature of our language capacity, and Bickerton's hypothesis is consistent with this emphasis. But it is more than that. **Task specificity** refers to the notion that the cognitive processes associated with language use are not general purpose problem-solving processes but are instead restricted to language. Bickerton goes a step further: not only is the language bioprogram specific to language but it is itself highly specific—a prepackaged, ready-to-go linguistic system.

Parameter Setting

Bickerton's language bioprogram may be thought of as a specific instance of a general innate mechanism called **parameter setting.** The notion of parameters plays a key role in the concept of a universal grammar (Chomsky, 1981). In this view, grammar can be defined in terms of a set of parameters corresponding to each of the subsystems of the language (binding, government, and so on), with each parameter having a finite (usually small) number of possible settings. Various combinations of these parameter settings then yield all of the languages of the world. According to Chomsky, children are born with the knowledge of the parameters and their settings. The task of acquiring a language is then reduced to identifying which parameter settings apply to one's native language.

One parameter is called the **head parameter** and has been discussed by Cook (1988). Each phrase in the language has one element that is most essential, which is called the head. It is the noun in noun phrases and the verb in verb phrases. The head parameter specifies the position of the head within the phrase. In English noun phrases, the head noun occurs first. In sentence (5), for example, the head *the man* appears to the left of the phrase *with the bow tie*. It turns out that the head also appears first in verb phrases, as shown, for example, in sentence (6); here the head *liked* occurs before *him*. This is also true of adjectives in adjective phrases, as in sentence (7), and prepositions in prepositional phrases, as in sentence (8):

(5) the man with the bow tie
(6) liked him
(7) nice to see
(8) to the bank

Once we know that English is a head-first language, we know that this principle applies to all of the types of phrases in the language.

In contrast, in Japanese, the heads appear last rather than first. Thus, the verb appears last in sentence (9), which means *I Japanese am*.

(9) Watashi wa nihonjin desu.

Once again, this is a general characteristic of Japanese. For example, Japanese has postpositions rather than prepositions, as in sentence (10), which means *Japan in*.

(10) Nihon ni

Another parameter is the **null-subject parameter** (sometimes called the **pro-drop parameter**). As we discussed in Chapter 2, it is grammatically acceptable in languages such as Italian and Spanish to drop the subject of a sentence. In other languages, such as English, this is not permitted. This parameter, then, has two values: subject and null-subject. Hyams (1986) has argued that children are born with this parameter set to the null-subject value. This initial setting is called the **default value**—the child proceeds on the assumption that this value is correct unless given contrary evidence. If the null-subject is the default value, then children learning English would be expected to initially drop their subjects just as Italian and Spanish children (correctly) do. Hyams cited examples from L. Bloom (1970) that indicate that errors such as this do occur as in sentences (11) through (14):

(11) Play it.
(12) Eating cereal.
(13) Shake hands.
(14) See window.

Hyams assumes that as children are exposed to examples of well-formed English sentences, they adjust this parameter to the subject setting.

An alternative interpretation of these sentences is that young children have difficulty producing complete sentences (L. Bloom, 1970; P. Bloom, 1990). P. Bloom argues that children omit all constituents, not just subjects. In addition, he found that children were more likely to have shorter verb phrases when they included subjects in their utterances than when they didn't. This suggests that children have difficulty expressing all of the elements of their sentences, and so these elements compete for limited processing capacity. Hyams's view has also been criticized by Valian (1990), who argues that children begin with both values of the null-subject parameter.

These points certainly pose some problems for Hyams's model. However, despite these criticisms, the general class of parameter setting models remain attractive because parameters address a fundamental aspect of the acquisition process—that children rapidly acquire their native language despite enormous differences among languages. The general answer given by parameter setting models—that children are born with the settings and thus need only learn which setting their language is—would greatly simplify the language learning process for children. Any model that can explain how children do so much so quickly deserves to be taken seriously. However, the details of parameter setting models (such as whether the child begins with one value or two and whether there are different weights assigned to different values) may need further study.

The subset principle   Another way to think about how these parameter settings may be made is through what Pinker (1990) calls the **subset principle.** First think about languages as subsets of one another. Consider word order. English is a very strict word-order language, Russian allows a small set of admissible orders, and the aborigine language Warlpiri allows an almost total scrambling of word order within a clause. The idea of a subset is that Russian could be considered a subset of Warlpiri with somewhat more restricted word order. In the same way, with respect to word order, English may be considered a subset of Russian.

The question that arises is how children determine which system applies to their native language. Children must induce this system from the evidence presented to them. However, as we saw in the case of lexical induction, there are a great many possibilities and thus an apparent need to constrain the induction process in some way. Pinker argues that at the grammatical level these constraints are provided by the language itself. The subset principle is that children begin to search through possible languages by beginning with the smallest subset available (that is, most restrictive language). If there is no evidence from their linguistic input that this is their native language, they proceed to the next largest subset, until they find a match.

This principle allows for some testable developmental predictions. If fixed word order is the default value, then children all over the world should begin their linguistic careers by producing utterances that adhere to strict word order. If their native language is English, this would produce word orders that are similar to English. But if their native language has a freer word order, it would produce undergeneration (failure to use all of the orders permissible in the language). If, instead, children use free word order as the default value, then overgeneration (production of impermissible word orders) would occur in English but not in a free word-order language. These predictions are shown in Table 12-4.

Table 12-4. Predictions of Two Hypotheses about Children's Default
Assumptions about Word-Order Freedom

	Fixed-Constituent-Order Language	*Free-Constituent-Order Language*
Fixed order as default	No overgeneration	Undergeneration possible
Free order as default	Overgeneration possible	No undergeneration

Source: S. Pinker, "Language Acquisition," in D. N. Osherson and H. Lasnik (eds.), *Invitation to Cognitive Science.* Vol. 1, *Language* (Cambridge, MA: MIT Press, 1990), pp. 199–241.

According to Pinker (1990), the evidence is consistent with the notion that children use fixed word order as the default value and, therefore, with the subset principle. Children learning fixed-word-order languages generally stick to the orders used by their parents. Children learning free-word-order languages appear to use only some of the permissible orders of their language, at least in certain circumstances. Although more work needs to be done, the subset principle is a plausible account of how children deal with the tremendous number of possible languages they might consider.

The Issue of Negative Evidence

One important feature of the way in which the subset principle was formulated deals with the distinction between positive and negative evidence. At the grammatical level, positive evidence is evidence that a particular utterance is grammatical in the language that the child is learning; negative evidence is evidence that a particular utterance is ungrammatical. Children receive positive evidence when they are exposed to an utterance that is not corrected or otherwise indicated as inappropriate. Children receive negative evidence when someone indicates that a particular utterance is ungrammatical or inappropriate.

Pinker (1990) argues that it would be very difficult to acquire a language from positive evidence alone. This notion was based, in part, on some computer simulation studies of language learning done some time ago (see Gold, 1967). This work assumed that children use linguistic evidence to construct hypotheses about the language they are learning, much as a linguist would use such evidence to learn about a language in a foreign land. Gold found that when he wrote a program in which the computer received only positive evidence, it failed to adequately acquire the language. This was presumably because positive evidence is consistent with a great number of different grammars. Without knowing what is ungrammatical in a language, it is impossible to rule out some of the various competing grammars.

However, Pinker (1990) has claimed that, on the whole, parents do not provide sufficient negative evidence to enable a child to learn a language. He argues that although negative evidence is sometimes present, it is not systematically and consistently available to all children acquiring a language, and yet all normal children do acquire a language. Therefore, innate mechanisms, such as the subset principle, are needed to constrain the child's search processes. Pinker's argument is:

A. Positive evidence alone is consistent with too many competing grammars.
B. Negative evidence, which could constrain the problem space, is not generally available.
C. Therefore, some constraints must be innate.

This is another form of the poverty of the stimulus argument (Chapter 1). If we accept A, the argument rests on B. Let us then look at the research on negative evidence.

One often-cited study on this point was performed by Brown and Hanlon (1970), who examined parents' responses to various well-formed and ill-formed child utterances. The researchers were particularly interested in parents' explicit statements of approval or disapproval of child utterances. The parents in this study did little to correct their children's syntactic errors, although they sometimes corrected their children on semantic errors (when the children's statements were not true). Brown and Hanlon concluded that there was not "even a shred of evidence that approval and disapproval are contingent on syntactic correctness" (p. 47).

These results have been replicated and extended by Hirsh-Pasek, Treiman, and Schneiderman (1984), who studied 40 mother/child dyads where the children were 2 to 5 years of age. They replicated Brown and Hanlon's results with regard to the relative absence of explicit approval and disapproval of child utterances. However, they also examined implicit parental responses, such as when the mother repeated a child utterance with corrected syntax. The researchers found that these responses were more likely after an ill-formed child utterance than a well-formed child utterance, at least for the 2-year-olds. Thus, there are some subtle cues in parental responses to child speech that might assist the child's language development.

However, the results of this study are limited in several respects. First, there were no significant effects at 3 to 5 years, when children are acquiring many complex constructions that might conceivably be affected by parental input. Also, Hirsh-Pasek and colleagues were careful to point out that although their results show that subtle cues are sometimes present, there is no evidence (yet) that children actually capitalize on these cues. We know from other studies (for example, McNeill, 1966) that children are not always receptive to adult observations on their grammar.

On balance, these results leave the force of the nativist argument largely intact. Although negative evidence is present and may assist language development, research has not shown that it is necessary. Language, under normal rearing conditions, is quite robust: children from even poor environments acquire a mastery of their native language. This contrast between the poverty of the stimulus and the robustness of the child's language remains the most sound justification for innate mechanisms.

Summary

Several lines of evidence have been presented to support the assumption of innate mechanisms in language acquisition. Studies of creole language suggest that we have a linguistic backup system, the language bioprogram, which springs into action when language input is limited. The bioprogram may be thought of as a specific instance of the general concept of parameter setting. Some evidence has been presented that child learners have initial preferences in the parameter settings, although this point has been disputed. Finally, the argument has been made that there is insufficient negative evidence for children to induce the grammar of their native language and that, therefore, some innate constraints must guide this process.

Review Questions

1. Distinguish between necessary and sufficient conditions.
2. Describe the case study of Genie, and summarize her language progress.
3. Identify phonological, syntactic, semantic, and pragmatic characteristics of motherese.
4. Why might maternal yes/no questions be related with the child's acquisition of verb auxiliaries?
5. Define and illustrate operating principles.
6. Define induction.
7. Summarize the research on object permanence and language development.
8. Distinguish between creoles and pidgins.
9. Give one example of parameter setting.
10. Discuss the issue of negative evidence in language acquisition and the evidence that is germane to it.

Thought Questions

1. Critically evaluate the view that Victor was abandoned because he was mentally retarded or autistic.
2. When discussing Slobin's operating principles, I commented that it is not clear that they are independent of language or apply to other cognitive domains. Can you think of any domains in which these principles might apply?
3. Based on all of the research discussed in the chapter, what can you conclude regarding whether environmental, cognitive, or innate factors are necessary or sufficient? Explain your answer.

part *5*

Language in Perspective

13

Biological Foundations of Language

- Different language skills are represented in different parts of the brain. Individuals who have sustained brain damage often show deficits only in selected aspects of language.
- Studies of split-brain patients and normal individuals reveal that the left hemisphere of the brain controls language, especially syntactic processes and language production, for most people. The right hemisphere is essentially mute but plays a role in comprehension and in the pragmatic aspects of language.
- Studies of the evolution of language have examined hand preferences, brain specialization, and vocal tract specialization in nonhuman primates. Fossil records of vocal tract anatomy suggest that the capacity for speech is a recent evolutionary development.
- Although they do not use language in their natural environment, chimpanzees can be taught sign language. The degree of similarity between chimpanzee language and child language is a matter of considerable debate.

Introduction

Throughout this text, we have examined language from a psycholinguistic viewpoint—how individuals comprehend, produce, and acquire language. In the last two chapters, I will attempt to place these processes in a broader perspective. In this chapter, we will examine language processes from a biological viewpoint. In Chapter 14, we will look at language as a cultural phenomenon.

From a biological perspective, language has been regarded as special in the sense that it is a dividing line between humans and other species. The emergence of language occurred only recently in our evolutionary history, and the set of forces that led to this extraordinary development are not yet clear. We do know that part of the story concerns the evolution of brain mechanisms specialized for language functions. Language behavior, like all behavior, is mediated by brain structures, but because language is extremely subtle and multifaceted, it has a particularly complex representation in the brain. Although speculation about the brain has been going on for centuries, scientific knowledge about the brain and language has only accumulated in the last century or so.

It is important to know about the biology of language for two reasons. First, the study of brain regions related to language clarifies our previous discussion of language comprehension and production. We will learn that various aspects of our language capacity are not mere abstractions but rather have separate and specifiable representations in the brain. Second, the study of the biological foundations of language enriches our discussion of language acquisition. If specialized brain mechanisms enable children to acquire language, then how much language is possible in species, such as nonhuman primates, which lack these mechanisms?

This chapter is organized into three sections. In the first section, we look into cases of individuals who have suffered brain damage to the language regions of the brain. The second section addresses the nature of hemisphere differences in language and other functions, first with respect to human brains and later with respect to animals. The chapter concludes with a section that speculates on the evolutionary pressures that led to human language and assesses the studies that have attempted to teach language to chimpanzees.

Brain Mechanisms and Language

Some of the most significant insights into the biological foundations of language have come from individuals who have suffered damage to portions of the brain regions associated with language functions. These unfortunate individuals typically display uneven patterns of language behavior, with some functions spared and others dramatically impaired or even eliminated. A language disorder produced by brain damage is called an **aphasia.** As you might imagine, these "experiments of nature" vary tremendously in terms of the exact site of the brain damage and the corresponding behavioral patterns. Nevertheless, we begin by examining some of the more common forms of aphasia.

Major Types of Aphasia

Broca's aphasia   The disorder **Broca's aphasia,** also known as **expressive aphasia,** was discovered by and named after the French surgeon Paul Broca. Broca studied individuals who, after a stroke or accident, displayed halting, agrammatic speech. These individuals were often unable to express themselves by more than a single word at a time. Moreover, some parts of their speech were more affected than others: content words such as nouns and verbs were usually well preserved, whereas function words such as adjectives and articles were not. This dysfunction leads to impoverished speech, such as in the following excerpt, in which a patient is attempting to explain that he came to the hospital for dental surgery:

> Yes . . . ah . . . Monday . . er . . . Dad and Peter H. . . . (his own name), and Dad . . . er . . . hospital . . . and ah . . . Wednesday. . . . Wednesday, nine o'clock . . . and oh . . . Thursday . . . ten o'clock, ah doctors . . . two . . . an' doctors. . . . and er . . . teeth . . . yah. (Goodglass & Geschwind, 1976, p. 408)

In contrast, the individuals' ability to comprehend language appears to be less impaired than that of producing it.

The clear difficulty in articulating speech by Broca's aphasics might lead us to believe that its agrammatic nature is due to a voluntary economy of effort. That is, since articulation is so difficult—they speak slowly and often confuse related sounds—perhaps Broca's aphasics are trying to save effort by expressing only the most important words. Although this factor may have some role in the disorder, it is not the most important feature since many Broca's aphasics do no better after repeated efforts at self-correction. Moreover, the writing of these patients is usually at least as impaired as their speech, and individual words out of grammatical context are usually spared. These considerations suggest that the main feature of this disorder is the loss of the ability to express grammatical relationships, either in speech or in writing.

This pattern of deficits is usually found in individuals who have sustained damage to the frontal regions of the left hemisphere of the brain. Figure 13-1 shows some of the main functional areas of the cerebral hemispheres; this is a view of the left side (hemisphere). As you can see, the visual centers lie at the back of the brain in what is called the **occipital lobe.** The auditory regions in both hemispheres lie at the sides of the brain known as the **temporal lobes.** Motor centers controlling facial and speech muscles are located in the middle region of the brain, called the **parietal lobe,** with different points corresponding to different muscle groups. The **somatosensory regions,** which mediate our sense of touch, are also located in the parietal lobe, just behind the motor areas.

Figure 13-2 shows some of the areas specifically related to language functions. **Broca's area** is adjacent to the motor cortex and is part of the frontal lobe, which is intimately involved in processes such as thought, reasoning, judgment, and initiative. Although it is likely that Broca's area plays an important role in the process of speech production, it is overly simplistic to conclude that there is a one-to-one correspondence between brain regions and behavioral processes. Rather, these syndromes are best viewed as the operation of the brain tissue that remains (Jackson, 1882, cited in Goodglass & Geschwind, 1976).

Wernicke's aphasia   A few years after Broca's discovery, a young surgeon named Carl Wernicke discovered a different form of aphasia, which now bears his name. **Wernicke's aphasia,** which is sometimes called **receptive aphasia,** is associated

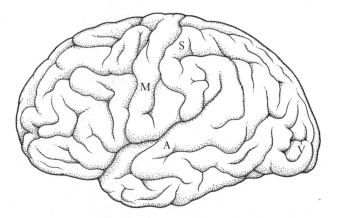

Figure 13-1.   Location of the primary motor and sensory regions on the cortex; M = motor, S = somatosensory, V = visual, and A = auditory. [From H. Goodglass and N. Geschwind, "Language Disorders (Aphasia)," in E. C. Carterette and M. P. Friedman (eds.), *Handbook of Perception.* Vol. 7, *Language and Speech* (New York: Academic Press, 1976), pp. 389–428.]

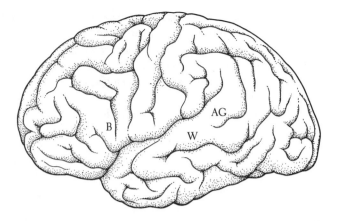

Figure 13-2. Location of the principal language areas on the cortex; B = Broca's area, W = Wernicke's area, AG = angular gyrus. [From H. Goodglass and N. Geschwind, "Language Disorders (Aphasia)," in E. C. Carterette and M. P. Friedman (eds.), *Handbook of Perception.* Vol. 7, *Language and Speech* (New York: Academic Press, 1976), pp. 389–428.]

with speech that is fluent but of no informational value, as in the following example:

> Well this is . . . mother is away here working her work out o'here to get her better, but when she's looking, the two boys looking in the other part. One their small tile into her time here. She's working another time because she's getting, too. . . . (Goodglass & Geschwind, 1976, p. 410)

Moreover, comprehension is also impaired. Broca's aphasics are generally able to demonstrate comprehension of simple sentences such as *Touch your knee* by performing nonverbal actions, whereas Wernicke's aphasics often have difficulty and will touch another, albeit related, part (such as an ankle). The brain regions associated with Wernicke's aphasia are typically located in the temporal lobe of the left hemisphere, adjacent to the auditory centers of the brain (see Figure 13-2).

Conduction aphasia   What do you think might be the behavior of an individual who has both Broca's and Wernicke's areas intact but has lost the main connection between them? Geschwind has found individuals with this brain deficit, called **conduction aphasia,** and they appear to be able to understand and produce speech. However, they are unable to repeat what they have just heard. Geschwind (1965) reports the case of an individual who, unable to repeat the word *president,* came up with *I know who that is—Kennedy,* which was a true statement at the time.

Other aphasias   The impression that we get when reading about such cases is that our language functions may often be broken down quite selectively, with comprehension damage and not production damage, or just the opposite. The literature on aphasia contains a rich variety of cases, many of which are baffling, but most of which fit this impression of discrete, separable language functions. Some of these language disturbances, although rare, are of great importance in enabling us to construct a model of normal language functioning.

One rare form of aphasia is called **pure word deafness.** Behaviorally, such individuals are unable to comprehend language in the auditory modality, although they are still capable of comprehending visual language and of producing language in either modality. Anatomically, there is damage to the auditory nerve, which sends messages to the auditory centers in the left hemisphere. In addition, there is a loss of those portions of the **corpus callosum** (the thick band of fibers that connect the two hemispheres) that send messages from the auditory region in the right hemisphere to the language areas, particularly Wernicke's area, in the left hemisphere. The result is that neither the left nor the right auditory center can transmit information to the language regions, so even though patients can hear some words, they cannot comprehend them.

Another interesting form of aphasia is called **alexia,** which is the dissociation (disconnection) of the visual regions from the language areas. In its most severe form, alexia prevents even the recognition of individual letters or matching of script and print (Goodglass & Geschwind, 1976). Damage to the angular gyrus leads to both alexia and **agraphia,** the inability to write. It is thought that the angular gyrus serves as an association area in the brain that connects one region with another. In particular, it is important for the association of visual stimuli with linguistic symbols, which influences both reading and writing. Alexia also sometimes occurs without agraphia; in one case (Dejerine, 1892, cited in Geschwind, 1965), damage to the visual cortex on the left side was coupled with an injury to the portion of the corpus callosum that connected an intact right visual area with the language areas on the left (Figure 13-3). Thus, visual stimuli are isolated from Wernicke's area, so that affected individuals can write but cannot read what they have written (Benson & Geschwind, 1969)!

Implications for Normal Language Processing

Comprehension and production   Geschwind (1972) has organized many of the available facts on aphasia and formulated a general model of normal language functioning. The proposal is shown in Figure 13-4.

Consider a simple situation in which we see something and then make a verbal comment about it. According to the model, the visual input is first sent to the visual regions of the brain and then to the angular gyrus. The message then goes to Wernicke's area, which creates a meaningful sequence of linguistic units and transmits it to Broca's area via the **arcuate fasciculus,** the primary pathway between the two areas. In Broca's area, the message is translated into motor commands that are sent to the speech muscles and finally articulated. If we felt a stimulus instead of seeing it, the sequence would begin in the somatosensory regions, go to the angular gyrus, and then to Wernicke's and Broca's areas. In a conversation, auditory input is transmitted to the auditory regions, then on to Wernicke's and Broca's regions.

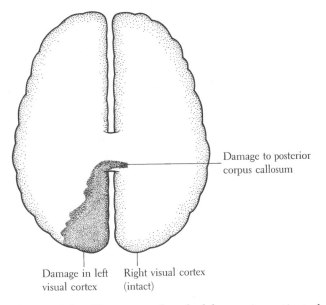

Figure 13-3. The pattern of cerebral damage in a patient who had alexia without agraphia. [From T. S. Brown and P. M. Wallace, *Physiological Psychology* (New York: Academic Press, 1980).]

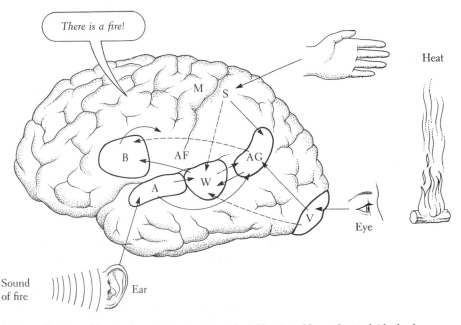

Figure 13-4. Pathways for language; known (solid line) and hypothetical (dashed line) pathways for language are shown; A = auditory area, V = visual area, S = somatosensory area, M = motor area, AG = angular gyrus, W = Wernicke's area, B = Broca's area, AF = arcuate fasciculus. [From R. A. McFarland, *Physiological Psychology: The Biology of Human Behavior* (Palo Alto, CA: Mayfield, 1981).]

Let us see whether this model illuminates our understanding of aphasic language. Injury to Broca's area presumably would lead to the halting, agrammatic speech characterisic of such patients because of a disruption in the process of translating sequences into motor commands but would leave comprehension intact. Injury to Wernicke's area would presumably disrupt comprehension mainly, but if the arcuate fasciculus and Broca's area were intact, the patient would speak fluently but in a manner that would be informationally empty. If only the arcuate fasciculus were damaged, the behavioral deficit for the patient would be in relating what she heard to what she should say, which shows up as conduction aphasia. In each of these cases, the model does a good job of explaining some of the major clinical impressions of aphasic language.

The model also bears on the question of whether an aphasic patient can recover some aspect of lost language ability through a secondary route when the primary route has been damaged. Recall that in conduction aphasia an individual responded *Kennedy* when unable to repeat *president.* How might this have occurred? One possibility is that with repetition precluded by damage to the arcuate fasciculus, a secondary route from Wernicke's area to the angular gyrus and then another from the angular gyrus to Broca's area may be involved (see Figure 13-4). Since the angular gyrus serves as an association area in the brain, it makes some sense that the patient, unable to supply the exact word, was able to recover an associated word.

The speech of Wernicke's aphasics has been found to contain many irrelevant associations. This is known as **paragrammatic speech.** Although excerpts of Wernicke's speech often sound like random combinations of words, it may be that the speech is disorganized as the patient shifts topics to an associatively related theme every few seconds. If so, a greater involvement of the angular gyrus in language processing after damage to Wernicke's area may explain the paragrammatic flavor of the speech of Wernicke's patients. In normal brains, these irrelevant associations would be inhibited by Wernicke's region. Thus, as noted before, the resulting behavioral performance is not simply the outcome of the regions that are injured but of the combined effect of partially damaged mechanisms with those that remain intact.

Syntax and semantics   Let us now look at neurolinguistic research that has clarified the role of syntactic and semantic processes in various aphasias. The traditional view has been that Broca's aphasia is a production deficit and Wernicke's a comprehension deficit. The implicit assumption is that the underlying language representation is intact with Broca's patients but that they have difficulty putting appropriately formulated linguistic messages into words. That is, they conceptualize sentences normally but have difficulty translating them into productive speech.

Clearly, data regarding the comprehension abilities of Broca's aphasics would be extremely useful here. Broca's aphasics have often been viewed as having normal comprehension, but there are good reasons for questioning this assumption. For one, many of the tests of comprehension have been extremely global in nature and do not clarify the respective roles of syntactic and semantic processes in comprehension. For another, it is possible to disguise deficits in comprehension somewhat more easily than deficits in production.

The latter point was brought out in a study by Caramazza and Zurif (1976), who examined comprehension capacities in Broca's, Wernicke's, and conduction aphasics. Patients heard a sentence and then had to choose which of two pictures corresponded to the sentence. Some sentences, such as (1), contained nouns that are nonreversible:

(1)　　The book that the girl is reading is yellow.

Here, knowing that girls read books but not vice versa is sufficient to understand the sentence correctly. In contrast, in a sentence such as (2), it is semantically possible for either the horse or the bear to be doing the kicking:

(2)　　The horse that the bear is kicking is brown.

In reversible sentences, we must process the syntactic structure carefully to arrive at the correct interpretation.

How did the three aphasic groups fare on this test? Wernicke's aphasics did poorly on both types of sentences, in agreement with their known difficulties with comprehension. More interestingly, both Broca's aphasics and conduction aphasics performed very well on nonreversible sentences, but their performance fell to chance levels on the reversible sentences. These results suggest that both groups suffer from subtle syntactic deficits in comprehension that are revealed once semantic cues are eliminated. Caramazza and Zurif suggest that Broca's area may be necessary in order to perform some syntactic operations; syntactic deficits may thus appear in conduction aphasics as a result of the dissociation of Wernicke's and Broca's areas.

Our understanding of syntactic ability in Broca's aphasics has been sharpened further by a report by Linebarger, Schwartz, and Saffran (1983). They gave four Broca's patients a series of sentences and asked them to judge whether the sentences were grammatical or not. Overall, the patients did surprisingly well. Their performance was particularly good on structurally deformed sentences such as (3). However, they were less adept at recognizing the unacceptability of sentences with an inappropriate pronoun, such as (4):

(3)　　*How many did you see birds in the park?
(4)　　*The little boy fell down, didn't it?

These results suggest that Broca's aphasics may be better at constructing syntactic representations during comprehension than previously believed but are deficient in using these representations during comprehension. It may be, for instance, that they can reach this level of syntactic understanding only when given the luxury of time afforded in the acceptability task, and that they can't compute syntactic representations quickly enough to help in normal comprehension.

New studies have also clarified the nature of language representation in Wernicke's patients. Wernicke's aphasics have difficulties in word finding that are well documented. Such individuals often report, when asked to name an object that they know, that they know what it is but can't seem to find the name. Experimental studies typically find very poor performance in naming tasks by Wernicke's aphasics.

Caramazza and Berndt (1978) argue that in addition to such word-retrieval problems, these aphasics also suffer from impairment in the semantic structure itself. The clearest evidence comes from a study in which Wernicke's aphasics were asked to make judgments about groups of three words at a time and then asked to indicate which two of the words were most similar to each other. Unlike Broca's aphasics and normal individuals, Wernicke's aphasics did poorly on this test, even though they had demonstrated knowledge of the definitions of the nouns on a pretest. When presented with a triad such as *mother, husband, shark*, Broca's and normal individuals tended to choose the first two, indicating knowledge of the semantic feature human/animal. Wernicke's aphasics tended to group words in terms of the affective characteristics of situations that are related to the words (for example, *mother* and *cook* are grouped on the basis that the patient's mother was a good cook). Thus, Wernicke's aphasics have difficulties that go beyond finding words; the semantic structure itself seems to be impaired.

Summary

The data from aphasic cases are important in psycholinguistics for they demonstrate dissociations between various linguistic functions that would be difficult if not impossible to find in other ways. There was no reason to think that a person would be able to write without being able to read or be able to speak and understand speech without being able to repeat what was heard, before these cases were reported.

Current research reveals at least three major types of aphasia. Broca's aphasia results from damage to a region in the left hemisphere near the motor cortex and leads to deficits in language production and syntactic analysis. Wernicke's aphasia is due to injury to an area adjacent to the auditory cortex in the left hemisphere and is associated with deficits in comprehension and semantic organization. Conduction aphasia results from dissociation of an intact Broca's area from an intact Wernicke's area and leads to a deficit in repetition. Thus, the distinctions noted throughout this book between comprehension and production and between syntax and semantics are not mere conceptual distinctions but relate in specifiable ways to the organization of the brain.

Lateralization of Language Processes

There has been a great deal of interest in the functions of the left and right hemispheres of the brain in recent decades, and part of that interest extends to the lateralization of language functioning. The term **lateralization** refers to the tendency for a given psychological function to be served by one hemisphere, with the other hemisphere either incapable or less capable of performing the function. We will begin by discussing individuals who have had a "split-brain" operation, then turn to normal individuals, and finally to lateralization in animals.

Split-Brain Research

A consistent finding in the research on aphasia was that language deficits are associated with damage to the left hemisphere of the brain more often than to the right hemisphere. Moreover, we have known for some time, from studies of animals, that communication between the hemispheres may be disrupted by severing the corpus callosum. In the animal studies, one hemisphere could be taught a specific task, then the other hemisphere could be tested. Typically, little or no learning was found in the other hemisphere, indicating little or no transfer of information between the hemispheres.

In the 1940s, these two lines of research converged in a dramatic way with the emergence of the split-brain operation. In this operation, human patients had their corpus callosum severed as a means of preventing the spread of epilepsy from one side of the brain to the other. The earliest reports (see Springer & Deutsch, 1989) gave little indication of what was to come. The patients' everyday behavior was virtually unaffected, and postsurgical testing revealed no obvious deficits. The surgery, by the way, produced relief from epileptic seizures in some patients but not others.

In the next two decades, more sophisticated and subtle research methods began to tell a far different story. In order to understand these studies, you must know some anatomical details of the two hemispheres. Figure 13-5 shows the visual pathways to the brain. Notice that the left visual field sends information to a portion of each retina in such a way that the information ultimately ends up in the right hemisphere. With an intact corpus callosum, this information then crosses over to the left hemisphere. Similarly, information from the right visual field projects to the left hemisphere. Information in the middle of the visual field projects to both hemispheres.

Similar arrangements exist in the auditory and tactile systems. The nervous system in humans is predominantly **contralateral,** which means that one half of the brain controls the other half of the body. This contralateral structure allows investigators to test more precisely the functions of the two hemispheres in the split-brain patient by presenting stimuli to just one side of the brain and observing the resulting behavior. The goal of these studies is to determine what skills are lateralized to one or the other side of the brain.

We are now in a position to examine some of the studies of split-brain patients. In one, a patient was shown a picture of a spoon in her left visual field and was asked what she saw. She replied, *No, nothing.* Then she was asked to select with her left hand the object from an array that was out of sight, and she correctly picked out the spoon from a group of common objects. When asked what she was holding, she responded *Nothing.* When asked to reach for the object with her right hand, she performed at a chance level, as likely to pick up a straw or a pencil as a spoon (Sperry, 1968).

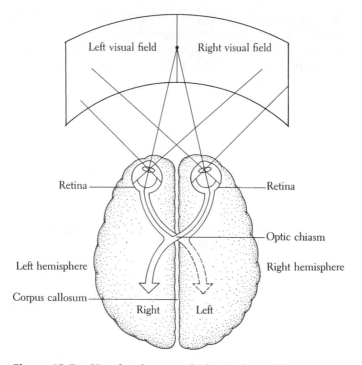

Figure 13-5.   Visual pathways to the hemispheres. [From S. P. Springer and G. Deutsch, *Left Brain, Right Brain,* 3rd ed. (New York: W. H. Freeman, 1989).]

These results can be interpreted in light of the way information gets processed by the two hemispheres. When a stimulus is presented to the left visual field, the right hemisphere of a split-brain patient becomes aware of the stimulus and is able to communicate that awareness in nonverbal ways, such as grabbing an object with the left hand, which is controlled by the right hemisphere. Since speech is predominantly controlled by the left hemisphere, the patient is unable to describe what she has seen. Moreover, the right hand is incompetent to find the correct object because the left hemisphere does not "know" what the object is.

Although the right hemisphere has a limited ability to perform language skills, it is more skilled at tasks that require spatial analysis. In one study, patients viewed line drawings of shapes such as triangles and squares that had been cut up into pieces. They had to reach behind a screen, feel three solid forms, and determine the ones that the fragmented figure would make if its pieces were reunited. The left hand proved to be very accurate at this task, but the right hand performed poorly (Nebes, 1972). This task requires the patient to construct a concept of a whole stimulus from its parts, a skill at which the right hemisphere excels. Related studies have shown that the right hemisphere is better than the left hemisphere in tasks that require the understanding and manipulation of spatial relationships, such as in drawing (Gazzaniga & LeDoux, 1978) and in dealing with geometric arrays (Franco & Sperry, 1977).

Returning to language in the right hemisphere, several studies have clarified the nature of right-hemisphere language skills. It is clear that certain aspects of language are better represented in the right hemisphere than others. Gazzaniga and Hillyard (1971) presented split-brain patients with simple pictures depicting visual scenes. After the scene, the subject was auditorily presented with two sentences and asked which one correctly described the picture. On this test, the patients proved to be incapable of distinguishing between sentences (5) and (6). Further testing revealed that these subjects could not deal properly with the future tense by distinguishing between sentences (7) and (8) or with the difference between singular and plural nouns in sentences (9) and (10). The single grammatical feature they dealt with properly was that of affirmative versus negative sentences as in (11) and (12):

(5) The boy kisses the girl.

(6) The girl kisses the boy.

(7) The girl is drinking.

(8) The girl will drink.

(9) The dog jumps over the fence.

(10) The dogs jump over the fence.

(11) The girl is sitting.

(12) The girl is not sitting.

These results are even more impressive when compared with the generally successful performance of these subjects on tests that required only comprehension of a single noun. That is, they correctly responded to *boy* and *girl*. In contrast, there was little or no evidence that the subjects could respond properly to verbs; when presented with verbal commands, such as *tap, smile,* and *frown*, the patients remained mute. It appears that the right hemisphere has, at best, very rudimentary syntactic mechanisms but that the mechanisms needed to retrieve single words from semantic memory are much better developed.

In addition to syntactic deficits relative to the left hemisphere, the right hemisphere also shows phonetic deficits. The right hemisphere may be capable of matching the sounds of words, as complete auditory images, to meanings but is deficient in the phonetic analysis of these sounds. For example, the right hemisphere might comprehend the meanings of *ache* and *lake* without knowing that they rhyme (Levy, 1974).

Reports on split-brain patients have also shown that the right hemisphere, although it may possess some abilities to comprehend language, is seriously deficient in language production (Gazzaniga & Sperry, 1967). However, aphasic patients with damage to the left hemisphere also experience difficulty in making nonverbal oral movements such as retracting the lips, clenching the teeth, and protruding the lips (Mateer & Kimura, 1977). It may be that the left hemisphere is specialized to perform sequences of motor acts, especially those involving the tongue and the jaw, but that such motor specialization is not specific to language production (Corballis, 1980; Sussman & MacNeilage, 1975).

The emerging picture of right-hemisphere language is that it is organized along different cognitive lines than left-hemisphere language. The right hemisphere is weak in syntactic and expressive skills, but less so in terms of semantic processes and comprehension. As Zaidel (1978) puts it:

> The LH [left hemisphere], in accordance with Chomsky's view, does seem to possess an innate and highly specialized linguistic mechanism whose paradigmatic functions are phonetic and syntactic encoding and analysis. The RH [right hemisphere], on the other hand, represents the limited linguistic competence that can be acquired by a more general purpose (nonlinguistic) cognitive apparatus through repeated exposure to experience and the formation of associations. (p. 196)

Lateralization in Normal Brains

Research on the representation of language and nonverbal functions in the intact brain has increased dramatically in the last few decades as techniques for studying the normal brain have been developed and refined. The visual-field task used with split-brain patients has also been used frequently with normal individuals. Another commonly used technique, referred to as a **dichotic-listening** task, involves the simultaneous presentation of different stimuli to the two ears. Initially developed by Broadbent (1954) to study attention, the technique was first used to examine ear differences and hemisphere differences by Kimura (1961). Kimura (1964) found that recall of verbally presented materials such as digits was superior in the right ear and that recognition of nonverbal stimuli such as melodies was better in the left ear.

The anatomical details of the auditory system are similar to, but somewhat more complex than, those of the visual system. Specifically, input from the right ear not only projects to the left hemisphere (the contralateral pathway) but also to the right hemisphere (the **ipsalateral** pathway). To account for dichotic-listening results, Kimura proposed that the contralateral pathways are stronger than the ipsalateral connections and that under the competing conditions of dichotic presentation, the former "block" the latter. Dichotic studies of split-brain patients indicate highly exaggerated right-ear advantages for speech stimuli: normal performance by the right ear with chance performance by the left ear. The failure of the left ear is due to two factors. First, the contralateral pathway (left ear to right hemisphere) is not helpful since the corpus callosum is not present to facilitate transfer to the left hemisphere. Second, the ipsalateral pathway (left ear to left hemisphere) is blocked or suppressed by the contralateral pathway. Thus, the left ear does poorly on this task. Kimura's model of performance under dichotic listening conditions with speech and nonspeech stimuli appears to fit both normal and split-brain data.

Nevertheless, the distinction between linguistic and nonverbal stimuli is unsatisfactory as a basis for predicting which hemisphere will control processing. One reason is that these terms are vague and imprecise; it is unclear what features of linguistic or nonlinguistic stimuli are important in influencing hemispheric control. As an example, studies of dichotic listening have been extended in an important way to nonmeaningful speech. Shankweiler and Studdert-Kennedy (1967) found right-ear advantages with nonsense syllables such as *ba* and *pa* played backward. Similarly, Zurif and Sait (1970) found a right-ear advantage for nonsense words, but only when they were arranged in a syntactically acceptable manner, as in *The wak jud shendily*. It appears that meaning is not necessary to elicit left-hemispheric processing of speech stimuli.

Conversely, sometimes right-ear advantages fail to occur with speech stimuli on dichotic tasks. The most prominent case is the failure to find right-ear advantages for vowels, although results for consonants have been found consistently (see, for example, Shankweiler & Studdert-Kennedy, 1967). It has been suggested (Darwin, 1973) that this difference is due to the greater length of vowels than consonants, since it is known that the degree of ipsalateral suppression is greater for shorter sounds than for longer ones.

Even more striking are cases in which linguistic stimuli that typically evoke right-ear advantages occasionally produce left-ear advantages. A case in point is a study by Darwin (1969, cited in Darwin, 1973) in which the subjects had to make judgments about pitch contours presented dichotically. They had to decide which two of four patterns—rising, falling, rising then falling, or falling then rising—had occurred. The subjects demonstrated a left-ear advantage for these stimuli, even when the contours amounted to a word. Darwin concludes that right-ear advantages are not invariably associated with linguistic stimuli. Specifically, they do not occur if the task is not linguistically significant.

This result has been replicated and extended by Wood (1975), who measured both reaction time and **evoked potentials,** the electrical activity of the brain immediately after the presentation of a stimulus. When the task was nonlinguistic (subjects had to make a judgment about the pitch of a speech sound), greater right-hemisphere activity was found. However, when the task was linguistic (to recognize the sound), the evoked potential was greater in the left hemisphere. Moreover, the linguistic task led to longer reaction times. Since the stimuli were identical in the two conditions, this result clearly shows that the stimulus factors alone are insufficient to determine hemispheric processing.

Bever (1980) has argued that the left hemisphere prefers to process information in a relational manner, whereas the right hemisphere uses a holistic mode of processing. **Holistic processing** involves the activation of a single mental representation of a stimulus; **relational processing** involves the activation of at least two distinct representations along with some relation between the two. An example might be listening to music. We can listen expansively to a piece of classical music, simply being moved by the music. Alternatively, we can attend to the same piece in a more relational (or analytic) manner, identifying different portions of the composition and the relations between them.

If this view is correct, then we ought to see some right-ear advantages for nonspeech stimuli when processed in a relational manner. Indeed, Bever and Chiarello (1974) found right-ear advantages on musical tasks for experienced musicians but not for nonmusicians. According to Bever, experienced musicians have developed relational processing strategies for organizing musical stimuli that are not available to the novice. Consistent with this interpretation, no differences have been found between the left ears of musicians and nonmusicians; the greater right-ear advantages for musical stimuli in musicians are due to the improved performance of their right ears.

Further support for the processing distinction between the hemispheres comes from studies of deaf individuals who had suffered strokes. Poizner, Klima, and Bellugi (1987) studied deaf persons who suffered strokes to either the right or the left hemisphere. These individuals raise an interesting question. If we regard the left hemisphere as specialized for language and the right hemispere for spatial skills, then where would we expect to find the brain mechanisms for American Sign Language, which is a spatial language? According to Poizner and colleagues, deaf signers have their language skills in the left hemisphere. If the left hemisphere is damaged by stroke, these individuals have impairments in language function similar to aphasic patients, but their nonlinguistic spatial skills (drawing, painting, and so on) are spared. If the right hemisphere is injured, nonlinguistic spatial skills are severely disrupted, but ASL remains intact.

Furthermore, Poizner and colleagues found that the regions in the left hemisphere associated with language use in ASL are similar (although not identical) to those for speech. One patient who suffered a stroke that included Broca's area displayed halting, agrammatic signing. Another, who suffered damage to Wernicke's area, had difficulty with comprehension and displayed paragrammatic language.

The distinction between relational and holistic processing appears to provide a good account of all of these results. When stimuli are processed in a relational nature, the left hemisphere assumes control. This is typically the case in language processing (including the processing of a spatial language) and may occur in some individuals with nonspeech stimuli such as music. In contrast, when stimuli are processed holistically, the right hemisphere prevails. This is ordinarily the case for nonlinguistic spatial stimuli and, for most people, musical stimuli.

Contributions of the Right Hemisphere

So far I have emphasized the talents of the left hemisphere and the ineptness of the right hemisphere. However, the right hemisphere also has some talents in the linguistic realm. Normal individuals use the skills of both hemispheres to comprehend and produce language, so we need to examine some of the ways that the two hemispheres interact during language use.

It appears that the right hemisphere is better prepared than the left to appreciate some of the pragmatic aspects of language. Kaplan, Brownell, Jacobs, and Gardner (1990) examined the ability of individuals with right-hemisphere brain damage to interpret conversational remarks. The subjects heard short vignettes that described the performance of one character and the relationship between two characters and then interpreted an utterance from one of the characters. Some of the utterances were literally true and some were literally false. For instance, in one vignette, Mark was playing golf poorly, and Hal said, *You sure are a good golfer,* which was literally false. The interpretation of this utterance is in part based on the relationship between the two men. When it was friendly, the comment might be taken as a white lie intended to encourage a friend, but when the relationship was hostile, it could be taken as a sarcastic statement. Kaplan and colleagues found that individuals with right-hemisphere damage were as adept as control subjects in interpreting the literally true sentences but were poorer at identifying the pragmatic intent of literally false utterances. In particular, they had difficulty integrating information about the performance with information about the characters' relationship.

Bihrle, Brownell, Powelson, and Gardner (1986) examined comprehension of humorous material by individuals with right- or left-hemisphere damage. Individuals with either right- or left-hemisphere damage were presented with three frames from a cartoon and had to select the final frame that would be most humorous. Right-hemisphere patients did more poorly than left-hemisphere patients on this task. More important, they made different kinds of errors. Right-hemisphere patients erred by selecting an ending that, although it was funny, was unrelated to the previous frames. In contrast, left-hemisphere patients selected an ending that was appropriate in content but not humorous. Similar results occurred with a verbal analog of the cartoon task. Bihrle and her colleagues conclude that the right hemisphere is adept at detecting surprise, whereas the left hemisphere is better at preserving coherence. Appreciation of humor depends, then, on both hemispheres.

Similar conclusions have come from studies of the lexicon. Remember that, in Chapter 5, we found that although all of the meanings of an ambiguous word are briefly entertained, inappropriate meanings are rapidly suppressed. Burgess and Simpson (1988) found that this pattern of performance is more characteristic of the left hemisphere than the right hemisphere. Using normal subjects, they presented the left and right hemispheres with a lexical decision task in which the letter strings were preceded by a lexically ambiguous prime word. The target words were related either to the dominant or the subordinate meaning of the ambiguous word. When stimuli were presented in the right visual field, the researchers found that the dominant meaning was immediately facilitated by the prime word, whereas there was less facilitation for the subordinate meaning, especially when the period between the prime and target words was increased. When stimuli were presented in the left visual field, the dominant meaning again showed immediate facilitation, but the inappropriate meaning was not suppressed and in fact increased in activation over time. Burgess and Simpson conclude that automatic spreading activation occurs in both hemispheres, but only the left hemisphere engages in controlled processing (that is, in suppression of inappropriate meanings).

Chiarello (1991) reviewed similar studies and concludes that both hemispheres play a role in the interpretation of word meanings. Chiarello suggests that we have two semantic systems, one in each hemisphere, which we use to interpret linguistic meaning. In the realm of lexical ambiguity, it appears that the left hemisphere makes a rapid commitment to a particular meaning whereas the right hemisphere maintains alternative meanings for a longer period of time. If so, the two hemispheres may play complementary roles in the comprehension of lexically ambiguous words. The efficiency of the left hemisphere may be an asset in most situations but when the wrong meaning has been selected (as in garden path sentences), the correct meaning may be more accessible in the right hemisphere.

The broader point is that language processes depend upon the joint functioning of both cerebral hemispheres. Chiarello (1991) concludes that "a consideration of the available neuropsychological data leads one to the view that processes subserved by each of the two cerebral hemispheres are necessary for the proper interpretation of words in context. One is not enough" (p. 274).

Lateralization in Other Species

It was once thought that laterality was exclusively human, but we now have several documented cases of the lateralization of species-specific vocalizations. One study (Petersen, Beecher, Zoloth, Moody, & Stebbins, 1978) investigated the perception of vocalizations in Japanese macaque monkeys. The investigators presented the vocalizations to either the left or the right ear. All five macaques showed better performance when the vocalizations were given to the right ear. Only one of the five monkeys from other species showed a right-ear advantage for macaque sounds. These results suggest the exciting possibility that human lateralization of speech is part of a larger pattern in which a number of species show lateralization on the left half of the brain for important, species-specific sounds.

This view is reinforced by some impressive work on bird song. Nottebohm (1970) has pointed out that three basic developmental sequences may be observed with young birds. In the first type, the bird develops a normal song even if it is completely isolated at birth and deafened at hatching. Examples of this type are chickens and ring doves. In a second type, the bird will develop the normal song if isolated but not if deafened. Song sparrows are an example. Finally, in the third variety, either isolation or deafening at an early age produces an abnormal song; chaffinches and white-crowned sparrows fit this pattern.

Nottebohm has found a number of analogs to human speech in this third type of songbird. First, these birds go through a period of "subsong," similar to human babbling, in which the song is distinct from the adult version in a number of ways. Second, birds in different areas learn different dialects of the same song. Third, the consequences of deafening the bird are different at different ages. If the bird is deafened before it has begun to sing, it develops a highly abnormal song. If, however, the deafening is delayed until after the song has developed, it has no effect on the motor output.

Finally, Nottebohm has found that the left half of the brain is more intimately involved than the right half in the songs of chaffinches. The major structure of the vocal system of the chaffinch is called the **syrinx,** and each side of it is connected by the hypoglossus nerve to each side of the brain. (Here, the connection is ipsalateral, with the left hypoglossus connected to the left half of the brain.) Nottebohm found that when the left hypoglossus was severed, the nature of the song was seriously disrupted, with some parts missing and replaced by unstructured bursts of noise. The same operation on the right side leaves the song intact.

What can we learn about human language by studying macaques and songbirds? Certainly, the sounds to which they respond are of no direct relevance to human beings, just as our speech is irrelevant to them. Yet they suggest that human lateralization of speech is not an isolated event in the animal kingdom and that the brain mechanisms underlying speech may have evolved in ways that are analogous to how similar structures in other species have evolved. In the final section of the chapter, we will examine more closely the evolution of lateralization and language.

Summary

Studies of split-brain patients clarify the respective roles of the left and right hemispheres in the use of language. The left hemisphere is more linguistically sophisticated than the right, especially in the areas of syntactic and phonetic processing. The right hemisphere is more adept at understanding individual words and in comprehending pragmatic aspects of language such as indirect speech acts.

Studies with normal individuals of dichotic listening typically reveal right-ear advantages for speech stimuli and left-ear advantages for nonspeech stimuli. Nevertheless, speech sometimes elicits left-ear advantages, and right-ear advantages for musical stimuli have been found. The distinction between holistic and relational processing appears to capture a salient difference in how the two hemispheres do their work.

Lateralization is not limited to humans, or even to primates. Japanese macaque monkeys show lateralization of species-specific vocalizations, and anatomical arrangements in songbirds are analogous to those in humans. This evidence suggests that human lateralization for speech is part of a larger evolutionary pattern.

Language in Evolutionary Context

We tend to think more often in terms of features that distinguish us from other animals rather than elements of similarity. Language, and the specialized equipment for perceiving and producing it, seems to be qualitatively different from the communication systems found elsewhere in the animal kingdom. Yet, from a biological perspective, all behavior may be understood as related to a series of evolutionary antecedents. In some cases, as in the progressive enlargement of an organ over time, the change is quantitative. Other times, as with language, it appears to be qualitative. Although this difference does not mean that it is impossible to find antecedents of modern language in our evolutionary past, it does make the task more difficult.

The sheer complexity of language makes it improbable that a single event or mutation could have caused so complex a change in behavior. Rather, language probably evolved from the convergence of various evolutionary events. In this section of the chapter, we first examine some of the ideas that have been proposed regarding the evolution of language and lateralization of the brain for language functions. Then we pursue the question of whether other species, such as chimpanzees, could possibly learn a human or humanlike language from the perspective afforded by these evolutionary considerations.

Evolution of Language and Lateralization

We have two primary means of examining questions related to the evolution of language. One is to do behavioral studies of other animals, such as nonhuman primates. The goal here is to identify similarities and differences between animals in the areas of communication skills and lateralization of brain function. The other is to examine the fossil record, which provides clues regarding the behavior of our evolutionary ancestors.

Field studies of animal communicative behavior indicate that our closest evolutionary neighbors lack anything resembling a language in their natural habitat. Most primate communication systems comprise a relatively small number of fixed signals consisting of vocal or gestural displays. Typically, each signal serves a different function. Alarm calls, mating displays, submissive gestures, and food-related calls are among the most common (see Altmann, 1967). There is little doubt that these communication systems fall well short of the properties generally associated with human language, such as arbitrariness and duality of patterning (see Chapter 2).

Studies of handedness in nonhuman primates are more enlightening. MacNeilage, Studdert-Kennedy, and Lindblom (1987) reviewed studies of hand preference and concluded that several primate species have a left-hand preference for simple reaching and a right-hand preference for manipulation of objects. MacNeilage and colleagues argue that left-hand (right hemisphere) specialization developed first, followed by right-hand (left hemisphere) specialization. The authors suggest that both preferences arose out of the demands of feeding. According to this view, the right hand stabilized the animal so that the left hand could reach for food.

This theory is appealing without being fully convincing. It is appealing because food gathering is the kind of selection pressure upon which evolutionary accounts typically are based. It is, for example, more difficult to explain why there would be selection for a left hemisphere that uses relational processing and a right hemisphere that uses holistic processing. What survival advantage would that confer? According to MacNeilage and colleagues, the initial specialization is for manual function, with cognitive differences coming later. This hypothesis is consistent with results that indicate that the left hemisphere in humans is specialized for certain nonlinguistic motor functions, as we saw earlier in the chapter (Mateer & Kimura, 1977). If the left hemisphere is specialized to perform sequences of motor acts, this specialization may be traced, ultimately, to sequences in food-gathering behaviors.

Nonetheless, the data upon which the theory rests are not completely convincing. Many studies of hand preference in nonhuman primates found very weak differences between the hands, and some found no differences at all. MacNeilage and his colleagues acknowledge this point, but argue that when task differences (such as reaching versus reaching and manipulating, field versus laboratory studies) are taken into account, the results are more consistent. Nonetheless, the results are weak. In one reaching study, 30 animals exhibited a left-hand preference, 16 a right-hand preference, and 36 no preference at all. This is a far cry from the human case, in which approximately 90% of individuals are right-handed.

An alternative view is presented by Corballis (1989), who suggests that both the human pattern of right-handedness and the left-cerebral representation of language may go back as far as 2 to 3 million years ago. As for handedness, Corballis reviews studies that have examined the patterns of wear in tools and concludes that the majority of tool users were right-handed as far back as 1.9 million years ago. In addition, anatomical analysis of skulls from this period suggests that lateralization of the brain for language may have been present at the same time. Corballis cites the work of Tobias, who found anatomical asymmetries suggesting the existence of Broca's and possibly Wernicke's areas. It has been known for some time that a region in the left temporal lobe, close to Wernicke's area, is typically larger than the corresponding region in the right temporal lobe (Geschwind & Levitsky, 1968). It now appears that similar anatomical asymmetries existed perhaps 2 to 3 million years ago.

In contrast, the capacity for speech came much later. As we saw in Chapter 4, when we produce sounds, air is expelled from the lungs and sent through the structures of the vocal tract (see Figure 4-1). We can change the shape of the vocal tract by altering the position of our lips, jaw, tongue, and larynx. The shape and flexibility of our vocal tract are required for the range of sounds found in contemporary languages.

A crucial evolutionary development is the enlargement of the pharyngeal area that lies above the larynx and just below the mouth. In newborn humans and adult chimpanzees, the larynx exits directly into the mouth, whereas in adult humans, it exits into the pharynx. This anatomical difference greatly influences the number of sounds that can be produced. For example, newborns and chimpanzees are physically incapable of producing the vowels [a], [i], and [u], sounds that are found in a wide variety of languages.

Lieberman (1973, 1991) has examined reconstructions of the vocal tracts of various hominids, the evolutionary family that includes modern humans. In particular, after examining Neanderthal fossils, he concluded that Neanderthals had vocal tracts that were similar to those of human newborns. Although they were apparently capable of producing some speech, they probably lacked the mobility to produce the range of vowel sounds found in modern language. On the basis of these and other fossil analyses, Lieberman (1991) suggests that a functionally modern human vocal tract may have emerged only 125,000 years ago. These findings imply that speech is a relatively recent evolutionary development, more recent than hand preference and brain lateralization.

Speculation about what our ancestors might or might not have been able to do or say is just that—speculation. The best thinking currently available suggests that a combination of factors (the emergence of hand preferences, the lateralization of the brain, and the development of the modern vocal tract) converged in the evolution of language. Although the exact line of development is not clear, the net effect of all of these changes is a form of communication that is qualitatively distinct from that possessed by present-day primates. Of course, the fact that nonhuman primates do not have language does not necessarily mean that they are incapable of learning and using language. There have been a number of attempts to teach language to chimpanzees and other nonhuman primates, and these have aroused considerable interest and debate.

Teaching Language to Nonhuman Primates

Attempts to teach language (or a languagelike system of communication) to other primates may be divided into three groups. In the first group, attempts were made to teach speech to chimpanzees (Hayes & Hayes, 1952; Kellogg & Kellogg, 1933). As we have seen, the vocal apparatus of chimpanzees is not suited to produce speech sounds, and consequently these studies proved very little. In the Hayes's study, the chimpanzee was able to learn only two words in 2 years of training.

A second group involved programs in which the communication system was not clearly defined in linguistic terms. Premack (1971) used tokens with symbols on them to teach a chimpanzeee named Sarah some logical concepts. Although Sarah was able to demonstrate a number of aspects of complex cognition, the results are of uncertain importance to the issue of whether apes can acquire a language because it has not been demonstrated that these symbols have the power or flexibility of human language. Similar considerations apply to the work of Rumbaugh (1977) and his associates, who used a computer to teach a chimpanzee, Lana, to produce and respond to messages. Once again, the linguistic status of the "language" is not known.

A third group of programs has taken advantage of the obvious manual dexterity of these animals to teach them American Sign Language. B. T. and R. A. Gardner (1969, 1975; Gardner, Gardner, & Van Cantfort, 1989) pioneered this work with studies of Washoe, a chimpanzee. Similar work has been carried out in other laboratories with chimpanzees, gorillas, and an orangutan. The Gardners themselves replicated the study with Washoe with four other chimpanzees that they reared from birth, Moja, Pili, Tatu, and Dar. Since ASL is commonly regarded as a full-fledged language, albeit with a grammar different from English (see Chapter 2), and since the Gardners' program, unlike most others, is analogous to the circumstances in which a child would be naturally exposed to language, I will focus on their efforts here.

The conditions under which Washoe was "trained" to use ASL are similar to those of children learning language. American Sign Language was used or modeled in a variety of contexts such as eating dinner, playing, and so on. Although the adult models presumably used correct ASL with Washoe, there was no explicit attempt to teach her the rules of ASL as such. Rather, sign language was used to communicate with her.

The evidence of Washoe's language development is in many respects quite remarkable. She quickly acquired a number of signs and learned to use them correctly. Moreover, she was productive in her use of signs. When she didn't know the name of an object she was trying to convey, she invented one. An example was her invention of the sign *waterbird*, combining two previously learned signs, *water* and *bird*, to refer to a swan (Linden, 1975). Additionally, Washoe demonstrated the appropriate generality in her learning of various signs. When she mastered the term *open*, she applied it spontaneously to a number of new contexts (opening the door, the window, and so on). In rigorous tests, Washoe and her successors in the Gardner laboratory demonstrated the ability to sign the names of common objects far better than simply by chance (see Figure 13-6).

It seems that Washoe mastered at least a rudimentary understanding of the semantics of individual lexical items. Whether or not she correctly understood the syntax of ASL is another matter. In general, Washoe tended to put signs together in a wide variety of different orders, apparently using sentences such as (13) and (14) interchangeably (Brown, 1970):

(13) Roger tickle Washoe.

(14) Washoe tickle Roger.

Individual words go only so far, of course. It is primarily through syntax that we acquire a truly productive linguistic system. These observations suggest that Washoe did not master word order, an important syntactic device in English and many other languages.

The Gardners found better syntactic performance when Washoe was given a task in which she had to respond to *wh-* questions (B. T. Gardner & R. A. Gardner, 1975). Questions such as those in sentences (15) through (17) call for responses from a particular grammatical category. For example, (15) calls for a noun, and (16) requires a noun referring to a location:

(15) Who are you?

(16) Where is the box?

(17) When is dinner?

Washoe gave a response from the correct grammatical category 84% of the time in this task, a level of performance that even exceeded that of children just beginning to produce two-word utterances (Washoe's stage of development at that time). This suggests that Washoe had greater syntactic knowledge than was evident in her own language output (see Figure 13-6).

Several criticisms have been raised regarding these studies of chimpanzee language skills. For example, Terrace, Petitto, Sanders, and Bever (1979) have questioned whether the sentences of Washoe and other chimpanzees were creative or whether they had been merely prompted by the human trainer. Terrace and colleagues closely examined videotapes of Washoe and of a chimpanzee they worked with, whom they called Neam Chimpsky (or Nim for short). These researchers found that 39% of Nim's utterances were either imitations of adjacent human utterances or reductions of such utterances. In many instances, Nim interrupted teachers while they were making signs. Thus, there seems to be some question whether or not Nim was combining words in novel, rule-governed ways or whether she was merely imitating the utterances of those around her. Seidenberg and Petitto (1979) have raised similar points.

A. *Susan N.*: What that?
Washoe: Dirty

B. *Greg G.*: What that?
Washoe: Hammer

C. *Tom T.*: What that?
Moja: Tree

D. *Susan N.*: What that?
Washoe: Lollipop

E. *Susan N.*: Whose that?
Washoe: Mine

F. *Washoe*: Gimme

Figure 13-6. Chimpanzees signing about objects. A–D: of different objects, replies to "What that?" D–F: of the same object, sequentially, replies to (D) "What that?" then (E) "Whose?" then (F) stands up and signs "Gimme" of the object. [From R. A. Gardner, T. E. Van Cantfort, and B. T. Gardner, "Categorical Replies to Categorical Questions by Cross-fostered Chimpanzees," *American Journal of Psychology* 105 (1992):27–57.]

On the other hand, O'Sullivan and Yeager (1989) contend that Nim's communicative and linguistic skills were limited by the type of training she received. Unlike the naturalistic circumstances in which humans taught ASL to Washoe, Terrace trained Nim in a laboratory setting. O'Sullivan and Yeager tested Nim's performance under two conditions, a training condition and a conversational condition. In the training condition, designed to replicate the conditions used by Terrace, Nim was given drills in naming objects. In the conversational condition, which was similar to the procedure followed by the Gardners, Nim was observed in more unstructured interactions. The investigators found that the number of spontaneous (that is, not imitative) utterances was far greater in the conversational session (60%) than in the training session (14%). In addition, interruptions by Nim were three times more likely in the training session. Although these results support O'Sullivan and Yeager's contention, it should be noted that their training results were based on a single 8-minute session.

More recent studies have included chimpanzees teaching ASL to younger chimpanzees without human intervention (Fouts, Fouts, & Van Cantfort, 1989). Fouts and his colleagues examined whether Washoe was able to pass on her signing skills to her adopted son Loulis, who was 10 months old when he arrived at Washoe's home. Loulis was reared in somewhat unusual circumstances in that although Washoe and other chimpanzees were allowed to sign to him, the humans present were not. In a sense, Loulis was deprived of human signing. Nonetheless, Loulis acquired 17 different signs by 29 months, and by 63 months his vocabulary had grown to 47 signs.

What conclusions can be drawn from these studies? Certainly, chimpanzees are capable of acquiring certain aspects of human language, and can transmit sign language from one generation to the next without human intervention. Moreover, as the training sessions become more relaxed and conversational, the language skills appear all the more impressive. To put the matter in some perspective, however, we should bear in mind that Loulis had a vocabulary of 47 signs at 63 months and normal children have acquired approximately 14,000 words by 72 months (Carey, 1978). Thus, although recent work has cast chimpanzee language skills in a more positive light, there remain significant differences between their skills and those of normal children.

These differences can be interpreted in at least two ways. It is possible that as research with chimpanzees advances further, the gap between chimpanzee and child language will be reduced substantially. Another possibility is that the pattern of strengths and weaknesses found in chimpanzee language to date are accurate indicators of their linguistic ability. We have seen that the specialized left hemisphere plays a major role in language use and language acquisition in humans. When an intact left hemisphere is not available—as with Genie, aphasic patients, and split-brain patients tested on their right hemisphere—language acquisition is slow, and syntactic skills in particular are weak. On the basis of these observations, we might expect that a chimpanzee attempting to acquire language without benefit of these neurological mechanisms would also show relatively slow acquisition and difficulties with syntactic structure.

Finally, recent research with bonobos (pygmy chimpanzees or *Pan paniscus*) should be mentioned. Bonobos use gestures and vocalizations more often in their natural habitat than the chimpanzees (*Pan troglodytes*) we have been discussing. Bonobos are also thought to be more intelligent than chimpanzees and possibly better prepared to acquire language. Savage-Rumbaugh, McDonald, Sevcik, Hopkins, and Rubert (1986) studied symbolic communication in two pygmy chimpanzees and found that they did not need explicit training to acquire associations between symbols and objects. In addition, one 5-year-old pygmy chimpanzee, Kanzi, preserved word order most of the time (Greenfield & Savage-Rumbaugh, 1991). Future work with this species should shed further light on syntactic skills in nonhuman primates.

Summary

The complexity of present-day language suggests that a convergence of evolutionary developments, rather than a single event, led to its emergence. Three factors were discussed: hand preference, structural differences between the left and right hemispheres of the brain, and the capacity for speech. Although some studies have found hand preferences in nonhuman primates, the results are relatively weak. Fossil records are consistent with the notion that both handedness and anatomical differences between the hemispheres existed approximately 2 million years ago. The emergence of a specialized vocal tract is a more recent evolutionary event.

Studies that have attempted to teach sign language to chimpanzees have produced some impressive results. Chimpanzees are capable of acquiring signs and using them appropriately. However, even when the mode of communication is well adapted to the animals' manual skills, syntactic skills are acquired slowly. Research that is just beginning with pygmy chimpanzees may clarify the language capabilities of nonhuman primates.

Review Questions

1. Distinguish among Broca's aphasia, Wernicke's aphasia, and conduction aphasia in terms of the brain regions involved and the language performance that is observed.
2. According to Geschwind's model, what sequence of brain regions would be involved if you (a) heard a sentence and then responded to it orally or (b) saw a sentence then spoke it?
3. What evidence suggests that Broca's patients suffer from syntactic deficits?
4. Explain how lateralization of language skills is tested in split-brain patients and in normal individuals.
5. Summarize the research that has been done on language and the right hemisphere.
6. Under what circumstances might language stimuli elicit a left-ear advantage in normal right-handed individuals?

7. Summarize the evidence for lateralization of sounds in animals other than humans.

8. What evidence exists regarding the capacity for speech in Neanderthals?

9. Why did the Gardners use American Sign Language in their studies with Washoe?

10. Discuss studies in which chimpanzees teach ASL to younger chimpzanees without human intervention.

Thought Questions

1. What might happen if a person who was bilingual in Spanish and English suffered an injury to Broca's area? Would both languages be affected or just one? Why? What aspects of language might be affected?

2. Assume that your grandfather has had a stroke and is greatly limited in his ability to articulate meaningful speech. How might you determine his comprehension skills?

3. If one hemisphere dominates the other on a task for which it is clearly more qualified, does this mean that the hemisphere "knows" its abilities and disabilities? How might you tell?

4. Attempts to prove that chimpanzees or other animals can acquire language inevitably suffer from the difficulties associated with defining language. Suppose you wanted to prove (or disprove) the point. How would you go about it? What aspects of language would you choose to teach?

14

Language, Culture, and Cognition

- The Whorf hypothesis states that the structure of a language determines a native speaker's world view. Different languages are assumed to lead to different world views.
- Psychological studies of the Whorf hypothesis have examined whether lexical and grammatical differences between languages influence various nonlinguistic cognitive processes.
- Studies of color terms have not provided strong support for the Whorf hypothesis. Other studies of the lexicon are more consistent with the hypothesis.
- The presence of a grammatical distinction in a language may increase the ease of some cognitive processes. However, the absence of such distinctions does not prevent these processes.

Introduction

In this chapter we explore the interrelationships among language, culture, and cognition. The central notion—that individuals with different linguistic and cultural backgrounds think differently—is not far from our everyday experience. If you have had the opportunity to engage in a conversation with a person whose native language is not English, you may have found that communication breaks down at times and that there are concepts that are not easily translated into another language. Or, if you happen to be a fluent bilingual (or multilingual), you may agree with those bilinguals and multilinguals who insist that they think differently in each of their languages.

There are a number of intriguing questions here. Is there a particular style of thinking that is "natural" for speakers of each language? If so, is it possible for a person to think in a different way, one that is not "natural" for that individual? Is this style of thinking imparted by the language, the culture, or both? Or have we overestimated the differences among languages and cultures: Will we find, upon deeper inspection, fundamental similarities in thought processes in individuals with diverse linguistic and cultural backgrounds?

These questions have engaged the attention of anthropologists, linguists, and psychologists. We will begin by examining the ideas of scholars who have studied this issue, then turn to experimental research that bears on these questions.

The Whorf Hypothesis

The view that language shapes thought is most often associated with the work of Benjamin Lee Whorf. Whorf received his degree in chemical engineering from the Massachusetts Institute of Technology and worked throughout his life for an insurance company as a fire-prevention engineer. He had a number of avocations, however. He had a strong interest in the relationship between science and religion, and ultimately religion led him to language. He was initially self-taught in linguistics, but eventually studied American Indian linguistics with the prominent anthropologist Edward Sapir at Yale University.

Sapir (1921) had earlier suggested that languages are diverse in the way that they structure reality, but had not fully developed the thesis that these linguistic differences might facilitate certain modes of thought. This was a position that Whorf developed in a series of articles between 1925 and 1941, many of which are included in Carroll (1956). The notion that language shapes thought patterns is commonly referred to as the **Whorf hypothesis,** although it is also called the **Sapir-Whorf hypothesis,** to acknowledge the role of Whorf's mentor.

Linguistic Determinism and Relativity

The Whorf hypothesis consists of two parts, linguistic determinism and linguistic relativity. **Linguistic determinism** refers to the notion that a language determines certain nonlinguistic cognitive processes. That is, learning a language changes the way a person thinks. **Linguistic relativity** refers to the claim that the cognitive processes that are determined are different for different languages. Thus, speakers of different languages are said to think in different ways.

Whorf's reasoning on these matters is revealed in a famous quote:

> We dissect nature along lines laid down by our native languages. The categories and types that we isolate from the world of phenomena we do not find there because they stare every observer in the face; on the contrary, the world is presented in a kaleidoscopic flux of impressions which has to be organized by our minds—and this means largely by the linguistic systems in our minds. We cut nature up, organize it into concepts, and ascribe significances as we do, largely because we are parties to an agreement to organize it in this way—an agreement that holds throughout our speech community and is codified in the patterns of our language. The agreement is, of course, an implicit and unstated one, BUT ITS TERMS ARE ABSOLUTELY OBLIGATORY; we cannot talk at all except by subscribing to the organization and classification of data which the agreement decrees. (Carroll, 1956, pp. 213–214)

There are several notions here. One is that languages "carve up" reality in different ways. Another is that these language differences are covert or unconscious; that is, we are not consciously aware of the way in which we classify objects. Third, these language differences influence our world view. These are profound ideas, but not ones easily amenable to experimental test. Let us begin by looking, as Whorf did, at linguistic examples from various languages that seem to bear on his thesis.

Some Whorfian Examples

Whorf provided a number of examples that were designed to show that linguistic determinism and relativity were valid concepts. They can be broadly organized into lexical and grammatical examples.

Lexical examples We may begin by considering the concept of differentiation. **Differentiation** refers to the number of words in a given domain (for example, colors, birds, fruits, and so on) in a lexicon. A more highly differentiated domain has more words that express finer distinctions, such as subtle shades of color. Whorf argued that languages differ in the domains that are most differentiated. That is, all languages show high degrees of differentiation in some domains and low degrees in others. The implication is that greater degrees of differentiation are related to culturally significant concepts.

For example, Whorf noted that in the American Indian language of Hopi there is but one word that covers everything that flies except birds (for example, the same word for insects, airplanes, aviators, and so on). The Hopi speaker calls all of these disparate objects by the same name without any apparent difficulty. Whorf argued that although this class might seem very broad to us, so would our word *snow* to an Eskimo:

> We have the same word for falling snow, snow on the ground, snow packed hard like ice, slushy snow, wind-driven flying snow—whatever the situation may be. To an Eskimo, this all-inclusive word would be almost unthinkable; he would say that falling snow, slushy snow, and so on, are sensuously and operationally different, different things to contend with; he uses different words for them and for other kinds of snow. (Carroll, 1956, p. 216)

Whorf suggested that there is no "natural" way to carve up reality; different languages do it in quite different ways.

Whorf's observations about Eskimo words for snow have recently been criticized by Martin (1986; see also Pullum, 1991). Martin claims that Whorf and subsequent writers (for example, Brown, 1958) greatly exaggerated the lexical differences between Eskimo and English. The number of words in a lexicon varies with how one defines a word. If we only count root words (bound morphemes), we will get one number, but if we count each suffixed version of each root word, the estimate will rise dramatically. Martin suggests that the failure to attend to the rich morphological system of the Eskimo language led Whorf and others to the myth that Eskimos have vastly more words for snow than English speakers. It appears that when morphology is taken into account, Eskimos have perhaps a dozen words for snow (Pullum, 1991). But then English has quite a few as well, including *slush, avalanche, blizzard,* and *powder.* It is not clear that Eskimos have a more highly differentiated snow domain than English speakers.

Whatever the final consensus on Eskimo snow words might be, the more general notion that languages differ in the degree to which they differentiate various lexical domains does not seem to be at issue. The question is whether these differences lead to differences in thinking. Whorf suggested that they did, in the sense that when we encounter a particular word on a regular basis, it may influence our habitual thought patterns (that is, the kind of thought process that comes easily or naturally to an individual).

Whorf gave an example based on his work experience in which he sought explanations for the start of fires. Initially, he only considered physical causes, such as defective wiring. Over time, however, he came to think that psychological causes were important: the meaning of a situation to an individual often was directly related to the onset of the fire. And this meaning was often in the form of linguistic meaning, such as the meaning typically conveyed by particular words:

> Thus, around a storage of what are called "gasoline drums," behavior will tend to a certain type, that is, great care will be exercised; while around a storage of what are called "empty gasoline drums," it will tend to be different—careless, with little repression of smoking or of tossing cigarette stubs about. Yet the "empty" drums are perhaps the most dangerous, since they contain explosive vapor. Physically the situation is hazardous, but the linguistic analysis according to regular analogy must employ the word 'empty,' which inevitably suggests lack of hazard. (Carroll, 1956, p. 135)

Whorf offered this as evidence of linguistic determinism, of the power of words to influence thought processes. We are careless because of the word *empty*. Note also that Whorf emphasized "regular" analogy: we come to this (precarious) interpretation of experience based on habitual experience with words. It is something that occurs slowly, over time, seeping into our mental framework. Whorf did not say that we couldn't avoid this pattern of thought and treat the empty drums with proper respect (obviously he did); but this is a different, more active pattern of thought.

Grammatical examples   Although some of Whorf's lexical examples, such as his comments on Eskimo, have generated a considerable amount of discussion, it appears that he was more interested in the grammatical differences among languages.

In English, we come to respect the difference between nouns and verbs as a fundamental distinction. Nouns refer to long-lasting and stable events, such as *horse* and *man*, whereas verbs refer to short-lived actions, such as *hit* and *run*. And yet, Whorf asked, why then do we classify temporary events such as *lightning* and *spark* as nouns? And why are *dwell*, *persist*, and *continue* verbs? In Hopi, *lightning* is a verb because events of brief duration must be verbs. Whorf also mentioned Nootka, a language used on Vancouver Island, in which all words seem to be treated as verbs. This is just one indication of how grammatical characteristics vary from language to language.

Another example of grammatical diversity concerns the extent to which a language uses word order or morphology to signal meaning. In English, the vast majority of sentences use a subject-verb-object (SVO) order, and in most of these the first noun is the agent and the second the patient. This order is adhered to rather rigidly. If the verb is intransitive (one that does not take an object), the remainder of the sequence holds (SV). Similarly, when the first noun is deleted, it is very often replaced by a pronoun; other languages allow deletion of the subject more often. The major exception to the standard order is the question form. The consistency of word order in English makes it a reliable cue for sentence interpretation (MacWhinney, Bates, & Kliegl, 1984). For a speaker of English, languages that violate the SVO order may seem unnatural.

Many other languages use morphology more extensively than word order to signal meaning. As we saw in Chapter 2, the major English grammatical morphemes are number, tense, person, and aspect. In Spanish, nouns are marked for grammatical gender. This distinction does not correspond to a semantic distinction (that is, masculine versus feminine objects) but is simply a formal property of the language that its users must acquire.

On the other hand, some of the grammatical distinctions that are found in other languages do appear to be semantically significant. Several Indian languages conjugate verbs for validity. For example, consider sentence (1):

(1)   John is chopping wood.

In Wintu, there would be one inflection attached to the verb if there were direct visual evidence of this fact, another if it were gossip, and still another if it were a regular event (Lee, 1938, cited in Brown, 1958). This suggests, as Brown (1958, p. 254) puts it, that Wintu speakers must have "a continuing grasp of the evidence" of their assertions.

Whorf believed that grammatical distinctions such as these exert an effect on not just the way individuals think but also their overall world view. In English, there is a distinction between what Whorf called **individual nouns** (more commonly called **count nouns**) and **mass nouns.** Count nouns refer to bodies with definite outlines (for example, a tree, a stick, a hill), whereas mass nouns refer to objects without clear boundaries (for example, air, water, rain). Linguistically, the distinction is that count nouns take the plural morpheme, whereas mass nouns cannot. Thus, we can speak of *trees, sticks,* and *hills,* but not *airs, waters,* and *rains.* In addition, count nouns take the singular indefinite article (*a*) but mass nouns do not. In contrast, in Hopi, there are no mass nouns.

Although we cannot pluralize English mass nouns directly, we can do so by the use of a phrase of the form count noun + of + mass noun. That is, we cannot say *waters* or *sands* but can say *bodies of water* or *buckets of sand.* But this form of expression, according to Whorf, has cognitive consequences since it leads us to think of some objects as being "containers" (form) that hold "contents" (substance or matter). This distinction between form and substance is not a necessary feature of objective reality; rather, the English language imposes the distinction upon reality. For example, even though some objects, such as butter and meat, have clear boundaries, they are treated grammatically as mass nouns (for example, *two sticks of butter,* not *two butters*). Thus, Whorf suggested that English speakers think of objects as consisting of form and substance because of this grammatical distinction.

A basic question to ask at this juncture is whether Whorf's arguments are convincing. Most psychologists have not been convinced. There are several reasons for this. A. H. Bloom (1981) has suggested that Whorf's views, because they emphasized cognitive structures, did not square well with the behavioristic tradition in psychology prevalent at the time that Whorf was writing. It is also true that the relativism that Whorf emphasized did not fit well with the rationalistic approach to language subsequently advocated by Chomsky, which emphasizes linguistic universals. A third reason is more methodological. In order to test the Whorf hypothesis, we need to assess language and cognition independently of each other. In particular, we need to assess (nonlinguistic) cognitive processes independently of the linguistic features that are presumed, in the Whorf hypothesis, to influence them. Whorf discussed many linguistic distinctions but provided no real evidence of their cognitive consequences. In the remainder of this chapter, we will discuss the various experimental tests that have been done of the Whorf hypothesis.

Summary

The Whorf hypothesis states that the way we think about the world is shaped by our language. This hypothesis consists of two parts. Linguistic determinism states that languages determine (nonlinguistic) thought processes, and linguistic relativity states that the resulting thought processes vary from language to language. Although Whorf provided many lexical and grammatical examples of how language may influence cognition, he did not present convincing evidence for his hypothesis.

Lexical Influences on Cognition

Experimental tests of the Whorf hypothesis fall into two groups: those that examine the lexical level and those at the grammatical level. Before looking at these studies, however, let us consider what is needed in order to test the linguistic relativity hypothesis.

Testing the Whorf Hypothesis

Any study that attempts to test the hypothesis that differences in language determine differences in thinking must, at the outset, define the three key terms. First, we need to define what we mean by "differences in language." This has been done in two ways. One way is to compare a language that linguistically marks a particular conceptual distinction with a language that does not. Thus, the presence or absence of the explicit linguistic marking is the language difference of interest. Although most studies have approached the problem in this way, another possibility is to compare two languages that mark the same distinction in different ways. This comparison focuses not on whether a language marks a concept, but rather how it does so. As we have seen, English marks number through the use of the plural morpheme. One comparison would be another language that does not mark number; another would be a language that marks number in a different way.

Second, we need to define "differences in thinking" in a satisfactory manner. It is obviously difficult to measure a person's world view. But it should be kept in mind that Whorf was especially interested in those aspects of thinking that indicated a habitual mode of thought. Lucy (1992b) defines habitual thought as "routine ways of attending to objects and events, categorizing them, remembering them, and perhaps even reflecting upon them" (p. 7). The mode is contrasted with specialized thought, which comprises cognitive routines or structures that are restricted either to certain subgroups within a culture (such as technical specialists) or to certain domains (such as kinship or illness). As we will see, psychologists and anthropologists have studied a wide range of cognitive processes, including form perception, color perception, mathematical thinking, and logical reasoning. As we discuss these studies, you might consider whether they better represent habitual or specialized modes of thought.

Finally, we need to clarify what is meant by saying that languages "determine" thought. The Whorf hypothesis can be interpreted in at least two different ways. The strong version states that language determines cognition; that is, the presence of linguistic categories creates cognitive categories. In this view, the presence of terms to refer to different objects that move through the air produces the cognitive ability to discriminate between birds and airplanes. Although some of Whorf's comments suggest that he believed in the strong version of linguistic determinism, recent interpreters of his work have claimed that he did not (see, for example, the discussion in Schwanenflugel, Blount, & Lin, 1991). In any event, there is no evidence for the strong version.

Alternatively, a weak version of the hypothesis states that the presence of linguistic categories influences the ease with which various cognitive operations are performed. That is, certain thought processes may be more accessible or more easily performed by members of one linguistic community relative to those of a different linguistic community. As Hockett (1954) expresses it, "Languages differ not so much as to what *can* be said in them, but rather as to what it is *relatively easy* to say" (p. 122). It is this version that has guided most of the research that we will discuss.

Color Terms

At the lexical level, much work has been done on words for color. This is, in part, due to the fact that languages differ tremendously in their differentiation of the color domain. Some languages, such as English, have many color terms, and others have as few as two. It thus seems natural to ask whether speakers of such disparate languages perceive and think of color in fundamentally similar or different ways.

Codability   A concept that has figured in much of the research on color cognition is **codability**. Brown (1958) defined codability as the length of a verbal expression. As we saw in our discussion of differentiation, some languages have single words to refer to a particular object or event, whereas others do not. If one's language does not have a specific word for the occasion, the speaker can still make the reference but will need to do so by some combination of words. Relative to the case in which a single word serves the purpose, the phrase is, in Brown's terms, less codable.

Brown (1958) suggested a relationship between the frequency of usage of a verbal expression, its length (codability), and the ease with which it may be utilized. The relationship between frequency and length is captured in what is called **Zipf's law.** Some time ago, Zipf (1935) examined Chinese, Latin, and English and found that the length of a word is negatively correlated with its frequency of usage. That is, the more frequently a word is used in a language, the shorter the word (measured either in phonemes or syllables). There are many examples of Zipf's law in English. Whenever technological innovations are introduced in society, their initial, cumbersome names become shortened for easy reference (for example, *videocamera-videocassette recorder* becomes *camcorder*). It may be that the differences in the differentiation of domains that Whorf found are a special instance of Zipf's law. For instance, it may be that in cultures in which an object is referred to extremely often, it is referred to by a single, brief name; when it is moderately frequent, by a longer name; and when it is infrequently referred to, by a phrase.

The relationship between codability and ease of expression has been studied in several experiments. In an early study, Brown and Lenneberg (1954) examined the responses of college students to 24 different colors. The colors were identified beforehand by a set of judges who were asked to look at a series of color chips and determine which was the best instance of the color in question. The judges produced a list of 8 central colors, with 16 other colors included for comparison. The 24 colors were shown to the students, one at a time, and they were asked to name the colors, with their reaction time to naming the colors being measured. Brown and Lenneberg found that colors that evoked long names (that is, those less codable) were named with hesitation, with disagreement from one person to another, and with inconsistency from one time to another.

Crosslinguistic studies   These results suggest that the presence of a brief verbal expression in a language influences certain cognitive processes. However, to evaluate the notion of linguistic determinism, we need to study the effects of color terms in different languages. Color terms in various languages have been investigated by Berlin and Kay (1969). They found that although the number of color terms in a language varied quite a bit from language to language, there was an underlying order. They found that every language has a small number of basic color terms. These are terms that consist of only one morpheme (for example, *blue* versus *blue green*) are not contained within another color (for example, *crimson* is contained within the category of *red*), and are not restricted to a small number of objects (for example, *blond* is restricted mainly to hair color). Furthermore, each language draws its basic color terms from the following list of 11 names: *white, black, red, yellow, green, blue, brown, purple, pink, orange,* and *gray.* In addition, Berlin and Kay found that these 11 terms formed a hierarchy. Some languages, such as English, use all 11, whereas others use as few as 2. When a language has just 2 terms, it is not a random selection, but always *black* and *white* (sometimes translated as *dark* and *light*). When a language has a third term, it is always *red*. The entire hierarchy looks like this:

Black
White $\rightarrow$ Red $\rightarrow$ Yellow
Green $\rightarrow$ Blue $\rightarrow$ Brown $\rightarrow$ Purple
Pink
Orange
Grey

Thus, a language with 4 terms has *black, white, red,* and either *yellow* or *green*. A language with 7 terms has all of these plus *blue* and *brown*. In general, Berlin and Kay found a remarkable degree of universal structure in color terms.

Building upon the work of Berlin and Kay, Rosch (formerly Heider) performed several studies with the Dani, a New Guinea people whose language consists of only two color terms, one for black and one for white. Rosch was particularly interested in what Berlin and Kay referred to as **focal colors,** the most representative example of various basic colors (such as the most blueish blue). Rosch argues that focal colors are more perceptually salient than nonfocal colors and that this salience, in turn, influences the codability and memorability of a color. Rosch (Heider, 1972) tested Dani and U.S. subjects on a task in which they were presented with color chips and later asked to name them. Rosch found that although Americans performed better on the whole, both groups' memory for focal colors was better than for nonfocal ones. In a subsequent study, Rosch (1973) demonstrated that the Dani learned the names for color categories when focal colors were at the center of the categories. Apparently, Dani learn and remember colors much as we do despite the extreme differences in color vocabulary.

The irony in these results is that the study of color terms began as an attempt to demonstrate the validity of the Whorf hypothesis. Rosch's studies do not support the hypothesis of linguistic relativity; rather, they turn it on its head:

> In short, far from being a domain well suited to the study of the effects of language on thought, the color space would seem to be a prime example for the influence of underlying perceptual-cognitive factors on the formation and reference of linguistic categories. (Heider, 1972, p. 20)

These studies have led some researchers (for example, Clark & Clark, 1977) to conclude that there is little support for the Whorf hypothesis. However, more recent work has questioned both Rosch's conclusions regarding color cognition as well as the generality of the color domain.

Lucy and Shweder (1979) argue that the focal colors used by Heider (1972) were more perceptually discriminable than the nonfocal colors. While focality is an intrinsic property of a color, discriminability is relative to the surrounding colors. When they controlled for discriminability, Lucy and Shweder found no differences between focal and nonfocal colors in a short-term recognition memory experiment, although they found differences in long-term recognition.

Kay and Kempton (1984) compared the performance of English speakers with individuals who spoke Tarahumara, a Mexican Indian language that does not have the blue and green color terms. They presented subjects with triads of colors in which two items were clear examples of blue and green and the third member was between the two. The subjects were then asked to decide if the third chip was closer to the first or to the second color. English speakers sharply distinguished between chips on one side of the blue-green border and those on the other side, whereas speakers of Tarahumara did not do so. In a second study, Kay and Kempton demonstrated that if English speakers were induced to call the intermediate chip both blue and green, the effect disappeared. Thus, the perception of colors appears to be dependent upon the terms we use to refer to them.

These results suggest that under some circumstances the manner in which we perceive and perhaps remember colors is related to the linguistic terms we use to refer to them. It is also related to the perceptual salience of colors themselves. It may not be that one set of factors, linguistic or perceptual, is reducible to the other but that both factors influence our color cognition.

Other Lexical Categories

Recent work by Schwanenflugel and colleagues suggests that there are clear cross-cultural differences in a number of lexical categories and that these differences might be related to language differences. Schwanenflugel and Rey (1986) examined lexical categories in Spanish- and English-speaking monolinguals living in southern Florida. The subjects were given instances of 12 different lexical categories, such as birds, colors, fruits, musical instruments, and weapons. For each category, the subjects were asked to rate a series of instances for typicality and for familiarity. There were 18 to 34 instances in each category. The results showed a moderately strong (.64) correlation between the English and Spanish typicality ratings. However, of greater interest was the fact that the correlations varied tremendously from category to category, with the strongest being for parts of the human body (.94) and the weakest for birds (.16). Both groups of subjects agreed that head, arm, and leg were more typical body parts than hair, tooth, and nail. But English speakers regarded robin as the second most-typical bird (after eagle) whereas Spanish speakers rated robin as 24th most typical out of 27 instances. In contrast, Spanish speakers rated canary as most typical, but it was 16th on the English list.

These are interesting results but, as Schwanenflugel has acknowledged, it is not clear that language differences are responsible for them. Another possibility is cultural familiarity. Schwanenflugel and Rey found that cultural familiarity played a role in the subject ratings of typicality, and when this factor was taken into account, the typicality correlations between languages increased (from .64 to .73). Thus, part of the reason why Spanish speakers rate canaries as more typical than English speakers do is because Spanish speakers are more familiar with them.

Is there any indication, then, that language differences play a role in these category judgments? Schwanenflugel, Blount, and Lin (1991) suggest that the language used to describe category members may influence how we think about various instances. In English, we have various hedges that may be applied to words to indicate the degree to which they are representative of their category (Lakoff, 1972). For instance, we might say sentence (2), but sentence (3) is decidedly odd:

> **(2)**   Loosely speaking, a bat is a bird.
> **(3)**   Loosely speaking, a robin is a bird.

In the terms used in Chapter 5, a bat has some of the characteristic features of birds but not the defining features. In contrast, compare sentences (4) and (5):

> **(4)**   Technically speaking, a tomato is a fruit.
> **(5)**   Technically speaking, an apple is a fruit.

Here, the hedge is appropriate for *tomato* but not for *apple*; *tomato* shares the defining but not the characteristic features of *fruit*. These observations suggest that linguistic devices that signal degree-of-category representativeness may influence the perception of category instances. Schwanenflugel and colleagues (1991) discuss some of the devices used in Tarahumara and in Chinese. For example, in Tarahumara, a bound modifier indicating degree of typicality must be attached to color terms. One modifier is used for colors that are highly typical, another for those that are somewhat typical, and a third for those that are only slightly typical. Devices such as these might well influence the manner in which individuals retrieve and think about category members.

Number Terms

There is one further set of studies that are relevant to how the lexicon may influence thought processes. Some recent studies by Miura (1987; Miura & Okamoto, 1989) look at how lexical differences in number names may influence children's conceptualization of numbers and, ultimately, their mathematics achievement. Miura examined some linguistic differences between Asian languages (Chinese, Korean, and Japanese) and English. The linguistic distinction here is not whether the different languages name numbers, but how they do so. According to Miura, in Asian languages, number names follow a base-10 number system. For example, the number 11 is read as *ten one*, 17 as *ten seven*, 20 as *two tens*, and 43 as *four tens three*. The numbers 14 and 40, which when spoken sound similar in English, are quite different in the Asian tongues: 14 is spoken as *ten four*, and 40 as *four tens*.

Miura (1987) studied first-grade children from the United States and Japan. The children were shown how to use a set of base-10 blocks to represent numbers. The set consisted of white unit blocks and purple ten's blocks equivalent to 10 unit blocks stuck together. On the first trial, the children were asked, in their native language, to read a number on a card and then to show that number in the blocks. After doing this for five numbers, they were given a second trial. They were reminded of the equivalence of 10 unit blocks and 1 ten block and were then asked to show each number in another way.

Miura distinguished three approaches to the task. A canonical approach was one that placed no more than 9 unit blocks in the one's position, such as using 4 ten's blocks and 2 unit blocks for 42. A noncanonical approach was one that used some combination of ten's blocks and more than 9 unit blocks, such as 3 ten's blocks and 12 unit blocks for 42. Finally, a one-to-one collection used only unit blocks, such as 42 unit blocks.

The results indicated that Japanese children were more than twice as likely as U.S. children to use canonical approaches on the first trial. The U.S. children tended to use one-to-one collections on the first trial. When prodded to generate a second approach, the U.S. children developed canonical approaches on the second trial. Miura also found that Japanese children used more noncanonical approaches than U.S. children. Miura has found similar results using Korean and Chinese first-graders.

Miura concludes that Asian children understand place value better as a result of the way that Asian languages represent numbers. Moreover, these cognitive differences in the representation of number may be related to subsequent mathematics achievement (Miura & Okamoto, 1989). Although cultural differences in socialization may play a role as well, Miura stresses that the way one thinks about numbers is fundamentally different in Chinese versus English. That is, it is not simply that Asian children do better on mathematics tasks; they approach the tasks differently as well.

Summary

There is some evidence for Whorf's hypothesis at the lexical level. Languages differ in the number of color terms they employ and the ease with which a given color term can be expressed. Although Rosch's studies indicate that certain focal colors are more perceptually salient for both Dani and U.S. subjects, her results do not preclude the existence of language effects as well. Subsequent studies suggest that language influences the perception and perhaps the memory of color.

Recent studies indicate that Spanish and English speakers differ somewhat in how they perceive different conceptual categories. In addition, children learning Asian languages conceptualize numbers differently than children learning English. The extent to which either of these results reflects language influences or broader cultural influences is not clear.

Grammatical Influences on Cognition

We have seen that there is some evidence for the Whorf hypothesis at the lexical level. What about the differences in grammatical categories across languages? Do these influence how we perceive the world?

Form Perception

A study by Carroll and Casagrande (1958) compared Navaho and English. They observed that in Navaho, the form of the verb for handling an object varies with the form or shape of the object. The verb varies if the object is a long flexible object (such as a piece of string) versus a long rigid object (such as a stick) or a flat flexible object (such as a cloth). On the basis of this grammatical distinction, Carroll and Casagrande proposed that Navaho-speaking children would learn to discriminate the forms of objects at an earlier age than their English-speaking peers.

Carroll and Casagrande used an object triads test, in which the child had to pick which of two objects, of three presented, went best together. For example, a child might be presented with a yellow stick and a piece of blue rope of comparable size. The child would then be shown a yellow rope and asked which of the first two it went best with. Thus, it is possible to determine if the children were focusing more on color or form. Carroll and Casagrande compared children who spoke Navaho with children who spoke English but came from the same reservation and lived in similar circumstances. The interesting result was that the Navaho children did group the objects on the basis of form at an earlier age than the English-speaking children did.

But this was not all. Carroll and Casagrande also tested English-speaking children in a Boston suburb and discovered that they performed similarly to the Navaho children. The researchers speculate that certain aspects of the environment of the white suburban children, such as playing with puzzles and toys, can cause an English-speaking child to attend to form at an early age. These results seem to generally support Whorf's view that the grammatical distinctions in a language may influence or determine certain cognitive processes. But the observations from the suburban children suggest that even if grammatical categories determine qualities of thought, they are not the only determinants. Other attributes of the child's environment may serve the same function.

Counterfactual Reasoning

A. H. Bloom (1981) has conducted some interesting but controversial studies on the differences between how Chinese and English speakers reason. He was particularly interested in **counterfactual reasoning,** which is the ability to reason about an event that is contrary to fact. For instance, imagine a situation in which several people are waiting for John; he is late, and the group, as a consequence, is late to the movies. The English language has the subjunctive mood, shown in (6), which enables us to discuss various states of affairs that we know to be false:

(6) If John had come earlier, they would have arrived at the movies on time. (Adapted from Bloom, 1981, p. 19)

In contrast, the Chinese language does not have a specific form, such as the subjunctive, to express a counterfactual meaning. Bloom's thesis was that since the Chinese language does not explicitly mark the counterfactual, Chinese speakers would experience greater difficulties with counterfactual reasoning. He presented several anecdotes of conversations with Chinese speakers that appear to support this assertion. For instance, when Chinese speakers were asked sentence (7), they refused to answer the question, saying that the government hadn't:

(7) If the Hong Kong government were to pass a law requiring that all citizens born outside of Hong Kong make weekly reports of their activities to the police, how would you react? (Bloom, 1981, p. 13)

When they were asked to imagine that the government had and then respond, the speakers protested that this manner of thinking was "unnatural," "unChinese," or "Western."

Let us look at Bloom's hypothesis more closely. Bloom does not argue that Chinese speakers are incapable of reasoning counterfactually; he simply states that such reasoning is more difficult for them. According to Bloom, the English subjunctive signals direct entry into the counterfactual realm. In contrast, the sentences used to express the counterfactual in Chinese are potentially more ambiguous in that they depend upon the context in which the utterance is made. A Chinese expression of the counterfactual is shown in sentence (8):

(8) If I am the U.S. president, then I will think before I speak. (Au, 1983, p. 157)

Note that this sentence can be interpreted as an implication (if/then) or as a counterfactual. The counterfactual interpretation only holds if the listener knows that the speaker is not the U.S. president. According to Bloom, when hearing (8), Chinese speakers must integrate their previous knowledge with the initial premise (*I am the U.S. president*) and then negate this premise before relating it to the if/then statement. In effect, the reasoning would have to be something like this: if A, then B; I know that A is not true, but if it were, then B would be true. This is a complex form of reasoning, with several steps. Thus, on the basis of this analysis of Chinese and English, Bloom predicted that Chinese speakers would make more errors in counterfactual reasoning than English speakers.

Bloom then conducted several studies to test this prediction. In one, Chinese and U.S. college students were presented with a story that involved a Greek philosopher who did not know Chinese, but if he had, he would have been influenced by Chinese culture and logic. One version of the story could be interpreted in either a counterfactual (that is, if he had known Chinese, he would have integrated the best features of Greek and Chinese systems) or a noncounterfactual way (that is, he did not read the Chinese works but they were translated for him). The subjects were then asked a series of questions to assess their understanding of the stories. Bloom found that although 98% of the U.S. students interpreted the story counterfactually, only 6% of the Chinese students did so. When given a second version of the story, in which the story was incoherent unless one made a counterfactual interpretation, 59% of the Chinese and 96% of the Americans interpreted the story counterfactually. Bloom concluded that the presence or absence of explicit marking of the counterfactual in one's language influences the facility with which one uses this mode of thought.

Bloom's conclusions have been called into question by Au (1983, 1984) and Liu (1985). Au, a native speaker of Chinese, argues that Bloom's stories are not idiomatic in Chinese, even though the stories were written by a Chinese speaker (under Bloom's direction) and then translated into English, rather than vice versa. Au tested Chinese students on revised versions of Bloom's studies and found much better performance. Au concluded that Bloom's studies provide no support for the Whorf hypothesis.

Bloom (1984) responded by challenging both the subjects and the materials in Au's studies. Even though Au's subjects were native Chinese speakers, they had taken English as a Second Language classes for 12 years. Bloom noted that the students were effectively bilingual, rendering them irrelevant to the issue. Bloom also contended that Au's stories were too concrete and simple. Since Bloom had contended that differences in processing were more likely to emerge with abstract, complex materials, the strong performance of Chinese students on the concrete stories is, again, not directly relevant to Bloom's thesis. In short, Bloom argues that the different results found by Au could be interpreted in ways that are still favorable to his hypothesis.

Finally, Liu (1985) attempted to assess the two points made by Bloom (1984). Liu used a sample of Chinese students who, unlike the bilinguals studied by Au, had very little exposure to or proficiency in English. In addition, Liu used both the abstract story constructed by Bloom and the concrete one favored by Au. Liu found a strong developmental trend in the ability to reason counterfactually. The youngest students in her sample, fourth-graders, did very poorly (less than 20% correct) whereas the oldest, eleventh-graders, did quite well (about 80% correct). In addition, most of the students performed better on the concrete story. Liu concluded that these age and story differences could not be attributable to the availability of a linguistic marker such as the subjunctive, and yet the absence of a distinct marker did not hamper Chinese students' ability to reason counterfactually.

Although Liu's study was well designed, it does not refute Bloom's thesis. Liu did not include a sample of English students, so there is no direct test of Bloom's hypothesis that English speakers would outperform Chinese speakers. Liu has shown that developmental maturity and story complexity influence the counterfactual reasoning of Chinese students and that under certain conditions Chinese students can perform better than Bloom's Chinese sample did. But Bloom's contention was that English speakers would more easily reason counterfactually, not that Chinese speakers could not do so. It would appear that a direct comparison of Chinese and English monolinguals on a reasonably complex, yet idiomatic, set of materials would be in order.

What do we learn from all of these studies? On the specific matter of Chinese and English differences in counterfactual reasoning, unfortunately, there are no clear conclusions. Some variables that influence reasoning have been uncovered, but precisely how they affect the alleged language difference is not clear.

However, we may learn something of more general interest regarding how to test the Whorf hypothesis. One point is certainly the difficulty in securing materials that are appropriate and comparable in the languages being studied. This is a troublesome feature of the Bloom–Au debate. Au claims that Bloom's materials are not idiomatic in her native language, whereas the native speakers that Bloom consulted believed the materials were appropriate. Perhaps Bloom's consultants differed from Au in linguistic or cultural background. In any event, in the absence of agreement regarding the appropriateness of the materials, it is difficult to interpret their results.

There are also problems to be considered on the cognitive side. As noted earlier, Whorf was principally interested in habitual modes of thought. Lucy (1992b) suggests that counterfactual reasoning is more specialized than habitual since it is probably more accessible to those with higher levels of education. It thus remains to be seen whether Whorfian effects can be observed when more habitual forms of thought are assessed.

Cognitive Representation of Number

Some recent studies have turned to an aspect of language that is somewhat closer to Whorf's original concerns—how languages grammatically mark number. Lucy (1992a) contrasted number marking in English and Yucatec Maya, an indigenous language spoken in southeastern Mexico. Noun phrases may be distinguished by the presence or absence of two semantic features, animacy and discreteness (see Figure 14-1). **Animacy** refers to whether the referent of the noun phrase is alive or not. **Discreteness** refers to whether the referent is an object with definite outlines or boundaries. Using these features, a dog is + animate; a shovel is − animate, + discrete; and mud is − animate, − discrete. (Since discreteness is embedded within − animacy, there is no + animate, − discrete.) In English, the plural is obligatorily applied to the first two groups (which we call count nouns), but not to the third (which we call mass nouns). That is, we say *persons* and *shovels*, but not *muds*. In Yucatec, the plural is (optionally) applied to + animate noun phrases, but not to the other two groups. Thus, the major distinction in English is between discrete and nondiscrete objects, whereas in Yucatec it is between animate and inanimate objects.

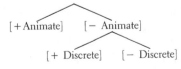

[+ Animate]   [− Animate]

[+ Discrete]   [− Discrete]

Figure 14-1. Semantic features pertaining to plural marking in Yucatec Maya and English. [From J. A. Lucy, *Grammatical Categories and Cognition: A Case Study of the Linguistic Relativity Hypothesis* (Cambridge, England: Cambridge University Press, 1992).]

In addition, the Yucatec lexicon has words that refer to a range of meanings that would be subdivided into different lexical items in English. For instance, the word *che'* is used to refer to a number of objects of various shapes, all of which are made out of wood (tree, stick, board, and so on). Similarly, *hú'un* can refer to a type of tree, to the bark of the tree, to paper, or even to items made of paper such as books.

Lucy hypothesized two cognitive consequences of these linguistic differences. First, since the plural is used with greater regularity and for a wider array of referents in English, he hypothesized that English speakers should habitually attend to the number of various objects of reference more than Yucatec speakers did. This should lead English speakers to specify the number of objects, especially inanimate objects, more often than Yucatec speakers. Second, he hypothesized that English speakers would be more sensitive to shape than to substance, whereas Yucatec speakers would be just the opposite. English speakers would attend to shape because it distinguishes discrete objects from nondiscrete objects. Yucatec speakers would attend less to shape because their language does not mark the discrete/nondiscrete distinction, and they would attend more to substance because of the presence of lexical items based on substance or material.

Lucy assessed cognitive processes in a series of 12 experimental tasks. In several, the subjects were presented with pictures (line drawings) depicting various scenes of Yucatec everyday life. The pictures included different objects in various numbers (for example, three pigs, one hen, and so on). The subjects (adult Mayan men between 18 and 45 years of age and college-aged U.S. men) were asked to do such things as verbally describe the pictures and recall the pictures. As expected, the English speakers specified the number of inanimate objects more frequently than the Yucatec speakers did. Also as expected, there were no differences between speakers in the frequency with which they specified the number of animate beings or nondiscrete substances.

Lucy also had a series of tasks in which the subjects were presented with three objects and asked to judge which two were most similar. In one study, the original object was a cardboard box and then the subjects were given two other objects, a plastic box (shape alternative) and a piece of cardboard (material alternative), and asked to determine which alternative was most similar to the original. Their judgments tended to follow the linguistic classifications for each language. English speakers regarded the two boxes as most similar, whereas Yucatec speakers regarded the piece of cardboard as most similar to the cardboard box. English speakers grouped together those alternatives that are treated the same way linguistically (that is, with the plural morpheme). In contrast, Yucatec speakers attended to substance more than shape.

Lucy's work is important in several respects. First, he has contrasted two grammatical treatments of number and how they may lead to different ways of thinking about objects. In contrast, several earlier approaches have identified a grammatical feature that is present in one language but not another. The latter approach tends to implicitly endorse the view that one language is deficient relative to another, whereas the comparative approach taken by Lucy merely implies that languages are different. In retrospect, much of the discussion of Bloom's research may have been related to this aspect of his work (but see Bloom, 1981, pp. 15–16). Second, Lucy used a number of different cognitive tasks. Many earlier studies used a single task and tended to reduce the broad Whorfian concerns of differences in world view to a single narrow experimental task. The use of multiple tasks makes sense in most psycholinguistic studies; it is more important, and perhaps even vital, in tests of the Whorf hypothesis.

Final Observations

The status of the Whorf hypothesis depends upon what we take it to mean. If the claim is that the presence of a language feature determines a mode of thought that cannot be attained in any other way, then the hypothesis is surely wrong. However, the weak version of the Whorf hypothesis may be tenable. We have seen a parallel between the results of recent studies at the lexical level and those at the grammatical. Whereas earlier studies did not provide any evidence for the Whorf hypothesis, recent work suggests otherwise. One reason may be that researchers are just beginning to find adequate ways of exploring a hypothesis as far reaching and yet as subtle as the Whorf hypothesis. We have seen that there are some major obstacles in terms of the selection of subjects, the preparation of materials, and the assessment of cognition. It is also necessary to tease apart the influences of language and culture on cognition. It appears that as researchers find ways to effectively grapple with these problems, the results are becoming more supportive of Whorf's hypothesis.

One final point. Several of the studies discussed in this chapter have focused on the percentage of errors as the measure of cognitive performance. However, as Hunt and Agnoli (1991) point out, there are much more subtle measures of cognition available. We have seen throughout this book that certain linguistic variables, such as the presence of multiple meanings in a lexically ambiguous word, may influence the speed of performance but not necessarily the number of errors. Hunt and Agnoli suggest that cognitive measures such as reaction time have not been utilized very often in studies of the Whorf hypothesis. This is unfortunate because effects of the sort that Whorf had in mind may be rather subtle. Further research using more sophisticated measures of cognition may yet provide evidence for what Bloom called "the linguistic shaping of thought."

Summary

At the grammatical level, the distinctions employed by a language may influence the ease with which a speaker can adopt a particular mode of thought. Certain modes of thought may be easier to attain or appear more natural for speakers of some languages, although they are by no means unattainable for speakers of other languages. On balance, these studies provide some support for the weak version of the Whorf hypothesis.

Review Questions

1. Identify the two parts of the Whorf hypothesis.
2. Define differentiation.
3. What conclusions did Whorf draw from his study of count and mass nouns in English?
4. Distinguish between the strong and weak versions of the linguistic determinism view.
5. Discuss the role of codability in color cognition.
6. Discuss Rosch's color studies and the conclusions that she drew.
7. What relationship did Miura find between language and mathematical skills?
8. What conclusions can be drawn from the Carroll and Casagrande study?
9. What criticisms have been made of the Bloom study?
10. Describe Lucy's studies of grammatical number marking in Yucatec and English.

Thought Questions

1. The publication manual of the American Psychological Association and other style manuals endorse the elimination of sexist language. Based on the material discussed in this chapter, do you think that the reduction of sexist language will influence the thoughts or attitudes of individuals who comply with these standards?
2. How might the distinction between automatic and controlled processes (see Chapter 3) be used to test the Whorf hypothesis?
3. Choose one or more of the studies designed to test the Whorf hypothesis and critically evaluate it. Is the study a fair test of the hypothesis? Why or why not?

Glossary

Acknowledgement A **speech act** in which the speaker expresses feelings for the listener. An example is *I'm sorry I was rude and hurt you.*

Acoustic phonetics The branch of phonetics that specifies the acoustic characteristics associated with each speech sound.

Active voice A sentence in which the surface structure subject is also the deep structure or logical subject of the sentence, such as *The woman scolded the child.*

Affricate A consonant that begins with complete closure of the **vocal tract** followed by gradual release of air pressure, such as the *ch* in *church.*

Agent The thematic or semantic role corresponding to an individual who performs a given action, such as *the manager* in *The manager opened the store.*

Agrammatic speech Speech in which there is a lack of grammatical structure, such as the absence of grammatical **morphemes** and **function words.**

Agraphia An **aphasia** characterized by the inability to write.

Alexia An **aphasia** characterized by the inability to comprehend written or printed words.

Alveolar A consonant articulated at the alveolar ridge, such as the *d* in *dog.*

Ambiguity A property of language in which a word or sentence may be interpreted in more than one way. See also **deep-structure ambiguity, lexical ambiguity,** and **phrase-structure ambiguity.**

American Sign Language (ASL) The form of sign language used in this country. It is a complete language distinct from oral languages.

Anaphor A linguistic expression that refers back to prior information in **discourse.**

Anaphoric reference A form of **reference cohesion** in which one linguistic expression refers back to prior information in **discourse.**

Animacy A semantic feature denoting whether an object is alive or not.

Antecedent Prior information in **discourse.**

Anticipation A speech error in which a later word or sound takes the place of an earlier one.

Anticipatory coarticulation Type of **coarticulation** in which the shape of the vocal tract for a given speech sound is influenced by upcoming sounds.

Anticipatory retracing   **Self-repair** in which the speaker traces back to some point prior to an error. Previously correct material is repeated along with the corrected material. See also **fresh start, instant repair.**

Antonymy   A semantic relationship in which two words mean the opposite of one another.

Aphasia   A language or speech disorder caused by brain damage.

Arbitrariness   A feature of language in which there is no direct resemblance between words and their **referents.**

Arcuate fasciculus   The primary pathway in the brain between **Wernicke's area** and **Broca's area.**

Argument   The portion of a **proposition** that refers to the person or thing that is doing something.

Articulatory phonetics   The branch of phonetics that specifies the articulatory gestures associated with each speech sound.

Aspiration   A puff of air that accompanies the production of certain speech sounds. Aspiraton is phonemic in some languages but not in English.

Assertion   A communicative act in which a person draws the attention of another person to a particular object. For example, a child showing a toy to an adult as if to say *This is mine.* Assertions may be made through words or gestures.

Assimilation   A phonological process in which one speech sound is replaced by another that is similar to sounds elsewhere in the utterance.

Associative chain theory   A theory, favored by behaviorists, which explains the formulation of a sentence as a chain of associations between the individual words in the sentence.

Attempt-suppressing signal   A cue given by a speaker to indicate to a listener that he/she is not finished.

Auditory level   A level of speech perception in which the speech signal is represented in terms of frequency, intensity, and temporal attributes.

Automaticity   A property of cognitive processes that do not require any processing capacity.

Automatic process   An activity that does not require any processing capacity.

Auxiliary verb   A "helping verb." A verb such as *is, do,* or *can* used in conjunction with the main verb in a sentence, such as *Jim is gardening this afternoon.*

Baby talk   See **motherese.**

Background   In discourse processing, information that was introduced or discussed earlier and is no longer the focus of discussion.

Basic child grammar   The grammatical characteristics of early child language found in numerous languages, such as telegraphic speech.

Basic color term   A term that refers to color and that is only one **morpheme,** not contained within another color, and not restricted to a small number of **referents.**

Basic level term   A term that refers to a category in which there are broad similarities among exemplars.

Behaviorism   The doctrine that states that the proper concern of psychology should be the objective study of behavior rather than the study of the mind.

Bilabial   A consonant articulated at the mouth, such as the *b* in *big.*

Binaural perception A procedure in which the same stimulus is presented simultaneously to the two ears.

Binding theory A component of **government-binding theory** that pertains to how linguistic expressions such as pronouns are related to their antecedents in **discourse**.

Blend A speech error in which two or more words are combined.

Bottom-up process A process in which lower level processes are carried out without influence from higher level processes (for example, perception of **phonemes** being uninfluenced by the words in which they appear).

Bound morpheme A unit of meaning that exists only when combined, or bound, to a **free morpheme**.

Bridging A process in which the listener or reader draws inferences to build a "bridge" between the current utterance and preceding utterances.

Broca's aphasia An **aphasia** characterized by deficits in language production (also called **expressive aphasia**).

Broca's area A brain region in the frontal lobe of the left hemisphere. Damage to this region leads to **Broca's aphasia**.

Cataphoric reference A form of **reference cohesion** in which one linguistic expression refers to information yet to be introduced in discourse.

Categorical perception The inability to discriminate sounds within a phonemic category.

Category-size effect The fact that it takes longer to semantically verify a statement of the form *An A is a B* if B is a larger semantic category.

Characteristic feature A **semantic feature** common to a given lexical entry but not strictly definitional. For example, a characteristic feature of birds is that they can fly.

Child-directed speech Speech addressed to children. See also **motherese**.

Chunking Grouping individual pieces of information into larger units. A **short-term memory** strategy.

Coalescence A phonological process in which **phonemes** from different syllables are combined into a single syllable.

Coarticulation The process of articuating more than one speech sound at a time.

Codability The length of a verbal expression.

Code switching Switching from one dialect or language to another.

Cognitive constraint A bias that children are assumed to use to infer the meanings of words.

Cognitive economy A characteristic of semantic memory in which information is only represented once within a **semantic network**.

Cognitive science The branch of science devoted to the study of the mind; consists of the fields of psychology, artificial intelligence, neuroscience, linguistics, philosophy, and adjacent disciplines.

Coherence The degree to which different parts of a text are connected to one another. Coherence exists at both local and global levels of **discourse**.

Cohesion Local **coherence** relations between adjacent sentences in **discourse**.

Commissive   A speech act in which the speaker is obligated, by virtue of the speech act, to do something. An example is *I'll return the book by Tuesday.*

Communicative competence   The skill associated with using a language appropriately and effectively in various social situations.

Complement   A noun phrase that includes a verb. For example, *you sat down* in *I see you sat down.*

Complex sentence   A sentence that expresses more than one **proposition.**

Comprehension monitoring   Self-assessment of one's degree of comprehension.

Conduction aphasia   An **aphasia** characterized by the inability to repeat what one has heard.

Conjunctive cohesion   A form of **cohesion** in which we express a relationship between sentences or phrases by using conjunctions such as *and, or,* and *but.*

Connected discourse   See **discourse.**

Connectionist model   A model of cognitive/linguistic processes that assumes (1) a vast, interconnected network of information nodes in which each node influences and is influenced by a large number of adjacent nodes and (2) parallel processing of information. (Also called **parallel distributed processing.**)

Connotation   The aspect of meaning suggested by a word but not strictly part of the word's dictionary definition. See also **denotation.**

Consonant   A speech sound in which the **vocal tract** is partially or fully closed during production.

Constative   A speech act in which the speaker expresses a belief with the intention of creating the same belief in the listener. An example is *Sally reported the incident to the police.*

Constituent   A grammatical unit, such as a noun or verb phrase.

Content word   A word (such as a noun, a verb, or an adjective) that plays a primary role in the meaning of a sentence. See also **function word.**

Context-conditioned variation   The fact that the acoustic parameters associated with a given speech sound vary with its phonetic context.

Context effect   The finding in **semantic verification** studies that filler items influence the verification times of target items.

Contextualized language   Language related to the immediate context.

Contralateral   The arrangement in the nervous system in which one half of the brain controls the other half of the body.

Controlled process   An activity that requires processing capacity.

Convention   A shared assumption about communication.

Coordination   A sentence in which two or more simple sentences are linked by a coordinating expression, such as *and, or,* or *but.* For example, *Lake Superior is beautiful but it is cold.*

Copula   The verb *to be* used as the main verb in a sentence, such as *Jim is wonderful.*

Coreferential   An arrangement in which two or more linguistic expressions (proper names, pronouns, and so on) refer to the same individual.

Corpus callosum   A band of fibers that connects the two cerebral hemispheres.

Counterfactual reasoning   The ability to reason about an event that is contrary to fact.

Count noun   A noun that takes the plural **morpheme** and refers to an object with clear boundaries, such as a stick (also called **individual nouns**).

Creole   The language developed by children who have been exposed to a **pidgin** as their native language.

Decontextualized language   Language that is separated, in time or place, from its **referent**.

Deep structure   The level of linguistic structure, assumed in transformational grammar, which expresses the underlying semantic meaning of a sentence.

Deep-structure ambiguity   A form of ambiguity in which a sentence may be derived from two different **deep structures**.

Default value   The value of a parameter that a child is hypothesized to be born with.

Deferred imitation   Imitation of a behavior that was observed some time earlier.

Defining feature   A **semantic feature** that must be present for an instance to be a member of a category.

Denotation   The dictionary definition of a word. See also **connotation**.

Dental   A consonant articulated at the teeth, such as the *th* in *thin*.

Derivation   The series of linguistic rules needed to generate a sentence.

Derivational theory of complexity   The theory, now discredited, which states that the psychological complexity of a sentence is directly proportional to the length of its derivation.

Descriptive adequacy   The extent to which a **grammar** can provide a structural description of a sentence. See also **explanatory adequacy, observational adequacy**.

Determiner   A part of speech that quantifies or specifies a count noun, such as *the* in *The cat ate the plant*.

Dichotic listening   An experimental task in which different stimuli are simultaneously presented to the two ears.

Differentiation   The number of words in a semantic domain.

Directive   A speech act in which the speaker tries to influence a listener's behavior. An example is *The student asked the professor to delay the exam*.

Discontinuous constituent   A grammatical constituent in which some elements are separated, such as *picked* and *up* in *George picked the baby up*.

Discourse   A group of sentences combined in a meaningful manner.

Discreteness   A **semantic feature** denoting whether or not an object has definite outlines or boundaries. For example, a tree is + discrete whereas air is − discrete.

Displacement   A feature of language in which words are separated in space and time from their **referents**.

Distinctive feature   The specification of the differences between speech sounds in terms of individual contrasts.

Duality of patterning   A feature of a communication system in which a small number of meaningless units can be combined into a large number of meaningful units.

Duplex perception   An experimental technique in which **formant** transitions are presented to one ear and **steady states** to the other.

Elaboration   The process of relating incoming information to information already stored in **permanent memory.**

Ellipsis   A form of **cohesion** in which a previous item is dropped from subsequent sentences but its presence is assumed.

Empiricism   The branch of philosophy that emphasizes the use of controlled observation and the belief that experience shapes human behavior.

Episode   A component of a **story grammar.**

Episodic memory   The division of **permanent memory** in which personally experienced information is stored.

Everyday style   A style of conversation during psychotherapy in which the client recounts events from everyday life in an objective manner.

Evoked potential   Measurement of electrical activity in a region of the brain following presentation of a stimulus.

Exchange   A speech error in which two sounds or words change places with one another.

Explanatory adequacy   The extent to which a **grammar** can explain the facts of language acquisition. See also **descriptive adequacy, observational adequacy.**

Explicit knowledge   Knowledge of how to perform various acts. See also **tacit knowledge.**

Expressive style   A style of child language characterized by low noun/pronoun ratio, poor articulation, clear intonation, and relatively long utterances.

Eye/voice span   The lag between eye position and voice when reading aloud, about six or seven words.

False recognition error   When a subject believes that an item was presented during a study although it wasn't.

Family resemblance   The notion that members of a category may resemble one another in the manner that members of a family resemble one another. That is, no single feature is necesssary but members typically share several features.

Family style   A style of conversation during psychotherapy in which the client recounts events from family life, usually in an emotion-laded manner.

Feature level   A level of written language perception in which a visual stimulus is represented in terms of the physical features that comprise a letter of the alphabet, such as a vertical line, a curved line, and so on.

Felicity condition   A condition that must be present for a **speech act** to be understood as sincere or valid.

Feral children   Children who have grown up without human companionship in the wild.

Fis phenomenon   When a child mispronounces a word, yet correctly distinguishes between child and adult versions of that word.

Fixation   The time spent focused at a given location during reading. The time between eye movements.

Focal color   The most representative example of a **basic color.**

Foreground   In **discourse** processing, information that is currently being discussed or explained.

Formant   A concentrated band of energy found in the sound spectrograms of **phonemes.**

Formant transition   A rapid increase or decrease in frequency at the beginning of a **formant.**

Free morpheme   A unit of meaning that can stand alone.

Fresh start   **Self-repair** in which the speaker replaces the original syntactic structure with a new one. See also **anticipatory retracing, instant repair.**

Fricative   A consonant in which the **vocal tract** is partially closed during articulation, such as the *f* in *fat*.

Function word   A word, such as an article, preposition, or conjunction, which plays a secondary role in the meaning of a sentence. See also **content word.**

Garden path sentence   A sentence in which the comprehender assumes a particular meaning of a word or phrase but discovers later that the assumption was incorrect, forcing the comprehender to backtrack and reinterpret the sentence.

Genre   A category of **discourse** characterized by a particular form or content, such as the genre for fairy tales.

Given information   Information that the speaker assumes is already known by the listener.

Given/new strategy   A comprehension strategy in which utterances are analyzed into given and new components and the new information is stored in memory with previously received given information.

Government-binding theory   A theory of language that assumes that language consists of a set of modules, each dedicated to a different aspect of language knowledge.

Grammar   In linguistics, a theory of language or set of hypotheses about how language is organized.

Grapheme   A printed letter of the alphabet.

Ground   In metaphor, the implied similarity between **tenor** and **vehicle.**

Habituation   The decline in a response to a stimulus following repeated presentation of the stimulus.

Head parameter   A grammatical feature that specifies the position of the head of a phrase (noun in noun phrase, verb in verb phrase, and so on).

Holistic processing   A style of processing, associated with the right cerebral hemisphere, which is global in nature.

Holophrase   A one-word utterance used by a child to express more than the meaning attributed to the word by adults.

Hyponymy   A semantic relationship in which a word is a superordinate, coordinate, or subordinate of another.

Iconicity   A characteristic of language in which words resemble their **referents.**

Idiomorph   A sound or sound sequence used consistently by a child to refer to someone or something, even though it is not the sound sequence conventionally used in the language for that purpose.

Illocutionary force   In **speech act** theory, the action that is performed by a speaker in uttering a sentence.

Immediacy principle   The principle that we immediately interpret words as we encounter them.

Implication   A semantic relationshp in which if one linguistic expression is true, then another must be. For example, if *John is a bachelor* is true, then *John is not married* must be.

Incompatibility   A semantic relationship in which a word contradicts another.

Incremental processing   The notion that we are planning one portion of our utterance as we articulate another portion.

Index of Productive Syntax   A measure of later syntactic development. It is computed by counting the occurrence of various types of sentence constructions in a child's language.

Indirect speech act   A **speech act** in which the literal utterance meaning is not the same as the speaker's meaning.

Induction   A process of reasoning from the specific to the general. For instance, if all of the specific horses we have seen are brown, then we might induce that all horses are brown.

Inference   A **proposition** that is drawn by the listener or reader.

Initiation-reply-evaluation sequence   A form of **discourse** used in classrooms in which the teacher asks a student a question, the student answers, and the teacher evaluates the answer.

Instantiation   Identifying a general term with a specific meaning.

Instant repair   **Self-repair** in which the speaker traces back to an error, which is then replaced with the correct word. See also **anticipatory retracing, fresh start.**

Internal lexicon   The storage of lexical information in memory.

Interruption   A period of simultaneous speech more than one word prior to the speaker's projected completion point. See also **overlap.**

Intersection search   The process of retrieving information from a **semantic network.**

Interview style   A style of conversation during psychotherapy in which jargon terms such as *relationship* or *interpretation* are used.

Intonation   The use of pitch to signal meaning.

Intonational contour   A pattern of pitch changes characteristic of an utterance as a whole, such as the rising intonation often found in questions.

Ipsalateral   The arrangement in the nervous system in which one half of the brain controls the same side of the body.

Isolated children   Children who have grown up without normal human interactions.

Language bioprogram   A hypothesized innate **grammar** that is used by children whose environmental exposure to language is limited. The bioprogram is assumed to be suppressed in children whose language environment is normal.

Language bioprogram hypothesis   The hypothesis that children whose environmental exposure to language is limited use a backup linguistic system.

Laryngeal system   The system of muscles that determines whether a speech sound is voiced or voiceless.

Late closure strategy   A strategy used in **parsing.** It states that, wherever possible, we prefer to attach new items to the current constituent.

Lateralization   The extent to which a given psychological function is served by one hemisphere of the brain. Functions primarily served by one hemisphere are said to be lateralized to that hemisphere.

Letter level   The level of written language perception in which a visual stimulus is represented as a letter of the alphabet.

Levels effect   In discourse memory, the finding that higher level **propositions** are retained better than lower level propositions.

Lexical access   The process of activating lexical items from **semantic memory.**

Lexical ambiguity   A form of ambiguity in which a word has more than one meaning.

Lexical bias effect   The finding that speech errors more commonly result in true words than would be expected by chance.

Lexical cohesion   The use of reiteration, **synonymy, hyponymy,** and other semantic relationships to link successive sentences in **discourse.**

Lexical decision task   An experimental task in which a subject sees a string of letters and must rapidly decide if the string is a word or not.

Lexical-functional grammar   A **grammar** in which structural relationships are built into enriched lexical entries rather than with **transformational rules.**

Lexical-insertion rule   A rule that governs how lexical entries are inserted into a tree structure during the derivation of a sentence.

Lexicon   The vocabulary of a language. See also **internal lexicon.**

Linguistic determinism   The hypothesis that languages determine nonlinguistic cognitive processes, such as the perception of shapes.

Linguistic productivity   The ability to create or comprehend an infinite number of new sentences that are grammatically correct (also called **linguistic creativity**).

Linguistic relativity   The hypothesis that the cognitive processes determined by language vary from language to language.

Linguistics   The branch of science that studies the origin, structure, and use of language.

Locutionary act   In **speech act** theory, the act of saying something.

Longitudinal investigation   A method of studying child development in which a small number of children are studied over a period of years.

Long-term memory   See **permanent memory.**

Macrostructure   The global **coherence** relationships in discourse.

Manner of articulation   How a speech sound is articulated (for example, **stop, fricative,** and so on).

Manual English   A manual version of English, as in fingerspelling the letters of the English alphabet. See also **American Sign Language.**

Mass noun   A noun that does not take the plural **morpheme** and that refers to objects without clear boundaries, such as air.

Mean length of utterance in morphemes   An index of children's language growth. It is computed by dividing the number of **morphemes** by the number of utterances.

Mental model   A mental representation of some aspect of the world.

Metalinguistic awareness   The ability to think of language as an object.

Metaphor   A form of language in which a word or phrase that literally denotes one idea is interpreted to mean a different one and suggests a similarity between the two. For example, *My head is an apple without a core.*

Metaphorical switching A form of code switching from one language or dialect to another in which the basis for the switch is a change in the conversational topic.

Microstructure The local **coherence** relationships in **discourse.**

Minimal attachment principle A strategy used in **parsing.** It states that we prefer attaching new items into the **phrase marker** being constructed using the fewest syntactic nodes consistent with the rules of the language.

Minimal response An utterance such as *uh huh* or *um hmm* made by a listener during a conversation. Ordinarily, minimal responses are taken as displays of interest in a speaker's topic.

Mispronunciation detection An experimental task in which subjects are presented auditorily with tapes that occasionally include mispronounced words. The subject's task is to detect the mispronunciations.

Modularity The degree to which language processing is independent of general cognitive processes such as memory and reasoning. Also refers to the degree to which an aspect of language is independent of other aspects of language. For example, **parsing** may be thought of as modular if there is a syntactic processor that operates independently of semantic and discourse processes.

Morpheme The smallest unit of meaning in a language.

Morphology The system of word-forming elements and processes in a language.

Motherese A form of adult-to-child speech characterized by relatively simple utterances, concrete referents, exaggerated intonation patterns, and a high proportion of directive utterances.

Mutual exclusivity bias A cognitive constraint in which children assume that an object is ordinarily not given two different names.

Nasal A **consonant** in which air flows through the nasal cavity, as in the *n* in *nail.*

Nativism An approach to language acquisition that emphasizes the innate organization of language.

Necessary condition A condition that must be present in order for a specified event to occur.

Negative evidence Evidence that a particular linguistic expression (a word or sentence) is inappropriate or unacceptable. Negative evidence may be presented explicitly (*No, that's not a cow, that's a dog*) or implicitly (such as when adults repeat child utterances with corrections).

Neurolinguistics The study of how linguistic information is processed in the brain.

New information Information that is assumed that the listener or reader does not know.

Null-subject parameter A grammatical feature that specifies whether or not a language permits sentences without subjects (also called the **pro-drop parameter**).

Object permanence The awareness that objects that can no longer be seen still exist.

Observational adequacy The extent to which a **grammar** can distinguish between acceptable and unacceptable strings of words. See also **descriptive adequacy, explanatory adequacy.**

Operating principle A preferred way of taking in or operating on information.

Original word game A game in which adults teach children the names of words. Children point to an object and say *What's that?* and the adult supplies the name.

Orthography The representation of a sound by written or printed symbols.

Ostensive definition The process of defining a word by pointing to its **referent.**

Overextension When a child uses a word to refer to a larger set of **referents** than an adult would. For example, calling a round clock a *moon.*

Overlap A period of simultaneous speech during the last word of a speaker's projected closing. See also **interruption.**

Overregularization When a child applies a linguistic rule to cases that are exceptions to the rule. For example, saying *goed* instead of *went.*

Paragrammatic speech Speech that is fluent but not coherent and that contains many irrelevant associations.

Parallel distributed processing model See **connectionist model.**

Parallel processing When two or more processes take place at the same time.

Parallel transmission The notion that different **phonemes** of the same syllable are encoded into the speech signal simultaneously.

Parameter (1) In **government-binding theory,** a grammatical feature that is "set" in different ways in different languages. See also **head parameter, null-subject parameter.** (2) In **American Sign Language,** a dimension along which signs may differ, such as hand configuration, movement, and location.

Parameter setting In **government-binding theory,** the notion that children are born with grammatical **parameters** that are "preset" to certain values. Language acquisition is seen as a matter of resetting these parameters to the values of one's native language.

Parsing The process of breaking a string of words into grammatical categories.

Partial report technique A technique for studying the **sensory stores.** Subjects are briefly presented with an array of stimuli and asked to report only a portion of the array.

Particle-movement transformation A **transformational rule** that accounts for the movement of particles such as *up* around noun phrases.

Passive transformation A **transformational rule** that transforms the **deep structure** of an active sentence into the **passive voice.**

Passive voice A sentence in which the **surface structure** subject is the **deep structure** or logical object of the action, such as in *The child was scolded by the mother.*

Patient A thematic or semantic role corresponding to the individual acted upon, such as *the elderly man* in *The neighborhood frightened the elderly man.*

Pattern recognition A process of matching information in the **sensory stores** with information retrieved from **permanent memory.**

Perlocutionary effect In **speech act** theory, the effect of a speech act on a listener.

Permanent memory Memory that is essentially permanent (also called **long-term memory**). Includes **semantic** and **episodic memory.**

Perseveration A speech error in which an earlier word or sound intrudes on a later one.

Perseveratory coarticulation The type of **coarticulation** in which the shape of the **vocal tract** for a given speech sound is influenced by previous sounds.

Phone The minimal unit of sound.

Phoneme   The minimal unit of sound that contributes to meaning.

Phoneme monitoring   An experimental task in which subjects listen for a particular **phoneme** while comprehending a passage and being timed for how long it takes them to monitor the phoneme.

Phonemic restoration   A **top-down process** in which the listener uses the context to restore **phonemes** missing from the speech signal.

Phonemic similarity effect   The observation that speech errors and targets are phonemically similar.

Phonetic level   A level of **speech perception** in which the speech signal is represented in terms of acoustic cues, such as **formant transitions.**

Phonetics   The study of speech sounds.

Phonetic trading relations   The notion that different acoustic cues have trade-off effects on speech perception.

Phonological bias technique   A method of inducing speech errors by having a subject read a series of words with similar phonological patterns.

Phonological level   A level of **speech perception** in which the speech signal is converted into a **phoneme,** and phonological rules are applied to the sound sequence.

Phonology   The sound system of a language, including the rules determining how different **phonemes** may be arranged in a word.

Phrase marker   A tree diagram that represents the **phrase structure** of a sentence.

Phrase structure   The hierarchical organization of sentences into phrases.

Phrase-structure ambiguity   A form of ambiguity in which a sentence has multiple meanings that may be revealed by regrouping the sentence constituents.

Phrase-structure rule   A rule that "rewrites" one constituent into one or more constituents. For example, a verb phrase may be rewritten as a verb and a noun phrase.

Pidgin   An auxiliary language that is created when speakers of mutually unintelligible languages are in close contact.

Place of articulation   The location within the vocal tract where articulation of a speech sound is produced (for example, **bilabial, alveolar,** and so on).

Positive evidence   Evidence that a particular linguistic expression (a word or sentence) is appropriate or acceptable. Positive evidence may be presented explicitly (when someone approves of another's word or utterance) or implicitly (for example, when a person responds to another's utterance without explicitly commenting on its appropriateness).

Poverty of stimulus argument   The argument, made by **nativists,** that the environmental input presented to children is too weak and degenerate to account for the child's language acquisition.

Power semantic   The use of different forms of speech that mark power asymmetries.

Pragmatics   The social rules underlying language use.

Predicate   The portion of a **proposition** that refers to the action.

Preemption principle   The principle that the speech of a child's linguistic environment preempts or suppresses the **language bioprogram.**

Pretend play   The use of an object in a playful or unconventional manner, such as using a toy rake to comb a doll's hair.

Priming An experimental procedure in which one word is presented in advance of another, target word, which reduces the time needed to retrieve or activate the target word.

Problem of invariance The fact that there is no one-to-one correspondence between speech cues and perception.

Processing capacity The overall amount of mental capacity available for various tasks or activities.

Proposition A unit of meaning consisting of a predicate (verb, adjective, or conjunction) plus one or more arguments (noun or pronoun). Simple sentences express a single proposition whereas complex sentences express more than one proposition.

Prosodic factors Factors such as intonation and stress that are superimposed on speech segments (also called **suprasegmentals**).

Prototype The best or most typical member of a category.

Psycholinguistics The study of the comprehension, production, and acquisition of language.

Pure word deafness An **aphasia** in which a person is unable to comprehend language in the auditory modality. Comprehension of visual language and production in both modalities is normal.

Rate normalization The process of taking the rate of speech into consideration when using acoustic cues during speech perception.

Rationalism The philosophical tradition that emphasizes the use of argument and the belief that innate knowledge guides human behavior.

Readability The degree to which a text is comprehensible to a reader. It may be measured by examining the number of **propositions** or ideas a reader has retained per unit of reading time.

Reading span task A measure of **working memory** capacity during reading. Subjects read aloud a series of sentences and then try to recall the last word in each sentence. The number of words recalled is the measure of the subject's reading span.

Recipient A semantic or thematic role referring to the person to whom something is given (for example, *Susan* in *John gave the flower to Susan*).

Recursive rule A rule that applies to its own output, such as a rule for self-embedded sentences.

Reduction A phonological process in child language in which one or more **phonemes** are deleted. Also called cluster reduction because consonant clusters are often reduced, such as saying *take* for *steak*.

Reduplicated babbling A form of babbling in which infants use the same sounds over and over, as in *gagagaga*.

Reduplication A phonological process in which the repetition of one syllable is used to mark a multisyllabic word (for example, *dada* for *daddy*).

Reference The relationship between a linguistic expression and a person, object, or event in the world.

Reference cohesion A form of **cohesion** in which the information needed to interpret a linguistic expression is found elsewhere in the text. See also **anaphoric reference, cataphoric reference.**

Referent The person, object, or event to which a linguistic expression refers.

Referential communication task   An experimental task in which the subject must formulate a message about an object in the environment (as opposed to one's thoughts or feelings).

Referential style   The style of child language that emphasizes a high ratio of nouns to pronouns, clear articulation, and an emphasis on naming.

Regression   Backward eye movement during reading.

Reinstatement search   The time-consuming process in which antecedents are retrieved from **permanent memory** into **working memory** in order to comprehend a current sentence.

Relational processing   A style of processing, associated with the left hemisphere, which emphasizes the analysis of whole units into parts.

Relative clause   A *wh*-clause that modifies a noun. For example, *that you found* in *Show me the book that you found.*

Repetition rule   The notion in **discourse** analysis that **propositions** that repeat the arguments of prior propositions are subordinated to them.

Request   A communicative act in which a person attempts to influence the behavior of another. For example, a child pointing at a milk bottle in order to be given some. Requests may occur in words or gestures.

Respiratory system   The system of muscles that regulates the flow of air from the lungs to the **vocal tract**.

Retention interval   The time between when information is presented and when it is to be recalled.

Saccade   An eye movement during reading.

Schema   A structure in **semantic memory** that specifies the expected series of events.

Schizophrenia   A form of mental illness that is characterized by disorders of thought processes, flattened affect, bizarre behaviors, and sometimes delusional thinking.

Self-repairs   Self-correction of speech errors.

Semantic bootstrapping   The process of using **semantics** to acquire **syntax**.

Semantic complexity   The complexity of the ideas expressed in a sentence or phrase (also called **conceptual complexity**). See also **syntactic complexity**.

Semantic differential   A tool for measuring the associative meanings of words by asking people to rate words on dimensions such as good/bad and strong/weak.

Semantic feature   A component of meaning in words. Words are marked by the presence or absence of various semantic features. For example, a giraffe is + animate but a building is − animate.

Semantic memory   The portion of **permanent memory** that contains organized knowledge of words, concepts, symbols, and objects. See also **internal lexicon**.

Semantic network   A model of **semantic memory** in which words are represented as nodes and connected to other nodes by various semantic relationships.

Semantic priming   An experimental task in which a context stimulus leads to the activation of a target stimulus.

Semantics   The domain of language that pertains to the meanings of words and sentences.

Semantic verification task   An experimental task in which subjects view sentences of the form *An A is a B* and rapidly decide if the sentence is true or false.

Sense   The relationship a word has with other words in the **lexicon.**

Sensory stores   The initial memory system for sensory stimuli. There is a separate store for each sense (vision, audition, and so on).

Serial processing   Processes that occur one at a time.

Shadowing   An experimental task in which subjects repeat what they hear.

Shift   A speech error in which a speech sound or word moves from one location to another.

Short-term memory   The memory system that holds information for about 30 seconds. See also **working memory.**

Situational model   A **mental model** of **discourse.**

Situational switching   Code switching in different social situations.

Sociolinguistics   The study of how language functions in social situations.

Solidarity semantic   The use of different forms of speech to convey friendship between individuals.

Sound spectrogram   A visual representation of the speech signal.

Sound spectrograph   A device that is used to create a sound.

Span of fixation   The size of the area from which a reader picks up visual information.

Speaker normalization   The process of taking the pitch of the speaker into account when using acoustic cues during speech perception.

Speech act   An utterance with an **illocutionary force.**

Speech perception   The process of using acoustic information to arrive at a recognition of the speech sounds in a message.

Spreading activation   The process by which one node in a **semantic network,** when active, activates related nodes.

Steady state   The portion of a **formant** that is of relatively constant frequency.

Stop   A consonant in which the **vocal tract** is completely closed, building up air pressure, and then abruptly released, such as in the *b* in *bat.*

Story grammar   The mental representation (**schema**) of an expected series of events in a story.

Stress   The emphasis given to a word or syllable during the articulation of a sentence (for example, *black-BIRD* versus *BLACK-bird*).

Structure-dependence   The fact that linguistic rules apply to grammatical structures (or constituents) rather than to individual words.

Subset principle   The notion that languages may be considered as subsets of one another.

Substitution   A form of **cohesion** in which one word is replaced by another as an alternative to repeating the first word. Also, a speech error or phonological process in which one sound or word replaces another.

Sufficient condition   A condition that, if present, ensures that a specified event will occur.

Supralaryngeal system   The system of muscles that manipulates the size and shape of the **vocal tract.**

Suprasegmentals   Prosodic factors, such as stress and intonational patterns, which lie "on top of" speech segments.

Surface structure   The level of syntactic structure, assumed in transformational grammar, which is closer to the phonetic specification of an utterance.

Synonymy   A semantic relationship in which two or more words have a similar meaning.

Syntactic complexity   The complexity of the grammatical operations required to express an idea in a given language; also called **formal complexity**. See also **semantic complexity**.

Syntax   The domain of language that pertains to the grammatical arrangement of words in a sentence.

Syrinx   The major structure in the vocal system of the chaffinch.

Tachistoscope   A machine that presents visual stimuli for very brief periods of time.

Tacit knowledge   Knowledge of how to perform an act. See also **explicit knowledge**.

Tag question   A question that is "tagged" onto a declarative sentence, such as *isn't it* in *It sure is cold in here, isn't it?*

Task specificity   The notion that certain cognitive processes are restricted to language and are not employed in other intellectual domains.

Taxonomic bias   A cognitive constraint in which children assume that a word refers to a class of individuals rather than to a single person or animal.

Tenor   The topic of a **metaphor**.

Top-down process   A process in which higher levels influence lower levels of processing. For example, the perception of **phonemes** may be influenced by the words in which they appear.

TRACE model   A **connectionist model** of speech perception.

Transformational rule   A rule that transforms one phrase structure into another by adding, deleting, or moving grammatical constituents (also called **transformation**).

Truth conditions   The conditions that need to be present in the world in order for a sentence to be true.

Turn-yielding signal   A set of cues given by a speaker to indicate that he/she is ready to yield the floor.

Typicality effect   The fact that it takes longer to verify a statement of the form *An A is a B* when A is not typical or characteristic of B.

Underextension   When a child uses a word in a more limited way than adults do (for example, refusing to call a taxi a *car*).

Variegated babbling   A form of babbling consisting of syllable strings with varying consonants and vowels.

Vehicle   What is predicated of the topic in a **metaphor**.

Velar   A consonant articulated at the velum, such as the *c* in *collar*.

Verb of possession   A verb pertaining to possession, such as *give, spend*, and *buy*.

Visual field task   An experimental task in which visual stimuli are presented to either the right or the left visual field.

Vocal cords   Two bands of muscular tissue in the larynx that vibrate during the production of speech sounds (also called vocal folds).

Vocal tract   The structures above the larynx that participate in speech production, principally the mouth (oral cavity) and nose (nasal cavity) regions.

Voice onset time   The period of time from when a consonant is released until the vocal cords vibrate.

Voicing   Whether or not the vocal cords are vibrating when air from the lungs passes over them. If the cords are vibrating, the speech sound is called voiced; if not, voiceless.

Vowel   A speech sound in which the vocal tract is open during production.

Wernicke's aphasia   An **aphasia** characterized by fluent speech that is not informational and by disorders of comprehension (also called **receptive aphasia**).

Wernicke's area   A brain region in the temporal lobe of the left hemisphere. Damage to this region leads to Wernicke's aphasia.

Whole object bias   A cognitive constraint in which children assume that a word refers to an entire object, not a part of it.

Whorf hypothesis   The hypothesis that languages shape thought processes (also called the **Sapir-Whorf hypothesis**). See also **linguistic determinism, linguistic relativity.**

Wh-**question**   A question beginning with *who, what, where, when,* or *how.*

Word level   A level of written language perception in which a visual stimulus is represented as a familiar word.

Word salad   A sentence that is grammatically jumbled.

Word-superiority effect   An experimental finding that it is easier to perceive a letter in a word context than in isolation.

Working memory   A form of memory with both storage and processing functions. Working memory is used to hold information for a short period of time as well as to perform various operations on the stored information.

Yes/no question   A question that can be answered with a *yes* or *no* answer.

Zipf's law   The fact that the length of a word is negatively correlated with its frequency of use.

References

Abrahamsen, A. A. (1982). Recasting the language-cognition question in a non-Piagetian process model framework: A reply to van Kleeck. *Merrill-Palmer Quarterly, 28*, 437–443.

Adams, M. J. (1979). Models of word recognition. *Cognitive Psychology, 11*, 133–176.

Allen, P. A., & Madden, D. J. (1990). Evidence for a parallel input serial analysis model of word processing. *Journal of Experimental Psychology: Human Perception and Performance, 16*, 48–64.

Allington, R. L., & Strange, M. (1977). Effects of grapheme substitutions in connected text upon reading behaviors. *Visible Language, 11*, 285–297.

Altmann, S. A. (1967). The structure of primate social communication. In S. A. Altmann (Ed.), *Social communication among primates* (pp. 325–362). Chicago: University of Chicago Press.

Andersen, E. S. (1984). The acquisition of sociolinguistic knowledge: Some evidence from children's verbal role play. *Western Journal of Speech Communication, 48*, 125–144.

Anderson, J. R. (1976). *Language, memory, and thought*. Hillsdale, NJ: Erlbaum.

Anderson, J. R. (1983). A spreading activation theory of memory. *Journal of Verbal Learning and Verbal Behavior, 22*, 261–295.

Anderson, R. C., & Ortony, A. (1975). On putting apples into bottles—A problem of polysemy. *Cognitive Psychology, 7*, 167–180.

Armstrong, S. L., Gleitman, L. R., & Gleitman, H. (1983). What some concepts might not be. *Cognition, 13*, 263–308.

Asch, S. E., & Nerlove, H. (1960). The development of double function terms in children: An exploratory investigation. In B. Kaplan & S. Wapner (Eds.), *Perspectives in psychological theory: Essays in honor of Heinz Werner* (pp. 47–60). New York: International Universities Press.

Aslin, R. N., Pisoni, D. B., Hennessy, B. L., & Perey, A. J. (1981). Discrimination of voice onset time by human infants: New findings and implications for the effects of early experience. *Child Development, 52*, 1135–1145.

Au, T. K. (1983). Chinese and English counterfactuals: The Sapir-Whorf hypothesis revisited. *Cognition, 15*, 155–187.

Au, T. K. (1984). Counterfactuals: In reply to Alfred Bloom. *Cognition, 17*, 289–302.

Austin, J. L. (1962). *How to do things with words.* New York: Oxford University Press.

Baars, B. J. (1980). On eliciting predictable speech errors in the laboratory. In V. A. Fromkin (Ed.), *Errors in linguistic performance* (pp. 307–318). New York: Academic Press.

Baars, B. J., Motley, M. T., & MacKay, D. G. (1975). Output editing for lexical status in artificially elicited slips of the tongue. *Journal of Verbal Learning and Verbal Behavior, 14,* 382–391.

Bach, K., & Harnish, R. M. (1979). *Linguistic communication and speech acts.* Cambridge, MA: MIT Press.

Baggett, P. (1975). Memory for explicit and implicit information in picture stories. *Journal of Verbal Learning and Verbal Behavior, 14,* 538–548.

Ball, E. W., & Blachman, B. A. (1991). Does phoneme awareness training in kindergarten make a difference in early word recognition and developmental spelling? *Reading Research Quarterly, 25,* 49–66.

Baron, J., & Thurston, I. (1973). An analysis of the word-superiority effect. *Cognitive Psychology, 4,* 207–228.

Barrett, M. D. (1982). The holophrastic hypothesis: Conceptual and empirical issues. *Cognition, 11,* 47–76.

Bartlett, F. C. (1932). *Remembering: A study in experimental and social psychology.* Cambridge, England: Cambridge University Press.

Bates, E., Camaioni, L., & Volterra, V. (1975). The acquisition of performatives prior to speech. *Merrill-Palmer Quarterly, 21,* 205–226.

Bates, E., Masling, M., & Kintsch, W. (1978). Recognition memory for aspects of dialogue. *Journal of Experimental Psychology: Human Learning and Memory, 4,* 187–197.

Beattie, G. (1983). *Talk: An analysis of speech and non-verbal behaviour in conversation.* Milton Keynes, England: Open University Press.

Beattie, G. W. (1981). Interruption in conversational interaction, and its relation to the sex and status of the interactants. *Linguistics, 19,* 15–35.

Bellinger, D. C., & Gleason, J. B. (1982). Sex differences in parental directives to young children. *Sex Roles, 8,* 1123–1139.

Bellugi, U. (1988). The acquisition of a spatial language. In F. S. Kessel (Ed.), *The development of language and language researchers: Essays in honor of Roger Brown* (pp. 153–185). Hillsdale, NJ: Erlbaum.

Bellugi, U., Bihrle, A., Jernigan, T., Trauner, D., & Doherty, S. (1990). Neuropsychological, neurological, and neuroanatomical profile of Williams Syndrome. *American Journal of Medical Genetics Supplement, 6,* 115–125.

Bellugi, U., & Fischer, S. (1972). A comparison of sign language and spoken language. *Cognition, 1,* 173–200.

Bellugi, U., & Studdert-Kennedy, M. (Eds.) (1980). *Signed and spoken language: Biological constraints on linguistic form.* Weinheim, Germany/Deerfield Beach, FL: Verlag Chemie.

Bennett-Kastor, T. (1983). Noun phrases and coherence in child narratives. *Journal of Child Language, 10,* 135–149.

Benson, D. F., & Geschwind, N. (1969). The alexias. In P. J. Vinken & G. W. Bruyn (Eds.), *Handbook of clinical neurology* (Vol. 4, pp. 112–140). Amsterdam: North-Holland.

Berko, J. (1958). The child's learning of English morphology. *Word, 14,* 150–177.

Berko, J., & Brown, R. (1960). Psycholinguistic research methods. In P. H. Mussen (Ed.), *Handbook of research methods in child development* (pp. 517–557). New York: Wiley.

Berlin, B., & Kay, P. (1969). *Basic color terms: Their universality and evolution.* Berkeley and Los Angeles: University of California Press.

Berman, R. A. (1985). The acquisition of Hebrew. In D. I. Slobin (Ed.), *The crosslinguistic study of language acquisition: Vol. 1. The data* (pp. 255–371). Hillsdale, NJ: Erlbaum.

Berwick, R. C., & Weinberg, A. S. (1983). The role of grammars in models of language use. *Cognition, 13,* 1–61.

Best, C. T., McRoberts, G. W., & Sithole, N. M. (1988). Examination of perceptual reorganization for nonnative speech contrasts: Zulu click discrimination by English-speaking adults and infants. *Journal of Experimental Psychology: Human Perception and Performance, 14,* 345–360.

Best, C. T., Morrongiello, B., & Robson, R. (1981). Perceptual equivalence of acoustic cues in speech and nonspeech perception. *Perception & Psychophysics, 29,* 191–211.

Bever, T. G. (1970). The cognitive basis for linguistic structures. In J. R. Hayes (Ed.), *Cognition and the development of language* (pp. 279–362). New York: Wiley.

Bever, T. G. (1980). Broca and Lashley were right: Cerebral dominance is an accident of growth. In D. Caplan (Ed.), *Biological studies of mental processes* (pp. 186–230). Cambridge, MA: MIT Press.

Bever, T. G., & Chiarello, R. J. (1974). Cerebral dominance in musicians and nonmusicians. *Science, 185,* 537–539.

Bickerton, D. (1981). *Roots of language.* Ann Arbor, MI: Karoma Publishers.

Bickerton, D. (1983). Creole languages. In S-Y. Wang (Ed.), *The emergence of language: Development and evolution* (pp. 59–69). New York: W. H. Freeman.

Bickerton, D. (1984). The language bioprogram hypothesis. *The Behavioral and Brain Sciences, 7,* 173–221.

Bihrle, A. M., Brownell, H. H., Powelson, J. A., & Gardner, H. (1986). Comprehension of humorous and nonhumorous materials by left and right brain-damaged patients. *Brain and Cognition, 5,* 399–411.

Black, J. B., & Bower, G. H. (1979). Episodes as chunks in narrative memory. *Journal of Verbal Learning and Verbal Behavior, 18,* 309–318.

Bleuler, E. (1950). *Dementia praecox or the group of schizophrenias* (J. Zinkin, Trans.). New York: International Universities Press. (Original work published 1911)

Blom, J-P., & Gumperz, J. J. (1972). Social meaning in linguistic structure: Code-switching in Norway. In J. J. Gumperz & D. Hymes (Eds.), *Directions in sociolinguistics: The ethnography of communication* (pp. 407–434). New York: Holt, Rinehart & Winston.

Bloom, A. H. (1981). *The linguistic shaping of thought: A study in the impact of language on thinking in China and the West.* Hillsdale, NJ: Erlbaum.

Bloom, A. H. (1984). Caution—the words you use may affect what you say: A response to Au. *Cognition, 17,* 275–287.

Bloom, L. (1970). *Language development: Form and function in emerging grammars.* Cambridge, MA: MIT Press.

Bloom, L. (1973). *One word at a time: The use of single word utterances before syntax.* The Hague: Mouton.

Bloom, L., & Lahey, M. (1978). *Language development and language disorders.* New York: Wiley.

Bloom, L., Lahey, J., Hood, L., Lifter, K., & Fiess, K. (1980). Complex sentences: Acquisition of syntactic connectives and the semantic relations they encode. *Journal of Child Language, 7,* 235–261.

Bloom, L., Lightbown, P., & Hood, L. (1975). Structure and variation in child language. *Monographs of the Society for Research in Child Development, 40*(2, Serial No. 160).

Bloom, L., Rocissano, L., & Hood, L. (1976). Adult-child discourse: Developmental interaction between information processing and linguistic knowledge. *Cognitive Psychology, 8,* 521–552.

Bloom, P. (1990). Subjectless sentences in child language. *Linguistic Inquiry, 21,* 491–504.

Bloomfield, L. (1914). An introduction to the study of language. New York: Henry Holt & Co.

Bloomfield, L. (1933). *Language.* New York: Henry Holt & Co.

Blumenthal, A. L. (1970). *Language and psychology: Historical aspects of psycholinguistics.* New York: Wiley.

Blumenthal, A. L. (1987). The emergence of psycholinguistics. *Synthese, 72,* 313–323.

Blumstein, S. E., & Stevens, K. N. (1979). Acoustic invariance in speech production: Evidence from measurements of the spectral characteristics of stop consonants. *Journal of the Acoustical Society of America, 66,* 1001–1017.

Bock, J. K. (1982). Toward a cognitive psychology of syntax: Information processing contributions to sentence formulation. *Psychological Review, 89,* 1–47.

Bock, J. K., & Cutting, J. C. (1992). Regulating mental energy: Performance units in language production. *Journal of Memory and Language, 31,* 99–127.

Bohannon, J. N., & Marquis, A. L. (1977). Children's control of adult speech. *Child Development, 48,* 1002–1008.

Bolinger, D. (1975). *Aspects of Language* (2nd ed.). New York: Harcourt Brace Jovanovich.

Bolinger, D. L., & Gerstman, L. J. (1957). Disjuncture as a cue to constructs. *Word, 13,* 246–255.

Bonvillian, J. D., Orlansky, M. D., & Novack, L. L. (1983). Developmental milestones: Sign language acquisition and motor development. *Child Development, 54,* 1435–1445.

Borke, H. (1975). Piaget's mountains revisited: Changes in the egocentric landscape. *Developmental Psychology, 11,* 240–243.

Bower, G. H., & Morrow, D. G. (1990). Mental models in narrative comprehension. *Science, 247,* 44–48.

Bowerman, M. (1973). Structural relationship in children's utterances: Syntactic or semantic? In T. E. Moore (Ed.), *Cognitive development and the acquisition of language* (pp. 197–213). New York: Academic Press.

Boysson-Bardies, B. de, Halle, P., Sagart, L., & Durand, C. (1989). A crosslinguistic investigation of vowel formants in babbling. *Journal of Child Language, 6,* 1–17.

Bradley, L., & Bryant, P. E. (1983). Categorizing sounds and learning to read: A causal connection. *Nature, 301,* 419–421.

Braine, M. D. S. (1963). The ontogeny of English phrase structure: The first phase. *Language, 39,* 1–13.

Braine, M. D. S. (1976). Children's first word combinations. *Monographs of the Society for Research in Child Development, 41*(1, Serial No. 164).

Bransford, J. D., Barclay, J. R., & Franks, J. J. (1972). Sentence memory: A constructive versus interpretive approach. *Cognitive Psychology, 3,* 193–209.

Bransford, J. D., & Johnson, M. K. (1973). Consideration of some problems of comprehension. In W. G. Chase (Ed.), *Visual information processing* (pp. 383–438). New York: Academic Press.

Bresnan, J. (1978). A realistic transformational grammar. In J. Bresnan, M. Halle, & G. A. Miller (Eds.), *Linguistic theory and psychological reality* (pp. 1–59). Cambridge, MA: MIT Press.

Britt, M. A., Perfetti, C. A., Garrod, S., & Rayner, K. (1992). Parsing in discourse: Context effects and their limits. *Journal of Memory and Language, 31*, 293–314.

Britton, B. K., Meyer, B. J. F., Simpson, R., Holdredge, T. S., & Curry, C. (1979). Effects of the organization of text on memory: Tests of two implications of a selective attention hypothesis. *Journal of Experimental Psychology: Human Learning and Memory, 5*, 496–506.

Broadbent, D. E. (1954). The role of auditory localization in attention and memory span. *Journal of Experimental Psychology, 47*, 191–196.

Brown, R. (1958). *Words and things.* Glencoe, IL: Free Press.

Brown, R. (1970). The first sentences of child and chimpanzee. In R. Brown, *Psycholinguistics* (pp. 208–231). New York: Free Press.

Brown, R. (1973a). *A first language: The early stages.* Cambridge, MA: Harvard University Press.

Brown, R. (1973b). Schizophrenia, language, and reality. *American Psychologist, 28*, 395–403.

Brown, R., & Bellugi, U. (1964). Three processes in the child's acquisition of syntax. In E. H. Lenneberg (Ed.), *New directions in the study of language* (pp. 131–161). Cambridge, MA: MIT Press.

Brown, R., & Ford, M. (1961). Address in American English. *Journal of Abnormal and Social Psychology, 62*, 375–385.

Brown, R., & Gilman, A. (1960). The pronouns of power and solidarity. In T. A. Sebeok (Ed.), *Style in language* (pp. 253–276). New York: MIT Press/Wiley.

Brown, R., & Hanlon, C. (1970). Derivational complexity and the order of acquisition in child speech. In J. R. Hayes (Ed.), *Cognition and the development of language* (pp. 11–53). New York: Wiley.

Brown, R. W., & Lenneberg, E. H. (1954). A study in language and cognition. *Journal of Abnormal and Social Psychology, 49*, 454–462.

Brown, T. S., & Wallace, P. M. (1980). *Physiological psychology.* New York: Academic Press.

Bruce, D. J. (1964). The analysis of word sounds by young children. *British Journal of Educational Psychology, 34*, 158–170.

Bruner, J. S. (1975). The ontogenesis of speech acts. *Journal of Child Language, 2*, 1–19.

Burgess, C., & Simpson, G. B. (1988). Cerebral hemispheric mechanisms in the retrieval of ambiguous word meanings. *Brain and Language, 33*, 86–103.

Cairns, H. S., & Cairns, C. E. (1976). *Psycholinguistics: A cognitive view of language.* New York: Holt, Rinehart & Winston.

Cairns, H. S., & Kamerman, J. (1975). Lexical information processing during sentence comprehension. *Journal of Verbal Learning and Verbal Behavior, 14*, 170–179.

Caplan, D. (1987). *Neurolinguistics and linguistic aphasiology: An introduction.* Cambridge, England: Cambridge University Press.

Caplan, D., & Chomsky, N. (1980). Linguistic perspectives on language development. In D. Caplan (Ed.), *Biological studies of mental processes* (pp. 97–105). Cambridge, MA: MIT Press.

Caramazza, A., & Berndt, R. S. (1978). Semantic and syntactic processes in aphasia: A review of the literature. *Psychological Bulletin, 85,* 898–918.

Caramazza, A., & Zurif, E. B. (1976). Dissociation of algorithmic and heuristic processes in language comprehension: Evidence from aphasia. *Brain and Language, 3,* 572–582.

Carey, S. (1978). The child as word learner. In M. Halle, J. Bresnan, & G. A. Miller (Eds.), *Linguistic theory and psychological reality* (pp. 264–293). Cambridge, MA: MIT Press.

Carpenter, P. A., & Just, M. A. (1989). The role of working memory in language comprehension. In D. Klahr & K. Kotovsky (Eds.), *Complex information processing: The impact of Herbert A. Simon* (pp. 31–68). Hillsdale, NJ: Erlbaum.

Carroll, J. B. (Ed.). (1956). *Language, thought, and reality: Selected writings of Benjamin Lee Whorf.* Cambridge, MA: MIT Press.

Carroll, J. B., & Casagrande, J. B. (1958). The function of language classifications in behavior. In E. E. Maccoby, T. M. Newcomb, & E. L. Hartley (Eds.), *Readings in social psychology* (pp. 18–31). New York: Holt, Rinehart & Winston.

Case, R., Kurland, M., & Goldberg, J. (1982). Operational efficiency and the growth of short-term memory span. *Journal of Experimental Child Psychology, 33,* 386–404.

Catford, J. C., Jusczyk, P. W., Klatt, D. H., Liberman, A. M., Remez, R. E., & Stevens, K. N. (1991). Panel discussion: The motor theory and alternative accounts. In I. G. Mattingly & M. Studdert-Kennedy (Eds.), *Modularity and the motor theory of speech perception* (pp. 175–195). Hillsdale, NJ: Erlbaum.

Cattell, J. M. (1886). The time taken up by cerebral operations. *Mind, 11,* 220–242, 377–392, 524–538.

Cazden, C. B. (1965). *Environmental assistance to the child's acquisition of grammar.* Unpublished doctoral dissertation, Harvard University, Cambridge, MA.

Cazden, C. B. (1968). The acquisition of noun and verb inflections. *Child Development, 39,* 433–448.

Cazden, C. B. (1976). Play with language and meta-linguistic awareness: One dimension of language experience. In J. S. Bruner, A. Jolly, & K. Sylva (Eds.), *Play: Its role in development and evolution* (pp. 603–608). New York: Basic Books.

Cazden, C. B. (1986). Classroom discourse. In M. C. Wittrock (Ed.), *Handbook of research on teaching* (3rd ed., pp. 432–463). New York: Macmillan.

Chafe, W. L. (1972). Discourse structure and human knowledge. In R. O. Freedle & J. B. Carroll (Eds.), *Language comprehension and the acquisition of knowledge* (pp. 41–69). Washington, DC: V. H. Winston.

Chaika, E. (1974). A linguist looks at "schizophrenic" language. *Brain and Language, 1,* 257–276.

Chaika, E. (1982). A unified explanation for the diverse structural deviations reported for adult schizophrenics with disrupted speech. *Journal of Communication Disorders, 15,* 167–189.

Chaney, C. (1992). Language development, metalinguistic skills, and print awareness in 3-year-old children. *Applied Psycholinguistics, 13,* 485–514.

Chapman, L. J., Chapman, J. P., & Miller, G. A. (1964). A theory of verbal behavior in schizophrenia. In B. A. Maher (Ed.), *Progress in experimental personality research* (Vol. 1, pp. 49–77). New York: Academic Press.

Cherry, L., & Lewis, M. (1976). Mothers and two-year-olds: A study of sex-differentiated aspects of verbal interaction. *Developmental Psychology, 12,* 278–282.

Cherry, L. J. (1978). A sociolinguistic approach to the study of teacher expectations. *Discourse Processes, 1,* 373–394.

Chiarello, C. (1991). Interpretation of word meanings by the cerebral hemispheres: One is not enough. In P. J. Schwanenflugel (Ed.), *The psychology of word meaning* (pp. 251–278). Hillsdale, NJ: Erlbaum.

Chomsky, N. (1957). *Syntactic structures.* The Hague: Mouton.

Chomsky, N. (1959). Review of *Verbal Behavior* by B. F. Skinner. *Language, 35,* 26–58.

Chomsky, N. (1965). *Aspects of the theory of syntax.* Cambridge, MA: MIT Press.

Chomsky, N. (1966). *Cartesian linguistics: A chapter in the history of rationalist thought.* New York: Harper & Row.

Chomsky, N. (1968). *Language and mind.* New York: Harcourt Brace Jovanovich.

Chomsky, N. (1975). *Reflections on language.* New York: Pantheon.

Chomsky, N. (1980). *Rules and representations.* New York: Columbia University Press.

Chomsky, N. (1981). *Lectures on government and binding.* Dordrecht, Holland: Foris.

Chukovsky, K. (1963). *From two to five* (M. Merton, Trans.). Berkeley and Los Angeles: University of California Press.

Clark, H. H. (1974). Semantics and comprehension. In T. A. Sebeok (Ed.), *Current trends in linguistics, Vol. 12: Linguistics and adjacent arts and sciences* (pp. 1291–1428). The Hague: Mouton.

Clark, H. H. (1977). Bridging. In P. N. Johnson-Laird & P. C. Wason (Eds.), *Thinking: Readings in cognitive science* (pp. 411–420). Cambridge, England: Cambridge University Press.

Clark, H. H., & Clark, E. V. (1977). *Psychology and language: An introduction to psycholinguistics.* New York: Harcourt Brace Jovanovich.

Clark, H. H., & Haviland, S. E. (1977). Comprehension and the given-new contract. In R. O. Freedle (Ed.), *Discourse production and comprehension* (pp. 1–40). Norwood, NJ: Ablex.

Clark, H. H., & Lucy, P. (1975). Understanding what is meant from what is said: A study in conversationally conveyed requests. *Journal of Verbal Learning and Verbal Behavior, 14,* 56–72.

Clark, H. H., & Sengul, C. J. (1979). In search of referents for nouns and pronouns. *Memory & Cognition, 7,* 35–41.

Cohen, B. D., Nachmani, G., & Rosenberg, S. (1974). Referent communication disturbances in acute schizophrenia. *Journal of Abnormal Psychology, 83,* 1–13.

Cole, R. A. (1973). Listening for mispronunciations: A measure of what we hear during speech. *Perception & Psychophysics, 13,* 153–156.

Cole, R. A., & Scott, B. (1974). Toward a theory of speech perception. *Psychological Review, 81,* 348–374.

Collins, A., Warnock, E. H., & Passafiume, J. J. (1975). Analysis and synthesis of tutorial dialogues. In G. H. Bower (Ed.), *The psychology of learning and motivation: Advances in research and theory* (Vol. 9, pp. 49–87). New York: Academic Press.

Collins, A. M., Adams, M. J., & Pew, R. W. (1978). Effectiveness of an interactive map display in tutoring geography. *Journal of Educational Psychology, 70,* 1–7.

Collins, A. M., & Loftus, E. F. (1975). A spreading-activation theory of semantic processing. *Psychological Review, 82,* 407–428.

Collins, A. M., & Quillian, M. R. (1969). Retrieval time from semantic memory. *Journal of Verbal Learning and Verbal Behavior, 8,* 240–247.

Collins, A. M., & Quillian, M. R. (1970). Does category size affect categorization time? *Journal of Verbal Learning and Verbal Behavior, 9,* 432–438.

Collins, A. M., & Quillian, M. R. (1972). Experiments on semantic memory and language comprehension. In L. W. Gregg (Ed.), *Cognition in learning and memory* (pp. 117–137). New York: Wiley.

Condon, W. S., & Sander, L. W. (1974). Synchrony demonstrated between movements of the neonate and adult speech. *Child Development, 45,* 456–462.

Connine, C. M. (1987). Constraints on interactive processes in auditory word recognition: The role of sentence context. *Journal of Memory and Language, 26,* 527–538.

Connine, C. M., & Clifton, C., Jr. (1987). Interactive use of lexical information in speech perception. *Journal of Experimental Psychology: Human Perception and Performance, 13,* 291–299.

Conrad, C. (1972). Cognitive economy in semantic memory. *Journal of Experimental Psychology, 92,* 149–154.

Cook, M. (1977). Gaze and mutual gaze in social encounters. *American Scientist, 65,* 328–333.

Cook, V. J. (1988). *Chomsky's universal grammar: An introduction.* Cambridge, MA: Basil Blackwell.

Cook-Gumperz, J., & Gumperz, J. J. (1982). Communicative competence in educational perspective. In L. C. Wilkinson (Ed.), *Communicating in the classroom* (pp. 13–24). New York: Academic Press.

Corballis, M. C. (1980). Laterality and myth. *American Psychologist, 35,* 284–295.

Corballis, M. C. (1989). Laterality and human evolution. *Psychological Review, 96,* 492–505.

Corrigan, R. (1979). Cognitive correlates of language: Differential criteria yield differential results. *Child Development, 50,* 617–631.

Craik, F. I. M., & Lockhart, R. S. (1972). Levels of processing: A framework for memory research. *Journal of Verbal Learning and Verbal Behavior, 11,* 671–684.

Crain, S., & Steedman, M. (1985). On not being led up the garden path: The use of context by the psychological syntax processor. In D. R. Dowty, L. Kartunnen, & A. M. Zwicky (Eds.), *Natural language parsing: Psychological, computational, and theoretical perspectives* (pp. 320–358). Cambridge, England: Cambridge University Press.

Cromwell, R. L. (1975). Assessment of schizophrenia. *Annual Review of Psychology, 26,* 593–619.

Crystal, D. (1987). *The Cambridge encyclopedia of language.* Cambridge, England: Cambridge University Press.

Cuetos, F., & Mitchell, D. C. (1988). Cross-linguistic differences in parsing: Restrictions on the use of the Late Closure strategy in Spanish. *Cognition, 30,* 73–105.

Curtiss, S. (1977). *Genie: A psycholinguistic study of a modern-day "wild child."* New York: Academic Press.

Curtiss, S. (1981). Dissociations between language and cognition: Cases and implications. *Journal of Autism and Developmental Disorders, 11,* 15–30.

Curtiss, S., Fromkin, V., Krashen, S., Rigler, D., & Rigler, M. (1974). The linguistic development of Genie. *Language, 50*, 528–554.

Dale, P. S. (1976). *Language development: Structure and function* (2nd ed.). New York: Holt, Rinehart & Winston.

Daneman, M., & Carpenter, P. A. (1980). Individual differences in working memory and reading. *Journal of Verbal Learning and Verbal Behavior, 19*, 450 466.

Daneman, M., & Tardif, T. (1987). Working memory and reading skill re-examined. In M. Coltheart (Ed.), *Attention and performance. Vol. XII: The psychology of reading* (pp. 492–508). Hillsdale, NJ: Erlbaum.

Danks, J. H. (1977). Producing ideas and sentences. In S. Rosenberg (Ed.), *Sentence production: Developments in research and theory* (pp. 229–258). Hillsdale, NJ: Erlbaum.

Darwin, C. J. (1973). Ear differences and hemispheric specialization. In F. O. Schmidt & F. G. Worden (Eds.), *The neurosciences: Third study program* (pp. 57–63). Cambridge, MA: MIT Press.

Darwin, C. J., Turvey, M. T., & Crowder, R. G. (1972). An auditory analogue of the Sperling partial report procedure: Evidence for brief auditory storage. *Cognitive Psychology, 3*, 255–267.

DeCasper, A. J., & Fifer, W. P. (1980). Of human bonding: Newborns prefer their mothers' voices. *Science, 208*, 1174–1176.

DeCasper, A. J., & Spence, M. J. (1986). Prenatal maternal speech influences newborns' perception of speech sounds. *Infant Behavior and Development, 9*, 133–150.

Deese, J. (1978). Thought into speech. *American Psychologist, 66*, 314–321.

Deese, J. (1980). Pauses, prosody, and the demands of production in language. In H. W. Dechert & M. Raupach (Eds.), *Temporal variables in speech: Studies in honour of Freda Goldman-Eisler*. The Hague: Mouton.

Dell, G. S. (1985). Positive feedback in hierarchical connectionist models: Applications to language production. *Cognitive Science, 9*, 3–23.

Dell, G. S. (1986). A spreading-activation theory of retrieval in sentence production. *Psychological Review, 93*, 283–321.

Dell, G. S. (1988). The retrieval of phonological forms in production: Tests of predictions from a connectionist model. *Journal of Memory and Language, 27*, 124–142.

Dell, G. S., & Reich, P. A. (1981). Stages in sentence production: An analysis of speech error data. *Journal of Verbal Learning and Verbal Behavior, 20*, 611–629.

Della Corte, M., Benedict, H., & Klein, D. (1983). The relationship of pragmatic dimensions of mothers' speech to the referential-expressive distinction. *Journal of Child Language, 10*, 35–43.

Dempster, F. N. (1981). Memory span: Sources of individual and developmental differences. *Psychological Bulletin, 89*, 63–100.

Demuth, K. (1990). Subject, topic, and Sesotho passive. *Journal of Child Language, 17*, 67–84.

Denes, P. B., & Pinson, E. N. (1963). *The speech chain: The physics and biology of spoken language*. Baltimore, MD: Bell Telephone Laboratories.

DePaulo, B. M., & Bonvillian, J. D. (1978). The effect on language development of the special characteristics of speech addressed to children. *Journal of Psycholinguistic Research, 7*, 189–211.

DeStefano, J. S., Pepinsky, H. B., & Sanders, T. S. (1982). Discourse rules for literacy learning in a classroom. In L. C. Wilkinson (Ed.), *Communicating in the classroom* (pp. 101–129). New York: Academic Press.

de Villiers, J. G., & de Villiers, P. A. (1973). A cross-sectional study of the acquisition of grammatical morphemes in child speech. *Journal of Psycholinguistic Research, 2,* 267–278.

de Villiers, J. G., & de Villiers, P. A. (1978). *Language acquisition.* Cambridge, MA: Harvard University Press.

de Villiers, J. G., & de Villiers, P. A. (1985). The acquisition of English. In D. I. Slobin (Ed.), *The crosslinguistic study of language acquisition: Vol. I. The data* (pp. 27–139). Hillsdale, NJ: Erlbaum.

Diamond, A. (1985). Development of the ability to use recall to guide action, as indicated by infants' performance on A$\overline{B}$. *Child Development, 56,* 868–863.

Diehl, R. L., Souther, A. F., & Convis, C. L. (1980). Conditions on rate normalization in speech perception. *Perception & Psychophysics, 27,* 435–443.

Dooling, D. J., & Lachman, R. (1971). Effects of comprehension on retention of prose. *Journal of Experimental Psychology, 88,* 216–222.

Dore, J. (1975). Holophrases, speech acts and language universals. *Journal of Child Language, 2,* 21–40.

Dosher, B. A., & Corbett, A. T. (1982). Instrument inferences and verb schemata. *Memory & Cognition, 10,* 531–539.

DuBois, B. L., & Crouch, I. (1977). The question of tag questions in women's speech: They don't really use more of them, do they? *Language in Society, 4,* 289–294.

Du Bois, J. W. (1974). *Syntax in mid-sentence* (Berkeley Studies in Syntax and Semantics Vol. I: III.1–III.23). Berkeley: University of California, Institute of Human Learning and Department of Linguistics.

Duncan, S., Jr., (1972). Some signals and rules for taking speaking turns in conversations. *Journal of Personality and Social Psychology, 23,* 283–292.

Edelsky, C. (1976). The acquisition of communicative competence: Recognition of linguistic correlates of sex roles. *Merrill-Palmer Quarterly, 22,* 47–59.

Eimas, P. D., Miller, J. L., & Jusczyk, P. W. (1987). On infant speech perception and the acquisition of language. In S. Harnad (Ed.), *Categorical perception: The groundwork of cognition* (pp. 161–195). Cambridge, England: Cambridge University Press.

Eimas, P. D., Siqueland, E. R., Jusczyk, P., & Vigorito, J. (1971). Speech perception in infants. *Science, 171,* 303–306.

Ellis, A. W. (1980). On the Freudian theory of speech errors. In V. A. Fromkin (Ed.), *Errors in linguistic performance* (pp. 123–131). New York: Academic Press.

Elman, J. L., & McClelland, J. L. (1988). Cognitive penetration of the mechanisms of perception: Compensation for coarticulation of lexically restored phonemes. *Journal of Memory and Language, 27,* 143–165.

Ervin, S. M. (1964). Imitation and structural change in children's language. In E. H. Lenneberg (Ed.), *New directions in the study of language* (pp. 163–189). Cambridge, MA: MIT Press.

Fantz, R. L. (1963). Pattern vision in newborn infants. *Science, 140,* 296–297.

Feldman, C. F., & Wertsch, J. V. (1976). Context dependent properties of teachers' speech. *Youth and Society, 7,* 227–258.

Feldman, H., Goldin-Meadow, S., & Gleitman, L. (1978). Beyond Herodotus: The creation of language by linguistically deprived deaf children. In A. Lock (Ed.), *Action, symbol, and gesture: The emergence of language* (pp. 351–414). New York: Academic Press.

Fernald, A., & Kuhl, P. (1987). Acoustic determinants of infant preference for motherese speech. *Infant Behavior and Development, 10,* 279–293.

Ferreira, F., & Clifton, C., Jr. (1986). The independence of syntactic processing. *Journal of Memory and Language, 25,* 348–368.

Fillenbaum, S. (1966). Memory for gist: Some relevant variables. *Language and Speech, 9,* 217–227.

Fitch, H. L., Halwes, T., Erickson, D. M., & Liberman, A. M. (1980). Perceptual equivalence of two acoustic cues for stop-consonant manner. *Perception & Psychophysics, 27,* 343–350.

Fodor, J. A. (1975). *The language of thought.* New York: Thomas Y. Crowell.

Fodor, J. A. (1983). *The modularity of mind: An essay on faculty psychology.* Cambridge, MA: MIT Press.

Fodor, J. A., Bever, T. G., & Garrett, M. F. (1974). *The psychology of language: An introduction to psycholinguistics and generative grammar.* New York: McGraw-Hill.

Fodor, J. A., Garrett, M., & Bever, T. G. (1968). Some syntactic determinants of sentential complexity, II: Verb structure. *Perception & Psychophysics, 3,* 453–461.

Folven, R. J., & Bonvillian, J. D. (1991). The transition from nonreferential to referential language in children acquiring American Sign Language. *Developmental Psychology, 27,* 806–816.

Ford, M., Bresnan, J., & Kaplan, R. M. (1982). A competence-based theory of syntactic closure. In J. Bresnan (Ed.), *The mental representation of grammatical relations* (pp. 727–796). Cambridge, MA: MIT Press.

Forster, K. I. (1976). Accessing the mental lexicon. In R. J. Wales & E. Walker (Eds.), *New approaches to language mechanisms* (pp. 257–287). Amsterdam: North-Holland.

Forster, K. I. (1979). Levels of processing and the structure of the language processor. In W. E. Cooper & E. C. T. Walker (Eds.), *Sentence processing* (pp. 27–85). Hillsdale, NJ: Erlbaum.

Foss, D. J. (1969). Decision processes during sentence comprehension: Effects of lexical item difficulty and position upon decision times. *Journal of Verbal Learning and Verbal Behavior, 8,* 457–462.

Foss, D. J. (1970). Some effects of ambiguity upon sentence comprehension. *Journal of Verbal Learning and Verbal Behavior, 9,* 699–706.

Foss, D. J., & Hakes, D. T. (1978). *Psycholinguistics: An introduction to the psychology of language.* Englewood Cliffs, NJ: Prentice-Hall.

Foss, D. J., & Jenkins, C. M. (1973). Some effects of context on the comprehension of ambiguous sentences. *Journal of Verbal Learning and Verbal Behavior, 12,* 577–589.

Fouts, R. S., Fouts, D. H., & Van Cantfort, T. E. (1989). The infant Loulis learns signs from cross-fostered chimpanzees. In R. A. Gardner, B. T. Gardner, & T. E. Van Cantfort (Eds.), *Teaching sign language to chimpanzees* (pp. 280–292). Albany, NY: SUNY Press.

Fowles, B., & Glanz, M. E. (1977). Competence and talent in verbal riddle comprehension. *Journal of Child Language, 4,* 433–452.

Franco, L., & Sperry, R. W. (1977). Hemisphere lateralization for cognitive processing of geometry. *Neuropsychologia, 15,* 107–113.

Frazier, L. (1987). Sentence processing: A tutorial review. In M. Coltheart (Ed.), *Attention and performance: Vol. XII. The psychology of reading* (pp. 559–586). Hillsdale, NJ: Erlbaum.

Frazier, L., & Fodor, J. D. (1978). The sausage machine: A new two-stage parsing model. *Cognition, 6,* 291–325.

Frazier, L., & Rayner, K. (1982). Making and correcting errors during sentence comprehension: Eye movements in the analysis of structurally ambiguous sentences. *Cognitive Psychology, 14,* 178–210.

Freud, S. (1963). *Introductory lectures on psycho-analysis* (Parts I and II) (J. Strachey, Trans.). London: Hogarth Press. (Original work published 1916–1917)

Frishberg, N. (1975). Arbitrariness and iconicity: Historical change in American Sign Language. *Language, 51,* 696–719.

Fromkin, V., & Rodman, R. (1974). *An introduction to language.* New York: Holt, Rinehart & Winston.

Fromkin, V. A. (1971). The non-anomalous nature of anomalous utterances. *Language, 47,* 27–52.

Fromkin, V. A. (Ed.). (1973). *Speech errors as linguistic evidence.* The Hague: Mouton.

Fromkin, V. A. (1975). A linguist looks at "A linguist looks at 'schizophrenic language'." *Brain and Language, 2,* 498–503.

Fromkin, V. A. (Ed.). (1980). *Errors in linguistic performance.* New York: Academic Press.

Fry, D. B., Abramson, A. S., Eimas, P. D., & Liberman, A. M. (1962). The identification and discrimination of synthetic vowels. *Language and Speech, 5,* 171–189.

Furrow, D., Nelson, K., & Benedict, H. (1979). Mothers' speech to children and syntactic development: Some simple relationships. *Journal of Child Language, 6,* 423–442.

Galambos, S. J., & Hakuta, K. (1988). Subject-specific and task-specific characteristics of metalinguistic awareness in bilingual children. *Applied Psycholinguistics, 9,* 141–162.

Gamst, G. (1982). Memory for conversation: Toward a grammar of dyadic conversation. *Discourse Processes, 5,* 33–51.

Gardner, B. T., & Gardner, R. A. (1975). Evidence for sentence constituents in the early utterances of child and chimpanzee. *Journal of Experimental Psychology: General, 104,* 244–267.

Gardner, H. (1974). Metaphors and modalities: How children project polar adjectives onto diverse domains. *Child Development, 45,* 84–91.

Gardner, R. A., & Gardner, B. T. (1969). Teaching sign language to a chimpanzee. *Science, 165,* 664–672.

Gardner, R. A., Gardner, B. T., & Van Cantfort, T. E. (Eds.). (1989). *Teaching sign language to chimpanzees.* Albany, NY: SUNY Press.

Garrett, M. F. (1975). The analysis of sentence production. In G. H. Bower (Ed.), *The psychology of learning and memory: Advances in research and theory* (Vol. 9, pp. 133–177). New York: Academic Press.

Garrett, M. F. (1980). The limits of accommodation. In V. A. Fromkin (Ed.), *Errors in linguistic performance* (pp. 263–271). New York: Academic Press.

Garrett, M. F. (1988). Processes in language production. In F. J. Newmeyer (Ed.), *Linguistics: The Cambridge Survey: Vol. III. Language: Psychological and biological aspects* (pp. 69–96). Cambridge, England: Cambridge University Press.

Garvey, C. (1975). Requests and responses in children's speech. *Journal of Child Language, 2,* 41–63.

Gazzaniga, M. S., & Hillyard, S. A. (1971). Language and speech capacity of the right hemisphere. *Neuropsychologia, 9,* 273–280.

Gazzaniga, M. S., & LeDoux, J. E. (1978). *The integrated mind.* New York: Plenum.

Gazzaniga, M. S., & Sperry, R. W. (1967). Language after section of the cerebral commissures. *Brain, 90,* 131–148.

Gee, J. P. (1989). Two styles of narrative construction and their linguistic and educational implications. *Discourse Processes, 12,* 287–307.

Gelman, R. (1978). Cognitive development. *Annual Review of Psychology, 29,* 297–332.

Gentner, D. (1975). Evidence for the psychological reality of semantic components: The verbs of possession. In D. A. Norman, D. E. Rumelhart, & the LNR Research Group (Eds.), *Explorations in cognition* (pp. 211–246). San Francisco: W. H. Freeman.

Geschwind, N. (1965). Disconnexion syndromes in animals and man. *Brain, 88,* 237–294, 585–644.

Geschwind, N. (1972, April). Language and the brain. *Scientific American,* pp. 76–83.

Geschwind, N., & Levitsky, W. (1968). Human brain: Left-right asymmetries in temporal speech regions. *Science, 161,* 186–187.

Gibb, C., & Randall, P. E. (1988). Metalinguistic abilities and learning to read. *Educational Research, 30,* 135–141.

Gibbs, R. W. (1979). Contextual effects in understanding indirect requests. *Discourse Processes, 2,* 1–10.

Gildea, P., & Glucksberg, S. (1983). On understanding metaphor: The role of context. *Journal of Verbal Learning and Verbal Behavior, 22,* 577–590.

Gleason, J. B., & Greif, E. B. (1983). Men's speech to young children. In B. Thorne, C. Kramarae, & N. Henley (Eds.), *Language, gender, and society* (pp. 140–150). Rowley, MA: Newbury House.

Gleitman, L. R., Gleitman, H., & Shipley, E. F. (1972). The emergence of the child as grammarian. *Cognition, 1,* 137–164.

Gleitman, L. R., Newport, E. L., & Gleitman, H. (1984). The current status of the motherese hypothesis. *Journal of Child Language, 11,* 43–79.

Gleitman, L. R., & Rozin, P. (1977). The structure and acquisition of reading I: Relations between orthographies and the structure of language. In A. S. Reber & D. L. Scarborough (Eds.), *Toward a psychology of reading: The proceedings of the CUNY conference* (pp. 1–53). Hillsdale, NJ: Erlbaum.

Glenn, C. G. (1978). The role of episodic structure and of story length in children's recall of simple stories. *Journal of Verbal Learning and Verbal Behavior, 17,* 229–247.

Glucksberg, S., & Danks, J. H. (1975). *Experimental psycholinguistics: An introduction.* Hillsdale, NJ: Erlbaum.

Glucksberg, S., Gildea, P., & Bookin, H. B. (1982). On understanding nonliteral speech: Can people ignore metaphors? *Journal of Verbal Learning and Verbal Behavior, 21,* 85–98.

Glucksberg, S., & Keysar, B. (1990). Understanding metaphorical comparisons: Beyond similarity. *Psychological Review, 97,* 3–18.

Glucksberg, S., Krauss, R. M., & Weisberg, R. (1966). Referential communication in nursery school children: Method and some preliminary findings. *Journal of Experimental Child Psychology, 3,* 333–342.

Gold, E. (1967). Language identification in the limit. *Information and Control, 10,* 447–474.

Goldfield, B. A. (1987). The contribution of child and caregiver to referential and expressive language. *Applied Psycholinguistics, 8,* 267–280.

Goldin-Meadow, S. (1982). The resilience of recursion: A study of a communication system developed without a conventional language model. In E. Wanner & L. R. Gleitman (Eds.), *Language acquisition: The state of the art* (pp. 51–77). Cambridge, England: Cambridge University Press.

Goldin-Meadow, S., & Mylander, C. (1990). Beyond the input given: The child's role in the acquisition of language. *Language, 66,* 323–355.

Goodglass, H., & Geschwind, N. (1976). Language disorders (aphasia). In E. C. Carterette & M. P. Friedman (Eds.), *Handbook of perception: Vol. 7. Language and speech* (pp. 389–428). New York; Academic Press.

Goodluck, H., & Tavakolian, S. (1982). Competence and processing in children's grammar of relative clauses. *Cognition, 11,* 1–27.

Gopnik, A. (1984). The acquisition of *gone* and the development of the object concept. *Journal of Child Language, 11,* 273–292.

Gordon, D., & Lakoff, G. (1975). Conversational postulates. In P. Cole & J. L. Morgan (Eds.), *Syntax and semantics: Vol. 3. Speech acts* (pp. 83–106). New York: Seminar Press.

Graesser, A. C., Hoffman, N. L., & Clark, L. F. (1980). Structural components of reading time. *Journal of Verbal Learning and Verbal Behavior, 19,* 135–151.

Greene, J. (1972). *Psycholinguistics: Chomsky and psychology.* Harmondsworth, Middlesex, England: Penguin.

Greenfield, P. M. (1982). The role of perceived variability in the transition to language. *Journal of Child Language, 9,* 1–12.

Greenfield, P. M., & Savage-Rumbaugh, E. S. (1991). Imitation, grammatical development, and the invention of protogrammar by an ape. In N. A. Krasnegor, D. M. Rumbaugh, R. L. Schiefelbusch, & M. Studdert-Kennedy (Eds.), *Biological and behavioral determinants of language development* (pp. 235–258). Hillsdale, NJ: Erlbaum.

Greenfield, P. M., & Smith, J. H. (1976). *The structure of communication in early language development.* New York: Academic Press.

Greenspoon, J. (1955). The reinforcing effect of two spoken sounds on the frequency of two responses. *American Journal of Psychology, 68,* 409–416.

Grice, H. P. (1975). Logic and conversation. In P. Cole & J. L. Morgan (Eds.), *Syntax and semantics: Vol. 3. Speech acts* (pp. 41–58). New York: Seminar Press.

Grosjean, F. (1979). A study in timing in a manual and a spoken language: American Sign Language and English. *Journal of Psycholinguistic Research, 8,* 379–405.

Grosjean, F., & Lane, H. (1981). Temporal variables in the perception and production of spoken and sign languages. In P. D. Eimas & J. L. Miller (Eds.), *Perspectives on the study of speech* (pp. 207–237). Hillsdale, NJ: Erlbaum.

Gur, R. E. (1978). Left hemisphere dysfunction and left hemisphere overactivation in schizophrenia. *Journal of Abnormal Psychology, 87,* 226–238.

Haber, R. N., & Hershenson, M. (1973). *The psychology of visual perception.* New York: Holt, Rinehart & Winston.

Haberlandt, K., Berian, C., & Sandson, J. (1980). The episode schema in story processing. *Journal of Verbal Learning and Verbal Behavior, 19,* 635–650.

Hakuta, K. (1986). *Mirror of language: The debate on bilingualism.* New York: Basic Books.

Halliday, M. A. K., & Hasan, R. (1976). *Cohesion in English.* London: Longman.

Hanson, V. L., & Bellugi, U. (1982). On the role of sign order and morphological structure in memory for American Sign Language sentences. *Journal of Verbal Learning and Verbal Behavior, 21,* 621–633.

Harding, C. G. (1982). Development of the intention to communicate. *Human Development, 25,* 140–151.

Harris, R. J. (1977). Comprehension of pragmatic implications in advertising. *Journal of Applied Psychology, 62,* 603–608.

Harris, R. J., & Monaco, G. E. (1978). The psychology of pragmatic implication: Information processing between the lines. *Journal of Experimental Psychology: General, 107,* 1–22.

Hasher, L., & Zacks, R. T. (1979). Automatic and effortful processes in memory. *Journal of Experimental Psychology: General, 108,* 356–388.

Haviland, S. E., & Clark, H. H. (1974). What's new? Acquiring new information as a process in comprehension. *Journal of Verbal Learning and Verbal Behavior, 13,* 512–521.

Hayes, K. J., & Hayes, C. (1952). Imitation in a home-raised chimpanzee. *Journal of Comparative and Physiological Psychology, 45,* 450–459.

Healy, A. F., Oliver, W. L., & McNamara, T. P. (1987). Detecting letters in continuous text: Effects of display size. *Journal of Experimental Psychology: Human Perception and Performance, 13,* 279–290.

Heider, E. R. (1972). Universals in color naming and memory. *Journal of Experimental Psychology, 93,* 10–20.

Henderson, A., Goldman-Eisler, F., & Skarbek, A. (1966). Sequential temporal patterns in spontaneous speech. *Language and Speech, 9,* 207–216.

Hicks, D. (1990). Narrative skills and genre knowledge: Ways of telling in the primary school grades. *Applied Psycholinguistics, 11,* 83–104.

Hicks, D. (1991). Kinds of narrative: Genre skills among first graders from two communities. In A. McCabe & C. Peterson (Eds.), *Developing narrative structure* (pp. 55–87). Hillsdale, NJ: Erlbaum.

Hirsh-Pasek, K., Reeves, L. M., & Golinkoff, R. (1993). Words and meaning: From primitives to complex organization. In J. B. Gleason & N. B. Ratner (Eds.), *Psycholinguistics* (pp. 133–197). Orlando, FL: Harcourt Brace Jovanovich.

Hirsh-Pasek, K., Treiman, R., & Schneiderman, M. (1984). Brown and Hanlon revisited: Mothers' sensitivity to ungrammatical forms. *Journal of Child Language, 11,* 81–88.

Hockett, C. F. (1954). Chinese versus English: An exploration of the Whortion theses. In H. Hoijer (Ed.), *Language in culture* (pp. 106–123). Chicago: University of Chicago Press.

Hockett, C. F. (1966). The problem of universals in language. In J. H. Greenberg (Ed.), *Universals of language* (2nd ed., pp. 1–29). Cambridge, MA: MIT Press.

Hoff-Ginsburg, E., & Shatz, M. (1982). Linguistic input and the child's acquisition of language. *Psychological Bulletin, 92,* 3–26.

Hoffman, R. E. (1986). Tree structures, the work of listening, and schizophrenic discourse: A reply to Beveridge and Brown. *Brain and Language, 27,* 385–392.

Hoffman, R. E., Hogben, G. L., Smith, H., & Calhoun, W. F. (1985). Message disruptions during syntactic processing in schizophrenia. *Journal of Communication Disorders, 18,* 183–202.

Hoffman, R. E., Kirstein, L., Stopek, S., & Cicchetti, D. V. (1982). Apprehending schizophrenic discourse: A structural analysis of the listener's task. *Brain and language, 15,* 207–233.

Hogaboam, T. W., & Perfetti, C. A. (1975). Lexical ambiguity and sentence comprehension. *Journal of Verbal Learning and Verbal Behavior, 14,* 265–274.

Horgan, D. (1981). Learning to tell jokes: A case study of metalinguistic abilities. *Journal of Child Language, 8,* 217–224.

Hubel, D. H., & Wiesel, T. N. (1965). Receptive fields and functional architecture in two nonstriate visual areas (18 and 19) of the cat. *Journal of Neurophysiology, 28,* 229–289.

Huey, E. B. (1968). *The psychology and pedagogy of reading.* Cambridge, MA: MIT Press. (Original work published 1908)

Hunt, E., & Agnoli, F. (1991). The Whorfian hypothesis: A cognitive psychology perspective. *Psychological Review, 98,* 377-389.

Huttenlocher, J., Haight, W., Bryk, A., Seltzer, M., & Lyons, T. (1991). Early vocabulary growth: Relation to language input and gender. *Developmental Psychology, 27,* 236–248.

Hyams, N. M. (1986). *Language acquisition and the theory of parameters.* Dordrecht, Holland: Reidel.

Ianco-Worrall, A. D. (1972). Bilingualism and cognitive development. *Child Development, 43,* 1390–1400.

Jaffe, J., & Feldstein, S. (1970). *Rhythms of dialogue.* New York: Academic Press.

Jakobson, R., Fant, C. G. M., & Halle, M. (1969). *Preliminaries to speech analysis.* Cambridge, MA: MIT Press. (Original work published 1951)

James, D. (1972). Some aspects of the syntax and semantics of interjections. In P. Peranteau, J. N. Levi, & G. C. Phares (Eds.), *Papers from the Eighth Regional Meeting of the Chicago Linguistic Society* (pp. 162–172). Chicago: Chicago Linguistics Society.

James, W. (1890). *The principles of psychology* (Vol. I). New York: Henry Holt & Co.

Jefferson, G. (1972). Side sequences. In D. Sudnow (Ed.), *Studies in social interaction* (pp. 294–338). New York: Free Press.

Johnson, M. K., Bransford, J. D., & Solomon, S. K. (1973). Memory for tacit implications of sentences. *Journal of Experimental Psychology, 98,* 203–205.

Johnson, N. F. (1975). On the function of letters in word identification: Some data and a preliminary model. *Journal of Verbal Learning and Verbal Behavior, 14,* 17–29.

Johnson-Laird, P. N. (1983). *Mental models.* Cambridge, MA: Harvard University Press.

Johnson-Laird, P. N. (1988a). *The computer and the mind: An introduction to cognitive science.* Cambridge, MA: Harvard University Press.

Johnson-Laird, P. N. (1988b). How is meaning mentally represented? In U. Eco, M. Santambrogio, & P. Violi (Eds.), *Meaning and mental representations* (pp. 99–118). Bloomington: Indiana University Press.

Johnson-Laird, P. N., Herrmann, D. J., & Chaffin, R. (1984). Only connections: A critique of semantic networks. *Psychological Bulletin, 96,* 292–315.

Johnston, J. C., & McClelland, J. L. (1980). Experimental tests of a hierarchical model of word identification. *Journal of Verbal Learning and Verbal Behavior, 19,* 503–524.

Johnston, J. R., & Slobin, D. I. (1979). The development of locative expressions in English, Italian, Serbo-Croatian, and Turkish. *Journal of Child Language, 6,* 529–545.

Jusczyk, P. W. (1992). Developing phonological categories from the speech signal. In C. A. Ferguson, L. Menn, & C. Stoel-Gammon (Eds.), *Phonological development: Models, research, and implications* (pp. 17–64). Timonium, MD: York Press.

Just, M. A., & Carpenter, P. A. (1976). Eye fixations and cognitive processes. *Cognitive Psychology, 8,* 441–480.

Just, M. A., & Carpenter, P. A. (1980). A theory of reading: From eye fixations to comprehension. *Psychological Review, 87*, 329–354.

Just, M. A., & Carpenter, P. A. (1987). *The psychology of reading and language comprehension.* Boston: Allyn & Bacon.

Kaplan, J. A., Brownell, H. H., Jacobs, J. R., & Gardner, H. (1990). The effects of right hemisphere damage on the pragmatic interpretation of conversational remarks. *Brain and Language, 38*, 315–333.

Kay, P., & Kempton, W. (1984). What is the Sapir-Whorf hypothesis? *American Anthropologist, 86*, 65–79.

Keenan, E. O. (1974). Conversational competence in children. *Journal of Child Language, 1*, 163–183.

Keenan, J. M., MacWhinney, B., & Mayhew, D. (1977). Pragmatics in memory: A study of natural conversation. *Journal of Verbal Learning and Verbal Behavior, 16*, 549–560.

Kellogg, W. N., & Kellogg, L. A. (1933). *The ape and the child: A study of environmental influence upon early behavior.* New York: Whittlesey House.

Kempen, G., & Hoenkamp, E. (1987). An incremental procedural grammar for sentence formulation. *Cognitive Science, 11*, 201–258.

Kess, J. F. (1991). On the developing history of psycholinguistics. *Language Sciences, 13*, 1–20.

Kimball, J. (1973). Seven principles of surface structure parsing in natural language. *Cognition, 2*, 15–47.

Kimura, D. (1961). Cerebral dominance and the perception of verbal stimuli. *Canadian Journal of Psychology, 15*, 166–171.

Kimura, D. (1964). Left-right differences in the perception of melodies. *Quarterly Journal of Experimental Psychology, 16*, 355–358.

Kintsch, W. (1974). *The representation of meaning in memory.* Hillsdale, NJ: Erlbaum.

Kintsch, W. (1988). The role of knowledge in discourse comprehension: A construction-integration model. *Psychological Review, 95*, 163–182.

Kintsch, W., & Bates, E. (1977). Recognition memory for statements from a classroom lecture. *Journal of Experimental Psychology: Human Learning and Memory, 3*, 150–159.

Kintsch, W., & Keenan, J. (1973). Reading rate and retention as a function of the number of propositions in the base structure of sentences. *Cognitive Psychology, 5*, 257–274.

Kintsch, W., Kozminsky, E., Streby, W. J., McKoon, G., & Keenan, J. M. (1975). Comprehension and recall of text as a function of content variables. *Journal of Verbal Learning and Verbal Behavior, 14*, 196–214.

Kintsch, W., & van Dijk, T. A. (1978). Toward a model of text comprehension and production. *Psychological Review, 85*, 363–394.

Kintsch, W., & Vipond, D. (1979). Reading comprehension and readability in educational practice and psychological theory. In L. G. Nilsson (Ed.), *Perspectives on memory research* (pp. 329–365). Hillsdale, NJ: Erlbaum.

Klima, E. S., & Bellugi, U. (1966). Syntactic regularities in the speech of children. In J. Lyons & R. J. Wales (Eds.), *Psycholinguistics papers* (pp. 183–208). Edinburgh, Scotland: Edinburgh University Press.

Klima, E. S., & Bellugi, U. (1979). *The signs of language.* Cambridge, MA: Harvard University Press.

Kozminsky, E. (1977). Altering comprehension: The effects of biasing titles on text comprehension. *Memory & Cognition, 5*, 482–490.

Kreutzer, M. A., Leonard, S. C., & Flavell, J. H. (1975). An interview study of children's knowledge about memory. *Monographs of the Society for Research in Child Development, 40*(1, Serial No. 159).

Kuczaj, S. A., II, & Brannick, N. (1979). Children's use of the *wh* question modal auxiliary placement rule. *Journal of Experimental Child Psychology, 28*, 43–67.

Kuhl, P. K. (1987). The special-mechanisms debate in speech research: Categorization tests on animals and infants. In S. Harnad (Ed.), *Categorical perception: The groundwork of cognition* (pp. 355–386). Cambridge, England: Cambridge University Press.

Labov, W. (1969). The logic of nonstandard English. *Georgetown Monographs on Language and Linguistics, 22*, 1–43.

Labov, W. (1970). The study of language in its social context. *Studium Generale, 23*, 30–87.

Labov, W., & Fanshel, D. (1977). *Therapeutic discourse: Psychotherapy as conversation.* New York: Academic Press.

Lakoff, G. (1972). Hedges: A study of meaning criteria and the logic of fuzzy concepts. In *Papers from the Eighth Regional Meeting of the Chicago Linguistics Society* (pp. 183–228). Chicago: Chicago Linguistics Society.

Lakoff, R., (1975). *Language and woman's place.* New York: Harper & Row.

Landauer, T. K., & Meyer, D. E. (1972). Category size and semantic-memory retrieval. *Journal of Verbal Learning and Verbal Behavior, 11*, 539–549.

Lane, H. (1976). *The wild boy of Aveyron.* Cambridge, MA: Harvard University Press.

Lane, H., Boyes-Braem, P., & Bellugi, U. (1976). Preliminaries to a distinctive feature analysis of handshapes in American Sign Language. *Cognitive Psychology, 8*, 263–289.

Lashley, K. S. (1951). The problem of serial order in behavior. In L. A. Jeffress (Ed.), *Cerebral mechanisms in behavior* (pp. 112–136). New York: Wiley.

Lasky, R. E., Syrdal-Lasky, A., & Klein, R. E. (1975). VOT discrimination by four to six and a half month old infants from Spanish environments. *Journal of Experimental Child Psychology, 20*, 215–225.

Lasnik, H. (1990). Syntax. In D. N. Osherson & H. Lasnik (Eds.), *An invitation to cognitive science: Vol. 1. Language* (pp. 5–21). Cambridge, MA: MIT Press.

Lenneberg, E. H. (1964). A biological perspective of language. In E. H. Lenneberg (Ed.), *New directions in the study of language* (pp. 65–88). Cambridge, MA: MIT Press.

Lenneberg, E. H. (1967). *Biological foundations of language.* New York: Wiley.

Lesgold, A. M., Roth, S. F., & Curtis, M. E. (1979). Foregrounding effects in discourse comprehension. *Journal of Verbal Learning and Verbal Behavior, 18*, 291–308.

Levelt, W. J. M. (1983). Monitoring and self-repair in speech. *Cognition, 14*, 41–104.

Levelt, W. J. M. (1989). *Speaking: From intention to articulation.* Cambridge, MA: MIT Press.

Levy, J. (1974). Cerebral asymmetries as manifested in split-brain man. In M. Kinsbourne & W. L. Smith (Eds.), *Hemispheric disconnection and cerebral function.* Springfield, IL: Charles C Thomas.

Liberman, A. M. (1970). The grammars of speech and language. *Cognitive Psychology, 1*, 301–323.

Liberman, A. M. (1982). On finding that speech is special. *American Psychologist, 37*, 148–167.

Liberman, A. M., Cooper, F. S., Shankweiler, D. P., & Studdert-Kennedy, M. (1967). Perception of the speech code. *Psychological Review, 74,* 431–461.

Liberman, A. M., Harris, K. S., Hoffman, H. S., & Griffith, B. C. (1957). The discrimination of speech sounds within and across phoneme boundaries. *Journal of Experimental Psychology, 54,* 358–368.

Liberman, A. M., & Mattingly, I. G. (1985). The motor theory of speech perception revised. *Cognition, 21,* 1–36.

Liberman, I. Y., Shankweiler, D., Fischer, F. W., & Carter, B. (1974). Explicit syllable and phoneme segmentation in the young child. *Journal of Experimental Child Psychology, 18,* 201–212.

Lieberman, P. (1965). On the acoustic basis of the perception of intonation by linguists. *Word, 21,* 40–54.

Lieberman, P. (1967). *Intonation, perception, and language.* Cambridge, MA: MIT Press.

Lieberman, P. (1973). On the evolution of language: A unified view. *Cognition, 2,* 59–94.

Lieberman, P. (1991). *Uniquely human: The evolution of speech, thought, and selfless behavior.* Cambridge, MA: Harvard University Press.

Lieven, E. M., Pine, J. M., & Barnes, H. D. (1992). Individual differences in early vocabulary development: Redefining the referential-expressive distinction. *Journal of Child Language, 19,* 287–310.

Lima, S. D. (1987). Morphological analysis in sentence reading. *Journal of Memory and Language, 26,* 84–99.

Limber, J. (1973). The genesis of complex sentences. In T. E. Moore (Ed.), *Cognitive development and the acquisition of language* (pp. 169–185). New York: Academic Press.

Linden, E. (1974). *Apes, men, and language.* New York: Dutton.

Lindsley, J. R. (1975). Producing simple utterances: How far ahead do we plan? *Cognitive Psychology, 7,* 1–19.

Linebarger, M. C., Schwartz, M. F., & Saffran, E. M. (1983). Sensitivity to grammatical structure in so-called agrammatic aphasics. *Cognition, 13,* 361–392.

Liu, L. G. (1985). Reasoning counterfactually in Chinese: Are there any obstacles? *Cognition, 21,* 239–270.

Lounsbury, F. G. (1965). Transitional probability, linguistic structure, and systems of habit-family hierarchies. In C. E. Osgood & T. Sebeok (Eds.), *Psycholinguistics: A survey of theory and research problems* (pp. 93–101). Bloomington: Indiana University Press. (Original work published 1954)

Lucy, J. A. (1992a). *Grammatical categories and cognition: A case study of the linguistic relativity hypothesis.* Cambridge, England: Cambridge University Press.

Lucy, J. A. (1992b). *Language diversity and thought: A reformulation of the linguistic relativity hypothesis.* Cambridge, England: Cambridge University Press.

Lucy, J. A., & Shweder, R. A. (1979). Whorf and his critics: Linguistic and nonlinguistic influences on color memory. *American Anthropologist, 81,* 581–615.

Lundberg, I., Frost, J., & Petersen, O-P. (1988). Effects of an extensive program for stimulating phonological awareness in preschool children. *Reading Research Quarterly, 23,* 263–284.

Lyons, J. (1968). *Introduction to theoretical linguistics.* Cambridge, England: Cambridge University Press.

MacDonald, J., & McGurk, H. (1978). Visual influences on speech perception processes. *Perception & Psychophysics, 24,* 253–257.

MacKay, D. G. (1978). Derivational rules and the internal lexicon. *Journal of Verbal Learning and Verbal Behavior, 17*, 61–71.

MacKay, D. G. (1982). The problems of flexibility, fluency, and speed-accuracy trade-off in skilled behavior. *Psychological Review, 89*, 483–506.

MacKay, D. G. (1987). *The organization of perception and action: A theory for language and other cognitive skills.* New York: Springer-Verlag.

Macnamara, J. (1972). Cognitive basis of language learning in infants. *Psychological Review, 79*, 1–13.

MacNeilage, P. (1991). Comment: The gesture as a unit in speech perception theories. In I. G. Mattingly & M. Studdert-Kennedy (Eds.), *Modularity and the motor theory of speech perception* (pp. 61–67). Hillsdale, NJ: Erlbaum.

MacNeilage, P., & Ladefoged, P. (1976). The production of speech and language. In E. C. Carterette & M. P. Friedman (Eds.), *Handbook of perception: Vol. 7. Language and speech* (pp. 75–120). New York: Academic Press.

MacNeilage, P., Studdert-Kennedy, M. G., & Lindblom, B. (1987). Primate handedness reconsidered. *The Behavioral and Brain Sciences, 10*, 247–303.

MacWhinney, B., Bates, E., & Kliegl, R. (1984). Cue validity and sentence interpretation in English, German, and Italian. *Journal of Verbal Learning and Verbal Behavior, 23*, 127–150.

Maher, B. (1972). The language of schizophrenia: A review and interpretation. *British Journal of Psychiatry, 120*, 3–17.

Mandler, J. M. (1984). *Stories, scripts, and scenes: Aspects of schema theory.* Hillsdale, NJ: Erlbaum.

Mandler, J. M., & Johnson, N. S. (1977). Remembrance of things parsed: Story structure and recall. *Cognitive Psychology, 9*, 111–151.

Mandler, J. M., Scribner, S., Cole, M., & DeForest, M. (1980). Cross-cultural invariance in story recall. *Child Development, 51*, 19–26.

Mann, V. A., Madden, J., Russell, J. M., & Liberman, A. (1981). Further investigation into the influence of preceding liquids on stop consonant perception. *Journal of the Acoustical Society of America, 69* (Suppl. 1), S91 (Abstract).

Mann, V. A., & Repp, B. H. (1981). Influence of preceding fricative on stop consonant perception. *Journal of the Acoustical Society of America, 69*, 548–558.

Mannes, S. M., & Kintsch, W. (1987). Knowledge organization and text organization. *Cognition and Instruction, 4*, 91–115.

Maratsos, M. (1982). The child's construction of grammatical categories. In E. Wanner & L. R. Gleitman (Eds.), *Language acquisition: The state of the art* (pp. 240–266). Cambridge, England: Cambridge University Press.

Maratsos, M. P. (1973). Nonegocentric communication abilities in preschool children. *Child Development, 44*, 697–700.

Maratsos, M. P. (1974). Children who get worse at understanding the passive: A replication of Bever. *Journal of Psycholinguistic Research, 3*, 65–74.

Maratsos, M. P., & Chalkley, M. A. (1980). The internal language of children's syntax: The ontogenesis and representation of syntactic categories. In K. E. Nelson (Ed.), *Children's language* (Vol. 2, pp. 127–214). New York: Gardner Press.

Markman, E. M. (1977). Realizing that you don't understand: A preliminary investigation. *Child Development, 48*, 986–992.

Markman, E. M. (1979). Realizing that you don't understand: Elementary children's awareness of inconsistencies. *Child Development, 50,* 643–655.

Markman, E. M. (1981). Comprehension monitoring. In W. P. Dickson (Ed.), *Children's oral communication skills* (pp. 61–84). New York: Academic Press.

Markman, E. M. (1989). *Categorization and naming in children.* Cambridge, MA: MIT Press.

Markman, E. M., & Hutchinson, J. E. (1984). Children's sensitivity to constraints on word meaning: Taxonomic versus thematic relations. *Cognitive Psychology, 16,* 1–27.

Markman, E. M., & Wachtel, G. F. (1988). Children's use of mutual exclusivity to constrain the meanings of words. *Cognitive Psychology, 20,* 121–157.

Marshall, J. C. (1980). On the biology of language acquisition. In D. Caplan (Ed.), *Biological studies of mental processes* (pp. 106–148). Cambridge, MA: MIT Press.

Marslen-Wilson, W. D., & Welsh, A. (1978). Processing interactions and lexical access during word recognition in continuous speech. *Cognitive Psychology, 10,* 29–63.

Martin, J. G. (1972). Rhythmic (hierarchical) versus serial structure in speech and other behavior. *Psychological Review, 79,* 487–509.

Martin, L. (1986). "Eskimo words for snow": A case study in the genesis and decay of an anthropological example. *American Anthropologist, 88,* 418–423.

Masur, E. F. (1982). Mothers' responses to infants' object-related gestures: Influence on lexical development. *Journal of Child Language, 9,* 23–30.

Mateer, C., & Kimura, D. (1977). Impairment of nonverbal oral movements in aphasia. *Brain and Language, 4,* 262–276.

Mattingly, I. G. (1972). Reading, the linguistic process, and linguistic awareness. In J. F. Kavanaugh & I. G. Mattingly (Eds.), *Language by ear and by eye: The relationships between speech and reading* (pp. 133–147). Cambridge, MA: MIT Press.

Mattingly, I. G., Liberman, A. M., Syrdal, A. K., & Halwes, T. (1971). Discrimination in speech and nonspeech modes. *Cognitive Psychology, 2,* 131–157.

McCabe, A., & Peterson, C. (1991). Getting the story: A longitudinal study of parental styles in eliciting narratives and developing narrative skill. In A. McCabe and C. Peterson (Eds.), *Developing narrative structure* (pp. 217–253). Hillsdale, NJ: Erlbaum.

McCauley, R. N. (1987). The not so happy story of the marriage of linguistics and psychology, or why linguistics has discouraged psychology's recent advances. *Synthese, 72,* 341–353.

McClelland, J. L. (1985). Putting knowledge in its place: A scheme for programming parallel processing structures on the fly. *Cognitive Science, 9,* 113–146.

McClelland, J. L., & Elman, J. L. (1986). Interactive processes in speech perception: The TRACE model. In J. L. McClelland, D. E. Rumelhart, & the PDP Research Group (Eds.), *Parallel distributed processing: Vol. 2. Psychological and biological models* (pp. 58–121). Cambridge, MA: MIT Press.

McClelland, J. L., & Rumelhart, D. E. (1981). An interactive activation model of context effects in letter perception: Part 1. An account of basic findings. *Psychological Review, 88,* 375–407.

McClelland, J. L., Rumelhart, D. E., and the PDP Research Group (1986). *Parallel distributed processing: Explorations in the microstructure of cognition: Vol. 2. Psychological and biological models.* Cambridge, MA: MIT Press.

McCloskey, M. (1980). The stimulus familiarity problem in semantic memory research. *Journal of Verbal Learning and Verbal Behavior, 19,* 485–502.

McCloskey, M., & Glucksberg, S. (1979). Decision processes in verifying category membership statements: Implications for models of semantic memory. *Cognitive Psychology, 11*, 1–37.

McFarland, R. A. (1981). *Physiological psychology: The biology of human behavior*. Palo Alto, CA: Mayfield.

McGhee, P. E. (1979). *Humor: Its origin and development*. San Francisco: W. H. Freeman.

McGurk, H., & MacDonald, J. (1976). Hearing lips and seeing voices. *Nature, 264*, 746–748.

McKoon, G. (1977). Organization of information in text memory. *Journal of Verbal Learning and Verbal Behavior, 16*, 247–260.

McKoon, G., & Ratliff, R. (1980). Priming in item recognition: The organization of propositions in memory for text. *Journal of Verbal Learning and Verbal Behavior, 19*, 369–386.

McKoon, G., & Ratliff, R. (1981). The comprehension processes and memory structures involved in instrumental inference. *Journal of Verbal Learning and Verbal Behavior, 20*, 671–682.

McKoon, G., & Ratliff, R. (1992). Inference during reading. *Psychological Review, 99*, 440–466.

McMillan, J. R., Clifton, A. K., McGrath, D., & Gale, W. S. (1977). Women's language: Uncertainty or interpersonal sensitivity and emotionality? *Sex Roles, 3*, 545–559.

McNeill, D. (1966). Developmental psycholinguistics. In F. Smith & G. A. Miller (Eds.), *The genesis of language: A psycholinguistic approach* (pp. 15–84). Cambridge, MA: MIT Press.

McNeill, D. (1970). *The acquisition of language: The study of developmental psycholinguistics*. New York: Harper & Row.

Meadow, K. P. (1980). *Deafness and child development*. Berkeley, CA: University of California Press.

Mehan, H. (1979). *Learning lessons: Social organization in the classroom*. Cambridge, MA: Harvard University Press.

Mehler, J., Jusczyk, P., Lambertz, G., Halsted, N., Bertoncini, J., & Amiel-Tison, C. (1988). A precursor of language acquisition in young infants. *Cognition, 29*, 143–178.

Meier, R. P., & Newport, E. L. (1990). Out of the hands of babes: On a possible sign advantage in language acquisition. *Language, 66*, 1–23.

Menn, L., and Stoel-Gammon, C. (1993). Phonological development: Learning sounds and sound patterns. In J. B. Gleason (Ed.), *Language development* (3rd ed., pp. 65–113). New York: Macmillan.

Merriman, W. E., & Bowman, L. L. (1989). The mutual exclusivity bias in children's word learning. *Monographs of the Society for Research in Child Development, 54*(3–4, Serial No. 220).

Merritt, M. (1982). Distributing and directing attention in primary classrooms. In L. C. Wilkinson (Ed.), *Communicating in the classroom* (pp. 223–244). New York: Academic Press.

Mervis, C. B., & Mervis, C. A. (1982). Leopards are kitty-cats: Object labeling by mothers for their thirteen-month-olds. *Child Development, 53*, 267–273.

Meyer, B. J. F. (1975). *The organization of prose and its effects on memory*. Amsterdam: North-Holland.

Meyer, B. J. F., Brandt, D. M., & Bluth, G. J. (1980). Use of top-level structure in text: Key for reading comprehension of ninth-grade students. *Reading Research Quarterly, 16,* 72–103.

Meyer, D. E., & Schvaneveldt, R. W. (1971). Facilitation in recognizing pairs of words: Evidence of a dependence between retrieval operations. *Journal of Experimental Psychology, 90,* 227–234.

Michaels, S. (1981). "Sharing time": Children's narrative styles and differential access to literacy. *Language in Society, 10,* 423–442.

Michaels, S. (1991). The dismantling of narrative. In A. McCabe & C. Peterson (Eds.), *Developing narrative structure* (pp. 303–351). Hillsdale, NJ: Erlbaum.

Miller, G. A. (1979). Images and models, similes and metaphors. In A. Ortony (Ed.), *Metaphor and thought* (pp. 202–250). Cambridge, England: Cambridge University Press.

Miller, G. A. (1990). Linguists, psychologists, and the cognitive sciences. *Language, 66,* 317–322.

Miller, G. A., & Chomsky, N. (1963). Finitary models of language users. In R. D. Luce, R. R. Bush, & E. Galanter (Eds.), *Handbook of mathematical psychology* (Vol. 2, pp. 419–491). New York: Wiley.

Miller, G. A., Heise, G. A., & Lichten, W. (1951). The intelligibility of speech as a function of the context of the test materials. *Journal of Experimental Psychology, 41,* 329–335.

Miller, G. A., & Isard, S. (1963). Some perceptual consequences of linguistic rules. *Journal of Verbal Learning and Verbal Behavior, 2,* 217–228.

Miller, G. A., & Nicely, P. A. (1955). An analysis of perceptual confusions among some English consonants. *Journal of the Acoustical Society of America, 27,* 338–352.

Miller, J. F., & Chapman, R. S. (1981). The relation between age and mean length of utterance in morphemes. *Journal of Speech and Hearing Research, 24,* 154–161.

Miller, J. L. (1981). Effects of speaking rate on segmental distinctions. In P. D. Eimas & J. L. Miller (Eds.), *Perspectives on the study of speech* (pp. 39–74). Hillsdale, NJ: Erlbaum.

Miller, J. R., & Kintsch, W. (1980). Readability and recall of short prose passages: A theoretical analysis. *Journal of Experimental Psychology: Human Learning and Memory, 6,* 335–354.

Miller, W., & Ervin, S. (1964). The development of grammar in child language. In U. Bellugi & R. Brown (Eds.), The acquisition of language (pp. 9–34). *Monographs of the Society for Research in Child Development, 29*(1, Serial No. 92).

Mitchell, D. C. (1987). Lexical guidance in human parsing: Locus and processing characteristics. In M. Coltheart (Ed.), *Attention and performance: Vol. XII. The psychology of reading* (pp. 601–618). Hillsdale, NJ: Erlbaum.

Miura, I. T. (1987). Mathematics achievement as a function of language. *Journal of Educational Psychology, 79,* 79–82.

Miura, I. T., & Okamoto, Y. (1989). Comparisons of U.S. and Japanese first graders' cognitive representation of number and understanding of place value. *Journal of Educational Psychology, 81,* 109–113.

Moerk, E. L. (1980). Relationships between parental input frequencies and children's language acquisition: A reanalysis of Brown's data. *Journal of Child Language, 7,* 105–118.

Moerk, E. L. (1981). To attend or not to attend to unwelcome reanalyses? A reply to Pinker. *Journal of Child Language, 8,* 627–631.

Morrow, D. G., Bower, G. H., & Greenspan, S. L. (1989). Updating situational models during narrative comprehension. *Journal of Memory and Language, 28*, 292–312.

Morton, J. (1969). Interaction of information in word recognition. *Psychological Review, 76*, 165–178.

Morton, J. (1979). Word recognition. In J. Morton & J. C. Marshall (Eds.), *Psycholinguistics 2: Structures and processes.* (pp. 108–156). Cambridge, MA: MIT Press.

Motley, M. T. (1980). Verification of "Freudian slips" and semantic prearticulatory editing via laboratory-induced spoonerisms. In V. A. Fromkin (Ed.), *Errors in linguistic performance* (pp. 133–147). New York: Academic Press.

Motley, M. T. (1987, February). What I meant to say. *Psychology Today*, pp. 24–28.

Motley, M. T., Baars, B. J., & Camden, C. T. (1983). Experimental verbal slip studies: A review and an editing model of language encoding. *Communication Monographs, 50*, 79–101.

Murphy, C. M. (1978). Pointing in the context of a shared activity. *Child Development, 49*, 371–380.

Nakazima, S. (1975). Phonemicization and symbolization in language development. In E. H. Lenneberg and E. Lenneberg (Eds.), *Foundations of language development* (Vol. 1, pp. 181–187). New York: Academic Press.

Nebes, R. D. (1972). Dominance of the minor hemisphere in commissurotomized man on a test of figural unification. *Brain, 95*, 633–638.

Neisser, U. (1964, June). Visual search. *Scientific American*, pp. 94–102.

Nelson, K. (1973). Structure and strategy in learning to talk. *Monographs of the Society for Research in Child Development, 38*(1–2, Serial No. 149).

Nelson, K. (1975). The nominal shift in semantic-syntactic development. *Cognitive Psychology, 7*, 461–479.

Nelson, K. (1981). Individual differences in language development: Implications for development and language. *Developmental Psychology, 17*, 170–187.

Nelson, K. E. (1976). Facilitating children's syntax acquisition. *Developmental Psychology, 13*, 101–107.

Nelson, K. E., Carskaddon, G., & Bonvillian, J. D. (1973). Syntax acquisition: Impact of experimental variation in adult verbal interaction with the child. *Child Development, 44*, 497–504.

Newkirk, D., Klima, E. S., Pedersen, C. C., & Bellugi, U. (1980). Linguistic evidence from slips of the hand. In V. A. Fromkin (Ed.), *Errors in linguistic performance* (pp. 165–197). New York: Academic Press.

Newmeyer, F. J. (1986). *Linguistic theory in America* (2nd ed.). Orlando, FL: Academic Press.

Newport, E. L. (1990). Maturational constraints on language learning. *Cognitive Science, 14*, 11–28.

Newport, E. L., & Ashbrook, E. F. (1977). The emergence of semantic relations in ASL. *Papers and Reports on Child Language Development, 13*, 16–21.

Newport, E. L., Gleitman, H., & Gleitman, L. R. (1977). Mother, I'd rather do it myself: Some effects and non-effects of maternal speech style. In C. E. Snow & C. A. Ferguson (Eds.), *Talking to children: Language input and language acquisition* (pp. 109–149). Cambridge, England: Cambridge University Press.

Newport, E. L., & Meier, R. P. (1985). The acquisition of American Sign Language. In D. I. Slobin (Ed.), *The crosslinguistic study of language acquisition: Vol. 1. The data* (pp. 881–938). Hillsdale, NJ: Erlbaum.

Ninio, A. (1980). Ostensive definition in vocabulary teaching. *Journal of Child Language, 7*, 565–573.

Ninio, A., & Bruner, J. (1978). The achievement and antecedents of labelling. *Journal of Child Language, 5*, 1–15.

Noble, C. E., & McNeely, D. A. (1957). The role of meaningfulness (*m*) in paired-associate learning. *Journal of Experimental Psychology, 53*, 16–22.

Nooteboom, S. (1980). Speaking and unspeaking: Detection and correction of phonological and lexical errors in spontaneous speech. In V. A. Fromkin (Ed.), *Errors in linguistic performance* (pp. 87–95). New York: Academic Press.

Norman, D. A., Rumelhart, D. E., & the LNR Research Group (1975). *Explorations in cognition.* San Francisco: W. H. Freeman.

Nottebohm, F. (1970). Ontogeny of bird song. *Science, 167*, 950–956.

Ojemann, G. A. (1983). Brain organization for language from the perspective of electrical stimulation mapping. *The Behavioral and Brain Sciences, 2*, 189–230.

Oller, D. K. (1974). Simplification as the goal of phonological processes in child speech. *Language Learning, 24*, 299–303.

Oller, D. K. (1980). The emergence of the sounds of speech in infancy. In G. Yeni-Komshian, J. F. Kavanaugh, & C. A. Ferguson (Eds.), *Child phonology: Vol. 1. Production* (pp. 93–112). New York: Academic Press.

Orlansky, M. D., & Bonvillian, J. D. (1984). The role of iconicity in early sign language acquisition. *Journal of Speech and Hearing Disorders, 49*, 287–292.

Ortony, A. (1975). Why metaphors are necessary and not just nice. *Educational Theory, 25*, 45–53.

Ortony, A., Schallert, D. L., Reynolds, R. E., & Antos, S. J. (1978). Interpreting metaphors and idioms: Some effects of context on comprehension. *Journal of Verbal Learning and Verbal Behavior, 17*, 465–477.

Osgood, C. E. (1971). Where do sentences come from? In D. D. Steinberg & L. A. Jakobovits (Eds.), *Semantics: An interdisciplinary reader in philosophy, linguistics, and psychology* (pp. 497–529). Cambridge, England: Cambridge University Press.

Osgood, C. E., & Bock, J. K. (1977). Salience and sentencing: Some production principles. In S. Rosenberg (Ed.), *Sentence production: Developments in research and theory* (pp. 89–140). Hillsdale, NJ: Erlbaum.

Osgood, C. E., & Sebeok, T. A. (Eds.). (1965). *Psycholinguistics: A survey of theory and research problems.* Bloomington: Indiana University Press. (Original work published 1954)

Osgood, C. E., Suci, G. J., & Tannenbaum, P. H. (1957). *The measurement of meaning.* Urbana: University of Illinois Press.

Osherson, D. N., & Markman, E. (1975). Language and the ability to evaluate contradictions and tautologies. *Cognition, 3*, 213–226.

O'Sullivan, C., & Yeager, C. P. (1989). Communicative context and linguistic competence: The effects of social setting on a chimpanzee's conversational skill. In R. A. Gardner, B. T. Gardner, & T. E. Van Cantfort (Eds.), *Teaching sign language to chimpanzees* (pp. 269–279). Albany, New York: SUNY Press.

Pavel, T. G. (1986). *Fictional words.* Cambridge, MA: Harvard University Press.

Pavy, D. (1968). Verbal behavior in schizophrenia: A review of recent studies. *Psychological Bulletin, 70,* 164–178.

Peters, A. M. (1977). Language learning strategies: Does the whole equal the sum of the parts? *Language, 53,* 560–573.

Petersen, M. R., Beecher, M. D., Zoloth, S. R., Moody, D. B., & Stebbins, W. C. (1978). Neural lateralization of species-specific vocalizations by Japanese macaques. *(Macaca fuscata). Science, 202,* 324–327.

Peterson, C., & Dodsworth, P. (1991). A longitudinal analysis of young children's cohesion and noun specification in narratives. *Journal of Child Language, 18,* 397–415.

Peterson, C., & McCabe, A. (1983). *Developmental psycholinguistics: Three ways of looking at a child's narrative.* New York: Plenum.

Petitto, L. A. (1988). "Language" in the prelinguistic child. In F. S. Kessel (Ed.), *The development of language and language researchers: Essays in honor of Roger Brown* (pp. 187–221). Hillsdale, NJ: Erlbaum.

Petitto, L. A., & Marentette, P. F. (1991). Babbling in the manual mode: Evidence for the ontogeny of language. *Science, 251,* 1493–1496.

Piaget, J. (1952). *The origins of intelligence in children* (M. Cook, Trans.). New York: International Universities Press.

Piaget, J. (1962). *Play, dreams, and imitation in childhood* (C. Gattegno & F. M. Hodgson, Trans.). New York: Norton.

Piaget, J., & Inhelder, B. (1967). *The child's conception of space* (F. J. Langdon & J. L. Lunzer, Trans.). New York: Norton. (Original work published 1948)

Pichert, J. W., & Anderson, R. C. (1977). Taking different perspectives on a story. *Journal of Educational Psychology, 69,* 309–315.

Pinker, S. (1981). On the acquisition of grammatical morphemes. *Journal of Child Language, 8,* 477–484.

Pinker, S. (1984). *Language learnability and language development.* Cambridge, MA: Harvard University Press.

Pinker, S. (1987). The bootstrapping problem in language acquisition. In B. MacWhinney (Ed.), *Mechanisms of language acquisition* (pp. 399–441). Hillsdale, NJ: Erlbaum.

Pinker, S. (1990). Language acquisition. In D. N. Osherson & H. Lasnik (Eds.), *An invitation to cognitive science: Vol. 1. Language* (pp. 199–241). Cambridge, MA: MIT Press.

Pinker, S., & Prince, A. (1988). On language and connectionism: Analysis of a parallel distributed processing model of language acquisition. In S. Pinker & J. Mehler (Eds.), *Connections and symbols* (pp. 73–193). Cambridge, MA: MIT Press.

Pisoni, D. B. (1973). Auditory and phonetic memory codes in the discrimination of consonants and vowels. *Perception & Psychophysics, 13,* 253–260.

Pisoni, D. B. (1978). Speech perception. In W. K. Estes (Ed.), *Handbook of learning and cognitive processes: Vol. 6. Linguistic functions in cognitive theory* (pp. 167–233). Hillsdale, NJ: Erlbaum.

Pittenger, R. E., Hockett, C. F., & Danehy, J. J. (1960). *The first five minutes: A sample of microscopic interview analysis.* Ithaca, NY: Paul Martineau.

Poizner, H., Klima, E. S., & Bellugi, U. (1987). *What the hands reveal about the brain.* Cambridge, MA: MIT Press.

Polanyi, L. (1989). *Telling the American story: A structural and cultural analysis of conversational storytelling.* Cambridge, MA: MIT Press.

Pollack, I., & Pickett, J. M. (1964). Intelligibility of excerpts from fluent speech: Auditory vs. structural context. *Journal of Verbal Learning and Verbal Behavior, 3,* 79–84.

Potter, J. M. (1980). What was the matter with Dr. Spooner? In V. A. Fromkin (Ed.), *Errors in linguistic performance* (pp. 13–34). New York: Academic Press.

Pratt, M. W., & MacKenzie-Keating, S. (1985). Organizing stories: Effects of development and task difficulty on referential cohesion in narrative. *Developmental Psychology, 21,* 350–356.

Pratt, M. W., Scribner, S., & Cole, M. (1977). Children as teachers: Developmental studies of instructional communication. *Child Development, 48,* 1475–1481.

Premack, D. (1971). Language in chimpanzee? *Science, 172,* 808–822.

Prinz, P. M., & Prinz, E. A. (1979). Simultaneous acquisition of ASL and spoken English (In a hearing child of a deaf mother and hearing father). Phase I: Early lexical development. *Sign Language Studies, 25,* 283–296.

Pullum, G. K. (1991). *The great Eskimo vocabulary hoax and other irreverent essays on the study of language.* Chicago: University of Chicago Press.

Pylyshyn, Z. W. (1972). Competence and psychological reality. *American Psychologist, 27,* 546–552.

Pylyshyn, Z. W. (1973). The role of competence theories in cognitive psychology. *Journal of Psycholinguistic Research, 2,* 21–50.

Quigley, S. P., & King, C. M. (1982). The language development of deaf children and youth. In S. Rosenberg (Ed.), *Handbook of applied psycholinguistics* (pp. 429–475). Hillsdale, NJ: Erlbaum.

Quine, W. V. O. (1960). *Word and object.* Cambridge, MA: MIT Press.

Rand, T. C. (1974). Dichotic release from masking for speech. *Journal of the Acoustical Society of America, 55,* 678–680.

Rayner, K. (1975). The perceptual span and peripheral cues in reading. *Cognitive Psychology, 7,* 65–81.

Rayner, K., Carlson, M., & Frazier, L. (1983). The interaction of syntax and semantics during sentence processing: Eye movements in the analysis of semantically biased sentences. *Journal of Verbal Learning and Verbal Behavior, 22,* 358–374.

Rayner, K., & Duffy, S. A. (1986). Lexical complexity and fixation times in reading: Effects of word frequency, verb complexity, and lexical ambiguity. *Memory & Cognition, 14,* 191–201.

Reber, A. S. (1987). The rise and (surprisingly rapid) fall of psycholinguistics. *Synthese, 72,* 325–339.

Reder, L. M., & Anderson, J. R. (1980). A comparison of texts and their summaries: Memorial consequences. *Journal of Verbal Learning and Verbal Behavior, 19,* 121–134.

Reich, P. A. (1986). *Language development.* Englewood Cliffs, NJ: Prentice-Hall.

Reicher, G. M. (1969). Perceptual recognition as a function of meaningfulness of stimulus material. *Journal of Experimental Psychology, 81,* 275–280.

Rescorla, L. A. (1980). Overextension in early language development. *Journal of Child Language, 7,* 321–335.

Richman, H. B., & Simon, H. A. (1989). Context effects in letter perception: Comparison of two theories. *Psychological Review, 96,* 417–432.

Rieger, C. J., III (1975). Conceptual memory and inference. In R. C. Schank (Ed.), *Conceptual information processing* (pp. 157–288). Amsterdam: North-Holland.

Rips, L. J., Shoben, E. J., & Smith, E. E. (1973). Semantic distance and the verification of semantic relations. *Journal of Verbal Learning and Verbal Behavior, 12,* 1–20.

Rips, L. J., Smith, E. E., & Shoben, E. J. (1978). Semantic composition in sentence verification. *Journal of Verbal Learning and Verbal Behavior, 17,* 375–401.

Robinson, W. P. (1972). *Language and social behavior.* Middlesex, England: Penguin.

Rochester, S., & Martin, J. R. (1979). *Crazy talk: A study in the discourse of schizophrenic speakers.* New York: Plenum.

Rodgon, M. M. (1976). *Single-word usage, cognitive development, and the beginnings of combinatorial speech.* Cambridge, England: Cambridge University Press.

Rosch, E. (1977). Linguistic relativity. In P. N. Johnson-Laird & P. C. Wason (Eds.), *Thinking: Readings in cognitive science* (pp. 501–519). Cambridge, England: Cambridge University Press.

Rosch, E., & Mervis, C. B. (1975). Family resemblances: Studies in the internal structure of categories. *Cognitive Psychology, 7,* 573–605.

Rosch, E., Mervis, C. B., Gray, W. D., Johnson, D. M., & Boyes-Braem, P. (1976). Basic objects in natural categories. *Cognitive Psychology, 8,* 382–439.

Rosch, E. H. (1973). On the internal structure of perceptual and semantic categories. In T. E. Moore (Ed.), *Cognitive development and the acquisition of language* (pp. 111–144). New York: Academic Press.

Rosenberg, S. (1982). The language of the mentally retarded: Development, processes, and intervention. In S. Rosenberg (Ed.), *Handbook of applied psycholinguistics* (pp. 329–392). Hillsdale, NJ: Erlbaum.

Rosenblum, T., & Pinker, S. A. (1983). Word magic revisited: Monolingual and bilingual children's understanding of the word-object relationship. *Child Development, 54,* 773–780.

Rozin, P., Bressman, B., & Taft, M. (1974). Do children understand the basic relationship between speech and writing? The mow-motorcycle test. *Journal of Reading Behavior, 6,* 327–334.

Rubenstein, H., Garfield, L., & Milliken, J. A. (1970). Homographic entries in the internal lexicon. *Journal of Verbal Learning and Verbal Behavior, 9,* 487–494.

Rubin, G. S., Becker, C. A., & Freeman, R. H. (1979). Morphological structure and its effect on visual word recognition. *Journal of Verbal Learning and Verbal Behavior, 18,* 757–767.

Rumbaugh, D. M. (Ed.). (1977). *Language learning by a chimpanzee: The Lana project.* New York: Academic Press.

Rumelhart, D. E. (1970). A multicomponent theory of the perception of briefly exposed visual displays. *Journal of Mathematical Psychology, 7,* 191–218.

Rumelhart, D. E. (1975). Notes on a schema for stories. In D. G. Bobrow & A. M. Collins (Eds.), *Representation and understanding* (pp. 211–236). New York: Academic Press.

Rumelhart, D. E. (1977). Understanding and summarizing brief stories. In D. LaBerge & S. J. Samuels (Eds.), *Basic processes in reading: Perception and comprehension* (pp. 265–303). Hillsdale, NJ: Erlbaum.

Rumelhart, D. E., & McClelland, J. L. (1986). On learning the past tenses of English verbs. In J. L. McClelland, D. E. Rumelhart, & the PDP Research Group (Eds.), *Parallel distributed processing: Vol. 2. Psychological and biological models* (pp. 216–271). Cambridge, MA: MIT Press.

Rumelhart, D. E., McClelland, J. L., & the PDP Research Group (1986). *Parallel distributed processing: Explorations in the microstructure of cognition: Vol. 1. Foundations.* Cambridge, MA: MIT Press.

Rymer, R. (1993). *Genie: An abused child's flight from silence.* New York: HarperCollins.

Sachs, J. (1976). The development of speech. In E. C. Carterette & M. P. Friedman (Eds.), *Handbook of perception: Vol. 7. Language and speech* (pp. 145–172). New York: Academic Press.

Sachs, J. (1993). The emergence of intentional communication. In J. B. Gleason (Ed.), *The development of language* (3rd ed., pp. 39–64). New York: Macmillan.

Sachs, J. S. (1967). Recognition memory for syntactic and semantic aspects of connected discourse. *Perception & Psychophysics, 2,* 437–442.

Sachs, J. S. (1974). Memory in reading and listening to discourse. *Memory & Cognition, 2,* 95–100.

Sacks, H., Schegloff, E. A., & Jefferson, G. (1974). A simplest systematics for the organization of turn-taking in conversation. *Language, 50,* 696–735.

Samuel, A. G. (1981). Phonemic restoration: Insights from a new methodology. *Journal of Experimental Psychology: General, 110,* 474–494.

Sapir, E. (1921). *Language: An introduction to the study of speech.* New York: Harcourt, Brace, and Company.

Savage-Rumbaugh, E. S., McDonald, K., Sevcik, R. A., Hopkins, W. D., & Rubert, E. (1986). Spontaneous symbol acquisition and communicative use by pygmy chimpanzees (*Pan paniscus*). *Journal of Experimental Psychology: General, 115,* 211–235.

Scarborough, H. S. (1990). Index of productive syntax. *Applied Psycholinguistics, 11,* 1–22.

Schank, R. C. (1977). Rules and topics in conversation. *Cognitive Science, 1,* 421–441.

Schegloff, E. A. (1972). Sequencing in conversational openings. In J. J. Gumperz & D. Hymes (Eds.), *Directions in sociolinguistics: The ethnography of communication* (pp. 346–380). New York: Holt, Rinehart & Winston.

Schlefen, A. E. (1973). *Communicational structure: Analysis of a psychotherapy transaction.* Bloomington: Indiana University Press.

Schwanenflugel, P. J., Blount, B. G., & Lin, P.-J. (1991). Cross-cultural aspects of word meanings. In P. J. Schwanenflugel (Ed.), *The psychology of word meanings* (pp. 71–90). Hillsdale, NJ: Erlbaum.

Schwanenflugel, P. J., & Rey, M. (1986). The relationship between category typicality and concept familiarity: Evidence from Spanish- and English-speaking monolinguals. *Memory & Cognition, 14,* 150–163.

Scotton, C. M. (1976). Strategies of neutrality: Language choice in uncertain situations. *Language, 52,* 919–941.

Searle, J. R. (1969). *Speech acts: An essay in the philosophy of language.* Cambridge, England: Cambridge University Press.

Searle, J. R. (1975). Indirect speech acts. In P. Cole & J. L. Morgan (Eds.), *Syntax and semantics: Vol. 3. Speech acts* (pp. 59–82). New York: Seminar Press.

Searle, J. R. (1979). Metaphor. In A. Ortony (Ed.), *Metaphor and thought* (pp. 92–123). Cambridge, England: Cambridge University Press.

Seidenberg, M. S., & Petitto, L. A. (1979). Signing behavior in apes: A critical review. *Cognition, 7,* 177–215.

Seidenberg, M. S., Tanenhaus, M. K., Leiman, J. M., & Bienkowski, M. (1982). Automatic access of the meanings of ambiguous words in context: Some limitations of knowledge-based processing. *Cognitive Psychology, 14,* 489–537.

Shankweiler, D., & Studdert-Kennedy, M. (1967). Identification of consonants and vowels presented to left and right ears. *Quarterly Journal of Experimental Psychology, 19,* 59–63.

Shapiro, L. P., Nagel, H. N., & Levine, B. A. (1993). Preferences for a verb's complements and their use in sentence processing. *Journal of Memory and Language, 32,* 96–114.

Shapiro, L. P., Zurif, E. B., & Grimshaw, J. (1989). Verb processing during sentence comprehension: Contextual impenetrability. *Journal of Psycholinguistic Research, 18,* 223–243.

Shattuck-Hufnagel, S. (1979). Speech errors as evidence for a serial-ordering mechanism in sentence production. In W. E. Cooper & E. C. T. Walker (Eds.), *Sentence processing: Psycholinguistic studies presented to Merrill Garrett* (pp. 295–342). Hillsdale, NJ: Erlbaum.

Shattuck-Hufnagel, S., & Klatt, D. H. (1979). The limited use of distinctive features and markedness in speech production: Evidence from speech error data. *Journal of Verbal Learning and Verbal Behavior, 18,* 41–55.

Shatz, M. (1978). On the development of communicative understandings: An early strategy for interpreting and responding to messages. *Cognitive Psychology, 10,* 271–301.

Shatz, M., & Gelman, R. (1973). The development of communication skills: Modifications in the speech of young children as a function of listener. *Monographs of the Society for Research in Child Development, 38*(5, Serial No. 152).

Shields, J. L., McHugh, A., & Martin, J. G. (1974). Reaction time to phoneme targets as a function of rhythmic cues in continuous speech. *Journal of Experimental Psychology, 102,* 250–255.

Shipley, E. F., Smith, C. S., & Gleitman, L. R. (1969). A study in the acquisition of language: Free responses to commands. *Language, 45,* 322–342.

Shultz, T. R. (1974). Development of the appreciation of riddles. *Child Development, 45,* 100–105.

Simpson, G. B. (1984). Lexical ambiguity and its role in models of word recognition. *Psychological Bulletin, 96,* 316–340.

Sinclair, A. (1982). Some recent trends in the study of language development. *International Journal of Behavioral Development, 5,* 413–431.

Singer, M. (1990). *Psychology of language: An introduction to sentence and discourse processes.* Hillsdale, NJ: Erlbaum.

Singer, M., Andrusiak, P., Reisdorf, P., & Black, N. L. (1992). Individual differences in bridging inference processes. *Memory & Cognition, 20,* 539–548.

Skinner, B. F. (1957). *Verbal behavior.* New York: Appleton-Century-Crofts.

Slobin, D. I. (1970). Universals of grammatical development in children. In G. B. Flores D'Arcais & W. J. M. Levelt (Eds.), *Advances in psycholinguistics* (pp. 174–186). Amsterdam: North-Holland.

Slobin, D. I. (1971). *Psycholinguistics.* Glenview, IL: Scott, Foresman.

Slobin, D. I. (1973). Cognitive prerequisites for the development of grammar. In C. A. Ferguson & D. I. Slobin (Eds.), *Studies of child language development* (pp. 175–208). New York: Holt, Rinehart & Winston.

Slobin, D. I. (1985a). Crosslinguistic evidence for the language-making capacity. In D. I. Slobin (Ed.), *The crosslinguistic study of language acquisition: Vol. 2. Theoretical issues* (pp. 1157–1256). Hillsdale, NJ: Erlbaum.

Slobin, D. I. (Ed.). (1985b). *The crosslinguistic study of language acquisition: Vol. 1. The data.* Hillsdale, NJ: Erlbaum.

Smith, C. L., & Tager-Flusberg, H. (1982). Metalinguistic awareness and language development. *Journal of Experimental Child Psychology, 34,* 449–468.

Smith, E. E. (1978). Theories of semantic memory. In W. K. Estes (Ed.), *Handbook of learning and cognitive processes: Vol. 6. Linguistic functions in cognitive theory* (pp. 1–56). Hillsdale, NJ: Erlbaum.

Smith, E. E., Shoben, E. J., & Rips, L. J. (1974). Structure and process in semantic memory: A featural model for semantic decisions. *Psychological Review, 81,* 214–241.

Smith, E. E., & Spoehr, K. T. (1974). The perception of printed English: A theoretical perspective. In B. H. Kantowitz (Ed.), *Human information processing: Tutorials in performance and cognition* (pp. 231–275). Hillsdale, NJ: Erlbaum.

Smith, N. V. (1973). *The acquisition of phonology: A case study.* Cambridge, England: Cambridge University Press.

Snodgrass, J. G., & Jarvella, R. J. (1972). Some linguistic determinants of word classification times. *Psychonomic Science, 27,* 220–222.

Snow, C. E. (1977). The development of conversation between mothers and babies. *Journal of Child Language, 4,* 1–22.

Snow, C. E. (1979). The role of social interaction in language acquisition. In W. A. Collins (Ed.), *Minnesota symposium on child psychology* (Vol. 12, pp. 157–182). Hillsdale, NJ: Erlbaum.

Snow, C. E., Barnes, W. S., Chandler, J., Goodman, I. F., & Hemphill, L. (1991). *Unfulfilled expectations: Home and school influences on literacy.* Cambridge, MA: Harvard University Press.

Sperry, R. W. (1968). Hemisphere deconnection and unity in conscious awareness. *American Psychologist, 23,* 723–733.

Sperling, G. (1960). The information available in brief visual presentations. *Psychological Monographs, 74*(11, Whole No. 48).

Springer, S. P., & Deutsch, G. (1989). *Left brain, right brain* (3rd ed.). New York: W. H. Freeman.

Sridhar, S. N. (1989). Cognitive structures in language production: A crosslinguistic study. In B. MacWhinney & E. Bates (Eds.), *The crosslinguistic study of sentence processing* (pp. 209–224). Cambridge, England: Cambridge University Press.

Staff. (1992, November 2). Perspectives. *Newsweek,* p. 43.

Stanovich, K. E. (1980). Toward an interactive compensatory model of individual differences in the development of reading fluency. *Reading Research Quarterly, 16,* 32–71.

Stanovich, K. E., Cunningham, A. E., & Cramer, B. B. (1984). Assessing phonological awareness in kindergarten children: Issues of task comparability. *Journal of Experimental Child Psychology, 38,* 175–190.

Stanovich, K. E., & West, R. F. (1989). Exposure to print and orthographic processing. *Reading Research Quarterly, 24,* 402–433.

Stark, R. E. (1980). Stages of speech development in the first year of life. In G. H. Yeni-Komshian, J. F. Kavanaugh, & C. A. Ferguson (Eds.), *Child phonology: Vol. 1. Production* (pp. 73–92). New York: Academic Press.

Stein, N. L., & Glenn, C. G. (1979). An analysis of story comprehension in elementary school children. In R. O. Freedle (Ed.), *New directions in discourse processing* (pp. 53–120). Norwood, NJ: Ablex.

Stemberger, J. P. (1985). An interactive activation model of language production. In A. W. Ellis (Ed.), *Progress in the psychology of language* (Vol. 1, pp. 143–186). Hillsdale, NJ: Erlbaum.

Stillings, N. A., Feinstein, M. H., Garfield, J. L., Rissland, E. L., Rosenbaum, D. A., Weisler, S. E., & Baker-Ward, L. (1987). *Cognitive science: An introduction.* Cambridge, MA: MIT Press.

Stokoe, W. C., Casterline, D. C., & Croneberg, C. G. (1976). A *dictionary of American Sign Language on linguistic principles.* Silver Spring, MD: Linstok Press.

Streeter, L. A. (1976). Language perception of two-month-old infants shows effects of both innate mechanisms and experience. *Nature, 259,* 39–41.

Studdert-Kennedy, M. (1974). The perception of speech. In T. A. Sebeok (Ed.), *Current trends in linguistics* (Vol. 12, pp. 2349–2385). The Hague: Mouton.

Studdert-Kennedy, M. (1975). The nature and function of phonetic categories. In F. Restle, R. M. Shiffrin, J. Castellan, & D. B. Pisoni (Eds.), *Cognitive theory* (Vol. 1, pp. 5–22). Potomac, MD: Erlbaum.

Studdert-Kennedy, M. (1976). Speech perception. In N. J. Lass (Ed.), *Contemporary issues in experimental phonetics* (pp. 243–293). New York: Academic Press.

Studdert-Kennedy, M., & Shankweiler, D. (1970). Hemispheric specialization for speech perception. *Journal of the Acoustical Society of America, 48,* 579–594.

Sulin, R. A., & Dooling, D. J. (1974). Intrusion of a thematic idea in retention of prose. *Journal of Experimental Psychology, 103,* 255–262.

Sussman, H. M., & MacNeilage, P. F. (1975). Hemispheric specialization for speech production and perception in stutterers. *Neuropsychologia, 13,* 19–26.

Sussman, H. M., & Westbury, J. R. (1981). The effects of antagonistic gestures on temporal and amplitude parameters of anticipatory labial coarticulation. *Journal of Speech and Hearing Research, 24,* 16–24.

Sutton-Smith, B. (1981). *The folkstories of children.* Philadelphia: University of Philadelphia Press.

Swinney, D. A. (1979). Lexical access during sentence comprehension: (Re)consideration of context effects. *Journal of Verbal Learning and Verbal Behavior, 18,* 645–659.

Taft, M. (1981). Prefix stripping revisited. *Journal of Verbal Learning and Verbal Behavior, 20,* 289–297.

Taft, M., & Forster, K. I. (1975). Lexical storage and retrieval of prefixed words. *Journal of Verbal Learning and Verbal Behavior, 14,* 638–647.

Tager-Flusberg, H. (1993). Putting words together: Morphology and syntax in the preschool years. In J. B. Gleason (Ed.), *The development of language* (3rd ed., pp. 151–193). New York: Macmillan.

Tanenhaus, M. K. (1988). Psycholinguistics: An overview. In F. J. Newmeyer (Ed.), *Linguistics: The Cambridge survey: Vol. 3. Language: Psychological and biological aspects* (pp. 1–37). Cambridge, England: Cambridge University Press.

Tannen, D. (1990). *You just don't understand: Women and men in conversation.* New York: Ballatine.

Taraban, R., & McClelland, J. L. (1988). Constituent attachment and thematic role assignment in sentence processing: Influences of content-based expectations. *Journal of Memory and Language, 27,* 597–632.

Taylor, S. E., Frackenpohl, H., & Pettee, J. L. (1960). *Grade level norms for the components of the fundamental reading skill* (EDL Research and Information Bulletin No. 3). Huntington, NY: Educational Development Laboratories.

Terrace, H. S., Petitto, L. A., Sanders, R. J., & Bever, T. G. (1979). Can an ape create a sentence? *Science, 206,* 891–902.

Thorndyke, P. W. (1977). Cognitive structures in comprehension and memory of narrative discourse. *Cognitive Psychology, 9,* 77–110.

Tomasello, M., & Farrar, M. J. (1984). Cognitive bases of lexical development: Object permanence and relational words. *Journal of Child Language, 11,* 477–493.

Tulving, E. (1972). Episodic and semantic memory. In E. Tulving & W. Donaldson (Eds.), *Organization in memory* (pp. 381–403). New York: Academic Press.

Tulving, E., & Thomson, D. M. (1973). Encoding specificity and retrieval processes in episodic memory. *Psychological Review, 80,* 352–373.

Tyler, L. K., & Marslen-Wilson, W. D. (1977). The on-line effects of semantic context on syntactic processing. *Journal of Verbal Learning and Verbal Behavior, 16,* 683–692.

Underwood, B. J. (1966). *Experimental psychology* (2nd ed.). New York: Appleton-Century-Crofts.

Valian, V. (1990). Null subjects: A problem for parameter-setting models of language acquisition. *Cognition, 35,* 105–122.

van Dijk, T. A., & Kintsch, W. (1983). *Strategies of discourse comprehension.* New York: Academic Press.

Van Kleeck, A. (1982). The emergence of linguistic awareness: A cognitive framework. *Merrill-Palmer Quarterly, 28,* 237–265.

Verbrugge, R. R., & McCarrell, N. S. (1977). Metaphoric comprehension: Studies in reminding and resembling. *Cognitive Psychology, 9,* 494–533.

Verplanck, W. S. (1955). The control of the content of conversation: Reinforcement of statements of opinion. *Journal of Abnormal and Social Psychology, 51,* 668–676.

Wanner, E. (1974). *On remembering, forgetting, and understanding sentences.* The Hague: Mouton.

Warren, R. M. (1970). Perceptual restoration of missing speech sounds. *Science, 167,* 392–393.

Warren, R. M., & Warren, R. P. (1970, December). Auditory illusions and confusions. *Scientific American,* pp. 30–36.

Watt, W. C. (1970). On two hypotheses concerning psycholinguistics. In J. R. Hayes (Ed.), *Cognition and the development of language* (pp. 137–220). New York: Wiley.

Werker, J. F., Gilbert, J. H. V., Humphrey, K., & Tees, R. C. (1981). Developmental aspects of cross-language speech perception. *Child Development, 52,* 349–355.

Werker, J. F., & Pegg, J. E. (1992). Infant speech perception and phonological acquisition. In C. A. Ferguson, L. Menn, & C. Stoel-Gammon (Eds.), *Phonological development: Models, research, and implications* (pp. 285–311). Timonium, MD: York Press.

Werker, J. F., & Tees, R. C. (1984). Cross-language speech perception: Evidence for perceptual reorganization during the first year of life. *Infant Behavior and Development, 7,* 49–63.

Wessells, M. G. (1982). *Cognitive psychology.* New York: Harper & Row.

West, C., & Zimmerman, D. H. (1977). Women's place in everyday talk: Reflections on parent-child interaction. *Social Problems, 24,* 521–529.

West, C., & Zimmerman, D. H. (1985). Gender, language, and discourse. In T. A. van Dijk (Ed.), *Handbook of discourse analysis: Vol. 4. Discourse analysis in society* (pp. 103–124). New York: Academic Press.

Whaley, C. P. (1978). Word non-word classification time. *Journal of Verbal Learning and Verbal Behavior, 17,* 143–154.

Wheeler, D. D. (1970). Processes in word recognition. *Cognitive Psychology, 1,* 59–85.

Whitney, P., Ritchie, B. G., & Clark, M. B. (1991). Working-memory capacity and the use of elaborative inferences in text comprehension. *Discourse Processes, 14,* 133–145.

Wilkinson, L. C. (Ed.). (1982). *Communicating in the classroom.* New York: Academic Press.

Wilkinson, L. C., & Calculator, S. (1982). Effective speakers: Students' use of language to request and obtain information and action in the classroom. In L. C. Wilkinson (Ed.), *Communicating in the classroom* (pp. 85–99). New York: Academic Press.

Wilkinson, L. C., Clevenger, M., & Dollaghan, C. (1981). Communication in small instructional groups: A sociolinguistic approach. In W. P. Dickson (Ed.), *Children's oral communication skills* (pp. 207–240). New York: Academic Press.

Winner, E., Rosenstiel, A. K., & Gardner, H. (1976). The development of metaphoric understanding. *Developmental Psychology, 12,* 289–297.

Wittgenstein, L. (1953). *Philosophical investigations* (G. E. M. Anscombe, Trans.). New York: Macmillan.

Wood, C. C. (1975). Auditory and phonetic levels of processing in speech perception: Neurophysiological and information-processing analyses. *Journal of Experimental Psychology: Human Perception and Performance, 104,* 3–20.

Woodworth, R. S. (1938). *Experimental psychology.* New York: Henry Holt & Co.

Yekovich, F. R., & Walker, C. H. (1978). Identifying and using referents in sentence comprehension. *Journal of Verbal Learning and Verbal Behavior, 17,* 265–277.

Zaidel, E. (1978). Lexical organization in the right hemisphere. In P. A. Buser & A. Rougeul-Buser (Eds.), *Cerebral correlates of conscious experience* (pp. 177–197). Amsterdam: North-Holland.

Zhurova, L. Ye. (1973). The development of analysis of words into their sounds by preschool children. In C. A. Ferguson & D. I. Slobin (Eds.), *Studies of child language development* (pp. 141–154). New York: Holt, Rinehart & Winston.

Zimmerman, D. H., & West, C. (1975). Sex roles, interruptions, and silences in conversation. In B. Thorne & N. Henley (Eds.), *Language and sex: Differences and dominance* (pp. 105–129). Rowley, MA: Newbury House.

Zipf, G. K. (1935). *The psycho-biology of language: An introduction to dynamic philology.* Boston: Houghton Mifflin.

Zurif, E. B., & Sait, P. E. (1970). The role of syntax in dichotic listening. *Neuropsychologia, 8,* 239–244.

Author Index

Subject Index

A

Accommodation, 197–198, 214
Acoustic phonetics, 74–77
Active search model of internal lexicon, 119, 123
Active voice, 37, 42
Advertising, inferences in, 148–149
Agraphia, 348–349
Alexia, 348–349
Ambiguity:
  deep-structure, 37
  lexical, 122–125
  phrase-structure, 26
American Sign Language (ASL):
  brain mechanisms in, 358
  child acquisition of, 281–284
  chimpanzee acquisition of, 364–368
  grammatical features of, 29–35
  memory for, 146
  parameters of, 31–32
  production of, 211–217
Anaphoric reference, 157–158
Animal communication, 362 (see also Chimpanzees, language in)
Aphasia:
  agraphia, 348–349
  alexia, 348–349
  Broca's, 345–346, 350–352
  comprehension and production in, 348–350
  conduction, 347, 351
  definition of, 9–10
  pure word deafness, 348
  syntax and semantics in, 350–352
  Wernicke's, 10, 346–347, 350–352
Arbitrariness, 30–31, 283
Arcuate fasciculus, 348
Articulatory phonetics:
  manner of articulation, 71–72
  place of articulation, 71
  voicing, 72–73
Aspect, grammatical marking of, 27, 33
Aspiration, 23–24
Assertion, in prelinguistic communication, 258
Assimilation, 266
Associative chain theory, 14
Attempt-suppressing signal, 224
Attentional processes, 83–84
Automatic level of speech processing, 78
Automatic processes, 56–57, 125, 316

B

Babbling, 264–265
  in American Sign Language, 282
Baby talk (see Motherese)
Basic child grammar, 275
Basic color terms, 379–391
Behaviorism, 13–14
Binding theory, 43–45
Blend, 192–193
Bottom-up processing, 12, 55–56, 316
Bound morphemes, 27
Brain:
  language and, 10, 345–352, 358
  lateralization of function in, 352–361
Bridging, 160, 245
Broca's aphasia, 345–346, 350–352

C

Cataphoric reference, 157
Categorical perception:
  in adults, 79–83
  consonants versus vowels, 81
  definition of, 80
  in infants, 261–264

D

Credits

Page 2. Photo courtesy of Spencer Grant/Stock, Boston.

Page 64. Photo courtesy of Elizabeth Crews.

Page 66. Photo courtesy of Joseph Schuyler/Stock, Boston.

Page 75. Photo courtesy of AT&T Bell Laboratories.

Pages 162 and 164 (excerpt on page 162 and Table 7.2 on page 164). Adapted from "Memory for Prose," by W. Kintsch et al., *The Structure of Human Memory*, edited by C. N. Cofer. W. H. Freeman and Company. Copyright © 1976.

Pages 176 and 177 (Table 7.3 on page 176 and list on page 177). From *Stories, Scripts, and Scenes: Aspects of Schema Theory*, by J. M. Mandler. Copyright © 1984 by Lawrence Erlbaum Associates.

Page 186. Photo courtesy of Judy Canty/Stock, Boston.

Page 235. Photo courtesy of Jon Riley/Tony Stone Images.

Page 250. Photo courtesy of Richard B. Levine.

Page 270. Photo courtesy of Elizabeth Crews.

Page 309. Photo courtesy of Debora Carroll.

Page 313. Photo courtesy of Elizabeth Crews/Stock, Boston.

Page 340. Photo courtesy of Richard B. Levine.

Page 366. Photo courtesy of R. A. Gardner and B. T. Gardner.

TO THE OWNER OF THIS BOOK:

I hope that you have found *Psychology of Language*, Second Edition, useful. So that this book can be improved in a future edition, would you take the time to complete this sheet and return it? Thank you.

School and address: _____

Department: _____

Instructor's name: _____

_____

1. What I like most about this book is: _____

_____

2. What I like least about this book is: _____

_____

_____

3. My general reaction to this book is: _____

_____

4. The name of the course in which I used this book is: _____

_____

5. Were all of the chapters of the book assigned for you to read? _____

    If not, which ones weren't? _____

6. In the space below, or on a separate sheet of paper, please write specific suggestions for improving this book and anything else you'd care to share about your experience in using the book.

_____

_____

_____

_____

_____

_____

_____

Optional:

Your name: _____   Date: _____

May Brooks/Cole quote you, either in promotion for *Psychology of Language*, Second Edition, or in future publishing ventures?

    Yes: _____   No: _____

    Sincerely,

    David W. Carroll

- -

FOLD HERE

BUSINESS REPLY MAIL

FIRST CLASS   PERMIT NO. 358   PACIFIC GROVE, CA

POSTAGE WILL BE PAID BY ADDRESSEE

ATT: *David W. Carroll*

**Brooks/Cole Publishing Company
511 Forest Lodge Road
Pacific Grove, California 93950-9968**

- -

FOLD HERE